P9-CDM-326

S·O·U·R·C·E·S

NOTABLE SELECTIONS IN

Educational Psychology

EDITED BY

RHETT DIESSNER
Lewis-Clark State College

STACY SIMMONS
Lewis-Clark State College

TOURO COLLEGE LIBRARY
Kings Hwy

WITHDRAWN

Dushkin/McGraw-Hill

A Division of The McGraw-Hill Companies

KH

To the Landegg Academy Community and its rector,
Dr. Hossain Danesh, with love and gratitude.

© 2000 by Dushkin/McGraw-Hill, A Division of The McGraw-Hill Companies,
Guilford, Connecticut 06437

Copyright law prohibits the reproduction, storage, or transmission in any form by any
means of any portion of this publication without the express written permission of
Dushkin/McGraw-Hill and of the copyright holder (if different) of the part of the
publication to be reproduced. The Guidelines for Classroom Copying endorsed by
Congress explicitly state that unauthorized copying may not be used to create, to
replace, or to substitute for anthologies, compilations, or collective works.

Manufactured in the United States of America

First Edition

123456789FGRFGR3210

Library of Congress Cataloging-in-Publication Data
  Main entry under title:
    Sources: notable selections in educational psychology/edited by Rhett Diessner and
    Stacy Simmons.—1st ed.
    Includes bibliographical references and index.
    1. Educational psychology. I. Diessner, Rhett, *comp.* II. Simmons, Stacy, *comp.*

                                                                                370.15
  0-07-232334-5   ISSN: 1525-3732

 Printed on Recycled Paper

2/16/06

Preface

Like most fields of human endeavor, there are different theoretical orientations and schools of educational psychology. Our orientation to educational psychology is primarily as applied human development. We feel that teaching children and youth is about applying developmental psychology; that is, teachers are by necessity developmental psychologists. Education and schooling is about explicitly guiding the development of human beings. This position is very similar to John Dewey's, one of America's greatest philosopher-psychologist-educators. Another orientation to educational psychology is based on the question, What can the field of psychology offer to teachers and students? Psychologists' contributions to the field of intelligence and testing and measurement have been immense, as has their research in learning theory and motivation. These contributions are to be found in every standard educational psychology text, and excerpts from primary sources on these topics can be found in this text.

Chapter 2, Cross-Cultural, Religious, Spiritual, and Ethical Foundations, includes excerpts from texts that are not common to mainstream educational psychology texts. Besides giving some unique flavor to this book, the selections are included for several important reasons: One, about 80 percent of the students who take educational psychology courses become public school teachers. As our planet shrinks, teachers throughout America and Canada are encountering children of Hindu, Jewish, Christian, Islamic, Buddhist, Muslim, and Bahá'í backgrounds in their classes. For teachers to understand their diverse students' psyches, they need some background on the worldview that informs and creates those students' mental worlds. Two, teachers and psychologists themselves have their own views of psychology, and their own convictions concerning the basic human nature of their students are influenced by their own belief systems. They need to appreciate the diversity and relativity of their cultural foundations. And three, the methods of educational psychology and the methods of teaching school vary as a function of culture, and cultures vary as a function of the belief systems that influence them.

Sources: Notable Selections in Educational Psychology is an introductory-level college text containing 40 carefully edited selections that have shaped the study of educational psychology and our contemporary understanding of it. Included here are the works of a wide range of distinguished scientists, researchers, theoreticians, and philosophers of educational psychology. Each selection contains topics that are central to this field. The selections included here come from the fields of psychology, anthropology, philosophy, religion, computer science, and pedagogy, and they are well suited to courses that want to examine, in depth, educational psychology topics through primary sources. Each selection is preceded by a headnote that establishes the relevance of the selection and provides biographical information about the author.

Perhaps the greatest tension and the longest ongoing debate in educational psychology has been between the behaviorist and the constructivist orientations to learning. Behaviorists emphasize the influence of the external environment through reinforcement, and constructivists emphasize the internal world and students' constructing their own minds. Behaviorist positions found in this text range from Edward L. Thorndike, at the dawn of American educational psychology, to B. F. Skinner, to neobehaviorists such as Robert M. Gagné, Herbert A. Simon, Lee Canter, and Albert Bandura (although Bandura may be closer to the constructivist pole at the point in his career represented by his excerpt). The constructivist thread in this book begins with John Dewey, Maxine Greene, and Jean Piaget, and goes on through Lev Vygotsky, Lawrence Kohlberg, and Jerome S. Bruner.

We hope that this text will enhance the joy of learning for students who peruse it.

ORGANIZATION OF THE BOOK.   The selections are organized topically around the major areas of study in the field of educational psychology. Part 1 includes selections on the Foundations of Educational Psychology; Part 2, Cognitive Development and Intelligence; Part 3, Social and Moral Development; Part 4, Approaches to Learning; Part 5, Methods and Evaluation of Teaching; Part 6, Motivation and Classroom Management; and Part 7, Special Needs and Socioeconomic Issues.

ON THE INTERNET.   Each part in this book is preceded by an *On the Internet* page. This page provides a list of Internet site addresses that are relevant to the part as well as a description of each site.

A WORD TO THE INSTRUCTOR.   An *Instructor's Manual With Test Questions* (multiple-choice and essay) is available through the publisher for instructors using *Sources: Notable Selections in Educational Psychology* in the classroom.

ACKNOWLEDGMENTS   Rhett wishes to thank those educational psychologists who have had the greatest impact on his psychological development: Ruth, Rand, Wendy, Naeem, Sokrates, Larry, Kurt, Michael, and Julio. He also thanks David Dean, former list manager of the Sources series at Dushkin/McGraw-Hill, for guiding him through his first *Sources* text (*Sources: Notable Selections in Human Development*) and for launching him into this volume. His gratitude goes to senior developmental editor David Brackley, who has helped him through both books; thanks for the continuity! Commendation is due Professor Scott Coleman for his assistance with chapter 2. Rhett especially thanks his students at Lewis-Clark State College and Landegg Academy. He also appreciates the sabbatical leave given him by LCSC and the generous scholar-in-residence support from Landegg Academy, which allowed him to complete this text in a timely and most pleasant manner.

Stacy would like to thank her family for their ongoing support, Jennifer and Laura for their inspiration, and especially Dr. Diessner, for allowing her the honor of assisting him.

Rhett Diessner
Lewis-Clark State College

Stacy Simmons
Lewis-Clark State College

Contents

Preface   *i*

PART ONE   *Foundations of Educational Psychology   1*

CHAPTER 1   Theoretical Background to Educational Psychology   3

1.1   **JOHN DEWEY,** from *John Dewey on Education: Selected Writings,* ed. Reginald D. Archambault   3

"[S]ince education is a rational process, that is a process in harmony with the laws of psychical development, it is plain that the educator needs not and should not depend upon vague inductions from a practice not grounded upon principles."

1.2   **MAXINE GREENE,** from "Metaphors and Multiples: Representation, the Arts, and History," *Phi Delta Kappan*   14

"Few educators today can escape the impact of cultural diversity or the sounds of newly audible 'voices' seldom attended to before."

1.3   **WILLIAM JAMES,** from *Talks to Teachers on Psychology: And to Students on Some of Life's Ideals*   28

"In the general activity and uprising of ideal interests which every one with an eye for fact can discern all about us in American life, there is perhaps no more promising feature than the fermentation which for a dozen years or more has been going on among the teachers."

1.4   **EDWARD L. THORNDIKE,** from *Educational Psychology, vol. 2: The Psychology of Learning*   33

"We may roughly distinguish in human learning (1) connection-forming of the common animal type, as when a ten-months-old-baby learns to beat a drum, (2) connection-forming involving ideas, as when a two-year-old learns to think of his mother upon hearing the word, or to say candy when he thinks of the thing, (3) analysis or abstraction, as when the student of music learns to respond to an overtone in a given sound, and (4) selective thinking or reasoning, as when the school pupil learns the meaning of a Latin sentence by using his knowledge of the rules of syntax and meanings of the word-roots."

1.5   **CAROL GILLIGAN,** from *In a Different Voice: Psychological Theory and Women's Development*   41

"Conceptions of the human life cycle represent attempts to order and make coherent the unfolding experiences and perceptions, the changing wishes and realities of everyday life. But the nature of such conceptions depends in part on the position of the observer."

CHAPTER 2   Cross-Cultural, Religious, Spiritual, and Ethical Foundations 50

2.1   **KRISHNA,** from The Bhagavad Gita, trans. Juan Mascaró   50

"When the sage climbs the heights of Yoga, he follows the path of work; but when he reaches the heights of Yoga, he is in the land of peace."

2.2   **MOSES,** from The Holy Bible   54

"I *am* the LORD thy God, which have brought thee out of the land of Egypt, out of the house of bondage."

2.3   **K'UNG FU-TZU (CONFUCIUS),** from *The Great Learning,* in Wing-Tsit Chan, comp. and trans., *A Source Book in Chinese Philosophy* 58

"The Way of learning to be great (or adult education) consists in manifesting the clear character, loving the people, and abiding . . . in the highest good."

2.4   **JESUS CHRIST,** from The Holy Bible   66

"And the Pharisees and scribes murmured, saying, This man receiveth sinners, and eateth with them."

2.5   **MUHAMMAD,** from The Koran, trans. M. H. Shakir   71

"Thus does Allah, the Mighty, the Wise, reveal to you, and (thus He revealed) to those before you. His is what is in the heavens and what is in the earth, and He is the High, the Great."

2.6   **'ABDU'L-BAHÁ,** from *The Promulgation of Universal Peace*   76

"The greatest attainment in the world of humanity has ever been scientific in nature. It is the discovery of the realities of things. Inasmuch as I find myself in the home of science—for this is one of the great universities of the country and well known abroad—I feel a keen sense of joy."

PART TWO   *Cognitive Development and Intelligence*   83

3.1   **JEAN PIAGET,** from *Six Psychological Studies,* trans. Anita Tenzer   85

" 'The Thought of the Young Child' is an enormous subject, which I have studied for more than forty years without yet having covered it, and it may be approached from many points of view. I shall consider three of them."

3.2   **DAVID WECHSLER,** from *Wechsler Intelligence Scale for Children*   92

"The *Wechsler Intelligence Scale for Children* will be found to differ from other individual tests of intelligence for children in several important ways. The first is its complete renunciation of the concept of mental age as a basic measure of intelligence. This concept, originally introduced by Binet in 1908, has had great influence particularly in this country, and has remained practically unchanged, if not unchallenged, as the ultimate basis for appraising intellectual capacity."

3.3   **ROBERT J. STERNBERG,** from "What Does It Mean to Be Smart?" *Educational Leadership*   99

"Creativity and the practical application of information—ordinary common sense or 'street smarts'—are two... abilities that go unappreciated and unrecognized. They are simply not considered relevant to conventional education."

3.4   **HOWARD GARDNER AND KATHY CHECKLEY,** from "The First Seven... and the Eighth: A Conversation With Howard Gardner," *Educational Leadership*   106

"Howard Gardner's theory of multiple intelligences, described in *Frames of Mind* (1985), sparked a revolution of sorts in classrooms around the world, a mutiny against the notion that human beings have a single, fixed intelligence."

3.5   **HOSSAIN B. DANESH AND WILLIAM S. HATCHER,** from "Errors in Jensen's Analysis," *World Order*   115

"In the December 1973 issue of *Psychology Today,* Professor Arthur Jensen has undertaken to expound directly, unequivocally, and in more or less popular terms his convictions about race and intelligence as measured by IQ tests. We feel strongly that there are a number of errors in Jensen's analysis presented in this article, some subtle and some quite blatant."

PART THREE   *Social and Moral Development*   125

CHAPTER 4   Emotional and Social Development   127

4.1   **ERIK ERIKSON**, from *Childhood and Society,* 2d ed.   127

"The first demonstration of social trust in the baby is the ease of his feeding, the depth of his sleep, the relaxation of his bowels."

4.2   **JAMES E. MARCIA,** from "Development and Validation of Ego-Identity Status," *Journal of Personality and Social Psychology*   138

"Ego identity and identity diffusion... refer to polar outcomes of the hypothesized psychosocial crisis occurring in late adolescence."

CHAPTER 5   Value and Moral Development   149

5.1   **LAWRENCE KOHLBERG,** from "The Child as a Moral Philosopher," *Psychology Today*   149

"Inspired by Jean Piaget's pioneering effort to apply a structural approach to moral development, I have gradually elaborated over the years of my study a typological scheme describing general structures and forms of moral thought which can be defined independently of the specific content of particular moral decisions or actions."

5.2   **JOHN R. SNAREY,** from "Cross-Cultural Universality of Social–Moral Development: A Critical Review of Kohlbergian Research," *Psychological Bulletin*   161

"The aspect of Kohlberg's theory that has been most difficult for many social scientists to accept is the claim that the development of moral reasoning about the social environment follows a universal invariant sequence, toward the same universal ethical principles, in all cultural settings."

5.3   **NEL NODDINGS,** from "Teaching Themes of Care," *Phi Delta Kappan*   177

"Some educators today—and I include myself among them—would like to see a complete reorganization of the school curriculum. We would like to give a central place to the questions and issues that lie at the core of human existence. One possibility would be to organize the curriculum around themes of care—caring for self, for intimate others, for strangers and global others, for the natural world and its nonhuman creatures, for the human-made world, and for ideas."

PART FOUR   *Approaches to Learning*   187

6.1   **B. F. SKINNER,** from "The Science of Learning and the Art of Teaching," *Harvard Educational Review*   189

"Recent improvements in the conditions which control behavior in the field of learning are of two principal sorts. The Law of Effect has been taken seriously; we have made sure that effects *do* occur and that they occur under conditions which are optimal for producing the changes called learning."

6.2   **ROBERT M. GAGNÉ AND WALTER DICK,** from "Instructional Psychology," *Annual Review of Psychology*   200

"The Gagné-Briggs... theory of instruction... begins with a taxonomic framework of learning outcomes considered essential for an understanding of human learning as it occurs in instructional settings."

6.3   **ALBERT BANDURA,** from "Social Cognitive Theory," in Ross Vasta, ed., *Annals of Child Development, vol. 6*   209

"Learning from models may take varied forms, including new behavior patterns, judgmental standards, cognitive competencies, and generative rules for creating new forms of behavior."

CHAPTER 7   Cognitive and Constructivist Learning Theory   216

7.1   **JEROME S. BRUNER,** from "The Act of Discovery," *Harvard Educational Review*   216

"The immediate occasion for my concern with discovery—and I do not restrict discovery to the act of finding out something that before was unknown to mankind, but rather include all forms of obtaining knowledge for oneself by the use of one's own mind—the immediate occasion is the work of the various new curriculum projects that have grown up in America during the last six or seven years. For whether one speaks to mathematicians or physicists or historians, one encounters repeatedly an expression of faith in the powerful effects that come from permitting the student to put things together for himself, to be his own discoverer."

7.2   **LEV VYGOTSKY,** from "The Development of Academic Concepts in School Aged Children," in René van der Veer and Jaan Valsiner, eds., *The Vygotsky Reader,* trans. Theresa Prout and René van der Veer   228

"The topic of the development of academic concepts in school aged children is first and foremost a practical problem of enormous, even primary, importance from the point of view of the difficulties which schools face in connection with providing children with an academic education."

CHAPTER 8   Information Processing   237

8.1   **HERBERT A. SIMON,** from "The Information Processing Explanation of Gestalt Phenomena," *Computers in Human Behavior*   237

"A central goal of contemporary information processing psychology is to explain the cognitive processes that occur in the course of various kinds of human thinking, learning, and problem solving."

8.2   **ENDEL TULVING,** from "How Many Memory Systems Are There?" *American Psychologist*   246

"The picture, or the hypothesis, depicts memory as consisting of a number of systems, each system serving somewhat different purposes and operating according to somewhat different principles. Together they form the marvelous capacity that we call by the single name of *memory*, the capacity that permits organisms to benefit from their past experiences."

PART FIVE   *Methods and Evaluation of Teaching*   255

CHAPTER 9   Methods and Models of Teaching   257

9.1   **NEL NODDINGS,** from "A Morally Defensible Mission for Schools in the Twenty-First Century," *Phi Delta Kappan*   257

"Our society does not need to make its children first in the world in mathematics and science. It needs to care for its children."

9.2   **ROBERT E. SLAVIN,** from "Synthesis of Research on Cooperative Learning," *Educational Leadership*   266

"There was once a time when it was taken for granted that a quiet class was a learning class, when principals walked down the hall expecting to be able to hear a pin drop. Today, however, many schools are using programs that foster the hum of voices in classrooms. These programs, called *cooperative learning*, encourage students to discuss, debate, disagree, and ultimately to teach one another."

9.3   **F. CLARK POWER ET AL.,** from *Lawrence Kohlberg's Approach to Moral Education*   281

"The Cluster School of Cambridge, Massachusetts, had the distinction of being the site for the first application of the just community approach to a school setting."

10.1 **ROBERT L. LINN,** from "Educational Testing and Assessment: Research Needs and Policy Issues," *American Psychologist*   289

"The role of testing in discussions of American education is ubiquitous. Testing is often a prominent subject in the arguments of educational reformers. Test results are used to document the need for reform, and tests are frequently regarded as powerful instruments of change."

10.2 **GRANT WIGGINS,** from "Assessment: Authenticity, Context, and Validity," *Phi Delta Kappan*   301

"There is an inescapable tension between the challenges presented by contextualized performance and conventional, large-scale, generic testing. Understanding is not cued knowledge: performance is never the sum of drills; problems are not exercises; mastery is not achieved by the unthinking application of algorithms."

PART SIX   *Motivation and Classroom Management*   325

CHAPTER 11   Motivation and Discipline   327

11.1 **ABRAHAM H. MASLOW,** from *Motivation and Personality,* 3rd ed.   327

"This [selection] is an attempt to formulate a positive theory of motivation that will ... conform to the known facts, clinical and observational as well as experimental. It derives most directly, however, from clinical experience. This theory is in the functionalist tradition of James and Dewey, and is fused with the holism of Wertheimer, Goldstein, and Gestalt psychology and with the dynamism of Freud, Fromm, Horney, Reich, Jung, and Adler. This integration or synthesis may be called a holistic-dynamic theory."

11.2 **JERE BROPHY,** from "Teacher Praise: A Functional Analysis," *Review of Educational Research*   336

"Most educational psychologists and other sources of advice to classroom teachers stress the value of reinforcement of good conduct and successful performance, and single out teacher praise as a particularly valuable and desirable form of such reinforcement. Until recently, my own thinking and research was no exception."

11.3 **LEE CANTER,** from "Assertive Discipline—More Than Names on the Board and Marbles in a Jar," *Phi Delta Kappan*   349

"About a year ago I was on an airline flight, seated next to a university professor. When he found out that I had developed the Assertive Discipline program, he said, 'Oh, that's where all you do is write the kids' names on the board when they're bad and drop marbles in the jar when they're good.'"

PART SEVEN *Special Needs and Socioeconomic Issues* *357*

CHAPTER 12 Special Needs 359

12.1 **DANIEL J. RESCHLY,** from "Identification and Assessment of Students With Disabilities," *The Future of Children* 359

"The two main purposes of identification and assessment of students with disabilities are to determine whether they are eligible for special education services and, if they are eligible, to determine what those services will be."

12.2 **JOSEPH S. RENZULLI,** from "What Makes Giftedness? Reexamining a Definition," *Phi Delta Kappan* 373

"Throughout recorded history and undoubtedly even before records were kept, people have always been interested in men and women who display superior ability."

CHAPTER 13 Socioeconomic and Cultural Issues 385

13.1 **MARGE SCHERER AND JONATHAN KOZOL,** from "On Savage Inequalities: A Conversation With Jonathan Kozol," *Educational Leadership* 385

"The schools, not surprisingly, are utterly impoverished. East St. Louis High School, one of the two schools I visited, had a faint smell of water rot and sewage because not long before I visited, the entire school system had been shut down after being flooded with sewage from the city's antiquated sewage system."

13.2 **JOHN U. OGBU,** from "Understanding Cultural Diversity and Learning," *Educational Researcher* 394

"Cultural diversity has become a household phrase in education, especially minority education. I suspect, however, that there is some misunderstanding about what it means and its relevance to minority education."

Acknowledgments *409*

Index *412*

PART ONE

Foundations of Educational Psychology

Chapter 1   Theoretical Background to Educational Psychology   3

Chapter 2   Cross-Cultural, Religious, Spiritual, and Ethical Foundations
50

On the Internet . . .

Sites appropriate to Part One

The Center for Dewey Studies at Southern Illinois University at Carbondale was established in 1961 as the "Dewey Project." It is the international focal point for research on Dewey's life and work.

```
http://www.siu.edu/~deweyctr/
```

These pages contain a biography of William James, excerpts from his *Talks to Teachers*, information on his psychological and educational work, and related links.

```
http://www.emory.edu/EDUCATION/mfp/
    james.html
```

Professor emeritus Maxine Greene has donated her professional papers and publications to the Milbank Memorial Library of Teachers College, Columbia University, which also contains the world's largest and richest collection of materials on the educating professions.

```
http://lweb.tc.columbia.edu/cs/na/
    greene1.html
```

Relevant to Carol Gilligan's work, the American Association of University Women is a national organization that promotes education and equity for all women and girls. Learn about the issues facing women in education and read about research on gender bias and on paths to gender equity at this site.

```
http://www.aauw.org
```

CHAPTER 1

Theoretical Background to Educational Psychology

1.1 JOHN DEWEY

What Psychology Can Do for the Teacher

John Dewey is a likely contender for the title "America's greatest philosopher," but he was also an extraordinary psychologist and educator. In 1884 he received his doctorate in philosophy from Johns Hopkins University in Baltimore, Maryland. He then taught at the University of Michigan and the University of Minnesota before accepting a position at the University of Chicago in 1894. There Dewey started an experimental (or laboratory) school, using somewhat radical educational methods, which brought him fame and made him a center of controversy.

Dewey was a leader in the functional school of psychology, and his paper "The Reflex Arc Concept in Psychology" is acclaimed as the seminal paper in this school. It is noteworthy that this paper set the stage to debunk the use of the stimulus-response unit as central to psychological theory. Dewey lamented that reducing human behavior to a basic sensory-motor description was not meaningful. He asserted that the organism was not a passive receiver of stimuli but an active perceiver. Dewey cogently argued, having been influenced by Charles Darwin, that behavior should be studied in terms of adaptation to the environment. Dewey recommended

3

that psychologists accept the study of the total organism as it functions in its environment as the proper unit of analysis in psychological research. His functional and pragmatic philosophy held that ideas are plans for action arising in response to reality and its problems; the purpose of the human intellect is to consciously make behavioral responses that enable the organism to function and progress in its world.

The following selection was originally published in *The Psychology of Number* in 1895. It has been excerpted from the anthology *John Dewey on Education* edited by Reginald D. Archambault (University of Chicago Press). It is a good introduction to Dewey's progressive education approach, which has influenced theory and practice in educational psychology for a century.

Key Concept: psychology and experience

*T*he value of any fact or theory as bearing on human activity is, in the long run, determined by practical application—that is, by using it for accomplishing some definite purpose. If it works well—if it removes friction, frees activity, economizes effort, makes for richer results—it is valuable as contributing to a perfect adjustment of means to end. If it makes no such contribution it is practically useless, no matter what claims may be theoretically urged in its behalf. To this the question of the relation between psychology and education presents no exception. The value of a knowledge of psychology in general, or of the psychology of a particular subject, will be best made known by its fruits. No amount of argument can settle the question once for all and in advance of any experimental work. But, since education is a rational process, that is a process in harmony with the laws of psychical development, it is plain that the educator need not and should not depend upon vague inductions from a practice not grounded upon principles. Psychology can not dispense with experience, nor can experience, if it is to be rational, dispense with psychology. It is possible to make actual practice less a matter of mere experiment and more a matter of reason; to make it contribute directly and economically to a rich and ripe, because rational, experience. And this the educational psychologist attempts to do by indicating in what directions help is likely to be found; by indicating what kind of psychology is likely to help and what is not likely; and, finally, by indicating what valid reasons there are for anticipating any help at all.

I. As to the last point suggested, that psychology *ought* to help the educator, there can be no disagreement. In the *first place* the study of psychology has a high *disciplinary* value for the teacher. It develops the power of connected thinking and trains to logical habits of mind. These qualities, essential though they are in thorough teaching, there is a tendency to undervalue in educational methods of the present time when so much is made of the accumulation of facts and so little of their organization. In our eager advocacy of "facts and things" we are apparently forgetting that these are comparatively worthless, either as stored knowledge or for developing power, till they have been subjected to the discriminating and formative energy of the intelligence. Unrelated facts are not knowledge any more than the words of a dictionary are connected thoughts.

And so the work of getting "things" may be carried to such an extent as to burden the mind and check the growth of its higher powers. There may be a surfeit of things with the usual consequence of an impaired mental digestion. It is pretty generally conceded that the number of facts memorized is by no means a measure of the amount of power developed; indeed, unless reflection has been exercised step by step with observation, the mass of power gained may turn out to be inversely proportional to the multitude of facts. This does not mean that there is any opposition between reflection and true observation. There can not be observation in the best sense of the word without reflection, nor can reflection fail to be an effective preparation for observation.

It will be readily admitted that this tendency to exalt facts unduly may be checked by the study of psychology. Here, in a comparatively abstract science, there *must* be reflection—abstraction and generalization. In nature study we gather the facts, and we *may* reflect upon the facts: in mind study we must reflect in order to get the facts. To observe the subtle and complex facts of mind, to discriminate the elements of a consciousness never the same for two successive moments, to give unity of meaning to these abstract mental phenomena, demands such concentration of attention as must secure the growth of mental power—power to master, and not be mastered by, the facts and ideas of whatever kind which may be crowding in upon the mind; to resolve a complex subject into its component parts, seizing upon the most important and holding them clearly defined and related in consciousness; to take, in a word, any "chaos" of experience and reduce it to harmony and system. This analytic and relating power, which is an essential mark of the clear thinker, is the prime qualification of the clear teacher.

But, in the *second place*, the study of psychology is of still more value to the teacher in its bearing upon his *practical* or strictly professional training.

Every one grants that the primary aim of education is the training of the powers of intelligence and will—that the object to be attained is a certain quality of character. To say that the purpose of education is "an increase of the powers of the mind rather than an enlargement of its possessions"; that education is a science, the science of the formation of character; that character means a measure of mental power, mastery of truths and laws, love of beauty in nature and in art, strong human sympathy, and unswerving moral rectitude; that the teacher is a trainer of mind, a former of character; that he is an artist above nature, yet in harmony with nature, who applies the science of education to help another to the full realization of his personality in a character of strength, beauty, freedom—to say this is simply to proclaim that the problem of education is essentially an ethical and psychological problem. This problem can be solved only as we know the true nature and destination of man as a rational being, and the rational methods by which the perfection of his nature may be realized. Every aim proposed by the educator which is not in harmony with the intrinsic aim of human nature itself, every method or device employed by the teacher that is not in perfect accord with the mind's own workings, not only wastes time and energy, but results in positive and permanent harm; running counter to the true activities of the mind, it certainly distorts and may possibly destroy them. To the educator, therefore, the only solid ground of assurance that he is not setting up impossible or artificial aims, that he is not using ineffective and perverting methods, is a clear and definite knowledge of the normal end and the normal forms of mental action. To know these things is to be a true psychologist and a true moralist, and to have the essential qualifications of the true educationist. Briefly, only psychology and ethics can take education out of its purely empirical and rule-of-thumb stage. Just as a knowledge of mathematics and mechanics have wrought marvelous improvements in all the arts of construction; just as a knowledge of steam and electricity has made a revolution in modes of communication, travel, and transportation of commodities; just as a knowledge of anatomy, physiology, pathology has transformed medicine from empiricism to applied science, so a knowledge of the structure and functions of the human being can alone elevate the school from the position of a mere workshop, a more or less cumbrous, uncertain, and even baneful institution, to that of a vital, certain, and effective instrument in the greatest of all constructions—the building of a free and powerful character.

Without the assured methods and results of science there are just three resources available in the work of education.

1. The first is *native tact and skill*, the intuitive power that comes mainly from sympathy. For this personal power there is absolutely no substitute. "Any one can keep school," perhaps, but not every one can teach school any more than every one can become a capable painter, or an able engineer, or a skilled artist in any direction. To ignore native aptitude, and to depend wholly, or even chiefly, upon the knowledge and use of "methods," is an error fatal to the best interests of education; and there can be no question that many schools are suffering frightfully from ignoring or undervaluing this paramount qualification of the true teacher. But in urging the need of psychology in the preparation of the teacher there is no question of ignoring personal power or of finding a substitute for personal magnetism. It is only a question of providing the best opportunities for the exercise of native capacity—for the fullest development and most fruitful application of endowments of heart and brain. Training and native outfit, culture and nature, are never opposed to each other. It is always a question, not of suppressing or superseding, but of cultivating native instinct, of training natural equipment to its ripest development and its richest use. A Pheidias does not despise learning the principles necessary to the mastery of his art, nor a Beethoven disregard the knowledge requisite for the complete technical skill through which he gives expression to his genius. In a sense it is true that the great artist is born, not made; but it is equally true that a scientific insight into the technics of his art *helps* to make him. And so it is with the artist teacher. The greater and more scientific his knowledge of human nature, the more ready and skilful will be his application of principles to varying circumstances, and the larger and more perfect will be the product of his artistic skill.

But the genius in education is as rare as the genius in other realms of human activity. Education is, and forever will be, in the hands of ordinary men and women; and if psychology—as the basis of scientific insight into human nature—is of high value to the few who possess genius, it is indispensable to the many who have not genius. Fortunately for the race, most persons, though not "born" teachers, are endowed with some "genial impulse," some native instinct and skill for education; for the cardinal requisite in this endowment is, after all, sympathy with human life and its aspirations. We are all born to be educators, to be parents, as we are not born to be engineers, or sculptors, or musicians, or painters. Native capacity for education is therefore much more common than native capacity for any other calling. Were it not so, human society could not hold together at all. But in most people this native sympathy is either dormant or blind and irregular in its action; it needs to be awakened, to be cultivated, and above all to be intelligently directed. The instinct to walk, to speak, and the like are imperious instincts, and yet they are not wholly left to "nature"; we do not assume that they will take care of themselves; we stimulate a guide, we supply them with proper conditions and material for their development. So it must be with this instinct, so common yet at present so comparatively ineffective, which lies at the heart of all educational efforts, the instinct to help others in their struggle for self-mastery and self-expression. The very fact that this instinct is so strong, and all but universal, and that the happiness of the individual and of the race so largely depends upon its development and intelligent guidance, gives greater force to the demand that its growth may be fostered by favourable conditions; and that it may be made certain and reasonable in its action, instead of being left blind and faltering, as it surely will be without rational cultivation.

To this it may be added that native endowment can work itself out in the best possible results only when it works under right conditions. Even if scientific insight were not a necessity for the true educator himself, it would still remain a necessity for others in order that they might not obstruct and possibly drive from the profession the teacher possessed of the inborn divine light, and restrict or paralyze the efforts of the teacher less richly endowed. It is the mediocre and the bungler who can most readily accommodate himself to the conditions imposed by ignorance and routine; it is the higher type of mind and heart which suffers most from its encounter with incapacity and ignorance. One of the greatest hindrances to true educational progress is the reluctance of the best class of minds to engage in educational work precisely because the general standard of ethical and psychological knowledge is so low that too often high ideals are belittled and efforts to realize them even vigorously opposed. The educational genius, the earnest teacher of any class, has little to expect from an indifference, or a stolidity, which is proof alike against the facts of experience and the demonstrations of science.

2. The Second Resource is *experience*. This, again, is necessary. Psychology is not a short and easy path that renders personal experience superfluous. The real question is: What kind of experience shall it be? It is in a way perfectly true that only by teaching can one become a teacher. But not any and every sort of thing which passes for teaching or for "experience" will make a teacher any more than simply sawing a bow across violin strings will make a violinist. It is a certain quality of practice, not mere practice, which produces the expert and the artist. Unless the practice is based upon rational principles, upon insight into facts and their meaning, "experience" simply fixes incorrect acts into wrong habits. Nonscientific practice, even if it finally reaches sane and reasonable results—which is very unlikely—does so by unnecessarily long and circuitous routes; time and energy are wasted that might easily be saved by wise insight and direction at the outset.

The worst thing about empiricism in every department of human activity is that it leads to a blind observance of rule and routine. The mark of the empiric is that he is helpless in the face of new circumstances; the mark of the scientific worker is that he has power in grappling with the new and the untried; he is master of principles which he can effectively apply under novel conditions. The one is a slave of the past, the other is a director of the future. This attachment to routine, this subservience to empiric formula, always reacts into the character of the empiric; he becomes hour by hour more and more a mere routinist and less and less an artist. Even that which he has once learned and applied with some interest and intelligence tends to become more and more mechanical, and its application more and more an unintelligent and unemotional procedure. It is never brightened and quickened by adaptation to new ends. The machine teacher, like the empiric in every profession, thus becomes a stupefying and corrupting influence in his surroundings; he himself becomes a mere tradesman, and makes his school a mere machine shop.

3. The Third Resource is *authoritative instruction in methods and devices*. At present, the real opposition is not between native skill and experience on the one side, and psychological methods on the other; it is rather between devices picked up no knows how, methods inherited from a crude past, or else invented, *ad hoc*, by educational quackery—and methods which can be rationally justified —devices which are the natural fruit of knowing the mind's powers and the ways in which it works and grows in assimilating its proper nutriment. The mere fact that there are so many methods current, and constantly pressed upon the teacher as the acme of the educational experience of the past, or as the latest and best discovery in pedagogy, makes an absolute demand for some standard by which they may be tested. Only knowledge of the principles upon which all methods are based can free the teacher from dependence upon the educational nostrums which are recommended like patent medicines, as panaceas for all educational ills. If a teacher is one fairly initiated into the real workings of the mind, if he realizes its normal aims and methods, false devices and schemes can have no attraction for him; he will not swallow them "as silly people swallow empirics' pills"; he will reject them as if by instinct. All new suggestions, new methods, he will submit to the infallible test of science; and those which will further his work he can adopt and rationally apply, seeing clearly their place and bearings, and the conditions under which they can be most effectively employed. The difference between being overpowered and used by machinery and being able to use the machinery is precisely the difference between methods externally inculcated and methods freely adopted, because of insight into the psychological principles from which they spring.

Summing up, we may say that the teacher requires a sound knowledge of ethical and psychological principles—first, because such knowledge, besides its indirect value as forming logical habits of mind, is necessary to secure the full use of native skill; secondly, because it is necessary in order to attain a perfected experience with the least expenditure of time and energy; and thirdly, in order that the educator may not be at the mercy of every sort of doctrine and device, but may have his own standard by which to test the many methods and expedients constantly urged upon him, selecting those which stand the test and rejecting those which do not, no matter by what authority or influence they may be supported.

II. We may now consider more positively how psychology is to perform this function of developing and directing native skill, making experience rational and hence prolific of the best results, and providing a criterion for suggested devices.

Education has two main phases which are never separated from each other, but which it is convenient to distinguish. One is concerned with the organization and workings of the school as part of an organic whole; the other, with the adaptation of this school structure to the individual pupil. This difference may be illustrated by the difference in the attitude of the school board or minister of education or superintendent, whether state, county, or local, to the school, and that of the individual teacher within the school. The former (the administrators of an organized system) are concerned more with the constitution of the school as a whole; their survey takes in a wide field, extending in some cases from the kindergarten to the university throughout an entire country, in other cases from the primary school to the high or academic school in a given town or city. Their chief business is with the organization and management of the school, or system of schools, upon certain general principles. What shall be the end and means of the entire institution? What subjects shall be studied? At what stage shall they be introduced, and in what sequence shall they follow one another—that is, what shall be the arrangement of the school as to its various parts in time? Again, what shall be the correlation of studies and methods at every period? Shall they be taught as different subjects? in departments? or shall methods be sought which shall work them into an organic whole? All this lies, in a large measure, outside the purview of the individual teacher; once within the institution he finds its purpose, its general lines of work, its constitutional structure, as it were, fixed for him. An individual may choose to live in France, or Great Britain, or the United States, or Canada; but after he has made his choice, the general conditions under which he shall exercise his citizenship are decided for him. So it is, in the main, with the individual teacher.

But the citizen who lives within a given system of institutions and laws finds himself constantly called upon to act. He must adjust his interests and activities to those of others in the same country. There is, at the same time, scope for purely individual selection and application of means to ends, for unfettered action of strong personality, as well as opportunity and stimulus for the free play and realization of individual equipment and acquisition. The better the constitution, the system which he can not directly control, the wider and freer and more potent will be this sphere of individual action. Now, the individual teacher finds his duties within the school as an entire institution; he has to adapt this organism, the subjects taught, the modes of discipline, etc., to the individual pupil. Apart from this personal adaptation on the part of the individual teacher, and the personal assimilation on the part of the individual pupil, the general arrangement of the school is purely meaningless; it has its object and its justification in this individual realm. Geography, arithmetic, literature, etc., may be provided in the curriculum, and their order, both of sequence and coexistence, laid down; but this is all dead and formal until it comes to the intelligence and character of the individual pupil, and the individual teacher is *the medium through which it comes.*

Now, the bearing of this upon the point in hand is that psychology and ethics have to subserve these two functions. These functions, as already intimated, can not be separated from each other; they are simply the general and the individual aspects of school life; but for purposes of study, it is convenient and even important to distinguish them. We may consider psychology and ethics from the standpoint of the light they throw upon the organization of the school as a whole—its end, its chief methods, the order and correlation of studies—and we may consider from the standpoint of the service they can perform for the individual teacher in qualifying him to use the prescribed studies and methods intelligently and efficiently, the insight they can give him into the workings of the individual mind, and the relation of any given subject to that mind.

Next to positive doctrinal error within the pedagogy itself, it may be said that the chief reason why so much of current pedagogy has been either practically useless or even practically harmful is the failure to distinguish these two functions of psychology. Considerations, principles, and maxims that derive their meaning, so far as they have any meaning, from their reference to the organization of the whole institution, have been presented as if somehow the individual teacher might derive from them specific information and direction as to how to teach particular subjects to particular pupils; on the other hand, methods that have their value (if any) as simple suggestions to the individual teacher as to how to accomplish temporary ends at a particular time have been presented as if they were eternal and universal laws of educational polity. As a result the teacher is confused; he finds himself expected to draw particular practical conclusions from very vague and theoretical educational maxims (e.g., proceed from the whole to the part, from the concrete to the abstract), or he finds himself expected to adopt as rational principles what are mere temporary expedients. It is, indeed, advisable that the teacher should understand, and even be able to criticise, the general principles upon which the whole educational system is formed and administered. He is not like a private soldier in an army, expected merely to obey, or like a cog in a wheel, expected merely to respond to and transmit external energy; he must be an intelligent medium of action. But only confusion can result from trying to get principles or devices to do what they are not intended to do—to adapt them to purposes for which they have no fitness.

In other words, the existing evils in pedagogy, the prevalence of merely vague principles upon one side and of altogether too specific and detailed methods (expedients) upon the other, are really due to failure to ask what psychology is called upon to do, and upon failure to present it in such a form as will give it undoubted value in practical applications.

III. This brings us to the positive question: In what forms can psychology best do the work which it ought to do?

1. *The Psychical Functions Mature in a Certain Order.*—When development is normal the appearance of a certain impulse or instinct, the ripening of a certain interest, always prepares the way for another. A child spends the first six months of his life in learning a few simple adjustments; his instincts to reach,

to see, to sit erect assert themselves, and are worked out. These at once become tools for further activities; the child has now to use these acquired powers as means for further acquisitions. Being able, in a rough way, to control the eye, the arm, the hand, and the body in certain positions in relation to one another, he now inspects, touches, handles, throws what comes within reach; and thus getting a certain amount of physical control, he builds up for himself a simple world of objects.

But his instinctive bodily control goes on asserting itself; he continues to gain in ability to balance himself, to coordinate, and thus control, the movements of his body. He learns to manage the body, not only at rest, but also in motion—to creep and to walk. Thus he gets a further means of growth; he extends his acquaintance with things, daily widening his little world. He also, through moving about, goes from one thing to another—that is, makes simple and crude *connections* of objects, which become the basis of subsequent relating and generalizing activities. This carries the child to the age of twelve or fifteen months. Then another instinct, already in occasional operation, ripens and takes the lead—that of imitation. In other words, there is now the attempt to adjust the activities which the child has already mastered to the activities which he sees exercised by others. He now endeavors to make the simple movements of hand, of vocal organs, etc., already in his possession the instruments of reproducing what his eye and his ear report to him of the world about him. Thus he learns to talk and to repeat many of the simple acts of others. This period lasts (roughly) till about the thirtieth month. These attainments, in turn, become the instruments of others. The child has now control of all his organs, motor and sensory. The next step, therefore, is to relate these activities to one another consciously, and not simply unconsciously as he has hitherto done. When, for example, he sees a block, he now sees in it the possibility of a whole series of activities, of throwing, building a house, etc. The head of a broken doll is no longer to him the mere thing directly before his senses. It symbolizes "some fragment of his dream of human life." It arouses in consciousness an entire group of related actions; the child strokes it, talks to it, sings it to sleep, treats it, in a word, as if it were the perfect doll. When this stage is reached, that of ability to see in a partial activity or in a single perception, a whole system or circuit of relevant actions and qualities, the imagination is in active operation; the period of symbolism, of recognition of meaning, of significance, has dawned.

But the same general process continues. Each function as it matures, and is vigorously exercised, prepares the way for a more comprehensive and a deeper conscious activity. All education consists in seizing upon the dawning activity and in presenting the material, the conditions, for promoting its best growth —in making it work freely and fully towards its proper end. Now, even in the first stages, the wise foresight and direction of the parent accomplish much, far more indeed than most parents are ever conscious of; yet the activities at this stage are so simple and so imperious that, given any chance at all, they work themselves out in some fashion or other. But when the stage of conscious recognition of meaning, of conscious direction of action, is reached, the process of development is much more complicated; many more possibilities are opened to the parent and the teacher, and so the demand for proper conditions and direction becomes indefinitely greater. Unless the right conditions and direction are supplied, the activities do not freely express themselves; the weaker are thwarted and die out; among the stronger an unhappy conflict wages and results in abnormal growth; some one impulse, naturally stronger than others, asserts itself out of all proportion, and the person "runs wild," becomes wilful, capricious, irresponsible in action, and unbalanced and irregular in his intellectual operations.

Only knowledge of the order and connection of the stages in the development of the psychical functions can, negatively, guard against these evils, or, positively, insure the full meaning and free, yet orderly or law-abiding, exercise of the psychical powers. In a word, education itself is precisely the work of supplying the conditions which will enable the psychical functions, as they successively arise, to mature and pass into higher functions in the freest and fullest manner, and this result can be secured only by knowledge of the process—that is, only by a knowledge of psychology.

The so-called psychology, or pedagogical psychology, which fails to give this insight, evidently fails of its value for educational purposes. This failure is apt to occur for one or the other of two reasons: either because the psychology is too vague and general, not bearing directly upon the actual evolution of psychical life, or because, at the other extreme, it gives a mass of crude, particular, undigested facts, with no indicated bearing or interpretations:

1. The psychology based upon a doctrine of "faculties" of the soul is a typical representative of the first sort, and educational applications based upon it are necessarily mechanical and formal; they are generally but plausible abstractions, having little or no direct application to the practical work of the classroom. The mind having been considered as split up into a number of independent powers, pedagogy is reduced to a set of precepts about the "cultivation" of these powers. These precepts are useless, in the first place, because the teacher is confronted not with abstract faculties, but with living individuals. Even when the psychology teaches that there is a unity binding together the various faculties, and that they are not really separate, this unity is presented in a purely external way. It is not shown in what way the various so-called faculties are the expressions of one and the same fundamental process. But, in the second place, this "faculty" psychology is not merely negatively useless for the educator, it is positively false, and therefore harmful in its effects. The psychical reality is that continuous growth, that unfolding of a single functional principle already referred to. While perception, memory, imagination and judgment are not present in complete form from the first, one physical activity is present, which, as it becomes more developed and complex, manifests itself in these processes as stages of its growth. What the educator requires, therefore, is not vague information about these mental powers in general, but a clear knowledge of the underlying single activity and of the conditions under which it differentiates into these powers.

2. The value for educational purposes of the mere presentation of unrelated facts, of anecdotes of child life, or even of particular investigations into certain details, may be greatly exaggerated. A great deal of material which, even if intelligently collected, is simply data for the scientific specialist, is often presented as if educational practice could be guided by it. Only *interpreted* material, that which reveals general principles or suggests the lines of growth to which the educator has to adapt himself, can be of much practical avail; and

the interpreter of the facts of the child mind must begin with knowing the facts of the adult mind. Equally in mental evolution as in physical, nature makes no leaps. "The child is father of the man" is the poetic statement of a psychologic fact.

3. *Every Subject Has Its Own Psychological Place and Method.*—Every special subject, geography, for instance, represents a certain grouping of facts, classified on the basis of *the mind's attitude towards these facts.* In the thing itself, in the actual world, there is organic unity; there is no division in the facts of geology, geography, zoölogy, and botany. These facts are not externally sorted out into different compartments. They are all bound up together; the facts are many, but the thing is *one*. It is simply some interest, some urgent need of man's activities, which discriminates the facts and unifies them under different heads. *Unless the fundamental interest and purpose which underlie this classification are discovered and appealed to, the subject which deals with it can not be presented along the lines of least resistance and in the most fruitful way.* This discovery is the work of psychology. In geography, for example, we deal with certain classes of facts, not merely in themselves, but from the standpoint of their influence in the development and modification of human activities. A mountain range or a river, treated simply as mountain range or river, gives us geology; treated in relation to the distribution of genera of plants and animals, it has a biological interpretation; treated as furnishing conditions which have entered into and modified human activities —grazing, transportation of commodities, fixing political boundaries, etc.—it acquires a geographical significance.

In other words, the unity of geography is a certain unity of human action, a certain human interest. Unless, therefore, geographical data are presented in such a way as to appeal to this interest, the method of teaching geography is uncertain, vacillating, confusing; it throws the movement of the child's mind into lines of great, rather than of least, resistance, and leaves him with a mass of disconnected facts and a feeling of unreality in presence of which his interest dies out. All method means adaptation of means to a certain end; if the end is not grasped there is no rational principle for the selection of means; the method is haphazard and empirical—a chance selection from a bundle of expedients. But the elaboration of this interest, the discovery of the concrete ways in which the mind realizes it, is unquestionably the province of psychology. There are certain definite modes in which the mind images to itself the relation of environment and human activity in production and exchange; there is a certain order of growth in this imagery; to know this is psychology; and, once more, to know this is to be able to direct the teaching of geography rationally and fruitfully, and to secure the best results, both in culture and discipline, that can be had from the study of the subject.

Metaphors and Multiples: Representation, the Arts, and History

Maxine Greene was born in 1917. She finished her liberal arts degree in 1938 at Barnard College in New York and later received her M.A. (1949) and Ph.D. (1955) from New York University, studying literary analysis and philosophy. She was an instructor at NYU from 1949 to 1956, then taught at Montclair State College in New York for one year and later at Brooklyn College of the City University of New York. In 1965 Greene settled into her professorship at Teachers College, Columbia University. She is one of the great "integrators" in the field of education, entwining a pedagogy of awareness with aesthetics into a lived philosophy of teaching. She has been called a "positive existentialist" in her optimistic insistence that philosophy be "thought-in-action." Her work in applied educational psychology is based on her philosophy of teaching students to live the "good life," with the teacher's role being that of a facilitator of child development.

Appointed in 1975 to the William F. Russell Endowed Professorship at Teachers College, Columbia University, Greene now holds that position as emeritus. Among her honors is a Phi Delta Kappan Educator of the Year, the presidency of the American Educational Research Association, election to the National Academy of Education, and a Kappa Delta Gamma Best Educational Book of the Year Award. Having written scores of articles, her best-known book may be *Teacher as Stranger: Educational Philosophy for the Modern Age* (Wadsworth, 1973), and some of her best philosophy of educational psychology is reflected in *The Dialectic of Freedom* (Teachers College Press, 1988).

The following selection comes from "Metaphors and Multiples: Representation, the Arts, and History," *Phi Delta Kappan* (January 1997). It summarizes and exemplifies Greene's commitment to the integration of such disparate fields as cognitive development, art, literature, and history.

14

Key Concept: integration of the arts in teaching

*F*ew educators today can escape the impact of cultural diversity or the sounds of newly audible "voices" seldom attended to before. The implications for our conceptions of curriculum content are considerable. Questions are raised about the American tradition, about the American Dream, about what can and should be transmitted to the changing populations in our schools. In addition, with a growing awareness of multiple meanings in the various areas of study, teachers and administrators are beginning to seek out alternative ways of representing what is known and what the young are expected to respect and understand. Educators who have not been exposed to the nuances of changing approaches to the history of ideas and the history of the schools are unlikely to respond well to the challenges that increasing diversity now poses for them.

The exploration that follows arises out of my experience over the years in engaging teachers-to-be in personal as well as collaborative inquiries into the historical contexts of American public education. I have sometimes thought of our joint efforts as an open-ended adventure into the landscapes of the past. Because I have always believed that the symbol systems we associate with the several arts ought to be included in attempts to make meaning, I have made use of a range of literary works, paintings, and other art forms, as well as the more standard list of works in American history, educational and curriculum history, and so on.

In the process of our inquiries, we have found our perspectives opening, as imagination is released and one-dimensional explanations give way to a notion of multiple realities. We have discovered a new energy in posing questions in the light of lived situations and from articulated vantage points. At once, we have discovered and rediscovered the pleasures that come from reflective encounters with works of art. Class dialogues have been enriched, and unexpected possibilities for research have emerged.

As will be seen, this mode of teaching and curriculum-making does not lead to final answers. My aim is not to achieve certainty or to recapture some golden age of unassailable "truth." My aim is to awaken teachers-to-be to the ongoing quest for meaning in our history. If they can become the kinds of teachers who can enlist their students in that quest, then their involvement with the problem of representation will have been worthwhile.

The thinkers of the 18th-century European Enlightenment took it for granted that every question had only one possible answer. They were convinced that, if they could represent the world correctly, they would be able to order it rationally and control it. What they conceived to be the correct representation had primarily to do with the use of logic, mathematics, or science (known then as "natural philosophy"). Like the "rationalists" in Wallace Stevens' "Six Significant Landscapes," they tended to think "in square rooms":

> Looking at the floor,
> Looking at the ceiling.
> They confine themselves
> To right-angled triangles.
> If they tried rhomboids,
> Cones, waving lines, ellipses—

> As, for example, the ellipse of the half-moon—
> Rationalists would wear sombreros.[1]

To turn their backs on clearly defined forms would threaten the accuracy of their rendering. Certainly, to let their attention wander to the particularity of the half-moon would undermine their dependence on the generalized, perhaps even on the universal.

The ordered universe of Newton allowed these 18th-century rationalists to "see" and provided sanction for such texts as the Declaration of Independence and the Bill of Rights. Theirs was a predictable, knowable universe. To grasp it was to be convinced of unerring human progress and of the ultimate attainment of freedom and equality.

We have only to consult the first inaugural address of Thomas Jefferson to be reminded of the confidence in a forward and upward movement that defined the Enlightenment. Of course, Jefferson did acknowledge "an overruling Providence, which by all its dispensations proves that it delights in the happiness of man here and his greater happiness hereafter."[2] Ceremonial and poetic, the address evokes images of the "Heavenly City," the "New Canaan," and the "City on the Hill." But all of this depended upon a rationalist's single-minded rendering of the way things objectively were. For the Enlightenment intellectual and for many philosophers of the 19th century, knowledge signified "accuracy of representation."[3] Out of what was thought to be *the* accurate representation came what [postmodern French philosopher] Jean-Francois Lyotard has described as a "grand narrative" used to legitimate knowledge claims and a range of practices at various moments in history.[4]

Most of us are familiar with the "grand narrative" that purportedly offers us a sweeping account of the way things are and have been in America. It has to do with individualism and the ongoing triumph of the Adamic personality born into a New World that he has the right to conquer, to exploit, and to use. It has to do with the link between dignity and independence, between merit and material success. Lyotard writes about the presumed unanimity among rational minds when it comes to the legitimacy of certain kinds of knowledge and the validity of certain institutions. He speaks of a "hero of knowledge" working toward a "good ethico-political end." Of course, he means the Enlightenment notion of the "rational man," entitled to dominate the culture's conversation.

Not surprisingly, many of the same themes are to be found in the arguments for free common schools early in the 19th century. Horace Mann's reports are obviously affected by what is known as the Enlightenment Project. Mann wrote:

> I believe in the existence of a great, immutable principle of natural law, or natural ethics—a principle antecedent to all human institutions and incapable of being abrogated by any ordinances of man—a principle of divine origin, clearly legible in the ways of Providence as those ways are manifested in the order of nature and in the history of the race—which provides the absolute right of every human being that comes into the world to an education, and which, of course, proves the correlative duty of every government to see that the means of education are provided by all.[5]

Mann could not but see this as the consequence of a consensus of all rational men, and it was a sanction to be used for educating the young "to perform all domestic, social, civil, and moral duties." He wrote that "education... is the great equalizer of the conditions of men—the balance wheel of the social machinery... it gives each man the independence and the means, by which he can resist the selfishness of other men."[6]

Even as we appreciate the call for universal education and its absorption into the "grand narrative," we have to remember that the claims and promises were being made at the time of the rise of capitalism, child labor, a competitive and often brutal free market, and exclusion of ethnic minorities from the common school. In many ways, these actualities were obscured by the vision created by the "grand narrative." Mann's call for universal education was responding to a unitary kind of representation of the world—law-governed, fundamentally beneficent, infused with the hereditary values of middle-class white males. It was also responding to one particular *form* of representation: a mode of rhetoric used by natural philosophers, statesmen, and certain ministers, all of whom inhabited a public space that they felt they were defining and in which they felt ineluctably at home.

As the century went on and the traditional rationalism slowly wed itself to the methods of a rapidly advancing empirical science, a more and more technical, formalized kind of representation became common. If there were differences in form, they were differences that could be expressed mathematically and statistically. Feeding into a society increasingly ruled by technical expertise, this purportedly "scientific" rendering of reality became even more authoritative than what had preceded it—in part because it was so difficult to translate into ordinary language and in part because it seemed to spring from some nameless place.

Unaware that science ought to be understood as just one of the culture's symbol systems used in constructing meaning, most people (including schoolpeople) were unable to realize that there were multiple ways of "worldmaking."[7] Nor did they see that knowledge cannot be exclusively—or even primarily—a matter of "determining what is true." The so-called hero of knowledge, certainly into the late 20th century, continued to insist that there was one "right" version of reality—the version resulting from controlled empirical inquiry. A heterogeneity of narratives, like an approach to understanding that takes multiple perspectives, was seen as blatant relativism that eroded the authority of single-stranded representation. The same charges were leveled at the sounding of silenced voices or the effort to give diverse forms of human expression full play.

For all that, in this country and in Europe, a stubborn recognition of diversity was becoming evident. We might remember Nathaniel Hawthorne's metaphor having to do with the "machine in the garden"[8] and the way it cut through the blandness of the faith in progress. We might also recall Ralph Waldo Emerson's description of cracks in the "social edifice" and of the "invasion of Nature by Trade with its Money, its Steam, its Railroad, [which] threatens to upset the balance of man."[9] And then there was Henry David Thoreau, who said, "We are acquainted with a mere pellicle of the globe on which we live. Most have not delved six feet below the surface, nor leaped as many above it. We know not where we are. Beside, we are sound asleep nearly half our time. Yet we esteem ourselves wise and have an established order on the surface."[10] Moreover, Thoreau was not simply posing a challenge to the certainties of rationalism. In the next moment he was shifting perspective by focusing on an insect crawling among the pine needles and trying to stay out of sight. It made him think of "the greatest Benefactor and Intelligence that stands over me the human insect"—certainly a vision quite at odds with that of "rational man" at the center of the universe.

There were women's voices, too, in the 19th century—many of them demanding recognition as reasonable beings entitled to equality with men. Margaret Fuller, condemning the laws that gave men rights over their wives and children, rejected the ordinary distinctions between the sexes and, by so doing, subverted in some sense the notion of the male "hero of knowledge." She wrote, "What woman needs is not *as* a woman to act or rule, but as a nature to grow, as an intellect to discern, as a soul to live freely and unimpeded, to unfold such powers as were given her when we left our common home."[11] The abolitionist Sojourner Truth had gone further not long before. At a women's rights meeting she argued against those who kept stressing the gender of Jesus and the frailty of women, and she announced that women were not inherently weak or helpless. Indeed, she said, Jesus came from "God and a woman—*man* had nothing to do with it." And then she thundered that she could outwork, outeat, and outlast any man and challenged, "Ain't I a woman?"[12]

Still another voice, that of Frederick Douglass, set forth a range of lived experiences that clearly called the "grand narrative" into question. Douglass focused on the year of 1838 and the climactic restlessness he suffered during that last period of his enslavement. It happens that 1838 was the year after Horace Mann became secretary of the Massachusetts Board of Education and the year after Emerson delivered his "American Scholar" address. In their different idioms, both white men had heralded the freedoms that might survive the erosions of "Trade," conformity, and human greed. Describing that year in his life, Douglass said, "I could see no reason why I should, at the end of each week, put the reward of my toil into the purse of my master. When I carried to him my weekly wages, he would, after counting the money, look me in the face with a robber-like fierceness and ask, 'Is that all?'"[13] In later accounts of his slave years, Douglass deliberately chose a more conventional voice, trying to meet "the audience expectations of white America... increasingly Douglass's America."[14] Reading the various versions of Douglass' autobiography, we become conscious again of how differing modes of representation, differing symbol systems, release a variety of divergent meanings.

The point is that the purportedly "accurate" picture or narrative was beginning to seem less accurate to those conscious of divergent representations of the way things actually were. The assurance of universal freedom and equality, the promise of a social balance wheel, the conception of a Providence that delighted in the happiness of man—all became the stuff of what Sacvan Bercovitch calls the "ritual of consensus."[15] That consensus, allegedly evolving from the unanimity of rational opinion, had to do with the need to control the "revolutionary impulse" once so important to the nation's founding. It had to do with reliance on the laws of righteousness, on acceptance of existing hierarchies, on compliance with the ethic of honest work and success.

Clearly, such a consensus was a dominant influence on conceptions of what should be taught in schools, what should be communicated through textbooks, and what should be learned. It showed itself in the generally sober and optimistic rhetoric of the schoolmen—latter-day Puritan apostles of the American Dream.

I was first introduced to the history of American education as a history of a kind of blessed pilgrimage, destined to lead to a promised land. Some years ago, I was abruptly struck by the contrast between the viewpoint of the education reformers, who seemed to have brought down the tablets from the mountain and to have charted the way through the wilderness, and that of the imaginative writers of the same period. Paying particular heed to the novelists at first, I became preoccupied with the darkness of so many of their visions, the tragic sense that seemed to infuse so much of what they wrote. What fascinated me was the dichotomy between those who appeared to me to be purveyors of the American Dream and spokespersons for training and social control and those who, participants in the same culture, saw the ambiguity and tension, the questions that could never be resolved.

For instance, I attributed the contrast between Horace Mann and Nathaniel Hawthorne in large measure to the difference between nondiscursive and discursive communication, between poetry or fiction and the rhetoric of the advocate. I saw Hawthorne transmuting his own lived experiences into the kind of language that would enable readers to "see" as they would not otherwise have seen, to make new connections with their experience that would disclose new meanings in their lives. Knowing that it made a difference that Mann had a Calvinist background, a long involvement with prison reform and the temperance movement, and a strong commitment to education as a mode of conversion and awakening, I nevertheless saw him as someone distancing himself from his experience. I saw him speaking with the authority of detached rationality and righteousness, strictly assuming that there was one incontrovertible truth above all others. To present them together in a course or in a text (or to present Mark Twain and Francis Parker, Herman Melville and John Dewey, or Toni Morrison and Julia Richman) would be to permit students to take new perspectives on their own culture, to integrate somehow the personal and the public, and to allow lived life to shed light on classroom practice.

It was clear enough from interactions in my classes that what Dewey called the "realm of meanings" was opening for my students and for those who read my work. Dewey wrote that "the realm of meanings is wider than that of true-and-false meanings; it is more urgent and more fertile.... Poetic meanings, moral meanings, a large part of the goods of life are matters of richness and freedom of meanings, rather than of truth; a large part of our life is carried on in a realm of meanings to which truth and falsity as such are irrelevant."[16] The proper task of philosophy, he said, had to do with "liberating and clarifying" meanings, and students seek "meanings and shades of meaning" far more than they seek knowledge of systems or a store of ultimate truths.

I must stress that what Dewey thought of as a truth/meaning was "in the keeping of the best available methods of inquiry and testing as to matters-of-fact"—in other words, in the keeping of science. But Dewey kept warning against giving it a "monopolistic" role in the realms of meaning. Scientific truth differed, obviously, from what the men of the Enlightenment (depending primarily on logic and reason) thought to be truth, but there was and is still an emphasis on "accuracy" that derives from dependence on a dominant mode of representation oriented toward "testing as to matters-of-fact." Using novels and poetry, I discovered ways of doing justice to whatever might be called the historical record or the "facts," while working for the liberation and clarification of meanings regarding teaching and the school.

An experience with teaching one of Hawthorne's short stories made me begin to understand the ways in which the *form* of representation feeds the life of meaning. It was not simply a notion of an alternative way of seeing that was important, I began to realize. It was the whole mystery of imaginative literature, the cultural symbol system being tapped, and, in particular, the power of metaphor.

The story was "The May-Pole of Merry Mount," that tale of two colonies in old New England, the emblem of one being a maypole and of the other, a whipping post.[17] The story begins with the wedding of the Lord and Lady of the May on midsummer eve, with a "wild throng"—masked figures, a real bear, a counterfeit Indian hunter, a priest with vine leaves in his hair—dancing around the maypole. The climax comes when the Puritans from the nearby colony come to "establish their jurisdiction over the gay sinners... and make it a land of clouded visages, of hard toil, of sermon and psalm, forever." They chop down the maypole, take the dancers prisoner, and permit the Lord and Lady of the May to go "heavenward, supporting each other along the difficult path which it was their lot to tread, and never waste one regretful thought on the vanities of Merry Mount."

Hawthorne claims, of course, that he has taken authentic pages from history and that there was indeed a Cavalier colony called Mt. Wollaston. It is at least possible, therefore, that the story could be taught as a version of history, with some elaborations. Whether or not it stemmed from some authentic record, however, it is presented as a created world, an "as-if" world to be brought into existence only as it becomes an object of its readers' experience. This requires an act of imagination, a deliberate bracketing out for a time of the ordinary and the taken-for-granted. Readers who lend their own lives to what happens, who shape the stuff of their experience in accord with the story's symbolic development, who recognize it as a "denotative and expressive symbol" that reaches beyond itself may find perspectives opening and dimensions of experience disclosing themselves in wholly unpredictable ways.

The implications in this story for a conception of socialization can hardly be ignored. At the most literal level, there is the whole matter of deciding what is being sacrificed when play time and dance time give way to the demands of responsibility. Because readers, in order to open the work, must engage personally with it, their consciousness of agency becomes—or ought to become—

a matter of existential choosing when a world of "systematized gaiety," where the primary occupations are dancing and raising flowers, is made to give way to a life of work.

In this kind of fiction, of course, there can be no clear-cut either/ors. Looking through the perspectives made available by the work—those of the priest, the dancers with fool's caps on their heads, the London minstrels exiled in "gay despair," the saddened Lady of the May who fancies all the mirth unreal, the zealot Governor Endicott, the "straggling savage" the Puritans wanted to shoot down, the unfortunate in the stocks made to dance around the whipping post— readers look upon a world of almost endless variety. There are contradictions, gaps, views from the margin, views from the center; the ordered field thought accurate in its logical or rational representation is now a field of multiplicities. Moreover, the ending holds neither truth nor resolution; like other works of art (and unlike logical arguments) it comes to no firm conclusion. Readers can only attend, perceive particulars, respond emotionally, and interpret what they find against the backgrounds of their own lives—made abruptly more visible and more readable than before. It is as if a world opens through the reading of a work of art; readers may see their worlds through it in such a way that horizons broaden and the world seems new, ready to be questioned and explored.

The referential paths are multiple, as Nelson Goodman says, and, as they are pursued, meanings may be made. The larger drama of the tale, which is a drama of expulsion as much as of conquest, cannot but summon up the story of the Fall. The beribboned tree, the maypole, has taken root in a problematic Eden, a pagan land of barbarian dancers, which may or may not be real. The Puritan colonists, in their extreme defensiveness against what they perceive as a wilderness of heathens that threatens a subversion of ordered society, reach out to impose their own notions of hard work and control. When we read this story, we may come to think of the "fall" from childhood into adulthood and of its dramatization in books like *The Catcher in the Rye* and even in such articulations as Sigmund Freud's *Civilization and Its Discontents*.

I discovered, as any teacher might, that a concentration on metaphor (in this case, with the maypole and the whipping post as examples) made far more difference to the students' search for meaning than an emphasis on divergent conceptions of reality, enlightening though they clearly are. A metaphor enables us to understand one thing better by likening it to what it is not. For Hannah Arendt, the metaphor of "bridging the abyss between inward and invisible mental activities and the world of appearances was certainly the greatest gift language could bestow on thinking."[18] A metaphor not only involves a reorientation of consciousness, it also enables us to cross divides, to make connections between ourselves and others, and to look through other eyes. Cynthia Ozick describes the role of metaphor:

> Metaphor is compelled to press hard on language and storytelling; it inhabits language at its most concrete. As the shocking extension of the unknown into our most intimate, most feeling, most private selves, metaphor is the enemy of abstraction.... Think how ironic your life would be if you passed through it without the power of connection! Novels, those vessels of irony and connection, are nothing if not metaphors. The great novels transform experience into idea because it is

the way of metaphor to transform memory into a principle of continuity. By "continuity" I mean nothing less than literary seriousness, which is unquestionably a branch of life-seriousness.[19]

Only the kind of engagement that allows a novel's meanings to be *achieved* by consciousness (not found, not simply named) can become "serious" in that way and, in becoming serious, become a form of representation.

When I think back over American history and literature, other metaphors come to mind—all of them deepening and expanding the meanings to be discovered in the changing narratives of America's social and educational past. There is the overwhelming presence of *Moby Dick* and the quest of the *Pequod* under the domination of the archetypal individual, Captain Ahab. Human diversity, human inequality, the pressures of "cash," isolation, the frail cords of community, the eternal mystery of "whiteness," the danger of the vortex —all are there, interrelated, demanding attention of the reader, and forever unfinished.

"The path to my fixed purpose," says Captain Ahab, "is laid with iron rails, whereon my soul is grooved to run. Over unsounded gorges, through the rifled hearts of mountains, under torrents' beds, unerringly I rush! Naught's an obstacle, naught's an angle to the iron way."[20] Only from the symbol system associated with the arts could something like this outlook emerge. Only an artist, it has always seemed to me, could release meanings like this from the stored-up meanings of an industrializing society, order them as never before, and shock readers into an awareness of, among other things, what it signifies to experience oneself so grooved and at once so manically in charge, so dreadfully free. Later, the same Ahab continues:

> Close! Stand close to me, Starbuck; let me look into a human eye; it is better than to gaze into sea or sky; better than to gaze upon God. By the green land; and by the bright hearth-stone! This is the magic glass, man; I see my wife and my child in thine eye. No, no; stay on board, on board! ... lower not when I do; when branded Ahab gives chase to Moby Dick. That hazard shall not be thine. No, no! not with the faraway home I see in that eye![21]

There is a shift here, away from "totalized" representations of things; there is a shift that might hold a haunting answer for those willing and daring to "see." Also casting its long shadow over American literature, there is the haunting and troublesome image of the steamboat bulling up the channel in the fog in *The Adventures of Huckleberry Finn:*

> We could hear her pounding along, but we didn't see her good till she was close. She aimed right for us. Often they do that and try to see how close they can come without touching; sometimes the wheel bites off a sweep, and then the pilot sticks his head out and laughs, and thinks he's mighty smart. Well, here she comes, and we said she was going to try and shave us; but she didn't seem to be sheering off a bit. She was a big one, and she was coming in a hurry too, looking like a black cloud with rows of glowworms around it; but all of a sudden she bulged out, big and scary, with a long row of wide-open furnace doors shining like red-hot teeth, and her monstrous bows and guards hanging right over us. There was a yell at

us, and a jingling of bells to stop the engines, a powwow of cussing, and whistling of steam—and as Jim went overboard on one side and I on the other, she came smashing right through the raft.[22]

There is the concreteness of it: the fog; Jim and Huck with their flickering lanterns; the steamboatmen, "who never cared much for raftsmen"; the almost final separation of Jim and Huck. But there are also those referential strands, perhaps evoking for a teacher the economic and technological forces that dominate so much of what is asked for and account for so much that cannot be achieved. There are the intimations of impersonality, of indifference, which call on us sternly to comprehend what is happening and to say in our own voices what it means. There is, in fact, a not too strange resemblance between that metaphor and one of the central metaphors in F. Scott Fitzgerald's *The Great Gatsby:*

> His parents were shiftless and unsuccessful farm people—his imagination had never really accepted them as his parents at all. The truth was that Jay Gatsby of West Egg, Long Island, sprang from his Platonic conception of himself. He was a son of God—a phrase which, if it means anything, means just that—and he must be about His Father's business, the service of a vast, vulgar, and meretricious beauty. So he invented just the sort of Jay Gatsby that a seventeen-year-old boy would be likely to invent, and to this conception he was faithful to the end.[23]

None of this description is directly presented as an exposure or a debunking of the radiant American Dream or of notions of "accuracy" with regard to times past. I have been working to engage students with literary works and, as time has gone on, with paintings and music and film, in order to enable them to perceive more, to hear more, to grasp more in their lives and in the surrounding world. Eager to counteract what Dewey called the "anesthetic" in life, I have wanted, as Dewey did, to release more and more people for reflective encounters with a range of works of art, works that have the potential to awaken, to move persons to see, to hear, and to feel in often unexpected ways. "The enemies of the esthetic," wrote Dewey, "are neither the practical nor the intellectual. They are the humdrum; slackness of loose ends; submission to convention in practice and intellectual procedure."[24] And, in *The Public and Its Problems*, he wrote:

> The function of art has always been to break through the crust of conventionalized and routine consciousness.... Poetry, the drama, the novel are proofs that the problem of presentation is not insoluble. Artists have always been the real purveyors of news, for it is not the outward happening in itself which is new, but the kindling by it of emotion, perception and appreciation.[25]

Without a similar kind of kindling, it is difficult to think of teaching as opening possibilities.

As time has gone on, I have tried to purvey the news—in Dewey's sense —by making use of paintings and even film and dance in the teaching of educational history. Beginning frequently with the Hudson River School of painters, with their large canvases and strange sublimity, we have tried to move imaginatively from the precise specificity of their foregrounds to the vaporous skies of their backgrounds. We have taken heed of the artists' own accounts of the call to render the landscapes as "God's notebook." We have attended to the oddly diminished and formally dressed human figures and to the blasted trees that appear symbolically in so many works.

Moving through the genre paintings at length to the works of Winslow Homer and Thomas Eakins, often drawing the observers into the play of paint and the pulsation of forms, we have gone beyond moralism—and often, verbal explication—to gain a sense of how it was in America, in its clinics and salons, its boxing rings, its fishing villages, its cotton fields. Later, moving into the "Ashcan" city paintings of the 20th century, discovering what happened during and after the Armory Show, moving through social realism and abstract expressionism, we have been more and more concerned about vantage points and varied interpretations and the multiple modes of rendering the faces of a fluid, sometimes shadowed, sometimes deeply eroded world.

Thinking about our experiences now, I cannot but think of George Bellows' tenement streets, of Edward Hopper's coldly lit luncheonette, of William Gropper's caricatured politicians, of Romare Bearden's Harlem rooftops, of Jacob Lawrence's migrants to the north. Clifford Geertz, speaking of "art as a cultural system," reminds us that to explore such works is to come in touch with a particular sensibility. And then he tells us that such sensibility "is essentially a collective formation" and that its foundations are as wide as social existence and as deep. He makes the point that, for all the importance of the arts in strengthening social values, the primary connection between art and social life lies on a semiotic plane. Whether the signs' elements are Matisse's yellow jottings or the Yoruba's slash, they are "primary documents, not illustrations of conceptions already in force, but conceptions themselves that seek—or for which people seek—a meaningful place in a repertoire of other documents, equally Primary."[26]

Later, Geertz makes a point of great importance to me and my students when he locates the commonality among the arts in the fact that "certain activities everywhere seem specifically designed to demonstrate that ideas are visible, audible, and—one needs to make up a word here—tactible, that they can be cast in forms where the senses, and through the senses the emotions, can reflectively address them."[27] To be effective in the study of art, he believes that we ought to move beyond the consideration of signs as a means of communication or as codes to be deciphered to a consideration of those signs as modes of thought, as idioms to be interpreted. Geertz and those of us who seek to provoke our students to pursue meaning in several disciplines are concerned about their finding the meaning of things for the life that they lead.

Before I offer some concluding words about meaning, the artistic aesthetic, and the matter of representation, I want to turn once more to an instance of metaphor. This one is to be found in Toni Morrison's *Jazz*. It is a description of an event that becomes a metaphor, a ruling metaphor, as it sounds and returns like a theme in an extended piece of jazz. Violet, sitting in a Harlem drugstore playing with a spoon in a tall glass, begins thinking of her mother at a table, pretending to drink from a cup.

She didn't want to be like that. Oh never like that. To sit at the table, alone in the moonlight, sipping boiled coffee from a white china cup as long as it was there, and pretending to sip it when it was gone, waiting for morning when men came, talking low as though nobody was there but themselves, and picked around in our things, lifting out what they wanted—what was theirs, they said, although we cooked in it, washed sheets in it, sat on it, ate off it. That way after they had hauled away the plow, the scythe, the mule, the sow, the churn and the butter press. Then they came inside the house and all of us children put one foot on the other and watched. When they got to the table where our mother sat nursing an empty cup, they took the table out from under her and then, while she sat there alone, and all by herself like, cup in hand, they came back and tipped the chair she sat in. She didn't jump up right away, so they shook it a bit and since she still stayed seated —looking ahead at nobody—they just tipped her out of it like the way you get the cat off the seat if you don't want to touch it or pick it up in your arms. You tip it forward and it lands on the floor. No harm done if it's a cat because it has four legs. But a person, a woman, might fall forward and just stay there a minute looking at the cup, stronger than she is, unbroken at least and lying a bit beyond her hand. Just out of reach.[28]

Four years later, after her mother "got things organized," Rose Dear jumped in the well. And, indeed, suicide is one of the recurrent themes in this novel, in which the sounds of jazz are somehow captured in the language and in which the language and those sounds evoke an entire complex American world. In part a memory play, the novel reaches back to the days of slavery, then to efforts to survive in a fearsome South, then to the migration northward on the trains. Then to the rhythmic, contradictory life of the "artful City." Visualizations, nuances, layers of meaning—all to be brought alive by readers willing to enter that world, with its wonders, its questions, its injustices, its connections, its leaps of flame.

Yes, we need the sociologists' accounting and the researchers' documenting of lives in schools. And we need the demographers' listing of newcomers in the city and the evaluators' reports. There are conflicting claims of "accuracy" of representation; there is conflict about the very possibility of representation in a world of such diversity. Toni Morrison's prose suggests the endless complexity and the incompleteness of all explorations. It enables us to see and feel, as seldom before, the textures of lives surrounding the schools and mediated by the schools, things that cannot be captured by lists, tables, administrative reports, even personal stories. As important for me as any of these other symbol systems that purport to explain our existence is the heart-stopping vision of someone being tipped forward, someone on the verge. Finally, there is the phrase "just out of reach," which ought to resonate for teachers and everyone else trying to make sense of a culture that never stays the same.

The assurances and the promises of the Enlightenment Project that so influenced Mann can no longer buoy our hopes. The notion of a totally ordered world shows itself to have been an illusion, even if a useful one that provided sanctions for our nation's founding and for the founding of the common school. Too much in the self-righteous search for truth was excluded by that single-stranded point of view that claimed to come from above. It is not only that there were no ellipses and no rhomboids; it was not only that the rationalists never wore sombreros. Too many voices were ignored or silenced, and too many ways of seeing and saying were repressed.

Jerome Bruner, arguing for a cultural psychology with interpretation and meaning at its center, reminds us of a cognitive revolution that eventually gave rise to a cognitive science that attacked mental states, intentionality, subjectivity, and (crucially) the concept of agency.[29] Challenging the idea of essential truth and the old idea of a truth that "corresponds" to some reality "out there," Bruner is aware of the fear of relativism and of the dread that the foundations of our most cherished values and beliefs will cave in. He says that values inhere in commitment to "ways of life" and that ways of life in their complex interaction "constitute a culture." And then he argues that "the pluralism of modern life and the rapid changes it imposes... create conflicts in commitment, conflicts in values, and therefore conflicts about the 'rightness' of various claims to knowledge about values." He realizes that insistence on some notion of absolute value will do nothing to banish our basic uncertainties—or (I would add) to keep our consciousness from being on the verge. His primary argument is for "open-mindedness" in literature, philosophy, and the arts. That means "a willingness to construe knowledge and values from multiple perspectives" and an ongoing constructivist quest for reciprocity.[30]

In making central to our teaching the arts and the symbol systems that present them, we may render conscious the process of making meaning, a process that has much to do with the shaping of identity, the development of a sense of agency, and a commitment to a certain mode of *praxis*. Yes, we are ever on the verge. But to recognize that there is something "out of reach" is to commit oneself to the pursuit of possibility.

I choose to end by quoting Emily Dickinson, as I often do, because what she said helps so much in identifying the relation, perhaps the necessary relation, between the pursuit of meaning and engagement with the several arts. "The Possible's slow fuse is lit / By the imagination," she wrote.[31] And it is the imagination that empowers human beings to create and to engage consciously with works of art. As they do, the realms of meaning can only deepen and expand.

NOTES

1. Wallace Stevens, "Six Significant Landscapes," in *The Collected Poems of Wallace Stevens* (New York: Knopf, 1964), p. 75.

2. Thomas Jefferson, "First Inaugural Address," in Gordon C. Lee, ed., *Crusade Against Ignorance: Jefferson on Education* (New York: Teachers College Press, 1961), p. 52.

3. Richard Rorty, *Philosophy and the Mirror of Nature* (Princeton, N.J.: Princeton University Press, 1979), p. 12.

4. Jean-François Lyotard, *The Postmodern Condition: A Report on Knowledge* (Minneapolis: University of Minnesota Press, 1984), p. 16.

5. Horace Mann, "Tenth Annual Report [to the Massachusetts Board of Education], 1846," in Lawrence A. Cremin, ed., *The Republic and the School: Horace Mann on the Education of Free Men* (New York: Teachers College Press, 1959), p. 63.

6. Ibid., p. 87.

7. Nelson Goodman, *Languages of Art* (Indianapolis: Hackett, 1976), pp. 1–17.

8. Leo Marx, *The Machine in the Garden* (New York: Oxford University Press, 1976), p. 17.

9. Ralph Waldo Emerson, journal entry, in Joel Porte, ed., *Emerson's Journals* (Cambridge, Mass.: Harvard University Press, 1982), p. 45.

10. Henry David Thoreau, *Walden* (New York: New American Library, 1989), p. 349.

11. Margaret Fuller, quoted in Alice Felt Tyler, *Freedom's Ferment* (New York: Harper Torchbooks, 1962), p. 38.

12. Sojourner Truth, quoted in Paula Giddings, *When and Where I Enter* (New York: William Morrow, 1984), p. 64.

13. Frederick Douglass, *Narrative of the Life of an American Slave: Written by Himself*, Benjamin Quarles, ed. (Cambridge, Mass.: Harvard University Press, 1988), p. 137.

14. Eric J. Sundquist, *To Wake the Nation* (Cambridge, Mass.: Harvard University Press, 1993), p. 89.

15. Sacvan Bercovitch, *The American Jeremiad* (Madison: University of Wisconsin Press, 1980), pp. 132–41.

16. John Dewey, *Experience and Nature* (New York: Dover, 1958), p. 411.

17. Nathaniel Hawthorne, "The May-Pole of Merry Mount," in *Selected Tales and Sketches* (New York: Penguin Books, 1987), pp. 172–84.

18. Hannah Arendt, *The Life of the Mind: Thinking* (New York: Harcourt Brace Jovanovich, 1978), p. 105.

19. Cynthia Ozick, *Metaphor and Memory* (New York: Knopf, 1992), p. 282.

20. Herman Melville, *Moby Dick* (Berkeley, Calif.: Clarendon Press, 1981), p. 172.

21. Ibid., p. 545.

22. Mark Twain, *The Adventures of Huckleberry Finn* (New York: New American Library, 1935), p. 508.

23. F. Scott Fitzgerald, *The Great Gatsby* (Philadelphia: Franklin Press, 1974), p. 96.

24. John Dewey, *Art as Experience* (New York: Minton Balch; 1934), p. 40.

25. John Dewey, *The Public and Its Problems* (Athens, Ohio: Swallow Press, 1954), p. 184.

26. Clifford Geertz, *Local Knowledge* (New York: Basic Books, 1983), p. 101.

27. Ibid., p. 119.

28. Toni Morrison, *Jazz* (New York: Knopf, 1992), p. 98.

29. Jerome Bruner, *Acts of Meaning* (Cambridge, Mass.: Harvard University Press, 1990), p. 9.

30. Ibid., pp. 29–30.

31. Emily Dickinson, "The Gleam of a Heroic Act," in T. H. Johnson, ed., *The Complete Poems of Emily Dickinson* (Boston: Little, Brown, 1960), pp. 688–89.

Talks to Teachers on Psychology

William James (1842–1910) is considered one of America's greatest philosophers and one of the country's first psychologists. He was educated in both America and Europe and made frequent trips abroad, giving him a non-provincial sense of the world. His parents encouraged his pursuit of a scientific education, and he earned his M.D. from Harvard University in 1869. James took a teaching position at Harvard in 1872, and he taught the very first American university psychology course there in 1875. Although Germany's Wilhelm Wundt is often credited as the father of experimental psychology, James started his psychological research laboratory at Harvard in 1875, the same year that Wundt set up his in Leipzig. In 1890, after working on the book for 12 years, James completed *The Principles of Psychology,* often considered the first great psychology text.

Somewhat of a perfectionist, James was unhappy with *Principles of Psychology,* and, deciding that he had nothing more to offer the field of psychology, he began to focus on his highly influential work in pragmatic philosophy. Similar to John Dewey, his philosophy was considered "functionalist," and his writing is appraised as both deep and lucid. This concept of functionalism in James's psychology became the central principle of American psychology at that time, focusing on the naturalistic observation of how persons adapt to their environment.

Having been greatly influenced by Charles Darwin, James viewed psychology as a biological science and mental processes as functional activities of living creatures attempting to adapt themselves to the world of nature. He described mental life as in constant, fluid, unified change, and he coined his most famous phrase, "stream of consciousness," to denote it. James's theory of emotions continues to be cited in every introductory psychology textbook. He explained that the physical response of arousal precedes the appearance of any emotion and that the mind's interpretation of this bodily arousal causes the experienced emotion. For example, one sees a snake, one's heartbeat rapidly accelerates, and then one feels afraid. Danish psychologist Carl Lange published similar findings at the same time as James; thus, this theory is known as the James-Lange theory of emotion.

The following selection comes from a series of lectures that James gave to teachers of Cambridge, Massachusetts, in 1892. It was republished as

Key Concept: the functions of the stream of consciousness *William James*

THE CHILD AS A BEHAVING ORGANISM

I wish ... to [describe] the peculiarities of the stream of consciousness by asking whether we can in any intelligible way assign its *functions*.

It has two functions that are obvious: it leads to knowledge, and it leads to action.

Can we say which of these functions is the more essential?

An old historic divergence of opinion comes in here. Popular belief has always tended to estimate the worth of a man's mental processes by their effects upon his practical life. But philosophers have usually cherished a different view. "Man's supreme glory," they have said, "is to be a *rational* being, to know absolute and eternal and universal truth. The uses of his intellect for practical affairs are therefore subordinate matters. 'The theoretic life' is his soul's genuine concern." Nothing can be more different in its results for our personal attitude than to take sides with one or the other of these views, and emphasize the practical or the theoretical ideal. In the latter case, abstraction from the emotions and passions and withdrawal from the strife of human affairs would be not only pardonable, but praiseworthy; and all that makes for quiet and contemplation should be regarded as conducive to the highest human perfection. In the former, the man of contemplation would be treated as only half a human being, passion and practical resource would become once more glories of our race, a concrete victory over this earth's outward powers of darkness would appear an equivalent for any amount of passive spiritual culture, and conduct would remain as the test of every education worthy of the name.

It is impossible to disguise the fact that in the psychology of our own day the emphasis is transferred from the mind's purely rational function, where Plato and Aristotle, and what one may call the whole classic tradition in philosophy had placed it, to the so long neglected practical side. The theory of evolution is mainly responsible for this. Man, we now have reason to believe, has been evolved from infra-human ancestors, in whom pure reason hardly existed, if at all, and whose mind, so far as it can have had any function, would appear to have been an organ for adapting their movements to the impressions received from the environment, so as to escape the better from destruction. Consciousness would thus seem in the first instance to be nothing but a sort of super-added biological perfection,—useless unless it prompted to useful conduct, and inexplicable apart from that consideration.

Deep in our own nature the biological foundations of our consciousness persist, undisguised and undiminished. Our sensations are here to attract us or to deter us, our memories to warn or encourage us, our feelings to impel, and our thoughts to restrain our behavior, so that on the whole we may prosper and our days be long in the land. Whatever of transmundane metaphysical insight or of practically inapplicable aesthetic perception or ethical sentiment we may carry in our interiors might at this rate be regarded as only part of the incidental excess of function that necessarily accompanies the working of every complex machine.

I shall ask you now—not meaning at all thereby to close the theoretic question, but merely because it seems to me the point of view likely to be of greatest practical use to you as teachers—to adopt with me, in this course of lectures, the biological conception, as thus expressed, and to lay your own emphasis on the fact that man, whatever else he may be, is primarily a practical being, whose mind is given him to aid in adapting him to this world's life.

In the learning of all matters, we have to start with some one deep aspect of the question, abstracting it as if it were the only aspect; and then we gradually correct ourselves by adding those neglected other features which complete the case. No one believes more strongly than I do that what our senses know as 'this world' is only one portion of our mind's total environment and object. Yet, because it is the primal portion, it is the *sine qua non* of all the rest. If you grasp the facts about it firmly, you may proceed to higher regions undisturbed. As our time must be so short together, I prefer being elementary and fundamental to being complete, so I propose to you to hold fast to the ultra-simple point of view.

The reasons why I call it so fundamental can be easily told.

First, human and animal psychology thereby become less discontinuous. I know that to some of you this will hardly seem an attractive reason, but there are others whom it will affect.

Second, mental action is conditioned by brain action, and runs parallel therewith. But the brain, so far as we understand it, is given us for practical behavior. Every current that runs into it from skin or eye or ear runs out again into muscles, glands, or viscera, and helps to adapt the animal to the environment from which the current came. It therefore generalizes and simplifies our view to treat the brain life and the mental life as having one fundamental kind of purpose.

Third, those very functions of the mind that do not refer directly to this world's environment, the ethical utopias, aesthetic visions, insights into eternal truth, and fanciful logical combinations, could never be carried on at all by a human individual, unless the mind that produced them in him were also able to produce more practically useful products. The latter are thus the more essential, or at least the more primordial results.

Fourth, the inessential 'unpractical' activities are themselves far more connected with our behavior and our adaptation to the environment than at first sight might appear. No truth, however abstract, is ever perceived, that will not probably at some time influence our earthly action. You must remember that, when I talk of action here, I mean action in the widest sense. I mean speech, I mean writing, I mean yeses and noes, and tendencies 'from' things and tendencies 'toward' things, and emotional determinations; and I mean them in the future as well as in the immediate present. As I talk here, and you listen, it might seem as if no action followed. You might call it a purely theoretic process, with no practical result. But it *must* have a practical result. It cannot take place at all and leave your conduct unaffected. If not to-day, then on some far future day, you will answer some question differently by reason of what you are thinking now. Some of you will be led by my words into new veins of inquiry, into reading special books. These will develop your opinion, whether for or against. That opinion will in turn be expressed, will receive criticism from others in your environment, and will affect your standing in their eyes. We cannot escape our destiny, which is practical; and even our most theoretic faculties contribute to its working out.

These few reasons will perhaps smooth the way for you to acquiescence in my proposal. As teachers, I sincerely think it will be a sufficient conception for you to adopt of the youthful psychological phenomena handed over to your inspection if you consider them from the point of view of their relation to the future conduct of their possessor. Sufficient at any rate as a first conception and as a main conception. You should regard your professional task as if it consisted chiefly and essentially in *training the pupil to behavior*; taking behavior, not in the narrow sense of his manners, but in the very widest possible sense, as including every possible sort of fit reaction on the circumstances into which he may find himself brought by the vicissitudes of life.

The reaction may, indeed, often be a negative reaction. *Not* to speak, *not* to move, is one of the most important of our duties, in certain practical emergencies. "Thou shalt refrain, renounce, abstain!" This often requires a great effort of will power, and, physiologically considered, is just as positive a nerve function as is motor discharge.

EDUCATION AND BEHAVIOR

In our foregoing talk we were led to frame a very simple conception of what an education means. In the last analysis it consists in the organizing of *resources* in the human being, of powers of conduct which shall fit him to his social and physical world. An 'uneducated' person is one who is nonplussed by all but the most habitual situations. On the contrary, one who is educated is able practically to extricate himself, by means of the examples with which his memory is stored and of the abstract conceptions which he has acquired, from circumstances in which he never was placed before. Education, in short, cannot be better described than by calling it *the organization of acquired habits of conduct and tendencies to behavior*.

To illustrate. You and I are each and all of us educated, in our several ways; and we show our education at this present moment by different conduct. It would be quite impossible for me, with my mind technically and professionally organized as it is, and with the optical stimulus which your presence affords, to remain sitting here entirely silent and inactive. Something tells me that I am expected to speak, and must speak; something forces me to keep on speaking. My organs of articulation are continuously innervated by outgoing currents, which the currents passing inward at my eyes and through my educated brain have set in motion; and the particular movements which they make have their form and order determined altogether by the training of all my past years of lecturing and reading. Your conduct, on the other hand, might seem at first sight purely receptive and inactive,—leaving out those among you who happen to be taking notes. But the very listening which you are carrying on is itself a determinate kind of conduct. All the muscular tensions of your body are distributed in a peculiar way as you listen. Your head, your eyes, are fixed characteristically. And, when the lecture is over, it will inevitably eventuate in some stroke of behavior, as I said on the previous occasion: you may be guided differently in some special emergency in the schoolroom by words which I now let fall.—So it is with the impressions you will make there on your pupil. You should get into the habit of regarding them all as leading to the acquisition by him of capacities for behavior,—emotional, social, bodily, vocal, technical, or what not. And, this being the case, you ought to feel willing, in a general way, and without hair-splitting or farther ado, to take up for the purposes of these lectures with the biological conception of the mind, as of something given us for practical use. That conception will certainly cover the greater part of your own educational work.

If we reflect upon the various ideals of education that are prevalent in the different countries, we see that what they all aim at is to organize capacities for conduct. This is most immediately obvious in Germany, where the explicitly avowed aim of the higher education is to turn the student into an instrument for advancing scientific discovery. The German universities are proud of the number of young specialists whom they turn out every year,—not necessarily men of any original force of intellect, but men so trained to research that when their professor gives them an historical or philogical thesis to prepare, or a bit of laboratory work to do, with a general indication as to the best method, they can go off by themselves and use apparatus and consult sources in such a way as to grind out in the requisite number of months some little pepper-corn of new truth worthy of being added to the store of extant human information on that subject. Little else is recognized in Germany as a man's title to academic advancement than his ability thus to show himself an efficient instrument of research.

In England, it might seem at first sight as if the higher education of the universities aimed at the production of certain static types of character rather than at the development of what one may call this dynamic scientific efficiency. Professor Jowett, when asked what Oxford could do for its students, is said to have replied, "Oxford can teach an English gentleman how to *be* an English gentleman."

But, if you ask what it means to 'be' an English gentleman, the only reply is in terms of conduct and behavior. An English gentleman is a bundle of specifically qualified reactions, a creature who for all the emergencies of life has his line of behavior distinctly marked out for him in advance. Here, as elsewhere, England expects every man to do his duty.

1.4 EDWARD L. THORNDIKE

The Psychology of Learning

Edward L. Thorndike (1874–1949) received his bachelor's degree from Wesleyan University and then studied under William James (1842–1910) at Harvard University. He performed "comparative psychology," better known as animal research. When he moved on to Columbia University in New York City he continued his work with dogs, cats, and chickens. Thorndike became quite famous in the field of psychology for his "puzzle boxes," through which he studied animal intelligence. These findings were published in a monograph entitled *Animal Intelligence*. Thorndike received his doctorate in 1898 from Columbia University and continued to perform research and teach there for his entire career. He began applying his animal research methods to the study of children on the advice of James M. Cattell, who taught psychology at the University of Pennsylvania. For the next 50 years Thorndike's research and teaching activities centered upon human learning, education, and mental testing. He was quite successful in publishing many journal articles, books, and monographs.

Thorndike was an early behaviorist, emphasizing the study of observable behavior and ignoring conscious experience and mental or emotional states. He was a leader in the approach called "connectionism," focusing primarily on associations between situations and responses. He declared that stimulus-response units are the correct locus of psychological research and that they are the building blocks from which more complex behaviors are constructed.

Thorndike is well known for coining the phrase "law of effect," which had much in common with Ivan Pavlov's "law of reinforcement." Pavlov (1849–1936) gave credit to Thorndike's work, praising his careful research and claiming that he and Thorndike had simultaneous independent discoveries. Thorndike's work demonstrated that through trial-and-error learning response, tendencies are "stamped" into memory. He also found, through his work in the 1930s, that rewarding a response helps to more effectively stamp in the behavioral tendency. Perhaps surprisingly, Thorndike's studies showed that punishment did not have a comparable effect of stamping out the response tendency. What he did find was that the less often a response was used, the more likely the response tendency would weaken or disappear. The results of these studies are contained in his very popular text *Human Learning* (Century, 1931).

Thorndike's studies and theories of children, education, and psychology were written into a large two-volume work entitled *Educational Psychology* (Teachers College Press, 1913). The following selection is excerpted from chapters 3 and 4 of the second volume, *The Psychology of Learning.*

Key Concept: connection forming and analytic learning

ASSOCIATIVE LEARNING IN MAN

Varieties of Learning

We may roughly distinguish in human learning (1) connection-forming of the common animal type, as when a ten-months-old baby learns to beat a drum, (2) connection-forming involving ideas, as when a two-year-old learns to think of his mother upon hearing the word, or to say candy when he thinks of the thing, (3) analysis or abstraction, as when the student of music learns to respond to an overtone in a given sound, and (4) selective thinking or reasoning, as when the school pupil learns the meaning of a Latin sentence by using his knowledge of the rules of syntax and meanings of the word-roots.

Connection-forming of the common animal type occurs frequently in the acquisitions of early infancy, in 'picking up' swimming or skating undirected, in increasing the distance and precision of one's hits in golf or baseball by the mere try, try again method, and in similar unthinking improvement of penmanship, acting, literary style, tact in intercourse, and indeed almost every sort of ability. Such direct selection of responses to fit a situation, irrespective of ideas of either, appears in experimental studies of human learning.

Thus, a person absorbed in reading the copy, holding it in mind and getting it typewritten as fast as he can, will modify his responses to various elements in the situations met so as to write more efficiently, without thinking of the element in question, *or* of how he has responded to it, or of the change he is actually making in the response. . . .

Similarly a person whose general aim is to solve a mechanical puzzle may hit upon the solution, or some part of it, in the course of random fumbling, may hit upon it sooner in the next trial, and so progress in the learning—all with little help from ideas about the puzzle or his own movements. . . .

If the reader will trace, fairly rapidly, the outline of, say, a six-pointed star, looking only at the reflection of it and his hand given by a mirror, he will get a useful illustration of the animal-like learning by the gradual elimination of wrong responses. . . .

Learning is indeed theoretically, and perhaps in fact, possible without any other factors than a situation, an animal whose inner conditions it can change, the retention of certain of these conditions in the animal because they favor, and the abandonment of certain others of them because they disturb, the life-processes of the neurones concerned at the time. The bare fact of selective association of response to situation is all that is needed for certain cases of learning.

Other cases follow the same simple associative plan, save that *ideas* are terms in the associated series. The familiar mental arithmetic drills of childhood, wherein we were made to "Take 6, add 5, subtract 2, divide by 3, multiply by 5, add 9, divide by 6, and give the answer," differ from the long maze through which the chicks were put, essentially in that the situations, after the first 'Take 6,' and the responses, until final announcement of the answer, include ideas as components.

The formation of connections involving ideas accounts for a major fraction of 'knowledge' in the popular sense of the term. Words heard and seen, with their meanings, events with their dates, things with their properties and values, numerical problems, such as $9 + 3$ or $36 \div 4$, with their answers, persons with their characteristics, places with their adjuncts, and the like, make up the long list of situation-response bonds where one term, at least, is the inner condition in a man which we call an idea or judgment or the like.

Man learns also to isolate and respond to elements which for the lower animals remain inextricably imbedded in gross total situations. The furniture, conversation or behavior which to a dog are an undefined impression (such as the reader would have from looking at an unfamiliar landscape upside down or hearing a babel of Chinese speeches, or being submerged ten feet under water for the first time, or being half awakened in an unfamiliar room by an earthquake), become to man intelligible aggregates of separate 'things,' 'words,' or 'acts,' further defined and constituted by color, number, size, shape, loudness, and the many elements which man analyzes out of the gross total situations of life for individual response.

Of this analytic learning and also of the longer or shorter inferential and selective series, fuller account will be given later. The simpler connection-forming, without or with ideas as features of the situation or the response, is obviously the primary fact and will be considered first.

The Laws of Habit

This sort of learning, more or less well named connection-forming, habit-formation, associative memory and association, is an obvious consequence of the laws of readiness, exercise, and effect.... By it things are put together and kept together in behavior which have gone together, often enough or with enough resulting satisfaction, and are put apart and kept apart which have been separated long enough, or whose connection has produced enough annoyance. The laws of connection forming or association or habit furnish education with two obvious general rules:—(1) Put together what should go together and keep apart what should not go together. (2) Reward desirable connections and make undesirable connections produce discomfort. Or, in combined form: Exercise and reward desirable connections; prevent or punish undesirable connections. These psychological laws and educational rules for the learning process are among the elementary principles taught to beginners. They may seem so obvious as not to need statement even to beginners, much less here. But an examination of the literature of educational theory and practice and of the textbooks, courses of study, and classroom exercises of schools will prove that they are neglected or misunderstood and that a thoroughgoing practical use of them is almost never made.

Educational theorists neglect them when they explain learning in terms of general faculties, such as attention, interest, memory, or judgment, instead of multitudes of connections; or appeal to vague forces such as *learning, development, adaptation,* or *adjustment* instead of the defined action of the laws of exercise and effect; or assume that the mere presence of ideas of good acts will produce those acts.

School practice neglects them when it fancies that knowledge of the addition combinations in higher decades (that is, $17 + 9$, $23 + 5$, $38 + 4$, etc.) will come by magic after $7 + 9$, $3 + 5$, $8 + 4$, etc., are once known: or that the difficulty which pupils find in learning 'division by a fraction' will be prevented or cured by explanation of *why* one should 'invert and multiply' or 'multiply by the reciprocal.'...

LEARNING BY ANALYSIS AND SELECTION

Analysis and Selection in General

All learning is *analytic.* (1) The bond formed never leads from absolutely the entire situation or state of affairs at the moment. (2) Within any bond formed there are always minor bonds from parts of the situation to parts of the response, each of which has a certain degree of independence, so that if that part of the situation occurs in a new context, that part of the response has a certain tendency to appear without its old accompaniments. The convenient custom of symbolizing a bond as $S_1 \rightarrow R_1$, or $S_2 \rightarrow R_2$ always requires interpretation as $(S_{1a} + S_{1b} + S_{1c} + S_{1d} \ldots S_{1n}) \rightarrow (R_{1a} + R_{1b} + R_{1c} \ldots R_{1n})$. Of the elements of a situation some are analyzed out to affect the animal, while others are left; of those so abstracted for efficacy on learning and future behavior, one will be picked out by one neurone group, another by another; although these neurone-groups co-act in making connection with the further response to the situation, they do not co-act indissolubly as an absolute unit, but form preferential bonds.

The bond formed never leads from absolutely the entire state of affairs outside the animal, because the original sensitivities and attentivenesses always neglect certain elements of it, and because acquired interests emphasize the welcome to these or others....

Each total situation-response bond is composed of minor bonds from parts of the situation to parts of the response, because man's equipment of sensory neurones is such a set of analytical organs as it is, and because his connecting neurones are such a mechanism as they are for converging and distributing the currents of conduction set up in these sensory neurones. The action set up in sensory neurones by the sight of a smiling mother (call it S_{1a}) plus whatever accessories the total situation contains (call these S_{1b}, S_{1c}, etc.) is as a whole bound to the baby's response, say, of saying mamma in a certain happy way; but the bond from S_{1a} to the 'in a certain happy way' part of the response is somewhat

FIGURE 1   **37**

$$\times \diamondsuit \square = \text{bet}$$

$$\sqcap \vdash \triangle = \text{din}$$

$$\text{⊤L} \times = \text{rag}$$

Edward L.
Thorndike

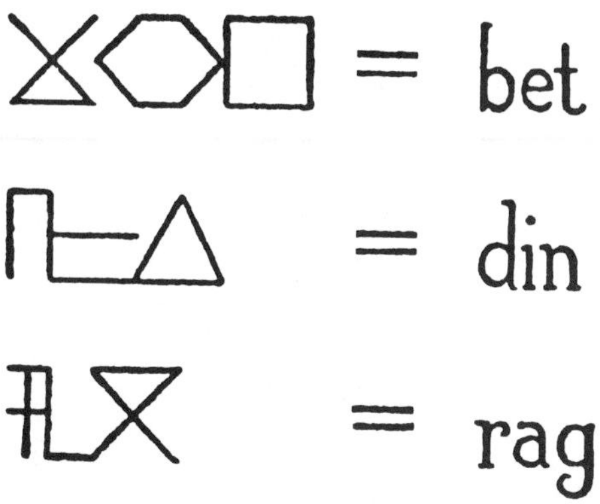

independent of other elements of the total bond. The degree of independence varies enormously. At one extreme is such great interdependence, or intimate co-action, or 'fusion,' in a total bond that the element in a new context retains almost nothing (nothing apparent to external observation) of the connecting tendency it had acquired in the old context. Thus let the reader memorize the three-pair vocabulary of Fig. 1 so that upon seeing anyone of the diagrams in a changed order, as in Fig. 2, he can give the associated word. Let him do this as quickly as possible. Let him then look at Fig. 3. It is not probable that he will connect the letters 't r a n d i g' with it, though the elements of which it is composed were, in order of reading, connected, in learning the other ten pairs, with t, r, a, n, d, i, g, respectively. At the other extreme is an independence or separateness of component bonds within the total bond such that the element in a new context evokes almost exactly its old associates. Thus let a man be taught to shut his eyes and open his right hand as a total response to the situation—*the field of vision changing from white to red, and simultaneously his right hand receiving a sharp prick.* Let him also be taught to keep his eyes open and to close his right hand as a total response to the situation—*the field of view changing from white to blue and his right hand receiving a cold moist bath.* These total bonds having been made, it is very likely that if his right hand received the same prick while the field of view changed from white to blue, he would open his right hand without shutting his eyes.

Consider now any part of a situation with which, as a whole, there is, by original nature or by the action of use, disuse, satisfaction and discomfort, some bond. When such a part happens alone[1] or in a new context, it does... what it can. It tends to provoke the total response that was bound to it; it tends especially to provoke the minor feature of that total response which was especially bound to it. If this special preferential bond is strong, it may become the dominant feature of the response to a situation composed of the old element *plus* a new context.

FIGURE 2

In the lower animals, and in very young children, the situations act more as gross totals; and the combination of connections which we call 'the' bond between the situation and its response acts more as a unit. So, to get a dog to perform a trick, say of jumping up on a box and begging, at the appropriate verbal command, it may be necessary to have not only the words, but also the voice, intonation, sight and smell of the one person; and if he jumps up on the box he may inevitably beg. But even in the lower animals cases of decided preferential bonds of elements in situations with parts of the responses thereto may be found in abundance. In all save stupid men, the training given by modern life results in the formation of an enormous number of bonds with separate elements of situations, some of them very, very subtle elements. This training results also in the power, given the appropriate mental set, of responding alike to an element in almost complete disregard of the contexts of the gross total situations in which it appears. Indeed, the intellectual life of man seems to consist as much in discriminating, abstracting, taking apart, as in associating or connecting. His procedure in learning geometry, grammar, physics or law seems in large measure almost the opposite of his procedure in habit-formation and memory. For a first step in the description of learning, such learning by analysis does need to be distinguished from the mere associative learning, though... the same fundamental mechanism accounts for both.

All man's learning, and indeed all his behavior, is *selective*. Man does not, in any useful sense of the words, ever absorb, or re-present, or mirror, or copy, a

FIGURE 3   **39**

*Edward L.
Thorndike*

situation uniformly. He never acts like a *tabula rasa* on which external situations write each its entire contribution, or a sensitive plate which duplicates indiscriminately whatever it is exposed to, or a galvanometer which is deflected equally by each and every item of electrical force. Even when he seems most subservient to the external situation—most compelled to take all that it offers and do all that it suggests—it appears that his sense organs have shut off important features of the situation from influencing him in any way comparable to that open to certain others, and that his original or acquired tendencies to neglect and attend have allotted only trivial power to some, and greatly magnified that of others.

All behavior is selective, but certain features of it are so emphatically so that it has been customary to contrast them sharply with the associative behavior which [was previously] described. A notable case is the acceptance of some one very subtle element of an outside event or an inner train of thought to determine further thought and action. In habit-formation, memory, and association by contiguity, the psychologist has declared, the situation determines the responses with little interference from the man, the bond leads from some one concrete thing or event as it is, and the laws of habit explain the process. In the deliberate choice of one or another feature of the present thought to determine thought's future course, on the other hand, the man directs the energy of the situation, the response which the situation itself would be expected to provoke does not come, and new faculties or powers of inference or reasoning have to be invoked.

Such a contrast is almost necessary for a first rough description of learning, and the distinction of such highly selective thinking from the concrete association of totals is useful throughout.... [H]owever,... learning by inference is not opposed to, or independent of, the laws of habit, but really is their necessary result under the conditions imposed by man's nature and training. A closer examination of selective thinking will show that no principles beyond the laws of readiness, exercise, and effect are needed to explain it; that it is only an extreme case of what goes on in associative learning as described under the 'piecemeal' activity of situations; and that attributing certain features of learning to mysterious faculties of abstraction or reasoning gives no real help toward understanding or controlling them.

It is true that man's behavior in meeting novel problems goes beyond, or even against, the habits represented by bonds leading from gross total situations and customarily abstracted elements thereof. One of the two reasons therefor, however, is simply that the finer, subtle, preferential bonds with subtler and less often abstracted elements go beyond, and at times against, the grosser and more usual ones. One set is as much due to exercise and effect as the other. The other reason is that in meeting novel problems the mental set or attitude is likely to be one which rejects one after another response as their unfitness to satisfy a certain desideratum appears. What remains as the apparent course of thought includes only a few of the many bonds which did operate, but which, for the most part, were unsatisfying to the ruling attitude or adjustment.

NOTES

1. It really never happens alone, being always a part of some total state of affairs. The *'alone'* means simply that it is a very distinct and predominant element of the total situation.

1.5 CAROL GILLIGAN

Woman's Place in Man's Life Cycle

Carol Gilligan was born in 1936 in New York City. She is currently a professor of human development at the Harvard Graduate School of Education. Originally, Gilligan was an English major at Swarthmore College in Swarthmore, Pennsylvania, where she was involved in the interpretation of texts. She transferred that skill and interest into the reading and interpreting of humans and their development. As a student at Harvard University, she followed American psychoanalyst Erik Erikson's work closely and became a research associate to psychologist Lawrence Kohlberg, copublishing on the topic of adolescent development. During her collaboration with Kohlberg, she noticed that females tended to respond in a qualitatively different way than males to the hypothetical moral dilemmas that Kohlberg used in his research. This led her to conclude that not only were the most influential developmental psychologists male (Sigmund Freud, Erikson, Jean Piaget, and Kohlberg) but that their theories contained a masculine bias. Data that were collected about women were either forced to fit into what was considered "normal" for a man's development or were considered aberrant.

Gilligan wrote several papers revealing this problem, which were later collected, revised, and included in the text *In a Different Voice: Psychological Theory and Women's Development,* first published by Harvard University Press in 1982. It immediately caught the attention of not only academics and psychologists but also the general public, becoming a nonfiction bestseller. The book has inspired a whole new generation of gender-related research and influenced a wide range of academic fields, from English literature to philosophy and education. In particular, it has inspired work on the "caring" classroom and school. Gilligan's work as an educational psychologist has come out in several journal articles and books, including *Mapping the Moral Domain: A Contribution of Women's Thinking to Psychological Theory and Education,* published by the Center for the Study of Gender, Education, and Human Development, Harvard University Graduate School of Education, and distributed by Harvard University Press (1988), as well as *Making Connections: The Relational Worlds of Adolescent Girls at Emma Willard School* (Harvard University Press, 1990).

The first chapter of Gilligan's *In a Different Voice* is excerpted below. An earlier version of "Woman's Place in Man's Life Cycle" was published in the *Harvard Educational Review*. It is a seminal paper on revisions in women's psychological development, and it has important implications for educational psychology.

Key Concept: women's distinct developmental path

*I*n the second act of *The Cherry Orchard*, Lopahin, a young merchant, describes his life of hard work and success. Failing to convince Madam Ranevskaya to cut down the cherry orchard to save her estate, he will go on in the next act to buy it himself. He is the self-made man who, in purchasing the estate where his father and grandfather were slaves, seeks to eradicate the "awkward, unhappy life" of the past, replacing the cherry orchard with summer cottages where coming generations "will see a new life." In elaborating this developmental vision, he reveals the image of man that underlies and supports his activity: "At times when I can't go to sleep, I think: Lord, thou gavest us immense forests, unbounded fields and the widest horizons, and living in the midst of them we should indeed be giants"—at which point, Madame Ranevskaya interrupts him, saying, "You feel the need for giants—They are good only in fairy tales, anywhere else they only frighten us."

Conceptions of the human life cycle represent attempts to order and make coherent the unfolding experiences and perceptions, the changing wishes and realities of everyday life. But the nature of such conceptions depends in part on the position of the observer. The brief excerpt from Chekhov's play suggests that when the observer is a woman, the perspective may be of a different sort. Different judgments of the image of man as giant imply different ideas about human development, different ways of imagining the human condition, different notions of what is of value in life.

At a time when efforts are being made to eradicate discrimination between the sexes in the search for social equality and justice, the differences between the sexes are being rediscovered in the social sciences. This discovery occurs when theories formerly considered to be sexually neutral in their scientific objectivity are found instead to reflect a consistent observational and evaluative bias. Then the presumed neutrality of science, like that of language itself, gives way to the recognition that the categories of knowledge are human constructions. The fascination with point of view that has informed the fiction of the twentieth century and the corresponding recognition of the relativity of judgment infuse our scientific understanding as well when we begin to notice how accustomed we have become to seeing life through men's eyes. . . .

The penchant of developmental theorists to project a masculine image, and one that appears frightening to women, goes back at least to Freud (1905), who built his theory of psychosexual development around the experiences of the male child that culminate in the Oedipus complex. In the 1920s, Freud struggled to resolve the contradictions posed for his theory by the differences in female anatomy and the different configuration of the young girl's early family relationships. After trying to fit women into his masculine conception, seeing them as envying that which they missed, he came instead to acknowledge, in the strength and persistence of women's pre-Oedipal attachments to their mothers, a developmental difference. He considered this difference in women's development to be responsible for what he saw as women's developmental failure.

Having tied the formation of the superego or conscience to castration anxiety, Freud considered women to be deprived by nature of the impetus for a clear-cut Oedipal resolution. Consequently, women's superego—the heir to the Oedipus complex—was compromised: it was never "so inexorable, so impersonal, so independent of its emotional origins as we require it to be in men." From this observation of difference, that "for women the level of what is ethically normal is different from what it is in men," Freud concluded that women "show less sense of justice than men, that they are less ready to submit to the great exigencies of life, that they are more often influenced in their judgments by feelings of affection or hostility" (1925, pp. 257–258).

Thus a problem in theory became cast as a problem in women's development, and the problem in women's development was located in their experience of relationships. Nancy Chodorow (1974), attempting to account for "the reproduction within each generation of certain general and nearly universal differences that characterize masculine and feminine personality and roles," attributes these differences between the sexes not to anatomy but rather to "the fact that women, universally, are largely responsible for early child care." Because this early social environment differs for and is experienced differently by male and female children, basic sex differences recur in personality development. As a result,"in any given society, feminine personality comes to define itself in relation and connection to other people more than masculine personality does" (pp. 43–44).

In her analysis, Chodorow relies primarily on Robert Stoller's studies which indicate that gender identity, the unchanging core of personality formation, is "with rare exception firmly and irreversibly established for both sexes by the time a child is around three." Given that for both sexes the primary caretaker in the first three years of life is typically female, the interpersonal dynamics of gender identity formation are different for boys and girls. Female identity formation takes place in a context of ongoing relationship since "mothers tend to experience their daughters as more like, and continuous with, themselves." Correspondingly, girls, in identifying themselves as female, experience themselves as like their mothers, thus fusing the experience of attachment with the process of identity formation. In contrast, "mothers experience their sons as a male opposite," and boys, in defining themselves as masculine, separate their mothers from themselves, thus curtailing "their primary love and sense of empathic tie." Consequently, male development entails a "more emphatic individuation and a more defensive firming of experienced ego boundaries." For boys, but not girls, "issues of differentiation have become intertwined with sexual issues" (1978, pp. 150, 166–167).

Writing against the masculine bias of psychoanalytic theory, Chodorow argues that the existence of sex differences in the early experiences of individuation and relationship "does not mean that women have 'weaker' ego boundaries than men or are more prone to psychosis." It means instead that "girls emerge from this period with a basis for 'empathy' built into their primary definition of self in a way that boys do not." Chodorow thus replaces Freud's negative and derivative description of female psychology with a positive and direct account of her own: "Girls emerge with a stronger basis for experiencing another's needs or feelings as one's own (or of thinking that one is so experiencing another's needs and feelings). Furthermore, girls do not define themselves in terms of the denial of preoedipal relational modes to the same extent as do boys. Therefore, regression to these modes tends not to feel as much as a basic threat to their ego. From very early, then, because they are parented by a person of the same gender . . . girls come to experience themselves as less differentiated than boys, as more continuous with and related to the external object-world, and as differently oriented to their inner object-world as well" (p. 167).

Consequently, relationships, and particularly issues of dependency, are experienced differently by women and men. For boys and men, separation and individuation are critically tied to gender identity since separation from the mother is essential for the development of masculinity. For girls and women, issues of femininity or feminine identity do not depend on the achievement of separation from the mother or on the progress of individuation. Since masculinity is defined through separation while femininity is defined through attachment, male gender identity is threatened by intimacy while female gender identity is threatened by separation. Thus males tend to have difficulty with relationships, while females tend to have problems with individuation. The quality of embeddedness in social interaction and personal relationships that characterizes women's lives in contrast to men's, however, becomes not only a descriptive difference but also a developmental liability when the milestones of childhood and adolescent development in the psychological literature are markers of increasing separation. Women's failure to separate then becomes by definition a failure to develop.

. . . [Janet] Lever extends and corroborates the observations of [Jean] Piaget in his study of the rules of the game, where he finds boys becoming through childhood increasingly fascinated with the legal elaboration of rules and the development of fair procedures for adjudicating conflicts, a fascination that, he notes, does not hold for girls. Girls, Piaget observes, have a more "pragmatic" attitude toward rules, "regarding a rule as good as long as the game repaid it" (p. 83). Girls are more tolerant in their attitudes toward rules, more willing to make exceptions, and more easily reconciled to innovations. As a result, the legal sense, which Piaget considers essential to moral development, "is far less developed in little girls than in boys" (p. 77).

The bias that leads Piaget to equate male development with child development also colors Lever's work. The assumption that shapes her discussion of results is that the male model is the better one since it fits the requirements for modern corporate success. In contrast, the sensitivity and care for the feelings of others that girls develop through their play have little market value and can even impede professional success. Lever implies that, given the realities of adult life, if a girl does not want to be left dependent on men, she will have to learn to play like a boy.

To Piaget's argument that children learn the respect for rules necessary for moral development by playing rule-bound games, Lawrence Kohlberg (1969) adds that these lessons are most effectively learned through the opportunities for role-taking that arise in the course of resolving disputes. Consequently, the moral lessons inherent in girls' play appear to be fewer than in boys'. Traditional girls' games like jump rope and hopscotch are turn-taking games, where competition is indirect since one person's success does not necessarily signify another's failure. Consequently, disputes requiring adjudication are less likely to occur. In fact, most of the girls whom Lever interviewed claimed that when a quarrel broke out, they ended the game. Rather than elaborating a system of rules for resolving disputes, girls subordinated the continuation of the game to the continuation of relationships. . . .

"Puberty," Freud says, "which brings about so great an accession of libido in boys, is marked in girls by a fresh wave of *repression*," necessary for the transformation of the young girls' "masculine sexuality" into the specifically feminine sexuality of her adulthood (1905, pp. 220–221). Freud posits this transformation on the girl's acknowledgment and acceptance of "the fact of her castration" (1931, p. 229). To the girl, Freud explains, puberty brings a new awareness of "the wound to her narcissism" and leads her to develop, "like a scar, a sense of inferiority" (1925, p. 253). Since in Erik Erikson's expansion of Freud's psychoanalytic account, adolescence is the time when development hinges on identity, the girl arrives at this juncture either psychologically at risk or with a different agenda.

The problem that female adolescence presents for theorists of human development is apparent in Erikson's scheme. Erikson (1950) charts eight stages of psychosocial development, of which adolescence is the fifth. The task at this stage is to forge a coherent sense of self, to verify an identity that can span the discontinuity of puberty and make possible the adult capacity to love and work. The preparation for the successful resolution of the adolescent identity crisis is delineated in Erikson's description of the cries that characterize the preceding four stages. Although the initial crisis in infancy of "trust versus mistrust" anchors development in the experience of relationship, the task then clearly becomes one of individuation. Erikson's second stage centers on the crisis of "autonomy versus shame and doubt," which marks the walking child's emerging sense of separateness and agency. From there, development goes on through the crisis of "initiative versus guilt," successful resolution of which represents a further move in the direction of autonomy. Next, following the inevitable disappointment of the magical wishes of the Oedipal period, children realize that to compete with their parents, they must first join them and learn to do what they do so well. Thus in the middle childhood years, development turns on the crisis of "industry versus inferiority," as the demonstration of competence becomes critical to the child's developing self-esteem. This is the time when children strive to learn and master the technology of their culture, in order to recognize themselves and to be recognized by others as capable of becoming adults. Next comes adolescence, the celebration of the autonomous, initiating, industrious self through the forging of an identity based on an ideology that can support and justify adult commitments. But about whom is Erikson talking?

Once again it turns out to be the male child. For the female, Erikson (1968) says, the sequence is a bit different. She holds her identity in abeyance as she prepares to attract the man by whose name she will be known, by whose status she will be defined, the man who will rescue her from emptiness and loneliness by filling "the inner space." While for men, identity precedes intimacy and generativity in the optimal cycle of human separation and attachment, for women these tasks seem instead to be fused. Intimacy goes along with identity, as the female comes to know herself as she is known, through her relationships with others.

Yet despite Erikson's observation of sex differences, his chart of life-cycle stages remains unchanged: identity continues to precede intimacy as male experience continues to define his life-cycle conception. But in this male life cycle there is little preparation for the intimacy of the first adult stage. Only the initial stage of trust versus mistrust suggests the type of mutuality that Erikson means by intimacy and generativity and Freud means by genitality. The rest is separateness, with the result that development itself comes to be identified with separation, and attachments appear to be developmental impediments, as is repeatedly the case in the assessment of women. . . .

In his elaboration of the identity crisis, Erikson (1968) cites the life of George Bernard Shaw to illustrate the young person's sense of being co-opted prematurely by success in a career he cannot wholeheartedly endorse. Shaw at seventy, reflecting upon his life, described his crisis at the age of twenty as having been caused not by the lack of success or the absence of recognition, but by too much of both: "I made good in spite of myself, and found, to my dismay, that Business, instead of expelling me as the worthless impostor I was, was fastening upon me with no intention of letting me go. Behold me, therefore, in my twentieth year, with a business training, in an occupation which I detested as cordially as any sane person lets himself detest anything he cannot escape from. In March 1876 I broke loose" (p. 143). At this point Shaw settled down to study and write as he pleased. Hardly interpreted as evidence of neurotic anxiety about achievement and competition, Shaw's refusal suggests to Erikson "the extraordinary workings of an extraordinary personality [coming] to the fore" (p. 144).

We might on these grounds begin to ask, not why women have conflicts about competitive success, but why men show such readiness to adopt and celebrate a rather narrow vision of success. . . .

"It is obvious," Virginia Woolf says, "that the values of women differ very often from the values which have been made by the other sex" (1929, p. 76). Yet, she adds, "it is the masculine values that prevail." As a result, women come to question the normality of their feelings and to alter their judgments in deference to the opinion of others. In the nineteenth century novels written by women, Woolf sees at work "a mind which was slightly pulled from the straight and made to alter its clear vision in deference to external authority." The same deference to the values and opinions of others can be seen in the judgments of twentieth century women. The difficulty women experience in finding or speaking publicly in their own voices emerges repeatedly in the form of qualification and self-doubt, but also in intimations of a divided judgment, a public assessment and private assessment which are fundamentally at odds.

Yet the deference and confusion that Woolf criticizes in women derive from the values she sees as their strength. Women's deference is rooted not only in their social subordination but also in the substance of their moral concern. Sensitivity to the needs of others and the assumption of responsibility for taking care lead women to attend to voices other than their own and to include in their judgment other points of view. Women's moral weakness, manifest in an apparent diffusion and confusion of judgment, is thus inseparable from women's moral strength, an overriding concern with relationships and responsibilities. The reluctance to judge may itself be indicative of the care and concern for others that infuse the psychology of women's development and are responsible for what is generally seen as problematic in its nature.

Thus women not only define themselves in a context of human relationship but also judge themselves in terms of their ability to care. Women's place in man's life cycle has been that of nurturer, caretaker, and helpmate, the weaver of those networks of relationships on which she in turn relies. But while women have thus taken care of men, men have, in their theories of psychological development, as in their economic arrangements, tended to assume or devalue that care. When the focus on individuation and individual achievement extends into adulthood and maturity is equated with personal autonomy, concern with relationships appears as a weakness of women rather than as a human strength (Miller, 1976).

The criticism that Freud makes of women's sense of justice, seeing it as compromised in its refusal of blind impartiality, reappears not only in the work of Piaget but also in that of Kohlberg. While in Piaget's account (1932) of the moral judgment of the child, girls are an aside, a curiosity to whom he devotes four brief entries in an index that omits "boys" altogether because "the child" is assumed to be male, in the research from which Kohlberg derives his theory, females simply do not exit. Kohlbert's (1958, 1981) six stages that describe the development of moral judgment from childhood to adulthood are based empirically on a study of eighty-four boys whose development Kohlberg has followed for a period of over twenty years. Although Kohlberg claims universality for his stage sequence, those groups not included in his original sample rarely reach his higher stages (Edwards, 1975; Holstein, 1976; Simpson, 1974). Prominent among those who thus appear to be deficient in moral development when measured by Kohlberg's scale are women, whose judgments seem to exemplify the third stage of his six-stage sequence. At this stage morality is conceived in interpersonal terms and goodness is equated with helping and pleasing others. This conception of goodness is considered by Kohlberg and Kramer (1969) to be functional in the lives of mature women insofar as their lives take place in the home. Kohlberg and Kramer imply that only if women enter the traditional arena of male activity will they recognize the inadequacy of this moral perspective and progress like men toward higher stages where relationships are subordinated to rules (stage four) and rules to universal principles of justice (stages five and six).

Yet herein lies a paradox, for the very traits that traditionally have defined the "goodness" of women, their care for and sensitivity to the needs of others, are those that mark them as deficient in moral development. In this version of moral development, however, the conception of maturity is derived from the study of men's lives and reflects the importance of individuation in their development. Piaget (1970), challenging the common impression that a developmental theory is built like a pyramid from its base in infancy, points out that a conception of development instead hangs from its vertex of maturity, the point toward which progress is traced. Thus, a change in the definition of maturity does not simply alter the description of the highest stage but recasts the understanding of development, changing the entire account.

When one begins with the study of women and derives developmental constructs from their lives, the outline of a moral conception different from that described by Freud, Piaget, or Kohlberg begins to emerge and informs a different description of development. In this conception, the moral problem arises from conflicting responsibilities rather than from competing rights and requires for its resolution a mode of thinking that is contextual and narrative rather than formal and abstract. This conception of morality as concerned with the activity of care centers moral development around the understanding of responsibility and relationships, just as the conception of morality as fairness ties moral development to the understanding of rights and rules....

Thus it becomes clear why a morality of rights and noninterference may appear frightening to women in its potential justification of indifference and unconcern. At the same time, it becomes clear why, from a male perspective, a morality of responsibility appears inconclusive and diffuse, given its insistent contextual relativism. Women's moral judgments thus elucidate the pattern observed in the description of the developmental differences between the sexes, but they also provide an alternative conception of maturity by which these differences can be assessed and their implications traced. The psychology of women that has consistently been described as distinctive in its greater orientation toward relationships and interdependence implies a more contextual mode of judgment and a different moral understanding. Given the differences in women's conceptions of self and morality, women bring to the life cycle a different point of view and order human experience in terms of different priorities.

The myth of Demeter and Persephone . . . was associated with the Eleusinian Mysteries celebrated in ancient Greece for over two thousand years....

Persephone, the daughter of Demeter, while playing in a meadow with her girlfriends, sees a beautiful narcissus which she runs to pick. As she does so, the earth opens and she is snatched away by Hades, who takes her to his underworld kingdom. Demeter, goddess of the earth, so mourns the loss of her daughter that she refuses to allow anything to grow. The crops that sustain life on earth shrivel up, killing men and animals alike, until Zeus takes pity on man's suffering and persuades his brother to return Persephone to her mother. But before she leaves, Persephone eats some pomegranate seeds, which ensures that she will spend part of every year with Hades in the underworld.

The elusive mystery of women's development lies in its recognition of the continuing importance of attachment in the human live cycle. Woman's place in man's life cycle is to protect this recognition while the developmental litany intones the celebration of separation, autonomy, individuation, and natural rights. The myth of Persephone speaks directly to the distortion in this view by reminding us that narcissism leads to death, that the fertility of the earth is in some mysterious way tied to the continuation of the mother-daughter relationship, and that the life cycle itself arises from an alternation between the world of women and that of men. Only when life-cycle theorists divide their attention and begin to live with women as they have lived with men will their vision encompass the experience of both sexes and their theories become correspondingly more fertile.

Carol Gilligan

CHAPTER 2 Cross-Cultural, Religious, Spiritual, and Ethical Foundations

2.1 KRISHNA

The Bhagavad Gita

Krishna is considered a manifestation of God—the incarnation, or avatar, of the god Vishnu. Krishna is likely a historical figure of approximately 1000 B.C.E. and is revered by followers of the Hindu religion. There are approximately 700 million Hindus in Southeast Asia but also approximately 1 million Hindus each in Europe, North America, South America, and Africa.

The Bhagavad Gita, or the Blessed Song, is a poem in Sanskrit that describes a conversation that Krishna has with Arjuna, who is a mortal prince. The Bhagavad Gita was included in a much larger (100,000 stanzas!) epic poem, the *Mahabharata,* in about the second century C.E. The Bhagavad Gita is taught in most Hindu-influenced schools and has a very powerful effect on the formation of the worldview and psychology of Hindu youth. The following selection is taken from the translation by Juan Mascaró and comprises all of chapter 6 of the Bhagavad Gita.

Key Concept: the Yogi

1. He who works not for an earthly reward, but does the work to be done, he is a Sanyasi,* he is a Yogi**: not he who lights not the sacred fire or offers not the holy sacrifice.

2. Because the Sanyasi of renunciation is also the Yogi of holy work; and no man can be a Yogi who surrenders not his earthly will.

3. When the sage climbs the heights of Yoga,† he follows the path of work; but when he reaches the heights of Yoga, he is in the land of peace.

4. And he reaches the heights of Yoga when he surrenders his earthly will: when he is not bound by the work of his senses, and he is not bound by his earthly works.

5. Arise therefore! And with the help of thy Spirit lift up thy soul: allow not thy soul to fall. For thy soul can be thy friend, and thy soul can be thine enemy.

6. The soul of man is his friend when by the Spirit he has conquered his soul; but when a man is not lord of his soul then this becomes his own enemy.

7. When his soul is in peace he is in peace, and then his soul is in God. In cold or in heat, in pleasure or pain, in glory or disgrace, he is ever in Him.

8. When, happy with vision and wisdom, he is master of his own inner life, his soul sublime set on high, then he is called a Yogi in harmony. To him gold or stones or earth are one.

9. He has risen on the heights of his soul. And in peace he beholds relatives, companions and friends, those impartial or indifferent or who hate him: he sees them all with the same inner peace.

10. Day after day, let the Yogi practise the harmony of soul: in a secret place, in deep solitude, master of his mind, hoping for nothing, desiring nothing.

11. Let him find a place that is pure and a seat that is restful, neither too high nor too low, with sacred grass and a skin and a cloth thereon.

12. On that seat let him rest and practise Yoga for the purification of the soul: with the life of his body and mind in peace; his soul in silence before the One.

13. With upright body, head, and neck, which rest still and move not; with inner gaze which is not restless, but rests still between the eye-brows;

14. With soul in peace, and all fear gone, and strong in the vow of holiness, let him rest with mind in harmony, his soul on me, his God supreme.

---

* [A Sanyasi, as Paramahansa Yogananda explains, is a "renunciant." Specifically, it can mean a monk or nun who has taken his or her final vows; more generally, it can mean the external practice of desireless and detachment from the material world.—Eds.]

** [A Yogi, as explained by Paramahansa Yogananda, is a truth-seeker who primarily concentrates on the meditative path to God.—Eds.]

† [Yoga are the divine meditative actions. Hatha yoga, which is popular in the West and involves a series of healthy postures, is only one aspect of Yoga.—Eds.]

52

*Chapter 2
Cross-Cultural,
Religious,
Spiritual, and
Ethical
Foundations*

15. The Yogi who, lord of his mind, ever prays in this harmony of soul, attains the peace of Nirvana,* the peace supreme that is in me.

16. Yoga is a harmony. Not for him who eats too much, or for him who eats too little; not for him who sleeps too little, or for him who sleeps too much.

17. A harmony in eating and resting, in sleeping and keeping awake: a perfection in whatever one does. This is the Yoga that gives peace from all pain.

18. When the mind of the Yogi is in harmony and finds rest in the Spirit within, all restless desires gone, then he is a Yukta,** one in God.

19. Then his soul is a lamp whose light is steady, for it burns in a shelter where no winds come.

20. When the mind is resting in the stillness of the prayer of Yoga, and by the grace of the Spirit sees the Spirit and therein finds fulfilment;

21. Then the seeker knows the joy of Eternity: a vision seen by reason far beyond what senses can see. He abides therein and moves not from Truth.

22. He has found joy and Truth, a vision for him supreme. He is therein steady: the greatest pain moves him not.

23. In this union of Yoga there is liberty: a deliverance from the oppression of pain. This Yoga must be followed with faith, with a strong and courageous heart.

24. When all desires are in peace and the mind, withdrawing within, gathers the multitudinous straying senses into the harmony of recollection,

25. Then, with reason armed with resolution, let the seeker quietly lead the mind into the Spirit, and let all his thoughts be silence.

26. And whenever the mind unsteady and restless strays away from the Spirit, let him ever and for ever lead it again to the Spirit.

27. Thus joy supreme comes to the Yogi whose heart is still, whose passions are peace, who is pure from sin, who is one with Brahman,† with God.

28. The Yogi who pure from sin ever prays in this harmony of soul soon feels the joy of Eternity, the infinite joy of union with God.

29. He sees himself in the heart of all beings and he sees all beings in his heart. This is the vision of the Yogi of harmony, a vision which is ever one.

30. And when he sees me in all and he sees all in me, then I never leave him and he never leaves me.

31. He who in this oneness of love, loves me in whatever he sees, wherever this man may live, in truth this man lives in me.

32. And he is the greatest Yogi he whose vision is ever one: when the pleasure and pain of others is his own pleasure and pain.

* [Nirvana is the state of complete extinction of self and causes the cycle of reincarnation to end.—Eds.]

** [A Yukta is one who is united with God, who is one with God.—Eds.]

† [Brahman is one of the names of God; it may be translated "Spirit" or "Holy Spirit."—Eds.]

33. Thou hast told me of a Yoga of constant oneness, O Krishna, of a communion which is ever one. But, Krishna, the mind is inconstant: in its restlessness I cannot find rest.
34. The mind is restless, Krishna, impetuous, self-willed, hard to train: to master the mind seems as difficult as to master the mighty winds.

Krishna

35. The mind is indeed restless, Arjuna: it is indeed hard to train. But by constant practice and by freedom from passions the mind in truth can be trained.
36. When the mind is not in harmony, this divine communion is hard to attain; but the man whose mind is in harmony attains it, if he knows and if he strives.

Arjuna

37. And if a man strives and fails and reaches not the End of Yoga, for his mind is not in Yoga; and yet this man has faith, what is his end, O Krishna?
38. Far from earth and far from heaven, wandering in the pathless winds, does he vanish like a cloud into air, not having found the path of God?
39. Be a light in my darkness, Krishna: be thou unto me a Light. Who can solve this doubt but thee?

Krishna

40. Neither in this world nor in the world to come does ever this man pass away; for the man who does the good, my son, never treads the path of death.
41. He dwells for innumerable years in the heaven of those who did good; and then this man who failed in Yoga is born again in the house of the good and the great.
42. He may even be born in a family of Yogis, where the wisdom of Yoga shines; but to be born in such a family is a rare event in this world.
43. And he begins his new life with the wisdom of a former life; and he begins to strive again, ever onwards towards perfection.
44. Because his former yearning and struggle irresistibly carries him onwards, and even he who merely yearns for Yoga goes beyond the words of books.
45. And thus the Yogi ever-striving, and with soul pure from sin, attains perfection through many lives and reaches the End Supreme.
46. Be thou a Yogi, Arjuna! Because the Yogi goes beyond those who only follow the path of the austere, or of wisdom, or of work.
47. And the greatest of all Yogis is he who with all his soul has faith, and he who with all his soul loves me.

Exodus and The Proverbs

Moses lived in the thirteenth century B.C.E. He was born in Egypt, and his Hebrew mother saved him from an Egyptian slaughter of male children by hiding him near a stream. Moses was found by Pharaoh's daughter and raised as a prince. He led an uprising of the Jews, who were slaves to the Egyptians, and helped them escape to Canaan (modern-day Israel). On the way he received revelation from God, including the Ten Commandments, which are excerpted here from his book Exodus. Exodus is one of the five books of the Torah, the main scripture of Judaism, and is among the first five books of the Bible in what Christians call the Old Testament. The influence of the Ten Commandments on the moral psychology and sociology of all Western civilization has been tremendous.

Solomon was king of Israel (ca. 961–922 B.C.E.) and was born son of David, also a famous king and prophet. Solomon's wealth and wisdom are legendary. He rebuilt a great temple in Jerusalem and forged political alliances with Egypt and Phoenicia. Solomon is credited with writing both the Song of Solomon and The Proverbs, a selection of which is also excerpted here. In it Solomon offers moral instruction to his son, a practice that has become a psychological model of teaching for Jewish teachers for thousands of years.

There are over 20 million Jews in the world, with 10 million in the United States, close to 2 million in Europe, and several million in both Russia and South Asia. The effects of the Torah and other books of the Bible on the psychology and worldview of the Jewish people cannot be overestimated; instruction from these texts has been the centerpiece of Jewish schools for 3,000 years, and the texts are still taught in the modern Yeshivas, or Jewish academies.

Key Concept: moral law and moral instruction

EXODUS

20

1. And God spake all these words, saying,
2. I *am* the LORD thy God, which have brought thee out of the land of Egypt, out of the house of bondage.
3. Thou shalt have no other gods before me.

4. Thou shalt not make unto thee any graven image, or any likeness of *any thing* that *is* in heaven above, or that *is* in the earth beneath, or that *is* in the water under the earth.

5. Thou shalt not bow down thyself to them, nor serve them: for I the LORD thy God *am* a jealous God, visiting the iniquity of the fathers upon the children unto the third and fourth *generation* of them that hate me;

6. And shewing mercy unto thousands of them that love me, and keep my commandments.

7. Thou shalt not take the name of the LORD thy God in vain; for the LORD will not hold him guiltless that taketh his name in vain.

8. Remember the sabbath day, to keep it holy.

9. Six days shalt thou labour, and do all thy work:

10. But the seventh day *is* the sabbath of the LORD thy God: *in it* thou shalt not do any work, thou, nor thy son, nor thy daughter, thy manservant, nor thy maidservant, nor thy cattle, nor thy stranger that *is* within thy gates:

11. For *in* six days the LORD made heaven and earth, the sea, and all that in them *is*, and rested the seventh day: wherefore the LORD blessed the sabbath day, and hallowed it.

12. ¶ Honour thy father and thy mother: that thy days may be long upon the land which the LORD thy God giveth thee.

13. Thou shalt not kill.

14. Thou shalt not commit adultery.

15. Thou shalt not steal.

16. Thou shalt not bear false witness against thy neighbour.

17. Thou shalt not covet thy neighbour's house, thou shalt not covet thy neighbour's wife, nor his manservant, nor his maidservant, nor his ox, nor his ass, nor any thing that *is* thy neighbour's.

18. ¶ And all the people saw the thunderings, and the lightnings, and the noise of the trumpet, and the mountain smoking: and when the people saw *it*, they removed, and stood afar off.

19. And they said unto Moses, Speak thou with us, and we will hear: but let not God speak with us, lest we die.

20. And Moses said unto the people, Fear not: for God is come to prove you, and that his fear may be before your faces, that ye sin not.

21. And the people stood afar off, and Moses drew near unto the thick darkness where God *was*.

22. ¶ And the LORD said unto Moses, Thus thou shalt say unto the children of Israel, Ye have seen that I have talked with you from heaven.

23. Ye shall not make with me gods of silver, neither shall ye make unto you gods of gold.

24. ¶ An altar of earth thou shalt make unto me, and shalt sacrifice thereon thy burnt offerings, and thy peace offerings, thy sheep, and thine oxen: in all places where I record my name I will come unto thee, and I will bless thee.

25. And if thou wilt make me an altar of stone, thou shalt not build it of hewn stone: for if thou lift up thy tool upon it, thou hast polluted it.

26. Neither shalt thou go up by steps unto mine altar, that thy nakedness be not discovered thereon....

THE PROVERBS

1

1. The proverbs of Solomon the son of David, king of Israel;
2. To know wisdom and instruction; to perceive the words of understanding;
3. To receive the instruction of wisdom, justice, and judgment, and equity;
4. To give subtilty to the simple, to the young man knowledge and discretion.
5. A wise *man* will hear, and will increase learning; and a man of understanding shall attain unto wise counsels:
6. To understand a proverb, and the interpretation; the words of the wise, and their dark sayings.
7. ¶ The fear of the LORD *is* the beginning of knowledge: *but* fools despise wisdom and instruction.
8. My son, hear the instruction of thy father, and forsake not the law of thy mother:
9. For they *shall be* an ornament of grace unto thy head, and chains about thy neck.
10. ¶ My son, if sinners entice thee, consent thou not.
11. If they say, Come with us, let us lay wait for blood, let us lurk privily for the innocent without cause:
12. Let us swallow them up alive as the grave; and whole, as those that go down into the pit:
13. We shall find all precious substance, we shall fill our houses with spoil:
14. Cast in thy lot among us; let us all have one purse:
15. My son, walk not thou in the way with them; refrain thy foot from their path:
16. For their feet run to evil, and make haste to shed blood.
17. Surely in vain the net is spread in the sight of any bird.
18. And they lay wait for their *own* blood; they lurk privily for their *own* lives.
19. So *are* the ways of every one that is greedy of gain; *which* taketh away the life of the owners thereof.
20. ¶ Wisdom crieth without; she uttereth her voice in the streets:
21. She crieth in the chief place of concourse, in the openings of the gates: in the city she uttereth her words, *saying,*
22. How long, ye simple ones, will ye love simplicity? and the scorners delight in their scorning, and fools hate knowledge?
23. Turn you at my reproof: behold, I will pour out my spirit unto you, I will make known my words unto you.

24. ¶ Because I have called, and ye refused; I have stretched out my hand, and no man regarded;
25. But ye have set at nought all my counsel, and would none of my reproof:
26. I also will laugh at your calamity; I will mock when your fear cometh;
27. When your fear cometh as desolation, and your destruction cometh as a whirlwind; when distress and anguish cometh upon you.
28. Then shall they call upon me, but I will not answer; they shall seek me early, but they shall not find me:
29. For that they hated knowledge, and did not choose the fear of the LORD:
30. They would none of my counsel: they despised all my reproof.
31. Therefore shall they eat of the fruit of their own way, and be filled with their own devices.
32. For the turning away of the simple shall slay them, and the prosperity of fools shall destroy them.
33. But whoso hearkeneth unto me shall dwell safely, and shall be quiet from fear of evil.

The Great Learning

Confucius was born in 551 B.C.E. His family name was K'ung and his personal name Ch'iu. *Fu-tzu* is Chinese for "Master," and "Confucius" is a latinized form of K'ung Fu-tzu, or "Master K'ung." The teachings of Confucius were often directed toward the practical side of learning and educational psychology. As historians of China say, if one were to characterize the Chinese way of life for the last two-and-a-half millennia, one would say it was "Confucian." Although the Maoist revolution attempted to replace Confucius's teachings with Marxist beliefs, it was only partially successful. There is now a resurgence of Confucian studies occurring in the Academies of China, as the influence of Mao wanes. There are about 1.2 billion people in China, and hundreds of millions of Chinese distributed throughout many other countries. To the degree that educational psychology is involved in the designing of curriculum and instruction, Confucius must be considered one of the most influential educational psychologists in world history.

The following selection comes from the classic essay *The Great Learning* which is one of four Confucian works included in a text called *The Four Books*. *The Four Books* is considered the greatest classic in all Chinese history; it was the basis of the civil service examinations in China for six centuries (A.D. 1313–1905). The Chinese title for *The Great Learning* is *Ta hsüeh,* and it may be translated as "adult development" or "higher education." At first glance a Westerner might say that this selection looks like political science, not a study of human development or educational psychology. As cross-cultural psychologists point out, however, the Chinese culture is a "collectivist" culture. The Chinese tend to look at the individual in a different context than Westerners do. The Chinese would not want to distinctly separate individual development from development of the society, as is common in the West.

The following selection comes from the textual arrangement and commentary of Chu Hsi (1130–1200 C.E.). He was one of the greatest Confucian philosophers, but Buddhism was also a major influence on him, as it was on all of China. It is unclear who actually wrote *The Great Learning,* although there is consensus among scholars that it is clearly a "Confucian" work. Some attribute its writing to Tseng Tzu, one of Confucius's pupils, or to Tzu Ssu, his grandson.

Key Concept: the way of the great learning

The Great Learning is originally ch. 42 of the Li chi *(Book of Rites). Not much attention was paid to it until the time of Ssu-ma Kuang (1019–1086), who wrote a commentary on it, treating it as a separate work for the first time. This commentary is now lost. Ch'eng Hao (Ch'eng Ming-tao, 1032–1085) and his younger brother Ch'eng I (Ch'eng I-ch'uan, 1033–1107) each rearranged the text. Chu Hsi did the same and, moreover, added a "supplement." He further divided the work into one "text" and ten "chapters of commentary," and contended that the former was Confucius' own words handed down by his pupil Tseng Tzu (505–c. 436 B.C.) and that the latter were the views of Tseng Tzu recorded by his pupils. There is no evidence for this contention. Recent scholars, equally without evidence, have dated the work as late as around 200 B.C. Regardless of its date and authorship, which has also been attributed to Confucius' grandson Tzu-ssu (492–431 B.C.), it was Chu Hsi who made it important in the last 800 years. He grouped it with the* Analects, *the* Book of Mencius, *and the* Doctrine of the Mean *as the "Four Books" and wrote commentaries on them. Since then they were honored as Classics, and from 1313 till 1905 they were the basis of civil service examinations. Thus they replaced the other Classics in importance and influence.*

The Way of learning to be great (or adult education) consists in manifesting the clear character, loving the people, and abiding *(chih)* in the highest good.

Only after knowing what to abide in can one be calm. Only after having been calm can one be tranquil. Only after having achieved tranquility can one have peaceful repose. Only after having peaceful repose can one begin to deliberate. Only after deliberation can the end be attained. Things have their roots and branches. Affairs have their beginnings and their ends. To know what is first and what is last will lead one near the Way.

The ancients who wished to manifest their clear character to the world would first bring order to their states. Those who wished to bring order to their states would first regulate their families. Those who wished to regulate their families would first cultivate their personal lives. Those who wished to cultivate their personal lives would first rectify their minds. Those who wished to make their wills sincere would first extend their knowledge. The extension of knowledge consists in the investigation of things. When things are investigated, knowledge is extended; when knowledge is extended, the will becomes sincere; when the will is sincere, the mind is rectified; when the mind is rectified, the personal life is cultivated; when the personal life is cultivated, the family will be regulated; when the family is regulated, the state will be in order; and when the state is in order, there will be peace throughout the world. From the Son of Heaven down to the common people, all must regard cultivation of the personal life as the root or foundation. There is never a case when the root is in disorder and yet the branches are in order. There has never been a case when what is treated with great importance becomes a matter of slight importance or what is treated with slight importance becomes a matter of great importance.

60

Chapter 2
Cross-Cultural,
Religious,
Spiritual, and
Ethical
Foundations

Chu Hsi's Remark.   The above is the text in one chapter. It is the words of Confucius, handed down by Tseng Tzu. The ten chapters of commentary which follow are the views of Tseng Tzu and were recorded by his pupils. In the traditional version there have been some mistakes in its arrangement. Now follows the new version fixed by Master Ch'eng I, and in addition, having examined the contents of the text, I (Chu Hsi) have rearranged it as follows:

CHAPTERS OF COMMENTARY

1. In the "Announcement of K'ang" it is said, "He was able to manifest his clear character." In the "T'ai-chia" it is said, "He contemplated the clear Mandates of Heaven." In the "Canon of Yao" it is said, "He was able to manifest his lofty character." These all show that the ancient kings manifested their own character.

Chu Hsi's Remark.   The above first chapter of commentary explains manifesting the clear character.

2. The inscription on the bath-tub of King T'ang read, "If you can renovate yourself one day, then you can do so every day, and keep doing so day after day." In the "Announcement of K'ang," it is said, "Arouse people to become new." The *Book of Odes* says, "Although Chou is an ancient state, the mandate it has received from Heaven is new." Therefore, the superior man tries at all times to do his utmost [in renovating himself and others].

Chu Hsi's Remark.   The above second chapter of commentary explains the renovating of the people.

3. The *Book of Odes* says, "The imperial domain of a thousand *li* is where the people stay *(chih)*." The *Book of Odes* also says, "The twittering yellow bird rests *(chih)* on a thickly wooded mount." Confucius said, "When the bird rests, it knows where to rest. Should a human being be unequal to a bird?" The *Book of Odes* says, "How profound was King Wen! How he maintained his brilliant virtue without interruption and regarded with reverence that which he abided *(chih)*." As a ruler, he abided in humanity. As a minister, he abided in reverence. As a son, he abided in filial piety. As a father, he abided in deep love. And in dealing with the people of the country, he abided in faithfulness.

The *Book of Odes* says, "Look at that curve in the Ch'i River. How luxuriant and green are the bamboo trees there! Here is our elegant and accomplished prince. [His personal life is cultivated] as a thing is cut and filed and as a thing is carved and polished. How grave and dignified! How majestic and distinguished! Here is our elegant and accomplished prince. We can never forget him!" "As a thing is cut and filed" refers to the pursuit of learning. "As a thing is carved and polished" refers to self-cultivation. "How grave and how dignified" indicates precaution. "How majestic and distinguished" expresses awe-inspiring appearance. "Here is our elegant and accomplished prince. We can never forget him" means that the people cannot forget his eminent character and perfect virtue. The *Book of Odes* says, "Ah! the ancient kings are not forgotten." [Future] rulers deemed worthy what they deemed worthy and loved what they loved, while the common people enjoyed what they enjoyed and benefited from their beneficial arrangements. That was why they are not forgotten even after they passed away.

Chu Hsi's Remark. The above third chapter of commentary explains abiding in the highest good.

4. Confucius said, "In hearing litigations, I am as good as anyone. What is necessary is to enable people not to have litigations at all." Those who would not tell the truth will not dare to finish their words, and a great awe would be struck into people's minds. This is called knowing the root.

Chu Hsi's Remark. The above fourth chapter of commentary explains the root and the branches.

5. This is called knowing the root. This is called the perfecting of knowledge.

Chu Hsi's Remark. The above fifth chapter of commentary explains the meaning of the investigation of things and the extension of knowledge, which is now lost. I have ventured to take the view of Master Ch'eng I and supplement it as follows: The meaning of the expression "The perfection of knowledge depends on the investigation of things (*ko-wu*)" is this: If we wish to extend our knowledge to the utmost, we must investigate the principles of all things we come into contact with, for the intelligent mind of man is certainly formed to know, and there is not a single thing in which its principles do not inhere. It is only because all principles are not investigated that man's knowledge is incomplete. For this reason, the first step in the education of the adult is to instruct the learner, in regard to all things in the world, to proceed from what knowledge he has of their principles, and investigate further until he reaches the limit. After exerting himself in this way for a long time, he will one day achieve a wide and far-reaching penetration. Then the qualities of all things, whether internal or external, the refined or the coarse, will all be apprehended, and the mind, in its total substance and great functioning, will be perfectly intelligent. This is called the investigation of things. This is called the perfection of knowledge.

6. What is meant by "Making the will sincere" is allowing no self-deception, as when we hate a bad smell or love a beautiful color. This is called satisfying oneself. Therefore the superior man will always be watchful over himself when alone. When the inferior man is alone and leisurely, there is no limit to which he does not go in his evil deeds. Only when he sees a superior man does he then try to disguise himself, concealing the evil and showing off the good in him. But what is the use? For other people see him as if they see his very heart. This

62

*Chapter 2
Cross-Cultural,
Religious,
Spiritual, and
Ethical
Foundations*

is what is meant by saying that what is true in a man's heart will be shown in his outward appearance. Therefore the superior man will always be watchful over himself when alone. Tseng Tzu said, "What ten eyes are beholding and what ten hands are pointing to—isn't it frightening?" Wealth makes a house shining and virtue makes a person shining. When one's mind is broad and his heart generous, his body becomes big and is at ease. Therefore the superior man always makes his will sincere.

Chu Hsi's Remark.   The above sixth chapter of commentary explains the sincerity of the will.

7. What is meant by saying that cultivation of the personal life depends on the rectification of the mind is that when one is affected by wrath to any extent, his mind will not be correct. When one is affected by fear to any extent, his mind will not be correct. When he is affected by fondness to any extent, his mind will not be correct. When he is affected by worries and anxieties, his mind will not be correct. When the mind is not present, we look but do not see, listen but do not hear, and eat but do not know the taste of the food. This is what is meant by saying that the cultivation of the personal life depends on the rectification of the mind.

Chu Hsi's Remark.   The above seventh chapter of commentary explains the rectification of the mind in order to cultivate the personal life.

8. What is meant by saying that the regulation of the family depends on the cultivation of the personal life is this: Men are partial toward those for whom they have affection and whom they love, partial toward those whom they despise and dislike, partial toward those whom they fear and revere, partial toward those whom they pity and for whom they have compassion, and partial toward those whom they do not respect. Therefore there are few people in the world who know what is bad in those whom they love and what is good in those whom they dislike. Hence it is said, "People do not know the faults of their sons and do not know (are not satisfied with) the bigness of their seedlings." This is what is meant by saying that if the personal life is not cultivated, one cannot regulate his family.

Chu Hsi's Remark.   The above eighth chapter of commentary explains the cultivation of the personal life in order to regulate the family.

9. What is meant by saying that in order to govern the state it is necessary first to regulate the family is this: There is no one who cannot teach his own family and yet can teach others. Therefore the superior man (ruler) without going beyond his family, can bring education into completion in the whole state. Filial piety is that with which one serves his ruler. Brotherly respect is that with which one serves his elders, and deep love is that with which one treats the multitude. The "Announcement of K'ang" says, "Act as if you were watching over

an infant." If a mother sincerely and earnestly looks for what the infant wants, she may not hit the mark but she will not be far from it. A young woman has never had to learn about nursing a baby before she marries. When the individual families have become humane, then the whole country will be aroused toward humanity. When the individual families have been compliant, then the whole country will be aroused toward compliance. When one man is greedy or avaricious, the whole country will be plunged into disorder. Such is the subtle, incipient activating force of things. This is what is meant by saying that a single word may spoil an affair and a single man may put the country in order. (Sage-emperors) Yao and Shun led the world with humanity and the people followed them. (Wicked kings) Chieh and Chou led the world with violence and the people followed them. The people did not follow their orders which were contrary to what they themselves liked. Therefore the superior man must have the good qualities in himself before he may require them in other people. He must not have the bad qualities in himself before he may require others not to have them. There has never been a man who does not cherish altruism *(shu)* in himself and yet can teach other people. Therefore the order of the state depends on the regulation of the family.

The *Book of Odes* says, "How young and pretty is that peach tree! How luxuriant is its foliage! This girl is going to her husband's house. She will rightly order her household." Only when one has rightly ordered his household can he teach the people of the country. The *Book of Odes* says, "They were correct and good in their elder brothers. They were correct and good to their younger brothers." Only when one is good and correct to one's elder and younger brothers can one teach the people of the country. The *Book of Odes* says, "His deportment is all correct, and he rectifies all the people of the country." Because he served as a worthy example as a father, son, elder brother, and younger brother, therefore the people imitated him. This is what is meant by saying that the order of the state depends on the regulation of the family.

Chu Hsi's Remark. The above ninth chapter of commentary explains regulating the family to bring order to the state.

10. What is meant by saying that peace of the world depends on the order of the state is this: When the ruler treats the elders with respect, then the people will be aroused toward filial piety. When the ruler treats the aged with respect, then the people will be aroused toward brotherly respect. When the ruler treats compassionately the young and the helpless, then the common people will not follow the opposite course. Therefore the ruler has a principle with which, as with a measuring square, he may regulate his conduct.

What a man dislikes in his superiors, let him not show it in dealing with his inferiors; what he dislikes in those in front of him, let him not show it in preceding those who are behind; what he dislikes in those behind him, let him not show it in following those in front of him; what he dislikes in those on the right, let him not apply it to those on the left; and what he dislikes in those on the left, let him not apply it to those on the right. This is the principle of the measuring square.

64

*Chapter 2
Cross-Cultural,
Religious,
Spiritual, and
Ethical
Foundations*

The *Book of Odes* says, "How much the people rejoice in their prince, a parent of the people!" He likes what the people like and dislikes what the people dislike. This is what is meant by being a parent of the people. The *Book of Odes* says, "Lofty is the Southern Mountain! How massive are the rocks! How majestic is the Grand Tutor Yin (of Chou)! The people all look up to you!" Thus rulers of states should never by careless. If they deviate from the correct path, they will be cast away by the world. The Book of Odes] says, "Before the rulers of the Yin (Shang) dynasty lost the support of the people, they could have been counterparts of Heaven. Take warning from the Yin dynasty. It is not easy to keep the Mandate of Heaven." This shows that by having the support of the people, they have their countries, and by losing the support of the people, lose their countries. Therefore the ruler will first be watchful over his own virtue. If he has virtue, he will have the people with him. If he has the people with him, he will have the territory. If he has the territory, he will have wealth. And if he has wealth, he will have its use. Virtue is the root, while wealth is the branch. If he regards the root as external (or secondary) and the branch as internal (or essential), he will compete with the people in robbing each other. Therefore when wealth is gathered in the ruler's hand, the people will scatter away from him; and when wealth is scAttered [among the people], they will gather round him. Therefore if the ruler's words are uttered in an evil way, the same words will be uttered back to him in an evil way; and if he acquires wealth in an evil way, it will be taken away from him in an evil way. In the "Announcement of K'ang" it is said, "The Mandate of Heaven is not fixed or unchangeable." The good ruler gets it and the bad ruler loses it. In the *Book of Ch'u* it is said, "The State of Ch'u does not consider anything as treasure; it considers only good [men] as treasure. Uncle Fan (maternal uncle to a prince of Chin in exile) said, 'Our exiled prince has no treasure; to be humane toward his parents in his only treasure.'" In the "Oath of Ch'in" it is said, "Let me have but one minister, sincere and single-minded, not pretending to other abilities, but broad and upright of mind, generous and tolerant toward others. When he sees that another person has a certain kind of ability, he is as happy as though he himself had it, and when he sees another man who is elegant and wise, he loves him in his heart as much as if he said so in so many words, thus showing that he can really tolerate others. Such a person can preserve my sons, and grandsons and the black-haired people (the common people). He may well be a great benefit to the country. But when a minister sees another person with a certain kind of ability, he is jealous and hates him, and when he sees another person who is elegant and wise, he blocks him so he cannot advance, thus showing that he really cannot tolerate others. Such a person cannot preserve my sons, grandsons, and the black-haired people. He is a danger to the country." It is only a man of humanity who can send away such a minister and banish him, driving him to live among the barbarian tribes and not allowing him to exist together with the rest of the people in the Middle Kingdom (China). This is what is meant by saying that it is only the man of humanity who can love or who can hate others. To see a worthy and not be able to raise him to office, or be able to raise him but not to be the first one to do so—that is negligence. To see bad men and not be able to remove them from office, or to be able to remove them but not to remove them as far away as possible—that is a mistake. To love what the people hate and to hate what the people love—that is to act contrary to human nature, and disaster will come to such a person. Thus we see that the ruler has a great principle to follow. He must attain it through loyalty and faithfulness and will surely lose it through pride and indulgence.

There is a great principle for the production of wealth. If there are many producers and few consumers, and if people who produce wealth do so quickly and those who spend it do so slowly, then wealth will always be sufficient. A man of humanity develops his personality by means of his wealth, while the inhumane person develops wealth at the sacrifice of his personality. There has never been a case of a ruler who loved humanity and whose people did not love righteousness. There has never been a case where the people loved righteousness and yet the affairs of the state have not been carried to completion. And there has never been a case where in such a state the wealth collected in the national treasury did not continue in the possession of the ruler.

The officer Meng-hsien said, "He who keeps a horse [one who has just become an official] and a carriage does not look after poultry and pigs. [The higher officials] who use ice [in their sacrifices] do not keep cattle and sheep. And the nobles who can keep a hundred carriages do not keep rapacious tax-gathering ministers under them. It is better to have a minister who robs the state treasury than to have such a tax-gathering minister. This is what is meant by saying that in a state financial profit is not considered real profit whereas righteousness is considered to be the real profit. He who heads a state or a family and is devoted to wealth and its use must have been under the influence of an inferior man. He may consider this man to be good, but when an inferior man is allowed to handle the country or family, disasters and injuries will come together. Though a good man may take his place, nothing can be done. This is what is meant by saying that in a state financial profit is not considered real profit whereas righteousness is considered the real profit.

Chu Hsi's Remark.   The above tenth chapter of commentary explains ordering the state to bring peace to the world. There are altogether ten commentary chapters. The first four generally discuss the principal topics and the basic import. The last six chapters discuss in detail the items and the required effort involved. Chapter five deals with the essence of the understanding of goodness and chapter six deals with the foundation of making the personal life sincere. These two chapters, especially, represent the immediate task, particularly for the beginning student. The reader should not neglect them because of their simplicity.

Luke and Matthew

Jesus Christ was born with the Hebrew name Yeshua bin Miriam to his mother Mary (Miriam) in about 4 B.C.E. in Bethlehem, Palestine. He began his teaching at about age 30, and he was martyred in 29 C.E. a few short years later. Jesus' instruction was very "psychological" both in its content and in his methodologies. He taught that the psyche—the soul—was eternal and of incomparable worth compared to the body. His use of parables as a teaching method is a powerful form of applied educational psychology. Christianity is the most widespread of religions, with 1.7 to 2 billion followers distributed throughout all countries. The teachings of Jesus have had a huge impact on the many Christian schools as well as the public and private schools throughout the Americas, Europe, Africa, Australia, and Asia.

The "educationally psychological" story, or parable, of the Prodigal Son is excerpted here from the Gospel of Luke, which was probably recorded by "Luke the physician," a companion of Paul, approximately 60 to 100 years after the crucifixion of Jesus. The Gospel of Matthew was recorded at approximately the same time and may have been compiled by the apostle Matthew. It contains Jesus' most famous teachings on love, as well as his most famous sermon, the Sermon on the Mount, both of which are excerpted here as well.

Key Concept: instruction in spiritual and moral development

LUKE

15

1. Then drew near unto him all the publicans and sinners for to hear him.
2. And the Pharisees and scribes murmured, saying, This man receiveth sinners, and eateth with them.
3. ¶ And he spake this parable unto them, saying,
4. What man of you, having an hundred sheep, if he lose one of them, doth not leave the ninety and nine in the wilderness, and go after that which is lost, until he find it?
5. And when he hath found *it*, he layeth *it* on his shoulders, rejoicing.
6. And when he cometh home, he calleth together *his* friends and neighbours, saying unto them, Rejoice with me; for I have found my sheep which was lost.

7. I say unto you, that likewise joy shall be in heaven over one sinner that repenteth, more than over ninety and nine just persons, which need no repentance.

8. ¶ Either what woman having ten pieces of silver, if she lose one piece, doth not light a candle, and sweep the house, and seek diligently till she find *it*?

9. And when she hath found *it,* she calleth *her* friends and *her* neighbours together, saying, Rejoice with me; for I have found the piece which I had lost.

10. Likewise, I say unto you, there is joy in the presence of the angels of God over one sinner that repenteth.

11. ¶ And he said, A certain man had two sons:

12. And the younger of them said to *his* father, Father, give me the portion of goods that falleth to *me.* And he divided unto them *his* living.

13. And not many days after the younger son gathered all together, and took his journey into a far country, and there wasted his substance with riotous living.

14. And when he had spent all, there arose a mighty famine in that land; and he began to be in want.

15. And he went and joined himself to a citizen of that country; and he sent him into his fields to feed swine.

16. And he would fain have filled his belly with the husks that the swine did eat: and no man gave unto him.

17. And when he came to himself, he said, How many hired servants of my father's have bread enough and to spare, and I perish with hunger!

18. I will arise and go to my father, and will say unto him, Father, I have sinned against heaven, and before thee,

19. And am no more worthy to be called thy son: make me as one of thy hired servants.

20. And he arose, and came to his father. But when he was yet a great way off, his father saw him, and had compassion, and ran, and fell on his neck, and kissed him.

21. And the son said unto him, Father, I have sinned against heaven, and in thy sight, and am no more worthy to be called thy son.

22. But the father said to his servants, Bring forth the best robe, and put it on him; and put a ring on his hand, and shoes on *his* feet:

23. And bring hither the fatted calf, and kill *it*; and let us eat, and be merry:

24. For this my son was dead, and is alive again; he was lost, and is found. And they began to be merry.

25. Now his elder son was in the field: and as he came and drew nigh to the house, he heard musick and dancing.

26. And he called one of the servants, and asked what these things meant.

27. And he said unto him, Thy brother is come; and thy father hath killed the fatted calf, because he hath received him safe and sound.

28. And he was angry, and would not go in: therefore came his father out, and intreated him.

68

*Chapter 2
Cross-Cultural,
Religious,
Spiritual, and
Ethical
Foundations*

29. And he answering said to *his* father, Lo, these many years do I serve thee, neither transgressed I at any time thy commandment: and yet thou never gavest me a kid, that I might make merry with my friends:
30. But as soon as this thy son was come, which hath devoured thy living with harlots, thou hast killed for him the fatted calf.
31. And he said unto him, Son, thou art ever with me, and all that I have is thine.
32. It was meet that we should make merry, and be glad: for this thy brother was dead, and is alive again; and was lost, and is found.

MATTHEW

5

1. And seeing the multitudes, he went up into a mountain: and when he was set, his disciples came unto him:
2. And he opened his mouth, and taught them, saying,
3. Blessed *are* the poor in spirit: for theirs is the kingdom of heaven.
4. Blessed *are* they that mourn: for they shall be comforted.
5. Blessed *are* the meek: for they shall inherit the earth.
6. Blessed *are* they which do hunger and thirst after righteousness: for they shall be filled.
7. Blessed *are* the merciful: for they shall obtain mercy.
8. Blessed *are* the pure in heart: for they shall see God.
9. Blessed *are* the peacemakers: for they shall be called the children of God.
10. Blessed *are* they which are persecuted for righteousness' sake: for theirs is the kingdom of heaven.
11. Blessed are ye, when *men* shall revile you, and persecute *you*, and shall say all manner of evil against you falsely, for my sake.
12. Rejoice, and be exceeding glad: for great *is* your reward in heaven: for so persecuted they the prophets which were before you.
13. ¶ Ye are the salt of the earth: but if the salt have lost his savour, wherewith shall it be salted? it is thenceforth good for nothing, but to be cast out, and to be trodden under foot of men.
14. Ye are the light of the world. A city that is set on an hill cannot be hid.
15. Neither do men light a candle, and put it under a bushel, but on a candlestick; and it giveth light unto all that are in the house.
16. Let your light so shine before men, that they may see your good works, and glorify your Father which is in heaven.
17. ¶ Think not that I am come to destroy the law, or the prophets: I am not come to destroy, but to fulfil.
18. For verily I say unto you, Till heaven and earth pass, one jot or one tittle shall in no wise pass from the law, till all be fulfilled.

19. Whosoever therefore shall break one of these least commandments, and shall teach men so, he shall be called the least in the kingdom of heaven: but whosoever shall do and teach *them,* the same shall be called great in the kingdom of heaven.

20. For I say unto you, That except your righteousness shall exceed the *righteousness* of the scribes and Pharisees, ye shall in no case enter into the kingdom of heaven.

21. ¶ Ye have heard that it was said of them of old time, Thou shalt not kill; and whosoever shall kill shall be in danger of the judgment:

22. But I say unto you, That whosoever is angry with his brother without a cause shall be in danger of the judgment: and whosoever shall say to his brother, Rā'-că, shall be in danger of the council: but whosoever shall say, Thou fool, shall be in danger of hell fire.

23. Therefore if thou bring thy gift to the altar, and there rememberest that thy brother hath ought against thee;

24. Leave there thy gift before the altar, and go thy way; first be reconciled to thy brother, and then come and offer thy gift.

25. Agree with thine adversary quickly, whiles thou art in the way with him; lest at any time the adversary deliver thee to the judge, and the judge deliver thee to the officer, and thou be cast into prison.

26. Verily I say unto thee, Thou shalt by no means come out thence, till thou hast paid the uttermost farthing.

27. ¶ Ye have heard that it was said by them of old time, Thou shalt not commit adultery:

28. But I say unto you, That whosoever looketh on a woman to lust after her hath committed adultery with her already in his heart.

29. And if thy right eye offend thee, pluck it out, and cast *it* from thee: for it is profitable for thee that one of thy members should perish, and not *that* thy whole body should be cast into hell.

30. And if thy right hand offend thee, cut it off, and cast *it* from thee: for it is profitable for thee that one of thy members should perish, and not *that* thy whole body should be cast into hell.

31. It hath been said, Whosoever shall put away his wife, let him give her a writing of divorcement:

32. But I say unto you, That whosoever shall put away his wife, saving for the cause of fornication, causeth her to commit adultery: and whosoever shall marry her that is divorced committeth adultery.

33. ¶ Again, ye have heard that it hath been said by them of old time, Thou shalt not forswear thyself, but shalt perform unto the Lord thine oaths:

34. But I say unto you, Swear not at all; neither by heaven; for it is God's throne:

35. Nor by the earth; for it is his footstool: neither by Jerusalem; for it is the city of the great King.

36. Neither shalt thou swear by thy head, because thou canst not make one hair white or black.

37. But let your communication be, Yea, yea; Nay, nay: for whatsoever is more than these cometh of evil.

Chapter 2
Cross-Cultural,
Religious,
Spiritual, and
Ethical
Foundations

38. ¶ Ye have heard that it hath been said, An eye for an eye, and a tooth for a tooth:
39. But I say unto you, That ye resist not evil: but whosoever shall smite thee on thy right cheek, turn to him the other also.
40. And if any man will sue thee at the law, and take away thy coat, let him have thy cloak also.
41. And whosoever shall compel thee to go a mile, go with him twain.
42. Give to him that asketh thee, and from him that would borrow of thee turn not thou away.
43. ¶ Ye have heard that it hath been said, Thou shalt love thy neighbour, and hate thine enemy.
44. But I say unto you, Love your enemies, bless them that curse you, do good to them that hate you, and pray for them which despitefully use you, and persecute you;
45. That ye may be the children of your Father which is in heaven: for he maketh his sun to rise on the evil and on the good, and sendeth rain on the just and on the unjust.
46. For if ye love them which love you, what reward have ye? do not even the publicans the same?
47. And if ye salute your brethren only, what do ye more *than others*? do not even the publicans so?
48. Be ye therefore perfect, even as your Father which is in heaven is perfect.

22

34. ¶ But when the Pharisees had heard that he had put the Săd'-dū-cees to silence, they were gathered together.
35. Then one of them, *which* was a lawyer, asked *him a question*, tempting him, and saying,
36. Master, which *is* the great commandment in the law?
37. Jesus said unto him, Thou shalt love the Lord thy God with all thy heart, and with all thy soul, and with all thy mind.
38. This is the first and great commandment.
39. And the second *is* like unto it, Thou shalt love thy neighbour as thyself.
40. On these two commandments hang all the law and the prophets.

2.5 MUHAMMAD

The Opening and The Counsel

Muhammad, whose name means "The Praised One," was born around 570 C.E. in the city of Mecca, Arabia. At the age of 25 he married Khadijah, who was a wealthy widow and who had been employing him as a trading agent for her caravans. At age 40 Muhammad received his first revelation of the Koran through the angel Gabriel. He began to preach to the Meccans that idol worship was wrong and that there was only one God, Allah. The Meccans' persecution of him caused him to leave for Medina with his followers. This emigration is called the "Hijrah," and the Islamic calendar dates from that time. Muhammad continued to reveal suras (chapters) of the Koran until his passing in 632 C.E.

The Koran has been the central focus of all elementary and secondary schools in Islamic countries. There are approximately 1 billion Muslims (some estimate more; for instance, there are at least 50 million Muslims in China, a fact that surprises most Westerners). There are over 3 million Muslims in North America. The name "Muslim" means a person who has surrendered to God and given complete submission to his will. The Koran has been the biggest influence in educational psychology in Islamic schools both in the curriculum and in methods of instruction. Muslim psychologists have extracted a stage theory of human development from the Koran: (1) nafs-i-ammarah (12:53, the primitive psyche, or psyche prone to evil); (2) nafs-i-lawwamah (75:2, the self-accusing psyche, the beginning of conscience in the psyche); (3) nafs-i-mulhamah (91:8, the inspired psyche, the mature and moral psyche); (4) nafs-i-mutma'innah (89:27, the psyche at peace); (5) nafs-i-raziah (89:27, the contented psyche, which has turned its will completely to God's will); and (6) nafs-i-marziyyah (89:27, the psyche approved of by God).

The following selection from the Koran consists of the first sura, "The Opening," and the 42d sura, "The Counsel."

Key Concept: submission of the psyche's (or soul's) will to God

71

THE OPENING

In the name of Allah, the Beneficent, the Merciful.

1.1 All praise is due to Allah, the Lord of the Worlds.
1.2 The Beneficent, the Merciful.
1.3 Master of the Day of Judgment.
1.4 Thee do we serve and Thee do we beseech for help.
1.5 Keep us on the right path.
1.6 The path of those upon whom Thou hast bestowed favors. Not (the path) of those upon whom Thy wrath is brought down, nor of those who go astray.

THE COUNSEL

In the name of Allah, the Beneficent, the Merciful.

42.1 Ha Mim.
42.2 Ain Sin Qaf.*
42.3 Thus does Allah, the Mighty, the Wise, reveal to you, and (thus He revealed) to those before you.
42.4 His is what is in the heavens and what is in the earth, and He is the High, the Great.
42.5 The heavens may almost rend asunder from above them and the angels sing the praise of their Lord and ask forgiveness for those on earth; now surely Allah is the Forgiving, the Merciful.
42.6 And (as for) those who take guardians besides Him, Allah watches over them, and you have not charge over them.
42.7 And thus have We revealed to you an Arabic Quran, that you may warn the mother city and those around it, and that you may give warning of the day of gathering together wherein is no doubt; a party shall be in the garden** and (another) party in the burning fire [hell].
42.8 And if Allah had pleased He would surely have made them a single community, but He makes whom He pleases enter into His mercy, and the unjust it is that shall have no guardian or helper.
42.9 Or have they taken guardians besides Him? But Allah is the Guardian, and He gives life to the dead, and He has power over all things.
42.10 And in whatever thing you disagree, the judgment thereof is (in) Allah's (hand); that is Allah, my Lord, on Him do I rely and to Him do I turn time after time.

* [Verses 1 and 2 comprise five disconnected letters from the Arabic alphabet. Many suras of the Koran start in a similar way, and there is no widespread agreement among Muslims as to what it symbolizes.—Eds.]

** [The garden is paradise, or Heaven.—Eds.]

42.11 The Originator of the heavens and the earth; He made mates for you from among yourselves, and mates of the cattle too, multiplying you thereby; nothing like a likeness of Him; and He is the Hearing, the Seeing.

42.12 His are the treasures of the heavens and the earth; He makes ample and straitens the means of subsistence for whom He pleases; surely He is Cognizant of all things.

42.13 He has made plain to you of the religion what He enjoined upon Nuh [Noah] and that which We have revealed to you and that which We enjoined upon Ibrahim [Abraham] and Musa [Moses] and Isa [Jesus] that keep to obedience and be not divided therein; hard to the unbelievers is that which you call them to; Allah chooses for Himself whom He pleases, and guides to Himself him who turns (to Him), frequently.

42.14 And they did not become divided until after knowledge had come to them out of envy among themselves; and had not a word gone forth from your Lord till an appointed term, certainly judgment would have been given between them; and those who were made to inherit the Book after them are most surely in disquieting doubt concerning it.

42.15 To this then go on inviting, and go on steadfastly on the right way as you are commanded, and do not follow their low desires, and say: I believe in what Allah has revealed of the Book, and I am commanded to do justice between you: Allah is our Lord and your Lord; we shall have our deeds and you shall have your deeds; no plea need there be (now) between us and you: Allah will gather us together, and to Him is the return.

42.16 And (as for) those who dispute about Allah after that obedience has been rendered to Him, their plea is null with their Lord, and upon them is wrath, and for them is severe punishment.

42.17 Allah it is Who revealed the Book with truth, and the balance, and what shall make you know that haply the hour be nigh?

42.18 Those who do not believe in it would hasten it on, and those who believe are in fear from it, and they know that it is the truth. Now most surely those who dispute obstinately concerning the hour are in a great error.

42.19 Allah is Benignant to His servants; He gives sustenance to whom He pleases, and He is the Strong, the Mighty.

42.20 Whoever desires the gain of the hereafter, We will give him more of that again; and whoever desires—the gain of this world, We give him of it, and in the hereafter he has no portion.

42.21 Or have they associates who have prescribed for them any religion that Allah does not sanction? And were it not for the word of judgment, decision would have certainly been given between them; and surely the unjust shall have a painful punishment.

42.22 You will see the unjust fearing on account of what they have earned, and it must befall them; and those who believe and do good shall be in the meadows of the gardens; they shall have what they please with their Lord: that is the great grace.

74

*Chapter 2
Cross-Cultural,
Religious,
Spiritual, and
Ethical
Foundations*

42.23 That is of which Allah gives the good news to His servants, (to) those who believe and do good deeds. Say: I do not ask of you any reward for it but love for my near relatives; and whoever earns good, We give him more of good therein; surely Allah is Forgiving, Grateful.

42.24 Or do they say: He has forged a lie against Allah? But if Allah pleased, He would seal your heart; and Allah will blot out the falsehood and confirm the truth with His words; surely He is Cognizant of what is in the breasts.

42.25 And He it is Who accepts repentance from His servants and pardons the evil deeds and He knows what you do;

42.26 And He answers those who believe and do good deeds, and gives them more out of His grace; and (as for) the unbelievers, they shall have a severe punishment.

42.27 And if Allah should amplify the provision for His servants they would certainly revolt in the earth; but He sends it down according to a measure as He pleases; surely He is Aware of, Seeing, His servants.

42.28 And He it is Who sends down the rain after they have despaired, and He unfolds His mercy; and He is the Guardian, the Praised One.

42.29 And one of His signs is the creation of the heavens and the earth and what He has spread forth in both of them of living beings; and when He pleases He is all-powerful to gather them together.

42.30 And whatever affliction befalls you, it is on account of what your hands have wrought, and (yet) He pardons most (of your faults).

42.31 And you cannot escape in the earth, and you shall not have a guardian or a helper besides Allah.

42.32 And among His signs are the ships in the sea like mountains.

42.33 If He pleases, He causes the wind to become still so that they lie motionless on its back; most surely there are signs in this for every patient, grateful one,

42.34 Or He may make them founder for what they have earned, and (even then) pardon most;

42.35 And (that) those who dispute about Our communications may know; there is no place of refuge for them.

42.36 So whatever thing you are given, that is only a provision of this world's life, and what is with Allah is better and more lasting for those who believe and rely on their Lord.

42.37 And those who shun the great sins and indecencies, and whenever they are angry they forgive.

42.38 And those who respond to their Lord and keep up prayer, and their rule is to take counsel among themselves, and who spend out of what We have given them.

42.39 And those who, when great wrong afflicts them, defend themselves.

42.40 And the recompense of evil is punishment like it, but whoever forgives and amends, he shall have his reward from Allah; surely He does not love the unjust.

42.41 And whoever defends himself after his being oppressed, these it is against whom there is no way (to blame).

42.42 The way (to blame) is only against those who oppress men and revolt in the earth unjustly; these shall have a painful punishment.

42.43 And whoever is patient and forgiving, these most surely are actions due to courage.

42.44 And whomsoever Allah makes err, he has no guardian after Him; and you shall see the unjust, when they see the punishment, saying: Is there any way to return?

42.45 And you shall see them brought before it humbling themselves because of the abasements, looking with a faint glance. And those who believe shall say: Surely the losers are they who have lost themselves and their followers on the resurrection day. Now surely the iniquitous shall remain in lasting chastisement.

42.46 And they shall have no friends to help them besides Allah; and— whomsoever Allah makes err, he shall have no way.

42.47 Hearken to your Lord before there comes the day from Allah for which there shall be no averting; you shall have no refuge on that day, nor shall it be yours to make a denial.

42.48 But if they turn aside, We have not sent you as a watcher over them; on you is only to deliver (the message); and surely when We make man taste mercy from Us, he rejoices thereat; and if an evil afflicts them on account of what their hands have already done, then-surely man is ungrateful.

42.49 Allah's is the kingdom of the heavens and the earth; He creates what He pleases; He grants to whom He pleases daughters and grants to whom He pleases sons.

42.50 Or He makes them of both sorts, male and female; and He makes whom He pleases barren; surely He is the Knowing, the Powerful.

42.51 And it is not for any mortal that Allah should speak to them, they could not bear to hear and they did not see.

42.52 And thus did We reveal to you an inspired book by Our command. You did not know what the Book was, nor (what) the faith (was), but We made it a light, guiding thereby whom We please of Our servants; and most surely you show the way to the right path:

42.53 The path of Allah, Whose is whatsoever is in the heavens and whatsoever is in the earth; now surely to Allah do all affairs eventually come.

The Promulgation of Universal Peace

'Abdu'l-Bahá, the son of Bahá'u'lláh, who initiated the Bahá'í movement, was the leader of the Bahá'í faith from 1892 until his passing in 1921. He was born in Tehran in 1844 and shared his father's progressive banishments and imprisonments throughout his childhood and youth, from Tehran to Baghdad to Constantinople (Istanbul) to Adrianople (Edirne) to the prison city of Akka, Palestine (Israel). Although never having the opportunity to attend school, he was erudite in Persian, Arabic, and Turkish languages and spent his life in service to the poor and oppressed. He was knighted by the British government after World War I for saving the lives of thousands of wartime starving people by donating his storehouses of grain to them.

Some of 'Abdu'l-Bahá's more popular texts that have been translated into English are *Some Answered Questions,* table talks with American intellectual Laura Clifford Barney (1908/1981); *Selections from the Writings of 'Abdu'l-Bahá* (1978); and *The Secret of Divine Civilization,* a treatise on political science (1882/1970). Although there are only approximately 6 to 7 million Bahá'ís, according to the *Encyclopedia Britannica 1988 Book of the Year,* theirs is the second most widespread religion in that Bahá'ís are found in every country in the world. There are several hundred Bahá'í schools worldwide, and they are heavily influenced in their curriculum and instructional design by the works of 'Abdu'l-Bahá.

Following multiple requests from American Bahá'ís, 'Abdu'l-Bahá visited America in 1912. He spoke in many churches, synagogues, and universities, including Howard University, Columbia University, Clark University, and Stanford University. These talks were collected and published as *The Promulgation of Universal Peace* (1925). The following selection comes from that book and is the text of his 1912 talk at Stanford University in Palo Alto, California, originally published in the Palo Altan newspaper.

Key Concept: education for peace

*T*he greatest attainment in the world of humanity has ever been scientific in nature. It is the discovery of the realities of things. Inasmuch as I find myself in the home of science—for [Leland Stanford Junior University] is one of the great universities of the country and well known abroad—I feel a keen sense of joy.

77

'Abdu'l-Bahá

The highest praise is due to men who devote their energies to science, and the noblest center is a center wherein the sciences and arts are taught and studied. Science ever tends to the illumination of the world of humanity. It is the cause of eternal honor to man, and its sovereignty is far greater than the sovereignty of kings. The dominion of kings has an ending; the king himself may be dethroned; but the sovereignty of science is everlasting and without end. Consider the philosophers of former times. Their rule and dominion is still manifest in the world. The Greek and Roman kingdoms with all their grandeur passed away; the ancient sovereignties of the Orient are but memories, whereas the power and influence of Plato and Aristotle still continue. Even now in schools and universities of the world their names are revered and commemorated, but where do we hear the names of bygone kings extolled? They are forgotten and rest in the valley of oblivion. It is evident that the sovereignty of science is greater than the dominion of rulers. Kings have invaded countries and achieved conquest through the shedding of blood, but the scientist through his beneficent achievements invades the regions of ignorance, conquering the realm of minds and hearts. Therefore, his conquests are everlasting. May you attain extraordinary progress in this center of education. May you become radiant lights flooding the dark regions and recesses of ignorance with illumination.

Inasmuch as the fundamental principle of the teaching of Bahá'u'lláh is the oneness of the world of humanity, I will speak to you upon the intrinsic oneness of all phenomena. This is one of the abstruse subjects of divine philosophy.

Fundamentally all existing things pass through the same degrees and phases of development, and any given phenomenon embodies all others. An ancient statement of the Arabian philosophers declares that all things are involved in all things. It is evident that each material organism is an aggregate expression of single and simple elements, and a given cellular element or atom has its coursings or journeyings through various and myriad stages of life. For example, we will say the cellular elements which have entered into the composition of a human organism were at one time a component part of the animal kingdom; at another time they entered into the composition of the vegetable, and prior to that they existed in the kingdom of the mineral. They have been subject to transference from one condition of life to another, passing through various forms and phases, exercising in each existence special functions. Their journeyings through material phenomena are continuous. Therefore, each phenomenon is the expression in degree of all other phenomena. The difference is one of successive transferences and the period of time involved in evolutionary process.

For example, it has taken a certain length of time for this cellular element in my hand to pass through the various periods of metabolism. At one period it was in the mineral kingdom subject to changes and transferences in the mineral state. Then it was transferred to the vegetable kingdom where it entered into different grades and stations. Afterward it reached the animal plane, appearing in forms of animal organisms until finally in its transferences and coursings it attained to the kingdom of man. Later on it will revert to its primordial elemen-

78

*Chapter 2
Cross-Cultural,
Religious,
Spiritual, and
Ethical
Foundations*

tal state in the mineral kingdom, being subject, as it were, to infinite journeyings from one degree of existence to another, passing through every stage of being and life. Whenever it appears in any distinct form or image, it has its opportunities, virtues and functions. As each component atom or element in the physical organisms of existence is subject to transference through endless forms and stages, possessing virtues peculiar to those forms and stations, it is evident that all phenomena of material being are fundamentally one. In the mineral kingdom this component atom or element possesses certain virtues of the mineral; in the kingdom of the vegetable it is imbued with vegetable qualities or virtues; in the plane of animal existence it is empowered with animal virtues —the senses; and in the kingdom of man it manifests qualities peculiar to the human station.

As this is true of material phenomena, how much more evident and essential it is that oneness should characterize man in the realm of idealism, which finds its expression only in the human kingdom. Verily, the origin of all material life is one and its termination likewise one. In view of this fundamental unity and agreement of all phenomenal life, why should man in his kingdom of existence wage war or indulge in hostility and destructive strife against his fellowman? Man is the noblest of the creatures. In his physical organism he possesses the virtues of the mineral kingdom. Likewise, he embodies the augmentative virtue, or power of growth, which characterizes the kingdom of the vegetable. Furthermore, in his degree of physical existence he is qualified with functions and powers peculiar to the animal, beyond which lies the range of his distinctive human mental and spiritual endowment. Considering this wonderful unity of the kingdoms of existence and their embodiment in the highest and noblest creature, why should man be at variance and in conflict with man? Is it fitting and justifiable that he should be at war, when harmony and interdependence characterize the kingdoms of phenomenal life below him? The elements and lower organisms are synchronized in the great plan of life. Shall man, infinitely above them in degree, be antagonistic and a destroyer of that perfection? God forbid such a condition!

From the fellowship and commingling of the elemental atoms life results. In their harmony and blending there is ever newness of existence. It is radiance, completeness; it is consummation; it is life itself. Just now the physical energies and natural forces which come under our immediate observation are all at peace. The sun is at peace with the earth upon which it shines. The soft breathing winds are at peace with the trees. All the elements are in harmony and equilibrium. A slight disturbance and discord among them might bring another San Francisco earthquake and fire. A physical clash, a little quarreling among the elements as it were, and a violent cataclysm of nature results. This happens in the mineral kingdom. Consider, then, the effect of discord and conflict in the kingdom of man, so superior to the realm of inanimate existence. How great the attendant catastrophe, especially when we realize that man is endowed by God with mind and intellect. Verily, mind is the supreme gift of God. Verily, intellect is the effulgence of God. This is manifest and self-evident.

For all created things except man are subjects or captives of nature; they cannot deviate in the slightest degree from nature's law and control. The colossal sun, center of our planetary system, is nature's captive, incapable of the least variation from the law of command. All the orbs and luminaries in this illimitable universe are, likewise, obedient to nature's regulation. Our planet, the earth, acknowledges nature's omnipresent sovereignty. The kingdoms of the mineral, vegetable and animal respond to nature's will and fiat of control. The great bulky elephant with its massive strength has no power to disobey the restrictions nature has laid upon him; but man, weak and diminutive in comparison, empowered by mind which is an effulgence of Divinity itself, can resist nature's control and apply natural laws to his own uses.

According to the limitations of his physical powers man was intended by creation to live upon the earth, but through the exercise of his mental faculties, he removes the restriction of this law and soars in the air like a bird. He penetrates the secrets of the sea in submarines and builds fleets to sail at will over the ocean's surface, commanding the laws of nature to do his will. All the sciences and arts we now enjoy and utilize were once mysteries, and according to the mandates of nature should have remained hidden and latent, but the human intellect has broken through the laws surrounding them and discovered the underlying realities. The mind of man has taken these mysteries out of the plane of invisibility and brought them into the plane of the known and visible.

It has classified and adapted these laws to human needs and uses, this being contrary to the postulates of nature. For example, electricity was once a hidden, or latent, natural force. It would have remained hidden if the human intellect had not discovered it. Man has broken the law of its concealment, taken this energy out of the invisible treasury of the universe and brought it into visibility. Is it not an extraordinary accomplishment that this little creature, man, has imprisoned an irresistible cosmic force in an incandescent lamp? It is beyond the vision and power of nature itself to do this. The East can communicate with the West in a few minutes. This is a miracle transcending nature's control. Man takes the human voice and stores it in a phonograph. The voice naturally should be free and transient according to the law and phenomenon of sound, but man arrests its vibrations and puts it in a box in defiance of nature's laws. All human discoveries were once secrets and mysteries sealed and stored up in the bosom of the material universe until the mind of man, which is the greatest of divine effulgences, penetrated them and made them subservient to his will and purpose. In this sense man has broken the laws of nature and is constantly taking out of nature's laboratory new and wonderful things. Notwithstanding this supreme bestowal of God, which is the greatest power in the world of creation, man continues to war and fight, killing his fellowman with the ferocity of a wild animal. Is this in keeping with his exalted station? Nay, rather, this is contrary to the divine purpose manifest in his creation and endowment.

If the animals are savage and ferocious, it is simply a means for their subsistence and preservation. They are deprived of that degree of intellect which can reason and discriminate between right and wrong, justice and injustice; they are justified in their actions and not responsible. When man is ferocious and cruel toward his fellowman, it is not for subsistence or safety. His motive is selfish advantage and willful wrong. It is neither seemly nor befitting that such a noble creature, endowed with intellect and lofty thoughts, capable of wonderful achievements and discoveries in sciences and arts, with potential for ever higher perceptions and the accomplishment of divine purposes in life,

80

*Chapter 2
Cross-Cultural,
Religious,
Spiritual, and
Ethical
Foundations*

should seek the blood of his fellowmen upon the field of battle. Man is the temple of God. He is not a human temple. If you destroy a house, the owner of that house will be grieved and wrathful. How much greater is the wrong when man destroys a building planned and erected by God! Undoubtedly, he deserves the judgment and wrath of God.

God has created man lofty and noble, made him a dominant factor in creation. He has specialized man with supreme bestowals, conferred upon him mind, perception, memory, abstraction and the powers of the senses. These gifts of God to man were intended to make him the manifestation of divine virtues, a radiant light in the world of creation, a source of life and the agency of constructiveness in the infinite fields of existence. Shall we now destroy this great edifice and its very foundation, overthrow this temple of God, the body social or politic? When we are not captives of nature, when we possess the power to control ourselves, shall we become captives of nature and act according to its exigencies?

In nature there is the law of the survival of the fittest. Even if man be not educated, then according to the natural institutes this natural law will demand of man supremacy. The purpose and object of schools, colleges and universities is to educate man and thereby rescue and redeem him from the exigencies and defects of nature and to awaken within him the capability of controlling and appropriating nature's bounties. If we should relegate this plot of ground to its natural state, allow it to return to its original condition, it would become a field of thorns and useless weeds, but by cultivation it will become fertile soil, yielding a harvest. Deprived of cultivation, the mountain slopes would be jungles and forests without fruitful trees. The gardens bring forth fruits and flowers in proportion to the care and tillage bestowed upon them by the gardener. Therefore, it is not intended that the world of humanity should be left to its natural state. It is in need of the education divinely provided for it. The holy, heavenly Manifestations of God have been the Teachers. They are the divine Gardeners Who transform the jungles of human nature into fruitful orchards and make the thorny places blossom as the rose. It is evident, then, that the intended and especial function of man is to rescue and redeem himself from the inherent defects of nature and become qualified with the ideal virtues of Divinity. Shall he sacrifice these ideal virtues and destroy these possibilities of advancement? God has endowed him with a power whereby he can even overcome the laws and phenomena of nature, wrest the sword from nature's hand and use it against nature itself. Shall he, then, remain its captive, even failing to qualify under the natural law which commands the survival of the fittest? That is to say, shall he continue to live upon the level of the animal kingdom without distinction between them and himself in natural impulses and ferocious instincts? There is no lower degree nor greater debasement for man than this natural condition of animalism. The battlefield is the acme of human degradation, the cause of the wrath of God, the destruction of the divine foundation of man.

Praise be to God! I find myself in an assemblage, the members of which are peace loving and advocates of international unity. The thoughts of all present are centered upon the oneness of the world of mankind, and every ambition is to render service in the cause of human uplift and betterment. I supplicate God that He may confirm and assist you, that each one of you may become a professor emeritus in the world of scientific knowledge, a faithful standard-bearer of peace and bonds of agreement between the hearts of men.

Fifty years ago Bahá'u'lláh declared the necessity of peace among the nations and the reality of reconciliation between the religions of the world. He announced that the fundamental basis of all religion is one, that the essence of religion is human fellowship and that the differences in belief which exist are due to dogmatic interpretation and blind imitations which are at variance with the foundations established by the Prophets of God. He proclaimed that if the reality underlying religious teaching be investigated all religions would be unified, and the purpose of God, which is love and the blending of human hearts, would be accomplished. According to His teachings if religious belief proves to be the cause of discord and dissension, its absence would be preferable; for religion was intended to be the divine remedy and panacea for the ailments of humanity, the healing balm for the wounds of mankind. If its misapprehension and defilement have brought about warfare and bloodshed instead of remedy and cure, the world would be better under irreligious conditions.

Bahá'u'lláh especially emphasized international peace. He declared that all mankind is the one progeny of Adam and members of one great universal family. If the various races and distinct types of mankind had each proceeded from a different original paternity—in other words, if we had two or more Adams for our human fathers—there might be reasonable ground for difference and divergence in humanity today; but inasmuch as we belong to one progeny and one family, all names which seek to differentiate and distinguish mankind as Italian, German, French, Russian and so on are without significance and sanction. We are all human, all servants of God and all come from Mr. Adam's family. Why, then, all these fallacious national and racial distinctions? These boundary lines and artificial barriers have been created by despots and conquerors who sought to attain dominion over mankind, thereby engendering patriotic feeling and rousing selfish devotion to merely local standards of government. As a rule they themselves enjoyed luxuries in palaces, surrounded by conditions of ease and affluence, while armies of soldiers, civilians and tillers of the soil fought and died at their command upon the field of battle, shedding their innocent blood for a delusion such as "we are Germans," "our enemies are French," etc., when, in reality, all are humankind, all belong to the one family and posterity of Adam, the original father. This prejudice or limited patriotism is prevalent throughout the world, while man is blind to patriotism in the larger sense which includes all races and native lands. From every real standpoint there must and should be peace among all nations.

God created one earth and one mankind to people it. Man has no other habitation, but man himself has come forth and proclaimed imaginary boundary lines and territorial restrictions, naming them Germany, France, Russia, etc. And torrents of precious blood are spilled in defense of these imaginary divisions of our one human habitation, under the delusion of a fancied and limited patriotism.

After all, a claim and title to territory or native land is but a claim and attachment to the dust of earth. We live upon this earth for a few days and then rest beneath it forever. So it is our graveyard eternally. Shall man fight for the tomb which devours him, for his eternal sepulcher? What ignorance could be

82

*Chapter 2
Cross-Cultural,
Religious,
Spiritual, and
Ethical
Foundations*

greater than this? To fight over his grave, to kill another for his grave! What heedlessness! What a delusion!

It is my hope that you who are students in this university may never be called upon to fight for the dust of earth which is the tomb and sepulcher of all mankind, but that during the days of your life you may enjoy the most perfect companionship one with another, even as one family—as brothers, sisters, fathers, mothers—associating together in peace and true fellowship.

PART TWO

Cognitive Development and Intelligence

Chapter 3 Cognition and Intelligence 85

On the Internet . . .

Sites appropriate to Part Two

The Jean Piaget Society, established in 1970, has an international, interdisciplinary membership of scholars, teachers, and researchers who are interested in exploring the nature of the developmental construction of human knowledge.

> http://www.piaget.org

Created by Branton Shearer, the Multiple Intelligences Developmental Assessment Scales (MIDAS) provides an efficient method of obtaining a descriptive assessment of a student's multiple intelligence profile. According to Howard Gardner, "the MIDAS represents the first effort to measure the multiple intelligences, which have been developed according to standard psychometric procedures."

> http://www.angelfire.com/oh/themidas/
> index.html

The Gardner School is dedicated to nurturing the unique potential of each child. In recognition of individuals' differing intelligences, learning styles, skills, and interests, the Gardner School provides all students with the appropriate opportunities, resources, and encouragement to develop and express their unique talents.

> http://www.gardnerschool.org/home.html

This is the home page of the Psychological Corporation, publisher of the Wechsler intelligence scales.

> http://www.hbtpc.com

CHAPTER 3 Cognition and Intelligence

3.1 JEAN PIAGET

The Thought of the Young Child

Swiss psychologist Jean Piaget (1896–1980) is considered the most influential developmental psychologist in Western history, and he has had a tremendous impact on educational psychology. His background deals with the scientific observation of organisms, having received his Ph.D. in zoology from the University of Neuchâtel in Switzerland in 1918. This helped Piaget become an astute researcher of the human child. His study of philosophy led him to examine the most fundamental categories of the developing human mind, as witnessed by the titles of a few of his many published texts: *The Language and Thought of the Child* (1923); *Judgment and Reasoning in the Child* (1924); *The Child's Conception of the World* (1926); *The Child's Conception of Physical Reality* (1927); *The Moral Judgement of the Child* (1932); *The Origins of Intelligence in the Child* (1936); *The Construction of Reality in the Child* (1937); *The Child's Conception of Time* (1946); *The Child's Conception of Movement and Speed* (1946), and *Psychology and Epistemology: Towards a Theory of Knowledge* (1970).

Piaget's life's work was focused on mapping the stages of cognitive development. He referred to his theory as "genetic epistemology," meaning the study of the emergence of the capacity "to know." His use of the term *genetic* does not simply mean the endowment of our genes. Piaget was both an "interactionist" and a "constructivist." He believed that children intentionally construct their own minds and are simultaneously influenced by their

85

genes and the environment while doing so. The selection included here was based on a lecture that Piaget gave at the University of London in 1963, in which he describes the transition from the preoperational to concrete operational stages of thought. It was first published in French in 1964, when Piaget was nearly 70 years old. It was later published in 1968 in Piaget's *Six Psychological Studies* translated by Anita Tenzer (Vintage Books).

Key Concept: cognitive-developmental stages

*T*he Thought of the Young Child" is an enormous subject, which I have studied for more than forty years without yet having covered it, and it may be approached from many points of view. I shall consider three of them:

1. Our studies show, first of all, in what respects the child differs from the adult, i.e., what the young child lacks in order to be able to reason like an average middle-class adult. It can be verified, for example, that certain logico-mathematical structures are not operative at all ages, hence are not innate.
2. Our studies show how cognitive structures are constructed. In this respect, child psychology may serve as an expository method for psychology in general, because to some extent the progressive formation of a structure furnishes its own explanation.
3. Our studies of the mode of construction of certain structures offer a response to certain questions posed by the philosophy of science. In this respect, child psychology can be extended into a "genetic epistemology."

1. THE CHILD AND THE ADULT

Let us start with the differences between the child and the adult. I maintained . . . that the child began by being "prelogical," not in the sense of a fundamental heterogeneity between the child and the adult, but in the sense of the necessity for a progressive construction of the logical structures. This hypothesis has been widely criticized, especially in Great Britain, and above all because my arguments were drawn from verbal thought. For example, it has been pointed out by . . . others (and in this respect with reason), that the child is more logical in action than in words. In general, I am little affected by critics, because they often do not understand an author's precise meaning when his contentions are far from accepted modes of thought, but the service which critics render is to impel a more prudent and more thoroughgoing analysis of the data.

When I myself had children I was better able to understand the role of action in the development of intelligence. In particular, I learned that actions were the starting point for the future *operations* of intelligence. An operation is an internalized action which becomes reversible and is coordinated with other operations into an integrated operational grouping. However, since operations materialize only toward seven or eight years of age, there is a long "preoperational" period of development which corresponds to what I used to call the "prelogical" period. (Operations themselves are formed in two successive stages: the "concrete" stage between seven and eleven years of age, and the "formal" or propositional stage, which appears only at age eleven to twelve years.)

Returning to the observations of my own children, I subjected the observation of infantile behavior to the same analysis which I first employed with respect to verbal behavior. I obtained—in a much more primitive and essential form—some of the same results I had previously obtained through language alone. For example, I had maintained that the thought of the young child was egocentric, not in the sense of a hypertrophy of the self, but in the sense of centration on his own point of view. There seemed to be an initial lack of differentiation among points of view, which necessitated a differentiation by means of *decentration* in order to arrive at objectivity. The study of the sensorimotor development of space at levels prior to the acquisition of language led to exactly the same conclusions. Development begins by the construction of a multiplicity of heterogeneous spaces (oral, tactile, visual, etc.), each of which is centered on the child's own body or perspective. Then, after a kind of miniature Copernican revolution, space finally becomes a general place that contains all objects including the child's own body. It is in this way that space becomes decentered during infancy.

There is no basic difference between verbal logic and the logic inherent in the coordination of actions, but the logic of actions is more profound and more primitive. It develops more rapidly and surmounts the difficulties it encounters more quickly, but they are the same difficulties of decentration as those which will appear later in the field of language.

The most universal manner in which the initial logic of the child differs from our own (but with a lag between its manifestations in action and its manifestations in language) is undoubtedly its *irreversibility* due to the initial absence of decentration, hence its lack of *conservations*. In effect, the logico-mathematical operations are, as we have seen, internalized, reversible actions (in the sense that each operation has an inverse, such as subtraction with respect to addition) coordinated into integrated groupings. The child first perceives by means of simple, one-way actions with centration on the *states* (and, above all, on the *final* states) without the decentration which alone permits the conceptualization of "transformations" as such. The basic consequence is that the conservation of objects, sets, quantities, etc., is not immediate before operational decentration is achieved. For example, a single object which leaves the perceptual field (hidden beneath a screen) only gradually acquires permanence at the sensorimotor level (eight to twelve months), and the number of objects in a collection whose form is modified is conserved, on the average, only toward seven or eight years.

The study of various forms of nonconservation, which we are still undertaking, shows that they do not result from a spontaneous tendency toward change (because the child is, on the contrary, above all a conservationist), but from an initial lack of reversible operations. For example, we [Piaget and Inhelder] have recently repeated and modified our early experiments on the nonconservation of liquid quantities (as this nonconservation is observed in the transfer of a liquid from receptacle A to a narrower and higher receptacle B). Before the transfer of liquids from one container A to another B, we first asked the subjects to anticipate (a) whether or not there would be conservation of the liquid and (b) how high the water would rise in receptacle B. Subjects from four to six years generally anticipated (a) that the quantity would remain the same, i.e., would be conserved, and (b) that the level itself was conserved. When the liquid was actually transferred, they were surprised to see that the level in receptacle B was higher than it was in A and, as a result, they concluded that there was nonconservation of the liquid quantity. It is true that certain children (very few) correctly predict the raised level in B (no doubt as a result of prior spontaneous experimentation) and then predict nonconservation. The following experiment clarifies these reactions. A child is given an empty glass A and a narrower empty glass B and is asked to pour liquid into A and into B so that there will be "the same amount to drink in each glass." The child will put exactly the same level of water into A and into B without bothering about the size of the glass. By contrast, after the age of six and a half to seven, the majority of children believe in the conservation of the liquid and can predict the difference in levels.

This repetition of early experiments shows that the basic reason for nonconservation has to do with the fact that the young child reasons only about *states* or static configurations and neglects *transformations* as such. In order to conceptualize these transformations, one must reason by means of reversible "operations" and these are built up only little by little by means of a progressive regulation of the compensations involved.

2. THE COGNITIVE STRUCTURES

This leads us to the second part of our study. How do the logico-mathematical, operational structures become constructed? It seems to me that the study of this construction gives child psychology an explanatory value which is of interest to psychology as a whole, in the sense that the genesis (or successive development, since they do not have absolute beginnings) of these structures is linked to the causality of the formative mechanisms. It is regrettable that in certain circles child psychologists have no contact with experimentalists and experimental psychologists ignore the child; the genetic dimension is necessary to explication in general.

The logico-mathematical operations derive from actions themselves, because they are the product of an abstraction which proceeds from the coordination of actions and not from the objects themselves. For example, the operations of "order" derive from the coordination of actions. To discern a certain order in a series of objects or events one must be capable of registering this order through actions (from ocular movements to manual reconstitution) which must themselves be ordered. Objective order is learned only through an order inherent in the actions themselves. A learning theorist... who worked with us for a year on experiments dealing with, among other things, the learning of order, found that to "learn" order, one must have a "counter" at one's disposition, which is equivalent to what I call an ordinated activity.

These operations are not, however, merely internalized actions. For operations to exist, these actions must become reversible and capable of being coordinated into integrated structures which can be expressed in such general algebraic terms as: "groupings," "groups," "lattices," etc.

The construction of structures is often effected in a complex and unexpected manner, as is demonstrable, for example, in the conceptualization of whole numbers. We studied this problem some time ago and have recently reverted to it.

We know that mathematicians hold two major types of hypotheses with respect to the construction of the whole numbers. On the one hand, according to the "intuitionists," number is constructed independently of logical structures and results from operational "intuitions" which are relatively primitive, such as the intuition of "n + 1." On the other hand, there are those who hypothesize that numerical structures are derived from logical structures. For example, in *Principia Mathematica*, [Alfred North] Whitehead and [Bertrand] Russell seek to reduce the cardinal number to the concept of class and the ordinal number to that of a transitive asymmetric relationship.

The psychological facts, however, do not accord with either of these hypotheses. In the first place, they show that all the elements of the number are logical in nature. There is no intuition of "n + 1" before a conservation of sets, based on operational inclusions (classifications) or seriations, is constructed. In the second place, these logical constituents give rise to a new synthesis in the case of the whole number, a synthesis which does not correspond to a simple composition of classes or to a simple serial composition but to both together. We are not dealing with a simple composition of classes, because if the qualities are abstracted (which is necessary in order to obtain a number) a factor of order (seriation) must be employed so that the units, which are now identical, can be distinguished. In addition, if the qualities are abstracted, the one-by-one correspondence which Russell employs for constructing class-by-class equivalencies, is no longer a qualified correspondence (a qualified element corresponding to another element of the same quality) but a unit correspondence which is already numerical, hence is begging the question. In short, the whole number is neither a simple system of class inclusions, nor a simple seriation, but an indissociable synthesis of inclusion and seriation. The synthesis derives from the abstraction of qualities and from the fact that these two systems (classification and seriation), which are distinct when their qualities are conserved, become fused as soon as their qualities are abstracted.

This construction of number seems somewhat heterodox from the point of view of logic, and the mathematician who did the English translation of my book, *The Child's Conception of Number*, asked me to delete from the English edition the formulas I had given at the end of the French edition because they seemed shocking to him and to English logicians. However, recently, an excellent logician, J. B. Grize provided a formalization of this psychological construction of the number which I had formulated through simple observation of the child. He presented it to our Symposia of The Center for the Study of Genetic Epistemology and logicians such as E. W. Beth and W. V. O. Quine, who were present at the Symposia, saw no problems in it except with respect to some possible ameliorations of detail. Thus a new explanation of the elaboration of number has been furnished by child psychology. Genetic psychology is therefore instructive not only with regard to the ways in which the child differs from the adult but also with regard to the construction of certain logico-mathematical structures which finally form a part of all the evolved forms of adult thought.

3. PSYCHOLOGY AND GENETIC EPISTEMOLOGY

A few final remarks remain to be made. In certain instances, the genetic study of the construction of concepts and operations provides a response to questions posed by the sciences with respect to their methods of knowledge. When this is the case, child psychology becomes extended into a "genetic epistemology."

I shall give one example, that of time and speed. At a philosophy of science meeting in 1928, Einstein asked me if, from a psychological point of view, the concept of speed developed as a function of time or whether it was built up independently of all duration or was even more primitive than the concept of duration. We know that in classical mechanics the concept of speed depends on duration, whereas from the relativist point of view, duration, by contrast, depends on speed. We therefore went to work, and our findings with respect to the development of the concept of speed were used by two French relativists in a new formulation of the concepts of speed and time.

Let us start with the concept of time. Time is manifested in two ways: through the successive order of events and the duration or interval between ordered events. In the young child it is easy to see that the estimation of ordinal relations (succession or simultaneity) depends on speed. For example, if two mannikins are set off at the same speed from the same line of departure on two parallel routes, the child will have no difficulty in recognizing that their respective departures and arrivals will be simultaneous. However, if one of the mannikins goes faster and thus arrives at a point farther away, the child will say that the departures are simultaneous but that the mannikins do not stop "at the same time." This is not a perceptual error, since the child recognizes that when one of the mannikins stops, the other does not continue.

Simultaneity does not make sense to the child in this instance, because he does not yet understand the "same time" concept for two movements of unequal speed. At around the age of six, on the average, the child will accept the simultaneity of arrival as well as departure, but from this he does not conclude that the durations of the trips were the same, since it seems to him that a longer route must require more time owing to his inability to coordinate simultaneity and temporal intervals. Analogous observations can be made with respect to psychological time (slow and fast work, etc.). Time appears to be a coordination of movements, inclusive of speeds ($t = d{:}s$), just as space is based on a coordination of displacements; i.e., movements independent of their speed.

As for the concept of speed, the classical formula $s = d{:}t$ makes sense if the duration t and the distance covered d correspond to simple intuitions which exist prior to the concept of speed. However, we have just seen that the estimation of duration t begins by depending on speed. Is there, then, an intuition of speed which is anterior to duration or at least independent of it? The intuition of speed is, in fact, found in the child in the form of an ordinal intuition based on overtaking. A moving object is judged to be more rapid than another when at a given moment the first object is behind and a moment or so later ahead of the other object. The intuition of overtaking is based on the temporal order (before and after) and on the spatial order (behind and in front), but it is not based on duration or on the distance traversed. Nevertheless, it furnishes an exact criterion of speed. At first, the child considers only the points of arrival, and thus for a long time he makes errors with respect to simple overtaking or partial overtaking. However, when he becomes adept at anticipating the course of perceived movements and of generalizing the concept of overtaking, he acquires an original ordinal concept of speed. It is also interesting to note that the perception of speed stems from the same ordinal relations and necessitates no reference to duration.

The results of this research, which was inspired by Einstein, were then utilized in the field of relativity. This occurred in the following manner. We know that in physics, even in relativistic physics, there is difficulty in defining duration and speed without running into a vicious circle. Speed is defined with reference to duration ($s = d:t$), and one can measure duration only by means of speed (astronomics, mechanics, etc.). Now two French physicists have tried to avoid this vicious circle in their reformulation of the theory of relativity by using our findings on the psychological formation of the concept of speed. Using our work on the genesis of this concept in the child, they developed the theory of ordinal speed or overtaking. With the help of a logarithmic law and an Abelian group, they constructed a theorem of addition of speeds, and from this they arrived at the Lorenz group and the initial principles of the theory of relativity.

The young child's thinking manifests considerable activity that is frequently original and unpredictable. It is remarkable not only by virtue of the way it differs from adult thinking but also by virtue of what it teaches us about the way in which rational structures are formed. Sometimes this may even lead to the clarification of certain obscure aspects of scientific thought.

The Rationale of the Children's Scale

David Wechsler (1896–1981) is one of the founding fathers of American clinical psychology and the creator of the most commonly used educational psychology intelligence test. He received his A.B. degree from the City College of New York in 1916 and earned his M.A. at Columbia University in 1917. For his master's thesis he studied Korsakoff's psychosis (a neurological disorder characterized by extreme amnesia present in a background of clear perception and full consciousness), thus contributing to the newly emerging field of experimental psychopathology. At that time the academic and experimental psychologists who made up the approximately 1,000-member American Psychological Association (APA) were not involved in the yet-to-be-created field of American psychotherapy. Wechsler was one of the first to move out of academia and venture into the field of applied, clinical, and educational psychology.

As the United States was preparing to enter World War I, Wechsler was able to gain firsthand experience working under experimental psychologist E. G. Boring at an army camp on Long Island. His work there involved scoring the Army Alpha test, which was based on a group-administered version of the Stanford-Binet intelligence test. The Army Alpha test had been developed by a few pioneer American psychologists. After actually conscripting in the army, Wechsler was assigned to the psychology unit at Fort Logan in Texas, where he tested recruits who required individual assessment because they did not read English. In addition to the Stanford-Binet test, which requires oral language, he gave them the Yerkes and Army Performance Scales, which are nonverbal tests of intelligence. He noticed from this experience that perfectly bright young men would have been classified as retarded on verbal intelligence tests, causing him to realize that the current definitions of intelligence were too narrow.

In 1920 Wechsler won a fellowship to the University of Paris, shortly after his army discharge. He studied under Henri Pieron and Louis Lapique in Paris and collected data on psychogalvanic responses and emotion, which later became the basis for his dissertation at Columbia University. At Columbia he moonlighted as a clinical psychologist in New York City's newly created Bureau of Child Guidance. Next he worked as the secretary of the Psychological Corporation, and he was a faculty member at New York University College of Medicine as well as the chief psychologist at Bellevue Psychiatric Hospital until 1967.

Wechsler completed his first innovative intelligence tests for adults in 1939, the Wechsler-Bellevue Scales. Later he developed the Wechsler Intelligence Scale for Children (WISC), the Wechsler Adult Intelligence Scale, and the Wechsler Preschool and Primary Scale of Intelligence. The WISC became the most widely used IQ test in history. The following selection comes from the introductory chapter of *Wechsler Intelligence Scale for Children,* published by the Psychological Corporation in 1949, which describes Wechsler's definition of intelligence and the multibattery tests that he created.

Key Concept: IQ and verbal and nonverbal intelligence

INTRODUCTION

The *Wechsler Intelligence Scale for Children* [WISC] has grown logically out of the *Wechsler-Bellevue Intelligence Scales* used with adolescents and adults. In fact, most of the items in the *WISC* are from Form II of the earlier scales, the main additions being new items at the easier end of each test to permit examination of children as young as five years of age.

Even though the materials overlap, the *WISC* is a distinct test from the *Wechsler-Bellevue Scales* and is independently standardized. The scales overlap in usefulness since both scales can be used with adolescents. However, it is expected that the *WISC* will be preferred in testing adolescents up through the age of fifteen years.

The examiner should also be warned that any proficiency he may have with the *Wechsler-Bellevue* does not permit him to assume that he has immediate skill in using the new Scale for children. Even when the same materials are used, the directions for presenting and the standards for scoring and assignment of weights and bonuses are quite different. The directions given [here] must be studied and mastered even by the long-experienced user of the *Wechsler-Bellevue.*

This new Children's Scale (as it probably will come to be known in everyday clinical parlance) has been standardized with exceptional care over a five-year period of experimental tryouts, field testing, and statistical analysis....

Clinical and statistical considerations also force the observation that the same test items or materials may have different psychological meaningfulness in the tests for adults and children. Object Assembly is one of the poorest adult tests in point of reliability and correlation with other tests. With children, this test is more reliable and relates more closely to the other tests of the Performance group. The clinical examiner who works with both adults and children is cautioned to avoid assuming that similar materials have the same clinical meaningfulness at all ages or that similar tests tap identical abilities at all ages. We just do not yet know the details of the relations of each test to all the components of intelligence at different ages. It is hoped that researches contributing to this general problem will be conducted with the new Scale.

ABANDONING THE MENTAL AGE

The *Wechsler Intelligence Scale for Children* will be found to differ from other individual tests of intelligence for children in several important ways. The first is its complete renunciation of the concept of mental age as a basic measure of intelligence. This concept, originally introduced by [French psychologist Alfred] Binet in 1908, has had great influence particularly in this country, and has remained practically unchanged, if not unchallenged, as the ultimate basis for appraising intellectual capacity.

Operationally defined, a mental age is first an arithmetical device for scoring tests in terms of a month-year notation and, second, a method of equating and comparing test scores. This equating is achieved by so grading the test items (whether in terms of difficulty or otherwise) that the average child of a given age will achieve a score which, when transmuted into a month-year notation, will equal his chronological age. A score so obtained is a mental age (MA). Thus, the average child of 6 may be expected to attain an MA of 6, the average child of 10, an MA of 10, and so on. So far this is straightforward. An MA is a definable level of test performance. If no further claims for it were made, the concept could be readily accepted as a practical method of defining levels of test performance. But much more is generally implied or subsumed. Mental age is considered to represent an absolute level of mental capacity, so that an MA of 6 means the same irrespective of whether it is obtained by a child of 6, 10 or 16. If all that is implied by this statement is that subjects of different ages can obtain the same test scores, it is true but so obvious. But if one also understands it to mean that their intelligence levels are identical, the statement is at best an assumption which has to be proved. In point of fact, both clinical and statistical evidence is clearly against such an assumption. Instructors in psychometrics have devoted many hours to teaching their pupils first that the MA is a *measure of mental level* (an MA of 7 is a mental level of 7 in all children attaining this rating) and then teaching them that this is not true after all (a 5-year-old with an MA of 7 has not the same kind of mind as a 10-year-old with an MA of 7).

Another problem of interpretation of the MA arises when one computes the IQ by the usual formula MA/CA = IQ. A child of 5 years with an MA of 6 has an IQ of 120. A child of 10 with an MA of 12 also has an IQ of 120. But the first child is advanced by one year of mental age while the second is advanced by two years of MA. This means that the IQ notation unaccompanied by a statement of the age at which the IQ is attained does not, as one is customarily told, eliminate the age factor. Hence, in giving a subject's IQ based on a mental age score, one must state his age when tested to make the IQ meaningful.

The difficulties in using mental ages first became apparent in the earlier attempts to define the adult norm. The perennial question was whether adult mental age should be 16 years (as set by Terman in the 1916 Stanford revision of the *Binet*) or some other age. This question has turned out to be pointless because the figure arrived at is essentially a function of the test used. Thus, if one defines the adult mental age as the age beyond which mean scores no longer increase, one can find tests whose mean scores stop increasing as early as age 12 and others that continue to increase with age up to 20 or 25. Furthermore, in stretching (or extrapolating, to use the statistical term) the concept of mental age, as was necessary in order to obtain equivalent MAs for superior test performances, the concept itself has been disregarded. A mental age which is not the equivalent of a mean score for an actual chronological age is a contradiction in terms. To obtain a mental age of 22 on a test whose mean adult norm is 15 years can only lead, as it has, to confusion.

Needless to say, the sophisticated test user can understand the three above limitations of the mental age and can accommodate this thinking about MAs and IQs, and his interpretations, to the difficulties. There is, indeed, considerable temptation to retain the MA because of its widespread usage in educational planning for children. For a while some psychologists may even feel uncomfortable without the MA as an intermediate step in their computing of IQs from raw scores. In the field of adolescent and adult testing the MA has all but disappeared. Even in educational testing with group tests the use of percentile ranks for a given age group has practically supplanted the IQs derived via MAs.

These are some of the reasons why the author decided to construct the *WISC* in such a manner that the confusions of the MA are avoided and the qualities of the IQ retained.

THE DEVIATION INTELLIGENCE QUOTIENT

One of the most important innovations in the standardization of the present Scale is that, for the first time on a comprehensive individually administered battery for use with children, IQs are obtained by comparing each subject's test performance not with a composite age group but exclusively with the scores earned by individuals in a single (that is, his or her own) age group.... Two points may ... be emphasized at this time. The first is that the new method, with one stroke, cuts away much of the underbrush which has encumbered the problem of the variability of the individual's IQ. By keeping the standard deviation of IQs identical from year to year, a child's obtained IQ does not vary unless his actual test performance as compared with his peers varies; if the standard deviations were not made identical, a child's obtained IQ might vary considerably from year to year, even though his relative ability remained constant. Apart from test unreliabilities, IQs obtained by successive retests with the *WISC* automatically give the subject's relative position in the age group to which he belongs at each time of testing. If any changes are observed they may be ascribed to changes in the subject and not in the structure of the test nor its standardization, since in IQ units the standard deviations as well as the means of all age groups are identical. It is no longer a matter of discovering how many children test above or below a given IQ in the population, since the deviation IQ is by definition dependent on the normal distribution of the test scores.

Each person tested is assigned an IQ which, at his age, represents his relative intelligence rating. This IQ, and all others similarly obtained, are deviation IQs since they indicate the amount by which a subject deviates above or below the average performance of individuals of his own age group. The IQ of 100 on the *WISC* is set equal to the mean total score for each age, and the standard deviation is set equal to 15 IQ points. In terms of percentile limits, the highest one per cent will have IQs of 135 and above, and the lowest one per cent IQs of 65 and below. The middle fifty per cent of children at each age will have IQs from 90 to 110.

The second point to be noted is that no attempt has been made to define *a priori* the social and clinical significance of any given IQ. The exact meaning of these deviation values, like any other measure of brightness, will become known through accumulating social statistics and clinical experience with both normal and clinical groups. As a matter of fact, the mean (100) and standard deviation (15) which have been chosen will give IQs which, on the whole, are fairly close numerically to IQs of other well-standardized tests like the *Stanford-Binet*. This will make comparison with IQs of other scales, at least at the numerical level, a not too unreasonable procedure. However, as the scales are not identical, individual interpretation must always be in terms of each test. Those accustomed to thinking in terms of percentiles will recognize, of course, that the deviation IQs are readily translated into percentile ranks....

THE GLOBAL CONCEPT OF INTELLIGENCE

Even more basic than the renunciation of the MA concept and the change in method of calculating the IQ is the extended definition of intelligence which, it is hoped, will emerge from the application of the Scale and which in point of fact forms the core of its rationale. Clinical experience and research in the past two decades have shown that it is not possible to identify or equate general intelligence with intellectual ability, however defined. Actually any and every test of intelligence measures something more, often a good deal more, than sheer intellectual ability—or any aspect of it, verbal, abstract, numerical, or even "g." Some of these other capacities, traits, etc., have been identified for some time and include, among other vectors, variables which have previously been called traits of temperament and personality, such as persistence, drive, energy level, etc. Moreover, it may be shown that the contributions which these factors make to the score of any intelligence test battery is a function of both the characteristics (contents) of the test and the circumstances under which it is administered.

It is possible by certain selective and statistical procedures to reduce the contribution of these factors, and that has generally been the aim of most authors of intelligence scales. This has usually been done in the hope of achieving "pure" measures of intellectual ability, which is a vain expectation. It turns out that the effect of such refinement, where approximated, has been to diminish rather than to increase the validity of the tests as effective measures of general intelligence. The reason for this is that while intellectual capacity (or any facet of it) may be a unitary trait or ability, general intelligence is not. In brief, intelligence is part of a larger whole, namely, personality itself. The theory underlying the *WISC* is that intelligence cannot be separated from the rest of the personality, and a deliberate attempt has been made to take into account the other factors which contribute to the total effective intelligence of the individual. This effort is reflected both in the composition of the Scale and, for the present, in the impartial weights attached to each test. No attempt has been made to get together a series of tests that measure "primary abilities" or to order them into a hierarchy of relative importance.

It is to be hoped that the point of view just advanced will help focus attention on the need for a broader concept of general intelligence than now obtains in psychometric circles. Of course, it is possible to continue measuring intelligence with a different orientation or indeed, as is not uncommon, with no orientation at all; but those who are already familiar with the *Wechsler-Bellevue Scales* know how much more useful a diagnostic instrument an intelligence test can be when some attention is paid to the nonintellective factors which modify and affect a subject's performance.

ORGANIZATION OF THE SCALE

The *WISC* consists of twelve tests which, like the adult scales, are divided into two subgroups identified as Verbal and Performance. Most of the verbal tests correlate better with each other than with tests of the performance group, and vice versa. But, while the tests identified as verbal and performance differ as these labels indicate, they each tap other factors, among them non-intellective ones, which cut across the groups to produce other classifications or categories that are equally important to consider in evaluating the individual's performance....

The tests of the Scale are grouped as follows—*Verbal:* Information, Comprehension, Arithmetic, Similarities, Vocabulary, Digit Span; *Performance:* Picture Completion, Picture Arrangement, Block Design, Object Assembly, Coding, Mazes.

In the standardization of the *WISC* all twelve tests were given to every subject; but in the interest of shortening the time required for an examination, the Scale has been reduced to ten tests. Ordinarily five Verbal and five Performance tests are administered to the subject, and the IQ tables are calculated on this basis. The two tests omitted in establishing the IQ tables are Digit Span in the Verbal and Mazes in the Performance part of the examination. The basis for omission of these tests was primarily their relatively low correlation with

TABLE 1

VERBAL	PERFORMANCE
1. General Information	6. Picture Completion
2. General Comprehension	7. Picture Arrangement
3. Arithmetic	8. Block Design
4. Similarities	9. Object Assembly
5. Vocabulary	10. Coding *or* Mazes

the other tests of the Scale and also, in the case of Mazes, the time factor. It is permissible to give all tests; indeed in clinical situations, their inclusion is strongly advised because of the qualitative and diagnostic data they add. Where all twelve tests are used, prorating is required before the IQs are computed....

In deciding which of the Performance tests could best be omitted from the battery, there were nearly as many reasons for leaving out the Coding test as there were for omitting Mazes. Although the Coding test was the one finally retained, it was also decided to permit the examiner to substitute Mazes in its stead if he so prefers. Accordingly, the final list of tests recommended for the ten-test Scale is [shown in Table 1].

Digit Span and Mazes (or Coding) are considered supplementary tests to be added when time permits, or used as alternate tests when some other test in the appropriate part is invalidated. A substitution may not, however, be made simply because a subject does poorly on a given test.

3.3 ROBERT J. STERNBERG

What Does It Mean to Be Smart?

Robert J. Sternberg (b. 1949) received his B.A. from Yale University in 1972 and his Ph.D. from Stanford University in California in 1975. Sternberg's first wave of well-received theory and research was on the "componential" theory of human intelligence. This theory was related to the "information processing" approach to psychology and viewed intelligence as made up of three interacting elementary informational processes: (1) knowledge-acquisition components, which learn how to solve problems; (2) metacomponents, which design, regulate, and evaluate problem-solving output; and (3) performance components, which enact the directions of the metacomponents and provide feedback to them.

In Sternberg's next wave of study and writing, he developed his "triarchic" theory of intelligence. Like the componential theory, intelligence was still considered to be made up of three interacting mental abilities: (1) relations to the external world (the environment); (2) relations to the internal world (thoughts, feelings, etc.); and (3) relations to the experience of the individual through application to the everyday world and to novel tasks and situations. In Sternberg's third major phase of research he emphasized the triarchic theory within the context of mental self-government. He concluded that intelligence is an interacting set of mechanisms, structures, and contents that empowers a person to conduct transactions with the self, others, and the environment.

Sternberg has been extraordinarily productive in publishing his works. Besides scores of journal articles, he has written, edited, or contributed to the books *Cognitive Psychology* (1998); *Defying the Crowd: Cultivating Creativity in a Culture of Conformity* (1995); *Encyclopedia of Human Intelligence* (1994); *In Search of the Human Mind* (1997); *Intelligence, Heredity, and Environment* (1997); *Intelligence, Instruction, and Assessment: Theory into Practice (Educational Psychology,* 1998; *Love Is a Story: A New Theory of Relationships* (1998); and many others.

The following selection comes from "What Does It Mean to Be Smart?" *Educational Leadership* (March 1997). In it, Sternberg describes the practical educational use of his theory in a schooling context as well as his latest work in the field of intelligence.

Key Concept: the four abilities: memory, analysis, creativity, and practicality

TOURO COLLEGE LIBRARY

*T*he most widely circulated newspaper in Connecticut recently carried a story on the meteoric rise of the president of one of the major banks in the state. I might have passed over the story with a glance had the name of the bank president not caught my eye. He was someone with whom I had gone to school from 1st grade right up through high school. What especially caught my attention, though, was that he had been a C student—someone who didn't seem to have much to offer.

Were the bank president an isolated case it might not be cause for alarm. But one cannot help wondering how many such students conclude that they really do not have much to contribute—in school or in the world at large—and so never try.

THE COST OF A CLOSED SYSTEM

Our system of education is, to a large degree, a closed system. Students are tested and classified in terms of two kinds of abilities—their ability to memorize information and, to a lesser extent, their ability to analyze it. They are also taught and assessed in ways that emphasize memory and analysis. As a result, we label students who excel in these patterns of ability as smart or able. We may label students who are weaker in these abilities as average or even slow or stupid.

The ability tests we currently use, whether to measure intelligence or achievement or to determine college admissions, also value memory and analytical abilities. These tests predict school performance reasonably well. They do so because they emphasize the same abilities that are emphasized in the classroom.

Thus, students who excel in memory and analytical abilities get good grades. Practically oriented learners, however, who are better able to learn a set of facts if they can see its relevance to their own lives, lose out. (Indeed, many teachers and administrators are themselves practical learners who simply tune out lectures or workshops they consider irrelevant to them.)

The consequences of this system are potentially devastating. Through grades and test scores, we may be rewarding only a fraction of the students who should be rewarded. Worse, we may be inadvertently disenfranchising multitudes of students from learning. In fact, when researchers have examined the lives of enormously influential people, whether in creative domains (Gardner 1993), practical domains (Gardner 1995), or both, they have found that many of these people had been ordinary—or even mediocre—students.

TEACHING IN ALL FOUR WAYS

At any grade level and in any subject, we can teach and assess in a way that enables students to use all four abilities (Sternberg 1994, Sternberg and Spear-

TABLE 1

Teaching for Four Abilities

Robert J. Sternberg

Type of Skill			
Memory	Analysis	Creativity	Practicality
Language Arts			
Remember what a gerund is or what the name of Tom Sawyer's aunt was.	Compare the function of a gerund to that of a participle, or compare the personality of Tom Sawyer to that of Huckleberry Finn.	Invent a sentence that effectively uses a gerund, or write a very short story with Tom Sawyer as a character.	Find gerunds in a newspaper or magazine article and describe how they are used, or say what general lesson about persuasion can be learned from Tom Sawyer's way of persuading his friends to whitewash Aunt Polly's fence.
Mathematics			
Remember a mathematical formula (Distance = Rate × Time).	Solve a mathematical word problem (using the D=RT formula).	Create your own mathematical word problem using the D=RT formula.	Show how to use the D=RT formula to estimate driving time from one city to another near you.
Social Studies			
Remember a list of factors that led up to the U.S. Civil War.	Compare, contrast, and evaluate the arguments of those who supported slavery versus those who opposed it.	Write a page of a journal from the viewpoint of a soldier fighting for one or the other side during the Civil War.	Discuss the applicability of lessons of the Civil War for countries today that have strong internal divisions, such as the former Yugoslavia.
Science			
Name the main types of bacteria.	Analyze the means the immune system uses to fight bacterial infections.	Suggest ways to cope with the increasing immunity bacteria are showing to antibiotic drugs.	Suggest three steps that individuals might take to reduce the likelihood of bacterial infections.

Swerling 1996. See also Sternberg and Williams 1996, Williams et al. 1996). In other words, we can ask students to

- Recall who did something, what was done, when it was done, where it was done, or how it was done;
- Analyze, compare, evaluate, judge, or assess;
- Create, invent, imagine, suppose, or design; and
- Use, put into practice, implement, or show use.

In physical education, for example, competitors need to learn and remember various strategies for playing games, analyze their opponents' strategies, create their own strategies, and implement those strategies on the playing field. Table 1 presents some examples of how teachers can do this in language arts, mathematics, social studies, and science.

When we use this framework, relatively few activities will end up requiring only one of these four abilities. On the contrary, most activities will be a mixture, as are the tasks we confront in everyday life. Notice that in this framework, instruction and assessment are closely related. Almost any activity that is used for the one can be used for the other.

In addition, no type of activity should be limited to students whose strength is in that area. On the contrary, we should teach all students in all four ways. In that way, each student will find at least some aspects of the instruction and assessment to be compatible with his or her preferred way of learning and other aspects to be challenging, if perhaps somewhat uncomfortable.

Teaching in all four ways also makes the teacher's job easier and more manageable. No teacher can individualize instruction and assessment for each student in a large class, but any teacher can teach in a way that meets all students' needs.

DOES THIS WORK IN PRACTICE?

In the summer of 1993, we conducted a study of high school students to test our hypothesis that students learn and perform better when they are taught in a way that at least partially matches their own strengths (Sternberg 1996; Sternberg and Clinkenbeard 1995; Sternberg et al. 1996). Known as the Yale Summer Psychology Program, the study involved 199 students from high schools across the United States and some from abroad.

Each school had nominated students for the program. Interested nominees then took a test designed to measure their analytical, creative, and practical abilities. The test included multiple-choice verbal, quantitative, and figural items, as well as analytical, creative, and practical essay items (Sternberg 1993). A sample of the items appears in Table 2.

We then selected the students who fit into one of five ability patterns: high analytical, high creative, high practical, high balanced (high in all three abilities), or low balanced (low in all three abilities). We based these judgments on both the individual student's patterns and the way these patterns compared to those of the other students.

We then placed each student into one of four differentiated instructional treatments. All included a morning lecture that balanced memory, analysis, creativity, and practical learning and thinking. All students used the same introductory psychology text (Sternberg 1995), which was also balanced among the four types of learning and thinking. The treatments differed, however, in the afternoon discussion sections. There, we assigned students to a section that emphasized either memory, analysis, creativity, or practical learning and thinking.

The critical feature of this design was that, based on their ability patterns, some students were matched and others mismatched to the instructional emphasis of their section. Another important feature was that all students received at least some instruction emphasizing each type of ability.

We assessed student achievement through homework assignments, tests, and an independent project. We assessed memory specifically through multiple-choice tests, and we evaluated analytical, creative, and practical abilities through essays. For the essays, we asked students questions such as "Discuss the advantages and disadvantages of having armed guards at school" (analysis); "Describe what your ideal school would be like" (creativity); and "Describe some problem you have been facing in your life and then give a practical solution" (practical use).

Because we assessed all students in exactly the same way, we could more easily compare the groups' performance. Had we used the more conventional forms of instruction and assessment, emphasizing memory and analysis, the creative and practical ability tests would probably not have told us much.

SOME SURPRISES

The study yielded many findings, but four stand out:

1. Students whose instruction matched their pattern of abilities performed significantly better than the others. Even by partially matching instruction to abilities, we could improve student achievement.

2. By measuring creative and practical abilities, we significantly improved our ability to predict course performance.

3. To our surprise, our four high-ability groups differed in their racial, ethnic, and socioeconomic composition. The high-analytic group was composed mostly of white, middle- to upper-middle-class students from well-known "good" schools. The high-creative and high-practical groups were much more diverse racially, ethnically, socioeconomically, and educationally. Our high-balanced group was in between. This pattern suggests that when we expand the range of abilities we test for, we also expand the range of students we identify as smart.

4. When we did a statistical analysis of the ability factors underlying performance on our ability test, we found no single general factor (sometimes called a g factor score or an IQ). This suggests that the general ability factor that has been found to underlie many conventional ability tests may not be truly general, but general only in the narrow range of abilities that conventional tests assess.

TABLE 2

Sample Multiple-Choice Questions from the Sternberg Triarchic Abilities Test

Analytical Verbal	The vip was green, so I started to cross the street. Vip most likely means: A. car B. sign C. light D. tree
Creative Quantitative	There is a new mathematical operation called graf. It is defined as follows: x graf $y = x + y$, if $x < y$ but x graf $y = x - y$, if otherwise. How much is 4 graf 7? A. -3 B. 3 C. 11 D. -11
Practical Figural (Students are shown a map)	After attending a performance at the theater, you need to drive to House A. If you want to avoid the traffic jam at the intersection of Spruce Avenue and Willow Street and take the shortest alternative route, you will drive A. west on Maple Avenue to Route 326. B. west on Pine Street to Hickory Street. C. east on Maple Avenue to Oak Street. D. east on Pine Street to Oak Street.

A CLEAR-EYED SENSE OF ACCOMPLISHMENT

By exposing students to instruction emphasizing each type of ability, we enable them to capitalize on their strengths while developing and improving new skills. This approach is also important because students need to learn that the world cannot always provide them with activities that suit their preferences. At the same time, if students are never presented with activities that suit them, they will never experience a sense of success and accomplishment. As a result, they may tune out and never achieve their full potential.

On a personal note, I was primarily a creative learner in classes that were largely oriented toward memorizing information. When in college, I took an introductory psychology course that was so oriented; I got a C, leading my instructor to suggest that I might want to consider another career path. What's more, that instructor was a psychologist who specialized in learning and memory! I might add that never once in my career have I had to memorize a book or lecture. But I have continually needed to think analytically, creatively, and practically in my teaching, writing, and research.

Success in today's job market often requires creativity, flexibility, and a readiness to see things in new ways. Furthermore, students who graduate with

A's but who cannot apply what they have learned may find themselves failing on the job.

Creativity, in particular, has become even more important over time, just as other abilities have become less valuable. For example, with the advent of computers and calculators, both penmanship and arithmetic skills have diminished in importance. Some standardized ability tests, such as the SAT, even allow students to use calculators. With the increasing availability of massive, rapid data-retrieval systems, the ability to memorize information will become even less important.

This is not to say that memory and analytical abilities are not important. Students need to learn and remember the core content of the curriculum, and they need to be able to analyze—to think critically about—the material. But the importance of these abilities should not be allowed to obfuscate what else is important.

In a pluralistic society, we cannot afford to have a monolithic conception of intelligence and schooling; it's simply a waste of talent. And, as I unexpectedly found in my study, it's no random waste. The more we teach and assess students based on a broader set of abilities, the more racially, ethnically, and socioeconomically diverse our achievers will be. We can easily change our closed system—and we should. We must take a more balanced approach to education to reach all of our students.

REFERENCES

Gardner, H. (1993) *Creating Minds.* New York: Basic Books.

Gardner, H. (1995). *Leading Minds.* New York: Basic Books.

Sternberg, R.J. (1993). "Sternberg Triarchic Abilities Test." Unpublished test.

Sternberg, R.J. (1994). "Diversifying Instruction and Assessment." The *Educational Forum* 59, 1: 47–53.

Sternberg, R.J. (1995). *In Search of the Human Mind.* Orlando, Fla.: Harcourt Brace College Publishers.

Sternberg, R.J. (1996). *Successful Intelligence.* New York: Simon & Schuster.

Sternberg, R.J., and P. Clinkenbeard. (May-June 1995). "A Triarchic View of Identifying, Teaching, and Assessing Gifted Children." *Roeper Review* 17, 4: 255–260.

Sternberg, R.J., M. Ferrari, P. Clinkenbeard, and E.L. Grigorenko. (1996). "Identification, Instruction, and Assessment of Gifted Children: A Construct Validation of a Triarchic Model." *Gifted Child Quarterly* 40: 129–137.

Sternberg, R.J., and L. Spear-Swerling. (1996). *Teaching for Thinking.* Washington, D.C.: American Psychological Association.

Sternberg, R.J., R.K. Wagner, W.M. Williams, and J.A. Horvath. (1995). "Testing Common Sense." *American Psychologist* 50, 11: 912–927.

Sternbeg, R.J., and W.M. Williams. (1996.) *How to Develop Student Creativity.* Alexandria, Va.: ASCD.

Williams, W.M., T. Blythe, N. White, J. Li, R.J. Sternberg, and H.I. Gardner. (1996). *Practical Intelligence for School: A Handbook for Teachers of Grades 5–8.* New York: Harper Collins.

The First Seven . . . and the Eighth

Howard Gardner was born in Scranton, Pennsylvania in 1943. He earned both his bachelor's and doctorate degrees from Harvard University and is currently a professor of human development at the Harvard Graduate School of Education. Gardner's book *Frames of Mind: The Theory of Multiple Intelligences* (Basic Books, 1983) has been influential in the ongoing debate concerning the nature of intelligence in both the field of psychology and in the popular press; it earned the Best Book Award from the American Psychological Association in 1984. Since the beginning of scientific psychology 100 years ago, researchers have been debating whether intelligence is best considered a single, broad, general ability (referred to as the "g-factor") or whether it is more accurately depicted as a set of specific abilities that are largely discrete and independent. In *Frames of Mind,* Gardner advanced a variety of strong evidence, ranging from physiological-psychological brain research to studies of precocity and genius, to demonstrate that there are at least seven basic different intelligences.

Gardner has been a prolific writer; he has published many journal articles and authored, edited and coauthored many texts, including *Art, Mind, and Brain: A Cognitive Approach to Creativity* (1984); *Artful Scribbles* (1989); *The Arts and Human Development: A Psychological Study of the Artistic Process* (1994); *Project Zero Frameworks for Early Childhood Education* (1998); *The Quest for Mind* (1981); and *To Open Minds: Chinese Clues to the Dilemma of Contemporary Education* (1989).

In the last 15 years Gardner's theory of multiple intelligences (TMI) has had a big impact on the practice of applied educational psychology in American schools as well as those of many other nations. School districts across America have been inspired with a vision of teaching to diverse forms of human intelligence. TMI has transformed curriculum and teaching methods in every part of the country, from preschool to college.

Recently, however, Gardner identified an eighth intelligence, the naturalistic. "The First Seven . . . and the Eighth: A Conversation With Howard Gardner," *Educational Leadership* (September 1997), from which the following selection has been taken, is one of the first publications in which Gardner mentions this new intelligence being added to his TMI. He is being interviewed by Kathy Checkley, who is a staff writer for *Update* and who has assisted in the development of the Association for Supervision and Curriculum Development's pilot online project on multiple intelligences and new CD-ROM *Exploring Our Multiple Intelligences.*

Key Concept: multiple intelligences

*H*oward Gardner's theory of multiple intelligences, described in Frames of Mind (1985), *sparked a revolution of sorts in classrooms around the world, a mutiny against the notion that human beings have a single, fixed intelligence. The fervor with which educators embraced his premise that we have multiple intelligences surprised Gardner himself. "It obviously spoke to some sense that people had that kids weren't all the same and that the tests we had only skimmed the surface about the differences among kids," Gardner said.*

Here Gardner brings us up-to-date on his current thinking on intelligence, how children learn, and how they should be taught.

How do you define intelligence?

Intelligence refers to the human ability to solve problems or to make something that is valued in one or more cultures. As long as we can find a culture that values an ability to solve a problem or create a product in a particular way, then I would strongly consider whether that ability should be considered an intelligence.

First, though, that ability must meet other criteria: Is there a particular representation in the brain for the ability? Are there populations that are especially good or especially impaired in an intelligence? And, can an evolutionary history of the intelligence be seen in animals other than human beings?

I defined seven intelligences (see box) in the early 1980s because those intelligences all fit the criteria. A decade later when I revisited the task, I found at least one more ability that clearly deserved to be called an intelligence.

That would be the naturalist intelligence. What led you to consider adding this to our collection of intelligences?

Somebody asked me to explain the achievements of the great biologists, the ones who had a real mastery of taxonomy, who understood about different species, who could recognize patterns in nature and classify objects. I realized that to explain that kind of ability, I would have to manipulate the other intelligences in ways that weren't appropriate.

So I began to think about whether the capacity to classify nature might be a separate intelligence. The naturalist ability passed with flying colors. Here are a couple of reasons: First, it's an ability we need to survive as human beings. We need, for example, to know which animals to hunt and which to run away from. Second, this ability isn't restricted to human beings. Other animals need to have a naturalist intelligence to survive. Finally, the big selling point is that brain evidence supports the existence of the naturalist intelligence. There are certain parts of the brain particularly dedicated to the recognition and the naming of what are called "natural" things.

How do you describe the naturalist intelligence to those of us who aren't psychologists?

The naturalist intelligence refers to the ability to recognize and classify plants, minerals, and animals, including rocks and grass and all variety of flora and fauna. The ability to recognize cultural artifacts like cars or sneakers may also depend on the naturalist intelligence.

Now, everybody can do this to a certain extent—we can all recognize dogs, cats, trees. But, some people from an early age are extremely good at recognizing and classifying artifacts. For example, we all know kids who, at age 3 or 4, are better at recognizing dinosaurs than most adults.

Darwin is probably the most famous example of a naturalist because he saw so deeply into the nature of living things.

Are there any other abilities you're considering calling intelligences?

Well, there may be an existential intelligence that refers to the human inclination to ask very basic questions about existence. Who are we? Where do we come from? What's it all about? Why do we die? We might say that existential intelligence allows us to know the invisible, outside world. The only reason I haven't given a seal of approval to the existential intelligence is that I don't think we have good brain evidence yet on its existence in the nervous system—one of the criteria for an intelligence.

You have said that the theory of multiple intelligences may be best understood when we know what it critiques. What do you mean?

The standard view of intelligence is that intelligence is something you are born with; you have only a certain amount of it; you cannot do much about how much of that intelligence you have; and tests exist that can tell you how smart you are. The theory of multiple intelligences challenges that view. It asks, instead, "Given what we know about the brain, evolution, and the differences in cultures, what are the sets of human abilities we all share?"

My analysis suggested that rather than one or two intelligences, all human beings have several (eight) intelligences. What makes life interesting, however, is that we don't have the same strength in each intelligence area, and we don't have the same amalgam of intelligences. Just as we look different from one another and have different kinds of personalities, we also have different kinds of minds.

This premise has very serious educational implications. If we treat everybody as if they are the same, we're catering to one profile of intelligence, the language-logic profile. It's great if you have that profile, but it's not great for the vast majority of human beings who do not have that particular profile of intelligence.

Howard Gardner and Kathy Checkley

The theory challenges the entire notion of IQ. The IQ test was developed about a century ago as a way to determine who would have trouble in school. The test measures linguistic ability, logical-mathematical ability, and, occasionally, spatial ability.

What the intelligence test does not do is inform us about our other intelligences; it also doesn't look at other virtues like creativity or civic mindedness, or whether a person is moral or ethical.

We don't do much IQ testing anymore, but the shadow of IQ tests is still with us because the SAT—arguably the most potent examination in the world —is basically the same kind of disembodied language-logic instrument.

The truth is, I don't believe there is such a general thing as scholastic aptitude. Even so, I don't think that the SAT will fade until colleges indicate that they'd rather have students who know how to use their minds well—students who may or may not be good test takers, but who are serious, inquisitive, and know how to probe and problem-solve. That is really what college professors want, I believe.

Can we strengthen our intelligences? If so, how?

We can all get better at each of the intelligences, although some people will improve in an intelligence area more readily than others, either because biology gave them a better brain for that intelligence or because their culture gave them a better teacher.

Teachers have to help students use their combination of intelligences to be successful in school, to help them learn whatever it is they want to learn, as well as what the teachers and society believe they have to learn.

Now, I'm not arguing that kids shouldn't learn the literacies. Of course they should learn the literacies. Nor am I arguing that kids shouldn't learn the disciplines. I'm a tremendous champion of the disciplines. What I argue against is the notion that there's only one way to learn how to read, only one way to learn how to compute, only one way to learn about biology. I think that such contentions are nonsense.

It's equally nonsensical to say that everything should be taught seven or eight ways. That's not the point of the MI theory. The point is to realize that any topic of importance, from any discipline, can be taught in more than one way. There are things people need to know, and educators have to be extraordinarily imaginative and persistent in helping students understand things better.

A popular activity among those who are first exploring multiple intelligences is to construct their own intellectual profile. It's thought that when teachers go through the process of creating such a profile, they're more likely to recognize and appreciate the intellectual strengths of their students. What is your view on this kind of activity?

My own studies have shown that people love to do this. Kids like to do it, adults like to do it. And, as an activity, I think it's perfectly harmless.

I get concerned, though, when people think that determining your intellectual profile—or that of someone else—is an end in itself.

You have to use the profile to understand the ways in which you seem to learn easily. And, from there, determine how to use those strengths to help you become more successful in other endeavors. Then, the profile becomes a way for you to understand yourself better, and you can use that understanding to catapult yourself to a better level of understanding or to a higher level of skill.

How has your understanding of the multiple intelligences influenced how you teach?

My own teaching has changed slowly as a result of multiple intelligences because I'm teaching graduate students psychological theory and there are only so many ways I can do that. I am more open to group work and to student projects of various sorts, but even if I wanted to be an "MI professor" of graduate students, I still have a certain moral obligation to prepare them for a world in which they will have to write scholarly articles and prepare theses.

Where I've changed much more, I believe, is at the workplace. I direct research projects and work with all kinds of people. Probably 10 to 15 years ago, I would have tried to find people who were just like me to work with me on these projects.

I've really changed my attitude a lot on that score. Now I think much more in terms of what people are good at and in putting together teams of people whose varying strengths complement one another.

How should thoughtful educators implement the theory of multiple intelligences?

Although there is no single MI route, it's very important that a teacher take individual differences among kids very seriously. You cannot be a good MI teacher if you don't want to know each child and try to gear how you teach and how you evaluate to that particular child. The bottom line is a deep interest in children and how their minds are different from one another, and in helping them use their minds well.

Now, kids can be great informants for teachers. For example, a teacher might say, "Look, Benjamin, this obviously isn't working. Should we try using a picture?" If Benjamin gets excited about that approach, that's a pretty good clue to the teacher about what could work.

The theory of multiple intelligences, in and of itself, is not going to solve anything in our society, but linking the multiple intelligences with a curriculum focused on understanding is an extremely powerful intellectual undertaking.

When I talk about understanding, I mean that students can take ideas they learn in school, or anywhere for that matter, and apply those appropriately in new situations. We know people truly understand something when they can represent the knowledge in more than one way. We have to put understanding up front in school. Once we have that goal, multiple intelligences can be a terrific handmaiden because understandings involve a mix of mental representations, entailing different intelligences.

Howard Gardner and Kathy Checkley

• Linguistic intelligence is the capacity to use language, your native language, and perhaps other languages, to express what's on your mind and to understand other people. Poets really specialize in linguistic intelligence, but any kind of writer, orator, speaker, lawyer, or a person for whom language is an important stock in trade highlights linguistic intelligence.

• People with a highly developed logical-mathematical intelligence understand the underlying principles of some kind of a causal system, the way a scientist or a logician does; or can manipulate numbers, quantities, and operations, the way a mathematician does.

• Spatial intelligence refers to the ability to represent the spatial world internally in your mind—the way a sailor or airplane pilot navigates the large spatial world, or the way a chess player or sculptor represents a more circumscribed spatial world. Spatial intelligence can be used in the arts or in the sciences. If you are spatially intelligent and oriented toward the arts, you are more likely to become a painter or a sculptor or an architect than, say, a musician or a writer. Similarly, certain sciences like anatomy or topology emphasize spatial intelligence.

• Bodily kinesthetic intelligence is the capacity to use your whole body or parts of your body—your hand, your fingers, your arms—to solve a problem, make something, or put on some kind of a production. The most evident examples are people in athletics or the performing arts, particularly dance or acting.

• Musical intelligence is the capacity to think in music, to be able to hear patterns, recognize them, remember them, and perhaps manipulate them. People who have a strong musical intelligence don't just remember music easily—they can't get it out of their minds, it's so omnipresent. Now, some people will say, "Yes, music is important, but it's a talent, not an intelligence." And I say, "Fine, let's call it a talent." But, then we have to leave the word intelligent out of all discussions of human abilities. You know, Mozart was damned smart!

• Interpersonal intelligence is understanding other people. It's an ability we all need, but is at a premium if you are a teacher, clinician, salesperson, or politician. Anybody who deals with other people has to be skilled in the interpersonal sphere.

(Continued on next page)

- Intrapersonal intelligence refers to having an understanding of yourself, of knowing who you are, what you can do, what you want to do, how you react to things, which things to avoid, and which things to gravitate toward. We are drawn to people who have a good understanding of themselves because those people tend not to screw up. They tend to know what they can do. They tend to know what they can't do. And they tend to know where to go if they need help.

- Naturalist intelligence designates the human ability to discriminate among living things (plants, animals) as well as sensitivity to other features of the natural world (clouds, rock configurations). This ability was clearly of value in our evolutionary past as hunters, gatherers, and farmers; it continues to be central in such roles as botanist or chef. I also speculate that much of our consumer society exploits the naturalist intelligences, which can be mobilized in the discrimination among cars, sneakers, kinds of makeup, and the like. The kind of pattern recognition valued in certain of the sciences may also draw upon naturalist intelligence.

People often say that what they remember most about school are those learning experiences that were linked to real life. How does the theory of multiple intelligences help connect learning to the world outside the classroom?

The theory of multiple intelligences wasn't based on school work or on tests. Instead, what I did was look at the world and ask, What are the things that people do in the world? What does it mean to be a surgeon? What does it mean to be a politician? What does it mean to be an artist or a sculptor? What abilities do you need to do those things? My theory, then, came from the things that are valued in the world.

So when a school values multiple intelligences, the relationship to what's valued in the world is patent. If you cannot easily relate this activity to something that's valued in the world, the school has probably lost the core idea of multiple intelligences, which is that these intelligences evolved to help people do things that matter in the real world.

School matters, but only insofar as it yields something that can be used once students leave school.

How can teachers be guided by multiple intelligences when creating assessment tools?

We need to develop assessments that are much more representative of what human beings are going to have to do to survive in this society. For example, I value literacy, but my measure of literacy should not be whether you can answer a multiple-choice question that asks you to select the best meaning of a paragraph. Instead, I'd rather have you read the paragraph and list four questions you have about the paragraph and figure out how you would answer those questions. Or, if I want to know how you can write, let me give you a stem and see whether you can write about that topic, or let me ask you to write an editorial in response to something you read in the newspaper or observed on the street.

The current emphasis on performance assessment is well supported by the theory of multiple intelligences. Indeed, you could not really be an advocate of multiple intelligences if you didn't have some dissatisfaction with the current testing because it's so focused on short-answer, linguistic, or logical kinds of items.

MI theory is very congenial to an approach that says: one, let's not look at things through the filter of a short-answer test. Let's look directly at the performance that we value, whether it's a linguistic, logical, aesthetic, or social performance; and, two, let's never pin our assessment of understanding on just one particular measure, but let's always allow students to show their understanding in a variety of ways.

You have identified several myths about the theory of multiple intelligences. Can you describe some of those myths?

One myth that I personally find irritating is that an intelligence is the same as a learning style. Learning styles are claims about ways in which individuals purportedly approach everything they do. If you are planful, you are supposed to be planful about everything. If you are logical-sequential, you are supposed to be logical-sequential about everything. My own research and observations suggest that that's a dubious assumption. But whether or not that's true, learning styles are very different from multiple intelligences. Multiple intelligences claims that we respond, individually, in different ways to different kinds of content, such as language or music or other people. This is very different from the notion of learning style.

You can say that a child is a visual learner, but that's not a multiple intelligences way of talking about things. What I would say is, "Here is a child who very easily represents things spatially, and we can draw upon that strength if need be when we want to teach the child something new." Another widely believed myth is that, because we have seven or eight intelligences, we should create seven or eight tests to measure students' strengths in each of those areas. That is a perversion of the theory. It's re-creating the sin of the single intelligence quotient and just multiplying it by a larger number. I'm personally against assessment of intelligences unless such a measurement is used for a very specific learning purpose—we want to help a child understand her history or his mathematics better and, therefore, want to see what might be good entry points for that particular child.

What experiences led you to the study of human intelligence?

It's hard for me to pick out a single moment, but I can see a couple of snapshots. When I was in high school, my uncle gave me a textbook in psychology. I'd never actually heard of psychology before. This textbook helped me understand color blindness. I'm color blind, and I became fascinated by the existence of plates that illustrated what color blindness was. I could actually explain why I couldn't see colors.

Another time when I was studying the Reformation, I read a book by Erik Erikson called *Young Man Luther* (1958).[1] I was fascinated by the psychological motivation of Luther to attack the Catholic Church. That fascination influenced my decision to go into psychology.

The most important influence was actually learning about brain damage and what could happen to people when they had strokes. When a person has a stroke, a certain part of the brain gets injured, and that injury can tell you what that part of the brain does. Individuals who lose their musical abilities can still talk. People who lose their linguistic ability still might be able to sing. That understanding not only brought me into the whole world of brain study, but it was really the seed that led ultimately to the theory of multiple intelligences. As long as you can lose one ability while others are spared, you cannot just have a single intelligence. You have to have several intelligences.

NOTES

1. See Erik Erikson, *Young Man Luther* (New York: W.W. Norton, 1958).

3.5 HOSSAIN B. DANESH AND
WILLIAM S. HATCHER

Errors in Jensen's Analysis

Hossain B. Danesh earned his M.D. in 1961 from the University of Isfahan in Iran. He completed his psychiatric residency at the University of British Columbia and the Illinois State Psychiatric Institute. For 30 years Danesh was in private practice as a psychiatrist in Canada. For 12 of those years he also taught psychiatry and family medicine at the University of Ottawa. He is currently the rector of Landegg Academy in Wienacht, Switzerland. His published texts include *The Violence-Free Society: A Gift for Our Children* (Canadian Association for Studies on the Baháví Faith, 1979), *Unity: The Creative Foundation of Peace* (Fitzhenry-Whiteside, 1986), *The Psychology of Spirituality* (Landegg Academy Press, 1994), and *The Violence-Free Family: Building Block of a Peaceful Civilization* (Bahai Studies Publications, 1995).

William S. Hatcher earned his docteur és sciences from the University of Neuchâtel, Switzerland, in 1963. In addition to holding visiting appointments at the École Polytechinque Fédéral in Switzerland and the University of Strasbourg in France, he is affiliated with Landegg Academy in Switzerland and the Steklov Institute for Mathematics in St. Petersburg, Russia. Hatcher has been a professor of mathematics at the Laval University in Quebec, Canada, since 1968. His published texts include *Absolute Algebra* (BSB Teubner, 1978), *The Logical Foundations of Mathematics* (Pergamon Press, 1982), *Logic and Logos: Essays on Science, Religion, and Philosophy* (G. Ronald, 1990), and *The Ethics of Authenticity* (International Moral Education Project, 1997).

In 1973 *Psychology Today* published a highly incendiary article, "The Differences Are Real," in which Arthur Jensen purported to prove that African Americans are genetically less intelligent than whites. Very similar in argument, and making liberal use of Jensen's work, is the book, *The Bell Curve: Intelligence and Class Structure in American Life* by Richard J. Herrnstein and Charles Murray (Free Press, 1994). The following selection from Danesh and Hatcher's article "Errors in Jensen's Analysis," *World Order* (Fall 1976) refutes the intent and logic of these divisive publications.

Key Concept: race and intelligence

*I*n the December 1973 issue of *Psychology Today*, Professor Arthur Jensen has undertaken to expound directly, unequivocally, and in more or less popular terms his convictions about race and intelligence as measured by IQ tests.[1] We feel strongly that there are a number of errors in Jensen's analysis presented in this article, some subtle and some quite blatant. Since none of the "responses" to Jensen's article contained in the same issue has taken up these points in a satisfactory way, we would like to present a brief discussion of some of them here. In order to avoid any possible charge of treating a modified or strawman version of Jensen's ideas, we will confine our remarks wholly to Jensen's *Psychology Today* article alone.

Under the heading "Culture-Fair Vs. Culture-Biased" Jensen attempts to disprove the claim that IQ differences can be attributed to culture-biased tests. In order to prove his point he suggests that he has undertaken a "rigorous study" and presents the following reasoning. He first makes the point that "the fact that the test is culture-*loaded* does not necessarily mean that it is culture-*biased*," even though he acknowledges that the comprehension of these items is directly related to culture. He then goes on to state that there are reputable culture-fair tests which measure the ability to generalize, to distinguish differences and similarities, to see relationships, but that blacks tend to perform better on the more culture-loaded tests while other minorities show the opposite trend. Among the other minorities mentioned as comparison groups by Jensen are Chinese, Mexican-Americans, Indians, and Eskimos.

In drawing conclusions from these observations Jensen omits a number of crucial facts and observations. One of the most important of these omitted variables is that of parental and family influence in early childhood. Indeed, there are similarities which are shared among Chinese, Mexican-Americans, Indians, and white Anglo middle-class Americans and which differentiate these groups sharply from the blacks. For the most part members of these former groups were all raised by their families; they have close bonds of affection between themselves and their parents; they receive encouragement, guidance, and values concurrent with their (respective) cultural values and points of view; they have the opportunity to identify with their people and thus be free of anxieties, deprivation, isolation, and rejection—while these latter are characteristic experiences of many black children.

One should ask Jensen whether in his studies the black children came from a similar family background as those of other children. Did they have a cohesive and close family? Or did they frequently come from broken homes with an absent father and perhaps a distracted, overwrought mother, laden with inferiority feelings, rage, and fears for the world into which her child is growing? Were they taught about the uniqueness of their culture, the splendor of their past, the stories of their nation and race?

Because black children live within the confines of white society, they are bombarded with the same cultural values as the white children through the strong influence of the mass media. But this "culture" is only a selective and disjointed input, directed, produced, and acted by the white majority. Indeed, this very "culture" teaches the black children their own inferiority. Since this is the only information they receive, it is not surprising that they do relatively better on the culture-loaded and verbal kinds of tests.

Furthermore, culture-fair tests are structured in the same way as culture-loaded tests in that they both use symbols to make sense out of life and the

*Hossain B.
Danesh and
William S.
Hatcher*

world. If a child is born into a family and culture where there are constant and specific norms, the child is able to make sense out of life, to construct a consistent model of the world. Lacking this initial successful model-building process, the individual often struggles for the rest of his life, piling layer upon layer of reinterpreted material on the false foundation. The effects of such early deprivation on the intellectual growth of the child are well documented.

Since the fact of the disastrous family structure of blacks is well-known to social scientists, Jensen's neglect of·this variable is particularly significant, for one would expect it to be among the most influential of the relevant cultural variables. Indeed, there is no more pervasive finding in the whole field of psychology than that of early parental influence on personality development (of which the intelligence is a part). These findings date from the beginning of the modern period and have continued to be confirmed in subsequent studies. And, as we have argued above, it is of even more particular significance with regard to the questions raised by Jensen concerning blacks.

Nor can one doubt the serious and widespread effect caused by racial prejudice and the negative self-image of the black American. The belief in the subhumanness of blacks was part of the black experience in America from the beginning. The multiplicity of cultural cues which the black child assimilates with every breath he takes—all telling him he is stupid and sometimes even rewarding him for acting so—cannot possibly be measured by any one-parameter system of measurement. In particular, one is certainly not going to neutralize this sort of massive education by such a trivial device as manipulating the race or color of the testing person or by giving a test in ghetto dialect. We find these examples of Jensen ludicrous in their oversimplification of cultural variables. Indeed, the word "cultural" is much too weak to carry the full weight of the educative process inflicted on blacks by whites.

Moreover, there are many examples of physical systems in which different variables reinforce each other, amplifying their total effect in such a way that *the outcome can never be predicted by varying each variable separately.* For example, it could be that the particular combination of disastrous family structure and socioeconomic disadvantage (to be discussed later) to which the black child is so widely subjected has a redoubling negative effect on IQ which is greater than the sum of each such condition acting separately. The highly probably occurrence of such "resonance" among purely environmental variables is never discussed by Jensen, nor does he seem to take it into account in drawing his conclusions or designing his experiments.

Although many other ethnic minorities such as Jews have been the object of prejudice in America and elsewhere, no such group in America has been an extraneous, highly visible minority *totally* cut off from its prior culture. The effect of this total deracination of the black by which he was reborn in a strange land as a chattel slave—as a physical object, no more, no less—cannot possibly be measured in such oversimplified terms as Jensen cites against the "environmental hypothesis."

In sum, we feel that Jensen neglects certain highly significant environmental variables (family structure and early parental influence, total cultural deracination, the accumulated effect of "learned inferiority") and that he fails to take into account the highly probable effect of resonance among environmental variables. It is not a question of "feeling sorry" for the plight of the black child (though we would not feel obliged to apologize for some such emotions). It is a question of serious logical and empirical omissions in Jensen's analysis of data and the design of experiments.

Not only are there neglected variables in Jensen's analysis, there are quite serious errors in the analysis given to some of the factors he does discuss. The most blatant is probably his discussion of the so-called " 'sociologist's fallacy.' " Jensen's argument here contains a serious non sequitur (or a circularity—it only depends on how Jensen would choose to defend his reasoning). His discussion, though terse, is highly confused; and we will examine it with care.

Jensen is concerned with refuting the validity of studies in which blacks and whites were matched for IQ according to socioeconomic status (abbreviated SES) and according to which the black-white IQ differential was substantially reduced. Jensen states: "Since whites and blacks differ in average socioeconomic status (SES), the matching of racial groups on SES variables such as education, occupation, and social class necessarily means that the black group is more highly selected in terms of whatever other traits and abilities correlate with SES, including intelligence."

There are several parts to this statement. We want to identify them for future analysis and reference. There is first the affirmation of an empirical fact of black-white difference in "average socioeconomic status." Let us call this (1). There is then a first conclusion from this "fact"—namely, that the black group is more "highly selected" according to certain other variables than the white one, and "necessarily" so. Call this (2). Finally, there is a second conclusion that intelligence (implicitly and crucially for Jensen's argument, *native* intelligence) is one of the variables with respect to which the black group is more highly selected. Call this second conclusion (3).

What Jensen presumably means when he speaks of whites and blacks as differing according to "average" SES is that, given the total black population as a sample space, on the one hand, and the total white population, on the other, there are proportionally fewer blacks in higher SE categories than whites. What this means in and of itself is precisely that the ratio of the number of blacks in higher SE categories to the total population of blacks is numerically smaller than is the corresponding ratio for the white case. It is most important to see, from the very beginning of this discussion, that nothing further can be drawn from this fact unless and until one determines the *de facto* criteria by which the black sample was determined—that is, the variables according to which the black sample is selective. One cannot simply presume that a sample is selective for some particular variable without furnishing evidence to support the affirmation.

Without such justification, the first conclusion (2) is already a non sequitur. For it does not follow from the pure logic of the situation that a given sample of a total sample space is necessarily selective according to any given variable because it is relatively smaller than some other sample.[2] A smaller sample could select, for instance, native intelligence in a random manner while a larger sample selected intelligence in a nonrandom way. Of course, it may happen, and frequently does, that a sample is in fact selective according to some given variable. But the simple logical point here is that the empirical fact of such se-lectivity has to be justified. It is not due to any inherent "necessity," logical or otherwise.

Of course, in (2) Jensen does not purport to identify the parameters along which the black sample is more selective. He only says that it is more selective according to "whatever other traits and abilities correlate with the given SES." But this statement by itself is just a tautology: any sample whatever is always selective according to those variables (if any) for which it is selective.

Finally, in (3) Jensen jumps to include, without justification, native intelli-gence as being one of the variables for which the black sample is more selective. He is arguing, in effect, that relatively brighter blacks are being matched against relatively dumber whites, thus accounting for the erasure of the black-white IQ differential when the comparison is made in this way.

Now *if* one begins with the *a priori* assumption that the average black-white IQ differential based on the total black and white populations (or on supposedly representative samples thereof) is due to genetic factors, the very fact that the comparison according to SE categories erases the difference will be evidence of the higher selectivity of the black samples according to native intelligence. But such an appeal is not open to Jensen as he is trying rather to establish independently the selectivity by intelligence of the black samples as an argument against the environmental thesis. To invoke here an assumption that the IQ differential is based on genetic factors would be to introduce a circularity in the argument.

This observation immediately raises another related question: To what ex-tent is IQ a reflection of native (genetically determined) intelligence? In partic-ular, if one assumes from the start that native intelligence is the prime variable being measured in IQ tests, the average black-white IQ differential is already complete and overwhelming proof of Jensen's thesis. No further arguments or proofs are necessary! But Jensen clearly states that our knowledge concerning the causes of the black-white IQ differential is uncertain and that the "issue" is "an open question, calling for much further scientific study." He, therefore, cannot hold it to have been established that IQ measures native intelligence.

Thus, even if IQ is found to be positively correlated with certain SE cate-gories, such a fact is not in itself evidence that native intelligence is. It further follows that, in lieu of independent justification of the assumption that the black SE categories are significantly *more* selective with respect to native intelligence than are the corresponding white ones, the reduction of the black-white IQ dif-ferential for matching SE categories must be interpreted as furnishing strong evidence for the environmental thesis. No other logical conclusion is possible.

Therefore, the crucial link in the chain of this apparently simple argument is that of justifying the implicit assumption Jensen makes that native intelli-gence is a selective criterion in determining SES for blacks and is positively correlated with SES, and more strongly so than for whites. (Notice that it is logically possible that different criteria determine the SE categories for the two races; thus we could not even argue naively from selectivity in the white case to that of the black.)

Let us now try to assess the justifiability of this assumption. Let us begin by focusing on the fact (1) and by asking the question: "To what is the average difference in socioeconomic status between blacks and whites due?" No one seriously debates the answer to that question. It is clearly that, from the beginning of their life on this continent, the blacks were crushed by a dominant and highly prejudiced white majority, first by a degrading chattel slavery and then, in the last one hundred years, by the exercise of numerous strategies to keep the blacks in the lowest possible SE categories. That any significant proportion of blacks have succeeded at all in achieving higher economic or social status in the face of such obstacles is in itself a miracle of human endurance.

But the important point here in terms of assessing the selection criteria of SES for blacks is the following: during the whole period from the beginning up until roughly the present hour, it was the whites who were "calling the shots." It, therefore, seems most reasonable that the blacks who succeeded (and who are thus now in the highest SE categories) are those who best conformed to the white image of blacks—that is, those who were docile, submissive, relatively unintelligent yes-men. These were "allowed" to succeed. These are the "Uncle Toms" that the newer generation of blacks have so strongly rejected as models for their own lives. Since the white notion that blacks are subhuman and not possessed of normal intelligence was part of the black experience from the beginning, as we have already observed in the preceding discussion, the more naturally intelligent blacks were consistently viewed as upstarts who "had airs" and who did not know their place. They were even more vigorously repressed than the average of blacks and have been so for a period of almost three hundred years. In other words, those blacks most capable of functioning in a white way in the white world were most consistently prevented from doing so. All of these well-known social facts, however unpleasant, are highly inconsistent with the assumption that native intelligence was a selective criterion in determining SES for blacks. The whites have, in effect, rendered the black dysfunctional (in the white world at any rate) and then observed that he was in fact dysfunctional.

Moreover, even within the white sample, the relationship between native intelligence and high SES seems tenuous at best. High status in America has traditionally meant success at making money. This ability seems most notably coupled with a certain aggressiveness, a certain kind of shrewdness, the ability to withstand certain kinds of stress and to take certain kinds of risks, and so on. A minimum of intelligence is undoubtedly necessary for success in business, but it is not at all clear that this minimum is not possessed by the person with an average (randomly selected) native intelligence which, when combined with the characteristics listed above, produces the successful individual.

Of course, since the Second World War it has become increasingly possible for people with high abstract intelligence (and without those other qualities) to make a decent living at being professors or the like. Thus a significant proportion of natively intelligent whites are certainly now to be found outside the lower SE categories. But this current fact does not mean that the sociological selection criterion which formed the category in the first place involved exceptional intelligence in any way: *a fortiori* for the blacks whose selection was determined by a still more complicated (and more irrational and anti-intellectual) criterion of conforming to white stereotypes.

Hossain B. Danesh and William S. Hatcher

Moreover, blacks with high native intelligence have not had the same opportunity to advance as whites and, therefore, are not likely to be found in as high SE categories as whites with the same native endowment. Also, it is clear that when one is primarily concerned with gut-level survival on a day-to-day basis, one would have no great inclination to devote himself to the abstract pursuits of the intellectual even if, under other conditions, he would be so fitted.

Of course, all these sociological observations do not, in themselves, prove that the black SE sample is not relatively more selective than the corresponding white ones as regards native intelligence. They do, however, constitute strong *prima facie* evidence that such is not the case. But the crucial logical point at issue here is that the burden of proof is on Jensen's shoulders, for it is he who asserts without justification that the black sample is in fact more selective. Lacking such justification, his argument against the SE matching studies is without any logical foundation.

Let us remark in passing that even the variable of educational level may have, in the American context especially, only the most indirect relationship to native intelligence with respect to the population as a whole. This is due in part to the prevailing values in our schools which tend to "turn off" many of the best and brightest students. Also, economic level (making money again) is probably the factor most directly related to educational level since it helps govern access to education and since extended formal education is part of the life style of the more affluent classes, and this independently of the intrinsic intellectual value or content of the education. Thus the variable of educational level is probably more correctly viewed as a function of economic status rather than as an independent variable; and economic status is, as we have suggested, only marginally related to native intelligence.

We do not insist on this last point but offer it only as a possibly interesting reflection.

Perhaps Jensen means to imply that performing at a certain economic level in society takes at least a minimal level of intelligence and that blacks must be more highly selected since, on the average, they score fifteen points lower than whites on IQ tests and are, therefore, in the majority, below this minimal level. But again, this argument is valid only if one attributes the average IQ difference to genetic factors in the first place, and this is the assumption Jensen must refute in order to avoid circularity in his argument.

Let us note also that social and economic variables (extreme poverty to put it simply) are among the major causative factors involved in brining about the disastrous family environment of large numbers of blacks (though not the only cause). Thus the relative stability of the home life of blacks with higher SE status is one possible cause of the higher IQ scores by blacks in these groups. It is, at any rate, totally consistent with the environmental explanation.

In the paragraph immediately following the statement quoted above Jensen pushes his reasoning one step further. In a statement which must be read to be believed he writes: "Those who cite the socioeconomic matching studies also fail to take account of the well-established genetic difference between social classes, which invalidates their comparison. For example, when the two races are matched for social background, the average skin color of the black group runs lighter in the higher SES groups. This difference indicates that genetic characteristics do vary with SES. Thus, SES matching of blacks and whites reduces the IQ difference not only because it controls for environmental differences, but because it tends to equalize genetic factors as well." Having failed to realize the lacuna in his argument of the previous paragraph, Jensen repeats a similar error here and further fails to realize that such a fact (if it is a fact) only serves to reinforce the interpretation that the SE selection criterion for blacks was determined by white prejudice more than anything else. For it is a fact, truly "well-established," that light-skinned blacks have always had an easier time in the white world than darker ones, and this obtains independently of *any* other factor. Less intelligent light-skinned blacks advanced much further than more intelligent darker ones. Thus lighter-skinned blacks in higher SE categories, though genetically closer to whites in general racial characteristics, *could still have been selected randomly (or even negatively) according to native intelligence.* Indeed, the known social facts of the situation reinforce this possibility. Yet Jensen steadfastly ignores this possibility and reasons naively from selectivity by skin color to selectivity for intelligence.

Clearly, no one doubts that individual native intelligence is primarily genetically determined. The point at issue is precisely whether, in the case under consideration, such genetic determination is linked to other casually observable genetically determined characteristics such as skin color. Jensen's reasoning here is thus question begging of the worst sort. (Could it be that he finds the opposite conclusion "unthinkable"?).

Indeed, without further justification, one cannot even take the lighter skins of blacks in higher SE categories (if this is established) as increasing the *probability* of a nonrandom selection with respect to native intelligence. This required, further justification leads back to the same question as before—namely, that of determining the *de facto* selection criterion for SES for blacks. But the fault in Jensen's skin-color argument remains in any case.

In a brief discussion of malnutrition and intelligence, Jensen acknowledges that malnutrition can affect intelligence but affirms "I have found no evidence that the degree of malnutrition associated with retarded mental development afflicts any major segment of the U.S. population." However, on page 12 of *Negro American Intelligence*, Thomas F. Pettigrew reports on studies concerning the effects of prenatal nutrition on IQ scores of young children.[3] In a sample of mothers from the lowest socioeconomic level, of which eighty percent were black, comparisons were made between a control group and a group fortified with iron and vitamin B complex. Children of mothers in the fortified group had a mean IQ at three years of age which was five full points above the children in the (unfortified) control group (103.4 to 98.4). It is also reported that the same researchers failed to find a similar effect among white mothers from a mountain area. This suggests that the black mothers were much more malnourished than the white sample from the mountain area. It also suggests strongly that malnutrition among blacks in America can and does attain degrees sufficient to affect IQ scores significantly.

Hossain B. Danesh and William S. Hatcher

On page 81 of his article Jensen states that it is not *a priori* unreasonable that genetics could produce significant differences in intelligence and that these differences could exist between two large population samples and that these differences could be positively correlated with other casually observable features such as skin color. To this any reasonable person must assent. After all, few things beyond logical contradictions are *a priori* unreasonable. But we are not operating *a priori*. We are operating *a posteriori*—after the fact of nearly three hundred years of the operation of many strong environmental factors any or all of which could, in various combinations, produce the effect which so impresses Jensen. We would say, then, that it is *a posteriori* most unreasonable that this effect (the average black-white IQ difference in America) is not largely or wholly due to environmental factors.

Of course, until the environmental hypothesis is conclusively proved or the genetic hypothesis disproved, we are left only with different degrees of reasonableness and not with a conclusively established explanation. And until there is such a conclusive resolution of the issue (which might, in fact, take generations of study), any person has a right to affirm publicly that the situation is inconclusive.

Jensen presents himself as saying nothing more than this, but in fact he is saying much more. When he says such things as "Most of the attempts to politicize the issue, I have found, come from the radical left. True liberals and humanists, on the other hand, want to learn the facts" or "I presented my research in a careful and dispassionate manner, hoping that it would stimulate rational discussion of the issue as well as further research. Much to my dismay, however, my article set off an emotional furor in the world of science," he is putting himself on the side of scientific objectivity and reasonableness and attributing emotional, pseudo-humanistic bias to those who object to his analyses.

Jensen strikes a pose of olympian objectivity as if he were a social scientist newly arrived from a distant planet, wholly detached from the culture he was observing. In fact, Jensen, as well as the writers of the present article, live, move, and have their being in the very white society which has inflicted such untold suffering on black people. Jensen must certainly be as aware as anyone else of these pervasive social facts (one wonders), yet his analyses consistently ignore their existence or their possible influence. Why? Is it because he thinks they truly do not matter, or does he feel somehow that "objectivity" requires that they be ignored? Perhaps, having already acquired the conviction, expressed in the title of his article, that there is a significant genetic difference, he has simply lost all interest in a careful (and possibly long and tedious) consideration of them.

Be this as it may, and whatever the ultimate resolution of the IQ controversy turns out to be, the lacunae and errors in Jensen's analysis of environmental factors stand to be corrected now.

PART THREE

Social and Moral Development

Chapter 4 Emotional and Social Development 127

Chapter 5 Value and Moral Development 149

On the Internet . . .

Sites appropriate to Part Three

Click to the *Journal of Moral Education* page for complete tables of contents of the latest issues.

```
http://www.tandf.co.uk/journals/
   alphalist.html
```

This is the official home page of the Association for Moral Education (AME), which is the world's largest organization of psychologists and educators devoted to moral development and education.

```
http://www.wittenberg.edu/ame/
```

Sponsored by the Yale-New Haven Teachers Institute, Ages in Stages: An Exploration of the Life Cycle based on Erik Erikson's Eight Stages of Human Development, by Margaret Krebs, includes a curriculum unit for high school teachers on this topic.

```
http://www.cis.yale.edu/ynhti/curriculum/
   guides/1980/1/80.01.04.x.html
```

CHAPTER 4 Emotional and Social Development

4.1 ERIK ERIKSON

Eight Ages of Man

Erik Erikson (1902–1994) was born in Germany, studied psychoanalysis under Sigmund Freud and his daughter Anna Freud in Vienna, and moved to America in 1933, taking a position at Harvard Medical School. He was the first child psychoanalyst in Boston, Massachusetts, and he worked at the Judge Baker Guidance Center and Massachusetts General Hospital. Erikson also performed research and taught at Yale University's Institute for Human Relations and its medical school in 1936. In 1939 he went to California and began a private practice associated with the University of California at Berkeley's Institute of Child Welfare. In the 1950s Erikson worked with emotionally disturbed youth at the Austen Riggs Center in Stockbridge, Massachusetts. And in the 1960s he was a professor of human relations at Harvard University. He retired in 1970.

Based on his observations of human development in Europe and America, including his studies among the Sioux in South Dakota and the Yurok in northern California, Erikson theorized that our social relationships are more influential on our development than the inner sexual tensions posited by Freud. He was also the first influential researcher in human development to emphasize stages of adult development beyond adolescence. Both Freud's psychosexual stages and Jean Piaget's cognitive-developmental stages end in puberty. Erikson, however, identified distinct stages of human functioning and interaction in early, middle, and late adulthood. His early childhood (initiative versus guilt), middle childhood (industry and competence versus inferiority), and adolescent (identity versus role confusion) stages of

127

socioemotional development have been guides to schoolteachers for several generations.

Erikson published many papers and books, including *Life History and the Historical Moment* (1975); *Insight and Responsibility: Lectures on the Ethical Implications of Psychoanalytic Insight* (W. W. Norton, 1964), *Identity and the Life Cycle* (International Universities Press, 1967), *Observations on the Yurok: Childhood and World Image* (Coyote Preess, 1943), *Gandhi's Truth: On the Origins of Militant Nonviolence* (W. W. Norton, 1969), and *Young Man Luther: A Study in Psychoanalysis and History* (W. W. Norton, 1962).

Erikson's theory of the eight stages of human development, spanning infancy to old age, was first published in his classic text *Childhood and Society* (W. W. Norton, 1950). In the following selection from the second edition of this text, he emphasizes the psychosocial "crises" that are the hallmarks of these stages. This revision of Freudian theory has inspired countless researchers, child psychologists, and educators in the last five decades. The stages he describes for early childhood, middle childhood, and adolescence are particularly helpful to public school teachers trying to understand the emotional needs of their students.

Key Concept: psychosocial stages

BASIC TRUST VS. BASIC MISTRUST

The first demonstration of social trust in the baby is the ease of his feeding, the depth of his sleep, the relaxation of his bowels. The experience of a mutual regulation of his increasingly receptive capacities with the maternal techniques of provision gradually helps him to balance the discomfort caused by the immaturity of homeostasis with which he was born. In his gradually increasing waking hours he finds that more and more adventures of the senses arouse a feeling of familiarity, of having coincided with a feeling of inner goodness. Forms of comfort, and people associated with them, become as familiar as the gnawing discomfort of the bowels. The infant's first social achievement, then, is his willingness to let the mother out of sight without undue anxiety or rage, because she has become an inner certainty as well as an outer predictability. Such consistency, continuity, and sameness of experience provide a rudimentary sense of ego identity which depends, I think, on the recognition that there is an inner population of remembered and anticipated sensations and images which are firmly correlated with the outer population of familiar and predictable things and people....

The firm establishment of enduring patterns for the solution of the nuclear conflict of basic trust versus basic mistrust in mere existence is the first task of the ego, and thus first of all a task for maternal care. But let it be said here that the amount of trust derived from earliest infantile experience does not seem to depend on absolute quantities of food or demonstrations of love, but rather on the quality of the maternal relationship. Mothers create a sense of trust in their children by that kind of administration which in its quality combines sensitive care of the baby's individual needs and a firm sense of personal trustworthiness within the trusted framework of their culture's life style. This forms the basis in the child for a sense of identity which will later combine a sense of being "all right," of being oneself, and of becoming what other people trust one will become. There are, therefore (within certain limits previously defined as the "musts" of child care), few frustrations in either this or the following stages which the growing child cannot endure if the frustration leads to the ever-renewed experience of greater sameness and stronger continuity of development, toward a final integration of the individual life cycle with some meaningful wider belongingness. Parents must not only have certain ways of guiding by prohibition and permission; they must also be able to represent to the child a deep, an almost somatic conviction that there is a meaning to what they are doing. Ultimately, children become neurotic not from frustrations, but from the lack or loss of societal meaning in these frustrations.

But even under the most favorable circumstances, this stage seems to introduce into psychic life (and become prototypical for) a sense of inner division and universal nostalgia for a paradise forfeited. It is against this powerful combination of a sense of having been deprived, of having been divided, and of having been abandoned—that basic trust must maintain itself throughout life.

Each successive stage and crisis has a special relation to one of the basic elements of society, and this for the simple reason that the human life cycle and man's institutions have evolved together. In this [essay] we can do little more than mention, after the description of each stage, what basic element of social organization is related to it. This relation is twofold: man brings to these institutions the remnants of his infantile mentality and his youthful fervor, and he receives from them—as long as they manage to maintain their actuality—reinforcement of his infantile gains.

The parental faith which supports the trust emerging in the newborn, has throughout history sought its institutional safeguard (and, on occasion, found its greatest enemy) in organized religion. Trust born of care is, in fact, the touchstone of the *actuality* of a given religion. All religions have in common the periodical childlike surrender to a Provider or providers who dispense earthly fortune as well as spiritual health; some demonstration of man's smallness by way of reduced posture and humble gesture; the admission in prayer and song of misdeeds, of misthoughts, and of evil intentions; fervent appeal for inner unification by divine guidance; and finally, the insight that individual trust must become a common faith, individual mistrust a commonly formulated evil, while the individual's restoration must become part of the ritual practice of many, and must become a sign of trustworthiness in the community.[1] ...[T]ribes dealing with one segment of nature develop a collective magic which seems to treat the Supernatural Providers of food and fortune as if they were angry and must be appeased by prayer and self-torture. Primitive religions, the most primitive layer in all religions, and the religious layer in each individual, abound with efforts at atonement which try to make up for vague deeds against a maternal matrix and try to restore faith in the goodness of one's strivings and in the kindness of the powers of the universe.

Each society and each age must find the institutionalized form of reverence which derives vitality from its world-image—from predestination to indeterminacy. The clinician can only observe that many are proud to be without religion whose children cannot afford their being without it. On the other hand, there are many who seem to derive a vital faith from social action or scientific pursuit. And again, there are many who profess faith, yet in practice breathe mistrust both of life and man.

AUTONOMY VS. SHAME AND DOUBT

In describing the growth and the crises of the human person as a series of alternative basic attitudes such as trust vs. mistrust, we take recourse to the term a "sense of," although, like a "sense of health," or a "sense of being unwell," such "senses" pervade surface and depth, consciousness and the unconscious. They are, then, at the same time, ways of *experiencing* accessible to introspection; ways of *behaving*, observable by others; and unconscious *inner states* determinable by test and analysis. It is important to keep these three dimensions in mind, as we proceed.

Muscular maturation sets the stage for experimentation with two simultaneous sets of social modalities: holding on and letting go. As is the case with all of these modalities, their basic conflicts can lead in the end to either hostile or benign expectations and attitudes. Thus, to hold can become a destructive and cruel retaining or restraining, and it can become a pattern of care: to have and to hold. To let go, too, can turn into an inimical letting loose of destructive forces, or it can become a relaxed "to let pass" and "to let be."

Outer control at this stage, therefore, must be firmly reassuring. The infant must come to feel that the basic faith in existence, which is the lasting treasure saved from the rages of the oral stage, will not be jeopardized by this about-face of his, this sudden violent wish to have a choice, to appropriate demandingly, and to eliminate stubbornly. Firmness must protect him against the potential anarchy of his as yet untrained sense of discrimination, his inability to hold on and to let go with discretion. As his environment encourages him to "stand on his own feet," it must protect him against meaningless and arbitrary experiences of shame and of early doubt. . . .

Shame is an emotion insufficiently studied, because in our civilization it is so early and easily absorbed by guilt. Shame supposes that one is completely exposed and conscious of being looked at: in one word, self-conscious. One is visible and not ready to be visible; which is why we dream of shame as a situation in which we are stared at in a condition of incomplete dress, in night attire, "with one's pants down." Shame is early expressed in an impulse to bury one's face, or to sink, right then and there, into the ground. But this, I think, is essentially rage turned against the self. He who is ashamed would like to force the world not to look at him, not to notice his exposure. He would like to destroy the eyes of the world. Instead he must wish for his own invisibility. This potentiality is abundantly used in the educational method of "shaming" used so exclusively by some primitive peoples. Visual shame precedes auditory guilt, which is a sense of badness to be had all by oneself when nobody watches and when everything is quiet—except the voice of the superego. Such shaming exploits an increasing sense of being small, which can develop only as the child stands up and as his awareness permits him to note the relative measures of size and power....

Doubt is the brother of shame. Where shame is dependent on the consciousness of being upright and exposed, doubt, so clinical observation leads me to believe, has much to do with a consciousness of having a front and a back —and especially a "behind." For this reverse area of the body, with its aggressive and libidinal focus in the sphincters and in the buttocks, cannot be seen by the child, and yet it can be dominated by the will of others. The "behind" is the small being's dark continent, an area of the body which can be magically dominated and effectively invaded by those who would attack one's power of autonomy and who would designate as evil those products of the bowels which were felt to be all right when they were being passed. This basic sense of doubt in whatever one has left behind forms a substratum for later and more verbal forms of compulsive doubting; this finds its adult expression in paranoiac fears concerning hidden persecutors and secret persecutions threatening from behind (and from within the behind).

This stage, therefore, becomes decisive for the ratio of love and hate, cooperation and willfulness, freedom of self-expression and its suppression. From a sense of self-control without loss of self-esteem comes a lasting sense of good will and pride; from a sense of loss of self-control and of foreign overcontrol comes a lasting propensity for doubt and shame....

We have related basic trust to the institution of religion. The lasting need of the individual to have his will reaffirmed and delineated within an adult order of things which at the same time reaffirms and delineates the will of others has an institutional safeguard in the *principle of law and order.* In daily life as well as in the high courts of law—domestic and international—this principle apportions to each his privileges and his limitations, his obligations and his rights. A sense of rightful dignity and lawful independence on the part of adults around him gives to the child of good will the confident expectation that the kind of autonomy fostered in childhood will not lead to undue doubt or shame in later life. Thus the sense of autonomy fostered in the child and modified as life progresses, serves (and is served by) the preservation in economic and political life of a sense of justice.

INITIATIVE VS. GUILT

There is in every child at every stage a new miracle of vigorous unfolding, which constitutes a new hope and a new responsibility for all. Such is the sense and the pervading quality of initiative. The criteria for all these senses and qualities are the same: a crisis, more or less beset with fumbling and fear, is resolved, in that the child suddenly seems to "grow together" both in his person and in his body. He appears "more himself," more loving, relaxed and brighter in his judgment, more activated and activating. He is in free possession of a surplus of energy which permits him to forget failures quickly and to approach what seems desirable (even if it also seems uncertain and even dangerous) with undiminished and more accurate direction. Initiative adds to autonomy the quality of undertaking, planning and "attacking" a task for the sake of being active and on the move, where before self-will, more often than not, inspired acts of defiance or, at any rate, protested independence....

The danger of this stage is a sense of guilt over the goals contemplated and the acts initiated in one's exuberant enjoyment of new locomotor and mental power: acts of aggressive manipulation and coercion which soon go far beyond the executive capacity of organism and mind and therefore call for an energetic halt on one's contemplated initiative. While autonomy concentrates on keeping potential rivals out, and therefore can lead to jealous rage most often directed against encroachments by younger siblings, initiative brings with it anticipatory rivalry with those who have been there first and may, therefore, occupy with their superior equipment the field toward which one's initiative is directed. Infantile jealousy and rivalry, those often embittered and yet essentially futile attempts at demarcating a sphere of unquestioned privilege, now come to a climax in a final contest for a favored position with the mother; the usual failure leads to resignation, guilt, and anxiety. The child indulges in fantasies of being a giant and a tiger, but in his dreams he runs in terror for dear life. This, then, is the stage of the "castration complex," the intensified fear of finding the (now energetically erotized) genitals harmed as a punishment for the fantasies attached to their excitement.

... [I]t is well to look back at the blueprint of the life-stages and to the possibilities of guiding the young of the race while they are young. And here we note that according to the wisdom of the ground plan the child is at no time more ready to learn quickly and avidly, to become bigger in the sense of sharing obligation and performance than during this period of his development. He is eager and able to make things cooperatively, to combine with other children for the purpose of constructing and planning, and he is willing to profit from teachers and to emulate ideal prototypes. He remains, of course, identified with the parent of the same sex, but for the present he looks for opportunities where work-identification seems to promise a field of initiative without too much infantile conflict or oedipal guilt and a more realistic identification based on a spirit of equality experienced in doing things together. At any rate, the "oedipal" stage results not only in the oppressive establishment of a moral sense restricting the horizon of the permissible; it also sets the direction toward the possible and the tangible which permits the dreams of early childhood to be attached to the goals of an active adult life, Social institutions, therefore, offer children of this age an *economic ethos,* in the form of ideal adults recognizable by their uniforms and their functions, and fascinating enough to replace, the heroes of picture book and fairy tale.

Thus the inner stage seems all set for "entrance into life," except that life must first be school life, whether school is field or jungle or classroom. The child must forget past hopes and wishes, while his exuberant imagination is tamed and harnessed to the laws of impersonal things—even the three R's. For before the child, psychologically already a rudimentary parent, can become a biological parent, he must begin to be a worker and potential provider. With the oncoming latency period, the normally advanced child forgets, or rather sublimates, the necessity to "make" people by direct attack or to become papa and mama in a hurry: he now learns to win recognition by producing things. He has mastered the ambulatory field and the organ modes. He has experienced a sense of finality regarding the fact that there is no workable future within the womb of his family, and thus becomes ready to apply himself to given skills and tasks, which go far beyond the mere playful expression of his organ modes or the pleasure in the function of his limbs. He develops a sense of industry—i.e., he adjusts himself to the inorganic laws of the tool world. He can become an eager and absorbed unit of a productive situation. To bring a productive situation to completion is an aim which gradually supersedes the whims and wishes of play....

In all cultures, at this stage, children receive some *systematic instruction,* although... it is by no means always in the kind of school which literate people must organize around special teachers who have learned how to teach literacy. In preliterate people and in non-literate pursuits much is learned from adults who become teachers by dint of gift and inclination rather than by appointment, and perhaps the greatest amount is learned from older children. Thus the *fundamentals of technology* are developed, as the child becomes ready to handle the utensils, the tools, and the weapons used by the big people. Literate people, with more specialized careers, must prepare the child by teaching him things which first of all make him literate, the widest possible basic education for the greatest number of possible careers. The more confusing specialization becomes, however, the more indistinct are the eventual goals of initiative; and the more complicated social reality, the vaguer are the father's and mother's role in it. School seems to be a culture all by itself, with its own goals and limits, its achievements and disappointment.

The child's danger, at this stage, lies in a sense of inadequacy and inferiority. If he despairs of his tools and skills or of his status among his tool partners, he may be discouraged from identification with them and with a section of the tool world. To lose the hope of such "industrial" association may pull him back to the more isolated, less tool-conscious familial rivalry of the oedipal time. The child despairs of his equipment in the tool world and in anatomy, and considers himself doomed to mediocrity or inadequacy. It is at this point that wider society becomes significant in its ways of admitting the child to an understanding of meaningful roles in its technology and economy. Many a child's development is disrupted when family life has failed to prepare him for school life, or when school life fails to sustain the promises of earlier stages....

On the other hand, this is socially a most decisive stage: since industry involves doing things beside and with others, a first sense of division of labor and of differential opportunity, that is, a sense of the *technological ethos* of a culture, develops at this time....

IDENTITY VS. ROLE CONFUSION

With the establishment of a good initial relationship to the world of skills and tools, and with the advent of puberty, childhood proper comes to an end. Youth begins. But in puberty and adolescence all samenesses and continuities relied on earlier are more or less questioned again, because of a rapidity of body growth which equals that of early childhood and because of the new addition of genital maturity. The growing and developing youths, faced with this physiological revolution within them, and with tangible adult tasks ahead of them are now primarily concerned with what they appear to be in the eyes of others as compared with what they feel they are, and with the question of how to connect the roles and skills cultivated earlier with the occupational prototypes of the day. In their search for a new sense of continuity and sameness, adolescents have to refight many of the battles of earlier years, even though to do so they must artificially appoint perfectly well-meaning people to play the roles of adversaries; and they are ever ready to install lasting idols and ideals as guardians of a final identity.

The integration now taking place in the form of ego identity is, as pointed out, more than the sum of the childhood identifications. It is the accrued experience of the ego's ability to integrate all identifications with the vicissitudes of the libido, with the aptitudes developed out of endowment, and with the opportunities offered in social roles. The sense of ego identity, then, is the accrued confidence that the inner sameness and continuity prepared in the past are matched by the sameness and continuity of one's meaning for others, as evidenced in the tangible promise of a "career."

The danger of this stage is role confusion.[2] Where this is based on a strong previous doubt as to one's sexual identity, delinquent and outright psychotic episodes are not uncommon. If diagnosed and treated correctly, these incidents do not have the same fatal significance which they have at other ages. In most instances, however, it is the inability to settle on an occupational identity which disturbs individual young people. To keep themselves together they temporarily overidentify, to the point of apparent complete loss of identity, with the heroes of cliques and crowds. This initiates the stage of "falling in love," which is by no means entirely, or even primarily, a sexual matter—except where the mores demand it. To a considerable extent adolescent love is an attempt to arrive at a definition of one's identity by projecting one's diffused ego image on another and by seeing it thus reflected and gradually clarified. This is why so much of young love is conversation....

INTIMACY VS. ISOLATION

The strength acquired at any stage is tested by the necessity to transcend it in such a way that the individual can take chances in the next stage with what was most vulnerably precious in the previous one. Thus, the young adult, emerging from the search for and the insistence on identity, is eager and willing to fuse his identity with that of others. He is ready for intimacy, that is, the capacity to commit himself to concrete affiliations and partnerships and to develop the ethical strength to abide by such commitments, even though they may call for significant sacrifices and compromises. Body and ego must now be masters of the organ modes and of the nuclear conflicts, in order to be able to face the fear of ego loss in situations which call for self-abandon: in the solidarity of close affiliations, in orgasms and sexual unions, in close friendships and in physical combat, in experiences of inspiration by teachers and of intuition from the recesses of the self. The avoidance of such experiences because of a fear of ego loss may lead to a deep sense of isolation and consequent self-absorption.

The counterpart of intimacy is distantiation: the readiness to isolate and, if necessary, to destroy those forces and people whose essence seems dangerous to one's own, and whose "territory" seems to encroach on the extent of one's intimate relations. Prejudices thus developed (and utilized and exploited in politics and in war) are a more mature outgrowth of the blinder repudiations which during the struggle for identity differentiate sharply and cruelly between the familiar and the foreign. The danger of this stage is that intimate, competitive, and combative relations are experienced with and against the selfsame people. But as the areas of adult duty are delineated, and as the competitive encounter, and the sexual embrace, are differentiated, they eventually become subject to that *ethical sense* which is the mark of the adult. . . .

GENERATIVITY VS. STAGNATION

In this [essay] the emphasis is on the childhood stages, otherwise the section on generativity would of necessity be the central one, for this term encompasses the evolutionary development which has made man the teaching and instituting as well as the learning animal. The fashionable insistence on dramatizing the dependence of children on adults often blinds us to the dependence of the older generation on the younger one. Mature man needs to be needed, and maturity needs guidance as well as encouragement from what has been produced and must be taken care of.

Generativity, then, is primarily the concern in establishing and guiding the next generation, although there are individuals who, through misfortune or because of special and genuine gifts in other directions, do not apply this drive to their own offspring. And indeed, the concept generativity is meant to include such more popular synonyms as *productivity* and *creativity*, which, however, cannot replace it.

It has taken psychoanalysis some time to realize that the ability to lose oneself in the meeting of bodies and minds leads to a gradual expansion of

135

ego-interests and to a libidinal investment in that which is being generated. Generativity thus is an essential stage on the psychosexual as well as on the psychosocial schedule. Where such enrichment fails altogether, regression to an obsessive need for pseudo-intimacy takes place, often with a pervading sense of stagnation and personal impoverishment. Individuals, then, often begin to indulge themselves as if they were their own—or one another's—one and only child; and where conditions favor it, early invalidism, physical or psychological, becomes the vehicle of self-concern. The mere fact of having or even wanting children, however, does not "achieve" generativity. In fact, some young parents suffer, it seems, from the retardation of the ability to develop this stage. The reasons are often to be found in early childhood impressions; in excessive self-love based on a too strenuously self-made personality; and finally (and here we return to the beginnings) in the lack of some faith, some "belief in the species," which would make a child appear to be a welcome trust of the community.

As to the institutions which safeguard and reinforce generativity, one can only say that all institutions codify the ethics of generative succession. Even where philosophical and spiritual tradition suggests the renunciation of the right to procreate or to produce, such early turn to "ultimate concerns," wherever instituted in monastic movements, strives to settle at the same time the matter of its relationship to the Care for the creatures of this world and to the Charity which is felt to transcend it.

If this were [an essay] on adulthood, it would be indispensable and profitable at this point to compare economic and psychological theories (beginning with the strange convergencies and divergencies of Marx and Freud) and to proceed to a discussion of man's relationship to his production as well as to his progeny.

EGO INTEGRITY VS. DESPAIR

Only in him who in some way has taken care of things and people and has adapted himself to the triumphs and disappointments adherent to being, the originator of others or the generator of products and ideas—only in him may gradually ripen the fruit of these seven stages. I know no better word for it than ego integrity. Lacking a clear definition, I shall point to a few constituents of this state of mind. It is the ego's accrued assurance of its proclivity for order and meaning. It is a post-narcissistic love of the human ego—not of the self—as an experience which conveys some world order and spiritual sense, no matter how dearly paid for. It is the acceptance of one's one and only life cycle as something that had to be and that, by necessity, permitted of no substitutions: it thus means a new, a different love of one's parents. It is a comradeship with the ordering ways of distant times and different pursuits, as expressed in the simple products and sayings of such times and pursuits....

The lack or loss of this accrued ego integration is signified by fear of death: the one and only life cycle is not accepted as the ultimate of life. Despair expresses the feeling that the time is now short, too short for the attempt to start another life and to try out alternate roads to integrity....

Each individual, to become a mature adult, must to a sufficient degree develop all the ego qualities mentioned, so that a wise Indian, a true gentleman, and a mature peasant share and recognize in one another the final stage of integrity. But each cultural entity, to develop the particular style of integrity suggested by its historical place, utilizes a particular combination of these conflicts, along with specific provocations and prohibitions of infantile sexuality. Infantile conflicts become creative only if sustained by the firm support of cultural institutions and of the special leader classes representing them. In order to approach or experience integrity, the individual must know how to be a follower of image bearers in religion and in politics, in the economic order and in technology, in aristocratic living and in the arts and sciences. Ego integrity, therefore, implies an emotional integration which permits participation by followership as well as acceptance of the responsibility of leadership.

Webster's Dictionary is kind enough to help us complete this outline in a circular fashion. Trust (the first of our ego values) is here defined as "the assured reliance on another's integrity," the last of our values. I suspect that Webster had business in mind rather than babies, credit rather than faith. But the formulation stands. And it seems possible to further paraphrase the relation of adult integrity and infantile trust by saying that healthy children will not fear life if their elders have integrity enough not to fear death.

NOTES

1. This is the communal and psychosocial side of religion. Its often paradoxical relation to the spirituality of the individual is a matter not to be treated briefly and in passing (see *Young Man Luther*). (E. H. E.)
2. See "The Problem of Ego-Identity," *J. Amer. Psa. Assoc.*, 4:56–121.

Development and Validation of Ego-Identity Status

James E. Marcia completed his Ph.D. in psychology at Ohio State University and went on to teach at Simon Fraser University in British Columbia. He became keenly interested in Erik Erikson's psychosocial stage theory, especially the adolescent stage, known as the identity versus role confusion stage. For his doctoral dissertation, Marcia decided to perform an empirical study in which he examined a method of assessing levels of achievement of ego identity, as described by Erikson.

By basing his work on Erikson's psychosocial stage theory, Marcia was placing himself in the Freudian, psychoanalytic tradition. Erikson borrowed Sigmund Freud's psychosexual concept of "ego" and transformed it into a social construct based on the ego's development of an "identity." Erikson framed identity as primarily coming from one's chosen career or profession but also as being greatly influenced by such factors as one's religious or sexual identification as well. Marcia then built upon Erikson's work by empirically delineating four different conditions, or statuses, of ego identity establishment.

Marcia condensed the results of his dissertation into journal article format, and it was published in the *Journal of Personality and Social Psychology* in 1966. This article, "Development and Validation of Ego-Identity Status," has since become a modern classic, and the following is an excerpt from it. At its core, this is scientific research into the age-old teenagers' question, "Who am I?"

Key Concept: identity statuses

*F*our modes of reacting to the late adolescent identity crisis were described, measured, and validated. Criteria for inclusion in 1 of 4 identity statuses were the presence of crisis and commitment in the areas of occupation and ideology. Statuses were determined for 86 college male Ss by means of individual interviews. Performance on a *stressful concept-attainment task, patters of goal setting, authoritarianism, and vulnerability to self-esteem change were dependent variables. Ss higher in ego identity performed best on the concept-attainment task; those in the status characterized by adherence to parental wishes set goals unrealistically high and subscribed significantly more to authoritarian values. Failure of the self-esteem condition to discriminate among the statuses was attributed to unreliability in self-esteem measurement.*

James E. Marcia

Ego identity and identity diffusion (Erikson, 1956, 1963) refer to polar outcomes of the hypothesized psychosocial crisis occurring in late adolescence. Erikson views this phase of the life cycle as a time of growing occupational and ideological commitment. Facing such imminent adult tasks as getting a job and becoming a citizen, the individual is required to synthesize childhood identifications in such a way that he can both establish a reciprocal relationship with his society and maintain a feeling of continuity within himself.

Previous studies have attempted to determine the extent of ego-identity achievement by means of an adjustment measure and the semantic differential technique (Bronson, 1959) a *Q*-sort measure of real-ideal-self discrepancy (Gruen, 1960), a measure of role variability based on adjective ranking (Block, 1961), and a questionnaire (Rasmussen, 1964). While these studies have investigated self-ratings on characteristics that should follow if ego identity has been achieved, they have not dealt explicitly with the psychosocial criteria for determining degree of ego identity, nor with testing hypotheses regarding direct behavioral consequences of ego identity.

To assess ego identity, the present study used measures and criteria congruent with Erikson's formulation of the identity crisis as a *psychosocial* task. Measures were a semi-structured interview and an incomplete-sentences blank. The interview (see Method section) was used to determine an individual's specific identity status: that is which of four concentration points along a continuum of ego-identity achievement best characterized him. The incomplete-sentences blank served as an overall measure of identity achievement. The criteria used to establish identity status consisted of two variables, crisis and commitment, applied to occupational choice, religion, and political ideology. Crisis refers to the adolescent's period of engagement in choosing among meaningful alternatives; commitment refers to the degree of personal investment the individual exhibits.

"Identity achievement" and "identity diffusion" are polar alternatives of status inherent in Erickson's theory. According to the criteria employed in this study, an identity-achievement subject has experienced a crisis period and is committed to an occupation and ideology. He has seriously considered several occupational choices and has made a decision on his own terms, even though his ultimate choice may be a variation of parental wishes. With respect to ideology, he seems to have reevaluated past beliefs and achieved a resolution that leaves him free to act. In general, he does not appear as if he would be overwhelmed by sudden shifts in his environment or by unexpected responsibilities.

The identity-diffusion subject may or may not have experienced a crisis period; his hallmark is a lack of commitment. He has neither decided upon an occupation nor is much concerned about it. Although he may mention a preferred occupation, he seems to have little conception of its daily routine and gives the impression that the choice could be easily abandoned should opportunities arise elsewhere. He is either uninterested in ideological matters or takes a smorgasbord approach in which one outlook seems as good to him as another and he is not averse to sampling from all.

Two additional concentration points roughly intermediate in this distribution are the moratorium and foreclosure statuses. The moratorium subject is *in* the crisis period with commitments rather vague; he is distinguished from the identity-diffusion subject by the appearance of an active struggle to make commitments. Issues often described as adolescent preoccupy him. Although his parents' wishes are still important to him, he is attempting a compromise among them, society's demands, and his own capabilities. His sometimes bewildered appearance stems from his vital concern and internal preoccupation with what occasionally appear to him to be unresolvable questions.

A foreclosure subject is distinguished by not having experienced a crisis, yet expressing commitment. It is difficult to tell where his parents' goals for him leave off and where his begin. He is becoming what others have prepared or intended him to become as a child. His beliefs (or lack of them) are virtually "the faith of his fathers living still." College experiences serve only as a confirmation of childhood beliefs. A certain rigidity characterizes his personality; one feels that if he were faced with a situation in which parental values were nonfunctional, he would feel extremely threatened.

Previous studies have found ego identity to be related to "certainty of self-conception" and "temporal stability of self-rating" (Bronson, 1959), extent of a subject's acceptance of a false personality sketch of himself (Gruen, 1960), anxiety (Block, 1961), and sociometric ratings of adjustment (Rasmussen, 1964). Two themes predominate in these studies: a variability-stability dimension of self-concept, and overall adjustment. In general, subjects who have achieved ego identity seem less confused in self-definition and are freer from anxiety.

Four task variables were used to validate the newly constructed identity statuses: a concept-attainment task administered under stressful conditions, a level of aspiration measure yielding goal-setting patterns, a measure of authoritarianism, and a measure of stability of self-esteem in the face of invalidating information.

The hypotheses investigated were these:

1. Subjects high in ego identity (i.e., identity-achievement status) will receive significantly lower (better) scores on the stressful concept-attainment task than subjects lower in ego identity. Subjects who have achieved an ego identity, with the internal locus of self-definition which that implies, will be less vulnerable to the stress conditions of evaluation apprehension and over-solicitousness (see Method section).
2. Subjects high in ego identity will set goals more realistically than subjects low in ego identity on a level of aspiration measure. The increment to overall ego strength following identity achievement should be reflected in the ego function of reality testing.

3. Subjects in the foreclosure status will endorse "authoritarian submission and conventionality" items to a greater extend than subjects in the other statuses.
4. There will be a significant positive relationship between ego identity measures and a measure of self-esteem.
5. Subjects high in ego identity will change less in self-esteem when given false information about their personalities than subjects low in ego identity.
6. There will be a significant relationship between the two measures of ego identity: the identity-status interview and the incomplete-sentences blank.

METHOD

Subjects

Subjects were 86 males enrolled in psychology, religion, and history courses at Hiram College.

Confederate Experimenters

Due to the possibility of contamination by subject intercommunication on a small campus, the study employed 10 confederate (task) experimenters who administered the concept-attainment task in one 12-hour period to all subjects. These task experimenters, 7 males and 3 females, were members of the author's class in psychological testing and had taken three or more courses in psychology. They had previously assisted in a pilot study, and had been checked twice by the author on their experimental procedure. The use of a sample of experimenters, none of whom were aware of the subjects' standings on crucial independent variables, also has advantages in terms of minimizing the effects of experimenter bias (Rosenthal, 1964).

Identity status. Identity status was established by means of a 15–30 minute semistructured interview. All interviews followed the same outline, although deviations from the standard form were permitted in order to explore some areas more thoroughly. In most cases, the criteria for terminating an interview involved the completion of the prescribed questions as well as some feeling of certainty on the interviewer's part that the individual had provided enough information to be categorized. Interviews were tape-recorded and then replayed for judging. Hence, each interview was heard at least twice, usually three or four times.

A scoring manual (Marcia, 1964) was constructed using both theoretical criteria from Erikson and empiracal criteria from a pilot study. Each subject was evaluated in terms of presence or absence of crisis as well as degree of commitment for three areas: occupation, religion, and politics—the latter two combined in a general measure of ideology. The interview judge familiarized himself with the descriptions of the statuses provided in the manual and sorted each interview into that pattern which it most closely resembled. Analysis of interjudge reliability for the identity statuses of 20 randomly selected subjects among three judges yielded an average percentage of agreement of 75. One of the judges was essentially untrained, having been given only the scoring manual and the 20 taped interviews.

A multiple question in the occupational area was:

How willing do you think you'd be to give up going into _____ if something better came along?

Examples of typical answers for the four statuses were:

[Identity achievement] Well, I might, but I doubt it. I can't see what "something better" would be for me.
[Moratorium] I guess if I knew for sure I could answer that better. It would have to be something in the general area—something related.
[Foreclosure] Not very willing. It's what I've always wanted to do. The folks are happy with it and so am I.
[Identity diffusion] Oh sure. If something better came along, I'd change just like that.

A sample question in the religious area was:

Have you ever had any doubts about your religious beliefs?
[Identity achievement] Yeah, I even started wondering whether or not there was a god. I've pretty much resolved that now, though. The way it seems to me is. . . .
[Moratorium] Yes, I guess I'm going through that now. I just don't see how there can be a god and yet so much evil in the world or . . . .
[Foreclosure] No, not really, our family is pretty much in agreement on those things.
[Identity diffusion] Oh, I don't know. I guess so. Everyone goes through some sort of stage like that. But it really doesn't bother me much. I figure one's about as good as the other!

Overall ego identity. The Ego Identity Incomplete Sentences Blank (EI-ISB) is a 23-item semistructured projective test requiring the subject to complete a sentence "expressing his real feelings" having been given a leading phrase. Stems were selected and a scoring manual designed (Marcia, 1964) according to behaviors which Erikson (1956) relates to the achievement of ego identity. Empirical criteria were gathered during a pilot study. Each item was scored 3, 2, or 1 and item scores summed to yield an overall ego-identity score. Two typical stems were: If one commits oneself _____ and, When I let myself go I _____. Scoring criteria for the latter stem are:

3—Nondisastrous self-abandonment. Luxuriating in physical release. For example, have a good time and do not worry about others' thoughts and standards, enjoy almost anything that has laughter and some physical activity involved, enjoy myself more.

2—Cautiousness, don't know quite what will happen, have to be careful. Defensive or trivial. For example, never know exactly what I will say or do, sleep, might be surprised since I don't remember letting myself go.

1—Goes all to pieces, dangerous, self-destructive, better not to. For example, think I talk too much about myself and my personal interests, tend to become too loud when sober and too melodramatic when drunk, sometimes say things I later regret.

Analysis of interscorer reliability for 20 protocols among three judges yielded an average item-by-item correlation of $r = .76$, an average total score correlation of $r = .73$, and an average percentage of agreement of 74.

Measures of Task Variables

Concept Attainment Task performance. The Concept Attainment Task (CAT) developed by Bruner, Goodnow, and Austin (1956) and modified by Weick (1964), requires the subject to arrive at a certain combination of attributes of cards. The subject may eliminate certain attributes by asking whether a card is positive or negative for the concept and he may guess the concept at any time. He is penalized 5 points for every request, 10 points for every guess, and 5 points for every 30 seconds that passes before he attains the concept. Level of aspiration was obtained by informing the subject of his previous time and asking him to estimate his time on the next problem.

Quality of performance on the CAT was assessed by the following measures: overall CAT scores (points for time plus points for requests and guesses), points for time alone, points for requests and guesses alone, number of "give-ups" (problems which the subject refused to complete). The main level of aspiration measure was attainment discrepancy or D score, the algebraic average of the differences between a subject's stated expectancy for a problem and his immediately preceding performance on a similar problem.

A combination of two stress conditions (stress defined here as externally imposed conditions which tend to impair performance) were used: evaluation apprehension and oversolicitousness. Evaluation apprehension refers to a subject's feeling that his standing on highly valued personal characteristics is to be exposed. The characteristic chosen for this study was intellectual competence, unquestionably salient for college students. Oversolicitousness was chosen as a logical complement to evaluation apprehension. It was assumed that unnecessary reassurance would validate and, hence, augment whatever anxiety the subject was experiencing.

Pilot study data indicated that the stress conditions were effective. Using the same task experimenters as in the final study, 56 subjects (27 males and 29 females) took the CAT under stress and nonstress (i.e., stress omitted) conditions. Each experimenter ran about 3 stress and 3 nonstress subjects. Stressed subjects performed significantly more poorly than nonstressed ones ($t = 2.61$, $df = 54$, $p < .02$).

Self-esteem change and authoritarianism. The Self-Esteem Questionnaire (SEQ-F) is a 20-item test developed by deCharms and Rosenbaum (1960) on which the subject indicates his degree of endorsement of statements concerning general feelings of self-confidence and worthiness.

In addition, statements reflecting authoritarian submission and conventionality, taken from the California F Scale (Adorno, Frenkel-Brunswik; Levinson, & Sanford, 1950), which were originally filler items, are used here as a dependent variable. The SEQ-F was administered twice, the first time in a classroom setting the second, during the experimental situation following an invalidated self-definition.

The treatment condition of "invalidated self-definition" (ISD) followed the CAT and directly preceded the second administration of SEQ-F. It consisted of giving the subject false information concerning the relationship between his alleged self-evaluation and his actual personality.

Procedure

Following is the experimental procedure: Subjects completed the EI-ISB and SEQ-F in class. Each subject was interviewed to determine his identity status. (This interviewing period lasted about 2 months.) On the day of the experiment, each subject went through the following conditions: *(a)* Administration of the CAT under stress by the task experimenter. *Evaluation apprehension* was created by the task experimenter's saying:

> By the way, I thought you might be interested to know that this test is related to tests of intelligence[1] and that it's been found to be one of the best single predictors of success in college. So of course, you'll want to do your very best.

Oversolicitousness was created during CAT performance by the task experimenter's hovering over the subject, asking him if he were comfortable, advising him not to "tense up," not to "make it harder on yourself." *(b)* Following the CAT, the subject was seated in the author's office where he was given either a positive or negative (randomly assigned) invalidated self-definition. The subject found the experimenter intently scanning a data sheet and was told:

> I've been looking over some of the data and it seems that while you consider yourself less [more] mature than other subjects, you actually come out as being more [less] mature. Is there any way you can account for this discrepancy? [Pause for the subject's response.] This seems to hold up also for self-confidence. It seems that you consider yourself as having less [more] self-confidence than other subjects, yet you actually come out having more [less].

(c) The subject was then sent to another room where he took the SEQ-F for the second time. The following day each subject received a postcard from the experimenter explaining the false information.

Performance on CAT

The relationship between the identity statuses and CAT performance was investigated....

For all three indices of CAT performance identity-achievement subjects perform significantly[2] better than identity-diffusion subjects (p's ranging from .01 to .05)* and identity achievement subjects perform significantly better than the other three statuses combined (p's ranging from .02 to .05)....

Comparing identity-achievement subjects with other subjects, significantly fewer instances of giving up on CAT problems are found for the identity-achievement subjects. This, together, with the previous findings concerning the relationship between identity status and CAT performance under stress, provides substantial confirmation of Hypothesis 1....

Level of Aspiration

The D, or attainment discrepancy score, reflects the difference between a subject's aspirations and his actual performance. An overall positive D score means that the subject tends to set his goals higher than his attainment; a negative D score means the opposite.

Inspection of original data revealed that no status obtained a negative average D score, the range being from 3.60 for identity achievement to 5.06 for foreclosure. Analysis of variance indicates a significant difference among statuses in D score($...p < .01$). The t tests... show the foreclosure subjects enhibiting higher D scores than identity-achievement subjects ($... p < .01$) and higher D scores than the other statuses combined ($...p < .001$). It appears that foreclosure subjects tend to maintain high goals in spite of failure.

Authoritarian Submission and Conventionality *(F)*

The t tests... show that foreclosure subjects received significantly higher F scores than identity-achievement subjects ($... p < .001$) and also significantly higher F scores than the other statuses combined ($... p < .001$).

Self-Esteem

The significant relationship found here was between EI-ISB scores and the initial SEQ ($... p < .01$). No significant differences among identity statuses for

---

* [When interpreting the statistical results, keep in mind that a probability level less than .05 ($p < .05$) indicates a statistically significant difference between or among the groups being tested. A probability level less than .01 ($p < .01$) gives one even more confidence in the results. A $p < .05$ means only 5 chances in 100 that there is not a true difference between groups; $p < .01$ means only 1 chance in 100 that there is not a true difference between groups; $p < .001$, only one chance in 1,000 that there is not a true difference between groups.—Eds.]

SEQ were found (. . . *ns* [not significant]). In addition, self-esteem appeared to be unrelated to authoritarian submission and conventionality (. . . *ns*) and to CAT performance (. . . *ns*).

Change in SEQ Following ISD

Although differences in the expected direction were found (i.e., identity achievement changed less than identity diffusion), these were not significant (. . . $p < .20$). Observer ratings of subjects' reactions to the invalidated self-definition indicated that this treatment condition was effective. The failure to obtain significant results may have been due to unreliability in the self-esteem measure engendered by the 2-month span between the first and second administration. There was a tendency for foreclosure subjects given negative information to show a greater decrease in self-esteem than identity-achievement subjects under similar conditions (. . . $p < .02$).

No relationship was found between EI-ISB scores and self-esteem change (. . . *ns*).

EI-ISB Scores and Identity Status

Two techniques were employed to assess the relationship between overall ego identity as measured by EI-ISB and identity status. These were an analysis of variance among the four statuses (. . . $p < .01$), and *t* tests among the individual statuses. . . .

Identity-achievement subjects received significantly higher EI-ISB scores than did identity-diffusion subjects (. . . $p < .001$), and the first three identity statuses taken together received significantly higher EI-ISB scores than did identity diffusion (. . . $p < .001$). Thus, the distinctive group with respect to EI-ISB scores appears to be identity diffusion. These findings lend some support to the hypothesized relationship between overall ego identity and identity status.

DISCUSSION

Of the two approaches to the measurement of ego identity, the interview, based on individual styles, was more successful than the incomplete-sentences test, which treated ego identity as a simple linear quality.

Particularly interesting was the relationship between such apparently diverse areas as performance in a cognitive task and commitment to an occupation and ideology. The interview and the CAT tapped two prime spheres of ego function: the infrapsychic, seen on the CAT which required the individual to moderate between pressing internal stimuli (stress-produced anxiety) and external demands (completion of the task), and the psychosocial, seen in the interview which evaluated the meshing of the individual's needs and capabilities with society's rewards and demands. The relationship between these two spheres contributes validity to both the identity statuses and to the generality of the construct, ego.

No confirmation of the hypothesis relating ego identity to resistance to change in self-esteem was obtained, possibly because the length of time between the first and second SEQ administration was 2 months. The variability in subjects' self-esteem over this period of time may have obscured differences due to treatment alone.

Following are experimentally derived profiles of each status:

1. Identity achievement. This group scored highest on an independent measure of ego identity and performed better than other statuses on a stressful concept attainment task—persevering longer on problems and maintaining a realistic level of aspiration. They subscribed somewhat less than other statuses to authoritarian values and their self-esteem was a little less vulnerable to negative information.
2. Moratorium. The distinguishing features of this group were its variability in CAT performance and its resemblance on other measures to identity achievement.
3. Foreclosure. This status' most outstanding characteristic was its endorsement of authoritarian values such as obedience, strong leadership, and respect for authority. Self-esteem was vulnerable to negative information and foreclosure subjects performed more poorly on a stressful concept-attainment task than did identity-achievement subjects. In addition, their response to failure on this task was unrealistic, maintaining, rather than moderating, unattained high goals. This behavior pattern is referred to by Rotter (1954) as "low freedom of movement [and is associated with] the achievement of superiority through identification [pp. 196–197]"—an apt description for one who is becoming his parents' alter ego.
4. Identity diffusion. While this status was originally considered the anchor point for high-low comparisons with identity achievement it occupied this position only in terms of EI-ISB scores. CAT performance was uniformly poorer than that of identity achievement, although not the lowest among the statuses. The identity-diffuse individuals to which Erikson refers and identity-diffusion subjects in this study may be rather different with respect to extent of psychopathology. A "playboy" type of identity diffusion may exist at one end of a continuum and a schizoid personality type at the other end. The former would more often be found functioning reasonably well on a college campus. While having tapped a rather complete range of adjustment in the other statuses, the extent of disturbance of an extreme identity diffusion would have precluded his inclusion in our sample. Hence, it is the foreclosure, and not the identity-diffusion, subject who occupies the lowest position on most task variables.

In conclusion, the main contribution of this study lies in the development, measurement, and partial validation of the identity statuses as individual styles of coping with the psychosocial task of forming an ego identity.

NOTES

1. In fact, intelligence test scores gleaned from the subjects' college files did correlate significantly with CAT performance ($r = 55$, $df = 82$, $p < .0005$). However, no significant relationship was found between intelligence and identity status.
2. All significance levels for t tests are based on two-tailed tests.

REFERENCES

ADORNO, T. W., FRENKEL-BRUNSWIK, E., LEVINSON, D. J., & SANFORD, R. N. *The authoritarian personality*. New York: Harper, 1950.

BLOCK, J. Ego identity, role variability, and adjustment. *Journal of Consulting Psychology*. 1961, **25**, 392–397.

BRONSON, G. W. Identity diffusion in late adolescents. *Journal of Abnormal and Social Psychology*, 1959, **59**, 414–417.

BRUNER, J. S., GOODNOW, I. J., & AUSTIN, G. A. *A study of thinking*. New York: Wiley, 1956.

DECHARMS, R., & ROSENBAUM, M. E. Status variables and matching behavior. *Journal of Personality*, 1960, **28**, 492–502.

ERIKSON, E. H. The problem of ego identity. *Journal of the American Psychoanalytic Association*, 1956, **4**, 56–121.

ERIKSON, E. H. *Childhood and society*. (2nd ed.) New York: Norton, 1963.

GRUEN, W. Rejection of false information about oneself as an indication of ego identity. *Journal of Consulting Psychology*, 1960, **24**, 231–233.

MARCIA, J. E. Determination and construct validity of ego identity status. Unpublished doctoral dissertation, Ohio State University, 1964.

RASMUSSEN, J. E. The relationship of ego identity to psychosocial effectiveness. *Psychological Reports*, 1964, **15**, 815–825.

ROSENTHAL, R. Experimenter outcome-orientation and the results of the psychological experiment. *Psychological Bulletin*, 1964, **61**, 405–412.

ROTTER, J. B. *Social learning and clinical psychology*. Englewood Cliffs, N. J. Prentice-Hall, 1954.

WEICK, K. E. Reduction of cognitive dissonance through task enhancement and effort expenditure. *Journal of Abnormal and Social Psychology*, 1964, **68**, 533–539.

CHAPTER 5 Value and Moral Development

5.1 LAWRENCE KOHLBERG

The Child as a Moral Philosopher

Lawrence Kohlberg (1927–1987) is considered the most influential of all psychologists who have studied and written about the psychology of moral development and moral education. He began his doctoral dissertation on stages of moral development at the University of Chicago in 1955 and completed the majority of his research as a professor at the Harvard Graduate School of Education. Kohlberg's theory coordinates both an ancient and a modern tradition; it is based upon the Socratic notion that justice is the end of all moral reasoning and on the Piagetian notion that development occurs in discrete qualitative stages. Whereas Jean Piaget posited developmental stages of scientific reasoning, Kohlberg applied Piaget's stages to the domain of moral reasoning.

Kohlberg's work also illustrates one of the most important research designs in developmental psychology and educational outcomes research: the *longitudinal design.* Kohlberg's initial sample was a group of 75 boys, aged 10 to 16. In the mid-1950s he asked these boys how to solve a series of moral dilemmas. The boys' responses were then stage-coded, based on the "structure" of their explanations. These boys were then reinterviewed with the same dilemmas every 3 to 5 years. They are still being contacted and interviewed now, 40 years later!

Kohlberg's work has been highly controversial, with much support and criticism from many quarters, including philosophers, feminists, anthropologists, educators, sociologists, and other psychologists. Nonetheless, most agree that his longitudinal data collection is one of the best storehouses of empirical data that the world has with regard to the ontogeny (individual development) of reasoning about justice. As an educational psychologist, Kohlberg extended educator John Dewey's work in democratizing schooling by creating "just community" schools in several places in Massachusetts and New York. Kohlberg worked from Dewey's lament that schools "told" students about democracy but did not let them live in democratic classrooms or schools.

Kohlberg published many articles in education, psychology, religion, and philosophy journals. He also authored or coauthored *Child Psychology and Childhood Education: A Cognitive-Developmental View* (Longman, 1987), *Lawrence Kohlberg's* Approach to Moral Education (Columbia University Press, 1989), *The Measurement of Moral Judgment*, 2 vols. (Cambridge University Press, 1987), *The Philosophy of Moral Development: Moral Stages and the Idea of Justice* (Harper & Row, 1981), and *Psychology of Moral Development: Essays on Moral Development* (Harper & Row, 1984). The following selection comes from "The Child as a Moral Philosopher," *Psychology Today* (1968). Kohlberg's explanation of the moral reasoning of children and youth is the most influential theory studied by schoolteachers with regard to the structure and development of moral thought in the twentieth century.

Key Concept: stages of moral reasoning

*H*ow can one study morality? Current trends in the fields of ethics, linguistics, anthropology and cognitive psychology have suggested a new approach which seems to avoid the morass of semantical confusions, value-bias and cultural relativity in which the psychoanalytic and semantic approaches to morality have foundered. New scholarship in all these fields is now focusing upon structures, forms and relationships that seem to be common to all societies and all languages rather than upon the features that make particular languages or cultures different.

For 12 years, my colleagues and I studied the same group of 75 boys, following their development at three-year intervals from early adolescence through young manhood. At the start of the study, the boys were aged 10 to 16. We have now followed them through to ages 22 to 28. In addition, I have explored moral development in other cultures—Great Britain, Canada, Taiwan, Mexico and Turkey.

Inspired by Jean Piaget's pioneering effort to apply a structural approach to moral development, I have gradually elaborated over the years of my study a typological scheme describing general structures and forms of moral thought which can be defined independently of the specific content of particular moral decisions or actions.

The typology contains three distinct levels of moral thinking, and within each of these levels distinguishes two related stages. These levels and stages may be considered separate moral philosophies, distinct views of the socio-moral world.

We can speak of the child as having his own morality or series of moralities. Adults seldom listen to children's moralizing. If a child throws back a few adult cliches and behaves himself, most parents—and many anthropologists and psychologists as well—think that the child has adopted or internalized the appropriate parental standards.

Actually, as soon as we talk with children about morality, we find that they have many ways of making judgments which are not "internalized" from the outside, and which do not come in any direct and obvious way from parents, teachers or even peers.

MORAL LEVELS

The *preconventional* level is the first of three levels of moral thinking; the second level is *conventional*, and the third *postconventional* or autonomous. While the preconventional child is often "well-behaved" and is responsive to cultural labels of good and bad, he interprets these labels in terms of their physical consequences (punishment, reward, exchange of favors) or in terms of the physical power of those who enunciate the rules and labels of good and bad.

This level is usually occupied by children aged four to 10, a fact long known to sensitive observers of children. The capacity of "properly behaved" children of this age to engage in cruel behavior when there are holes in the power structure is sometimes noted as tragic (*Lord of the Flies, High Wind in Jamaica*), sometimes as comic (Lucy in *Peanuts*).

The second or *conventional* level also can be described as conformist, but that is perhaps too smug a term. Maintaining the expectations and rules of the individual's family, group or nation is perceived as valuable in its own right. There is a concern not only with *conforming* to the individual's social order but in *maintaining*, supporting and justifying this order.

The *postconventional* level is characterized by a major thrust toward autonomous moral principles which have validity and application apart from authority of the groups or persons who hold them and apart from the individual's identification with those persons or groups.

MORAL STAGES

Within each of these three levels there are two discernable stages. At the preconventional level we have:

> **Stage 1:** Orientation toward punishment and unquestioning deference to superior power. The physical consequences of action regardless of their human meaning or value determine its goodness or badness.

Stage 2: Right action consists of that which instrumentally satisfies one's own needs and occasionally the needs of others. Human relations are viewed in terms like those of the marketplace. Elements of fairness, of reciprocity and equal sharing are present, but they are always interpreted in a physical, pragmatic way. Reciprocity is a matter of "you scratch my back and I'll scratch yours" not of loyalty, gratitude or justice.

And at the conventional level we have:

Stage 3: Good-boy–good-girl orientation. Good behavior is that which pleases or helps others and is approved by them. There is much conformity to stereotypical images of what is majority or "natural" behavior. Behavior is often judged by intention—"he means well" becomes important for the first time, and is overused, as by Charlie Brown in *Peanuts*. One seeks approval by being "nice."

Stage 4: Orientation toward authority, fixed rules and the maintenance of the social order. Right behavior consists of doing one's duty, showing respect for authority and maintaining the given social order for its own sake. One earns respect by performing dutifully.

At the postconventional level, we have:

Stage 5: A social-contract orientation, generally with legalistic and utilitarian overtones. Right action tends to be defined in terms of general rights and in terms of standards which have been critically examined and agreed upon by the whole society. There is a clear awareness of the relativism of personal values and opinions and a corresponding emphasis upon procedural rules for reaching consensus. Aside from what is constitutionally and democratically agreed upon, right or wrong is a matter of personal "values" and "opinion." The result is an emphasis upon the "legal point of view," but with an emphasis upon the possibility of *changing* law in terms of rational considerations of social utility, rather than freezing it in the terms of Stage 4 "law and order." Outside the legal realm, free agreement and contract are the binding elements of obligation. This is the "official" morality of American government, and finds its ground in the thought of the writers of the Constitution.

Stage 6: Orientation toward the decisions of conscience and toward self-chosen *ethical principles* appealing to logical comprehensiveness, universality and consistency. These principles are abstract and ethical (the Golden Rule, the categorical imperative); they are not concrete moral rules like the Ten Commandments. Instead, they are universal principles of *justice*, of the *reciprocity* and *equality* of human rights, and of respect for the dignity of human beings as *individual persons*.

UP TO NOW

In the past, when psychologists tried to answer the question asked of Socrates by Meno, "Is virtue something that can be taught (by rational discussion), or does it come by practice, or is it a natural inborn attitude?", their answers usually have been dictated, not by research findings on children's moral character, but by their general theoretical convictions.

Behavior theorists have said that virtue is behavior acquired according to their favorite general principles of learning. Freudians have claimed that virtue is superego-identification with parents generated by a proper balance of love and authority in family relations.

The American psychologists who have actually studied children's morality have tried to start with a set of labels—the "virtues" and "vices," the "traits" of good and bad character found in ordinary language. The earliest major psychological study of moral character, that of Hugh Hartshorne and Mark May in 1928–1930 focused on a bag of virtues including honesty, service (altruism or generosity), and self-control. To their dismay, they found that there were *no* character traits, psychological dispositions or entities which corresponded to words like honesty, service or self-control.

Regarding honesty, for instance, they found that almost everyone cheats some of the time, and that if a person cheats in one situation, it doesn't mean that he *will* or *won't* in another. In other words, it is not an identifiable character trait, *dis*honesty, that makes a child cheat in a given situation. These early researchers also found that people who cheat express as much or even more moral disapproval of cheating as those who do not cheat.

What Hartshorne and May found out about their bag of virtues is equally upsetting to the somewhat more psychological-sounding names introduced by psychoanalytic psychology: "superego-strength," "resistance to temptation," "strength of conscience," and the like. When recent researchers attempt to measure such traits in individuals, they have been forced to use Hartshorne and May's old tests of honesty and self-control and they get exactly the same results —"superego strength" in one situation predicts little to "superego strength" in another. That is, virtue-words like honesty (or superego-strength) point to certain behaviors with approval, but give us no guide to understanding them.

So far as one can extract some generalized personality factor from children's performance on tests of honesty or resistance to temptation, it is a factor of ego-strength or ego-control, which always involves non-moral capacities like the capacity to maintain attention, intelligent-task performance, and the ability to delay response. "Ego-strength" (called "will" in earlier days) has something to do with moral action, but it does not take us to the core of morality or to the definition of virtue. Obviously enough, many of the greatest evil-doers in history have been men of strong wills, men strongly pursuing immoral goals.

MORAL REASONS

In our research, we have found definite and universal levels of development in moral thought. In our study of 75 American boys from early adolescence on, these youths were presented with hypothetical moral dilemmas, all deliberately philosophical, some of them found in medieval works of casuistry.

On the basis of their reasoning about these dilemmas at a given age, each boy's stage of thought could be determined for each of 25 basic moral concepts or aspects. One such aspect, for instance, is "Motive Given for Rule Obedience or Moral Action." In this instance, the six stages look like this:

1. Obey rules to avoid punishment.
2. Conform to obtain rewards, have favors returned, and so on.
3. Conform to avoid disapproval, dislike by others.
4. Conform to avoid censure by legitimate authorities and resultant guilt.
5. Conform to maintain the respect of the impartial spectator judging in terms of community welfare.
6. Conform to avoid self-condemnation.

In another of these 25 moral aspects, the value of human life, the six stages can be defined thus:

1. The value of a human life is confused with the value of physical objects and is based on the social status or physical attributes of its possessor.
2. The value of a human life is seen as instrumental to the satisfaction of the needs of its possessor or of other persons.
3. The value of a human life is based on the empathy and affection of family members and others toward its possessor.
4. Life is conceived as sacred in terms of its place in a categorical moral or religious order of rights and duties.
5. Life is valued both in terms of its relation to community welfare and in terms of life being a universal human right.
6. Belief in the sacredness of human life as representing a universal human value of respect for the individual.

I have called this scheme a typology. This is because about 50 per cent of most people's thinking will be at a single stage, regardless of the moral dilemma involved. We call our types *stages* because they seem to represent an *invariant developmental sequence.* "True" stages come one at a time and always in the same order.

All movement is forward in sequence, and does not skip steps. Children may move through these stages at varying speeds, of course, and may be found half in and half out of a particular stage. An individual may stop at any given stage and at any age, but if he continues to move, he must move in accord with these steps. Moral reasoning of the conventional or Stage 3–4 kind never occurs before the preconventional Stage-1 and Stage-2 thought has taken place. No adult in Stage 4 has gone through Stage 6, but all Stage-6 adults have gone at least through 4.

While the evidence is not complete, my study strongly suggests that moral change fits the stage pattern just described. (The major uncertainty is whether all Stage 6s go through Stage 5 or whether these are two alternate mature orientations.)

As a single example of our findings of stage-sequence, take the progress of two boys on the aspect "The Value of Human Life." The first boy Tommy, is asked "Is it better to save the life of one important person or a lot of unimportant people?" At age 10, he answers "all the people that aren't important because one man just has one house, maybe a lot of furniture, but a whole bunch of people have an awful lot of furniture and some of these poor people might have a lot of money and it doesn't look it."

Clearly Tommy is Stage 1: he confuses the value of a human being with the value of the property he possesses. Three years later (age 13) Tommy's conceptions of life's value are most clearly elicited by the question, "Should the doctor 'mercy kill' a fatally ill woman requesting death because of her pain?" He answers, "Maybe it would be good to put her out of her pain, she'd be better off that way. But the husband wouldn't want it, it's not like an animal. If a pet dies you can get along without it—it isn't something you really need. Well, you can get a new wife, but it's not really the same."

Here his answer is Stage 2: the value of the woman's life is partly contingent on its hedonistic value to the wife herself but even more contingent on its instrumental value to her husband, who can't replace her as easily as he can a pet.

Three years later still (age 16) Tommy's conception of life's value is elicited by the same question, to which he replies: "It might be best for her, but her husband—it's a human life—not like an animal; it just doesn't have the same relationship that a human being does to a family. You can become attached to a dog, but nothing like a human you know."

Now Tommy has moved from a Stage 2 instrumental view of the woman's value to a Stage-3 view based on the husband's distinctively human empathy and love for someone in his family. Equally clearly, it lacks any basis for a universal human value of the woman's life, which would hold if she had no husband or if her husband didn't love her. Tommy, then, has moved step by step through three stages during the age 10–16. Tommy, though bright (I.Q. 120), is a slow developer in moral judgment. Let us take another boy, Richard, to show us sequential movement through the remaining three steps.

At age 13, Richard said about the mercy-killing, "If she requests it, it's really up to her. She is in such terrible pain, just the same as people are always putting animals out of their pain," and in general showed a mixture of Stage-2 and Stage-3 responses concerning the value of life. At 16, he said, "I don't know. In one way, it's murder, it's not a right or privilege of man to decide who shall live and who should die. God put life into everybody on earth and you're taking away something from that person that came directly from God, and you're destroying something that is very sacred, it's in a way part of God and it's almost destroying a part of God when you kill a person. There's something of God in everyone."

Here Richard clearly displays a Stage-4 concept of life as sacred in terms of its place in a categorical moral or religious order. The value of human life is universal, it is true for all humans. It is still, however, dependent on something else, upon respect for God and God's authority; it is not an autonomous human value. Presumably if God told Richard to murder, as God commanded Abraham to murder Isaac, he would do so.

At age 20, Richard said to the same question: "There are more and more people in the medical profession who think it is a hardship on everyone, the person, the family, when you know they are going to die. When a person is kept alive by an artificial lung or kidney it's more like being a vegetable than being a human. If it's her own choice, I think there are certain rights and privileges that go along with being a human being. I am a human being and have certain desires for life and I think everybody else does too. You have a world of which you are the center, and everybody else does too and in that sense we're all equal."

Richard's response is clearly Stage 5, in that the value of life is defined in terms of equal and universal human rights in a context of relativity ("You have a world of which you are the center and in that sense we're all equal"), and of concern for utility or welfare consequences.

THE FINAL STEP

At 24, Richard says: "A human life takes precedence over any other moral or legal value, whoever it is. A human life has inherent value whether or not it is valued by a particular individual. The worth of the individual human being is central where the principles of justice and love are normative for all human relationships."

This young man is at Stage 6 in seeing the value of human life as absolute in representing a universal and equal respect for the human as an individual. He has moved step by step through a sequence, culminating in a definition of human life as centrally valuable rather than derived from or dependent on social or divine authority.

In a genuine and culturally universal sense, these steps lead toward an increased *morality* of value judgment, where morality is considered as a form of judging, as it has been in a philosophic tradition running from the analyses of Kant to those of the modern analytic or "ordinary language" philosophers. The person at Stage 6 has disentangled his judgments of—or language about—human life from status and property values (Stage 1), from its uses to others (Stage 2), from interpersonal affection (Stage 3), and so on; he has a means of moral judgment that is universal and impersonal. The Stage-6 person's answers use moral words like "duty" or "morally right," and he uses them in a way implying universality, ideals, impersonality: He thinks and speaks in phrases like "regardless of who it was," or " ... I would do it in spite of punishment."

When I first decided to explore moral development in other cultures, I was told by anthropologist friends that I would have to throw away my culture-bound moral concepts and stories and start from scratch learning a whole new set of values for each new culture. My first try consisted of a brace of villages, one Atayal (Malaysian aboriginal) and the other Taiwanese.

My guide was a young Chinese ethnographer who had written an account of the moral and religious patterns of the Atayal and Taiwanese villages. Taiwanese boys in the 10–13 age group were asked about a story involving theft of food. A man's wife is starving to death but the store owner won't give the man any food unless he can pay, which he can't. Should he break in and steal some food? Why? Many of the boys said, "He should steal the food for his wife because if she dies he'll have to pay for her funeral and that costs a lot."

My guide was amused by these responses, but I was relieved: they were of course "classic" Stage-2 responses. In the Atayal village, funerals weren't such a big thing, so the Stage-2 boys would say, "He should steal the food because he needs his wife to cook for him."

This means that we need to consult our anthropologists to know what content a Stage-2 child will include in his instrumental exchange calculations, or what a Stage-4 adult will identify as the proper social order. But one certainly doesn't have to start from scratch. What made my guide laugh was the difference in form between the children's Stage-2 thought and his own, a difference definable independently of particular cultures.

[Figures] 1 and 2 indicate the cultural universality of the sequence of stages which we have found. [Figure] 1 presents the age trends for middle-class urban boys in the U.S., Taiwan and Mexico. At age 10 in each country, the order of use of each stage is the same as the order of its difficulty or maturity.

In the United States, by age 16 the order is the reverse, from the highest to the lowest, except that Stage 6 is still little-used. At age 13, the good-boy, middle stage (Stage 3), is not used.

The results in Mexico and Taiwan are the same, except that development is a little slower. The most conspicuous feature is that at the age of 16, Stage-5 thinking is much more salient in the United States than in Mexico or Taiwan. Nevertheless, it *is* present in the other countries, so we know that this is not purely an American democratic construct.

[Figure] 2 shows strikingly similar results from two isolated villages, one in Yucatan, one in Turkey. While conventional moral thought increases steadily from ages 10 to 16 it still has not achieved a clear ascendency over preconventional thought.

Trends for lower-class urban groups are intermediate in the rate of development between those for the middle-class and for the village boys. In the three divergent cultures that I studied, middle-class children were found to be more advanced in moral judgment than matched lower-class children. This was not due to the fact that the middle-class children heavily favored some one type of thought which could be seen as corresponding to the prevailing middle-class pattern. Instead, middle-class and working-class children move through the same sequences, but the middle-class children move faster and farther.

FIGURE 1

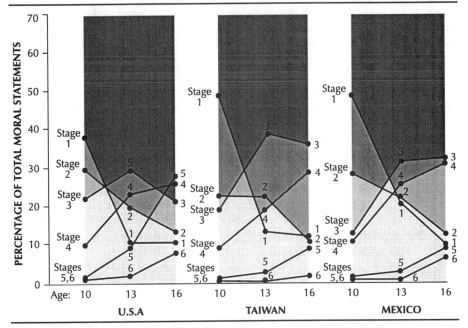

Note: Middle-class urban boys in the U.S., Taiwan and Mexico. At age 10 the stages are used according to difficulty. At age 13, Stage 3 is most used by all three groups. At age 16 U.S. boys have reversed the order of age 10 stages (with the exception of 6). In Taiwan and Mexico, conventional (3–4) stages prevail at age 16, with Stage 5 also little used.

This sequence is not dependent upon a particular religion, or any religion at all in the usual sense. I found no important differences in the development of moral thinking among Catholics, Protestants, Jews, Buddhists, Moslems and atheists. Religious values seem to go through the same stages as all other values.

TRADING UP

In summary, the nature of our sequence is not significantly affected by widely varying social, cultural or religious conditions. The only thing that is affected is the *rate* at which individuals progress through this sequence.

Why should there be such a universal invariant sequence of development? In answering this question, we need first to analyze these developing social concepts in terms of their internal logical structure. At each stage, the same basic moral concept or aspect is defined, but at each higher stage this definition is more differentiated, more integrated and more general or universal. When one's concept of human life moves from Stage 1 to Stage 2 the value of life becomes more differentiated from the value of property, more integrated (the value of life enters an organizational hierarchy where it is "higher" than property so

FIGURE 2

159

*Lawrence
Kohlberg*

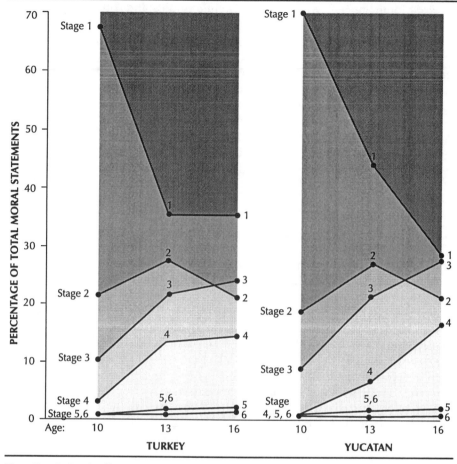

Note: Two isolated villages, one in Turkey, the other in Yucatan, show similar patterns in moral thinking. There is no reversal of order, and preconventional (1–2) thought does not gain a clear ascendancy over conventional stages at age 16.

that one steals property in order to save life) and more universalized (the life of any sentient being is valuable regardless of status or property). The same advance is true at each stage in the hierarchy. Each step of development then is a better cognitive organization than the one before it, one which takes account of everything present in the previous stage, but making new distinctions and organizing them into a more comprehensive or more equilibrated structure. The fact that this is the case has been demonstrated by a series of studies indicating that children and adolescents comprehend all stages up to their own, but not more than one stage beyond their own. And importantly, *they prefer this next stage.*

We have conducted experimental moral discussion classes which show that the child at an earlier stage of development tends to move forward when confronted by the views of a child one stage further along. In an argument between a Stage-3 and Stage-4 child, the child in the third stage tends to move toward or into Stage 4, while the Stage-4 child understands but does not accept the arguments of the Stage-3 child.

Moral thought, then, seems to behave like all other kinds of thought. Progress through the moral levels and stages is characterized by increasing differentiation and increasing integration, and hence is the same kind of progress that scientific theory represents. Like acceptable scientific theory—or like *any* theory or structure of knowledge—moral thought may be considered partially to generate its own data as it goes along, or at least to expand so as to contain in a balanced, self-consistent way a wider and wider experiential field. The raw data in the case of our ethical philosophies may be considered as conflicts between roles, or values, or as the social order in which men live.

THE ROLE OF SOCIETY

The social worlds of all men seem to contain the same basic structures. All the societies we have studied have the same basic institutions—family, economy, law, government. In addition, however, all societies are alike because they *are* societies—systems of defined complementary roles. In order to *play* a social role in the family, school or society, the child must implicitly take the role of others toward himself and toward others in the group. These role-taking tendencies form the basis of all social institutions. They represent various patternings of shared or complementary expectations.

In the preconventional and conventional levels (Stages 1–4), moral content or value is largely accidental or culture-bound. Anything from "honesty" to "courage in battle" can be the central value. But in the higher postconventional levels, Socrates, Lincoln, Thoreau and Martin Luther King tend to speak without confusion of tongues, as it were. This is because the ideal principles of any social structure are basically alike, if only because there simply aren't that many principles which are articulate, comprehensive and integrated enough to be satisfying to the human intellect. And most of these principles have gone by the name of justice.

Behavioristic psychology and psychoanalysis have always upheld the Philistine view that fine moral words are one thing and moral deeds another. Morally mature reasoning is quite a different matter, and does not really depend on "fine words." The man who understands justice is more likely to practice it.

In our studies, we have found that youths who understand justice act more justly, and the man who understands justice helps create a moral climate which goes far beyond his immediate and personal acts. The universal society is the beneficiary.

5.2 JOHN R. SNAREY

Cross-Cultural Universality of Social–Moral Development

John R. Snarey earned his Ed.D. at Harvard Graduate School of Education under Lawrence Kohlberg. He is currently a professor of human development and ethics at Emory University in Atlanta, Georgia. Snarey is best known for his cross-cultural research on moral judgment development and his longitudinal research on fathers. He is coeditor of *Conflict and Continuity: A History of Ideas on Social Equality and Human Development* (Harvard Educational Review, 1981) and the author of *How Fathers Care for the Next Generation: A Four-Decade Study* (Harvard University Press, 1993). He has received the Outstanding Human Development Research Award from the American Educational Research Association and the James D. Moran Award for Exceptional Research in Family Relations and Child Development.

The following selection is excerpted from Snarey's now-classic meta-analytic research paper "Cross-Cultural Universality of Social–Moral Development: A Critical Review of Kohlbergian Research," published in 1985 in the *Psychological Bulletin*. It gathers together empirical studies from more cultures than any other paper ever published concerning moral development and moral reasoning.

Key Concept: cross-cultural moral reasoning

*L*awrence Kohlberg's stage model of moral development... has attracted a great deal of positive attention from psychologists and educators. Not surprisingly, however, his work has also inspired considerable criticism and revisionism (cf. Gibbs, 1977; Gilligan, 1982; Kurtines & Grief, 1974; Rest, 1983). The aspect of Kohlberg's theory that has been most difficult for many social scientists to accept is the claim that the development of moral reasoning about the social environment follows a universal invariant sequence, toward the same universal ethical principles, in all cultural settings (cf. Bloom, 1977; Buck-Morss, 1975; Edwards, 1975, 1982; Guidon, 1978; Shweder, 1982a, 1982b;

161

Simpson, 1974; Sullivan, 1977). This article identifies the primary empirical assumptions underlying Kohlberg's claim of cross-cultural universality and clarifies the appropriate evidence necessary to judge the claim. It then presents a comprehensive examination of the available empirical evidence that has accumulated over the last 15 years and evaluates the support or lack of support indicated. The assumptions are discussed in evaluative order, from those that receive the most support to those that receive the least support.

ASSUMPTIONS AND HYPOTHESES

Kohlberg (1971) stated his claim for the cross-cultural universality of moral development as follows: "All individuals in all cultures use the same thirty basic moral categories, concepts, or principles, and all individuals in all cultures go through the same order or sequence of gross stage development, though they vary in rate and terminal point of development" (1971, p. 175). I believe that Kohlberg's claim implies at least five empirical assumptions, each of which may be understood as a testable hypothesis.

The first assumption is that moral development research has been conducted in a sufficiently wide range of sociocultural settings to jeopardize adequately the claim. It is not possible to conduct research in all cultures, of course, and one does not need to test all possible cultures to accept the claim as solidly based. How many cultures need to be studied to arrive at a reasonable degree of certainty is not easy to decide; the usual criteria of chance error may be misleading in this case. More important than number are the type and variety of cultural settings that are studied. The minimal requirement might be that research must be done in several non-Western and nonindustrialized traditional cultural groups in addition to Western European countries. Ideally, the cultural groups should be historically independent if each society is to serve as an independent unit of analysis (cf. Naroll & D'Andrade, 1963; Whiting, 1968). Further, the samples ideally should be internally diverse: they should include children, adolescents, and mature adults—both males and females—and all major levels of social stratification.

The second assumption is that all persons in all cultures inquire about the moral domain and, in doing so, ask the same basic kinds of questions or resort to the same basic issues. Kohlberg's model of moral development was constructed by presenting people with specific moral dilemmas and by asking specific moral questions. Do Kohlberg's dilemmas and the accompanying questions adequately sample the universe of moral dilemmas and questions? Do they reflect the general moral issues that people universally tend to set for themselves? Because the dilemmas and questions included in Kohlberg's interview obviously were not randomly selected, but reflect a prior understanding of moral issues, it is not obvious that these questions are universally shared.

The empirical data relevant to this second assumption include individual researchers' attempts to adapt the interview dilemmas and questions into a culturally or functionally equivalent form. This includes the relative success of

TABLE 1

Stages of Moral Development According to Kohlberg (1981)

John R. Snarey

Stage	What Is Considered to Be Right
Stage 1: Obedience and punishment orientation	To avoid breaking rules backed by punishment, obedience for its own sake, avoiding physical damage to persons and property
Stage 2: Instrumental purpose and exchange	Following rules only when it is to someone's immediate personal interest; acting to meet one's own interests and letting others do the same; right is an equal exchange, a good deal
Stage 3: Interpersonal accord and conformity	Living up to what is expected by people close to you or what people generally expect of people in your role; being good is important
Stage 4: Social accord and system maintenance	Fulfilling the actual duties to which you have agreed; laws are always to be upheld except in extreme cases where they conflict with other fixed social duties; right is also contributing to society, the group, or institution
Stage 5: Social contract, utility, individual rights	Being aware that people hold a variety of values and opinions, that most values and rules are relative to your group but should usually be upheld because they are the social contract; some nonrelative values and rights like life and liberty, however, must be upheld in any society regardless of the majority opinion
Stage 6: Universal ethical principles	Following self-chosen ethical principles; particular laws or social agreements are usually valid because they rest on such principles; when laws violate these principles, one acts in accordance with the principle; principles are universal principles of justice; the equality of human righrs and respect for the dignity of human beings as individual persons; the reason for doing right is the belief, as a rational person, in the validity of universal moral principles and a sense of personal commitment to them

Note. Stages 5 and 6 are not distinguished for research purposes; there is also a transition stage (e.g., 2/3) between each of the stages.

adapted versus nonadapted dilemmas, such as an interviewer's reported observations regarding the salience for subjects of the general issues contained within a particular dilemma. Further, because each dilemma essentially requires subjects to make a choice between two competing issues (e.g., life vs. law), culturally defined patterns in issue choices are important criteria for evaluating the degree to which Kohlbergian dilemmas adapt themselves to cultures that stress different issues. To the extent that the way the dilemmas and questions are understood parallels the stages of moral development, however, this proposition is closely related to the next assumption.

The third assumption is that stage development among individuals is found to be upwardly invariant in sequence and without significant regressions, regardless of cultural settings. In other words, all individuals in all cultures will follow the same stage sequence in a step-wise order, provided that their moral reasoning undergoes change. This particular assumption concerns only the order of appearance of the stages in individual development and not the presence of any one of the stages other than the first (cf. Kohlberg & Kramer, 1969). It does not state, for instance, that Stage 5 or any other stage will be achieved by every individual sooner or later, nor does it state that it will be found in every culture.

The hypothesis of a universal sequence would be supported if longitudinal testing reveals the same sequence, regardless of the cultural setting. Stage regressions and stage skipping would be evidence against the hypothesis. However, these empirical requirements cannot be understood as an absolute requirement, even for longitudinal studies. The reason is that Kohlberg has not constructed an error-free instrument, and regressions could be accounted for by measurement error if the frequency of regression is less than measurement error. Second, the time interval required for moving from one stage to the next varies between individuals, and probably between cultural groups and stages. Thus, data that suggest a skipped stage may in fact hide stage change if the interval between interview times was long enough to encompass two stage changes. Kuhn and Angeleu (1976) showed that 1 year was the minimum interval for observing clear changes in moral reasoning in a sample of children in the United States. In contrast, intervals of 3 years or less have also shown stage skipping to be extremely rare for adolescents and adults in the United States (Colby, Kohlberg, Gibbs, & Lieberman, 1983).

Cross-sectional testing can also provide valuable, although not conclusive, evidence if a properly selected sample is used (e.g., moderately large samples of age groups at approximately 3-year age intervals). Evidence in support of the proposition would be finding that all stages below the highest stage observed are also found in a particular cultural group and that, in each cultural group, higher stages correspond to older age groups. Evidence against this proposition would include nonordered or nonsequential relations between stage and age or the complete absence of a stage between the lowest and highest stages represented in the sample.

The fourth assumption is one to which Kohlberg himself is reluctant to assent, that the full range of moral stages, including the highest, should be found in all types of cultures. To be part of an empirical claim, all stages including the postconventional need to be present somewhere at some time. If this condition is met, however, Kohlberg and some of his developmentalist colleagues would claim that the overall stage model would be affirmed to be universal, and that only the rate and terminal point of development is culturally defined (cf. Broughton, 1978; Kohlberg, 1971; Lickona, 1969, 1976). Cross-cultural researchers, however, more often claim that the consistent absence of some stages in some types of cultures would indicate that the missing stages are culturally relative, the opposite of universal (Edwards, 1981; Simpson, 1974). Can one logically require that all cultural groups demonstrate all levels of moral reasoning in Kohlberg's model to establish its universality? The claim here is not that every individual should reach the highest stage, and it is not even that the highest stage should be found in every society studied. Rather, this proposition requires that all types of cultural groups (e.g., Western versus non-Western, urban versus folk) must demonstrate all levels of moral reasoning in Kohlberg's model to establish its universality. The failure to find a particular stage in all studies of a particular type of cultural group could indicate that the stage is culture specific, not universal. Of course, studies that include only adults cannot be required to find examples of the earliest stages, just as studies that include only children cannot be required to find the most mature stages present. One of the best test cases for the postconventional stages would be samples of adult subjects from non-Western, nonurban populations chosen because the other adult members of their society deemed them to be examples of unusual moral maturity. If the postconventional stages were absent among this last type of sample, then there would be grounds for doubting the universality of the full range of stages as they are presently defined.

The fifth assumption is that all instances of genuine moral reasoning in all cultures will correspond to one of the modes or stages of moral reasoning described by Kohlberg. This final proposition extends Kohlberg's set of stages to the most general applicability. Whereas some moral statements may fit more than one type, because later stages hierarchically incorporate earlier ones, no moral reasoning should be found for which none of the available stages or stage transitions is pertinent, because Kohlberg originally claimed that all individuals use the same basic concepts or principles. In other words, there is no wastebasket category. It is, of course, possible that moral statements may be found for which either the subject gives no explanation or the explanation is vague and brief. In this case, the available categories cannot be applied, not because they are inadequate as a set but because there is no clear or genuine moral judgment that can be interpreted. It is necessary, however, that clear criteria be provided to determine if the information given is inadequate or whether the available stage categories are insufficient. Otherwise, the meaning of *vague* or *incomplete* may be interpreted in such a way that Kohlberg's set of categories could never be proven false.

With this preface, the above proposition can be considered to be supported empirically if all moral judgments of a sample—regardless of culture (e.g., Western or non-Western) or of subculture (e.g., age, sex, and social-class subgroups)—are classifiable in one of the nine stages or stage transitions. In other words, all genuine moral responses given to Kohlberg's moral judgment interview can be scored according to the standardized scoring manual. Counterevidence to the hypothesis would be reports of moral judgments that are unscorable. If examples are reported from different studies, patterns in the various researchers' observations would be helpful in precisely defining areas of inadequacy in Kohlberg's theory. If the interview material in a particular study was usually readily scorable, however, the evidence of some unscorable material would necessarily jeopardize only this particular assumption. Any general theory can be valid and solidly supported and, at the same time, incomplete and open to modifications and additions....

FINDINGS AND DISCUSSION

Culturally Diverse Samples

Elizabeth Simpson was one of the first to point out a lack of cross-cultural diversity in moral development research:

> In his prolific writing [Kohlberg] does not make clear the empirical sources of his claims to universality in the empirical realm.... The evidence is suggestive but hardly conclusive enough for the use of those firm dogmatic "all's." Not that much work has been done. In one article, work in five cultures is referred to; in later work, still only twelve cultures are given as the basis for generalizing to mankind as a whole (1974, pp. 83, 86).

Kohlberg based his original claim of universality on the empirical findings of his research among children in five cultural settings—the United States, Taiwan, Turkey, urban Mexico, and a Yucatan village in Mexico. Although he presented graphs of the cross-sectional age trends from his research (1969), the details regarding sample size, interview translation procedure, or the means and range of scores have not been published prior to this present review. This free-wheeling approach to cross-cultural research thus, understandably, made it difficult for the claim to be evaluated or accepted.

The number of studies, however, has grown considerably. At present, 44 studies have been completed in 26 cultural areas (45 studies in 27 cultural areas if one includes, for comparative purposes, Kohlberg's original United States research). Longitudinal research has been carried out in the following countries: Bahamas, Canada (French), India, Indonesia, Israel (kibbutz), Turkey, and the United States. The remaining 20 cultural areas are represented only by cross-sectional studies: Alaska (Eskimos), England, Finland, Germany, Guatemala, Honduras, Hong Kong, Iran, Japan, Kenya, Mexico, New Zealand, Nigeria, New Guinea, Pakistan, Puerto Rico, Taiwan, Thailand, Yucatan, and Zambia....

Not surprisingly, the types of samples represented and the research methodology used within each study vary considerably. The 27 cultural areas vary in the degree to which they represent non-Western cultures: Approximately 22% of the cultural areas represent primarily Western European populations (e.g., Finland, Germany, New Zealand), 44% are non-European populations that have been influenced by the West (e.g., India, Japan, Taiwan), and 33% include tribal or village folk populations (e.g., Ladakh Indians, rural

Guatemalan Indians, Kalskagamuit Eskimos, rural Kenyan Kipsigis). The age groups studied also vary considerably: Approximately 30% of the 27 cultural areas included children, adolescents, and adults in the research, 18% included children and adolescents or adolescents and adults, and 52% included only children or adolescents or adults. Approximately 56% of the 27 cultural areas included both male and female subjects in at least one of the samples studied in that country.

If this research were begun from scratch, one might have selected 27 somewhat different countries to obtain a larger representation of non-Western traditional folk societies, including hunter–gatherer groups, and of noncapitalist societies, including Eastern European countries. The samples also do not necessarily represent societies that are historically independent (e.g., there is no longer a society that has not been influenced by the West to some degree). One also would prefer larger sample sizes, broader age ranges, and more uniformity in the scoring systems. Nevertheless, this being an imperfect world where cultural diversity is infinite and research time and money are finite, it seems reasonable to conclude that the diversity and number of cultures in which Kohlberg's model and measures have been applied are sufficient to evaluate the claim of cultural universality. The array generally compares favorably with cross-cultural research on other developmental theories, such as those of Erik Erikson, Jane Loevinger, and Jean Piaget (cf. Ashton, 1975; Dasen, 1972; Snarey & Blasi, 1980; Snarey, Kohlberg, & Noam, 1983).

Universal Moral Questions

Do Kohlberg's moral dilemmas and the accompanying questions adequately sample the universe of moral dilemmas or are they so culture-bound that they do not elicit a subject's best performance when the subject is from another culture? Do the moral issues contained in the dilemmas reflect the general issues that people, universally, tend to see as ethically relevant? Kohlberg argued that because the dilemmas focus on universal issues such as life, property, authority, and trust, they will represent real moral conflicts to anyone anywhere if suitable modifications are made in the content details of the dilemmas. Researchers have addressed this question on a number of levels to ensure that the interviews were culturally fair.

First, Kohlberg himself created three alternative forms of the standard interview. Each of the three forms contains three dilemmas. In each form, the first dilemma is based on the issues of life versus law, the second is based on the issues of conscience versus punishment, and the third is based on the issues of contract versus authority. The alternate interview reliability is quite high, and thus a researcher can choose which of the three different dilemmas for each of the three sets of moral issues will be included in a complete protocol. Although many researchers have simply used the three best-known dilemmas in the Form A interview, others have taken advantage of the alternative forms to select dilemmas that seemed to be the most relevant or most easily adapted to the culture in which they were conducting research.

...[M]ost researchers have also adapted the interview by translating it into the native language rather than attempting to interview subjects in English. Only six of the 45 studies clearly failed to make this minimal level of cultural adjustment (cf. Awa, 1979; Berry & Dasen, 1974; Cole & Scribner, 1974). Beyond literal translation, the majority of the studies also attempted to adapt the dilemmas so that the content was culturally relevant and the moral conflict was felt to be real. For instance, the names of the actors in the dilemmas have been changed to indigenous ones, the problem of stealing a drug to save a life has been changed to the problem of stealing food, and numerous other functional-equivalent translations have been undertaken (cf. Bredemeier, 1955; Mayers, 1974). Rachel Okonkuo (1983), for instance, found it necessary to adapt Dilemma III involving a father who unfairly asks his son for his savings so that the father can go on a fishing trip. Okonkuo's Nigerian subjects did not understand a fishing trip as a form of recreation but rather as a form of work by which to support one's family.... With the exception of 9 of the 45 studies, all researchers made this type of cultural adaptation when appropriate. Although researchers do not commonly comment on the perceived effectiveness of this adaptation process, they have been consistently positive when they do. Gorsuch and Barnes (1973) stated that "Carib children appeared to experience no more difficulty in formulating answers to most of the stories than did U.S. children of a similar age" (1973, p. 287). Vasudev (1983) similarly observed that "although the Heinz dilemma* is posed as a hypothetical dilemma, for many Indians it is an immediate and real dilemma. Heinz's predicament parallels mass deprivation, poverty and social injustice suffered by an overwhelming number of individuals" in India (1983, p. 5). Because of the open-ended or semiclinical nature of the interview, researchers also did not report that they encountered the typical problems found when administering a structured task or test to people who were not accustomed to interviews or tests.

Another area of possible testing bias involves the moral issues contained within each dilemma. Even if one selects the three seemingly most culturally relevant dilemmas from Kohlberg's set of nine, and even if one carefully translates and adapts the dilemmas to the culture, the underlying moral issues on which the dilemmas are based remain the same. This is both a weakness and a strength of Kohlberg's approach. On the one hand, as Simpson suggested, rather than constructing dilemmas "according to a series of issues which have been selected because they are deemed to have universal applicability" (1974, p. 96), the issues should grow more spontaneously out of the culture under study to ensure that they are truly salient issues in that particular society. On the other hand, a subject's score is not based on the issue chosen (e.g., life: "Steal the drug," or law: "Don't steal the drug"), but rather on the reasons given for why a choice is preferable. This allows subjects in a society that stresses the law issue more commonly to choose that issue without their stage score being

---

* [In Kohlberg's Heinz dilemma, Heinz's wife is dying. A druggist has developed a drug that might save her life, but he refuses to sell it to Heinz because the price of the drug is too high for Heinz to pay. Whether or not Heinz should steal the drug to save his wife's life is the crux of the dilemma.— Eds.]

penalized, whereas subjects from a society that stresses the life issue have the same freedom from penalty.

Studies that have examined the actual issue choices made by their subjects have often found that the choices are culturally patterned. Lei, for instance, found that his Taiwanese subjects chose the punishment issue twice as often as the conscience issue (Lei, 1980, p. 8). I found that kibbutz youth nearly always chose the life rather than the law issue in the husband–wife dilemma compared with a more even distribution in the United States, and that the kibbutz-born youth nearly always made the contract rather than the law choice in the father–son dilemma compared with Middle Eastern youths, who usually chose the authority issue and argued that the son should give his father the money (Snarey, 1982, pp. 288–316). Harkness similarly reported that the elders in a rural Kipsigis community in Kenya invariably responded to the father–son story by stating that the boy should give up the money to his father (Harkness, Edwards, & Super, 1981, p. 599). Nisan and Kohlberg (1982) also found that Turkish city subjects were more likely than Turkish village subjects to decide that one should not steal even if it was to save a human life. In each case, the differences in the issues choice appear to be attributable to cultural differences. For instance, in the kibbutz research it seemed predictable that kibbutz adolescents, who are raised communally, would be more likely than Middle Eastern youth, who are raised in patriarchal families, to question parental authority and to consider the father's request to be unfair. Thus, the issue choice contained within each dilemma seems to allow for cultural variation in the stress placed on particular issues while still searching for universals in the way people reason about the issues.

The most radical form of adjustment that has been attempted is to create completely new dilemmas in which both the content and issues are derived from the population under study. As admirable as this approach appears, the results of such nonstandardized interviews have not been reported to be significantly different from those of culturally adapted standardized dilemmas. To examine the possible cultural bias of the dilemmas, for instance, White created "a moral dilemma based upon the experiences directly relevant to the outislanders... and administered [it] to a portion of the sample" (White, Bushnell, & Regnemer, 1978, p. 63). He concluded that "it was apparent upon inspection of the participants' responses that there were no stage differences in their responses to that Bahamian dilemma and their responses to the standard Kohlberg dilemmas" (1978, p. 63). Although Kohlberg's interview cannot be culture free, it does appear to be reasonably culture fair when the content is creatively adapted and the subject is interviewed in the native language. Testing bias is still possible, however, and future researchers should pay closer attention to this general issue.

Invariant Sequence

This proposition requires that stage development be upwardly invariant in sequence, with stage regressions and skipping no greater than what can be accounted for by measurement error. . . .

Examining the cross-sectional stage distributions, the increase in modal stage, and in the upper limits of the stage range, with a parallel increase in the age of the subjects is usually clear and sometimes dramatic. In the 20 cultural areas in which only cross-sectional studies have been completed, 85% of the cases indicated an increase in modal stage, and an increase in the upper extreme of the stage range, with increases in age. The remaining 15% of the cases (India, Guatemala, Kenya) showed a regression in either the modal stage or the stage range, but never in both. Further, all three of these cross-sectional cases of apparent regression involved adult subjects in which one could expect to find greater variation, because development has slowed and individuals with different terminal points in development accumulate in the same adult-age cohorts. Regarding the issue of stage skipping, 100% of the cross-sectional studies found all major stages present between the lowest and highest stage in their distribution.

Despite the supportive nature of these cross-sectional findings, they are not adequate to test the hypothesis of invariant sequence. The hypothesis of invariant sequence can only be tested adequately by longitudinal research because it involves testing the same persons over time. The seven longitudinal studies reported strikingly similar findings. No regressions were reported in the three 1-to-2 year longitudinal studies (Bahamas, Canada, Indonesia). The three 9-to-20 year longitudinal studies (Israel, United States, Turkey) and the one 2-year longitudinal study (India) reported some regressions, and each is now examined.

In the Israeli kibbutz longitudinal study, which included both kibbutz-born and Middle-Eastern Israeli youths and adults, regressions occurred in 6.3% (6) of 96 longitudinal changes, using the customary 9-point scale, and in 7.3% (7) of the 96 cases using the most differentiated 13-point scale. In the United States study, which included both middle-class and working-class subjects, longitudinal regressions occurred in 5.2% (11) of the 209 longitudinal interviews using the 9-point scale and in 7.2% (14) using the 13-point scale. Saraswathi and Sundaresan's (1982) 2-year longitudinal study of boys in India reported that 12.7% (7) of the 55 longitudinal cases regressed in moral stage. Of these 7 cases, only 1 subject regressed a full stage, whereas the other 6 had half-stage or smaller regressions. Are these regressions significant? Colby, Kohlberg, Gibbs, and Lieberman (1983) reported test–retest error to be 19%, using the 9-point scale. Because test–retest reversals are always much higher than each case of longitudinal reversals, one could attribute the violations of longitudinal sequence to measurement error. Of course, some of the nonreversals might also be due to measurement error, but measurement error would not account for the overwhelming evidence of nonreversal. . . .

Full Stage Range

The fourth proposition requires that the full range of stages—including the preconventional (1, 1/2, 2), conventional (2/3, 3, 3/4, 4), and postconventional (4/5, 5)—be present in all types of cultures. It is often assumed that Stage 5, for instance, is common among middle-class men in the United States but absent among non-Westerners, the lower classes, and women. The following findings indicate that this belief is not fully correct.

... [I]n 67% of the 27 cross-cultural sample areas, some subjects were found reasoning at Stage 1; in 89% of the cultural samples, some subjects were found reasoning at Stage 2; in 100% of the cases, subjects were reported at Stage 2/3 or 3; in 89% of the cases, subjects were reported at Stage 3/4 or 4; and in 67% of the cases, some subjects were reported at Stage 4/5 or 5. Stages 2 to 4 are thus virtually universal but Stages 1 and 5 are represented in only 67% of the samples....

Stage 4/5 or 5 was present to some degree in 100% of the urban Western samples and in 91% of the urban non-Western societies. It was quite common, although the actual number of individuals within any particular sample was often low, ranging from 1 out of 20 Turkish city residents (5%) to 10 out of 12 subject in a selective sample of senior kibbutz members (83%). On the other hand, Stage 4/5 or 5 was absent in 100% of the 8 traditional tribal or village folk societies, both non-Western and Western. The available data thus suggest that the significant difference lies between folk versus urban societies rather than between Western versus non-Western societies (cf. Edwards, 1975; Redfield, 1956, 1962)....

Thirteen cross-cultural studies in 11 countries included both middle class and lower or working-class subjects. In nine cases statistically significant social-class differences were reported. Only one case reported finding no class effects (Taiwan); and in one case two studies reported class differences, whereas a third study did not (England). Because one of the English studies that reported differences had used a superior scoring system, it is possible to conclude that samples from 10 of the 11 countries showed significant class differences in moral development. Of the 10 cases in which class differences were reported, 100% found that upper middle- or middle-class subjects scored higher than lower class or working-class subjects. These findings are similar to the results of other research in the United States; class differences were common and virtually always favored the middle class (DeVos, 1983).

Seventeen cross-cultural studies in 15 countries included both male and female subjects. In 14 studies there were no significant sex differences. In the remaining 3 studies, a clear sex difference favoring males was found in only one case (England). The German study (Gielen, 1982) did not find any significant overall difference, but it was reported that females were more likely than males to score at Stage 3. In India, two studies did not find any significant sex differences and one did; because the latter study used a less reliable scoring system than the first two studies, it seems appropriate to conclude that the evidence against sex differences in moral judgment in India is stronger.

Thus to summarize, 3 of the 17 studies reported significant sex differences, only 1 of these 3 studies reported a clear sex difference, and no study that used the most reliable scoring system reported any significant sex differences. These cross-cultural findings are also similar to the results of other research in the United States. Walker (1984) reviewed 54 North American studies that had used Kohlberg's moral judgment interview and found that only eight cases of significant sex differences were reported. Walker concluded that sex differences in moral reasoning are found only in a minority of studies, and in each of these cases sex differences are confounded with differences in levels of education and occupation (i.e., indexes of social class). Sex differences were also less frequent when the current standardized scoring manual was used. However, in those few studies where sex differences were reported, they virtually always favored men. The most impressive argument for women's voices being incompletely represented in Kohlberg's scheme has been made by Carol Gilligan (1982). She cautioned, however, against generalizing her perspective to other cultures....

Why is Stage 5 a rare empirical phenomenon, and why is its distribution skewed toward particular types of societies and classes? Part of the answer may lie with the size of the adult samples; 6 of the 11 populations in the 28–60+ age range included fewer than 20 subjects each. It might be unreasonable to expect such small samples of adult moral reasoning to represent the population of moral reasoning instances. However, 6 of the 11 populations in the oldest age range were selected because they were thought to have a higher probability of including some subjects at the higher stages. Of these six, three did in fact include a substantial number of subjects at Stage 4/5 or 5 (India, kibbutz, Taiwan), but the other three selected populations did not go beyond Stage 3 or 3/4 (Kenyan village leaders, Tibetan monks, New Guinea village leaders). It is important to note that all three of the samples that included subjects scoring at the postconventional level were modern societies and two of them were urban, and all three of the selected samples that failed to score beyond the conventional level were traditional folk societies. Village leaders in Kenya and New Guinea did score significantly higher than nonleaders, suggesting that their fellow villagers recognized them as more morally mature; Tibetan monks, however, usually scored lower than lay Tibetans. However, the failure of all members of traditional folk societies, including leaders, to use Stage 4/5 or 5 reasoning suggests the additional possibility of a bias in the scoring system....

[T]his present review of the empirical studies does not support a supremacist view of North America. The United States sample did not rank first in mean moral maturity scores in any one of the five age divisions... Taiwanese, kibbutzniks, Indians, and Turkish subjects all ranked higher than parallel groups from the United States at one or more points in the life cycle.

Claims that Kohlberg's theory is completely ethnocentric and universal are not consistent with the empirical research. So, why do subjects from traditional folk societies never score at Stage 5? I would suggest a third perspective that avoids the extremes of the two previous positions, but also assimilates important aspects of these arguments. In brief, sociocultural systems should be expected to vary in modal stage of usage and should also be understood as fully equal. A key to this position is to distinguish between society and culture and to bring a developmental perspective to both. This classic distinction (Linton, 1945) has implicitly underlied the strongest previous critiques of Kohlberg's universality claim: Susan Buck-Morss' socioeconomic critique (1975) and Carolyn Edwards' social complexity critique (1975). The social features of sociocultural systems (e.g., demographics, sociotechnical complexity) vary tremendously, not only when comparisons are made between societies, but also within one society over time. As the distribution of age groups varies, for instance, one would expect the modal stage to vary accordingly. Further, even if some individuals in a society espouse principled morality, the social structure may hinder its acceptance or operationalization. For example, the social structure of most prisons is so inadequate that it makes it dangerous to reason beyond Stage 2, just as the social structure of the United States made it dangerous for Martin Luther King to reason beyond Stage 4 (cf. Kohlberg, 1981). Thus, social systems should be expected to differ in their modal stage or level of moral reasoning.

In contrast, a society's culture or world view provides each member with a rich pool of cultural values to digest cognitively. Cultural world views can, in fact, be reasoned about on any stage level. This phenomenon is visible, for instance, with regard to religious world views. The pool of cultural content is sufficiently rich in Judaism, Christianity, Hinduism, and other traditions that varying levels of sophistication within any particular tradition are possible despite important differences between it and other religions. Thus, one finds children making sense of God as a concrete person and theologians who make meaning within the same religious tradition by referring to a transcendent reality or the Ground of Being. An appealing counterargument to the position that cultural world views cannot be placed at a particular stage is to point to Nazi Germany as a clearly morally inferior culture. However, this misses the point. One can reason about one's nation on a Stage 4 or 5 level, as many citizens of modern Germany apparently do (Gielen, 1982) and as some German citizens did during Hitler's reign of terror (cf. Bonhoeffer, 1953; London, 1970), or one can reason about it on a Stage 2 level, as many Nazis obviously did (cf. Garbarino & Bronfenbrenner, 1976). Thus, although every society may not have a significant proportion of its population reasoning at the higher stages, every culture is capable of supporting higher stage reasoning.

When this third perspective is brought to bear on the previously reviewed research, one of the methodological problems is highlighted—the stage definitions and scoring manual are incomplete, especially for Stage 5. Although Kohlberg's preconventional and conventional stages are well based on empirical operative judgments rather than on philosophical ethical systems, this is only weakly true of the postconventional stages. Descriptions of higher stage reasoning are primarily based upon Kant, Rawls, and other Western philosophers. Of course, a system of philosophy common to the entire world does not exist, and the integration of all existing systems is not feasible. Thus, it is not surprising that Kohlberg's postconventional stage descriptions are incomplete. The stage model and scoring manual, nevertheless, should draw examples of reasoning at the higher stages from a wider range of cultural world views. As Elizabeth Simpson (1974) suggested regarding the value of life in Hindu philosophy, for instance, "It is not that life is not valued ... but that it is valued situationally in highly culturally specific ways" (p. 97). The cultural specificity of principled moral reasoning has not been adequately explored, and thus Kohlberg's stage schema and scoring system appear to misinterpret the presence of higher stage reasoning in some types of cultural groups. In sum, there is a need for a more pluralistic stage theory and for a scoring manual that is elaborated with culturally specific examples of formal principles from diverse cultures.

The cross-cultural elaboration of postconventional principles could, I believe, reveal Stage 5 to be a more common empirical phenomenon. Future researchers should seek to find negative results and alternative structures; future research needs to be maximally open to the possibility of discovering additional modes of moral reasoning, especially at the postconventional level (cf. Price-Williams, 1975). Such a constructive approach to future cross-cultural moral development research will result in a more adequate and pluralistic understanding of universality and variation in social–moral development. The current problems and future research strategies suggested by this review, of course, simply highlight the natural limitations of any scheme, including Kohlberg's. The significant shortcomings of Kohlberg's work should not overshadow its remarkable achievements.

REFERENCES

Ashton, P. (1975). Cross-cultural research: An experimental perspective. *Harvard Educational Review, 45*(4), 475–505.

Awa, N. (1979). Ethnocentric bias in development research. In M. Asante, E. Newmark, & C. Blake (Eds.), *Handbook of intercultural communication* (pp. 263–282). London: Sage.

Berry, J., & Dasen, P. (1974). *Culture and cognition.* London: Methuen.

Bloom, A. H. (1977). Two dimensions of moral reasoning: Social principledness and social humanism in cross-cultural perspective. *Journal of Social Psychology, 101*(1), 29–44.

Bonhoeffer, D. (1953). *Letters and papers from prison.* New York: Macmillan.

Bredemeier, H. (1955). The methodology of functionalism. *American Sociological Review, 20,* 173–180.

Broughton, J. (1978). The cognitive-developmental approach to morality: A reply to Kurtines and Grief. *Journal of Moral Education, 7*(2), 81–96.

Buck-Morss, S. (1975). Socioeconomic bias in Piaget's theory and its implications for the cross-cultural controversy. *Human Development, 18,* 35–49.

Colby, A., Kohlberg, L., Gibbs, J., & Lieberman, M. (1983). A longitudinal study of moral judgment. *Monographs of the Society for Research in Child Development, 48*(1–2), 1–124.

Cole, M., & Scribner, M. (1974). *Culture and thought.* New York: Wiley.

Dasen, P. R. (1972). Cross-cultural Piagetian research: A summary. *Journal of Cross-Cultural Psychology, 3,* 23–39.

DeVos, E. (1983). *Socioeconomic influences on moral reasoning: A structural developmental perspective.* Unpublished doctoral dissertation. Harvard University, Cambridge, MA.

Edwards, C. (1975). Societal complexity and moral development. *Ethos, 3,* 505–527.

Edwards, C. (1981). The comparative study of the development of moral judgment and reasoning. In R. Munroe, R. Munroe, & B. Whiting (Eds.), *Handbook of cross-cultural human development* (pp. 501–527). New York: Garland.

Edwards, C. (1982). Moral development in comparative cultural perspective. In D. Wagner & H. Stevenson (Eds.), *Cultural perspectives on child development* (pp. 248–278). San Francisco: Freeman.

Garbarino, J., & Bronfenbrenner, U. (1976). The socialization of moral judgment and behavior in cross-cultural perspective. In T. Lickona (Ed.), *Moral development and behavior* (pp. 70–83). New York: Holt, Rinehart & Winston.

Gibbs, J. (1977). Kohlberg's stages of moral development: A critique. *Harvard Educational Review, 47*(1), 43–61.

Gielen, U. (1982). *Moral reasoning in radical and nonradical German students.* Unpublished manuscript, St. Francis University, Brooklyn, NY.

Gilligan, C. (1982). *In a different voice.* Cambridge, MA: Harvard University Press.

Gorsuch, R., & Barnes, M. (1973). Stages of ethical reasoning and moral norms of Carib youths. *Journal of Cross-Cultural Psychology, 4,* 183–301.

Guidon, A. (1978). Moral development: A critique of Kohlberg's sequence. *University of Ottawa Quarterly, 48*(3), 232–263.

Harkness, S., Edwards, C., & Super, C. (1981). Social roles and moral reasoning: A case study in a rural African community. *Developmental Psychology, 17,* 595–603.

Kohlberg, L. (1969). Stage and sequence: The cognitive-developmental approach to socialization. In D. A. Goslin (Ed.), *Handbook of socialization theory and research* (pp. 347–480). Chicago: Rand McNally.

Kohlberg, L. (1971). From is to ought: How to commit the naturalistic fallacy and get away with it in the study of moral development. In L. Mischel (Ed.), *Cognitive development and epistemology* (pp. 151–284). New York: Academic Press.

Kohlberg, L. (1981). *The philosophy of moral development: Moral stages and the idea of justice: Vol. 1. Essays on moral development.* San Francisco: Harper & Row.

Kohlberg, L., & Kramer, R. (1969). Continuities and discontinuities in childhood and adult moral development. *Human Development, 12,* 93–120.

Kuhn, D., & Angeleu, J. (1976). An experimental study of the development of formal operational thought. *Child Development, 47,* 697–706.

Kurtines, W., & Grief, E. C. (1974). The development of moral thought: Review and evaluation of Kohlberg's approach. *Psychological Bulletin, 81,* 453–470.

Lei, T. (1980). *An empirical study of Kohlberg's theory and scoring system of moral judgment development in Chinese society.* Unpublished bachelor's thesis, National Taiwan University.

Lickona, T. (1969). Piaget misunderstood: A critique of the criticisms of his theory of moral development. *Merrill-Palmer Quarterly of Behavior and Development, 16,* 337–350.

Lickona, T. (Ed.) (1976). *Moral development and behavior: Theory, research, and social issues.* New York: Holt, Rinehart & Winston.

Linton, R. (1945). *The cultural background of personality.* New York: Appleton-Century-Crofts.

London, P. (1970). The rescuers: Motivational hypotheses about Christians who saved Jews from the Nazis. In J. Macaulay & L. Berkowitz (Eds.), *Altruism and helping behavior* (pp. 240–248). New York: Academic Press.

Mayers, M. K. (1974). *Christianity confronts culture.* Grand Rapids, MI: Zondervan.

Naroll, R., & D'Andrade, R. (1963). Two solutions to Galton's problem. *American Anthropologist, 65,* 1053–1067.

Nisan, M., & Kohlberg, L. (1982). Universality and variation in moral judgement: A longitudinal and cross-sectional study in Turkey. *Child Development, 53,* 865–876.

Okonkuo, R. (1983). *Moral development research in Nigeria: Preliminary report of a pilot study in progress.* Unpublished manuscript, Harvard University, Cambridge, MA.

Price-Williams, D. R. (1975). *Explorations in cross-cultural psychology.* San Francisco: Chandler & Sharp.

Redfield, R. (1956). *Peasant society and culture.* Chicago: University of Chicago Press.

Redfield, R. (1962). *Human nature and the study of society: The collected papers of Robert Redfield.* Chicago: University of Chicago Press.

Rest, J. (1983). Morality. In J. Flavell & E. Markman (Eds.), *Manual of child psychology: Vol. 3. Cognitive development* (pp. 556–629). New York: Wiley.

Saraswathi, T. S., & Sundaresan, J. (1982). *A short-term longitudinal study of the development of moral judgment in Indian Boys.* Unpublished manuscript, University of Baroda, Gujarat, India.

Shweder, R. (1982a). Beyond self-constructed knowledge: The study of culture and morality. *Merrill-Palmer Quarterly, 28,* 41–69.

Shweder, R. (1982b). Liberalism as destiny. *Contemporary Psychology, 27,* 421–424.

Simpson, E. L. (1974). Moral development research: A case study of scientific cultural bias. *Human Development, 17,* 81–106.

Snarey, J. (1982). The social and moral development of kibbutz founders and sabras: A longitudinal and cross-sectional cross-cultural study. (Doctoral dissertation, Harvard University, 1982). *Dissertation Abstracts International, 43*(10), 3416b. (University Microfilms No. 83–02, 435)

Snarey, J., & Blasi, J. (1980). Ego development among adult kibbutzniks: A cross-cultural application of Loevinger's theory. *Genetic Psychology Monographs, 102,* 117–157.

Snarey, J., Kohlberg, L., & Noam, G. (1983). Ego development in perspective: Structural stage, functional phase, and cultural age-period models. *Developmental Review, 3,* 303–338.

Sullivan, E. (1977). A study of Kohlberg's structural theory of moral development: A critique. *Human Development, 20,* 352–376.

Vasudev, J. (1983). *A study of moral reasoning at different life stages in India.* Unpublished manuscript. University of Pittsburgh, PA.

Walker, L. J. (1984). Sex differences in the development of moral reasoning: A critical review of the literature. *Child Development, 55,* 677–691.

White, C. B., Bushnell, N., & Regnemer, J. L. (1978). Moral development in Bahamian school children: A 3-year examination of Kohlberg's stages of moral development. *Developmental Psychology, 14,* 58–65.

Whiting, J. W. M. (1968). Methods and problems in cross-cultural research. In G. Lindzey & E. Aronson (Eds.) *The handbook of social psychology* (pp. 693–728). Reading, MA: Addison-Wesley.

5.3 NEL NODDINGS

Teaching Themes of Care

Nel Noddings earned her B.A. at Montclair State College and her M.A. at Rutgers University, both in New Jersey, and she received her Ph.D. in educational philosophy and theory from Stanford University in California. She taught from 1949 to 1952 at the Woodbury Grade School in New Jersey. Noddings's interest in mathematics led her from the elementary school to the high school, where she taught math and was the assistant principal at the Matawan Regional High School in New Jersey from 1958 to 1969. After earning her doctorate in 1973, she worked for one year as director of pre-collegiate education at the University of Chicago, then she took her current post as a professor at Stanford in 1977. Her interests in educational philosophy focus upon moral education, feminist ethics, and mathematics education.

Noddings's many awards include twice winning the Excellence in Teaching Award at Stanford; the Medal for Distinguished Service from Teachers College, Columbia University; and the Anne Roe Award from the Harvard Graduate School of Education. She has published over 100 articles as well as the texts *Philosophy of Education* (Westview Press, 1995), *Educating for Intelligent Belief or Unbelief* (Teachers College Press, 1993), and *Caring: A Feminine Approach to Ethics and Moral Education* (University of California Press, 1984).

Although Noddings is a philosopher of education, her views have a powerful influence on educational psychology. In particular, one of the most important intersections of philosophy and psychology is the question, "What is human nature?" Noddings argues that we must view humans most centrally as caring beings. Doing so re-creates both the curriculum and the psychological methods of teaching. She explains this briefly in the following selection from "Teaching Themes of Care," *Phi Delta Kappan* (May 1995).

Key Concept: teaching themes of care

*S*ome educators today—and I include myself among them—would like to see a complete reorganization of the school curriculum. We would like to give a central place to the questions and issues that lie at the core of human existence. One possibility would be to organize the curriculum around themes of care—caring for self, for intimate others, for strangers and global others, for the natural world and its nonhuman creatures, for the human-made world, and for ideas.[1]

A realistic assessment of schooling in the present political climate makes it clear that such a plan is not likely to be implemented. However, we can use the rich vocabulary of care in educational planning and introduce themes of care into regular subject-matter classes. In this article, I will first give a brief rationale for teaching themes of care; second, I will suggest ways of choosing and organizing such themes; and, finally, I'll say a bit about the structures required to support such teaching.

WHY TEACH CARING?

In an age when violence among schoolchildren is at an unprecedented level, when children are bearing children with little knowledge of how to care for them, when the society and even the schools often concentrate on materialistic messages, it may be unnecessary to argue that we should care more genuinely for our children and teach them to care. However, many otherwise reasonable people seem to believe that our educational problems consist largely of low scores on achievement tests. My contention is, first, that we should want more from our educational efforts than adequate academic achievement and, second, that we will not achieve even that meager success unless our children believe that they themselves are cared for and learn to care for others.

There is much to be gained, both academically and humanly, by including themes of care in our curriculum. First, such inclusion may well expand our students' cultural literacy. For example, as we discuss in math classes the attempts of great mathematicians to prove the existence of God or to reconcile a God who is all good with the reality of evil in the world, students will hear names, ideas, and words that are not part of the standard curriculum. Although such incidental learning cannot replace the systematic and sequential learning required by those who plan careers in mathematically oriented fields, it can be powerful in expanding students' cultural horizons and in inspiring further study.

Second, themes of care help us to connect the standard subjects. The use of literature in mathematics classes, of history in science classes, and of art and music in all classes can give students a feeling of the wholeness in their education. After all, why should they seriously study five different subjects if their teachers, who are educated people, only seem to know and appreciate one?

Third, themes of care connect our students and our subjects to great existential questions. What is the meaning of life? Are there gods? How should I live?

Fourth, sharing such themes can connect us person-to-person. When teachers discuss themes of care, they may become real persons to their students and so enable them to construct new knowledge. Martin Buber put it this way:

> Trust, trust in the world, because this human being exists—that is the most inward achievement of the relation in education. Because this human being exists, meaninglessness, however hard pressed you are by it, cannot be the real truth. Because

this human being exists, in the darkness the light lies hidden, in fear salvation, and in the callousness of one's fellow-man the great love.[2]

Finally, I should emphasize that caring is not just a warm, fuzzy feeling that makes people kind and likable. Caring implies a continuous search for competence. When we care, we want to do our very best for the objects of our care. To have as our educational goal the production of caring, competent, loving, and lovable people is not anti-intellectual. Rather, it demonstrates respect for the full range of human talents. Not all human beings are good at or interested in mathematics, science, or British literature. But all humans can be helped to lead lives of deep concern for others, for the natural world and its creatures, and for the preservation of the human-made world. They can be led to develop the skills and knowledge necessary to make positive contributions, regardless of the occupation they may choose.

CHOOSING AND ORGANIZING THEMES OF CARE

Care is conveyed in many ways. At the institutional level, schools can be organized to provide continuity and support for relationships of care and trust.[3] At the individual level, parents and teachers show their caring through characteristic forms of attention: by cooperating in children's activities, by sharing their own dreams and doubts, and by providing carefully for the steady growth of the children in their charge. Personal manifestations of care are probably more important in children's lives than any particular curriculum or pattern of pedagogy.

However, curriculum can be selected with caring in mind. That is, educators can manifest their care in the choice of curriculum, and appropriately chosen curriculum can contribute to the growth of children as carers. Within each large domain of care, many topics are suitable for thematic units: in the domain of "caring for self," for example, we might consider life stages, spiritual growth, and what it means to develop an admirable character; in exploring the topic of caring for intimate others, we might include units on love, friendship, and parenting; under the theme of caring for strangers and global others, we might study war, poverty, and tolerance; in addressing the idea of caring for the human-made world, we might encourage competence with the machines that surround us and a real appreciation for the marvels of technology. Many other examples exist. Furthermore, there are at least two different ways to approach the development of such themes: units can be constructed by interdisciplinary teams, or themes can be identified by individual teachers and addressed periodically throughout a year's or semester's work.

The interdisciplinary approach is familiar in core programs, and such programs are becoming more and more popular at the middle school level. One key to a successful interdisciplinary unit is the degree of genuinely enthusiastic support it receives from the teachers involved. Too often, arbitrary or artificial groupings are formed, and teachers are forced to make contributions that they themselves do not value highly. For example, math and science teachers are sometimes automatically lumped together, and rich humanistic possibilities may be lost. If I, as a math teacher, want to include historical, biographical, and literary topics in my math lessons, I might prefer to work with English and social studies teachers. Thus it is important to involve teachers in the initial selection of broad areas for themes, as well as in their implementation.

Such interdisciplinary arrangements also work well at the college level. I recently received a copy of the syllabus for a college course titled "The Search for Meaning," which was co-taught by an economist, a university chaplain, and a psychiatrist.[4] The course is interdisciplinary, intellectually rich, and aimed squarely at the central questions of life.

At the high school level, where students desperately need to engage in the study and practice of caring, it is harder to form interdisciplinary teams. A conflict arises as teachers acknowledge the intensity of the subject-matter preparation their students need for further education. Good teachers often wish there were time in the day to co-teach unconventional topics of great importance, and they even admit that their students are not getting what they need for full personal development. But they feel constrained by the requirements of a highly competitive world and the structures of schooling established by that world.

Is there a way out of this conflict? Imaginative, like-minded teachers might agree to emphasize a particular theme in their separate classes. Such themes as war, poverty, crime, racism, or sexism can be addressed in almost every subject area. The teachers should agree on some core ideas related to caring that will be discussed in all classes, but beyond the central commitment to address themes of care, the topics can be handled in whatever way seems suitable in a given subject.

Consider, for example, what a mathematics class might contribute to a unit on crime. Statistical information might be gathered on the location and number of crimes, on rates for various kinds of crime, on the ages of offenders, and on the cost to society; graphs and charts could be constructed. Data on changes in crime rates could be assembled. Intriguing questions could be asked: Were property crime rates lower when penalties were more severe—when, for example, even children were hanged as thieves? What does an average criminal case cost by way of lawyers' fees, police investigation, and court processing? Does it cost more to house a youth in a detention center or in an elite private school?

None of this would have to occupy a full period every day. The regular sequential work of the math class could go on at a slightly reduced rate (e.g., fewer textbook exercises as homework), and the work on crime could proceed in the form of interdisciplinary projects over a considerable period of time. Most important would be the continual reminder in all classes that the topic is part of a larger theme of caring for strangers and fellow citizens. It takes only a few minutes to talk about what it means to live in safety, to trust one's neighbors, to feel secure in greeting strangers. Students should be told that metal detectors and security guards were not part of their parents' school lives, and they should be encouraged to hope for a safer and more open future. Notice the words I've used in this paragraph: caring, trust, safety, strangers, hope. Each could be used as an organizing theme for another unit of study.

English and social studies teachers would obviously have much to contribute to a unit on crime. For example, students might read *Oliver Twist*, and they might also study and discuss the social conditions that seemed to promote crime in 19th-century England. Do similar conditions exist in our country today? The selection of materials could include both classic works and modern stories and films. Students might even be introduced to some of the mystery stories that adults read so avidly on airplanes and beaches, and teachers should be engaged in lively discussion about the comparative value of the various stories.

Science teachers might find that a unit on crime would enrich their teaching of evolution. They could bring up the topic of social Darwinism, which played such a strong role in social policy during the late 19th and early 20th centuries. To what degree are criminal tendencies inherited? Should children be tested for the genetic defects that are suspected of predisposing some people to crime? Are females less competent than males in moral reasoning? (Why did some scientists and philosophers think this was true?) Why do males commit so many more violent acts than females?

Teachers of the arts can also be involved. A unit on crime might provide a wonderful opportunity to critique "gangsta rap" and other currently popular forms of music. Students might profitably learn how the control of art contributed to national criminality during the Nazi era. These are ideas that pop into my mind. Far more various and far richer ideas will come from teachers who specialize in these subjects.

There are risks, of course, in undertaking any unit of study that focuses on matters of controversy or deep existential concern, and teachers should anticipate these risks. What if students want to compare the incomes of teachers and cocaine dealers? What if they point to contemporary personalities from politics, entertainment, business, or sports who seem to escape the law and profit from what seems to be criminal behavior? My own inclination would be to allow free discussion of these cases and to be prepared to counteract them with powerful stories of honesty, compassion, moderation, and charity.

An even more difficult problem may arise. Suppose a student discloses his or her own criminal activities? Fear of this sort of occurrence may send teachers scurrying for safer topics. But, in fact, any instructional method that uses narrative forms or encourages personal expression runs this risk. For example, students of English as a second language who write proudly about their own hard lives and new hopes may disclose that their parents are illegal immigrants. A girl may write passages that lead her teacher to suspect sexual abuse. A boy may brag about objects he has "ripped off." Clearly, as we use these powerful methods that encourage students to initiate discussion and share their experiences, we must reflect on the ethical issues involved, consider appropriate responses to such issues, and prepare teachers to handle them responsibly.

Caring teachers must help students make wise decisions about what information they will share about themselves. On the one hand, teachers want their students to express themselves, and they want their students to trust in and consult them. On the other hand, teachers have an obligation to protect immature students from making disclosures that they might later regret. There is a deep ethical problem here. Too often educators assume that only religious fundamentalists and right-wing extremists object to the discussion of emotionally and morally charged issues. In reality, there is a real danger of intrusiveness and lack of respect in methods that fail to recognize the vulnerability of students. Therefore, as teachers plan units and lessons on moral issues, they should anticipate the tough problems that may arise. I am arguing here that it is morally irresponsible to simply ignore existential questions and themes of care; we must attend to them. But it is equally irresponsible to approach these deep concerns without caution and careful preparation.

So far I have discussed two ways of organizing interdisciplinary units on themes of care. In one, teachers actually teach together in teams; in the other, teachers agree on a theme and a central focus on care, but they do what they can, when they can, in their own classrooms. A variation on this second way —which is also open to teachers who have to work alone—is to choose several themes and weave them into regular course material over an entire semester or year. The particular themes will depend on the interests and preparation of each teacher.

For example, if I were teaching high school mathematics today, I would use religious/existential questions as a pervasive theme because the biographies of mathematicians are filled with accounts of their speculations on matters of God, other dimensions, and the infinite—and because these topics fascinate me. There are so many wonderful stories to be told: Descartes' proof of the existence of God, Pascal's famous wager, Plato's world of forms, Newton's attempt to verify Biblical chronology, Leibnitz' detailed theodicy, current attempts to describe a divine domain in terms of metasystems, and mystical speculations on the infinite.[5] Some of these stories can be told as rich "asides" in five minutes or less. Others might occupy the better part of several class periods.

Other mathematics teachers might use an interest in architecture and design, art, music, or machinery as continuing themes in the domain of "caring for the human-made world." Still others might introduce the mathematics of living things. The possibilities are endless. In choosing and pursuing these themes, teachers should be aware that they are both helping their students learn to care and demonstrating their own caring by sharing interests that go well beyond the demands of textbook pedagogy.

Still another way to introduce themes of care into regular classrooms is to be prepared to respond spontaneously to events that occur in the school or in the neighborhood. Older teachers have one advantage in this area: they probably have a greater store of experience and stories on which to draw. However, younger teachers have the advantage of being closer to their students' lives and experiences; they are more likely to be familiar with the music, films, and sports figures that interest their students.

All teachers should be prepared to respond to the needs of students who are suffering from the death of friends, conflicts between groups of students, pressure to use drugs or to engage in sex, and other troubles so rampant in the lives of today's children. Too often schools rely on experts—"grief counselors" and the like—when what children really need is the continuing compassion and presence of adults who represent constancy and care in their lives. Artificially separating the emotional, academic, and moral care of children into tasks for specially designated experts contributes to the fragmentation of life in schools.

Of course, I do not mean to imply that experts are unnecessary, nor do I mean to suggest that some matters should not be reserved for parents or psychologists. But our society has gone too far in compartmentalizing the care of its children. When we ask whose job it is to teach children how to care, an appropriate initial response is "Everyone's." Having accepted universal responsibility, we can then ask about the special contributions and limitations of various individuals and groups.

SUPPORTING STRUCTURES

What kind of schools and teacher preparation are required, if themes of care are to be taught effectively? First, and most important, care must be taken seriously as a major purpose of schools; that is, educators must recognize that caring for students is fundamental in teaching and that developing people with a strong capacity for care is a major objective of responsible education. Schools properly pursue many other objectives—developing artistic talent, promoting multicultural understanding, diversifying curriculum to meet the academic and vocational needs of all students, forging connections with community agencies and parents, and so on. Schools cannot be single-purpose institutions. Indeed, many of us would argue that it is logically and practically impossible to achieve that single academic purpose if other purposes are not recognized and accepted. This contention is confirmed in the success stories of several inner-city schools.[6]

Once it is recognized that school is a place in which students are cared for and learn to care, that recognition should be powerful in guiding policy. In the late 1950s, schools in the U.S., under the guidance of James Conant and others, placed the curriculum at the top of the educational priority list. Because the nation's leaders wanted schools to provide high-powered courses in mathematics and science, it was recommended that small high schools be replaced by efficient larger structures complete with sophisticated laboratories and specialist teachers. Economies of scale were anticipated, but the main argument for consolidation and regionalization centered on the curriculum. All over the country, small schools were closed, and students were herded into larger facilities with "more offerings." We did not think carefully about schools as communities and about what might be lost as we pursued a curriculum-driven ideal.

Today many educators are calling for smaller schools and more family-like groupings. These are good proposals, but teachers, parents, and students should be engaged in continuing discussion about what they are trying to achieve through the new arrangements. For example, if test scores do not immediately rise, participants should be courageous in explaining that test scores were not the main object of the changes. Most of us who argue for caring in schools are intuitively quite sure that children in such settings will in fact become more competent learners. But, if they cannot prove their academic competence in a prescribed period of time, should we give up on caring and on teaching them to care? That would be foolish. There is more to life and learning than the academic proficiency demonstrated by test scores.

In addition to steadfastness of purpose, schools must consider continuity of people and place. If we are concerned with caring and community, then we must make it possible for students and teachers to stay together for several years so that mutual trust can develop and students can feel a sense of belonging in their "school-home."[7]

More than one scheme of organization can satisfy the need for continuity. Elementary school children can stay with the same teacher for several years, or they can work with a stable team of specialist teachers for several years. In the latter arrangement, there may be program advantages; that is, children taught by subject-matter experts who get to know them well over an extended period of time may learn more about the particular subjects. At the high school level, the same specialist teachers might work with students throughout their years in high school. Or, as Theodore Sizer has suggested, one teacher might teach two subjects to a group of 30 students rather than one subject to 60 students, thereby reducing the number of different adults with whom students interact each day.[8] In all the suggested arrangements, placements should be made by mutual consent whenever possible. Teachers and students who hate or distrust one another should not be forced to stay together.

A policy of keeping students and teachers together for several years supports caring in two essential ways: it provides time for the development of caring relations, and it makes teaching themes of care more feasible. When trust has been established, teacher and students can discuss matters that would be hard for a group of strangers to approach, and classmates learn to support one another in sensitive situations.

The structural changes suggested here are not expensive. If a high school teacher must teach five classes a day, it costs no more for three of these classes to be composed of continuing students than for all five classes to comprise new students—i.e., strangers. The recommended changes come directly out of a clear-headed assessment of our major aims and purposes. We failed to suggest them earlier because we had other, too limited, goals in mind.

I have made one set of structural changes sound easy, and I do believe that they are easily made. But the curricular and pedagogical changes that are required may be more difficult. High school textbooks rarely contain the kinds of supplementary material I have described, and teachers are not formally prepared to incorporate such material. Too often, even the people we regard as strongly prepared in a liberal arts major are unprepared to discuss the history of their subject, its relation to other subjects, the biographies of its great figures, its connections to the great existential questions, and the ethical responsibilities of those who work in that discipline. To teach themes of care in an academically effective way, teachers will have to engage in projects of self-education.

At present, neither liberal arts departments nor schools of education pay much attention to connecting academic subjects with themes of care. For example, biology students may learn something of the anatomy and physiology of mammals but nothing at all about the care of living animals; they may never be asked to consider the moral issues involved in the annual euthanasia of millions of pets. Mathematics students may learn to solve quadratic equations but never study what it means to live in a mathematicized world. In enlightened history classes, students may learn something about the problems of racism and colonialism but never hear anything about the evolution of childhood, the contributions of women in both domestic and public caregiving, or the connection between the feminization of caregiving and public policy. A liberal education that neglects matters that are central to a fully human life hardly warrants the name,[9] and a professional education that confines itself to technique does nothing to close the gaps in liberal education.

The greatest structural obstacle, however, may simply be legitimizing the inclusion of themes of care in the curriculum. Teachers in the early grades have long included such themes as a regular part of their work, and middle school educators are becoming more sensitive to developmental needs involving care. But secondary schools—where violence, apathy, and alienation are most evident—do little to develop the capacity to care. Today, even elementary teachers complain that the pressure to produce high test scores inhibits the work they regard as central to their mission: the development of caring and competent people. Therefore, it would seem that the most fundamental change required is one of attitude. Teachers can be very special people in the lives of children, and it should be legitimate for them to spend time developing relations of trust, talking with students about problems that are central to their lives, and guiding them toward greater sensitivity and competence across all the domains of care.

NOTES

1. For the theoretical argument, see Nel Noddings, *The Challenge to Care in Schools* (New York: Teachers College Press, 1992); for a practical example and rich documentation, see Sharon Quint, *Schooling Homeless Children* (New York: Teachers College Press, 1994).

2. Martin Buber, *Between Man and Man* (New York: Macmillan, 1965), p. 98.

3. Noddings, chap. 12.

4. See Thomas H. Naylor, William H. Willimon, and Magdalena R. Naylor, *The Search for Meaning* (Nashville, Tenn.: Abingdon Press, 1994).

5. For many more examples, see Nel Noddings, *Educating for Intelligent Belief and Unbelief* (New York: Teachers College Press, 1993).

6. See Deborah Meier, "How Our Schools Could Be," *Phi Delta Kappan*, January 1995, pp. 369–73; and Quint, op. cit.

7. See Jane Roland Martin, *The Schoolhome: Rethinking Schools for Changing Families* (Cambridge, Mass.: Harvard University Press, 1992).

8. Theodore Sizer, *Horace's Compromise: The Dilemma of the American High School* (Boston: Houghton Mifflin, 1984).

9. See Bruce Wilshire, *The Moral Collapse of the University* (Albany: State University of New York Press, 1990).

PART FOUR

Approaches to Learning

Chapter 6   Behavioral Learning Theory   189

Chapter 7   Cognitive and Constructivist Learning Theory   216

Chapter 8   Information Processing   237

On the Internet . . .

Sites appropriate to Part Four

The B. F. Skinner Foundation was established in 1987 to publish significant literary and scientific works on the analysis of behavior and to educate both professionals and the public about the science of behavior.

http://www.lafayette.edu/allanr/welcom.htm

The Los Angeles Open Charter School was started in 1977 by a group of parents and teachers who wanted an alternative to the "back-to-basics" approach that dominated the district at that time.

http://www.ed.gov/pubs/EdReformStudies/
    EdTech/opencharter.html

These pages offer advice on "best practices in education" regarding Lev Vygotsky as well as other links to his work in educational psychology.

http://www.bestpraceduc.org/people/
    LevVygotsky.html

This page links to some background information on Herbert Simon, the text of a speech he gave at Berkeley entitled "Literary Criticism: A Cognitive Approach," and over 30 essays in response to that work by a wide variety of commentators.

http://www.stanford.edu/group/SHR/4-1/
    text/toc.html

CHAPTER 6 Behavioral Learning Theory

6.1 B. F. SKINNER

The Science of Learning and the Art of Teaching

B. F. Skinner (1904–1990) was born in Pennsylvania, received his A.B. from Hamilton College in New York, and earned his master's and doctorate in psychology from Harvard University. He taught at the University of Minnesota from 1931 to 1943, and then at Indiana University until 1948. He then became a member of the Harvard faculty, where he stayed through retirement. Skinner is often called the most influential member of the behaviorist movement, which dominated American psychology for most of the twentieth century. He published many texts and research papers, including *The Behavior of Organisms* (1938), *Science and Human Behavior* (1953), *Verbal Behavior* (1957), *Walden Two* (1961), *Beyond Freedom and Dignity* (1971), and *About Behaviorism* (1974).

   Although Skinner is not considered primarily an educational psychologist, his work has been extraordinarily influential among school psychologists, school administrators, and classroom teachers. In fact, Skinner's version of behaviorism, along with that of the neobehaviorists, has become known as "learning theory" despite the many important and influential theories about learning that are nonbehavioristic. In particular, his explanation of *operant conditioning,* based on reinforcement and punishment, has been powerfully invoked to explain the acquisition of new behavior (learning) in the developing human. In the following selection from "The Science of Learning and the Art of Teaching," *Harvard Educational Review* (Spring 1954), Skinner describes his view of education.

Key Concept: reinforcement

*S*ome promising advances have recently been made in the field of learning. Special techniques have been designed to arrange what are called "contingencies of reinforcement"—the relations which prevail between behavior on the one hand and the consequences of that behavior on the other—with the result that a much more effective control of behavior has been achieved. It has long been argued that an organism learns mainly by producing changes in its environment, but it is only recently that these changes have been carefully manipulated. In traditional devices for the study of learning—in the serial maze, for example, or in the T-maze, the problem box, or the familiar discrimination apparatus—the effects produced by the organism's behavior are left to many fluctuating circumstances. There is many a slip between the turn-to-the-right and the food-cup at the end of the alley. It is not surprising that techniques of this sort have yielded only very rough data from which the uniformities demanded by an experimental science can be extracted only by averaging many cases. In none of this work has the behavior of the individual organism been predicted in more than a statistical sense. The learning processes which are the presumed object of such research are reached only through a series of inferences. Current preoccupation with deductive systems reflects this state of the science.

Recent improvements in the conditions which control behavior in the field of learning are of two principal sorts. The Law of Effect has been taken seriously; we have made sure that effects *do* occur and that they occur under conditions which are optimal for producing the changes called learning. Once we have arranged the particular type of consequence called a reinforcement, our techniques permit us to shape up the behavior of an organism almost at will. It has become a routine exercise to demonstrate this in classes in elementary psychology by conditioning such an organism as a pigeon. Simply by presenting food to a hungry pigeon at the right time, it is possible to shape up three or four well-defined responses in a single demonstration period—such responses as turning around, pacing the floor in the pattern of a figure-8, standing still in a corner of the demonstration apparatus, stretching the neck, or stamping the foot. Extremely complex performances may be reached through successive stages in the shaping process, the contingencies of reinforcement being changed progressively in the direction of the required behavior. The results are often quite dramatic. In such a demonstration one can *see* learning take place. A significant change in behavior is often obvious as the result of a single reinforcement.

A second important advance in technique permits us to maintain behavior in given states of strength for long periods of time. Reinforcements continue to be important, of course, long after an organism has learned *how* to do something, long after it has acquired behavior. They are necessary to maintain the behavior in strength. Of special interest is the effect of various schedules of intermittent reinforcement. Charles B. Ferster and the author are currently preparing an extensive report of a five-year research program, sponsored by the Office of Naval Research, in which most of the important types of schedules have been investigated and in which the effects of schedules in general have been reduced to a few principles. On the theoretical side we now have a fairly good idea of why a given schedule produces its appropriate performance. On the practical side we have learned how to maintain any given level of activity for daily periods limited only by the physical exhaustion of the organism and from day to day without substantial change throughout its life. Many of these effects would be traditionally assigned to the field of motivation, although the principal operation is simply the arrangement of contingencies of reinforcement.[1]

These new methods of shaping behavior and of maintaining it in strength are a great improvement over the traditional practices of professional animal trainers, and it is not surprising that our laboratory results are already being applied to the production of performing animals for commercial purposes. In a more academic environment they have been used for demonstration purposes which extend far beyond an interest in learning as such. For example, it is not too difficult to arrange the complex contingencies which produce many types of social behavior. Competition is exemplified by two pigeons playing a modified game of ping-pong. The pigeons drive the ball back and forth across a small table by pecking at it. When the ball gets by one pigeon, the other is reinforced. The task of constructing such a "social relation" is probably completely out of reach of the traditional animal trainer. It requires a carefully designed program of gradually changing contingencies and the skillful use of schedules to maintain the behavior in strength. Each pigeon is separately prepared for its part in the total performance, and the "social relation" is then arbitrarily constructed. The sequence of events leading up to this stable state are excellent material for the study of the factors important in nonsynthetic social behavior. It is instructive to consider how a similar series of contingencies could arise in the case of the human organism through the evolution of cultural patterns.

Cooperation can also be set up, perhaps more easily than competition. We have trained two pigeons to coordinate their behavior in a cooperative endeavor with a precision which equals that of the most skillful human dancers. In a more serious vein these techniques have permitted us to explore the complexities of the individual organism and to analyze some of the serial or coordinate behaviors involved in attention, problem solving, various types of self-control, and the subsidiary systems of responses within a single organism called "personalities." Some of these are exemplified in what we call multiple schedules of reinforcement. In general a given schedule has an effect upon the rate at which a response is emitted. Changes in the rate from moment to moment show a pattern typical of the schedule. The pattern may be as simple as a constant rate of responding at a given value, it may be a gradually accelerating rate between certain extremes, it may be an abrupt change from not responding at all to a given stable high rate, and so on. It has been shown that the performance characteristic of a given schedule can be brought under the control of a particular stimulus and that different performances can be brought under the control of different stimuli in the same organism. At a recent meeting of the American Psychological Association, Dr. Ferster and the author demonstrated a pigeon whose behavior showed the pattern typical of "fixed-interval" reinforcement in the presence of one stimulus and, alternately, the pattern typical of the very different schedule called "fixed ratio" in the presence of a second stimulus. In the laboratory we have been able to obtain performances appropriate to *nine* different schedules in the presence of appropriate stimuli in random alternation. When Stimulus 1 is present, the pigeon executes the performance appropriate to Schedule 1. When Stimulus 2 is present, the pigeon executes the performance appropriate to Schedule 2. And so on. This result is important because it makes the extrapolation of our laboratory results to daily life much more plausible. We are all constantly shifting from schedule to schedule as our immediate environment changes, but the dynamics of the control exercised by reinforcement remain essentially unchanged.

It is also possible to construct very complex *sequences* of schedules. It is not easy to describe these in a few words, but two or three examples may be mentioned. In one experiment the pigeon generates a performance appropriate to Schedule A where the reinforcement is simply the production of the stimulus characteristic of Schedule B, to which the pigeon then responds appropriately. Under a third stimulus, the bird yields a performance appropriate to Schedule C where the reinforcement in this case is simply the production of the stimulus characteristic of Schedule D, to which the bird then responds appropriately. In a special case, first investigated by L. B. Wyckoff, Jr., the organism responds to one stimulus where the reinforcement consists of the *clarification* of the stimulus controlling another response. The first response becomes, so to speak, an objective form of "paying attention" to the second stimulus. In one important version of this experiment, as yet unpublished, we could say that the pigeon is telling us whether it is "paying attention" to the *shape* of a spot of light or to its *color*.

One of the most dramatic applications of these techniques has recently been made in the Harvard Psychological Laboratories by Floyd Ratliff and Donald S. Blough, who have skillfully used multiple and serial schedules of reinforcement to study complex perceptual processes in the infrahuman organism. They have achieved a sort of psycho-physics without verbal instruction. In a recent experiment by Blough, for example, a pigeon draws a detailed dark-adaptation curve showing the characteristic breaks of rod and cone vision. The curve is recorded continuously in a single experimental period and is quite comparable with the curves of human subjects. The pigeon behaves in a way which, in the human case, we would not hesitate to describe by saying that it adjusts a very faint patch of light until it can just be seen.

In all this work, the species of the organism has made surprisingly little difference. It is true that the organisms studied have all been vertebrates, but they still cover a wide range. Comparable results have been obtained with pigeons, rats, dogs, monkeys, human children, and most recently, by the author in collaboration with Ogden R. Lindsley, human psychotic subjects. In spite of great phylogenetic differences, all these organisms show amazingly similar properties of the learning process. It should be emphasized that this has been achieved by analyzing the effects of reinforcement and by designing techniques which manipulate reinforcement with considerable precision. Only in this way can the behavior of the individual organism be brought under such precise control. It is also important to note that through a gradual advance to complex interrelations among responses, the same degree of rigor is being extended to behavior which would usually be assigned to such fields as perception, thinking, and personality dynamics.

From this exciting prospect of an advancing science of learning, it is a great shock to turn to that branch of technology which is most directly concerned with the learning process—education. Let us consider, for example, the teaching of arithmetic in the lower grades. The school is concerned with imparting to the child a large number of responses of a special sort. The responses are all verbal. They consist of speaking and writing certain words, figures, and signs which, to put it roughly, refer to numbers and to arithmetic operations. The first task is to shape up these responses—to get the child to pronounce and to write responses correctly, but the principal task is to bring this behavior under many sorts of stimulus control. This is what happens when the child learns to count, to recite tables, to count while ticking off the items in an assemblage of objects, to respond to spoken or written numbers by saying "odd," "even," "prime," and so on. Over and above this elaborate repertoire of numerical behavior, most of which is often dismissed as the product of rote learning, the teaching of arithmetic looks forward to those complex serial arrangements of responses involved in original mathematical thinking. The child must acquire responses of transposing, clearing fractions, and so on, which modify the order or pattern of the original material so that the response called a solution is eventually made possible.

Now, how is this extremely complicated verbal repertoire set up? In the first place, what reinforcements are used? Fifty years ago the answer would have been clear. At that time educational control was still frankly aversive. The child read numbers, copied numbers, memorized tables, and performed operations upon numbers to escape the threat of the birch rod or cane. Some positive reinforcements were perhaps eventually derived from the increased efficiency of the child in the field of arithmetic and in rare cases some automatic reinforcement may have resulted from the sheer manipulation of the medium—from the solution of problems or the discovery of the intricacies of the number system. But for the immediate purposes of education the child acted to avoid or escape punishment. It was part of the reform movement known as progressive education to make the positive consequences more immediately effective, but any one who visits the lower grades of the average school today will observe that a change has been made, not from aversive to positive control, but from one form of aversive stimulation to another. The child at his desk, filling in his workbook, is behaving primarily to escape from the threat of a series of minor aversive events—the teacher's displeasure, the criticism or ridicule of his classmates, an ignominious showing in a competition, low marks, a trip to the office "to be talked to" by the principal, or a word to the parent who may still resort to the birch rod. In this welter of aversive consequences, getting the right answer is in itself an insignificant event, any effect of which is lost amid the anxieties, the boredom, and the aggressions which are the inevitable by-products of aversive control.[2]

Secondly, we have to ask how the contingencies of reinforcement are arranged. When is a numerical operation reinforced as "right"? Eventually, of course, the pupil may be able to check his own answers and achieve some sort of automatic reinforcement, but in the early stages the reinforcement of being right is usually accorded by the teacher. The contingencies she provides are far from optimal. It can easily be demonstrated that, unless explicit mediating behavior has been set up, the lapse of only a few seconds between response and reinforcement destroys most of the effect. In a typical classroom, nevertheless, long periods of time customarily elapse. The teacher may walk up and down the aisle, for example, while the class is working on a sheet of problems, pausing here and there to say right or wrong. Many seconds or minutes intervene between the child's response and the teacher's reinforcement. In many cases—for example, when papers are taken home to be corrected—as much as 24 hours may intervene. It is surprising that this system has any effect whatsoever.

A third notable shortcoming is the lack of a skillful program which moves forward through a series of progressive approximations to the final complex behavior desired. A long series of contingencies is necessary to bring the organism into the possession of mathematical behavior most efficiently. But the teacher is seldom able to reinforce at each step in such a series because she cannot deal with the pupil's responses one at a time. It is usually necessary to reinforce the behavior in blocks of responses—as in correcting a work sheet or page from a workbook. The responses within such a block must not be interrelated. The answer to one problem must not depend upon the answer to another. The number of stages through which one may progressively approach a complex pattern of behavior is therefore small, and the task so much the more difficult. Even the most modern workbook in beginning arithmetic is far from exemplifying an efficient program for shaping up mathematical behavior.

Perhaps the most serious criticism of the current classroom is the relative infrequency of reinforcement. Since the pupil is usually dependent upon the teacher for being right, and since many pupils are usually dependent upon the same teacher, the total number of contingencies which may be arranged during, say, the first four years, is of the order of only a few thousand. But a very rough estimate suggests that efficient mathematical behavior at this level requires something of the order of 25,000 contingencies. We may suppose that even in the brighter student a given contingency must be arranged several times to place the behavior well in hand. The responses to be set up are not simply the various items in tables of addition, subtraction, multiplication, and division; we have also to consider the alternative forms in which each item may be stated. To the learning of such material we should add hundreds of responses concerned with factoring, identifying primes, memorizing series, using short-cut techniques of calculation, constructing and using geometric representations or number forms, and so on. Over and above all this, the whole mathematical repertoire must be brought under the control of concrete problems of considerable variety. Perhaps 50,000 contingencies is a more conservative estimate. In this frame of reference the daily assignment in arithmetic seems pitifully meagre.

The result of all this is, of course, well known. Even our best schools are under criticism for their inefficiency in the teaching of drill subjects such as arithmetic. The condition in the average school is a matter of wide-spread national concern. Modern children simply do not learn arithmetic quickly or well. Nor is the result simply incompetence. The very subjects in which modern techniques are weakest are those in which failure is most conspicuous, and in the wake of an ever-growing incompetence come the anxieties, uncertainties, and aggressions which in their turn present other problems to the school. Most pupils soon claim the asylum of not being "ready" for arithmetic at a given level or, eventually, of not having a mathematical mind. Such explanations are readily seized upon by defensive teachers and parents. Few pupils ever reach the stage at which automatic reinforcements follow as the natural consequences of mathematical behavior. On the contrary, the figures and symbols of mathematics have become standard emotional stimuli. The glimpse of a column of figures, not to say an algebraic symbol or an integral sign, is likely to set off—not mathematical behavior—but a reaction of anxiety, guilt, or fear.

The teacher is usually no happier about this than the pupil. Denied the opportunity to control via the birch rod, quite at sea as to the mode of operation of the few techniques at her disposal, she spends as little time as possible on drill subjects and eagerly subscribes to philosophies of education which emphasize material of greater inherent interest. A confession of weakness is her extraordinary concern lest the child be taught something unnecessary. The repertoire to be imparted is carefully reduced to an essential minimum. In the field of spelling, for example, a great deal of time and energy has gone into discovering just those words which the young child is going to use, as if it were a crime to waste one's educational power in teaching an unnecessary word. Eventually, weakness of technique emerges in the disguise of a reformulation of the aims of education. Skills are minimized in favor of vague achievements—educating for democracy, educating the whole child, educating for life, and so on. And there the matter ends; for, unfortunately, these philosophies do not in turn suggest improvements in techniques. They offer little or no help in the design of better classroom practices.

There would be no point in urging these objections if improvement were impossible. But the advances which have recently been made in our control of the learning process suggest a thorough revision of classroom practices and, fortunately, they tell us how the revision can be brought about. This is not, of course, the first time that the results of an experimental science have been brought to bear upon the practical problems of education. The modern classroom does not, however, offer much evidence that research in the field of learning has been respected or used. This condition is no doubt partly due to the limitations of earlier research. But it has been encouraged by a too hasty conclusion that the laboratory study of learning is inherently limited because it cannot take into account the realities of the classroom. In the light of our increasing knowledge of the learning process we should, instead, insist upon dealing with those realities and forcing a substantial change in them. Education is perhaps the most important branch of scientific technology. It deeply affects the lives of all of us. We can no longer allow the exigencies of a practical situation to suppress the tremendous improvements which are within reach. The practical situation must be changed.

There are certain questions which have to be answered in turning to the study of any new organism. What behavior is to be set up? What reinforcers are at hand? What responses are available in embarking upon a program of progressive approximation which will lead to the final form of the behavior? How can reinforcements be most efficiently scheduled to maintain the behavior in strength? These questions are all relevant in considering the problem of the child in the lower grades.

In the first place, what reinforcements are available? What does the school have in its possession which will reinforce a child? We may look first to the material to be learned, for it is possible that this will provide considerable automatic reinforcement. Children play for hours with mechanical toys, paints, scissors and paper, noise-makers, puzzles—in short, with almost anything which feeds back significant changes in the environment and is reasonably free of aversive properties. The sheer control of nature is itself reinforcing. This effect is not evident in the modern school because it is masked by the emotional responses generated by aversive control. It is true that automatic reinforcement from the manipulation of the environment is probably only a mild reinforcer and may need to be carefully husbanded, but one of the most striking principles to emerge from recent research is that the *net* amount of reinforcement is of little significance. A very slight reinforcement may be tremendously effective in controlling behavior if it is wisely used.

If the natural reinforcement inherent in the subject matter is not enough, other reinforcers must be employed. Even in school the child is occasionally permitted to do "what he wants to do," and access to reinforcements of many sorts may be made contingent upon the more immediate consequences of the behavior to be established. Those who advocate competition as a useful social motive may wish to use the reinforcements which follow from excelling others, although there is the difficulty that in this case the reinforcement of one child is necessarily aversive to another. Next in order we might place the good will and affection of the teacher, and only when that has failed need we turn to the use of aversive stimulation.

In the second place, how are these reinforcements to be made contingent upon the desired behavior? There are two considerations here—the gradual elaboration of extremely complex patterns of behavior and the maintenance of the behavior in strength at each stage. The whole process of becoming competent in any field must be divided into a very large number of very small steps, and reinforcement must be contingent upon the accomplishment of each step. This solution to the problem of creating a complex repertoire of behavior also solves the problem of maintaining the behavior in strength. We could, of course, resort to the techniques of scheduling already developed in the study of other organisms but in the present state of our knowledge of educational practices, scheduling appears to be most effectively arranged through the design of the material to be learned. By making each successive step as small as possible, the frequency of reinforcement can be raised to a maximum, while the possibly aversive consequences of being wrong are reduced to a minimum. Other ways of designing material would yield other programs of reinforcement. Any supplementary reinforcement would probably have to be scheduled in the more traditional way.

These requirements are not excessive, but they are probably incompatible with the current realities of the classroom. In the experimental study of learning it has been found that the contingencies of reinforcement which are most efficient in controlling the organism cannot be arranged through the personal mediation of the experimenter. An organism is affected by subtle details of contingencies which are beyond the capacity of the human organism to arrange. Mechanical and electrical devices must be used. Mechanical help is also demanded by the sheer number of contingencies which may be used efficiently in a single experimental session. We have recorded many millions of responses from a single organism during thousands of experimental hours. Personal arrangement of the contingencies and personal observation of the results are quite unthinkable. Now, the human organism is, if anything, more sensitive to precise contingencies than the other organisms we have studied. We have every reason to expect, therefore, that the most effective control of human learning will require instrumental aid. The simple fact is that, as a mere reinforcing mechanism, the teacher is out of date. This would be true even if a single teacher devoted all her time to a single child, but her inadequacy is multiplied many-fold when she must serve as a reinforcing device to many children at once. If the teacher is to take advantage of recent advances in the study of learning, she must have the help of mechanical devices.

The technical problem of providing the necessary instrumental aid is not particularly difficult. There are many ways in which the necessary contingencies may be arranged, either mechanically or electrically. An inexpensive device which solves most of the principal problems has already been constructed. It is still in the experimental stage, but a description will suggest the kind of instrument which seems to be required. The device consists of a small box about the size of a small record player. On the top surface is a window through which a question or problem printed on a paper tape may be seen. The child answers the question by moving one or more sliders upon which the digits 0 through 9 are printed. The answer appears in square holes punched in the paper upon which the question is printed. When the answer has been set, the child turns a knob. The operation is as simple as adjusting a television set. If the answer is right, the knob turns freely and can be made to ring a bell or provide some other conditioned reinforcement. If the answer is wrong, the knob will not turn. A counter may be added to tally wrong answers. The knob must then be reversed slightly and a second attempt at a right answer made. (Unlike the flash-card, the device reports a wrong answer without giving the right answer.) When the answer is right, a further turn of the knob engages a clutch which moves the next problem into place in the window. This movement cannot be completed, however, until the sliders have been returned to zero.

The important features of the device are these: Reinforcement for the right answer is immediate. The mere manipulation of the device will probably be reinforcing enough to keep the average pupil at work for a suitable period each day, provided traces of earlier aversive control can be wiped out. A teacher may supervise an entire class at work on such devices at the same time, yet each child may progress at his own rate, completing as many problems as possible within the class period. If forced to be away from school, he may return to pick up where he left off. The gifted child will advance rapidly, but can be kept from getting too far ahead either by being excused from arithmetic for a time or by being given special sets of problems which take him into some of the interesting bypaths of mathematics.

The device makes it possible to present carefully designed material in which one problem can depend upon the answer to the preceding and where, therefore, the most efficient progress to an eventually complex repertoire can be made. Provision has been made for recording the commonest mistakes so that the tapes can be modified as experience dictates. Additional steps can be inserted where pupils tend to have trouble, and ultimately the material will reach a point at which the answers of the average child will almost always be right.

If the material itself proves not to be sufficiently reinforcing, other reinforcers in the possession of the teacher or school may be made contingent upon the operation of the device or upon progress though a series of problems. Supplemental reinforcement would not sacrifice the advantages gained from immediate reinforcement and from the possibility of constructing an optimal series of steps which approach the complex repertoire of mathematical behavior most efficiently.

A similar device in which the sliders carry the letters of the alphabet has been designed to teach spelling. In addition to the advantages which can be gained from precise reinforcement and careful programming, the device will teach reading at the same time. It can also be used to establish the large and important repertoire of verbal relationships encountered in logic and science. In short, it can teach verbal thinking. As to content instruction, the device can be operated as a multiple-choice self-rater.

Some objections to the use of such devices in the classroom can easily be foreseen. The cry will be raised that the child is being treated as a mere animal and that an essentially human intellectual achievement is being analyzed in unduly mechanistic terms. Mathematical behavior is usually regarded, not as a repertoire of responses involving numbers and numerical operations, but as evidences of mathematical ability or the exercise of the power of reason. It is true that the techniques which are emerging from the experimental study of learning are not designed to "develop the mind" or to further some vague "understanding" of mathematical relationships. They are designed, on the contrary, to establish the very behaviors which are taken to be the evidences of such mental states or processes. This is only a special case of the general change which is under way in the interpretation of human affairs. An advancing science continues to offer more and more convincing alternatives to traditional formulations. The behavior in terms of which human thinking must eventually be defined is worth treating in its own right as the substantial goal of education.

Of course the teacher has a more important function than to say right or wrong. The changes proposed would free her for the effective exercise of that function. Marking a set of papers in arithmetic—"Yes, nine and six *are* fifteen; no, nine and seven *are not* eighteen"—is beneath the dignity of any intelligent individual. There is more important work to be done—in which the teacher's relations to the pupil cannot be duplicated by a mechanical device. Instrumental help would merely improve these relations. One might say that the main trouble with education in the lower grades today is that the child is obviously not competent and *knows it* and that the teacher is unable to do anything about it and *knows that too.* If the advances which have recently been made in our control of behavior can give the child a genuine competence in reading, writing, spelling, and arithmetic, then the teacher may begin to function, not in lieu of a cheap machine, but through intellectual, cultural, and emotional contacts of that distinctive sort which testify to her status as a human being.

Another possible objection is that mechanized instruction will mean technological unemployment. We need not worry about this until there are enough teachers to go around and until the hours and energy demanded of the teacher are comparable to those in other fields of employment. Mechanical devices will eliminate the more tiresome labors of the teacher but they will not necessarily shorten the time during which she remains in contact with the pupil.

A more practical objection: Can we afford to mechanize our schools? The answer is clearly yes. The device I have just described could be produced as cheaply as a small radio or phonograph. There would need to be far fewer devices than pupils, for they could be used in rotation. But even if we suppose that the instrument eventually found to be most effective would cost several hundred dollars and that large numbers of them would be required, our economy should be able to stand the strain. Once we have accepted the possibility and the necessity of mechanical help in the classroom, the economic problem can easily be surmounted. There is no reason why the school room should be any less mechanized than, for example, the kitchen. A country which annually produces millions of refrigerators, dish-washers, automatic washing-machines, automatic clothes-driers, and automatic garbage disposers can certainly afford the equipment necessary to educate its citizens to high standards of competence in the most effective way.

There is a simple job to be done. The task can be stated in concrete terms. The necessary techniques are known. The equipment needed can easily be provided. Nothing stands in the way but cultural inertia. But what is more characteristic of America than an unwillingness to accept the traditional as inevitable? We are on the threshold of an exciting and revolutionary period, in which the scientific study of man will be put to work in man's best interests. Education must play its part. It must accept the fact that a sweeping revision of educational practices is possible and inevitable. When it has done this, we may look forward with confidence to a school system which is aware of the nature of its tasks, secure in its methods, and generously supported by the informed and effective citizens whom education itself will create.

NOTES

1. The reader may wish to review Dr. Skinner's article, "Some Contributions of an Experimental Analysis of Behavior to Psychology as a Whole," *The American Psychologist*, 1953, 8, 69–78. Ed.

2. Skinner, B. F. *Science and Human Behavior*. New York: Macmillan, 1953.

Instructional Psychology

Robert M. Gagné was born in 1916, received his undergraduate degree from Yale University, and earned his doctoral degree in experimental psychology from Brown University in 1940. His first teaching post was at Connecticut College, after which he entered World War II as an aviation psychologist. In the air force Gagné developed assessments of the motor and perceptual functions of the air crews. For eight years he was technical director of two air force laboratories that studied methods of technical training. Later, from 1958 to 1962, Gagné was a professor of psychology at Princeton University. There he continued to extend his research on the acquisition of knowledge, learning hierarchies, and the learning and teaching of mathematics.

Gagné directed research at the American Institute for Research from 1962 to 1965, primarily focusing on the design and evaluation of educational procedures. Next, from 1966 to 1969, he was a professor of educational psychology at University of California, Berkeley, where he guided the establishment of a regional educational laboratory, supervised graduate students in educational research, and performed his own research on the learning of school subjects. Lastly, Gagné accepted a position as a professor of educational research in the College of Education at Florida State University. His research there concentrated on learning hierarchies related to school instruction and investigations of adult learning from television.

Some of Gagné's better-known works are *The Conditions of Learning and Theory of Instruction*, 4th ed. (Harcourt Brace, 1985), *Principles of Instructional Design* (Harcourt Brace Jovanovich, 1992), *Essentials of Learning for Instruction*, 2d ed. (Prentice Hall, 1988), and *Instructional Technology: Foundations* (Lawrence Erlbaum, 1987). The following selection is cowritten by Walter Dick, who is also a well-known educational psychologist and whose publications include *Instructional Planning: A Guide for Teachers* (Allyn & Bacon, 1996), *The Systematic Design of Instruction* (HarperCollins, 1996), *Planning Effective Instruction* (Prentice Hall, 1989), and *Topics in Measurement: Reliability and Validity* (1971). The following selection is from "Instructional Psychology," *Annual Review of Psychology* (1983) and summarizes some of Gagné's main contributions to educational psychology as well as the work of others in instructional psychology.

Key Concept: taxonomy of learning outcomes

Theories of instruction attempt to relate specified events comprising instruction to learning processes and learning outcomes, drawing upon knowledge generated by learning research and theory. Often instructional theories are prescriptive in the sense that they attempt to identify conditions of instruction which will optimize learning, retention, and learning transfer. Originators of such theories sometimes refer to Simon's (1969) description of "sciences of the artificial" as characteristic of their efforts. To be classified as theories, these formulations may be expected, at a minimum, to provide a rational description of causal relationships between procedures used to teach and their behavioral consequences in enhanced human performance. . . .

Gagné-Briggs

The Gagné-Briggs (1979) theory of instruction, based in part upon the work of Gagné (1977b), begins with a taxonomic framework of learning outcomes considered essential for an understanding of human learning as it occurs in instructional settings. Learning outcomes, conceived as acquired capabilities of human learners, are classified as (a) verbal information, (b) intellectual skills, (c) cognitive strategies, (d) motor skills, and (e) attitudes. Although independently derived, these categories have an approximate correspondence with those of Bloom and his co-workers (Bloom 1956). The first three of these categories also correspond with those in the psychology of cognition and learning, named respectively (a) declarative knowledge, (b) procedural knowledge, and (c) cognitive strategies (J. R. Anderson 1980, Bower 1975).

In addressing the matter of instruction, the Gagné-Briggs theory proposes that each of the categories of learning outcome requires a different set of conditions for optimizing learning, retention, and transferability. Optimal conditions include external events in the learner's immediate environment, usually called "instruction," and internal conditions acting through the learner's working memory, which have their origins largely in previous instruction (Gagné 1997b). It is the contention of this theory that traditional factors in learning, such as contiguity, exercise, and reinforcement, while of undoubted relevance, are much too general in their applicability to be of particular use in the design of instruction. Instead, internal and external conditions must be specified separately for the learning of verbal information, for intellectual skills, and for each of the other categories of learned capabilities.

The processes of learning assumed by the Gagné-Briggs theory are those included in the information-processing model of learning and memory, as described by Atkinson & Shiffrin (1968) and employed in essential aspects by several other memory theorists (Greeno & Bjork 1973). Prominent among these processes are attention, selective (feature) perception, short-term memory, rehearsal, long-term memory storage, and retrieval. Externally, reinforcement via informative feedback is also assumed (Atkinson & Wickens 1971, Estes 1972). From these processes are derived both the internal and external events which make possible effective learning and retention. Instruction is defined as a set of events external to the learner which are designed to support the internal processes of learning (Gagné 1977c). Specifically, these events are conceived as taking place in an approximately ordered sequence as follows: (*a*) gaining attention, (*b*) informing learner of the objective, (*c*) stimulating recall of prerequisites, (*d*) presenting the stimulus material, (*e*) providing "learning guidance," (*f*) eliciting the performance, (*g*) providing feedback, (*h*) assessing the performance, and (*i*) enhancing retention and transfer. While all of these events are considered to be involved in each act of learning, it is noted that as novice learners become more experienced, the events tend to be more frequently provided by the learners themselves rather than by external agents. As factors influencing learning, many of these events are included in other instructional theories (Bloom 1976, Merrill et al 1979) and share with them evidences of their individual causal effects.

Several characteristics of this prescriptive instructional model make it distinctive from others. In the first place, it is based upon identified aspects of information-processing theories of learning (Bower & Hilgard 1981), including the human modeling concept of Bandura (1969). The model does not attempt to propose new theory pertaining to learning and memory, but only to use existing theory as a basis for the conceptualization of instruction. [A particulate exception is the theory of learning hierarchies (Gagné 1968, 1977b).] Secondly, the theory is comprehensive in the sense that it attempts to include all of the kinds of learning outcomes to which instruction is usually addressed. This is the basic significance of the theory's proposal of five kinds of learning outcomes, including attitudes and motor skills as well as cognitive capabilities. A third distinctive feature is the fact that the theory provides a rational basis for instruction as a set of events which interact with internal learning processes, and also with previously acquired contents retrieved from the learner's long-term memory. The inclusion of these characteristics makes it possible for this theory to deal with instruction of many forms in a great variety of settings....

CONTRIBUTIONS OF COGNITIVE PSYCHOLOGY

By the time it has become entirely customary for research questions about the psychology of instruction to be phrased in terms of the concepts of cognitive psychology (Bower & Hilgard 1981, Estes 1975, 1976a,b, 1978a,b). Accordingly, instructional procedures are often described in the language of cognitive psychology, such as short-term and long-term memory, semantic encoding, retrieval, and the like (cf Gagné 1977b, Merrill et al 1981). During the period covered by this [selection], certain concepts of cognitive psychology have become prominent which are of undoubted relevance to instruction.

Cognitive Strategies

... [C]onsiderable research effort has been devoted to the investigation of cognitive strategies of learning and remembering. The effects of such strategies have been verified in connection with the learning of word pairs and lists (R. C. Anderson 1970, Bower 1970) as well as with prose learning (DiVesta et al 1973, Levin & Divine-Hawkins 1974). The technique of study skills described by Robinson (1946) called SQ3R has had remarkable durability, and appears in modified form in a... text on cognitive psychology (J. R. Anderson 1980). In recent years, more ambitious research projects have been undertaken to design training programs with the specific intention of teaching learning strategies and evaluating their effectiveness. Some of these efforts are described in a book edited by O'Neil (1978).

Dansereau (1978) describes a program designed by him and his co-workers to teach college students cognitive strategies of learning and retention. Instruction was developed for the following categories called *primary strategies:* (*a*) comprehension and retention strategies consisting of paraphrase-imagery, networking, and analysis of key ideas; and (*b*) retrieval and utilization strategies using such techniques as breaking questions down into subqueries and employing contextual cues. Other components were called *support strategies,* which included (*a*) cultivating a positive learning attitude, (*b*) concentration (coping with distractions), and (*c*) monitoring the progress of learning.

A number of additional varieties of learning strategies have been suggested, some of which continue under active investigation. Among these are elaboration strategies (Weinstein 1978), anxiety reduction and self-monitoring skills (Richardson 1978), goal imaging (Singer 1978), inferring deep-structure trace from surface structure (J. S. Brown et al 1978), and several varieties of self-programming skills (Rigney 1978). The work being done in this field of "learning strategies" has surely accomplished the identification of strategies that are learnable. Much additional research is needed to assess their effectiveness as components of instruction in the learning of educationally realistic tasks in the outcome categories of verbal knowledge and intellectual skills. Learning strategies enhance the effectiveness of learning and remembering of material such as word lists primarily because they make possible meaningfully organized encoding. Effective strategies for the learning of material which is itself meaningfully organized may be more difficult to discover, and their influence may turn out to be inherently weaker....

Metacognition

In a series of articles, Flavell (1976, 1978, Flavell & Wellman 1977) has described and exemplified a domain of intellectual functioning called metacognition. Although originally concerned with metamemory (Flavell & Wellman 1977, A. L. Brown 1978), the ideas have been elaborated to include a greater range of cognitive phenomena. The categories of knowledge about one's own cognition, according to Flavell, include *sensitivity,* knowing what situations call for intentional cognitive activity; *person variables,* knowledge of those attributes that influence learning and memory; a *task* category, referring to characteristics of the intellectual task which influence performance; and procedures for solution, or *strategies.* These metacognitive phenomena make possible cognitive

Robert M. Gagné and Walter Dick

monitoring (Flavell 1978, 1981) which can influence both the course and the outcome of cognitive activity. A comprehensive review of metacognitive effects, particularly as they pertain to learning and remembering, is by A. L. Brown (1978). Evidence is included on the effects of knowing one's knowledge state, of prediction of intellectual performance, of planning ability, and of checking and monitoring cognitive activities. Results of studies of training metacognitive sensitivity and strategies are also summarized and interpreted.

Obviously the concept of metacognition raises the sights of research on cognition well beyond the scope of work on traditional memory tasks. Knowledge of the conditions that affect the acquisition and employment of knowledge may be obtained through experience or as a result of deliberately planned instruction. Such knowledge can be used, presumably, as a basis from which to originate the cognitive strategies which affect the processes involved in learning, remembering, and thinking. Presumably, experienced learners and thinkers are accustomed to engaging in cognitive monitoring and in the use of (meta) cognitive strategies. Young children and other inexperienced learners can be trained to employ these strategies to good advantage, as the work of such investigators as Campione & Brown (1977), Belmont & Butterfield (1977), Markman (1977) and others has shown. Future research may be expected to illuminate further the specific nature of effective metacognitive strategies. . . .

APPLICATIONS OF INSTRUCTIONAL PSYCHOLOGY

Projects which employ psychological principles to solve applied problems are described in this section. The problems examined include those of selecting and sequencing appropriate content for inclusion in specialized curricula; second, improving the effectiveness of operational computer-assisted instruction systems; and third, improving teacher skills through inservice instruction. Each description includes a statement of the problem, a rationale for the psychological principle(s) employed, and the outcome of the project to date. In none of these studies can the outcomes be attributed solely to the principle identified; many factors have contributed to the solution of each problem.

Applications of Hierarchical Analysis

How should one identify and sequence intellectual skills? This problem arises when instructional materials are to be developed in areas in which no instruction previously existed, or that which existed was unsatisfactory, or, as in the case that follows, a new medium of instruction is employed.

Since 1970 the Ontario Institute for Studies in Education [OISE] has been involved with the schools and community colleges of Ontario in the cooperative development of computer-assisted instruction (CAI). In a recent report (Gershman & Sakamoto 1980), CAI instructional sequences were described for 30 of the most important topics in intermediate mathematics including arithmetic, algebra, probability, and measurement.

The development activities were conducted by joint teams consisting of OISE staff members and teachers from cooperating schools. Their basic approach was to cluster the skills to be taught into a terminal objective and one or more enabling objectives which represent skills that must be achieved in order to reach the terminal objective. The objectives form a hierarchical relationship in which subordinate skills must be achieved prior to the learning of superordinate skills (Gagné 1968).

This analytic approach was especially critical in this project because it provides not only the identification of skills and sequence for teaching them; it also provides a branching rationale for the CAI lessons. For example, in a typical lesson, students may be asked if they can perform the terminal objective. If they can, they are shown the subordinate skills and asked which is the most difficult one they can do. Students are then sequenced through the hierarchy based upon performance on tests embedded in the instruction. The hierarchy is also used as a major component of the sequential testing strategy. It is estimated that this technique reduces testing time by 50 percent.

The CAI mathematics curriculum which is based on the hierarchical analysis of each terminal objective was extensively evaluated during the 1979–80 academic year. From September to January over 2000 Ontario students in 18 schools spent an average of four hours to cover an average of seven topics. Great variability was found in the number of topics covered by the students. Pretest-posttest analyses indicate there were significant gains for both CAI and comparison non-CAI students in the same schools; however, the CAI students gained significantly more. Attitude questionnaire results showed that 94 percent of the students said CAI was "fun," "interesting," and 72 percent said they liked math better with CAI. Similar results have been reported for the other courses developed by the OISE staff.

The U.S. Navy also has found it useful to incorporate the use of hierarchical analysis into the curriculum development process. The need for added instruction in basic skills has resulted from the Navy's inability to attract personnel with aptitude scores high enough to qualify them for entry into initial job training programs. One response to the problem has been reported by Harding and his co-workers (1980). As contractors of the Navy Personnel Research and Development Center, they faced the task of identifying what basic skills should be taught to entering recruits in order to prepare them for the "A" (initial job training) Schools (JOBS program).

The research team's most successful approach to identifying needed skills was that of first identifying the major learning task in each of four A School curricula. Based on this analysis, tentative sets of skills were identified which appeared to be prerequisite to the skills that had to be learned in the A school. The types of skills that were tentatively identified were: find information in a table, add numbers, read a setting on a micrometer, comprehend a written passage, and solve word problems.

Hierarchical analysis procedures were used to identify subordinate basic skills which were prerequisite to those skills needed in the A Schools. The hierarchies served as the basic design component which resulted in the development of instructor guides, student guides, lesson summaries, practice exercises, overhead transparencies, and various evaluation instruments.

A preliminary evaluation of the JOBS program has been reported by Baker & Huff (1981). The performance of students entering the JOBS program was compared with that of those who chose not to enter it, and with students who were qualified directly to enter an A School. The students in the JOBS courses demonstrated gains of about 42 points from pre- to posttests, and 95 percent went on to complete the JOBS program successfully. Of the graduates of the program, 75 percent were able to graduate from A School. These percentages compare favorably with the qualified student graduation rate of 87 percent. Eight months after graduation, the qualified group had approximately three times as many fleet discharges as did the JOBS group. While the results are supportive of the JOBS program, an experimental study has not yet been conducted which includes JOBS-eligible students who do not get JOBS training but go directly to A School.

The OISE and JOBS projects are examples of two highly successful efforts which relied heavily on the hierarchical analysis of terminal objectives to identify the prerequisite subordinate skills and the appropriate sequence for those skills. Revisions of the hierarchies came about through the formative evaluation and revision of the instruction. The hierarchical approach, initially investigated as theory, appears to have served a very pragmatic role in these and many other instructional development projects.

REFERENCES

Anderson, J. R. 1980. *Cognitive Psychology and Its Implications.* San Francisco: Freeman. 503 pp.

Anderson, R. C. 1970. Control of student mediating processes during verbal learning and instruction. *Rev. Educ. Res.* 40: 349–69

Atkinson, R. C., Shiffrin, R. M. 1968. Human memory: A proposed system and its control processes. In *The Psychology of Learning and Motivation,* ed. K. W. Spence, J. T. Spence, 2: 89–195. New York: Academic. 249 pp.

Atkinson, R. C., Wickens, T. D. 1971. Human memory and the concept of reinforcement. In *The Nature of Reinforcement,* ed. R. Glaser, pp. 66–120. New York: Academic. 379 pp.

Baker, M., Huff, K. 1981. *The evaluation of a job-oriented basic skills training program—interim report.* Tech. Rep. 82–14, San Diego: Navy Pers. Res. Dev. Cent. 25 pp.

Bandura, A. 1969. *Principles of Behavior Modification.* New York: Holt, Rinehart & Winston. 677 pp.

Belmont, J. M., Butterfield, E. C. 1977. The instructional approach to developmental cognitive research. In *Perspectives on the Development of Memory and Cognition,* ed. R. V. Kail, J. W. Hagen, pp. 437–81. Hillsdale, NJ: Erlbaum. 498 pp.

Bloom, B. S., ed. 1956. *Taxonomy of Educational Objectives. Handbook I. Cognitive Domain.* New York: McKay

Bloom, B. S. 1976. *Human Characteristics and School Learning*. New York: McGraw-Hill. 284 pp.

Bower, G. H. 1970. Analysis of a mnemonic device. *Am. Psychol.* 58: 496–510

Bower, G. H. 1975. Cognitive psychology: An introduction. See Estes 1975, pp. 25–80

Bower, G. M., Hilgard, E. J. 1981. *Theories of Learning*. Englewood Cliffs, NJ: Prentice-Hall. 647 pp. 5th ed.

Brown, A. L. 1978. Knowing when, where, and how to remember: A problem of metacognition. See Glaser 1978a, pp. 77–165

Brown, J. S., Collins, A., Harris, G. 1978. Artificial intelligence and learning strategies. See O'Neil 1978, pp. 107–39

Campione, J. C., Brown, A. L. 1977. Memory and metamemory development in educable retarded children. See Belmont & Butterfield 1977, pp. 367–406

Dansereau, D. 1978. The development of a learning strategies curriculum. See O'Neil 1978, pp. 1–29

DiVesta, F. J., Schultz, C. B., Dangel, I. R. 1973. Passage organization and imposed learning strategies in comprehension and recall of connected discourse. *Mem. Cognit.* 1: 471–76

Estes, W. K. 1972. Reinforcement in human behavior. *Am. Sci.* 60: 723–29

Estes, W. K., ed. 1975. *Handbook of Learning and Cognitive Processes*, Vol. 1. *Introduction to Concepts and Issues*. Hillsdale, NJ: Erlbaum. 304 pp.

Estes, W. K., ed. 1976a. *Handbook of Learning and Cognitive Processes*, Vol. 3. *Approaches to Human Learning and Motivation*. Hillsdale, NJ: Erlbaum. 374 pp.

Estes, W. K., ed. 1976b. *Handbook of Learning and Cognitive Processes*, Vol. 4. *Attention and Memory*. Hillsdale, NJ: Erlbaum. 436 pp.

Estes, W. K., ed. 1978a. *Handbook of Learning and Cognitive Processes*, Vol. 5. *Human Information Processing*. Hillsdale, NJ: Erlbaum. 352 pp.

Estes, W. K., ed. 1978b. *Handbook of Learning and Cognitive Processes*, Vol. 6. *Linguistic Functions in Cognitive Theory*. Hillsdale, NJ: Erlbaum. 311 pp.

Flavell, J. H. 1976. Metacognitive aspects of problem solving. In *The Nature of Intelligence*, ed. L. B. Resnick. Hillsdale, NJ: Erlbaum. 364 pp.

Flavell, J. H. 1978. Metacognitive development. In *Structural/Process Theories of Complex Human Behavior*, ed. J. M. Scandura, C. J. Brainerd, pp. 213–45. Alphen a. d. Rijn, The Netherlands: Sijthoff & Hoordhoff. 612 pp.

Flavell, J. H. 1981. Cognitive monitoring. In *Children's Oral Communication Skills*, pp. 35–60. New York: Academic. 364 pp.

Flavell, J. H., Wellman, H. M. 1977. Metamemory. See Belmont & Butterfield 1977, pp. 437–81

Gagné, R. M. 1968. Learning hierarchies. *Educ. Psychol.* 6: 1–9

Gagné, R. M. 1977b. *The Conditions of Learning*. New York: Holt, Rinehart & Winston. 339 pp. 3rd ed.

Gagné, R. M. 1977c. Instructional programs. In *Fundamentals and Applications of Learning*, ed. M. H. Marx, M. E. Bunch, pp. 404–28. New York: Macmillan. 550 pp.

Gagné, R. M., Briggs, L. J. 1979. *Principles of Instructional Design*. New York: Holt, Rinehart & Winston. 321 pp. 2nd ed.

Gershman, J. S., Sakamoto, E. J. 1980. *Intermediate mathematics: CARE Ontario Assessment Instrument Pool*. Final Rep., Contract No. 206. Toronto: Ontario Inst. Stud. Educ. 141 pp.

Greeno, J. G., Bjork, R. A. 1973. Mathematical learning theory and the new "mental forestry." *Ann. Rev. Psychol.* 24: 81–116

Harding, S. R., Mogford, B., Melching, W. H., Showel, M. 1980. *The development of four job-oriented basic skills (JOBS) programs.* Final tech. rep., Northrop Services. San Diego: Navy Pers. Res. Dev. Cent. 57 pp.

Levin, J. R., Divine-Hawkins, P. 1974. Visual imagery as a prose learning process. *J. Reading Behav.* 6: 23–30

Markman, E. M. 1977. Realizing that you don't understand: A preliminary investigation. *Child Dev.* 48: 986–92

Merrill, M. D., Kelety, J. C., Wilson, B. 1981. Elaboration theory and cognitive psychology. *Instr. Sci.* 10: 217–37

Merrill, M. D., Reigeluth, C. M., Faust, G. W. 1979. The instructional quality profile: A curriculum evaluation and design tool. See O'Neil 1979b, pp. 165–204

O'Neil, H. F. Jr., ed. 1978. *Learning Strategies.* New York: Academic. 230 pp.

Richardson, F. 1978. Behavior modification and learning strategies. See O'Neil 1978, pp. 57–78

Rigney, J. W. 1978. Learning strategies: A theoretical perspective. See O'Neil 1978, pp. 165–205

Robinson, F. P. 1946. *Effective Study.* New York: Harper. 365 pp.

Simon, H. A. 1969. *The Sciences of the Artificial.* Cambridge, Mass: M.I.T. 123 pp.

Singer, R. N. 1978. Motor skills and learning strategies. See O'Neil 1978, pp. 79–106

Weinstein, C. E. 1978. Elaboration skills as a learning strategy. See O'Neil 1978, pp. 30–55

6.3 ALBERT BANDURA

Social Cognitive Theory

Albert Bandura was born in Canada in 1925 and earned his bachelor's degree from the University of British Columbia and his doctorate from the University of Iowa. He began teaching psychology at Stanford University in California in 1953. Initially working within the behaviorist paradigm, his work on observational learning through "vicarious reinforcement" substantially modified the traditional direct reinforcement theories of behaviorism. Bandura is considered the premier researcher on the topics of modeling and observational learning, which he initially summarized in his classic text *Social Learning Theory* (Prentice Hall, 1977). His own search for truth in psychology led him even farther afield from behaviorism, focusing on the internal cognitive events that mediate behavior and leading to his magnum opus, *Social Foundations of Thought and Action: A Social Cognitive Theory* (Prentice Hall, 1986).

Additionally, Bandura's research on human aggression and self-efficacy comprises some of the best-known works in the area of social psychology. His notion of "reciprocal determinism" is essential for any student of psychology to understand. Bandura explains how three broad domains dynamically, reciprocally, simultaneously, and constantly interact with one another and determine "causality." These domains are (1) internal variables, such as cognition, emotion, and genetic influences; (2) behavior itself; and (3) environmental variables. This reminds the student of psychology that no event has a single cause; rather, all events are determined by multiple causes. Every human thought has been influenced by the person's previous behavior and the environment, the environment has been influenced by human internal factors, and human behavior has been caused by both internal factors and the environment.

Observational learning is critical to schoolteachers and to school psychologists. Not only can understanding it lead to better direct instruction, but so much of the "hidden curriculum" is taught indirectly through students' observing others' behavior in schools. By refining our knowledge of the variables involved in observational learning, teachers can better teach such subjects as athletics, laboratory science, computer science, technology, art, music, etc. Additionally, as moral behavior is so highly influenced by models, the implications for observational learning in moral education is immense. The following excerpt comes from Bandura's chapter entitled "Social Cognitive Theory" in Ross Vasta, ed., *Annals of Child Development,* vol. 6 (JAI Press, 1989) and explicates the four basic processes of observational learning.

Key Concept: the four basic processes of observational learning

FIGURE 1

Subprocesses Governing Observational Learning

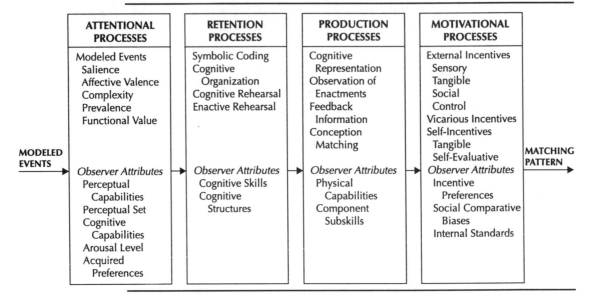

ATTENTIONAL PROCESSES	RETENTION PROCESSES	PRODUCTION PROCESSES	MOTIVATIONAL PROCESSES
Modeled Events Salience Affective Valence Complexity Prevalence Functional Value	Symbolic Coding Cognitive Organization Cognitive Rehearsal Enactive Rehearsal	Cognitive Representation Observation of Enactments Feedback Information Conception Matching	External Incentives Sensory Tangible Social Control Vicarious Incentives Self-Incentives Tangible Self-Evaluative
Observer Attributes Perceptual Capabilities Perceptual Set Cognitive Capabilities Arousal Level Acquired Preferences	*Observer Attributes* Cognitive Skills Cognitive Structures	*Observer Attributes* Physical Capabilities Component Subskills	*Observer Attributes* Incentive Preferences Social Comparative Biases Internal Standards

MODELED EVENTS → ... → MATCHING PATTERN

OBSERVATIONAL LEARNING

Learning from models may take varied forms, including new behavior patterns, judgmental standards, cognitive competencies, and generative rules for creating new forms of behavior. Observational learning is governed by four component subfunctions which are depicted in Figure 1. *Attentional processes* determine what people observe in the profusion of modeling influences and what information they extract from what they notice.

People cannot be much influenced by observed events if they do not remember them. A second major subfunction governing observational learning concerns *retention processes*. Retention involves an active process of transforming and restructuring the information conveyed by modeled events into rules and conceptions for memory representation. In the third subfunction in modeling—the *behavioral production process*—symbolic conceptions are translated into appropriate courses of action. This is achieved through a conception-matching process in which behavioral enactments are adjusted until they match the internal conception of the activity.

The fourth subfunction in modeling concerns *motivational processes*. Social cognitive theory distinguishes between acquisition and performance because people do not perform everything they learn. Performance of observationally learned behavior is influenced by three major types of incentive motivators—direct, vicarious, and self-produced. People are more likely to exhibit modeled behavior if it results in valued outcomes than if it has unrewarding or punishing effects. The observed cost and benefits accruing to others influence the performance of modeled patterns in much the same way as do directly experienced consequences. People are motivated by the successes of others who are similar to themselves, but are discouraged from pursuing courses of behavior that they have seen often result in adverse consequences. Personal standards of conduct provide a further source of incentive motivation. The evaluative reactions people generate to their own behavior regulate which observationally learned activities they are most likely to pursue. They express what they find self-satisfying and reject what they personally disapprove.

ABSTRACT MODELING

Modeling is not merely a process of behavioral mimicry. Highly functional patterns of behavior, which constitute the proven skills and established customs of a culture, may be adopted in essentially the same form as they are exemplified. There is little leeway for improvisation on how to drive automobiles or to perform arithmetic operations. However, in many activities, subskills must be improvised to suit varying circumstances. Modeling influences can convey rules for generative and innovative behavior as well. This higher-level learning is achieved through abstract modeling. Rule-governed behavior differs in specific content and other details but it contains the same underlying rule. For example, the modeled statements, "The dog is *being* petted," and "the window *was* opened" refer to different things but the linguistic rule—the passive form—is the same. In abstract modeling, observers extract the rule embodied in the specific behavior exhibited by others. Once they learn the rule, they can use it to generate new instances of behavior that go beyond what they have seen or heard. Much human learning is aimed at developing cognitive skills on how to gain and use knowledge for future use. Observational learning of thinking skills is greatly facilitated by modeling thought processes in conjunction with action strategies (Meichenbaum, 1984). Models verbalize their thought strategies as they engage in problem-solving activities. The ordinarily covert thoughts guiding the actions of the models are thus made observable and learnable by others.

Modeling has been shown to be a highly effective means of establishing abstract or rule-governed behavior. On the basis of modeled information, people acquire, among other things, judgmental standards, linguistic rules, styles of inquiry, information-processing skills, and standards of self-evaluation (Bandura, 1986; Rosenthal & Zimmerman, 1978). Evidence that generative rules of thought and conduct can be created through abstract modeling attests to the broad scope of observational learning.

DEVELOPMENT OF MODELING CAPABILITIES

Because observational learning involves several subfunctions that evolve with maturation and experiences, it depends upon prior development. When analyzed in terms of its constituent subfunctions, facility in observational learning is not primarily a matter of learning to imitate. Nor is it a discrete skill.

Rather, developing adeptness in observational learning involves acquiring multiple subskills in selective attention, cognitive representation, symbolic transformation, and anticipatory motivation.

Neonates possess greater modeling capabilities than is commonly believed. By several months of age, infants can and do model behavior with some consistency (Kaye, 1982; Meltzoff & Moore, 1983; Valentine, 1930). The development of proficiency in observational learning is grounded in social reciprocation. Infants possess sufficient rudimentary representational capacities and sensorimotor coordination to enable them to imitate elementary sounds and acts within their physical capabilities. Parents readily imitate a newborn's gestures and vocalizations from the very beginning, often in expressive ways that have been shown to facilitate modeling (Papousek & Papousek, 1977; Pawlby, 1977).

The newborn, whose means of communication and social influence are severely limited, learns that reciprocal imitation is an effective way of eliciting and sustaining parental responsiveness. Uzgiris (1984) has given considerable attention to the social function of imitation in infancy. Mutual imitation serves as a means of conveying interest and sharing experiences. Initially, parents tend to model acts that infants spontaneously perform. After the reciprocal imitation is established, parents are quick to initiate new response patterns for imitative sequences that help to expand their infant's competencies (Pawlby, 1977). Successful modeling of these more complicated patterns of behavior requires development of the major subfunctions that govern observational learning. It is to the developmental course of these subfunctions that we turn next.

ATTENTIONAL PROCESSES

Young children present certain attentional deficiencies that limit their proficiency in observational learning. They have difficulty attending to different sorts of information at the same time, distinguishing pertinent aspects from irrelevancies, and maintaining attention to ongoing events long enough to acquire sufficient information about them (Cohen & Salapatek, 1975; Hagen & Hale, 1973). They are easily distracted. With increasing experience, children's attentional skills improve in all of these respects.

In promoting observational learning, adults alter the behavior they model to compensate for the attentional limitations of children. With infants, parents gain their attention and give salience to the behavior they want to encourage by selectively imitating them. Parents tend to perform the reciprocated imitations in an exaggerated animated fashion that is well designed to sustain the child's attentiveness at a high level during the mutual modeling sequences (Papousek & Papousek, 1977). The animated social interplay provides a vehicle for channeling and expanding infants' attention in activities that go beyond those they have already mastered.

The attention-arousing value of the modeled acts, themselves, also influences what infants are likely to adopt. Infants are more attentive to, and imitate more often, modeled acts when they involve objects and sound accompaniments than when they are modeled silently and without objects to draw attention (Abravanel et al., 1976; Uzgiris, 1979). The more attention infants pay to the modeled activities, the more likely they are to adopt them. As infants' attentional capabilities increase, parents exhibit developmentally progressive activities for them to model.

REPRESENTATIONAL PROCESSES

In developing representational memory skills, children have to learn how to transform modeled information into symbolic forms and to organize it into easily remembered structures. They also have to learn how to use timely rehearsal to facilitate the retention of activities that are vulnerable to memory loss. It takes time for children to learn that they can improve their future performances by symbolizing and rehearsing their immediate experiences.

In the earliest period of development, experiences are probably retained mainly in imaginal modes of representation. Infants will model single acts, but they have difficulty reproducing coordinated sequences that require them to remember how several actions are strung together (McCall, Parke, & Kavanaugh, 1977). They often start the sequence right and simply forget what comes next. With experience, they become more skilled at delayed modeling. Indeed, infants even as young as 18 months will enact behavior learned from televised models after some time has elapsed. Delayed performances of this type require symbolic memory.

As children begin to acquire language they can symbolize the essential aspects of events in words for memory representation. It is not until children acquire some cognitive and linguistic skills that they can extract rules from modeled performances and make effective use of the more complex linguistic transformations (Rosenthal & Zimmerman, 1978). Children can improve their memory by instruction to anticipate, verbally code, and rehearse what they observe (Brown & Barclay, 1976). The vicarious memorial subskills can also be acquired through modeling. By observing the memory feats of others, children learn what information is worth coding, how events should be categorized, and more general strategies for processing information (Lamal, 1971; Rosenthal & Zimmerman, 1978).

PRODUCTION PROCESSES

Converting conceptions to appropriate actions requires development of transformational skills in intermodal guidance of behavior. Information in the symbolic mode must be translated into corresponding action modes. This involves learning how to organize action sequences, to monitor and compare behavioral enactments against the symbolic model, and to correct evident mismatches (Carroll & Bandura, 1985; 1989). When children must depend on what others tell them, because they cannot observe fully all of their own actions, detecting and correcting mismatches requires linguistic competencies. Deficiencies in any of these production subskills can create a developmental lag between comprehending and performing.

MOTIVATIONAL PROCESSES

Motivational factors that influence the use to which modeled knowledge is put undergo significant developmental changes. During infancy, imitation functions mainly to secure interpersonal responsiveness. Through mutual modeling with adults, infants enjoy playful intimacy and gain experience in social reciprocation. Before long parents cease mimicking their infant's actions, but they remain responsive to instances of infants adopting modeled patterns that expand their competencies. What continues to serve a social function for young infants changes into an instructional vehicle for parents. This transition requires infants to cognize, on the basis of observed regularities, the social effects their different imitations are likely to produce. To help infants to learn the functional value of modeling the parents make the outcomes salient, recurrent, consistent, and closely tied to the infant's actions (Papousek & Papousek, 1977). With increasing cognitive development, children become more skilled at judging probable outcomes of their actions. Such outcome expectations serve as incentives for observational learning.

What has incentive value for children also changes with experience. At the earliest level, infants and young children are motivated primarily by the immediate sensory and social effects of their actions. In the course of development, symbolic incentives signifying achievements, the exercise of mastery and self-evaluative reactions assume increasing motivational functions. Children soon learn that models are not only sources of social reward but also valuable sources of competencies for dealing effectively with the environment. The benefits of efficacious action and the personal satisfaction it brings become powerful incentives for modeling. Development thus increases the range and complexity of incentives that motivate children to gain knowledge through modeling and to use what they have learned.

When viewed from the developmental perspective of social cognitive theory, observational learning is part of a more general process of cognitive and social development. But observational learning is also one of the basic means by which cognitive competencies are developed and expanded. A comprehensive theory must, therefore, examine not only the cognitive mechanisms of observational learning, but also the social learning determinants of cognition.

REFERENCES

Abravanel, E., Levan-Goldschmidt, E., & Stevenson, M. B. (1976). Action imitation: The early phase of infancy. *Child Development, 47*, 1032–1044.

Bandura, A. (1986). *Social foundations of thought and action: A social cognitive theory.* Englewood Cliffs, NJ: Prentice-Hall, Inc.

Brown, A. L., & Barclay, C. R. (1976). The effects of training specific mnemonics on the metamnemonic efficiency of retarded children. *Child Development, 47*, 71–80.

Carroll, W. R., & Bandura, A. (1985). Role of timing of visual monitoring and motor rehearsal in observational learning of action patterns. *Journal of Motor Behavior, 17*, 269–281.

Carroll, W. R., & Bandura, A. (1989, in press). Representational guidance of action production in observational learning: A causal analysis. *Journal of Motor Behavior.*

Cohen, L. B., Salapatek, P. (1975). *Infant perception: From sensation to cognition: Vol. 1. Basic visual processes.* New York: Academic Press.

Hagen, J. W., & Hale, G. A. (1973). The development of attention in children. In A. D. Pick (Ed.), *Minnesota Symposium on Child Psychology* (Vol. 7, pp. 117–140). Minneapolis: University of Minnesota Press.

Kaye, K. (1982). *The mental and social life of babies: How parents create persons.* Chicago: University of Chicago Press.

Lamal, P. A. (1971). Imitation learning of information-processing. *Journal of Experimental Child Psychology, 12*, 223–227.

McCall, R. B., Parke, R. D., & Kavanaugh, R. D. (1977). Imitation of live and televised models by children one to three years of age. *Monograph of the Society for Research in Child Development, 42* (5, Serial No. 173).

Meichenbaum, D. (1984). Teaching thinking: A cognitive-behavioral perspective. In R. Glaser, S. Chipman, & J. Segal (Eds.), *Thinking and learning skills* (Vol. 2): *Research and Open Questions* (pp. 407–426). Hillsdale, NJ: Erlbaum.

Meltzoff, A. N., & Moore, M. K. (1983). The origins of imitation in infancy: Paradigm, phenomena, and theories. In L. P. Lipsitt & C. K. Rovee-Collier (Eds.), *Advances in infancy research* (Vol. 2, pp. 266–301). Norwood, NJ: Ablex Publishing.

Papousek, H., & Papousek, M. (1977). Mothering and the cognitive head-start: Psychobiological considerations. In H. R. Schaffer (Ed.), *Studies in mother-infant interaction.* London: Academic Press.

Pawlby, S. J. (1977). Imitative interaction. In H. R. Schaffer (Ed.), *Studies in mother-infant interaction.* London: Academic Press.

Rosenthal, T. L., & Zimmerman, B. J. (1978). *Social learning and cognition.* New York: Academic Press.

Uzgiris, I. C. (1979). The many faces of imitation in infancy. In L. Montada (Ed.), *Fortschritte der entwick lungpsychologie* (pp. 173–193). Stuttgart: Verlag W. Kohlhammer.

Uzgiris, I. C. (1984). Imitation in infancy: Its interpersonal aspects. In M. Perlmutter (Ed.), *The Minnesota symposia on child psychology* (Vol. 17, pp. 1–31). Hillsdale, NJ: Erlbaum.

Valentine, C. W. (1930). The psychology of imitation with special reference to early childhood. *British Journal of Psychology, 21*, 105–132.

CHAPTER 7 Cognitive and Constructivist Learning Theory

7.1 JEROME S. BRUNER

The Act of Discovery

Jerome S. Bruner was born in 1915 in New York. He earned his A.B. at Duke University in 1937 and his A.M. and Ph.D. at Harvard University in 1939 and 1941. He taught for many years at Harvard and more recently at the New School for Social Research in New York City.

Some of Bruner's better-known books are *Processes of Cognitive Growth: Infancy* (Clark University Press, 1968), *Acts of Meaning* (Harvard University Press, 1992), *Actual Minds, Possible Worlds* (Harvard University Press, 1986), *Child's Talk: Learning to Use Language* (W. W. Norton, 1983), and *On Knowing: Essays for the Left Hand* (Belknap Press of Harvard University Press, 1979).

Bruner's major theoretical work encompasses three central issues of human meaning: intentionality, thinking, and culture. For example, in his studies of infancy he demonstrated that the development of human action begins with a goal and ends with the means to achieve it. In Bruner's study of human language he showed that communication develops prior to the production of language. Infants are able to share meanings long before they begin using verbal language. He posits language as a tool of the thought processes. Language is a method of problem solving that also can be used to create meaning. This leads us to his view that children make, or construct, language rather than simply acquire or learn it.

Bruner's work on the ontogeny of thinking centers on the idea that human beings actively extract meaning from their interactions with others and with the world. He identified three critical modes of representation in meaning making: the enactive, the iconic, and the symbolic. For Bruner, knowledge is active and functional and requires a social or cultural context. He describes the "amplification systems" that each culture provides for each of the three modes of representation. As these amplifiers can vary greatly by culture, culture and cognitive development are closely linked in his theory.

Among schoolteachers Bruner is best known for his "discovery approach" to learning. He observed that students actively construct their own meaning out of the stimuli and materials provided by teachers. The following selection comes from Bruner's article on discovery learning, "The Act of Discovery," *Harvard Educational Review* (Winter 1961).

Key Concept: discovery learning

Maimonides, in his *Guide for the Perplexed*,[1] speaks of four forms of perfection that men might seek. The first and lowest form is perfection in the acquisition of worldly goods. The great philosopher dismisses such perfection on the ground that the possessions one acquires bear no meaningful relation to the possessor: "A great king may one morning find that there is no difference between him and the lowest person." A second perfection is of the body, its conformation and skills. Its failing is that is does not reflect on what is uniquely human about man: "he could [in any case] not be as strong as a mule." Moral perfection is the third, "the highest degree of excellency in man's character." Of this perfection Maimonides says: "Imagine a person being alone, and having no connection whatever with any other person; all his good moral principles are at rest, they are not required and give man no perfection whatever. These principles are only necessary and useful when man comes in contact with others." "The fourth kind of perfection is the true perfection of man; the possession of the highest intellectual faculties...." In justification of his assertion, this extraordinary Spanish-Judaic philosopher urges: "Examine the first three kinds of perfection; you will find that if you possess them, they are not your property, but the property of others.... But the last kind of perfection is exclusively yours; no one else owns any part of it."

It is a conjecture much like that of Maimonides that leads me to examine the act of discovery in man's intellectual life. For if man's intellectual excellence is the most his own among his perfections, it is also the case that the most uniquely personal of all that he knows is that which he has discovered for himself. What difference does it make, then, that we encourage discovery in the learning of the young? Does it, as Maimonides would say, create a special and unique relation between knowledge possessed and the possessor? And what may such a unique relation do for a man—or for a child, if you will, for our concern is with the education of the young?

The immediate occasion for my concern with discovery—and I do not restrict discovery to the act of finding out something that before was unknown

218

*Chapter 7
Cognitive and
Constructivist
Learning
Theory*

to mankind, but rather include all forms of obtaining knowledge for oneself by the use of one's own mind—the immediate occasion is the work of the various new curriculum projects that have grown up in America during the last six or seven years. For whether one speaks to mathematicians or physicists or historians, one encounters repeatedly an expression of faith in the powerful effects that come from permitting the student to put things together for himself, to be his own discoverer.

First, let it be clear what the act of discovery entails. It is rarely, on the frontier of knowledge or elsewhere, that new facts are "discovered" in the sense of being encountered as Newton suggested in the form of islands of truth in an uncharted sea of ignorance. Or if they appear to be discovered in this way, it is almost always thanks to some happy hypotheses about where to navigate. Discovery, like surprise, favors the well prepared mind. In playing bridge, one is surprised by a hand with no honors in it at all and also by hands that are all in one suit. Yet all hands in bridge are equiprobable: one must know to be surprised. So too in discovery. The history of science is studded with examples of men "finding out" something and not knowing it. I shall operate on the assumption that discovery, whether by a schoolboy going it on his own or by a scientist cultivating the growing edge of his field, is in its essence a matter of rearranging or transforming evidence in such a way that one is enabled to go beyond the evidence so reassembled to additional new insights. It may well be that an additional fact or shred of evidence makes this larger transformation of evidence possible. But it is often not even dependent on new information.

It goes without saying that, left to himself, the child will go about discovering things for himself within limits. It also goes without saying that there are certain forms of child rearing, certain home atmospheres that lead some children to be their own discoverers more than other children. These are both topics of great interest, but I shall not be discussing them. Rather, I should like to confine myself to the consideration of discovery and "finding-out-for-oneself" within an educational setting—specifically the school. Our aim as teachers is to give our student as firm a grasp of a subject as we can, and to make him as autonomous and self-propelled a thinker as we can—one who will go along on his own after formal schooling has ended. I shall return in the end to the question of the kind of classroom and the style of teaching that encourages an attitude of wanting to discover. For purposes of orienting the discussion, however, I would like to make an overly simplified distinction between teaching that takes place in the *expository mode* and teaching that utilizes the *hypothetical mode*. In the former, the decisions concerning the mode and pace and style of exposition are principally determined by the teacher as expositor; the student is the listener. If I can put the matter in terms of structural linguistics, the speaker has a quite different set of decisions to make than the listener: the former has a wide choice of alternatives for structuring, he is anticipating paragraph content while the listener is still intent on the words, he is manipulating the content of the material by various transformations, while the listener is quite unaware of these internal manipulations. In the hypothetical mode, the teacher and the student are in a more cooperative position with respect to what in linguistics would be called "speaker's decisions." The student is not a bench-bound listener, but is taking a part in the formulation and at times may play the principal role in it.

He will be aware of alternatives and may even have an "as if" attitude toward these and, as he receives information he may evaluate it as it comes. One cannot describe the process in either mode with great precision as to detail, but I think the foregoing may serve to illustrate what is meant.

Consider now what benefit might be derived from the experience of learning through discoveries that one makes for oneself. I should like to discuss these under four headings: (1) The increase in intellectual potency, (2) the shift from extrinsic to intrinsic rewards, (3) learning the heuristics of discovering, and (4) the aid to memory processing.

1. Intellectual potency.   If you will permit me, I would like to consider the difference between subjects in a highly constrained psychological experiment involving a two-choice apparatus. In order to win chips, they must depress a key either on the right or the left side of the machine. A pattern of payoff is designed such that, say, they will be paid off on the right side 70 per cent of the time, on the left 30 per cent, although this detail is not important. What is important is that the payoff sequence is arranged at random, and there is no pattern. I should like to contrast the behavior of subjects who think that there *is* some pattern to be found in the sequence—who think that regularities are discoverable—in contrast to subjects who think that things are happening quite by *chance*. The former group adopts what is called an "event-matching" strategy in which the number of responses given to each side is roughly equal to the proportion of times it pays off: in the present case R70: L30. The group that believes there is no pattern very soon reverts to a much more primitive strategy wherein *all* responses are allocated to the side that has the greater payoff. A little arithmetic will show you that the lazy all-and-none strategy pays off more if indeed the environment is random: namely, they win seventy per cent of the time. The event-matching subjects win about 70% on the 70% payoff side (or 49% of the time there) and 30% of the time on the side that pays off 30% of the time (another 9% for a total take-home wage of 58% in return for their labors of decision). But the world is not always or not even frequently random, and if one analyzes carefully what the event-matchers are doing, it turns out that they are trying out hypotheses one after the other, all of them containing a term such that they distribute bets on the two sides with a frequency to match the actual occurrence of events. If it should turn out that there is a pattern to be discovered, their payoff would become 100%. The other group would go on at the middling rate of 70%.

What has this to do with the subject at hand? For the person to search out and find regularities and relationships in his environment, he must be armed with an expectancy that there will be something to find and, once aroused by expectancy, he must devise ways of searching and finding. One of the chief enemies of such expectancy is the assumption that there is nothing one can find in the environment by way of regularity or relationship. In the experiment just cited, subjects often fall into a habitual attitude that there is either nothing to be found or that they can find a pattern by looking. There is an important sequel in behavior to the two attitudes, and to this I should like to turn now.

We have been conducting a series of experimental studies on a group of some seventy school children over the last four years. The studies have led us to

220

Chapter 7
Cognitive and
Constructivist
Learning
Theory

distinguish an interesting dimension of cognitive activity that can be described as ranging from *episodic empiricism* at one end to *cumulative constructionism* at the other. The two attitudes in the choice experiments just cited are illustrative of the extremes of the dimension. I might mention some other illustrations. One of the experiments employs the game of Twenty Questions. A child—in this case he is between 10 and 12—is told that a car has gone off the road and hit a tree. He is to ask questions that can be answered by "yes" or "no" to discover the cause of the accident. After completing the problem, the same task is given him again, though he is told that the accident had a different cause this time. In all, the procedure is repeated four times. Children enjoy playing the game. They also differ quite markedly in the approach or strategy they bring to the task. There are various elements in the strategies employed. In the first place, one may distinguish clearly between two types of questions asked: the one is designed for locating constraints in the problem, constraints that will eventually give shape to an hypothesis; the other is the hypothesis as question. It is the difference between, "Was there anything wrong with the driver?" and "Was the driver rushing to the doctor's office for an appointment and the car got out of control?" There are children who precede hypotheses with efforts to locate constraint and there are those who, to use our local slang, are "pot-shotters," who string out hypotheses non-cumulatively one after the other. A second element of strategy is its connectivity of information gathering: the extent to which questions asked utilize or ignore or violate information previously obtained. The questions asked by children tend to be organized in cycles, each cycle of questions usually being given over to the pursuit of some particular notion. Both within cycles and between cycles one can discern a marked difference on the connectivity of the child's performance. Needless to say, children who employ constraint location as a technique preliminary to the formulation of hypotheses tend to be far more connected in their harvesting of information. Persistence is another feature of strategy, a characteristic compounded of what appear to be two components: a sheer doggedness component, and a persistence that stems from the sequential organization that a child brings to the task. Doggedness is probably just animal spirits or the need for achievement—what has come to be called *n-ach*. Organized persistence is a maneuver for protecting our fragile cognitive apparatus from overload. The child who has flooded himself with disorganized information from unconnected hypotheses will become discouraged and confused sooner than the child who has shown a certain cunning in his strategy of getting information—a cunning whose principal component is the recognition that the value of information is not simply in getting it but in being able to carry it. The persistence of the organized child stems from his knowledge of how to organize questions in cycles, how to summarize things to himself, and the like.

Episodic empiricism is illustrated by information gathering that is unbound by prior constraints, that lacks connectivity, and that is deficient in organizational persistence. The opposite extreme is illustrated by an approach that is characterized by constraint sensitivity, by connective maneuvers, and by organized persistence. Brute persistence seems to be one of those gifts from the gods that make people more exaggeratedly what they are.[2]

Before returning to the issue of discovery and its role in the development of thinking, let me say a word more about the ways in which information may get transformed when the problem solver has actively processed it. There is first of all a pragmatic question: what does it take to get information processed into a form best designed to fit some future use? Take an experiment by Zajonc[3] as a case in point. He gives groups of subjects information of a controlled kind, some groups being told that their task is to transmit the information to others, others that it is merely to be kept in mind. In general, he finds more differentiation and organization of the information received with the intention of being transmitted than there is for information received passively. An active set leads to a transformation related to a task to be performed. The risk, to be sure, is in possible overspecialization of information processing that may lead to such a high degree of specific organization that information is lost for general use.

I would urge now in the spirit of an hypothesis that emphasis upon discovery in learning has precisely the effect upon the learner of leading him to be a constructionist, to organize what he is encountering in a manner not only designed to discover regularity and relatedness, but also to avoid the kind of information drift that fails to keep account of the uses to which information might have to be put. It is, if you will, a necessary condition for learning the variety of techniques of problem solving, of transforming information for better use, indeed for learning how to go about the very task of learning. Practice in discovering for oneself teaches one to acquire information in a way that makes that information more readily viable in problem solving. So goes the hypothesis. It is still in need of testing. But it is an hypothesis of such important human implications that we cannot afford not to test it—and testing will have to be in the schools.

2. Intrinsic and extrinsic motives.   Much of the problem in leading a child to effective cognitive activity is to free him from the immediate control of environmental rewards and punishments. That is to say, learning that starts in response to the rewards of parental or teacher approval or the avoidance of failure can too readily develop a pattern in which the child is seeking cues as to how to conform to what is expected of him. We know from studies of children who tend to be early over-achievers in school that they are likely to be seekers after the "right way to do it" and that their capacity for transforming their learning into viable thought structures tends to be lower than children merely achieving at levels predicted by intelligence tests. Our tests on such children show them to be lower in analytic ability than those who are not conspicuous in overachievement.[4] As we shall see later, they develop rote abilities and depend upon being able to "give back" what is expected rather than to make it into something that relates to the rest of their cognitive life. As Maimonides would say, their learning is not their own.

The hypothesis that I would propose here is that to the degree that one is able to approach learning as a task of discovering something rather than "learning about" it, to that degree will there be a tendency for the child to carry out his learning activities with the autonomy of self-reward or, more properly by reward that is discovery itself.

222

*Chapter 7
Cognitive and
Constructivist
Learning
Theory*

To those of you familiar with the battles of the last half-century in the field of motivation, the above hypothesis will be recognized as controversial. For the classic view of motivation in learning has been, until very recently, couched in terms of a theory of drives and reinforcement: that learning occurred by virtue of the fact that a response produced by a stimulus was followed by the reduction in a primary drive state. The doctrine is greatly extended by the idea of secondary reinforcement: any state associated even remotely with the reduction of a primary drive could also have the effect of producing learning. There has recently appeared a most searching and important criticism of this position, written by Professor Robert White,[5] reviewing the evidence of recently published animal studies, of work in the field of psychoanalysis, and of research on the development of cognitive processes in children. Professor White comes to the conclusion, quite rightly I think, that the drive-reduction model of learning runs counter to too many important phenomena of learning and development to be either regarded as general in its applicability or even correct in its general approach. Let me summarize some of his principal conclusions and explore their applicability to the hypothesis stated above.

> I now propose that we gather the various kinds of behavior just mentioned, all of which have to do with effective interaction with the environment, under the general heading of competence. According to Webster, competence means fitness or ability, and the suggested synonyms include capability, capacity, efficiency, proficiency, and skill. It is therefore a suitable word to describe such things as grasping and exploring, crawling and walking, attention and perception, language and thinking, manipulating and changing the surroundings, all of which promote an effective—a competent—interaction with the environment. It is true of course, that maturation plays a part in all these developments, but this part is heavily overshadowed by learning in all the more complex accomplishments like speech or skilled manipulation. I shall argue that it is necessary to make competence a motivational concept; there is *competence motivation* as well as competence in its more familiar sense of achieved capacity. The behavior that leads to the building up of effective grasping, handling, and letting go of objects, to take one example, is not random behavior that is produced by an overflow of energy. It is directed, selective, and persistent, and it continues not because it serves primary drives, which indeed it cannot serve until it is almost perfected, but because it satisfies an intrinsic need to deal with the environment.[6]

I am suggesting that there are forms of activity that serve to enlist and develop the competence motive, that serve to make it the driving force behind behavior. I should like to add to White's general premise that the *exercise* of competence motives has the effect of strengthening the degree to which they gain control over behavior and thereby reduce the effects of extrinsic rewards or drive gratification.

The brilliant Russian psychologist Vigotsky[7] characterizes the growth of thought processes as starting with a dialogue of speech and gesture between child and parent; autonomous thinking begins at the stage when the child is first able to internalize these conversations and "run them off" himself. This is a typical sequence in the development of competence. So too in instruction. The narrative of teaching is of the order of the conversation. The next move in the development of competence is the internalization of the narrative and its "rules of generation" so that the child is now capable of running off the narrative on his own. The hypothetical mode in teaching by encouraging the child to participate in "speaker's decisions" speeds this process along. Once internalization has occurred, the child is in a vastly improved position from several obvious points of view—notably that he is able to go beyond the information he has been given to generate additional ideas that can either be checked immediately from experience or can, at least, be used as a basis for formulating reasonable hypotheses. But over and beyond that, the child is now in a position to experience success and failure not as reward and punishment, but as information. For when the task is his own rather than a matter of matching environmental demands, he becomes his own paymaster in a certain measure. Seeking to gain control over his environment, he can now treat success as indicating that he is on the right track, failure as indicating he is on the wrong one.

In the end, this development has the effect of freeing learning from immediate stimulus control. When learning in the short run leads only to pellets of this or that rather than to mastery in the long run, then behavior can be readily "shaped" by extrinsic rewards. When behavior becomes more long-range and competence-oriented, it comes under the control of more complex cognitive structures, plans and the like, and operates more from the inside out. It is interesting that even Pavlov, whose early account of the learning process was based entirely on a notion of stimulus control of behavior through the conditioning mechanism in which, through contiguity a new conditioned stimulus was substituted for an old unconditioned stimulus by the mechanism of stimulus substitution, that even Pavlov recognized his account as insufficient to deal with higher forms of learning. To supplement the account, he introduced the idea of the "second signalling system," with central importance placed on symbolic systems such as language in mediating and giving shape to mental life. Or as Luria[8] has put it, "the first signal system [is] concerned with directly perceived stimuli, the second with systems of verbal elaboration." Luria, commenting on the importance of the transition from first to second signal system, says: "It would be mistaken to suppose that verbal intercourse with adults merely changes the contents of the child's conscious activity without changing its form.... The word has a basic function not only because it indicates a corresponding object in the external world, but also because it abstracts, isolates the necessary signal, generalizes perceived signals and relates them to certain categories; it is this systematization of direct experience that makes the role of the word in the formation of mental processes so exceptionally important."[9,10]

It is interesting that the final rejection of the universality of the doctrine of reinforcement in direct conditioning came from some of Pavlov's own students. Ivanov-Smolensky[11] and Krasnogorsky[12] published papers showing the manner in which symbolized linguistic messages could take over the place of the unconditioned stimulus and of the unconditioned response (gratification of hunger) in children. In all instances, they speak of these as *replacements* of lower, first-system mental or neural processes by higher order or second-system controls. A strange irony, then, that Russian psychology that gave us the notion of the conditioned response and the assumption that higher order activities are built up out of colligations or structurings of such primitive units,

224

*Chapter 7
Cognitive and
Constructivist
Learning
Theory*

rejected this notion while much of American learning psychology has stayed until quite recently within the early Pavlovian fold (see, for example, a recent article by Spence[13] in the *Harvard Educational Review* or Skinner's treatment of language[14] and the attacks that have been made upon it by linguists such as Chomsky[15] who have become concerned with the relation of language and cognitive activity). What is the more interesting is that Russian pedagogical theory has become deeply influenced by this new trend and is now placing much stress upon the importance of building up a more active symbolical approach to problem solving among children.

To sum up the matter of the control of learning, then, I am proposing that the degree to which competence or mastery motives come to control behavior, to that degree the role of reinforcement or "extrinsic pleasure" wanes in shaping behavior. The child comes to manipulate his environment more actively and achieves his gratification from coping with problems. Symbolic modes of representing and transforming the environment arise and the importance of stimulus-response-reward sequences declines. To use the metaphor that David Riesman developed in a quite different context, mental life moves from a state of outer-directedness in which the fortuity of stimuli and reinforcement are crucial to a state of inner-directedness in which the growth and maintenance of mastery become central and dominant.

3. Learning the heuristics of discovery. Lincoln Steffens,[16] reflecting in his *Autobiography* on his undergraduate education at Berkeley, comments that his schooling was overly specialized on learning about the known and that too little attention was given to the task of finding out about what was not known. But how does one train a student in the techniques of discovery? Again I would like to offer some hypotheses. There are many ways of coming to the arts of inquiry. One of them is by careful study of its formalization in logic, statistics, mathematics, and the like. If a person is going to pursue inquiry as a way of life, particularly in the sciences, certainly such study is essential. Yet, whoever has taught kindergarten and the early primary grades or has had graduate students working with him on their theses—I choose the two extremes for they are both periods of intense inquiry—knows that an understanding of the formal aspect of inquiry is not sufficient. There appear to be, rather, a series of activities and attitudes, some directly related to a particular subject and some of them fairly generalized, that go with inquiry and research. These have to do with the *process* of trying to find out something and while they provide no guarantee that the *product* will be any *great* discovery, their absence is likely to lead to awkwardness or aridity or confusion. How difficult it is to describe these matters—the heuristics of inquiry. There is one set of attitudes or ways of doing that has to do with sensing the relevance of variables—how to avoid getting stuck with edge effects and getting instead to the big sources of variance. Partly this gift comes from intuitive familiarity with a range of phenomena, sheer "knowing the stuff." But it also comes out of a sense of what things among an ensemble of things "smell right" in the sense of being of the right order of magnitude or scope or severity.

The English philosopher Weldon describes problem solving in an interesting and picturesque way. He distinguishes between difficulties, puzzles, and problems. We solve a problem or make a discovery when we impose a puzzle form on to a difficulty that converts it into a problem that can be solved in such a way that it gets us where we want to be. That is to say, we recast the difficulty into a form that we know how to work with, then work it. Much of what we speak of as discovery consists of knowing how to impose what kind of form on various kinds of difficulties. A small part but a crucial part of discovery of the highest order is to invent and develop models or "puzzle forms" that can be imposed on difficulties with good effect. It is in this area that the truly powerful mind shines. But it is interesting to what degree perfectly ordinary people can, given the benefit of instruction, construct quite interesting and what, a century ago, would have been considered greatly original models.

Now to the hypothesis. It is my hunch that it is only through the exercise of problem solving and the effort of discovery that one learns the working heuristic of discovery, and the more one has practice, the more likely is one to generalize what one has learned into a style of problem solving or inquiry that serves for any kind of task one may encounter—or almost any kind of task. I think the matter is self-evident, but what is unclear is what kinds of training and teaching produce the best effects. How do we teach a child to, say, cut his losses but at the same time be persistent in trying out an idea; to risk forming an early hunch without at the same time formulating one *so* early and with so little evidence as to be stuck with it waiting for appropriate evidence to materialize; to pose good testable guesses that are neither too brittle nor too sinuously incorrigible; etc., etc. Practice in inquiry, in trying to figure out things for oneself is indeed what is needed, but in what form? Of only one thing I am convinced. I have never seen anybody improve in the art and technique of inquiry by any means other than engaging in inquiry.

4. Conservation of memory.   I should like to take what some psychologists might consider a rather drastic view of the memory process. It is a view that in large measure derives from the work of my colleague, Professor George Miller.[17] Its first premise is that the principal problem of human memory is not storage, but retrieval. In spite of the biological unlikeliness of it, we seem to be able to store a huge quantity of information—perhaps not a full tape recording, though at times it seems we even do that, but a great sufficiency of impressions. We may infer this from the fact that recognition (i.e., recall with the aid of maximum prompts) is so extraordinarily good in human beings—particularly in comparison with spontaneous recall where, so to speak, we must get out stored information without external aids or prompts. The key to retrieval is organization or, in even simpler terms, knowing where to find information and how to get there.

Let me illustrate the point with a simple experiment. We present pairs of words to twelve-year-old children. One group is simply told to remember the pairs, that they will be asked to repeat them later. Another is told to remember them by producing a word or idea that will tie the pair together in a way that will make sense to them. A third group is given the mediators used by the second group when presented with the pairs to aid them in tying the pairs into working units. The word pairs include such juxtapositions as "chair-forest," "sidewalk-square," and the like. One can distinguish three styles of mediators

226

*Chapter 7
Cognitive and
Constructivist
Learning
Theory*

and children can be scaled in terms of their relative preference for each: *generic mediation* in which a pair is tied together by a superordinate idea: "chair and forest are both made of wood"; *thematic mediation* in which the two terms are imbedded in a theme or little story: "the lost child sat on a chair in the middle of the forest"; and *part-whole mediation* where "chairs are made from trees in the forest" is typical. Now, the chief result, as you would all predict, is that children who provide their own mediators do best—indeed, one time through a set of thirty pairs, they recover up to 95% of the second words when presented with the first ones of the pairs, whereas the uninstructed children reach a maximum of less than 50% recovered. Interestingly enough, children do best in recovering materials tied together by the form of mediator they most often use.

One can cite a myriad of findings to indicate that any organization of information that reduces the aggregate complexity of material by imbedding it into a cognitive structure a person has constructed will make that material more accessible for retrieval. In short, we may say that the process of memory, looked at from the retrieval side, is also a process of problem solving: how can material be "placed" in memory so that it can be got on demand?

We can take as a point of departure the example of the children who developed their own technique for relating the members of each word pair. You will recall that they did better than the children who were given by exposition the mediators they had developed. Let me suggest that in general, material that is organized in terms of a person's own interests and cognitive structures is material that has the best chance of being accessible in memory. That is to say, it is more likely to be placed along routes that are connected to one's own ways of intellectual travel.

In sum, the very attitudes and activities that characterize "figuring out" or "discovering" things for oneself also seems to have the effect of making material more readily accessible in memory.

NOTES

1. Maimonides, *Guide for the Perplexed* (New York: Dover Publications, 1956).

2. I should also remark in passing that the two extremes also characterize concept attainment strategies as reported in *A Study of Thinking* by J. S. Bruner *et al.* (New York: J. Wiley, 1956). Successive scanning illustrates well what is meant here by episodic empiricism; conservative focussing is an example of cumulative constructionism.

3. R. B. Zajonc (Personal communication, 1957).

4. J. S. Bruner and A. J. Caron, "Cognition, Anxiety, and Achievement in the Preadolescent," *Journal of Educational Psychology* (in press).

5. R. W. White, "Motivation Reconsidered: The Concepts of Competence," *Psychological Review,* LXVI (1959), 297–333.

6. *Ibid.,* pp. 317–318.

7. L. S. Vigotsky, *Thinking and Speech* (Moscow, 1934).

8. A. L. Luria, "The Directive Function of Speech in Development and Dissolution," *Word,* XV (1959), 341–464.

9. *Ibid.*, p. 12.

10. For an elaboration of the view expressed by Luria, the reader is referred to the forthcoming translation of L. S. Vigotsky's 1934 book being published by John Wiley and Sons and the Technology Press.

11. A. G. Ivanov-Smolensky, "Concerning the Study of the Joint Activity of the First and Second Signal Systems," *Journal of Higher Nervous Activity*, I (1951), 1.

12. N. D. Krasnogorsky, *Studies of Higher Nervous Activity in Animals and in Man*, Vol. I (Moscow, 1954).

13. K. W. Spence, "The Relation of Learning Theory to the Technique of Education," *Harvard Educational Review*, XXIX (1959), 84–95.

14. B. F. Skinner, *Verbal Behavior* (New York: Appleton-Century-Crofts, 1957).

15. N. Chomsky, *Syntactic Structure* (The Hague, The Netherlands: Mouton & Co., 1957).

16. L. Steffens. *Autobiography of Lincoln Steffens* (New York: Harcourt, Brace, 1931).

17. G. A. Miller, "The Magical Number Seven, Plus or Minus Two," *Psychological Review*, LXIII (1956), 81–97.

Development of Academic Concepts in School Aged Children

Lev Vygotsky (1896–1934) is generally considered the greatest Russian educational and developmental psychologist. He earned a degree in law from Moscow University but studied such disparate topics as linguistics, psychology, general social science, literature, and philosophy. Following graduation he taught psychology at a teacher's college in western Russia. This work brought Vygotsky in contact with children who had developmental and perceptual disabilities. His compassion for these children caused him to focus on cognitive-developmental psychology in his search to help them fulfill their potential through innovative educational methods. Later, Vygotsky accepted a position in Moscow at the Institute of Psychology. He was an authentic Marxist, aiming to help construct the new socialist state through a radically new psychology. Unfortunately he died of tuberculosis at the age of 38, only 10 years into his systematic research in developmental and educational psychology.

Vygotsky's *Thought and Language*, published posthumously in Russia in 1934, was too radical for the guardians of Soviet doctrine, and it was suppressed from 1936 to 1956; it was first published in English in 1962. Of focal concern to many psychologists is the development of "inner speech." Jean Piaget, early in his career, put forth that inner speech arises as egocentrism decreases; the behaviorists advocated that inner speech is simply nonobservable slight movements of the muscles related to speaking. Vygotsky, however, taking the notion of "consciousness" seriously, viewed "inner speech" as the internalization of human dialogue, which differed significantly from the approaches of both Piaget and the behaviorists.

Vygotsky also published the important text *Educational Psychology*, which was written while he was at Gomel's Teachers College in the early 1920s and published in Russian in 1926 (but not published in English until 1997). The following is excerpted from *The Vygotsky Reader*, edited by René van der Veer and Jaan Valsiner and translated by Theresa Prout and René van der Veer (Blackwell, 1994). It was originally published in Russian in 1934 as the introduction to a text subtitled *Investigation of the Question*

Key Concept: development of spontaneous (nonacademic) and nonspontaneous (academic) concepts

Lev Vygotsky

T he topic of the development of academic[1] concepts in school aged children is first and foremost a practical problem of enormous, even primary, importance from the point of view of the difficulties which schools face in connection with providing children with an academic education. At the same time, we are shocked by the scarcity of any available information on this subject. The theoretical side of this question is no less significant, because a study of the development of academic, i.e. authentic, reliable and true concepts, cannot fail to reveal the most profound, essential and fundamental laws which govern any type of process of concept formation. It is quite astonishing, in view of this fact, that this problem, which holds the key to the whole history of the child's intellectual development and which, one would think, should provide the starting point for any investigation of the thinking process in children, appears to have been neglected until very recently, to such an extent that the present experimental study, to which these pages are to serve as an introduction, is almost the very first attempt at a systematic investigation of this problem.

How do academic concepts develop in the mind of the child who undergoes school instruction? What are the relationships between the child's proper learning[2] and the acquisition of knowledge and the processes governing the internal development of an academic concept in the child's mind? Do they actually coincide and are they really only two sides of essentially one and the same process? Does the process of internal development of concepts follow the teaching/learning [*obuchenie*] process, like a shadow follows the object which casts it, never coinciding, but reproducing and repeating its movements exactly, or is it rather an immeasurably more complicated and subtle relationship which can only be explored by special investigations?

Contemporary child psychology offers only two answers to all these questions. The first says that, generally speaking, academic concepts do not have their own internal history and that they do not go through a process of development in the strict sense of that word, but that they are simply acquired, are taken in a ready-made state via processes of understanding, and are adopted by the child from the adult sphere of thinking and that, in essence, it should be possible to solve the whole problem of development of academic concepts by teaching the child academic facts and for the child to be able to assimilate the concepts. This is the most widespread and practical generally accepted view which, until very recently, has formed the basis of the educational and methodological theories of the various academic disciplines.

The inadequacy of this view is revealed as soon as it is brought face to face with any scientific criticism, and this becomes clear simultaneously both from the theoretical and the practical points of view. From investigations into the process of the formation of concepts, it is known that concepts do not simply

230

*Chapter 7
Cognitive and
Constructivist
Learning
Theory*

represent a concatenation of associative connections assimilated by the memory of an automatic mental skill, but a complicated and real act of thinking which cannot be mastered by simple memorization, and which inevitably requires that the child's thinking which cannot be mastered by simple memorization, and which inevitably requires that the child's thinking itself rise to a higher level in its internal development, to make the appearance of a concept possible within the consciousness. Research shows that, at any stage of its development, the concept represents an act of generalization when looked at from the psychological point of view. The most important result obtained from all the research in this field is the well established theory that concepts which are psychologically represented as word meanings, undergo development. The essence of this development is contained, first of all, in the transition from one generalization structure to another. Any word meaning at any age represents a generalization. However, the meanings of words develop. At the time when a child first acquires a new word connected with a definite meaning, the development of this word does not stop, but is only beginning. At first, it represents a generalization of the most elementary type and the child is only able to progress from the starting point to this generalization on this elemental level to ever higher types of generalization, depending on the level of his development, and this process is accomplished when real and proper concepts make an appearance.

This process of development of concepts or the meanings of words requires the development of a number of functions, such as voluntary attention, logical memory, abstraction, comparison and differentiation, and all these very complicated psychological processes cannot simply be taken on by the memory or just be learned and appropriated. Thus, from the theoretical point of view, one can hardly doubt the total inadequacy of the view which claims that a child acquires concepts in their finished state during the course of his schooling, and that they are mastered in the same way as any other intellectual skill.

However, from the practical point of view, the erroneousness of this view becomes revealed at every stage of the way. Educational experience, no less than theoretical research, teaches us that, in practice, a straightforward learning of concepts always proves impossible and educationally fruitless. Usually, any teacher setting out on this road achieves nothing except a meaningless acquisition of words, mere verbalization in children, which is nothing more than simulation and imitation of corresponding concepts which, in reality, are concealing a vacuum. In such cases, the child assimilates not concepts but words, and he fills his memory more than his thinking. As a result, he ends up helpless in the face of any sensible attempt to apply any of this acquired knowledge. Essentially, this method of teaching/learning [*obuchenie*] concepts, a purely scholastic and verbal method of teaching, which is condemned by everybody and which advocates the replacement of acquisition of living knowledge by the assimilation of dead and empty verbal schemes, represents the most basic failing in the field of education.

It was Leo Tolstoy, the great connoisseur of words and their meaning, who better than anyone recognized that a direct and simple communication of concepts from teacher to pupils, and a mechanical transference of the meanings of words from one head to another by using other words, was impossible—this impasse he had encountered in his own teaching experience.

Recounting these experiences whilst attempting to teach literary language to children by using translations of children's words into the language of fairy tales, and then from the language of fairy tales to a higher level, he came to the conclusion that pupils cannot be taught the literary language against their will, in the same way as they are taught French, by forcible explanations, memorizing and repetition. 'We must admit' he writes,

> that we have tried this more than once in the past two months and have always met with an insuperable distaste on the part of the pupils which has proved the wrongness of the path we took. In these experiments, I merely convinced myself that to explain the meanings of words and of speech is quite impossible, even for gifted teachers, not to speak of those explanations so beloved of ungifted teachers, that 'an assembly is a small Sanhedrin' and so on. In explaining any word, the word 'impression' for example, you either replace the word you explain by another word which is just as incomprehensible, or by a while series of words, the connection between which is just as incomprehensible as the word itself.[3]

Truth and falsehood are mixed in equal measure in Tolstoy's categorical statement. The true part of this statement is the conclusion which stems directly from experience and is known by every teacher who, like Tolstoy, is vainly struggling to explain the meaning of words. The truth of this theory, according to Tolstoy's own words, lies in the fact that almost always it is not the word itself which is unintelligible, but that the pupil lacks the concept which would be capable of expressing this word. The word is almost always available when the concept is ready.

The erroneous part of his statement is directly connected with Tolstoy's general views of the subject of teaching/learning [*obuchenie*] and it consists of the fact that it excludes any probability of this mysterious process being crudely interfered with, and strives to allocate the process of the development of concepts to the laws of its own internal strategy, and by doing so, he separates the whole process of concept development from the process of teaching and thus condemns teachers to an extreme state of passivity, as far as the problem of the development of concepts is concerned. This mistake is particularly conspicuous in his categorical formulation where he proclaims that 'any interference becomes a crude, clumsy force which retards the process of development'.[4]

However, even Tolstoy understood that not every interference holds up the process of concept development, but only the crude, instant, direct sort which follows a straight line, the shortest distance between two points, interference with the process of concept formation in the child's mind, which can produce nothing but harm. But more subtle, complex and more indirect teaching methods may interfere in the process of children's concept formation in such a way that they can lead this process forward and on to a higher plane. 'We must', says Tolstoy,

> give the pupil opportunities to acquire new concepts and words from the general sense of what is said. He will hear or read an incomprehensible word in an incomprehensible sentence once, then again in another sentence, and a new concept will begin dimly to present itself to him, and at length he will, by chance, feel the necessity of using that word, he will use it once, and word and concept become

232

*Chapter 7
Cognitive and
Constructivist
Learning
Theory*

his property. And there are thousands of other paths. But deliberately to present a pupil with new concepts and forms of language is, according to my conviction, as unnecessary and pointless as to teach a child to walk by means of the laws of equilibrium. Any such attempt carries a pupil not nearer to the appointed goal, but further away from it, as if a man should wish to help a flower to open out with his crude hand, should begin to unfold the petals, and crush everything around it.[5] . . .

It should be said right at the start, that the distinction drawn between everyday and academic concepts, which we have chosen as our starting point, and which we have developed in our working hypothesis, and in the entire formulation of this problem, which was dealt with in our research, is not only not generally accepted by contemporary psychology, but is seen as contradicting the widely held views on this subject. This is why it is in such dire need of elucidation and proof to uphold it.

We have already said above that at the present time there exist two answers to the question as to how academic concepts develop in the minds of school age children. The first of these answers, as has been said, fully denies the very presence of any process of an inner development of academic concepts which are acquired in school and we have already attempted to point out the unfoundedness of such a view. There still remains the other answer. This is the one that seems to be the most widely accepted at the present time. It says that the development of academic concepts in the minds of children in school, does not substantially differ from the development of all the remaining concepts which are being formed in the process of the child's personal experiences, and that, consequently, the very attempt to separate these two processes is a meaningless exercise. From this point of view, the process of development of academic concepts simply repeats the course of the development of everyday concepts in all its basic and essential features. But we must immediately ask ourselves what such a conviction can be based on.

If we look at the whole scientific literature on this subject, we will see that the subject of nearly all the research devoted to the problem of concept formation during childhood, invariably deals only with everyday concepts. All of the basic laws guiding the development of concepts in children are based on material about children's own everyday concepts. Later, without a thought, these laws are extended to the realm of the child's academic thinking,[6] and thus they are transferred directly to another sphere of concepts, ones which have formed in entirely different internal circumstances; and this happens simply as a result of the fact that the question of whether such an extended interpretation of experimental results limited to one single defined sphere of children's concepts, is right and valid, does not even enter the minds of these researchers.

We recognize that the most astute researchers, like Piaget, felt they had to deal with this question. As soon as they were faced with this problem, they felt obliged to draw a sharp line of demarcation between those conceptions of reality in children, where a decisive role is played by the workings of the child's own thinking, and those which have come into being as a result of the specific and determinant actions of facts which the child had acquired from his environment. Piaget designates the first type as spontaneous conceptions and the others as reactive ones.

Piaget[7] establishes that both these groups of children's conceptions or concepts have a lot in common: (1) they both reveal a tendency to resist suggestion; (2) they both are deeply rooted in the child's thinking; (3) they both disclose a definite common character among children of the same age; (4) they both remain in the child's consciousness for a long time, over a period of several years, and they gradually give way to new concepts instead of disappearing instantly, as suggested conceptions tend to do; and (5) they both become apparent in the child's very first correct replies.

All these signs which are common to both groups of children's concepts differentiate them from suggested conceptions and answers which a child is likely to produce under the influence of the suggestive force of the question.

In these basically correct ideas one can already find a full affirmation of the fact that academic concepts in children, which undoubtedly belong to the second group of children's concepts and which do not arise spontaneously, undergo a fundamental process of development. This is obvious from the five illustrations listed above.

Piaget concedes that research into this group of concepts may even become a legitimate and independent subject for a special study. In this respect he goes further and delves deeper than any other researchers. But at the same time, he follows false leads which tend to depreciate the correct parts of his arguments. Three such internally connected erroneous ideas in Piaget's thinking are of particular interest to us.

The first of these is that, whilst admitting the possibility of an independent investigation of non-spontaneous concepts in children, and at the same time as he points out that these concepts are deeply rooted in children's thinking, Piaget is still inclined towards the contrary assertion, according to which only the child's spontaneous concepts and his spontaneous ideas can serve as a source of direct knowledge about the qualitative uniqueness of children's thinking. According to Piaget, children's non-spontaneous concepts, which have been formed under the influence of adults who surround them, reflect not so much the characteristics of their own thinking, as the degree and type of assimilation on their part of adult thinking. At the same time, Piaget begins to contradict his own sound idea that, when a child assimilates a concept, he reworks it and in the course of this reworking, he imprints it with certain specific features of his own thoughts. However, he is inclined to apply this idea only to spontaneous concepts and he denies that it could equally be applied to non-spontaneous ones. It is in this completely unfounded conclusion where the first incorrect aspect of Piaget's theory lies concealed.

The second false premise flows directly from the first. Once it has been acknowledged that children's non-spontaneous concepts do not reflect any of the aspects of children's thinking as such, and that these aspects are only to be found in children's spontaneous concepts, by the same token we have to accept —as Piaget does—that there exists an impassable, solid and permanently fixed barrier which excludes any possibility of mutual influence among these two groups of concepts. Piaget is only able to differentiate between the spontaneous and the non-spontaneous concepts, but he is unable to see the facts which unite

234

*Chapter 7
Cognitive and
Constructivist
Learning
Theory*

them into a single system of concepts formed during the course of a child's mental development. He only sees the gap, not the connection. It is for this reason that he represents concept development as the mechanical coming together of two separate processes which have nothing to do with one another and which, as it were, flow along two completely isolated and divided channels.

These mistakes cause the theory to become entangled in another internal contradiction and this leads to the third one. On the one hand, Piaget admits that children's non-spontaneous concepts do not reflect any characteristics of children's thinking, and that this privilege belongs exclusively to spontaneous concepts. In that case he should agree that, in general, the understanding of the characteristics of children's thinking has no practical significance, as the non-spontaneous concepts are acquired completely independently of these characteristics. On the other hand, one of the basic points of his theory is the admission that the essence of a child's mental development consists of the progressive socialization of his thinking; one of the basic and most concentrated aspects of the formation process of non-spontaneous concepts is schooling, so the most important process of thought socialization for the development of a child as it makes its appearance during schooling turns out, as it were, not to have any connection with the child's own internal process of intellectual development. On the one hand, understanding of the process of the internal development of children's thinking has no significance for the clarification of the socialization process during the course of school education, and on the other, the socialization of child's thinking, which takes the foreground during the process of schooling, is in no way connected with the internal development of children's conceptions and concepts. . . .

To counter the first of these erroneous ideas, we can offer a suggestion with the opposite meaning, according to which one would expect that the development of non-spontaneous, particularly academic concepts, which we are justified in considering as representing a higher and most pure and significant type of non-spontaneous concept from the theoretical and practical point of view, should be able to reveal all their basic qualities which are characteristic of children's thinking, at any given stage of their development, when subjected to a special investigation. By putting forward this suggestion, we are basing ourselves on the simple premise previously developed, that academic concepts are not assimilated and learned by the child and are not taken up by memory, but arise and are formed with the help of the most extreme tension in the activity of his own thinking. And, with relentless inevitability, what emerges from this at the same time, is that the development of academic concepts should exhibit the peculiar characteristics of this high level of activity of children's thinking to the fullest extent. The results obtained from experimental studies entirely confirm this suggestion.

Against Piaget's second false idea, we can once again put forward a counter suggestion which has the opposite sense, according to which academic concepts in children, the purest type of non-spontaneous concepts, under investigation reveal not just certain features which are opposite to those which we know from the study of spontaneous concepts, but some which are common to both. The dividing line between these two types of concepts turns out to be highly fluid, passing from one side to the other an infinite number of times in the actual course of development. Right from the start it should be mentioned that the developments of spontaneous and academic concepts turn out as processes which are tightly bound up with one another and which constantly influence one another. On the other hand—this is how we have to develop our suggestions—the development of academic concepts should certainly be based on a certain degree of maturing of spontaneous concepts, which cannot be ignored in the process of formation of academic concepts, if for no other reason that direct experience teaches us that the development of academic concepts is only possible when the child's spontaneous concepts have reached a certain level peculiar to school age. Conversely, we have to suppose that the emergence of higher types of concepts, which academic concepts belong to, cannot remain without influence on the level of the previously formed spontaneous concepts, for the simple reason that both types of concepts are not encapsulated in the child's consciousness, are not separated from one another by an impermeable barrier, do not flow along two isolated channels, but are in the process of continual, unceasing interaction, which has to lead inevitably to a situation where generalizations, which have a higher structure and which are peculiar to academic concepts, should be able to elicit a change in the structure of spontaneous concepts. Whilst making this suggestion, we are basing ourselves on the fact that, whilst we are speaking about the development of spontaneous or academic concepts, what we really have in mind is the development of a single process of concept formation, which is happening under different internal and external conditions, but which remains unified in its nature and is not formed as a result of a struggle, conflict or any antagonism of two mutually exclusive forms of thinking. If we allow ourselves to anticipate the experimental results once again, they, too, entirely confirm this proposal.

Finally, we would counter the third idea by putting forward another assumption, which suggests that, so far as concept formation is concerned, not antagonism but relations of an infinitely more complex nature should exist between the processes of education and development. We should expect in advance that in the course of a special study, teaching/learning [*obuchenie*] will be revealed as one of the fundamental sources of the development of concepts in children and a powerful force which guides this process. In this proposal, we are basing ourselves on the generally accepted fact that teaching/learning [*obuchenie*] is a decisive factor during school age which determines the entire subsequent fate of the child's mental development, including the development of his concepts, as well as on the consideration that higher types of academic concepts cannot arise in the child's mind in any other way except out of already existing lower, rudimentary types of generalization, and that, under no circumstances, can they be deposited in the child's consciousness from the outside. Again our research confirms this third and last assumption, and thus allows us to put the question about using psychological research data on children's concepts applicable to teaching and training problems in a completely different way from Piaget.

1. The Russian term *nauchnoe ponjatie* is here rendered as 'academic concept' (i.e. concepts that emerge in children's use in conjunction with school education, in the context of academic curricular disciplines—in opposition to everyday concepts). An alternative (more widespread and literal) translation is 'scientific concept'.

2. In the Russian original: *protsessy sobstvenno obuchenija*, i.e. 'teaching/learning processes *per se*' (in contrast with acquisition of knowledge—*usvoenie znanija*).

3. This and the following quotes are taken from Leo Tolstoy's article 'The Yasnaya Polyana school in the months of November and December', which appeared in the January, March and April numbers of *Yasnaya Polyana* magazine in 1862. Yasnaya Polyana was the name of Tolstoy's estate where he started his experimental school for peasant children. See for the present text p. 123 of Pinch, A. and Armstrong, M,. (eds) 1982: *Tolstoy on Education: Tolstoy's educational writings 1861–62*. London: The Athlone Press.

4. See p. 123 of Pinch and Armstrong (1982).

5. Ibid., p. 125.

6. In the Russian original: *nauchnoe myshlenie*.

7. See Piaget, J. 1923: *Le langage et la penseé chez l'enfant*. Neuchatel: Delachaux et Niestlé. Translated into English as (1926) *The Language and Thought of the Child*. London: Kegan Paul.

CHAPTER 8 Information Processing

8.1 HERBERT A. SIMON

The Information Processing Explanation of Gestalt Phenomena

Herbert A. Simon was born in 1916 and earned his B.A. and Ph.D. degrees from the University of Chicago, focusing on political science and economics. His dissertation concerned decision making within organizations. This led Simon into the field of organizational psychology and the psychology of problem solving. He evolved into one of the main pioneers of the information processing approach to psychology.

Although now known as a leading psychologist, Simon remained involved in mathematical economics and organization theory. He is well known for putting forward his empirically based theory called "bounded rationality," which runs contra to other economists' overemphasizing economic man's mental processes. His work in this area earned him a 1978 Nobel Prize in economics. In the 1950s Simon, along with Allen Newell and J. C. Shaw, developed the first list-processing computer languages with the express purpose of building theory concerning human symbolic behavior. This led to the publication of their book *Human Problem Solving* (Prentice Hall, 1972). Simon and his colleagues later published *Models of Thought* (Yale University Press, 1979), in which they used information processing theory and modeling by computer programs to explain cognitive processes in human problem solving and problem understanding, the learning of language, and concept formation. Other influential texts of Simon's include *Models of My Life* (MIT Press, 1996) and *The Sciences of the Artificial,* 3rd ed. (MIT Press, 1996).

Simon has been a very active proselytizer of his theories and research findings. He has used his administrative post at Carnegie-Mellon University and his roles in the National Academy of Sciences, the National Research Council, and the President's Science Advisory Committee as platforms to advance the information-processing view of human cognition. He has also disseminated his ideas in scores of journal articles. The following selection comes from "The Information Processing Explanation of Gestalt Phenomena," *Computers in Human Behavior* (1986) and concerns using computers to model such complex human cognitive behavior as intuition.

Key Concept: information processing and intuition

A central goal of contemporary information processing psychology is to explain the cognitive processes that occur in the course of various kinds of human thinking, learning, and problem solving. These explanations frequently take the form of computer programs that simulate the actual thought process and that are tested for empirical validity by comparing program traces with the course of thought of human subjects, as revealed, say, by thinking-aloud protocols or records of eye movements.

There seems now to be considerable agreement, if not a perfect consensus, that such models can account for the thought processes that are observed in many kinds of relatively well-structured problem solving and learning situations. There continues to be considerable skepticism, however, as to how far computer simulations can capture such phenomena as insight, sudden "aha" experiences, learning with understanding, and other cognitive phenomena emphasized by Gestalt psychologists (Michael Wertheimer, 1985).

It is the purpose of this paper to show that a number of simulation programs already exist that provide veridical accounts of just these kinds of Gestalt phenomena in a variety of task environments. In successive sections of the paper, I will discuss insight, "aha" phenomena, and learning with understanding versus "mechanical" learning....

INSIGHT AND INTUITION

Before we can simulate a phenomenon like insight or intuition, or determine whether a proposed simulation of the phenomenon is veridical, we must provide an operational definition that permits us to decide when the phenomenon in question is present. One serious difficulty in testing Gestalt theories is that the concepts that play central roles in these theories are not often defined in terms of operations or measurements, but are usually assumed to be directly understood and observable. For example, I have been unable to discover in Max Wertheimer's *Productive Thinking* (1945) a definition of "insight." In the absence of such operational definitions, we must start from everyday usage of language and provide our own criteria for presence or absence of the phenomenon.

Definitions of Insight and Intuition

We begin with the dictionary definitions of insight and intuition. As a first approximation they are treated as synonyms, with the core meaning of "immediate apprehension or cognition." The second edition of Webster's unabridged dictionary then distinguishes them as follows: "Insight usually combines its original sense of seeing with the inner eye, or intuitively, with the later idea of seeing into the inner or hidden nature of things." Thus, we may treat insight as intuition that provides relatively deep understanding. "Immediate apprehension" is best treated as "sudden" rather than "instantaneous" apprehension, since an intuition or insight may occur after a person has been working on a problem for a long time. What makes the apprehension intuitive is that it involves a substantial change in understanding that occurs in a brief interval of time and without detectable explicit reasoning.

These definitions agree closely with the one given by Michael Wertheimer in the abstract of his recent paper on this topic (Wertheimer, 1985, p. 19). He speaks of "understanding, that is, grasping both what is crucial in any given problem and why it is crucial," then equates understanding with "this phenomenon of insight."

The verbal definitions help a little, but not much. To go the next step, we must ask under what circumstances we apply the terms "insight" and "intuition" to behavior that we observe. We ordinarily say that an act of insight has taken place when someone solves a problem or answers a question rather suddenly (but possibly following a short or long interval of puzzlement and effort) without being able to give an account of how the solution or answer was finally attained. We are more likely to use the term "insight" when it comes almost immediately upon presentation of the problem. In this section, I will use the two terms in this way, but in a later section will attend more specifically to the understanding that is supposed to be associated with insight.

As an example of intuition, if we present a physician with a set of symptoms and the physician immediately (e.g., within two seconds) makes the diagnosis, "measles," and if, when we ask him or her how the decision was reached, we receive only answers like, "I used my intuition," "I don't know," "It's a simple matter of medical judgment," "The symptoms are those we expect in measles," then we may say that the judgment has been reached intuitively. We will be particularly inclined to say it was intuitive if the subject cannot provide a veridical account of the steps of the problem solving, question answering, or recognition process that were used to arrive at the response. So, if we ask someone how he or she recognized that the person approaching on the street was Fred, a close friend, the response will seldom contain information that would allow anyone else to recognize Fred. It is notorious that taxonomists recognize common organisms, within their domain of specialization, within a second or two, and without making use of the formal criteria (often visible only under the microscope) that define these organisms in a taxonomic key.

Intuition as Recognition

If rapid response without ability to explain how the response came about is the indicator of intuition, then intuition is essentially synonymous with recognition. But recognition processes have long been modeled successfully by computer programs. For example, the EPAM [Elementary Perceiver and Memorizer] program (Feigenbaum, 1963; Feigenbaum & Simon, 1984) provides a model of the processes that occur during the performance of verbal learning tasks, and related tasks. When a stimulus is presented to EPAM, the program applies a sequence of tests to it, using the outcomes of the tests to sort it down a discrimination net until it is distinguished from alternative stimuli. (EPAM also contains learning processes for "growing" the discrimination net.)

The result of the discrimination or recognition process in EPAM is to place in short-term memory a symbol representing the stimulus that has been recognized. This symbol "points to," hence provides access to, knowledge about the stimulus that has been stored previously in long-term memory. However, no information is stored in short-term memory about the specific tests in EPAM's recognition net that led to the recognition. The recognition *process,* as distinguished from the *result* of that process, is not accessible to consciousness, hence cannot be reported. Because it is not accessible to consciousness, when the subject is asked how the recognition took place, he or she can only reply that it happened "intuitively." Moreover, the recognition process is rapid. At 10 msec per test, in a serial discrimination net with an average branching factor of four, recognition of a particular stimulus from among a million million—10^{12}—possibilities would take only 200 msec. Of course, a parallel discrimination net might be able to do the task even faster.

The EPAM model was extended by Simon and Gilmartin (1973) into the MAPP model, which simulates the intuitive recognition of patterns that takes place when experienced players—masters or grandmasters—look for a few seconds at a position on a chess board. Thus intuition (or recognition) provides a ready explanation of some of the apparently extraordinary memory feats of which experts are capable in their domain of expertise.

Patterns do not need to be identical to be recognized as the same by EPAM. Since EPAM tests only some portion of the features of a pattern, the exact tests depending on the structure of the discrimination net that has been grown, any set of patterns that agree with respect to these particular features will be recognized as the same pattern. Moreover, patterns belonging to the same class (e.g., all that are "cat-like") can be viewed as similar even if EPAM is able to discriminate among them on the basis of individual differences (e.g., this black cat and that marmalade cat). Hence EPAM can deal with similarity as well as identity of patterns.

The EPAM mechanism postulates that recognition is achieved by discriminating on the basis of features. The possibility of simulating recognition, hence intuition, by computer does not depend on the correctness of this particular postulate. It is equally feasible to build programs that recognize on the basis of the similarity of a stimulus to a prototypical stimulus for the concept, in the matter postulated by Rosch (1973).

On the basis on these models and experiments, it would appear that the process named "intuition" by Gestalt psychologists is none other than our familiar friend "recognition," and that recognition processes are readily modeled by computer programs.

It may be objected that I misunderstand what Gestaltists mean by "intuition." The mechanisms I have described certainly cover "the act of coming to direct knowledge or certainty without reasoning or inferring"—another entry under "intuition" in the Unabridged Dictionary. But Gestaltists also speak of "intuitive understanding," or "insight," which my examples have perhaps not encompassed. Intuitive understanding, hence insight, would appear to mean attaining understanding rapidly and without being able to report how the understanding was attained. Whether that process can be simulated by computer will be discussed when we come to the term "understanding."

THE "AHA" PHENOMENON

The "aha" phenomenon differs from other instances of problem solution by intuition or insight only in that the sudden solution is here preceded by a shorter or longer period during which the subject was unable to solve the problem, or even to seem to make progress towards its solution. "The "aha" may occur while the subject is working on the problem, or after the problem has been put aside for some period of "incubation." The incubation period may be a few minutes, but sudden problem solution after the problem has been set aside for some months has been reported (e.g., the celebrated anecdote of Poincaré about the circumstances of his discovery that the transformations that define Fuchsian functions are identical with those of non-Euclidean geometry).

Planning as Source of Sudden Insight

Koehler (1925), in his research on problem solving by apes, contrasted insightful problem solving, involving an "aha," with problem solving by trial and error. The phenomenal evidence was that the apes moved relatively suddenly from fruitless (literally!) attempts to reach their goal to a sequence of apparently purposeful, connected behaviors well designed to attain it (e.g., moving a box under a bunch of bananas, retrieving a stick, climbing on the box and knocking down the bananas).

The rapidity of the change in behavior can be attributed, as in our discussion of intuition and insight, to an act of recognition. However, attributing the change to recognition does not explain how the succession of means-ends connections underlying the successful solution plan was generated. But evidence exists that bears on this point too.

In problem solving studies by Newell and Simon (1972), subjects sometimes found solution plans in an abstract planning space, then returned to the original problem space to fill in the plans and reach the solution of the problem that was posed to them. At the moment when they had achieved a plan, and were about to return to the details of the original problem space, they frequently expressed an "aha"—an interjection indicating confidence that the road to the solution was now open. Since the plans that subjects constructed were not always executable when all the detailed conditions of the problem were reintroduced, these expressions of triumph were sometimes premature, but the failure of a plan does not affect our interpretation of the "aha." Koehler's apes, having arrived at a solution plan for reaching the bananas, could exhibit this same rapid transition from apparent stalemate and aimlessness to systematic execution of the plan. They could also sometimes arrive at plans that were not executable, for failure to take into account all of the conditions of the situation.

Planning of the kind that Newell and Simon describe has been simulated in the GPS [Global Positioning System] program (Newell & Simon, 1972, pp. 414–438), and Sacerdoti (1977) provides a more recent account of computer programs that plan. It would seem, then, that the "ahas" associated with success in discovering a plan for the solution of a problem can be and have been simulated by computer programs. Moreover, this feeling of confidence that a problem has been solved when a solution plan has been discovered, and prior to working out the actual details of the solution, appears to be a quite common form of the "aha" experience.

Sudden Insight After Incubation

The "aha" after incubation raises the question of how recognition could make a problem suddenly solvable that was not solvable before incubation. This question has most often been answered by postulating that incubation is an active (though unconscious) process that involves generating many potential solutions. When an actual solution (or a plausible one, for these "ahas" are also fallible) is attained, it comes to conscious attention.

But sudden problem solution after incubation can be explained without postulating that anything except forgetting goes on during the incubation period. The problem solver, who has been working towards specific subgoals, forgets during the period of inattention the Einstellung—the subgoals and other elements of immediate context that have been limiting the range of his or her attacks on the problem. Extracted by this forgetting from the current rut, and on resuming attention to the problem, the problem solver attacks it from a new angle, which happens now to be the right one. This alternative explanation of the post-incubation "aha" seems first to have been proposed by Woodworth (1938, pp. 38, 823), and it was later elaborated into a scheme that can be modeled on a computer (Simon, 1966). It has the advantage of parsimony over other explanations in that it employs a well-known mechanism, the Einstellung effect, and requires no essentially new hypotheses.

We see that the "aha" experience can be explained as an instance of recognition, and that both the "ahas" that occur as a product of successful planning

and those that accompany sudden discovery after incubation have been simulated by computer. Since these simulations derive from interpreting intuition
as recognition, it may be objected that we have still not explained "insightful"
intuition, that is, intuition with understanding. We turn to this topic next.

UNDERSTANDING

Again, the dictionary shows how difficult it is to give an operational definition
of the term, "understanding." Webster's Third New International Dictionary
equates understanding with such concepts as: "the act of grasping mentally,"
"the power of comprehending, analyzing, distinguishing, and judging," "the
condition of having attained full comprehension," "the faculty or ability of sub-
suming the particular under the general or of apprehending general relations of
particulars," "the power to make experience intelligible by bringing perceived
particulars under general concepts," "the capacity to formulate and apply to
experience concepts and categories, to judge, and to draw logical inferences."

Michael Wertheimer (1985) offers a characterization of understanding that
supplements the dictionary definitions. He says that "one test of whether learning [with understanding] has really happened is to check whether what has
been learned will generalize to a related task. . . . The transfer of learning is a
central issue for the Gestalt theorist" (p. 23).

Philosophy, from Plato to Kant and Hegel, has sought to distinguish between understanding and reason, the former implying a sudden, holistic grasp
of a situation, the latter a conscious step-by-step tracing of the relations among
its components. If we accept this distinction (and it appears that Gestalt psychologists usually use "understanding" in this narrower sense), then the notion
of suddenness of attainment is added to the notion of grasp. When I wish to
emphasize both elements, I will sometimes use the phrase "intuitive understanding"—which we have seen is very nearly synonymous with "insight."

Learning With Understanding

In Max Wertheimer's writings on problem solving and in other work by
Gestalt psychologists, much emphasis is placed upon the distinction between
learning by rote and learning with understanding. However difficult it may be
to operationalize this distinction, all experienced teachers are very aware of it
and persuaded of its importance. We all know that textbook material can be
(and often is) learned by rote without any understanding of its meaning. We
warn our students against rote learning, even though we are not always able to
tell them how to recognize it or exactly how to avoid it.

George Katona, in his *Organizing and Memorizing* (1940), provided some
experimental bases for distinguishing between rote learning and learning with
understanding. In a series of experiments, he showed that when some explanation is provided as to why a problem solution works, the solution is remembered better and transfers better to similar but non-identical problems than

when the solution is simply learned without explanation. Generalizing this finding, the route to distinguishing between these two forms of learning is to discover exactly what the subject has learned. And the way to discover what the subject has learned is to give him or her a variety of tasks, related in various ways to the learning task, and examine performance on these new tasks. As we have already seen, Wertheimer (1985) also emphasizes transfer as a key criterion of understanding.

As an example, consider the task in algebra of solving a simple linear equation in one unknown: $5x + 4 = 3x + 10$, say. We can test whether a student can recite the steps for solving this equation ("If there is a constant on the left side of the equation, you subtract it from both sides and collect similar terms. If there is a term in x on the right side, you subtract it from both sides and collect terms. If there is a term in x on the left with a coefficient different from unity, divide both sides by that coefficient").

Next, we can test whether the student can actually solve the equation. Some students who can recite the procedure correctly may not be able to carry it out, and some who can carry it out may not be able to recite it. Then, we can ask the student to check whether the right answer was obtained. Or we can ask him or her to state in words how the answer can be checked. Further, we can ask why the procedure followed to obtain the solution is valid—why it led to a value for x that satisfied the original equation.

Finally, we will certainly ask the student to solve a number of other equations that will yield to essentially the same method of solution as the original equation. If the original equation contained only integer coefficients, as in the example, we can test transfer to equations with rational or decimal coefficients. Although this is not an exhaustive list of tasks related to solving an equation (if the subjects were graduate students in mathematics, we could ask them about the underlying axiomatization of arithmetic and algebra), perhaps we would be willing to conclude that a student who can perform all of them correctly actually understands this topic in algebra to some degree of depth.

There is no great difficulty in constructing computer programs that can perform all of these tasks. In fact, Neves (1978) wrote and tested a program that not only could solve linear equations but also could *learn* to solve them by examining worked-out examples. By understanding the successive steps taken in the example to solve the problem, and understanding what contribution each step made toward the solution, Neves' program was able to construct a set of new instructions adequate for solving a wide range of algebra equations. . . .

CONCLUSION

Professor Wertheimer asks where the insight and understanding are in computer models. I have shown exactly where they are in my references to programs that exhibit the behaviors usually labelled "insightful" and "understanding." . . . He argues that a computer program cannot understand or learn, but must be provided in advance with its problem representation. But I have described existing computer programs (some of them more than a decade old) that can generate their own problem representations and can learn from examples.

Whether the mechanisms I have described correspond to the mechanisms Gestaltists have in mind when they use terms like "intuition," "insight," "understanding," "good Gestalt," ... is a question only Gestaltists can answer. But a vast body of empirical evidence now shows that the *phenomena* that have usually been singled out by Gestaltists as evidence for the presence of these processes can, in fact, be simulated by digital computers.

If we put aside our nostalgia for a rich, but largely non-operational, vocabulary, and when we focus instead on the observable processes of thought, we see that we are much further advanced in understanding these processes than Professor Wertheimer allows. We do not need to wait for the "computer of tomorrow or the day after tomorrow" to understand insight. The phenomena of insight are fully visible in the behavior of today's computers when they are programmed appropriately to simulate human thinking.

REFERENCES

Feigenbaum, E. A. (1963). Verbal learning and concept formation. In E. A. Feigenbaum & J. Feldman (Eds.), *Computers and Thought* (Part 2, section 2). New York: McGraw Hill.

Feigenbaum, E. A., & Simon, H. A. (1984). EPAM-like models of recognition and learning. *Cognitive Science*, **8,** 305–336.

Katona, G. (1940). *Organizing and memorizing.* New York: Columbia University Press.

Koehler, W. (1925). *The mentality of apes.* London: Kegan, Paul.

Neves, D. M. (1978). A computer program that learns algebraic procedures. *Proceedings of the 2nd Canadian Conference on Computational Studies of Intelligence.* Toronto.

Newell, A., & Simon, H. A. (1972). *Human problem solving.* Englewood Cliffs, NJ: Prentice Hall.

Rosch, E. (1973). On the internal structure of perceptual and semantic categories. In T. E. Moore (Ed.), *Cognitive development and the acquisition of language,* New York: Academic Press.

Sacerdoti, E. D. (1977). *A structure for plans and behavior.* New York: Elsevier.

Simon, H. A. (1966). Scientific discovery and the psychology of problem solving. In R. Colodny (Ed.), *Mind and cosmos.* Pittsburgh, PA: Pittsburgh University Press.

Simon, H. A., & Gilmartin, K. J. (1973). A simulation of memory for chess positions. In H. A. Simon *Models of thought* (Ch. 6.3). New Haven, CT: Yale University Press.

Wertheimer, M. (1945). *Productive thinking.* New York: Harper.

Wertheimer, M. (1985). A Gestalt perspective on computer simulations of cognitive processes. *Computers in Human Behavior,* **1,** 19–33.

Woodworth, R. S. (1938). *Experimental psychology.* New York: Holt.

How Many Memory Systems Are There?

Endel Tulving was born in 1927, attended the University of Heidelberg in Germany, and completed his B.A. at the University of Toronto in Canada. He earned his Ph.D. at Harvard University in 1957. Aside from five years at Yale University, he has spent his career at the University of Toronto.

Tulving is best known for his empirical and theoretical work in human memory, delving into issues of retrieval cues; subjective organization of memory; encoding specificity; and, perhaps most important, differentiating semantic from episodic memory. His work in long-term memory is collected in his text *Elements of Episodic Memory* (Oxford University Press, 1983). Tulving describes memory as an interaction between the memory trace (a subjective aspect; the encoding of a perceptual event) and the stimulus cue from the environment. This can be conceived as a unification of the past and the present to enable retrieval of a memory.

The following selection comes from Tulving's 1984 Distinguished Scientific Contribution Award address during the annual meeting of the American Psychological Association (APA). It was published in *American Psychologist* in 1985 and is a stimulating introduction to three major memory systems: procedural, episodic, and semantic.

Key Concept: procedural, episodic, and semantic memory systems

*S*olving puzzles in science has much in common with solving puzzles for amusement, but the two differ in important respects. Consider, for instance, the jigsaw puzzle that scientific activity frequently imitates. The everyday version of the puzzle is determinate: It consists of a target picture and jigsaw pieces that, when properly assembled, are guaranteed to match the picture. Scientific puzzles are indeterminate: The number of pieces required to complete a picture is unpredictable; a particular piece may fit many pictures or none; it may fit only one picture, but the picture itself may be unknown; or the hypothetical picture may be imagined, but its component pieces may remain undiscovered.

This article is about a current puzzle in the science of memory. It entails an imaginary picture and a search for pieces that fit it. The picture, or the hypothesis, depicts memory as consisting of a number of systems, each system serving somewhat different purposes and operating according to somewhat different principles. Together they form the marvelous capacity that we call by the single name of *memory*, the capacity that permits organisms to benefit from their past experiences. Such a picture is at variance with conventional wisdom that holds memory to be essentially a single system, the idea that "memory is memory." ...

PRETHEORETICAL CONSIDERATIONS

Why Multiple Memory Systems?

It is possible to identify several a priori reasons why we should break with long tradition (Tulving, 1984a) and entertain thoughts about multiple memory systems. I mention five here.

The first reason in many ways is perhaps the most compelling: No profound generalizations can be made about memory as a whole, but general statements about particular kinds of memory are perfectly possible. Thus, many questionable claims about memory in the literature, claims that give rise to needless and futile arguments, would become noncontroversial if their domain was restricted to parts of memory.

Second, memory, like everything else in our world, has become what it is through a very long evolutionary process. Such a process seldom forms a continuous smooth line, but is characterized by sudden twists, jumps, shifts, and turns. One might expect, therefore, that the brain structures and mechanisms that (together with their behavioral and mental correlates) go to make up memory will also reflect such evolutionary quirks (Oakley, 1983).

The third reason is suggested by comparisons with other psychological functions. Consider, for instance, the interesting phenomenon of *blindsight:* People with damage to the visual cortex are blind in a part of their visual field in that they do not see objects in that part, yet they can accurately point to and discriminate these objects in a forced-choice situation (e.g., Weiskrantz, 1980; Weiskrantz, Warrington, Sanders, & Marshall, 1974). Such facts imply that different brain mechanisms exist for picking up information about the visual environment. Or consider the massive evidence for the existence of two separate cortical pathways involved in vision, one mediating recognition of objects, the other their location in space (e.g., Mishkin, Ungerleider, & Macko, 1983; Ungerleider & Mishkin, 1982). If "seeing" things—something that phenomenal experience tells us is clearly unitary—is subserved by separable neural-cognitive systems, it is possible that learning and remembering, too, appear to be unitary only because of the absence of contrary evidence.

The fourth general reason derives from what I think is an unassailable assumption that most, if not all, of our currently held ideas and theories about mental processes are wrong and that sooner or later in the future they will be replaced with more adequate concepts, concepts that fit nature better (Tulving, 1979). Our task, therefore, should be to hasten the arrival of such a future.

Among other things, we should be willing to contemplate the possibility that the "memory-is-memory" view is wrong and look for a better alternative.

The fifth reason lies in a kind of failure of imagination: It is difficult to think how varieties of learning and memory that appear to be so different on inspection can reflect the workings of one and the same underlying set of structures and processes. It is difficult to imagine, for instance, that perceptual-motor adaptations to distorting lenses and their aftereffects (e.g., Kohler, 1962) are mediated by the same memory system that enables an individual to answer affirmatively when asked whether Abraham Lincoln is dead. It is equally difficult to imagine that the improved ability to make visual acuity judgments, resulting from many sessions of practice without reinforcement or feedback (e.g., Tulving, 1958), has much in common with a person's ability to remember the funeral of a close friend.

If we reflect on the limits of generalizations about memory, think about the twists and turns of evolution, examine possible analogies with other biological and psychological systems, believe that most current ideas we have about the human mind are wrong, and have great difficulty apprehending sameness in different varieties of learning and memory, we might be ready to imagine the possibility that memory consists of a number of interrelated systems. But what exactly do we mean by a *memory system*?

The Concept of System

We could think of a system simply as a set of correlated processes: Processes within a system are more closely related to one another than they are to processes outside the system. Such an abstract and relatively innocuous definition could be used by those students of memory who, for whatever reasons, are reluctant to consider biology when they think about psychology. It would not distort too many claims I will make about memory systems. However, a more concrete conceptualization—one that refers to the correlation of behavior and thought with brain processes and postulates the verifiable, real existence of memory systems (e.g., Tulving, 1984a)—is preferable because it points to stronger tests of such existence.

Memory systems constitute the major subdivisions of the overall organization of the memory complex. They are organized structures of more elementary operating components. An operating component of a system consists of a neural substrate and its behavioral or cognitive correlates. Some components are shared by all systems, others are shared only by some, and still others are unique to individual systems. Different learning and memory situations involve different concatenations of components from one or more systems. The relatedness of such situations in a natural classification scheme of learning and memory varies directly with the extent to which they entail identical components (Tulving, in press).

Although there is no one-to-one correspondence between tasks and systems (e.g., Kinsbourne, 1976; Tulving, in press), they are nonetheless systematically related: A given memory system makes it possible for organisms to perform memory tasks that entail operating components unique to that system. This means, among other things, that intervention with the operation of a system—even if it occurs through a single component of the system—affects all those learning and memory performances that depend on that system. The widespread but systematic effects of a single toxin or microorganisms, for example (Rozin, 1976), reflect the fact that many specific memory performances are subserved by the affected system.

Different systems have emerged at different stages in the evolution of the species, and they emerge at different stages in the development of individual organisms. Thus, they can be ordered from "lower" to "higher" systems (or from less to more advanced), provided that it is clearly understood that such attributions are meaningful only with respect to comparisons between combinations of systems, on the one hand, and individual systems alone, on the other (Schiller, 1952). When a new memory system with specialized novel capabilities evolves or develops, it enables the organism to increase the number, and the sophistication, of its memory functions. In this sense, the combination of the new system and the older ones is "higher," or more advanced than the older ones alone. As an analogy, we can think of an airplane with an autopilot as a more advanced or higher system than one without it, but we would not think of the autopilot alone as a higher system than the airplane.

PROCEDURAL, SEMANTIC, AND EPISODIC MEMORIES

A Ternary [Three-Part] Classification

Let me now switch gears and discuss a classification scheme according to which memory consists of three major systems. I will refer to them as procedural, semantic, and episodic, primarily for the sake of continuity with previous usage, although these are not necessarily the best terms. The three systems constitute what might be called a *monohierarchical* arrangement (cf. Engelien, 1971). The system at the lowest level of the hierarchy, procedural memory, contains semantic memory as its single specialized subsystem, and semantic memory, in turn, contains episodic memory as its single specialized subsystem. In this scheme, each higher system depends on, and is supported by, the lower system or systems, but it possesses unique capabilities not possessed by the lower systems.

Procedural memory enables organisms to retain learned connections between stimuli and responses, including those involving complex stimulus patterns and response chains, and to respond adaptively to the environment. Semantic memory is characterized by the additional capability of internally representing states of the world that are not perceptually present. It permits the organism to construct mental models of the world (Craik, 1943), models that can be manipulated and operated on covertly, independently of any overt behaviour. Episodic memory affords the additional capability of acquisition and retention of knowledge about personally experienced events and their temporal relations in subjective time and the ability to mentally "travel back" in time.

The monohierarchical relation among the systems means that only procedural memory can operate completely independently of the other systems. This necessarily happens when an organism does not possess either of the two more advanced systems, and it may happen with higher organisms when situations do not call for the use of the other systems. Semantic memory can function independently of episodic memory but not independently of procedural memory. And episodic memory depends on both procedural and semantic memory in its workings, although, as already mentioned, it also possesses its own unique capabilities. The monohierarchical arrangement also implies that certain kinds of double dissociations between learning and memory tasks are precluded (Tulving, in press)....

Each system differs in its methods of acquisition, representation, and expression of knowledge. Each also differs in the kind of conscious awareness that characterizes its operations. Let us briefly consider these differences, taking each in turn.

Acquisition in the procedural system requires overt behavioral responding, whereas covert responding—cognitive activity, or "mere observation"—may be sufficient for the other two. We could also say that the characteristic mode of learning is *tuning* in the procedural system, *restructuring* in the semantic system, and *accretion* in the episodic system, along the general lines suggested by Rumelhart and Norman (1978), as long as we keep in mind the implications of the monohierarchical relation among the systems.

The representation of acquired information in the procedural system is prescriptive rather than descriptive: It provides a blueprint for future action without containing information about the past (Dretske, 1982). It may be conceptualized in terms of the "stage-setting" metaphor of Bransford, McCarrell, Franks, and Nitsch (1977), a metaphor akin to Craik's (1983) suggestion that the consequences of learning may take the form of "subtle alterations of the system" (p. 345). It can also be specified in terms of changing probabilities of specific responses to specific stimuli (Mishkin, Malamut, & Bachevalier, 1984). When we are dealing with procedural memory, I agree with Bransford et al. (1977) and with Craik (1983) that it is inappropriate to talk about discrete "memory traces."

Representations in the semantic system, however, are different from those in the procedural system; they describe the world without prescribing any particular action. Representations in both the semantic and episodic systems are isomorphic with the information they represent (Dretske, 1982). Representations in episodic memory additionally carry information about the relations of represented events in the rememberer's personal identity as it exists in subjective time and space (e.g., Claparede, 1911/1951; Tulving, 1983).

Expression of knowledge (Spear, 1984) also differs in the three systems. Only direct expression is possible in procedural memory; overt responding according to a relatively rigid format determined at the time of learning is obligatory (Hirsch, 1974; Mishkin & Petri, 1984). On the other hand, acquired knowledge in both semantic and episodic memory can be expressed flexibly, in different behavioral forms. Such knowledge may manifest itself, under conditions far removed from those of original learning, in behaviors quite dissimilar to the behavior entailed in such learning. Overt behavior corresponding to actualized knowledge is only an optional form of expression. In episodic memory, the typical mode of "expression" of remembering is recollective experience, based on synergistic ecphory. It occurs when the organism is in the "retrieval mode" (Tulving, 1983) or has a particular "attitude" (Bartlett, 1932).

The three memory systems are characterized by different kinds of consciousness (Tulving, 1985). Procedural memory is associated with anoetic (nonknowing) consciousness, semantic memory with noetic (knowing) consciousness, and episodic memory with autonoetic (self-knowing) consciousness.…

Anoetic (nonknowing) consciousness represents one of the end points of the continuum: It refers to an organism's capability to sense and to react to external and internal stimulation, including complex stimulus patterns. Plants and very simple animals possess anoetic consciousness as do computers and learning machines that have knowledge and that can improve it (e.g., Hayes-Roth, Klahr, & Mostow, 1980).

Noetic (knowing) consciousness is an aspect of the semantic memory system. It makes possible introspective awareness of the internal and external world. We can say that the object of noetic consciousness is the organism's knowledge of its world. Noetic consciousness is to such knowledge as the knowledge is to the world. Lower animals, very young children, and people suffering from brain damage may lack episodic memory and autonoetic consciousness but may have fully developed noetic consciousness.

Autonoetic (self-knowing) consciousness is a necessary correlate of episodic memory. It allows an individual to become aware of his or her own identity and existence in subjective time that extends from the past through the present to the future. It provides the familiar phenomenal flavor of recollective experience characterized by "pastness" and subjective veridicality [truthfulness]. It can be impaired or lost without impairment or loss of other forms of consciousness.…

HOW MANY SYSTEMS?

The puzzle of memory systems is not and will not be an easy one to solve. Many difficulties have to be overcome before we can expect more rapid progress. We assume that both memory systems and memory tasks (performances, manifestations, achievements) are composed of, or can be broken down into, more elementary constituents (I have referred to them in this article as operating components), but we do not yet know how to relate one to the other in the world of empirical observations. In the absence of such rules of the game, interpretation of existing evidence from the point of view of multiple memory systems is uncertain and frustrating. The difficulty is compounded by the clever and inventive strategies that learners and remembers frequently use when confronted with laboratory tasks, strategies that drive wedges between what the experimenter thinks he or she is observing and what the observed organism is in fact doing. A familiar bane of learning and memory researchers is the omnipresent possibility that identical behaviors and responses are produced by different underlying processes and mechanisms. Sometimes crucial theoretical distinctions may depend on fine differences in observed patterns of data, requiring discriminations beyond the resolving power of conventional methodology.

How then, with few facts yet available to guide us and many intractable problems to damper our enthusiasm, can we expect to answer the question posed in the title of this article? We follow the same procedure that we use when we tackle other puzzles in our science: We exercise our imagination, trying to see beyond the visible horizons, reaching beyond what is given. As long as our imagination is eventually bridled and disciplined by nature's facts, we need not worry about thinking thoughts that transcend our knowledge.

Because I have discussed three systems in this article, in agreement with a number of other friends of multiple learning and memory systems, the answer "three" to our main question would not be entirely amiss at the present time. But if we try to imagine what might lie beyond our currently limited horizon we may decide that a better answer might be "at least three and probably many more."

Whether this or some other answer will prove to come closest to "carving nature at its joints" is something that only the future will show. What matters for the present is that the question is being asked by an increasing number of students of memory. There is no guarantee, of course, that just by asking the question we will get an answer that is acceptable to science. What is absolutely guaranteed, however, is that we will not get the answer unless we pose the question. We cannot solve puzzles that do not exist.

REFERENCES

Bartlett, F. C. (1932). *Remembering: A study in experimental and social psychology.* Cambridge, MA: University Press.

Bransford, J. D., McCarrell, N. S., Franks, J. J., & Nitsch, K. E. (1977). Toward unexplaining memory. In R. Shaw & J. Bransford (Eds.), *Perceiving, acting and knowing* (pp. 431–466). Hillsdale, NJ: Erlbaum.

Claparede, E. (1911). Reconnaissance et moiite. [Recognition and me-ness]. *Archives de Psychologie, 11,* 79–90. (English translation in D. Rapaport [Ed. and Trans.], *Organization and pathology of thought,* 1951, New York: Columbia University Press.)

Craik, K. (1943). *The nature of explanation.* Cambridge, MA: University Press.

Craik, F. I. M. (1983). On the transfer of information from temporary to permanent memory. *Philosophical Transactions of the Royal Society London, B302,* 341–359.

Dretske, F. (1982). The informational character of representations. *Behavioral and Brain Sciences, 5,* 376–377.

Engelien, G. (1971). *Der Begriff der Klassifikation* [The concept of classification]. Hamburg: Helmut Buske Verlag.

Hayes-Roth, F., Klahr, P., & Mostow, D. J. (1980, May). *Knowledge acquisition, knowledge programming, and knowledge refinement* (Report No. R-2540-NSF). Santa Monica, CA: Rand Corporation.

Hirsch, R. (1974). The hippocampus and contextual retrieval of information from memory: A theory. *Behavioral Biology, 12,* 421–444.

Kohler, I. (1962). Experiments with goggles. *Scientific American, 206,* 62–72.

Mishkin, M., Malamut, B., & Bachevalier, J. (1984). Memories and habits: Two neural systems. In G. Lynch, J. L. McGaugh, & N. M. Weinberger (Eds.), *The neurobiology of learning and memory* (pp. 65–77). New York: Guilford Press.

Mischkin, M., & Petri, H. L. (1984). Memories and habits: Some implications for the analysis of learning and retention. In L. Squire & N. Butters (Eds.), *Neuropsychology of memory* (pp. 287–296). New York: Guilford Press.

Mishkin, M., Ungerleider, L. G., & Macko, K. A. (1983). Object vision and spatial vision: Two cortical pathways. *Trends in Neurosciences, 6,* 414–417.

Oakley, D. A. (1983). The varieties of memory: A phylogenetic approach. In A. Mayes (Ed.), *Memory in animals and humans* (pp. 20–82). Wokingham, England: Van Nostrand Reinhold.

Rozin, P. (1976). The psychobiological approach to human memory. In M. R. Rosenzweig & E. L. Bennett (Eds.), *Neural mechanisms of learning and memory* (pp. 3–46). Cambridge, MA: MIT Press.

Rumelhart, D. E., & Norman, D. A. (1978). Accretion, tuning, and restructuring: Three modes of learning. In J. W. Cotton & R. Klatzky (Eds.), *Semantic factors in cognition* (pp. 37–53). Hillsdale, NJ: Erlbaum.

Schiller, F. (1952). Consciousness reconsidered. *Archives of Neurology and Psychiatry, 67,* 199–227.

Spear, N. E. (1984). Behaviors that indicate memory: Levels of expression. *Canadian Journal of Psychology, 38,* 348–367.

Tulving, E. (1958). The relation of visual acuity to convergence and accommodation. *Journal of Experimental Psychology, 55,* 530–534.

Tulving, E. (1979). Memory research: What kind of progress? In L.-G. Nilsson (Ed.), *Perspectives on memory research: Essays in honor of Uppsala University's 500th anniversary* (pp. 19–34). Hillsdale, NJ: Erlbaum.

Tulving, E. (1983). *Elements of episodic memory.* New York: Oxford University Press.

Tulving, E. (1984a). Multiple learning and memory systems. In K. M. J. Lagerspetz & P. Niemi (Eds.), *Psychology in the 1990's* (pp. 163–184). North Holland: Elsevier Science Publishers B. V.

Tulving, E. (1985). Memory and consciousness. *Canadian Psychology, 26,* 1–12.

Tulving, E. (in press). On the classification problem in learning and memory. In L.-G. Nilsson & T. Archer (Eds.), *Perspectives on learning and memory.* Hillsdale, NJ: Erlbaum, in press.

Ungerleider, L. G., & Mishkin, M. (1982). Two cortical visual systems. In D. J. Ingle, M. A. Goodale, & R. J. W. Mansfield (Eds.), *Analysis of visual behavior* (pp. 549–586). Cambridge, MA: MIT Press.

Weiskrantz, L. (1980). Varieties of residual experience. *Quarterly Journal of Experimental Psychology, 32,* 365–386.

Weiskrantz, L., Warrington, E. K., Sanders, M. D., & Marshall, J. (1974). Visual capacity in the hemianopic field following a restricted occipital ablation. *Brain, 97,* 709–728.

PART FIVE

Methods and Evaluation of Teaching

Chapter 9 Methods and Models of Teaching 257

Chapter 10 Evaluation, Measurement, and Testing 289

On the Internet . . .

Sites appropriate to Part Five

The Institute for the Academic Advancement of Youth is a comprehensive, university-based initiative that promotes the academic ability of children and youth throughout the world. Formally established at the Johns Hopkins University in 1979, it is a leading force in educational reform and improvement in the United States and abroad. Johns Hopkins is where Robert E. Slavin works, and there are many references to cooperative learning on these pages.

```
http://www.jhu.edu/~gifted/
```

This cooperative learning and conflict resolution site was developed by Drs. Roger and David Johnson, codirectors of the Cooperative Learning Center at the University of Minnesota.

```
http://www.newhorizons.org/
   trm_johnson.html
```

The Center of Learning, Assessment, and School Structure (CLASS) helps educators to build schools around the student's needs as a learner. The center provides consultations, in-service workshops, professional development seminars, and national conferences to improve the ways that educational goals and means are organized and assessed. It also provides a variety of printed materials, publications, and videotapes on student assessment and curriculum design. CLASS is headed by Grant Wiggins and is based in Pennington, New Jersey.

```
http://www.classnj.org
```

CHAPTER 9 Methods and Models of Teaching

9.1 NEL NODDINGS

A Morally Defensible Mission for Schools in the Twenty-First Century

Nel Noddings earned her B.A. at Montclair State College and her M.A. at Rutgers University, both in New Jersey, and she received her Ph.D. in educational philosophy and theory from Stanford University in California. She taught from 1949 to 1952 at the Woodbury Grade School in New Jersey. Noddings's interest in mathematics led her from the elementary school to the high school, were she taught math and was the assistant principal at the Matawan Regional High School in New Jersey from 1958 to 1969. After earning her doctorate in 1973, she worked for one year as director of pre-collegiate education at the University of Chicago, then she took her current post as a professor at Stanford in 1977. Her interests in educational philosophy focus upon moral education, feminist ethics, and mathematics education.

Noddings's many awards include twice winning the Excellence in Teaching Award at Stanford; the Medal for Distinguished Service from Teachers College, Columbia University; and the Anne Roe Award from the Harvard Graduate School of Education. She has published over 100 articles as well as the texts *Philosophy of Education* (Westview Press, 1995), *Educating for Intelligent Belief or Unbelief* (Teachers College Press, 1993), *The Challenge to Care in Schools: An Alernative Approach to Education* (Teachers College Press, 1992), *Women and Evil* (University of California Press, 1989), *Awakening the Inner Eye: Intuition in Education* (Teachers College, Columbia University, 1984), and *Caring: A Feminine Approach to Ethics and Moral Education* (University of California Press, 1984). She has also coedited *Stories Lives Tell: Narrative and Dialogue in Education* (Teachers College Press, 1991) and *Constructivist Views on the Teaching and Learning of Mathematics* (National Council of Teachers of Mathematics, 1990).

Although Noddings is a philosopher of education, her views have a powerful influence on educational psychology. Her approach to caring embraces "empathy," one of the most central psychological abilities, and the nurturing of the individual psyche. In the following selection, taken from "A Morally Defensible Mission for Schools in the Twenty-First Century," *Phi Delta Kappan* (January 1995), Noddings emphasizes creating a psychological climate in the classroom and in the school, in which the students explicitly learn to care for self, family and friends, distant others, animals, plants, the physical-cultural world, and ideas.

Key Concept: teaching as caring

Social changes in the years since World War II have been enormous. We have seen changes in work patterns, in residential stability, in styles of housing, in sexual habits, in dress, in manners, in language, in music, in entertainment, and—perhaps most important of all—in family arrangements. While schools have responded, albeit sluggishly, to technological changes with various additions to the curriculum and narrowly prescribed methods of instruction, they have largely ignored massive social changes. When they *have* responded, they have done so in piecemeal fashion, addressing isolated bits of the problem. Thus, recognizing that some children come to school hungry, schools provide meals for poor children. Alarmed by the increase in teenage pregnancies and sexually transmitted diseases, schools provide sex education. Many more examples could be offered, but no one of these nor any collection of them adequately meets the educational needs of today's students.

What do we want for our children? What do they need from education, and what does our society need? The popular response today is that students need more academic training, that the country needs more people with greater mathematical and scientific competence, that a more adequate academic preparation will save people from poverty, crime, and other evils of current society. Most of these claims are either false or, at best, only partly true. For example, we do *not* need more physicists and mathematicians; many people already highly trained in these fields are unable to find work. The vast majority of adults do *not* use algebra in their work, and forcing all students to study it is a simplistic response to the real issues of equity and mathematical literacy. Just as clearly, more education will not save people from poverty unless a sufficient number of unfortunate people either reject that education or are squeezed out of it. Poverty is a *social* problem. No person who does honest, useful work—regardless of his or her educational attainments—should live in poverty. A society that allows this to happen is not an educational failure; it is a moral failure.

Our society does not need to make its children first in the world in mathematics and science. It needs to care for its children—to reduce violence, to respect honest work of every kind, to reward excellence at every level, to ensure a place for every child and emerging adult in the economic and social world, to produce people who can care competently for their own families and contribute effectively to their communities. In direct opposition to the current emphasis on academic standards, a national curriculum, and national assessment, I have argued that our main educational aim should be to encourage the growth of competent, caring, loving, and lovable people.[1]

At the present time, it is obvious that our main educational purpose is not the moral one of producing caring people but a relentless—and, as it turns out, hapless—drive for academic adequacy. I am certainly not going to argue for academic *in*adequacy, but I will try to persuade readers that a reordering of priorities is essential. All children must learn to care for other human beings, and all must find an ultimate concern in some center of care: care for self, for intimate others, for associates and acquaintances, for distant others, for animals, for plants and the physical environment, for objects and instruments, and for ideas. Within each of these centers, we can find many themes on which to build courses, topical seminars, projects, reading lists, and dialogue.

Today the curriculum is organized almost entirely around the last center, ideas, but it is so poorly put together that important ideas are often swamped by facts and skills. Even those students who might find a genuine center of care in some arena of ideas—say mathematics or literature—are sorely disappointed. In trying to teach everyone what we once taught only a few, we have wound up teaching everyone inadequately. Further, we have not bothered to ask whether the traditional education so highly treasured was ever the best education for anyone.

I have argued that liberal education (defined as a set of traditional disciplines) is an outmoded and dangerous model of education for today's young. The popular slogan today is "All children can learn!" To insist, however, that all children should get the same dose of academic English, social studies, science, and mathematics invites an important question unaddressed by the sloganeers: Why should children learn what we insist they "can" learn? Is this the material people really need to live intelligently, morally, and happily? Or are arguments for traditional liberal education badly mistaken? Worse, are they perhaps mere political maneuverings?

My argument against liberal education is not a complaint against literature, history, physical science, mathematics, or any other subject. It is an argument, first, against an ideology of control that forces all students to study a particular, narrowly prescribed curriculum devoid of content they might truly care about. Second, it is an argument in favor of greater respect for a wonderful range of human capacities now largely ignored in schools. Third, it is an argument against the persistent undervaluing of skills, attitudes, and capacities traditionally associated with women. This last point is an argument that has been eloquently made by Jane Roland Martin. . . .

What do we want for our children? Most of us hope that our children will find someone to love, find useful work they enjoy or at least do not hate, establish a family, and maintain bonds with friends and relatives. These hopes are part of our interest in shaping an acceptable child.[2] What kind of mates, parents, friends, and neighbors will our children be?

I would hope that all our children—both girls and boys—would be prepared to do the work of attentive love. This work must be done in every family situation, whether the family is conventionally or unconventionally constituted. Both men and women, if they choose to be parents, should participate in the joys and responsibilities of direct parenting, of acting as psychological parent. Too often, women have complained about bearing this responsibility almost entirely. When men volunteer to help with child care or help with housework, the very language suggests that the tasks are women's responsibilities. Men "help" in tasks they do not perceive as their own. That has to change.

In education today, there is great concern about women's participation in mathematics and science. Some researchers even refer to something called the "problem of women and mathematics." Women's lack of success or low rate of participation in fields long dominated by men is seen as a problem to be treated by educational means. But researchers do not seem to see a problem in men's low rate of participation in nursing, elementary school teaching, or full-time parenting. Our society values activities traditionally associated with men above those traditionally associated with women.[3]

The new education I envision puts a very high valuation on the traditional occupations of women. Care for children, the aged, and the ill must be shared by all capable adults, not just women, and everyone should understand that these activities bring special rewards as well as burdens. Work with children can be especially rewarding and provides an opportunity to enjoy childhood vicariously. For example, I have often wondered why high school students are not more often invited to revisit the literature of childhood in their high school English classes. A careful study of fairy tales, augmented by essays on their psychology, might be more exciting and more generally useful than, for example, the study of *Hamlet*. When we consider the natural interest we have in ourselves—past, present, and future—it is clear that literature that allows us to look forward and backward is wonderful. Further, the study of fairy tales would provide opportunities for lessons in geography, history, art, and music.

Our children should learn something about life cycles and stages. When I was in high school, my Latin class read Cicero's essay "On Old Age." With all his talk of wisdom—of milk, honey, wine, and cheese; of meditating in the afternoon breeze—I was convinced that old age had its own romance. Looking at the present condition of many elderly people, I see more than enough horror to balance whatever romance there may be. But studies of early childhood, adulthood, and old age (with or without Latin) seem central to education for real life. Further, active association with people of all ages should be encouraged. Again, one can see connections with standard subjects—statistical studies in math; the history and sociology of welfare, medical care, and family life; geographical and cultural differences. We see, also, that the need for such studies has increased as a result of the social changes discussed earlier. Home life does not provide the experience in these areas that it once did.

Relations with intimate others are the beginning and one of the significant ends of moral life. If we regard our relations with intimate others as central in moral life, then we must provide all our children with practice in caring. Children can work together formally and informally on a host of school projects, and, as they get older, they can help younger children, contribute to the care of buildings and grounds, and eventually—under careful supervision—do volunteer work in the community. Looking at Howard Gardner's multiple intelligences, we see that children can contribute useful service in a wide variety of ways; some have artistic talents, some interpersonal gifts, some athletic or kinesthetic abilities, some spiritual gifts.[4]

A moral policy, a defensible mission, for education recognizes a multiplicity of human capacities and interests. Instead of preparing everyone for college in the name of democracy and equality, schools should instill in students a respect for all forms of honest work done well.[5] Preparation for the world of work, for parenting, and for civic responsibility is essential for all students. All of us must work, but few of us do the sort of work implied by preparation in algebra and geometry. Almost all of us enter into intimate relationships, but schools largely ignore the centrality of such interests in our lives. And although most of us become parents, evidence suggests that we are not very good at parenting—and again the schools largely ignore this huge human task.

When I suggest that a morally defensible mission for education necessarily focuses on matters of human caring, people sometimes agree but fear the loss of an intellectual mission for the schools. There are at least two powerful responses to this fear. First, anyone who supposes that the current drive for uniformity in standards, curriculum, and assessment represents an intellectual agenda needs to reflect on the matter. Indeed, many thoughtful educators insist that such moves are truly anti-intellectual, discouraging critical thinking, creativity, and novelty. Second, and more important from the perspective adopted here, a curriculum centered on themes of care can be as richly intellectual as we and our students want to make it. Those of us advocating genuine reform —indeed, transformation—will surely be accused of anti-intellectualism, just as John Dewey was in the middle of this century. But the accusation is false, and we should have the courage to face it down.

Examples of themes that are especially important to young people are love and friendship. Both can be studied in intellectual depth, but the crucial emphasis should be on the relevance of the subjects to self-understanding and growth. Friends are especially important to teenagers, and they need guidance in making and maintaining friendships.

Aristotle wrote eloquently on friendship, and he assessed it as central in moral life. In the *Nicomachean Ethics*, Aristotle wrote that the main criterion of friendship is that a friend wishes a friend well for his or her own sake. When we befriend others, we want good things for them not because those things may enhance our welfare but because they are good for our friends. Aristotle organized friendships into various categories: those motivated by common business or political purposes, those maintained by common recreational interests, and those created by mutual admiration of the other's virtue. The last was, for Aristotle, the highest form of friendship and, of course, the one most likely to endure.

How do friendships occur? What draws people together? Here students should have opportunities to see how far Aristotle's description will carry them. They should hear about Damon and Pythias, of course. But they should also examine some incongruous friendships: Huck and Jim in Mark Twain's *Adventures of Huckleberry Finn*; Miss Celie and Shug in Alice Walker's *Color Purple*; Lenny and George in John Steinbeck's *Of Mice and Men*; Jane and Maudie in Doris Lessing's *Diaries of Jane Somers*. What do each of these characters give to the friendship? Can friendship be part of a personal quest for fulfillment? When does a personal objective go too far and negate Aristotle's basic criterion?

Another issue to be considered is, When should moral principles outweigh the demands of friendship? The question is often cast this way, even though many of us find the wording misleading. What the questioner wants us to consider is whether we should protect friends who have done something morally wrong. A few years ago, there was a terrifying local example of this problem when a teenage boy killed a girl and bragged about it to his friends. His friends, in what they interpreted as an act of loyalty, did not even report the murder.

From the perspective of caring, there is no inherent conflict between moral requirements and friendship, because, as Aristotle teaches us, we have a primary obligation to promote our friends' moral growth. But lots of concrete conflicts can arise when we have to consider exactly what to do. Instead of juggling principles as we might when we say, "Friendship is more important than a little theft" or "Murder is more important than friendship," we begin by asking ourselves whether our friends have committed caring acts. If they have not, something has to be done. In the case of something as horrible as murder, the act must be reported. But true friends would also go beyond initial judgment and action to ask how they might follow through with appropriate help for the murderer. When we adopt caring as an ethical approach, our moral work has just begun where other approaches end. Caring requires staying-with, or what [Sara] Ruddick has called "holding." We do not let our friends fall if we can help it, and if they do, we hold on and pull them back up.

Gender differences in friendship patterns should also be discussed. It may be harder for males to reject relationships in which they are pushed to do socially unacceptable acts, because those acts are often used as tests of manhood. Females, by contrast, find it more difficult to separate themselves from abusive relationships. In both cases, young people have to learn not only to take appropriate responsibility for the moral growth of others but also to insist that others accept responsibility for their own behavior. It is often a fine line, and—since there are no formulas to assist us—we remain vulnerable in all our moral relations.

A transformation of the sort envisioned here requires organizational and structural changes to support the changes in curriculum and instruction. It requires a move away from the ideology of control, from the mistaken notion that iron-handed accountability will ensure the outcomes we identify as desirable. It won't just happen. We should have learned by now that both children and adults can accomplish wonderful things in an atmosphere of love and trust and that they will (if they are healthy) resist—sometimes to their own detriment— in environments of coercion.

Because I would like to present for discussion my basic recommendations for both structural and curricular changes, I will risk setting them forth here in a skeletal form. Of course, I cannot describe and defend the recommendations adequately in so brief a space, but here is a summary.

The traditional organization of schooling is intellectually and morally inadequate for contemporary society. We live in an age troubled by social problems that force us to reconsider what we do in schools. Too many of us think that we can improve education by merely designing a better curriculum, finding and implementing a better form of instruction, or instituting a better form of classroom management. These things won't work.

We need to give up the notion of a *single* ideal of the educated person and replace it with a multiplicity of models designed to accommodate the multiple capacities and interests of students. We need to recognize multiple identities. For example, an 11th-grader may be a black, a woman, a teenager, a Smith, an American, a New Yorker, a Methodist, a person who loves math, and so on. As she exercises these identities, she may use different languages, adopt different postures, and relate differently to those around her. But whoever she is at a given moment, whatever she is engaged in, she needs—as we all do—to be cared for. Her need for care may require formal respect, informal interaction, expert advice, just a flicker of recognition, or sustained affection. To give the care she needs requires a set of capacities in each of us to which schools give too little attention.

I have argued that education should be organized around themes of care rather than around the traditional disciplines. All students should be engaged in a general education that guides them in caring for self, intimate others, global others, plants, animals, the environment, objects and instruments, and ideas. Moral life so defined should be frankly embraced as the main goal of education. Such an aim does not work against intellectual development or academic achievement. Rather, it supplies a firm foundation for both.

How can we begin? Here is what I think we must do:

1. Be clear and unapologetic about our goal.   The main aim of education should be to produce competent, caring, loving, and lovable people.

2. Take care of affiliative needs.   We must keep students and teachers together (by mutual consent) for several years, and we must keep students together when possible. We should also strive to keep students in the same building for considerable periods of time and help students to think of the school as theirs. Finally, we must legitimize time spent in building relations of care and trust.

3. Relax the impulse to control.   We need to give teachers and students more responsibility to exercise judgment. At the same time we must get rid of competitive grading and reduce the amount of testing that we do. Those well-designed tests that remain should be used to assess whether people can competently handle the tasks they want to undertake. We also need to encourage teachers to explore material with students. We don't have to know everything to teach well.

In short, we need to define expertise more broadly and instrumentally. For example, a biology teacher should be able to teach whatever mathematics is involved in biology, while a social studies teacher should be able to teach whatever mathematics is required in that subject. We must encourage self-evaluation and teach students how to do it competently, and we must also involve students in governing their own classrooms and schools. Making such changes means that we accept the challenge to care by teaching well the things that students want to learn.

4. Get rid of program hierarchies. This will take time, but we must begin now to provide excellent programs for *all* our children. Programs for the noncollege-bound should be just as rich, desirable, and rigorous as those for the college-bound.

We must abandon uniform requirements for college entrance. What a student wants to do or to study should guide what is required by way of preparation. Here we should not worry greatly about students who "change their minds." Right now we are afraid that, if students prepare for something particular, they may change their minds and all that preparation will be wasted. Thus we busily prepare them uniformly for nothing. We forget that, when people have a goal in mind, they learn well and that, even if they change their minds, they may have acquired the skills and habits of mind they will need for further learning. The one essential point is that we give all students what all students need—genuine opportunities to explore the questions central to human life.

5. Give at least part of every day to themes of care. We should discuss existential questions—including spiritual matters—freely. Moreover, we need to help students learn to treat each other ethically by giving them practice in caring. We must help students understand how groups and individuals create rivals and enemies and help them learn how to "be on both sides." We should encourage a way of caring for animals, plants, and the environment that is consistent with caring for humans, and we should also encourage caring for the human-made world. Students need to feel at home in technical, natural, and cultural worlds, and educators must cultivate wonder and appreciation for the human-made world.

6. Teach students that caring in every domain implies competence. When we care, we accept the responsibility to work continuously on our competence so that the recipient of our care—person, animal, object, or idea—is enhanced. There is nothing mushy about caring. It is the strong, resilient backbone of human life.

NOTES

1. Nel Noddings, *The Challenge to Care in Schools* (New York: Teachers College Press, 1992).

2. Sara Ruddick, "Maternal Thinking," *Feminist Studies,* vol. 6, 1980, pp. 342-67.

3. For an extended and powerful argument on this issue, see Jane Roland Martin, *Reclaiming a Conversation* (New Haven, Conn.: Yale University Press, 1985).

4. Howard Gardner, *Frames of Mind* (New York: Basic Books, 1983).

5. John Gardner, *Excellence: Can We Be Equal and Excellent Too?* (New York: Harper, 1961).

Synthesis of Research on Cooperative Learning

Robert E. Slavin earned his B.A. in psychology in 1972 from Reed College in Portland, Oregon. In 1975 he earned his Ph.D. in social relations from Johns Hopkins University in Baltimore, Maryland. He is now a professor at Johns Hopkins University and codirector of the Center for Research on the Education of Students Placed at Risk. Slavin is a leading researcher in cooperative education, and his studies in this field earned him the American Educational Research Association's (AERA) Raymond B. Cattell Early Career Award for Programmatic and Research in 1986 and the Palmer O. Johnson Award for the best article in an AERA journal in 1988.

Slavin has authored and coauthored more than 180 articles and many books, including *Cooperative Learning: Theory, Research, and Practice*, 2d ed. (Allyn & Bacon, 1995), *Educational Psychology: Theory into Practice*, 4th ed. (Allyn & Bacon, 1994), *School and Classroom Organization* (Lawrence Erlbaum, 1989), *Effective Programs for Students at Risk* (Allyn & Bacon, 1989), *Preventing Early School Failure* (Allyn & Bacon, 1994), *Every Child, Every School: Success for All* (Corwin Press, 1996), and *Show Me the Evidence: Proven and Promising Programs for America's Schools* (Corwin Press, 1998).

Slavin's careful research indicates that cooperative learning improves the achievement of not only low- and medium-ability students but also high-ability students. Additionally, and perhaps more important, cooperative learning techniques have been shown to lower racial prejudice and improve the acceptance of "special education" students in the regular classroom. The following selection is an excellent summary of the research on cooperative education; it has been excerpted from "Synthesis of Research on Cooperative Learning," *Educational Leadership* (February 1991).

Key Concept: cooperative learning

*T*here was once a time when it was taken for granted that a quiet class was a learning class, when principals walked down the hall expecting to be able to hear a pin drop. Today, however, many schools are using programs that foster the hum of voices in classrooms. These programs, called *cooperative learning*, encourage students to discuss, debate, disagree, and ultimately to teach one another.

Cooperative learning has been suggested as the solution for an astonishing array of educational problems: it is often cited as a means of emphasizing thinking skills and increasing higher-order learning, as an alternative to ability grouping, remediation, or special education; as a means of improving race relations and acceptance of mainstreamed students; and as a way to prepare students for an increasingly collaborative work force. How many of these claims are justified? What effects do the various cooperative learning methods have on student achievement and other outcomes? Which forms of cooperative learning are most effective, and what components must be in place for cooperative learning to work?

To answer these questions, I've synthesized in this article the findings of studies of cooperative learning in elementary and secondary schools that have compared cooperative learning to traditionally taught control groups studying the same objectives over a period of at least four weeks (and up to a full school year or more). Here I present a brief summary of the effects of cooperative learning on achievement and noncognitive outcomes; for a more extensive review, see *Cooperative Learning: Theory, Research, and Practice* (Slavin 1990).

COOPERATIVE LEARNING METHODS

There are many quite different forms of cooperative learning, but all of them involve having students work in small groups or teams to help one another learn academic material. Cooperative learning usually supplements the teacher's instruction by giving students an opportunity to discuss information or practice skills originally presented by the teacher; sometimes cooperative methods require students to find or discover information on their own. Cooperative learning has been used—and investigated—in every imaginable subject in grades 2–12, and is increasingly used in college.

Small-scale laboratory research on cooperation dates back to the 1920s (see Deutsch 1949; Slavin 1977a); research on specific applications of cooperative learning to the classroom began in the early 1970s. At that time, four research groups, one in Israel and three in the U.S., began independently to develop and study cooperative learning methods in classroom settings.

Now researchers all over the world are studying practical applications of cooperative learning principles, and many cooperative learning methods have been evaluated in one or more experimental/control comparisons. The best evaluated of the cooperative models are described below (adapted from Slavin 1990). These include four Student Team Learning variations, Jigsaw, Learning Together, and Group Investigation.

Highlights of Research on Cooperative Learning

In cooperative learning, students work in small groups to help one another master academic material. There are many quite different forms of cooperative learning, and the effectiveness of cooperative learning (particularly for achievement outcomes) depends on the particular approach used.

- For enhancing student achievement, the most successful approaches have incorporated two key elements: group goals and individual accountability. That is, groups are rewarded based on the individual learning of all group members.
- When group goals and individual accountability are used, achievement effects of cooperative learning are consistently positive; 37 of 44 experimental/control comparisons of at least four weeks' duration have found significantly positive effects, and none have favored traditional methods.
- Achievement effects of cooperative learning have been found to about the same degree at all grade levels (2–12), in all major subjects, and in urban, rural, and suburban schools. Effects are equally positive for high, average, and low achievers.
- Positive effects of cooperative learning have been consistently found on such diverse outcomes as self-esteem, intergroup relations, acceptance of academically handicapped students, attitudes toward school, and ability to work cooperatively.

STUDENT TEAM LEARNING

Student Team Learning (STL) techniques were developed and researched at Johns Hopkins University. More than half of all experimental studies of practical cooperative learning methods involve STL methods.

All cooperative learning methods share the idea that students work together to learn and are responsible for one another's learning as well as their own. STL methods, in addition to this idea, emphasize the use of team goals and team success, which can only be achieved if all members of the team learn the objectives being taught. That is, in Student Team Learning the students' tasks are not to *do* something as a team but to *learn* something as a team.

Three concepts are central to all Student Team Learning methods: *team rewards, individual accountability,* and *equal opportunities for success.* Using STL techniques, teams earn certificates or other team rewards if they achieve above a designated criterion. The teams are not in competition to earn scarce rewards; all (or none) of the teams may achieve the criterion in a given week. *Individual accountability* means that the team's success depends on the individual learning of all team members. This focuses the activity of the team members on explaining concepts to one another and making sure that everyone on the team is ready for a quiz or other assessment that they will take without teammate help. *Equal opportunities for success* means that students contribute to their teams by improving over their own past performances. This ensures that high, average, and low achievers are equally challenged to do their best and that the contributions of all team members will be valued.

The findings of these experimental studies (summarized in this section) indicate that team rewards and individual accountability are essential elements for producing basic skills achievement (Slavin 1983a, 1983b, 1990). It is not enough to simply tell students to work together. They must have a reason to take one another's achievement seriously. Further, if students are rewarded for doing better than they have in the past, they will be more motivated to achieve than if they are rewarded based on their performance in comparison to others, because rewards for improvement make success neither too difficult nor too easy for students to achieve (Slavin 1980).

Four principal Student Team Learning methods have been extensively developed and researched. Two are general cooperative learning methods adaptable to most subjects and grade levels: Student Teams-Achievement Divisions (STAD) and Teams-Games-Tournament (TGT). The remaining two are comprehensive curriculums designed for use in particular subjects at particular grade levels: Team Assisted Individualization (TAI) for mathematics in grades 3–6 and Cooperative Integrated Reading and Composition (CIRC) for reading and writing instruction in grades 3–5.

Student Teams-Achievement Divisions (STAD)

In STAD (Slavin 1978, 1986), students are assigned to four-member learning teams mixed in performance level, sex, and ethnicity. The teacher presents a lesson, and then students work within their teams to make sure that all team members have mastered the lesson. Finally, all students take individual quizzes on the material, at which time they may *not* help one another.

Students' quiz scores are compared to their own past averages, and points are awarded based on the degree to which students can meet or exceed their own earlier performances. These points are then summed to form team scores, and teams that meet certain criteria earn certificates or other rewards. The whole cycle of activities, from teacher presentation to team practice to quiz, usually takes three to five class periods.

STAD has been used in a wide variety of subjects, from mathematics to language arts and social studies. It has been used from grade 2 through college. STAD is most appropriate for teaching well-defined objectives with single right answers, such as mathematical computations and applications, language usage and mechanics, geography and map skills, and science facts and concepts.

Teams-Games-Tournament (TGT)

Teams-Games-Tournament (DeVries and Slavin 1978; Slavin 1986) was the first of the Johns Hopkins cooperative learning methods. It uses the same teacher presentations and teamwork as in STAD, but replaces the quizzes with weekly tournaments. In these, students compete with members of other teams to contribute points to their team scores. Students compete at three-person "tournament tables" against others with similar past records in mathematics. A "bumping" procedure changes table assignments to keep the competition fair. The winner at each tournament table brings the same number of points to his or her team, regardless of which table it is; this means that low achievers (competing with other low achievers) and high achievers (competing with other higher achievers) have equal opportunities for success. As in STAD, high-performing teams earn certificates or other forms of team rewards. TGT is appropriate for the same types of objectives as STAD.

Team Assisted Individualization (TAI)

Team Assisted Individualization (TAI; Slavin et al. 1986) shares with STAD and TGT the use of four-member mixed ability learning teams and certificates for high-performing teams. But where STAD and TGT use a single pace of instruction for the class, TAI combines cooperative learning with individualized instruction. Also, where STAD and TGT apply to most subjects and grade levels, TAI is specifically designed to teach mathematics to students in grades 3–6 (or older students not ready for a full algebra course).

In TAI, students enter an individualized sequence according to a placement test and then proceed at their own rates. In general, team members work on different units. Teammates check each others' work against answer sheets and help one another with any problems. Final unit tests are taken without teammate help and are scored by student monitors. Each week, teachers total the number of units completed by all team members and give certificates or other team rewards to teams that exceed a criterion score based on the number of final tests passed, with extra points for perfect papers and completed homework.

Because students take responsibility for checking each others' work and managing the flow of materials, the teacher can spend most of the class time presenting lessons to small groups of students drawn from the various teams who are working at the same point in the mathematics sequence. For example, the teacher might call up a decimals group, present a lesson, and then send the students back to their teams to work on problems. Then the teacher might call the fractions group, and so on.

Cooperative Integrated Reading and Composition (CIRC)

The newest of the Student Team Learning methods is a comprehensive program for teaching reading and writing in the upper elementary grades called Cooperative Integrated Reading and Composition (CIRC) (Stevens et al. 1987). In CIRC, teachers use basal or literature-based readers and reading groups, much as in traditional reading programs. However, all students are assigned to teams composed of two pairs from two different reading groups. For example, a team might have two "Bluebirds" and two "Redbirds." While the teacher is working with one reading group, the paired students in the other groups are working on a series of cognitively engaging activities, including reading to one another, making predictions about how narrative stories will come out, summarizing stories to one another, writing responses to stories, and practicing spelling, decoding, and vocabulary. If the reading class is not divided into homogeneous reading groups, all students in the teams work with one another. Students work as a total team to master "main idea" and other comprehension skills. During language arts periods, students engage in writing drafts, revising and editing one another's work, and preparing for "publication" of team books.

In most CIRC activities, students follow a sequence of teacher instruction, team practice, team pre-assessments, and quizzes. That is, students do not take the quiz until their teammates have determined that they are ready. Certificates are given to teams based on the average performance of all team members on all reading and writing activities.

OTHER COOPERATIVE LEARNING METHODS

Jigsaw

Jigsaw was originally designed by Elliot Aronson and his colleagues (1978). In Aronson's Jigsaw method, students are assigned to six-member teams to work on academic material that has been broken down into sections. For example, a biography might be divided into early life, first accomplishments, major setbacks, later life, and impact on history. Each team member reads his or her section. Next, members of different teams who have studied the same sections meet in "expert groups" to discuss their sections. Then the students return to their teams and take turns teaching their teammates about their sections. Since the only way students can learn sections other than their own is to listen carefully to their teammates, they are motivated to support and show interest in one another's work.

Slavin (1986) developed a modification of Jigsaw at Johns Hopkins University and then incorporated it in the Student Team Learning program. In this method, called Jigsaw II, students work in four- or five-member teams as in TGT and STAD. Instead of each student's being assigned a particular section of text, all students read a common narrative, such as a book chapter, a short story, or a biography. However, each student receives a topic (such as "climate" in a unit on France) on which to become an expert. Students with the same topics meet in expert groups to discuss them, after which they return to their teams to teach what they have learned to their teammates. Then students take individual quizzes, which result in team scores based on the improvement score system of STAD. Teams that meet preset standards earn certificates. Jigsaw is primarily used in social studies and other subjects where learning from text is important.

David Johnson and Roger Johnson at the University of Minnesota developed the Learning Together models of cooperative learning (Johnson and Johnson 1987). The methods they have researched involve students working on assignment sheets in four- or five-member heterogeneous groups. The groups hand in a single sheet and receive praise and rewards based on the group product. Their methods emphasize team-building activities before students begin working together and regular discussions within groups about how well they are working together.

Group Investigation

Group Investigation, developed by Shlomo Sharan and Yael Sharan at the University of Tel-Aviv, is a general classroom organization plan in which students work in small groups using cooperative inquiry, group discussion, and cooperative planning and projects (Sharan and Sharan 1976). In this method, students form their own two- to six-member groups. After choosing subtopics from a unit being studied by the entire class, the groups further break their subtopics into individual tasks and carry out the activities necessary to prepare group reports. Each group then makes a presentation or display to communicate its findings to the the entire class.

RESEARCH ON COOPERATIVE LEARNING

Cooperative learning methods are among the most extensively evaluated alternatives to traditional instruction in use today. Outcome evaluations include:

- academic achievement,
- intergroup relations,
- mainstreaming,
- self-esteem,
- others.

Academic Achievement

More than 70 high-quality studies have evaluated various cooperative learning methods over periods of at least four weeks in regular elementary and secondary schools; 67 of these have measured effects on student achievement (see Slavin 1990). All these studies compared the effects of cooperative learning to those of traditionally taught control groups on measures of the same objectives pursued in all classes. Teachers and classes were either randomly assigned to cooperative or control conditions or matched on pretest achievement level and other factors.

Overall, of 67 studies of the achievement effects of cooperative learning, 41 (61 percent) found significantly greater achievement in cooperative than in control classes. Twenty-five (37 percent) found no differences, and in only one study did the control group outperform the experimental group. However, the effects of cooperative learning vary considerably according to the particular methods used. As noted earlier, two elements must be present if cooperative learning is to be effective: *group goals* and *individual accountability* (Slavin 1983a, 1983b, 1990). That is, groups must be working to achieve some goal or to earn rewards or recognition, and the success of the group must depend on the individual learning of every group member.

In studies of methods such as STAD, TGT, TAI, and CIRC, effects on achievement have been consistently positive; 37 out of 44 such studies (84 percent) found significant positive achievement effects. In contrast, only 4 of 23 studies (17 percent) lacking group goals and individual accountability found positive effects on student achievement. Two of these positive effects were found in studies of Group Investigation in Israel (Sharan et al. 1984; Sharan and Shachar 1988). In Group Investigation, students in each group are responsible for one unique part of the group's overall task, ensuring individual accountability. Then the group's overall performance is evaluated. Even though there are no specific group rewards, the group evaluation probably serves the same purpose.

Why are group goals and individual accountability so important? To understand this, consider the alternatives. In some forms of cooperative learning, students work together to complete a single worksheet or to solve one problem together. In such methods, there is little reason for more able students to take time to explain what is going on to their less able groupmates or to ask their opinions. When the group task is to *do* something, rather than to *learn* something, the participation of less able students may be seen as interference rather than help. It may be easier in this circumstance for students to give each other answers than to explain concepts or skills to one another.

In contrast, when the group's task is to ensure that every group member *learns* something, it is in the interests of every group member to spend time explaining concepts to his or her groupmates. Studies of students' behaviors within cooperative groups have consistently found that the students who gain most from cooperative work are those who give and receive elaborated explanations (Webb 1985). In contrast, Webb found that giving and receiving answers without explanations were *negatively* related to achievement gain. What group goals and individual accountability do is to motivate students to give explanations and to take one another's learning seriously, instead of simply giving answers.

Cooperative learning methods generally work equally well for all types of students. While occasional studies find particular advantages for high or low achievers, boys or girls, and so on, the great majority find equal benefits for all types of students. Sometimes teachers or parents worry that cooperative learning will hold back high achievers. The research provides absolutely no support for this claim; high achievers gain from cooperative learning (relative to high achievers in traditional classes) just as much as do low and average achievers (see Slavin, this issue, p. 63).

Research on the achievement effects of cooperative learning has more often taken place in grades 3–9 than 10–12. Studies at the senior high school level are about as positive as those at earlier grade levels, but there is a need for more research at that level. Cooperative learning methods have been equally successful in urban, rural, and suburban schools and with students of different ethnic groups (although a few studies have found particularly positive effects for black students; see Slavin and Oickle 1981).

Among the cooperative learning methods, the Student Team Learning programs have been most extensively researched and most often found instructionally effective. Of 14 studies of STAD and closely related methods, 11 found significantly higher achievement for this method than for traditional instruction, and two found no differences. For example, Slavin and Karweit (1984) evaluated STAD over an entire school year in inner-city Philadelphia 9th grade mathematics classes. Student performance on a standardized mathematics test increased significantly more than in either a mastery learning group or a control group using the same materials. Substantial differences favoring STAD have been found in such diverse subjects as social studies (e.g., Allen and Van Sickle 1984), language arts (Slavin and Karweit 1981), reading comprehension (Stevens, Slavin, Farnish, and Madden 1988), mathematics (Sherman and Thomas 1986), and science (Okebukola 1985). Nine of 11 studies of TGT found similar results (DeVries and Slavin 1978).

The largest effects of Student Team Learning methods have been found in studies of TAI. Five of six studies found substantially greater learning of mathematics computations in TAI than in control classes, while one study found no differences (see Slavin 1985b). Experimental control differences were still substantial (though smaller) a year after the students were in TAI (Slavin and Karweit 1985). In mathematics concepts and applications, one of three studies (Slavin et al. 1984) found significantly greater gains in TAI than control methods, while two found no significant differences (Slavin and Karweit 1985).

In comparison with traditional control groups, three experimental studies of CIRC have found substantial positive effects on scores from standardized tests of reading comprehension, reading vocabulary, language expression, language mechanics, and spelling (Madden et al. 1986, Stevens et al. 1987, Stevens et al. 1990). Significantly greater achievement on writing samples was also found favoring the CIRC students in the two studies which assessed writing.

Other than STL methods, the most consistently successful model for increasing student achievement is Group Investigation (Sharan and Sharan 1976). One study of this method (Sharan et al. 1984) found that it increased the learning of English as a foreign language, while Sharan and Shachar (1988) found positive effects of Group Investigation on the learning of history and geography. A third study of only three weeks' duration (Sharan et al. 1980) also found positive effects on social studies achievement, particularly on higher-level concepts. The Learning Together methods (Johnson and Johnson 1987) have been found instructionally effective when they include the assignment of group grades based on the average of group members' individual quiz scores (e.g., Humphreys et al. 1982, Yager et al. 1985). Studies of the original Jigsaw method have not generally supported this approach (e.g., Moskowitz et al. 1983); but studies of Jigsaw II, which uses group goals and individual accountability, have shown positive effects (Mattingly and VanSickle 1990, Ziegler 1981).

275

Robert E. Slavin

Intergroup Relations

In the laboratory research on cooperation, one of the earliest and strongest findings was that people who cooperate learn to like one another (Slavin 1977b). Not surprisingly, the cooperative learning classroom studies have found quite consistently that students express greater liking for their classmates in general as a result of participating in a cooperative learning method (see Slavin 1983a, 1990). This is important in itself and even more important when the students have different ethnic backgrounds. After all, there is substantial evidence that, left alone, ethnic separateness in schools does not naturally diminish over time (Gerard and Miller 1975).

Social scientists have long advocated interethnic cooperation as a means of ensuring positive intergroup relations in desegregated settings. Contact Theory (Allport 1954), which is in the U.S. the dominant theory of intergroup relations, predicted that positive intergroup relations would arise from school desegregation if and only if students participated in cooperative, equal-status interaction sanctioned by the school. Research on cooperative learning methods has borne out the predictions of Contact Theory. These techniques emphasize cooperative, equal-status interaction between students of different ethnic backgrounds sanctioned by the school (Slavin 1985a).

In most of the research on intergroup relations, students were asked to list their best friends at the beginning of the study and again at the end. The number of friendship choices students made outside their own ethnic groups was the measure of intergroup relations.

Positive effects on intergroup relations have been found for STAD, TGT, TAI, Jigsaw, Learning Together, and Group Investigation models (Slavin 1985b). Two of these studies, one on STAD (Slavin 1979) and one on Jigsaw II (Ziegler 1981), included follow-ups of intergroup friendships several months after the end of the studies. Both found that students who had been in cooperative learning classes still named significantly more friends outside their own ethnic groups than did students who had been in control classes. Two studies of Group Investigation (Sharan et al. 1984, Sharan and Shachar 1988) found that students' improved attitudes and behaviors toward classmates of different ethnic backgrounds extended to classmates who had never been in the same groups, and a study of TAI (Oishi 1983) found positive effects of this method on cross-ethnic interactions outside as well as in class. The U.S. studies of cooperative learning and intergroup relations involved black, white, and (in a few cases) Mexican-American students. A study of Jigsaw II by Ziegler (1981) took place in Toronto, where the major ethnic groups were Anglo-Canadians and children of recent European immigrants. The Sharan (Sharan et al. 1984, Sharan and Shachar 1988) studies of Groups Investigation took place in Israel and involved friendships between Jews of both European and Middle Eastern backgrounds.

Although ethnicity is a major-barrier to friendship, it is not so large as the one between physically or mentally handicapped children and their normal-progress peers. Mainstreaming, an unprecedented opportunity for handicapped children to take their place in the school and society, has created enormous practical problems for classroom teachers, and it often leads to social rejection of the handicapped children. Because cooperative learning methods have been successful in improving relationships across the ethnicity barrier—which somewhat resembles the barrier between mainstreamed and normal-progress students—these methods have also been applied to increase the acceptance of the mainstreamed student.

The research on cooperative learning and mainstreaming has focused on the academically handicapped child. In one study, STAD was used to attempt to integrate students performing two years or more below the level of their peers into the social structure of the classroom. The use of STAD significantly reduced the degree to which the normal-progress students rejected their mainstreamed classmates and increased the academic achievement and self-esteem of all students, mainstreamed as well as normal-progress (Madden and Slavin 1983). Similar effects have been found for TAI (Slavin et al. 1984), and other research using cooperative teams has also shown significant improvements in relationships between mainstreamed academically handicapped students and their normal-progress peers (Ballard et al. 1977, Cooper et al. 1980).

In addition, one study in a self-contained school for emotionally disturbed adolescents found that the use of TGT increased positive interactions and friendships among students (Slavin 1977a). Five months after the study ended, these positive interactions were still found more often in the former TGT classes than in the control classes. In a study in a similar setting, Janke (1978) found that the emotionally disturbed students were more on-task, were better behaved, and had better attendance in TGT classes than in control classes.

Self-Esteem

One of the most important aspects of a child's personality is his or her self-esteem. Several researchers working on cooperative learning techniques have found that these methods do increase students' self-esteem. These improvements in self-esteem have been found for TGT and STAD (Slavin 1990), for Jigsaw (Blaney et al. 1977), and for the three methods combined (Slavin and Karweit 1981). Improvements in student self-concepts have also been found for TAI (Slavin et al. 1984).

Other Outcomes

In addition to effects on achievement, positive intergroup relations, greater acceptance of mainstreamed students, and self-esteem, effects of cooperative learning have been found on a variety of other important educational outcomes. These include liking school, development of peer norms in favor of doing well academically, feelings of individual control over the student's own fate in school, and cooperativeness and altruism (see Slavin 1983a, 1990). TGT (DeVries and Slavin 1978) and STAD (Slavin 1978, Janke 1978) have been found to have positive effects on students' time-on-task. One study found that lower socioeconomic status students at risk of becoming delinquent who worked in cooperative groups in 6th grade had better attendance, fewer contacts with the police, and higher behavioral ratings by teachers in grades 7–11 than did control students (Hartley 1976). Another study implemented forms of cooperative learning beginning in kindergarten and continuing through the 4th grade (Solomon et al. 1990). This study found that the students who had been taught cooperatively were significantly higher than control students on measures of supportive, friendly, and prosocial behavior; were better at resolving conflicts; and expressed more support for democratic values.

USEFUL STRATEGIES

Returning to the questions at the beginning of this article, we now see the usefulness of cooperative learning strategies for improving such diverse outcomes as student achievement at a variety of grade levels and in many subjects, intergroup relations, relationships between mainstreamed and normal-progress students, and student self-esteem. Further, their widespread and growing use demonstrates that cooperative learning methods are practical and attractive to teachers. The history of the development, evaluation, and dissemination of cooperative learning is an outstanding example of the use of educational research to create programs that have improved the educational experience of thousands of students and will continue to affect thousands more.

REFERENCES

Allen, W. H., and R. L. Van Sickle, (1984). "Learning Teams and Low Achievers." *Social Education:* 60–64.

Allport, G. (1954). *The Nature of Prejudice.* Cambridge, Mass.: Addison-Wesley.

Aronson, E., N. Blaney, C. Stephan, J. Sikes, and M. Snapp. (1978). *The Jigsaw Classroom.* Beverly Hills, Calif.: Sage.

Ballard, M., L. Corman, J. Gottlieb, and M. Kauffman, (1977). "Improving the Social Status of Mainstreamed Retarded Children," *Journal of Educational Psychology* 69: 605–611.

Blaney, N. T., S. Stephan, D. Rosenfeld, E. Aronson, and J. Sikes, (1977). "Interdependence in the Classroom: A Field Study," *Journal of Educational Psychology* 69: 121–128.

Cooper, L., D. W. Johnson, R. Johnson, and F. Wilderson. (1980). "Effects of Cooperative, Competitive, and Individualistic Experiences on Interpersonal Attraction Among Heterogeneous Peers." *Journal of Social Psychology* 111: 243–252.

Deutsch, M. (1949). "A Theory of Cooperation and Competition." *Human Relations* 2: 129–152.

DeVries, D. L., and R. E. Slavin. (1978). "Teams-Games-Tournament (TGT): Review of Ten Classroom Experiments," *Journal of Research and Development in Education* 12: 28–38.

Gerard, H. B., and N. Miller (1975). *School Desegregation: A Long-Range Study.* New York: Plenum.

Hartley, W. (1976). *Prevention Outcomes of Small Group Education with School Children: An Epidemiologic Follow-Up of the Kansas City School Behavior Project,* Kansas City: University of Kansas Medical Center.

Humphreys, B., R. Johnson, and D. W. Johnson. (1982). "Effects of Cooperative, Competitive, and Individualistic Learning on Students' Achievement in Science Class." *Journal of Research in Science Teaching* 19: 351–356.

Janke, R. (April 1978). "The Teams-Games-Tournament (TGT) Method and the Behavioral Adjustment and Academic Achievement of Emotionally Impaired Adolescents." Paper presented at the annual convention of the American Educational Research Association, Toronto.

Johnson, D. W., and R. T. Johnson. (1987). *Learning Together and Alone.* 2nd ed. Englewood Cliffs, N.J.: Prentice-Hall.

Madden, N. A., and R. E. Slavin: (1983). "Cooperative Learning and Social Acceptance of Mainstreamed Academically Handicapped Students." *Journal of Special Education* 17: 171–182.

Madden, N. A., R. J. Stevens, and R. E. Slavin. (1986). *A Comprehensive Cooperative Learning Approach to Elementary Reading and Writing: Effects on Student Achievement.* Report No. 2. Baltimore, Md.: Center for Research on Elementary and Middle Schools, Johns Hopkins University.

Mattingly, R. M., and R. L. VanSickle. (1990). *Jigsaw II in Secondary Social Studies: An Experiment.* Athens, Ga.: University of Georgia.

Moskowitz, J. M., J. H. Malvin, G. A. Schaeffer, and E. Schaps. (1983). "Evaluation of a Cooperative Learning Strategy." *American Educational Research Journal* 20: 687–696.

Oishi, S. (1983). "Effects of Team-Assisted Individualization in Mathematics on Cross-Race Interactions of Elementary School Children." Doctoral diss., University of Maryland.

Okebukola, P. A. (1985). "The Relative Effectiveness of Cooperative and Competitive Interaction Techniques in Strengthening Students' Performance in Science Classes." *Science Education* 69: 501–509.

Sharan, S., and C. Shachar. (1988). *Language and Learning in the Cooperative Classroom.* New York: Springer.

Sharan, S., and Y. Sharan. (1976). *Small-group Teaching.* Englewood Cliffs, NJ: Educational Technology Publications.

Sharan, S., R. Hertz-Lazarowitz, and Z. Ackerman. (1980). "Academic Achievement of Elementary School Children in Small-group vs. Whole Class Instruction," *Journal of Experimental Education* 48: 125–129.

Sharan, S., P. Kussell, R. Hertz-Lazarowitz, Y. Bejarano, S. Raviv, and Y. Sharan. (1984). *Cooperative Learning in the Classroom: Research in Desegregated Schools.* Hillsdale, N.J.: Erlbaum.

Sherman, L. W., and M. Thomas. (1986). "Mathematics Achievement in Cooperative Versus Individualistic Goal-structured High School Classrooms." *Journal of Educational Research* 79: 169–172.

Slavin, R. E. (1977a). "A Student Team Approach to Teaching Adolescents with Special Emotional and Behavioral Needs." *Psychology in the Schools* 14: 77–84.

Slavin, R. E. (1977b). "Classroom Reward Structure: An Analytical and Practical Review." *Review of Educational Research* 47: 633–650.

Slavin, R. E. (1978). "Student Teams and Achievement Divisions." *Journal of Research and Development in Education* 12: 39–49.

Slavin, R. E. (1979). "Effects of Biracial Learning Teams on Cross-Racial Friendships." *Journal of Educational Psychology* 71: 381–387.

Slavin, R. E. (1983a). *Cooperative Learning.* New York: Longman.

Slavin, R. E. (1983b). "When Does Cooperative Learning Increase Student Achievement?" *Psychological Bulletin* 94: 429–445.

Slavin, R. E. (March 1985a). "Cooperative Learning: Applying Contact Theory in Desegregated Schools" *Journal of Social Issues* 41: 45–62.

Slavin, R. E. (1985b). "Team Assisted Individualization: A Cooperative Learning Solution for Adaptive Instruction in Mathematics." In *Adapting Instruction to Individual Differences,* edited by M. Wang and H. Walberg. Berkeley, Calif.: McCutchan.

Slavin, R. E. (1986). *Using Student Team Learning.* 3rd ed. Baltimore, Md.: Center for Research on Elementary and Middle Schools, Johns Hopkins University.

Slavin, R. E. (1990). *Cooperative Learning: Theory, Research, and Practice.* Englewood Cliffs, N.J.: Prentice-Hall.

Slavin, R. E. (February 1991). "Are Cooperative Learning and 'Untracking' Harmful to the Gifted?" *Educational Leadership* 48: 63–74.

Slavin, R. E., and N. Karweit. (1981). "Cognitive and Affective Outcomes of an Intensive Student Team Learning Experience." *Journal of Experimental Education* 50: 29–35.

Slavin, R. E., and N. Karweit. (1984). "Mastery Learning and Student Teams: A Factorial Experiment in Urban General Mathematics Classes." *American Educational Research Journal* 21: 725–736.

Slavin, R. E., and N. L. Karweit (1985). "Effects of Whole-Class, Ability Grouped, and Individualized Instruction on Mathematics Achievement." *American Educational Research Journal* 22: 351–367.

Slavin, R. E., M. Leavey, and N. A. Madden (1984). "Combining Cooperative Learning and Individualized Instruction: Effects on Student Mathematics Achievement Attitudes and Behaviors." *Elementary School Journal* 84: 409–422.

Slavin, R. E., M. B. Leavey, and N. A. Madden. (1986). *Team Accelerated Instruction-Mathematics.* Watertown, Mass.: Mastery Education Corporation.

Slavin, R. E., N. A. Madden, and M. B. Leavey. (1984). "Effects of Team Assisted Individualization on the Mathematics Achievement of Academically Handicapped and Nonhandicapped Students." *Journal of Educational Psychology* 76: 813–819.

Slavin, R. E., and E. Oickle. (1981). "Effects of Cooperative Learning Teams on Student Achievement and Race Relations: Treatment × Race Interactions." *Sociology of Education* 54: 174–180.

Solomon, D., M. Watson, E. Schaps, V. Battistich, and J. Solomon (1990). "Cooperative Learning as Part of a Comprehensive Classroom Program Designed to Promote Prosocial Development." In *Current Research on Cooperative Learning,* edited by S. Sharan, New York: Praeger.

Stevens, R. J., N. A. Madden, R. E. Slavin, and A. M. Farnish. (1987). "Cooperative Integrated Reading and Composition: Two Field Experiments." *Reading Research Quarterly* 22: 433–454.

Stevens, R. J., R. E. Slavin, and A. M. Farnish. (April 1990). "A Cooperative Learning Approach to Elementary Reading and Writing Instruction: Long-Term Effects." Paper presented at the annual convention of the American Educational Research Association, Boston.

Stevens, R. J., R. E., Slavin, A. M. Farnish, and N. A. Madden. (April 1988). "The Effects of Cooperative Learning and Direct Instruction in Reading Comprehension Strategies on Main Idea Identification." Paper presented at the annual convention of the American Educational Research Association, New Orleans.

Webb, N. (1985). "Student Interaction and Learning in Small Groups: A Research Summary." In *Learning to Cooperate, Cooperating to Learn*, edited by R. Slavin, S. Sharan, S. Kagan, R. Hertz-Lazarowitz, D. Webb, and R. Schmuck. New York: Plenum.

Yager, S., D. W. Johnson, and R. T. Johnson. (1985). "Oral Discussion, Group-to-Individual Transfer, and Achievement in Cooperative Learning Groups." *Journal of Educational Psychology* 77: 60–66.

Ziegler, S. (1981). "The Effectiveness of Cooperative Learning Teams for Increasing Cross-Ethnic Friendship: Additional Evidence." *Human Organization* 40: 264–268.

9.3 F. CLARK POWER ET AL.

A Week in the Life of Cluster

Lawrence Kohlberg (1927–1987) is considered the most influential of all psychologists who have studied and written about the psychology of moral development and moral education. He began his doctoral dissertation on stages of moral development at the University of Chicago in 1955 and completed the majority of his research as a professor at the Harvard Graduate School of Education (HGSE). It was at HGSE that he began his "applied" work in educational psychology through the creation of "just communities" in public schools. Many professional colleagues assisted Kohlberg in this work, including the coauthors of the following selection: F. Clark Power, a professor at Notre Dame University; Ann Higgins, now at New York's Fordham University; and Joseph Reimer.

The roots of Kohlberg's just community approach to the organization of schools are in Socrates's notion of the just city, as recorded by Plato in *The Republic* and in John Dewey's philosophy of democracy. As Dewey asserts, Americans preach about the benefits of democracy to their high school students, but they seldom let their students experience real democracy. Dewey urged high schools to be truly democratic, with students and teachers each having a vote. Kohlberg took this vision and made it a reality; his first attempt was as a consultant to an alternative high school in Cambridge, Massachusetts, called Cluster School. Its history is documented in the book from which the following selection has been taken, *Lawrence Kohlberg's Approach to Moral Education* (Columbia University Press, 1989).

Key Concept: the just community

*T*he Cluster School in Cambridge, Massachusetts, had the distinction of being the site for the first application of the just community approach for a school setting. An alternative school-within-a-school, Cluster was founded in 1974 and pioneered this approach for five years before being reorganized as K–100, a leadership program within the regular Cambridge high school (Cambridge Rindge and Latin School). It received much publicity from the Boston newspapers, *Newsweek,* and *Psychology Today.* In this [selection] we will present a description of the Cluster School as it embodied a developing just community approach. First we will focus briefly on the beginnings of the school and the evolution of its institutions and then concentrate primarily on the weekly functioning of the major institutions of the school. This portrait should convey how the theory of the just community was translated into daily practice.

THE BEGINNING OF CLUSTER

The Cluster School was born of the coincidence of two originally unrelated events. In the spring of 1975 [Lawrence] Kohlberg received grants from the Danforth and Kennedy foundations to undertake the training of high school teachers in developmental moral education and the just community approach. The grant application called for two programs in the Cambridge schools: one would train teachers in a variety of moral, discussion-based curricula, and another would create a just community school-within-a-school in one of the Cambridge high schools. The Cambridge schools were a particularly attractive setting because of the racial and social diversity in the student population. Kohlberg intended to have the first program precede the second by a year's time: but developments within the Cambridge schools led to a change in his schedule.

At the suggestion of the superintendent of the Cambridge schools, a group of parents invited Kohlberg to join them as a consultant in planning for a new alternative high school. The existing alternative school, the Pilot School, had grown from 60 to 180 students and had a waiting list of 55 applicants for the incoming freshmen class. A group of parents with children on that list had made the proposal to the school committee and won funding to plan for the new school, which would open that September. When Kohlberg joined the planning group of parents, teachers, and students, he took the opportunity to present his ideas on the just community, and they were interested enough to invite him to join a committee on governance. That committee came up with the following principles for governing the new school:

1. The school would be governed by direct democracy. All major issues would be discussed and decided at a weekly community meeting at which all members (students and teachers) would have one vote.
2. There would be additionally a number of standing committees to be filled by students, teachers, and parents.
3. A social contract would be drawn between members which would define everyone's responsibilities and rights.
4. Students and teachers would have the same basic rights, including freedom of expression, respect from others, and freedom from physical or verbal harm.

This plan was incorporated in a report which called for a new alternative school housed in three classrooms, with a half-day schedule and a curriculum based around a double-period, required core course, integrating English and social studies. The report was presented to the school committee, which approved opening the new alternative school in September. It would be called the Cluster School.

THE CLUSTER STAFF

Of the eight teachers from the Cambridge high school who applied for the eight half-time positions in Cluster, all were accepted. They were all veteran teachers; most were under the age of thirty. There were four men and four women, and all were white. As a group, they were articulate and self-assured and saw themselves as experienced teachers who had now been given the opportunity to put their beliefs to practice by establishing a new school-within-a-school. But, significantly, none had previous experience teaching in an alternative school, and had very little lead time to learn the ropes before Cluster opened. They, as the students, would have to do much of their learning in the course of running the school.

Most of the training occurred in evening meetings which the staff took turns hosting. While the major item of business was looking ahead to the community meeting, a significant amount of time was spent discussing problem students.... [E]ach staff member had a responsibility to monitor the overall progress of the students in their group. Since quite a few students came to Cluster with significant learning and adjustment problems, this was a very demanding role.

Cluster was different from the other alternative schools we studied in that there was no coordinator or principal. The Cluster faculty took turns representing the school at meetings within the parent high school and within the school system. Needless to say, this system of rotating representatives and of sharing responsibility for administrative chores proved to be somewhat inefficient. While all of the staff recognized this, a significant number of them consistently and passionately rejected Kohlberg's and others' suggestions of having a part-time administrator. They feared that if such a step were taken, their democratic character as a staff and as a school would be seriously compromised.

THE ROLE OF CONSULTANTS

Most of the Cluster faculty had not previously known Kohlberg or much about his educational writings, but intuitively agreed that democratic governance was the way to go at Cluster. They wanted Kohlberg as a consultant with the assurance he would not use the school as a research laboratory. He agreed to consult as long as the school was a participatory democracy and left the issue of research to be settled by student and faculty vote after the school had been established.

He wished not to come as the expert with the ready-made model to be applied, but to present a set of ideas, to see if there was interest in them, and then work *with* the participants to develop the model that would make most sense for Cluster. He expected that the governance structure would emerge and his previous experience with just community would be a helpful resource. As it turned out, he underestimated the extent to which he as consultant would initially be called upon to supply "hands-on" knowledge about how to run a democratic school.

From the beginning, several consultant researchers worked in Cluster with the approval of the staff. One of these, Elsa Wasserman, a former guidance counselor at Pilot School and one of the coordinators of the summer planning group, joined the staff in the second year. The coauthors, [F. Clark] Power and [Ann] Higgins, who joined Kohlberg during Cluster's third year, were less involved participants than Wasserman, although Higgins eventually became a voting member.

THE OPENING OF CLUSTER: FROM CHAOS
TO PARTIAL ORDER

Cluster opened in confusion. Classrooms were promised, but had to be located. Students (who, as planned, came mainly from Pilot's waiting list) had to be scheduled so they would take social studies, English, and physical education in Cluster and their other courses in the regular school. In spite of the chaos, all seemed to be going relatively smoothly until about a week into school, when the first community meeting was held. The community meeting . . . was the one time during the week when the whole school convened to discuss and decide democratically upon school policy. From the first week Kohlberg insisted that every member—student, teacher, and consultant, who would have one vote—should be required to attend. The meeting was scheduled as a regular part of the school's activities. This policy differed from that of other alternative schools, in which attendance at these meetings was not mandatory. Kohlberg argued at the time, "If you do not get the tough white and black kids coming to the community meetings, the intellectual kids will come and dialogue on boring issues with the staff and drive away the very kids who most need this experience."

At the first community meeting the main issue was the curriculum. The staff had listed a number of possible electives that could be offered during the last periods of the school day and wanted the students to choose among them. Toward the end of the meeting a student made the radical proposal that "everyone could leave before the close of school if they did not like the courses offered." A vote was taken and that proposal passed. The staff was stunned. This was democracy, but it also violated the rules of the Cambridge high school, which were operative for Cluster as well. At the last moment Kohlberg called out that that was only a straw vote and a real vote would have to be taken at the next meeting.

This tragicomic situation showed the staff that democracy was not going to be born of itself; it needed to be carefully nurtured. The students, or at least the majority, who had not been through the summer workshop, were coming to

Cluster because they wanted an alternative school and could not get into Pilot. They understood little about and had even less commitment to the democratic process. It was natural for them to view democratic governance as an opportunity to push the limits. The staff would have to structure democracy carefully if it were not to break down into anarchy.

THE CURRICULUM

... The core classes served to reinforce, complement, and expand upon the socio-cognitive learning that took place during small group and community meetings. Focusing on developing these capacities is in line with the idea of "development as the aim of education," which is opposed to a view of education that separates the "academic" learning of classes from the "experiential" learning of participatory governance. Kohlberg saw a need for school experience that as a whole represents real-life experience to the students and, in so doing, stimulates development. Class time should be an occasion to reflect upon real life and to expand one's view of real life by considering other perspectives and options. In turn, experiential learning should be challenging and thought provoking and have students wanting to know more about the concepts they have been employing. Thus "democracy," "community," "law," and "authority" were the subjects of both classes and meetings; and if in one context students thought *about* these concepts and in the other thought *through* these concepts, the net result was meant to be an integrated learning experience that promoted the students' cognitive, social, and moral development.

THE EMERGING JUST COMMUNITY APPROACH

As the complexities of starting a new school, planning a curriculum, and getting into place a system of governance became apparent, the faculty came to rely more heavily on Kohlberg's consultation and his previous experience with democratic governance. The teachers were learning under fire how to lead small groups, participate as *Madrichim* (moral leaders) in the community meetings, and integrate a developmental-democratic orientation into their classroom teaching. They met with Kohlberg in semiweekly consultations (after school hours) and at other odd hours during the school week, as circumstances dictated. One of the first opportunities for ad hoc consultation arose when several teachers arranged for their students to see a film shown at Harvard. The students agreed previous to going that they would not smoke cigarettes in the viewing room. But as soon as the lights went off, out came the butts. The teachers present did not react. Kohlberg, who was also present, had the film stopped and took the teachers out of the room. He told them that in a democracy it was crucial that the rules or agreements that the community makes be taken seriously. To sit by and watch the students violate the rules without reacting is to undercut the democratic authority of the community. The teachers agreed and upon reentering the room led a short discussion about smoking and upholding agreements. The film was then continued without interruption.

The staff were impressed by Kohlberg's serious attitude toward upholding the rules of the school. Some alternative schools allow such "expressive behaviors" as smoking to go by without much fuss. The "fuss" Kohlberg made had little to do with smoking per se, but had everything to do with what [French sociologist Emile] Durkheim calls respect for rules. The teachers learned quickly that without strengthening respect for rules, democratic governance will fail. For when adults cease to enforce the rules unilaterally, other means of social control have to come into play. In the just community mode, "the other means of social control" is the group that expects its members to live up to its agreements.

This incident also illustrates the relation between advocacy and the role of the consultant, Kohlberg, as consultant, advocated to the faculty a position based on the just community approach. They, agreeing with his point, in turn advocated a position to the students about the importance of upholding social agreements. The consultant by this model of intervention does not wait to be consulted; he or she takes an active, interventionist stance in relation to the staff. Similarly, the faculty intervened to raise the question about broken agreements. The objective in both interventions is for the second party to become more aware of their thinking and acting in the context of their effect on the community. The faculty were expected to learn "to take the perspective of the community" and ask, as Kohlberg did here, how the behavior of smoking is affecting the life of the community. Similarly, at least some of the students would learn to advocate to their peers a concern for how their behavior affects the community. The final decision, as to whether a given behavior should be changed in light of its effect on the community, is made democratically by the group as a whole; as in this case, when they had agreed by vote to see the film and not smoke while viewing it....

THE ENFORCEMENT OF RULES

In the spring of the first year enforcement became a central goal of the emerging just community approach. It was not difficult for students to learn to vote democratically for establishing rules, but as long as they expected that it would be the teachers who would enforce these rules, the basic authority structure of the school would remain unchanged and there would be no just community. What had to happen was for the community as a whole to own these rules and to insist upon everyone's upholding them....

ADVISER GROUPS

Adviser group meetings were held on Thursdays, sandwiched between the faculty meeting the night before and a community meeting the next day. The purpose of this scheduling was to prepare students and staff for the community meeting through a preliminary discussion of the proposal(s) on the agenda. Although adviser group meetings set the stage for the community meeting, this was not their only function. Adviser group meetings provided an opportunity for a small group of students and a teacher to socialize and share more personal concerns than those typically discussed in the community meeting....

287

F. Clark Power et al.

THE COMMUNITY MEETING

Participatory democratic governance was most clearly practiced at the community meeting. Each Friday at 10:50 A.M., the membership of the Cluster School would gather in the large double-classroom for the community meeting. Everyone—teachers, students, consultants, and researchers—was expected to be there; and almost everyone came. It was the only regular time during the week when the whole school was assembled, when everyone could see and hear each other. The meeting *was* community incarnate.

The meetings had a definite rhythm. They began slowly, almost incoherently, as people would gradually file into the large room and take seats along the walls. (It was an unwritten rule that no one sat in the middle of the room.) The rotating chairpersons, sitting on a desk in the front, would call for order, usually several times, before the proceedings could begin over the dull roar of the crowd. If there were any visitors present, they would stand, announce their names and reasons for coming, and receive by vote the community's welcome. Business would open with smaller agenda items that could be dealt with quickly so that the central issue of the day could be raised. Early in the discussion a proposal would be made suggesting a way to deal with the issue, and a straw vote would be taken to gauge how the members stood—for or against the proposal. Those in the minority on the straw vote would be first to present their views and reasons, followed by the majority. The stage was set for debating the merits of alternative options, raising questions, and trying to sway undecided voters to one's side. At their best the discussions would simmer with drama and even continue during the lunch break. But they were always goal-oriented. By 12:50 P.M. a final vote would be taken, and the community would have arrived by democratic process at a majority decision that would hopefully work in the community's best interest.

The community meeting functioned, in a sense, as Cluster's major ritual event. It "celebrated" Cluster as a community, and the proceedings were infused with references to "working together as a community." Participation in the meetings bound the members together as a group, and although there were suggestions from time to time that the meetings be held less often, the ritual quality of the meetings kept them anchored in their weekly spot. It was as if Cluster would not be Cluster without the community meetings.

The meetings also functioned, as did the adviser group meetings, as a context for moral discussion. Issues that arose were to be dealt with as "moral issues" and were to be discussed in rough accordance with the procedures of good moral discussion. Finally, the meetings were the occasions for communal decision making. All the other institutions led up to the community meeting.

There the whole community would establish the rules and policy of the school, which were to be implemented by the staff and students. The success of Cluster as a democratically governed, just community school depended on how well the community meeting functioned. It depended on the ability of the community, as led by its staff members, to arrive at decisions that would be judged as fair, motivate the actions of the members, and be enforceable in cases when deviation would occur. It was a tall order, but a lot of thought and planning went into making these meetings as effective a means as possible for democratically governing the school....

THE DISCIPLINE COMMITTEE [D.C.]

The D.C. had three functions: adjudicating fair punishments, mediating disputes between individuals in the community, and counseling students with disciplinary problems. The first of these functions was the primary one, as the name Discipline Committee suggests. The process of adjudicating fair punishments involved settling on the facts of the case, relating the case to a particular Cluster rule and stipulated punishment, and deciding on a particular punishment once all arguments had been heard....

CONCLUSION

Our introduction to the just community approach is now complete. We have sketched the evolution of the approach from Kohlberg's developmental research through the first year of Cluster School. In this [selection] we have described Cluster's major institutions: the community meeting, the adviser group, and the D.C. They provided the organizational framework for all the just community programs that followed.

CHAPTER 10 Evaluation, Measurement, and Testing

10.1 ROBERT L. LINN

Educational Testing and Assessment: Research Needs and Policy Issues

Robert L. Linn earned his A.B. from the University of California, Los Angeles, and received his M.A. and Ph.D. in 1965 from the University of Illinois at Urbana-Champaign, with a specialization in psychometrics. He worked as a senior research psychologist and director of developmental research at the Educational Testing Service and as a professor of education and psychology at the University of Illinois at Urbana-Champaign before moving to Colorado in 1987. Linn currently is the Distinguished Professor of Education at the University of Colorado at Boulder and codirector of the National Center for Research on Evaluation, Standards, and Student Testing. He is also chairperson of the National Research Council's Board on Testing and Assessment.

Linn has served as editor for the *Journal of Educational Measurement* and edited the text *Educational Measurement,* 3rd ed. (Oryx Press, 1993), and he coauthored *Measurement and Assessment in Teaching,* 7th ed. (Merrill, 1995). He has published approximately 200 journal articles and book chapters dealing with a wide range of theoretical and applied issues in educational measurement. Linn has received several awards for his contributions to the field, including the National Council on Measurement in Education Career Award and the American Educational Research Association Award for Distinguished Contributions to Educational Research. His "Educational Testing and Assessment: Research Needs and Policy Issues," *American Psychologist* (October 1986), which summarizes policy issues and research needs in educational testing and assessment, is excerpted here.

Key Concept: standardized testing

*T*he role of testing in discussions of American education is ubiquitous. Testing is often a prominent subject in the arguments of educational reformers. Test results are used to document the need for reform, and tests are frequently regarded as powerful instruments of change. Witness the recent barrage of reports on the status of education. One of the best known of these reports is *A Nation at Risk: The Imperative for Educational Reform,* issued by the National Commission on Excellence in Education (1983). In this report, test results, such as the frequently discussed decline in scores on the Scholastic Aptitude Test (Wirtz & Howe, 1977), were used as indicators of the malaise in education. The National Commission (1983) also pointed to tests as important tools that should be used to "(a) certify the student's credentials; (b) identify the need for remedial intervention; and (c) identify the opportunity for advanced or accelerated work" (p. 28).

Testing is also a subject of intense controversy. As the National Research Council's Committee on Ability Testing noted, some critics "see tests and testing as an example of science and technology run amok," whereas some proponents "argue that tests and testing offer the best hope of assuring fairness and objectivity in the treatment of all members of society" (Wigdor & Garner, 1982, p. 7). Furthermore, the sharp criticisms of and serious concerns about the overuse and misuse of tests currently coexist with widespread demands for and increased reliance on tests.

Neither the importance of testing's role in American education nor its controversial nature is new. For most of this century standardized tests have played a prominent role in the evaluation of educational programs and in the sorting of individuals for purposes of placement, selection, and certification. Given the importance of these functions to society and to the individuals affected by test-based decisions, it is hardly surprising that testing has frequently been at the center of public controversy since its rapid growth following World War I (Cronbach, 1975; Haney, 1981).

Despite the proliferation of tests, the numerous exchanges about the appropriate and inappropriate interpretations and uses of tests, and the substantial advances in the science of psychology, the statistical sophistication of psychometrics, and the technology supporting testing, the fundamental nature of the most widely used standardized tests has changed relatively little during the last half century. There have been technical changes, of course. Item response theory (e.g., Lord, 1980), for example, has provided a better foundation for designing tests, investigating item bias, estimating measurement error, and equating tests. It also has provided a foundation for the development of computerized adaptive tests. Matrix sampling coupled with item response theory has provided a more efficient means of conducting state and national assessments. However, these and other modifications have not resulted in major changes in the nature of the items that appear on the most widely used ability and achievement tests. Nor have they led to major alterations in the uses and interpretations of the scores or provided solutions to problems stemming from the limitations and misuses of test results.

Robert L. Linn

Scarr (1981) stated that "testing should always be used in the interests of the children tested" (p. 1159). This is a noble goal, but not one that is easily achieved. When test results are used to make instructional decisions for individual children it is rarely possible to know with certainty whether the best interests of those children have been served. Evidence that satisfies some observers that a particular use of a test is beneficial to children is often unconvincing to others with different values. For example, the fact that performance on ability tests is often substantially correlated with later achievement has been used as evidence to support long-term selection and tracking decisions. However, researchers such as Bloom (1976, 1980) reject this approach in favor of a focus on alterable cognitive entry characteristics and mastery learning.

An analysis of the history of educational testing by Resnick (1982) suggests that institutional concerns of school administrators may have played a more important role in the introduction of standardized tests than did evidence regarding the best interests of individual children. Efficiency was a major concern as the school population was increasing and becoming more diverse. Tracking some children into special classes for the mentally retarded and others into academic, general, and vocational programs seemed to provide the schools with a means of coping with the expanded population of students. Similarly, colleges and universities found that they could no longer rely on their familiarity with the characteristics of a relatively small number of feeder schools as a basis for admissions decisions, so the College Board was established to help them deal with this problem by developing standardized tests.

EXCELLENCE AND EQUITY

Efficiency is still a concern, but it is no longer the rallying cry of educational reformers. In the 1960s and 1970s, the focus was on questions of equity. Federal programs such as Head Start, Follow Through, and Title I of the Elementary and

Secondary Education Act of 1965 (PL 89-10) directed resources toward the educationally disadvantaged. The courts demanded, and Congress encouraged, school desegregation through the Emergency School Assistance Act of 1970 (PL 88-352). Testing played an important role in these programs—both in the identification of children who were eligible to receive services and in the mandated evaluations of the programs.

Special education, in particular, came under scrutiny during the 1970s. The principle of the least restrictive environment discouraged the segregation of children into separate classes. On the other hand, Section 504 of the Rehabilitation Act of 1973 (PL No 93-112) and the Education for All Handicapped Children Act of 1975 (PL 94-142) were intended "to ensure that the benefits of special educational programs are available to all who need them" (Heller, Holtzman, & Messick, 1982, p. 3). The disproportionate classification of minorities into separate special education classes and the role of intelligence tests in the placement process became major issues and led, in the case of *Larry P. v. Riles* (1980) to the banning of intelligence tests for the placement of children in special education in California.

During the last half of the 1970s, a new movement swept through education. From 1976 to 1980, the number of states requiring some form of minimum competency testing increased from 8 to 38 (Lerner, 1981). Popular opinion that many high school graduates lacked basic skills in reading, writing, and arithmetic focused attention on minimum performance standards and led legislators to turn to tests as enforcement mechanisms. Although the movement was not necessarily inconsistent with concerns for equity, these concerns were not the driving force.

By 1983, the concern for equity had receded further. "Excellence" had become the new rallying call. The focus in the rash of reports that appeared in 1983 was no longer on minimum standards. Higher order skills and achievement in the sciences and mathematics were judged to be inadequate. Schools were exhorted to increase requirements in core subjects, to raise standards, and to place more emphasis on advanced and accelerated programs for students. Colleges and universities were encouraged to raise their admissions requirements and their expectations for students. In the two years since the publication of *A Nation at Risk* (National Commission on Excellence in Education, 1983), there has been a flurry of activity in states, local districts, and universities directed toward increasing course requirements for high school graduation and college admission.

Although some have argued that "excellence cannot be allowed to become the new code word for a retreat from equity" (Gregory Anrig, cited in Hechinger 1984, p. C8), many would agree with Hechinger's (1984) conclusion that "demands for excellence have pushed concern for equity onto the back burner" (p. C8). There is at least a tension between the concerns for equity and excellence. This tension provides a context within which some major applications of testing, the current trends, and future research needs can be considered. A major emphasis in the following discussion is the ways in which research and testing methodology can contribute to the dual goals of excellence and equity.

Placement in Special Education

Views of the educational value of uses of IQ tests run the gamut from extremely positive to extremely negative. "The history of IQ tests can be told as one of psychology's greatest achievements (Herrnstein, 1973) or as one of its most shameful (Kamin, 1974)" (Scarr, 1981, p. 1159). The debates often have more to do with social values and views about the outcomes of test use and their interpretations than they do with the underlying science. Central to the debates are questions of bias, the disproportionate representation of minority children in special education classes, and the confusion of notions of fixed capacities with observed test performance.

Carroll and Horn (1981) have cautioned against confusing the science of human abilities with the technology of measurement: "Valid criticisms of particular applications of measurement are not, in general, criticisms of the science of ability measurement, and vice versa" (p. 1013). However, the two are easy to confuse. The development of IQ tests was a highly pragmatic undertaking. The fact that tests could be constructed that predicted subsequent academic achievement reasonably well had more to do with the tests' widespread acceptance and use than it did with any scientific understanding of cognitive processing. The result has been what Horn (in press) has referred to as a "mixture model of intelligence." Various cognitive tasks are combined in varying amounts to form a given measure. The resulting mixture may have utility, but it does not advance the scientific understanding of human abilities or their development....

There are at least three major research questions that need to be addressed in order to evaluate the appropriateness of using a test in making decisions about the placement of children in special education classes or the diagnosis of children who are eligible for educational services under the provisions of PL 94-142: (a) What is the validity of the diagnosis, and what contribution does the test make to a valid diagnosis? (b) What are the educational benefits of placing an identified child in a special class or program? (c) Does the test lead to bias in the decisions made regarding minorities? To some extent, these questions are interrelated and none is easily answered, but they are all crucial to evaluating the use of a test to place children....

The courts have already provided judgments regarding the question of bias. In *Larry P. v. Riles* (1980), IQ tests were judged to be biased because they showed group differences in performance. In *PASE v. Hannon* (1980), the Wechsler Intelligence Scale for Children, the Wechsler Intelligence Scale for Children —Revised, and the Stanford-Binet were judged to be unbiased based on Judge Grady's personal review of the tests. Neither conclusion had an adequate scientific base (Bersoff, 1981). Reschly (1981) has noted that IQ tests are only part of the placement process, and it is unclear that their elimination would reduce the disproportionate placement of minority children in special education classes. However, it is clear that better evidence is needed to support the claim that the tests contribute to fair and unbiased assessment and placement (Heller et al.,

1982). In short, a comprehensive validation program, along the lines described earlier, is needed.

Student Certification

Until recently, student certification in the form of high school diplomas was generally based on teacher grades and the completion of course requirements. Minimum competency testing (MCT) programs have added a new requirement for students in a number of states and local districts throughout the country. The purpose of this new requirement is clearly to improve education, as is exemplified by the legislation establishing one of the best known of the statewide MCT requirements in Florida. Florida's high school graduation test was the result of the state's Educational Accountability Act of 1976, which had as one of its clearly stated intents to give every student in the Florida public schools a "guarantee... that the system provides instructional programs which meet minimum performance standards comparable with the state's plan for education" (p. 1).

As is true of programs in other states, the test provided the tool for accomplishing the goal of ensuring that students had received certain minimum preparation. The focus is clearly on the outcomes rather than the process, although funds are generally made available to provide remedial instruction for students who fail to meet the minimum standards on their initial attempt at the test.

The use of MCT results to determine the award of high school diplomas sparked a heated debate among professional educators and researchers (e.g., Lerner, 1981; Madaus, 1981; Popham, 1981). It also led to new challenges of tests in the courts, the most notable of which was the *Debra P. v. Turlington* (1981) case. Florida's MCT requirement was challenged, in part, on the grounds of bias. A second key issue in *Debra P.*, however, was what has come to be known as "instructional validity." In May 1981, the U.S. Court of Appeals for the Fifth Circuit concluded that "the State may not deprive its high school seniors of the economic and educational benefits of a high school diploma until it has demonstrated that the SSAT II is a fair test of that which is taught in its classrooms" (*Debra P. v. Turlington*, 1981)....

Teacher Testing

Competency testing is not limited to elementary and secondary school students. Both practicing and prospective teachers are being required to pass tests. Furthermore, the purposes of such tests are no longer limited to initial certification. Practicing teachers in Arkansas and Texas must pass tests for recertification (Podemski & Lohr, 1985). Test results are part of the eligibility requirements for merit pay increases associated with Florida's Master Teacher Program (Fisher, Fry, Loewe, & Wilson, 1985). Satisfactory performance on the Pre-Professional Skills Test, published by the Educational Testing Service, was added to the requirements for entry into an approved teacher education program by the Texas State Board of Education (Popham & Yalow, 1983).

Teacher testing was common prior to the reforms of the 1920s and 1930s (Vold, 1985). The new spirit of reform has led to its reintroduction and the expansion of its use in the areas of recertification and merit pay. Proponents seem to assume that the tests provide a means of improving teacher effectiveness, enhancing professionalism, attracting more able students to teaching, and increasing public support for education. However, critics point to the lack of evidence supporting these assumptions (see, e.g., Pugach & Raths, 1983).

Although the debate about teacher testing is often more political than scientific in nature, validity is a key aspect of many of the arguments. Conclusions about the validity of using tests for teacher certification or recertification often depend on the kind of evidence that is assumed to be required. On one hand, those who assume that criterion-related evidence (e.g., correlations of teachers' performance on tests with ratings of classroom performance or with gains in student achievement) is required find little supporting evidence of validity (e.g., Darling-Hammond, Wise, & Pease, 1983; Medley, Coker, & Soar, 1984; Pugach & Raths, 1983; Quirk, Witten, & Weinberg, 1973). On the other hand, those who emphasize content-related evidence of validity (e.g., content ratings by teacher educators or practicing teachers) reach more positive conclusions (see, for example, Cross, 1985, for a listing of mostly unpublished studies of content-related validity).

A similar situation exists for licensing and certification examinations for many other occupations. As Kane (1982) has noted, licensure or certification test "scores can be interpreted as predictors of future performance in practice" or "as indicators of abilities that are critical for practice" (pp. 917–918). Criterion-related evidence is most relevant to the first interpretation, whereas content-related evidence and construct-related evidence are of primary importance for the second interpretation.

The evidence of validity that is most important to obtain depends on the intended purpose of the test. "The primary purpose of licensure or certification is to protect the public" (*Standards for Educational and Psychological Testing*, 1985, p. 63). In part, because this purpose is narrower than that of an employer who wants to use a test for selection, and, in part, because it is often not feasible to obtain adequate criterion-related evidence for licensure and certification tests, the recently published *Standards for Educational and Psychological Testing* (1985) emphasized the accumulation of content-related evidence "that is supplemented by evidence of the appropriateness of the construct being measured" (p. 63) for this use of tests.

From this perspective, the key requirement for teacher certification testing is to provide a rationale and supporting evidence that "the knowledge and skills being assessed are required for competent performance" (*Standards*, 1985, p. 64). Job analyses and analyses of the core curriculum required for prospective teachers should provide the primary basis of support for the claim that the tested knowledge and skills are necessary, albeit clearly not sufficient, for teaching. It may be concluded, for example, that knowledge of algebra is necessary to be a competent teacher of the subject, but it obviously does not follow that the subject matter knowledge implies that someone is competent to teach.

Additional evidence may be needed to support the other two uses of teacher tests mentioned earlier, that is, merit pay and entry into a teacher education program. For use in entry into a teacher education program, the usual standards for educational admissions tests are relevant. For merit pay use, evidence that the test scores are valid indicators of teaching superiority is needed.

Educational Assessment

The idea of assessing schooling by testing students is hardly new. Student performance on achievement tests played an important role in arguments of reformers in the 1920s. In the following decades, a wide variety of state and local testing programs were developed and used for monitoring student progress. However, educational assessment programs that were designed specifically to measure group performance rather than individual student achievement did not develop until the early 1960s.

Early state and local testing programs typically relied on traditional tests designed for the measurement of achievement of individual students and on a census approach to testing. Although this approach has the side benefit of providing schools and teachers with scores for individual students, it is highly inefficient if the goal of the assessment program is to obtain information only on group performance (e.g., average performance for a school, a district, a state, or the nation). For such a goal, sampling of both students and items is much more efficient.

Multiple-matrix sampling (Lord & Novick, 1968, chap. 11) provides the technical basis for modern assessment programs. Not only is it more efficient than a census approach to testing, but it can provide much more detailed information about the achievement of specific curricular objectives than could reasonably be obtained within the constraints of time available for testing if all items are administered to each student. A 40-item standardized test of arithmetic, for example, might include 8 or 10 specific objectives ranging from addition of whole numbers to division involving fractions. Such a test may be sufficient for obtaining a reliable global score of arithmetic achievement; however, only three or four items may be appropriate for the specific objective of division involving fractions. So few items per objective would provide inadequate guidance for possible changes in the curriculum....

The advantages to educational assessment programs of combining the power of multiple-matrix sampling and item response theory are clearly illustrated by the recent NAEP [National Assessment of Educational Progress] results for reading (Educational Testing Service, 1985). A new reading scale was defined that, for the first time, enables (a) comparisons across all four reading assessments conducted from 1971 to 1984 without concern for possible confounding effects of gradual changes in the item pool and (b) comparisons of the performance of 9-, 13-, and 17-year-old students on the same scale.

Educational assessment has evolved from an inefficient accumulation of scores on tests designed to provide global measures for individual students to a highly efficient, but separate, testing system based on the application of multiple-matrix sampling and item response theory. It would be desirable, however, to realize simultaneously the seemingly incompatible goals of obtaining measures that are useful for reporting the achievement of individual students and obtaining measures useful for reporting the achievement levels of groups with the broad coverage of subject-matter objectives provided by a well-designed assessment program. Current research on "the duplex design" by Bock and Mislevy (in preparation) promises to provide the necessary theoretical basis for meeting these dual goals. Using two-stage or adaptive testing procedures (Lord, 1980), duplex designs are expected to provide individually reliable scores and the detailed and comprehensive coverage needed for an assessment program from a single test administration.

Instructional Uses of Tests

It has been 50 years since Lindquist (1936) distinguished between tests designed to "rank students tested" and ones designed to "discover specific weaknesses, errors, or gaps in a student's achievement" (p. 20). Differentiating among students is important for tests whose goal is the prediction of relative standing. For example, if the goal is to predict which applicants to college will get the best grades, differentiation among test takers is essential. By contrast, a test that reliably rank orders students in terms of global test scores provides a teacher with relatively little information about the nature of a student's weaknesses, errors, or gaps. For example, the knowledge that a student scores, say, in the 10th percentile on a standardized arithmetic test suggests that the student has a general weakness in the area of arithmetic relative to his or her peers. However, such a score does not, by itself, indicate the source of the problem or what should be done to improve the student's level of achievement; that is, it lacks diagnostic information.

Most publishers of standardized achievement tests provide options for obtaining more detailed information. A variety of scores corresponding to highly specific instructional objectives (e.g., "can find sums to 18 using three addends") are provided by most publishers, along with suggested instructional activities to help correct identified weaknesses. However, because these highly specific scores are based on few items, they tend to have low reliabilities, and evidence supporting the valid use of the scores for making instructional decisions is rarely provided. For these and other reasons, a number of authors (e.g., Bejar, 1984) have concluded that standardized tests have relatively little impact on instruction....

Computer-administered tests. Using a computer to administer a test is not a new idea. Until recently, however, applications have been rare because of the high cost and limited availability of computer hardware and software. It is not necessary to review the rapidity with which these limitations are being overcome. Nor is it surprising that microcomputers have stimulated interest in computer-assisted testing in the past few years. A number of large-scale testing programs are exploring the use of computers to administer tests (e.g., the basic skill testing program at the Educational Testing Service, and the development of computerized adaptive tests for purposes of selection and classification by the

Department of Defense). Software for use in classroom testing is also appearing (Hsu & Nitko, 1984).

It seems likely that computers will be used in the classroom as well as in large-scale programs. The questions are, How will they be used? Can they lead to improvement in testing, and if so, how? Clearly, computers do not ensure better tests or wiser uses of the results. They do offer new capabilities, however....

CONCLUSION

Standardized testing has played a major role in education for most of this century. Despite frequent controversies, its role has continued to expand, and there are pressures for its continued growth. Although testing has served and can continue to serve important educational functions, we are still a long way from reaching Scarr's (1981) goal of ensuring that testing is "always... used in the interests of the children tested" (p. 1159). This goal implies the simultaneous pursuit of excellence and equity. Achieving this goal will require a better scientific understanding of cognitive processes and the construct validity of our measures of those processes. It will also require a better understanding of the consequences of the uses that are made of test results.

Testing needs to be more closely linked to instruction. Improving the link will require "a combined enterprise representing test design based on knowledge of human learning and performance, psychometric requirements, and studies of test use" (Curtis & Glaser, 1983, p. 144).

REFERENCES

Bejar, I. I. (1984). Educational diagnostic assessment. *Journal of Educational Measurement, 21,* 175–189.

Bersoff, D. N. (1981). Testing and the law. *American Psychologist, 36,* 1047–1056.

Bloom, B. S. (1976). *Human characteristics and school learning.* New York: McGraw-Hill.

Bloom, B. S. (1980). The new direction in educational research: Alterable variables. In W. B. Schrader (Ed.), *Measuring achievement: Progress over a decade. New directions for testing and measurement* (pp. 17–30). San Francisco: Jossey-Bass.

Bock, R. D., & Mislevy, R. J. (in preparation). *Theory of the duplex design.*

Carroll, J. B., & Horn, J. L. (1981). On the scientific basis of ability testing. *American Psychologist, 36,* 1012–1020.

Cronbach, L. J. (1975). Five decades of public controversy over mental testing. *American Psychologist, 30,* 1–14.

Cross, L. H. (1985). Validation of the NTE tests for certification decisions. *Educational Measurement: Issues and Practice, 4*(3), 7–10.

Curtis, M. E., & Glaser, R. (1983). Reading theory and the assessment of reading achievement. *Journal of Educational Measurement, 20,* 133–147.

Darling-Hammond, L., Wise, A. E., & Pease, S. R. (1983). Teacher evaluation in the organizational context: A review of the literature. *Review of Educational Research, 53,* 285–328.

Debra P. v. Turlington, 644 F. 2d 397 (5th Cir. 1981).

Educational Testing Service. (1985). *The reading report card: Progress toward excellence in our schools. Trends in reading over four national assessments.* Princeton, NJ: Author.

Education for All Handicapped Children Act of 1975, Pub. L. No. 94–142.

Emergency School Assistance Act of 1970. Pub. L. No. 88–352.

Fisher, T. H., Fry, B. V., Loewe, K. L., & Wilson, G. W. (1985). Testing teachers for merit pay purposes in Florida. *Educational Measurement: Issues and Practice, 4*(3), 10–12.

Green, B. F. (1983). Adaptive testing by computer. In R. B. Ekstrom (Ed.), *Measurement technology and individuality in education: New directions for testing and measurement* (pp. 5–12). San Francisco: Jossey-Bass.

Haney, W. (1981). Validity, vaudeville, and values: A short history of social concerns over standardized testing. *American Psychologist, 36,* 1021–1034.

Hechinger, F. M. (1984, November 20). A new elitism appears in higher education. *New York Times,* p. C8.

Heller, K. A., Holtzman, W. H., & Messick, S. (Eds). (1982). *Placing children in special education: A strategy for equity.* Washington, DC: National Academy Press.

Herrnstein, R. J. (1973). *IQ in the meritocracy.* Boston: Little, Brown.

Horn, J. L. (in press). Models of intelligence. In R. L. Linn (Ed.), *Intelligence: Measurement, theory, and public policy.* Champaign, IL: University of Illinois Press.

Hsu, T., & Nitko, A. J. (1984). *A comprehensive microcomputer system for classroom testing.* Unpublished manuscript, University of Pittsburgh, Pittsburgh, PA.

Kamin, L. J. (1974). *The science and politics of IQ.* Potomac, MD: Erlbaum.

Kane, M. T. (1982). The validity of licensure examinations. *American Psychologist, 37,* 911–918.

Larry, P. v. Riles, 495 F. Supp. 926 (N.D. Cal. 1979), *appeal docketed,* No. 80-4027 (9th Cir. Jan. 17, 1980).

Lerner, B. (1981). The minimum competence testing movement: Social, scientific, and legal implications. *American Psychologist, 36,* 1057–1066.

Lindquist, E. F. (1936). The theory of test construction. In H. E. Hawkes, E. F. Lindquist, & C. R. Mann (Eds.), *The construction and uses of achievement examinations* (pp. 1–53). Boston: Houghton Mifflin.

Lord, F. M. (1980). *Applications of item response theory to practical testing problems.* Hillsdale, NJ: Erlbaum.

Lord, F. M., & Novick, M. R. (1968). *Statistical theories of mental test scores.* Reading, MA: Addison-Wesley.

Madaus, G. F. (1981). NIE clarification hearing: The negative team's case. *Phi Delta Kappan, 63,* 92–94.

Medley, D. M., Coker, J., & Soar, R. S. (1984). *Measurement-based evaluation of teacher performance: An empirical approach.* New York: Longman.

National Commission on Excellence in Education. (1983). *A nation at risk: The imperative for educational reform.* Washington, DC: U.S. Government Printing Office.

PASE v. Hannon, 506 F. Supp. 831 (N. D. Ill. 1980).

Podemski, R. S., & Lohr, C. K. (1985). Why we are testing teachers: Some policy issues. *Educational Measurement: Issues and Practice, 4*(3), 20–22.

Popham, W. J. (1981). The case for minimum competency testing. *Phi Delta Kappan, 63,* 89–91.

Popham, W. J., & Yalow, E. S. (1983). *Appraising the Pre-Professional Skills Test for the state of Texas.* Culver City, CA: Instructional Objectives Exchange Assessment Associates.

Pugach, M. C., & Raths, J. D. (1983). Testing teachers: Analysis and recommendations. *Journal of Teacher Education, 34,* 37–43.

Rehabilitation Act of 1973, Pub. L. No. 93–112.

Quirk, T. J., Witten, B. J., & Weinberg, S. F. (1973). Review of studies of the concurrent and predictive validity of the National Teacher Examinations. *Review of Educational Research, 43,* 89–113.

Reschly, D. J. (1981). Psychological testing in educational certification and placement. *American Psychologist, 36,* 1094–1102.

Resnick, D. (1982). History of educational testing. In A. K. Wigdor & W. R. Garner (Eds.), *Ability testing: Uses, consequences, and controversies. Part II: Documentation section* (pp. 173–194). Washington, DC: National Academy Press.

Scarr, S. (1981). Testing for children: Assessment and the many determinants of intellectual competence. *American Psychologist, 36,* 1159–1166.

Standards for educational and psychological testing. (1985). Washington, DC: American Psychological Association.

Vold, D. J. (1985). The roots of teacher testing in America. *Educational Measurement: Issues and Practice, 4*(3), 5–7.

Wigdor, A. K., & Garner, W. R. (Eds.). (1982). *Ability testing: Uses, consequences, and controversies. Part I: Report of the Committee.* Washington, DC: National Academy Press.

Wirtz, W., & Howe, W. (1977). *On further examination: Report of the advisory panel on the Scholastic Aptitude Test score decline.* New York: College Entrance Examination Board.

10.2 GRANT WIGGINS

Assessment: Authenticity, Context, and Validity

Grant Wiggins earned his B.A. from St. John's College in Annapolis, Maryland, in 1972 and both his Ed.M., in 1982, and his Ed.D., in 1987, from the Harvard Graduate School of Education. From 1972 to 1981 he taught history, math, and philosophy at the Loomis Chaffee School in Windsor, Connecticut. From 1982 to 1985 he taught English at Buckingham Browne and Nichols School in Cambridge, Massachusetts. Wiggins was a research assistant to Carol Gilligan on the Adolescence Project at Harvard University (1982–1985) and later served as an adjunct professor in education at Brown University from 1985 to 1987.

Wiggins cofounded the Center on Learning, Assessment, and School Structure (CLASS), a not-for-profit educational organization in Pennington, New Jersey. He is currently president and director of programs for CLASS. CLASS consults with schools, districts, and state education departments on a variety of reform matters; organizes national conferences and workshops; and develops video, software, and print materials on assessment and curricular change. In particular, CLASS and Wiggins are best known for training teachers in performance and portfolio assessment.

There have always been critics of the multiple-choice (and true-false) testing methods employed by teachers, schools, and large testing organizations. There are many complaints that multiple-choice tests are "not like real life." Not only is Wiggins one of those critics, but he has moved beyond simple criticism to offering something better. He is offering teachers a more authentic and meaningful way of assessing student performance. His ideas on this topic are excerpted here from his article "Assessment: Authenticity, Context, and Validity," *Phi Delta Kappan* (November 1993).

Key Concept: authentic assessment

There is an inescapable tension between the challenges presented by contextualized performance and conventional, large-scale, generic testing. Understanding is not cued knowledge: performance is never the sum of drills; problems are not exercises; mastery is not achieved by the unthinking application of algorithms. In other words, we cannot be said to understand something unless we can employ our knowledge wisely, fluently, flexibly, and aptly in particular and diverse contexts. As Lauren Resnick has put it, the two key assumptions of conventional test design—the decomposability of knowledge into elements and the decontextualization of knowing (whereby it is assumed that if we know something we know it in any context)—are false.[1] It may in fact make better sense to think of understanding as being more like good judgment or a disposition than the possession of information.

In other words, something more than face validity is at stake. The simplest way to sum up the potential harm of our current tests is to say that we are not preparing students for real, "messy" uses of knowledge in context— the "doing" of a subject. Or, as one teacher expressed it to me a few years ago, "The trouble with kids today is that they don't know what to do when they don't know what to do." That is largely because all our testing is based on a simplistic stimulus/response view of learning.

Two key words in this analysis are *context* and *judgment.* Competent performance requires both. It makes no intellectual sense to test for "knowledge" as if mastery were an unvarying response to unambiguous stimuli. That would be like evaluating trial judges only on the basis of their knowledge of law or doctors only on the basis of their recall of biochemistry. What we should be assessing is the student's ability to prepare for and master the various "roles" and situations that competent professionals encounter in their work.

But we should keep the test-maker's dilemma in mind: fidelity to the criterion situations maximizes the complexity and ambiguity of the task requirements and maximizes the freedom to respond—both conditions that work against standardization and reliability. While this conflict between validity and reliability must never be construed as an either/or choice, it remains a design problem to be carefully negotiated.

Today, we are failing to negotiate the dilemma. Modern, professionally designed tests intended for national and state use tend to sacrifice validity for reliability. In other words, test-makers generally end up being more concerned with the precision of scores than with the intellectual value of the challenge. Thus the forms of testing and scoring used are indirect and generic, designed to minimize the ambiguity of tasks and answers.[2]

But such forms of testing simply do not tell us what we need to know: namely, whether students have the capacity to use wisely what knowledge they have. This is a judgment that we can make only through tasks that require students to "perform" in highly contextualized situations that are as faithful as possible to criterion situations.

Deeper educational issues underlie these concerns. To assume that tests should assess whether all students everywhere have the same "knowledge" is to short-circuit a vital educational dialogue in a pluralistic and diverse society. Genuine intellectual performance is inherently personalized, and the meanings, strengths, and aspirations that we derive from an education are inherently idiosyncratic. Common knowledge is not the aim of any robust education for lifelong learning. If competence is more like contextual insight and good judgment than inert knowledge, we will need to rethink our reliance on short-answer, unambiguous items and one-time tests.

We should be seeking a more robust and authentic construct of "understanding" and a more rigorous validation of tests against that construct. We can begin by keeping in mind that the aim of education is to help the individual become a competent intellectual performer, not a passive "selector" of orthodox and pre-fabricated answers.

WHAT IS PERFORMANCE?

The word *perform* in common parlance means to execute a task or process and to bring it to completion. Our ability to perform with knowledge can therefore be assessed only as we produce some work of our own, using a repertoire of knowledge and skills and being responsive to the particular tasks and contexts at hand.

One way to illustrate the difference between drilled skills and performance ability is with an anecdote from my soccer-coaching career. It is common in soccer and other sports to practice drills related to exploiting a numerical advantage on offense. Every coach routinely does what are called "2 on 1," "3 on 2," or "4 on 3" drills—drills in which the offense has the ball and a numerical advantage. But mastery of these drills does not automatically translate into mastery in a game, as the following tale reveals.

Once, during a game early in a season, one of my better players had a series of opportunities to exploit such a numerical advantage. I yelled from the sidelines, "2 on 1!" And she actually stopped dribbling the ball and yelled back at me, "I can't see it!"

That's the problem with testing by indirect items. Like soccer drills, test items are deliberately simplified and decontextualized. But the sum of the drills is never equal to fluid, effective, and responsive performance—no matter how complex or varied the drills. As all good athletes and coaches know, judgment and "anticipation" are essential elements of competence. Yet almost every major test (or set of textbook problems) is a *drill* test, not a performance test.

What we must keep asking is, What is the equivalent of the game in each subject? In other words, what does the "doing" of mathematics, history, science, or art look and feel like in context? And how can our tests better replicate authentic challenges and conditions instead of isolated drills? The simple answer is that all performance is highly contextual, involves constant judgment in adapting knowledge, and places an emphasis on habits of mind, not learnedness. Nor should this argument for authenticity be seen as applying only to older or more advanced students. If we want competent performance later, we need to introduce novices to that performance from day one. Only a deep and ancient prejudice about academic learning keeps us thinking that intellectual competence is achieved by accretion of knowledge and movement through simple logical elements to the complex whole—instead of movement from a *crude* grasp of the whole to a *sophisticated* grasp of the whole.

Consider the following test given in a U.S. history course after a unit on the Revolutionary War. It illustrates how a performance task to demonstrate understanding differs from a test of knowledge.

You are a prosecutor or a defense attorney in a trial brought by a parent group seeking to forbid purchase by your high school of a U.S. history textbook, excerpted below. (The book would be used as a *required supplement* to your current text, not in place of it.) You will present a 10-minute oral case (supported by a written summary of your argument), in pairs, to a jury, taking either side of the question, Is the book appropriate for school adoption and required reading? You will be assessed on how well you support your claim about the accounts in the text, in response to the question, Are the accounts biased, inaccurate, or merely different from our usual viewpoint? [The students are given an extended excerpt from the "textbook," actually a text used in China in 1970, along with the following questions to consider.]

1. What can be said to be the most likely political influences on the authors' point of view? What evidence is there of those influences? How do they affect the authors' choice of language? Does the language reflect bias or an acceptable (but different) point of view? Explain your reasoning.
2. Why does it make sense, given the authors' perspective, that they pay particular attention to a) the Committee of Correspondence, b) the contribution of women, and c) the plight of "Indians" and "Negroes"? Are the facts accurate? Do they warrant that much attention in your view, or does such selective emphasis suggest a biased treatment? (How are these topics treated in the current text, and is the treatment there less biased or selective?)
3. You will be judged on the accuracy, aptness, and convincing qualities of your documentation and on the rhetorical effectiveness of your case. Be fair, but be an effective speaker and writer! A six-point scoring scale will be used for each dimension to be assessed: persuasiveness of evidence, persuasiveness of argument, rhetorical effectiveness of speech, and support material.

Leaving aside the feasibility of using such tasks in large-scale assessments (though this is done in other countries), the question raised by such a task is, Isn't this what we mean by *performance?* Clearly, students must "do" history in order to master the task. Mere control over what was in the textbook would neither prepare students adequately for doing such a task nor adequately represent the "criterion situation" of "doing" history. To merely "understand" what the textbook said is neither to understand the events themselves nor to understand what it means to do historical research on such events. In fact, when I have used this task in some fine suburban high schools, many students have been stunned to discover that the passage disagrees with their own textbooks —a sure indication that they have not "understood" or "done" history.

All tests must always point toward and be "enabling" of adult performance, in the sense suggested by Robert Glaser: "To place tests in the service of learning in a marriage of cognitive and psychometric theory, we must consider assessment . . . as measures of skills and dispositions that are essential to further learning. Once mastered, the skills and knowledge of a domain can become enabling competencies for the future."[3] Thus we will need a better understanding of how understanding develops in a subject, as modeled by Harvard University psychologist William Perry's more general scheme for intellectual development in college.[4] Or, as Glaser has put it, "Modern learning theory is taking on the characteristics of a developmental psychology of performance changes.... In the future, achievement measurement will be designed to assess these changes."[5]

We must begin to do a better job of testing for emerging competence by moving backward from the ultimate criterion performance, even when the student's current knowledge is rudimentary. We need to generalize from such approaches as those of Berlitz and other immersion language courses, which get the learner speaking and listening in context immediately and working toward the ultimate criterion of fluent contextual performance.

Not all hands-on work involves performance. Doing simplistic tasks that merely "cue" us for the desired bit of knowledge is not a creative employment of knowledge and skill, but a drill or exercise out of context. Consider, for example, a task from the original hands-on science test given a few years ago to all fourth-graders in New York.

In the first of five "stations," the student is given a cup, water, a thermometer, and other instruments. The student is expected, among other things, to accurately measure the temperature of the water. Toward what end? To what degree of precision? No one measures anything *in general.* Are we simulating the measuring of body temperature or of roasts in the oven? Are we making gravy or medicine? Purpose and context *matter* in our assessment of skill.

The test also requires that the answer be correct within two degrees above or below the "actual" water temperature. But why two degrees? Why such generosity? (And why is the student not told of this tolerance margin?) With no consequence or purpose to the measuring, there can be no appropriate margin of error. (A better form of this task would be to choose a recipe that requires just the right temperature of a liquid for a specific result to occur.[6])

UNDERSTANDING AND HABITS OF MIND

Another way to see how contextual understanding might be better tested is to consider the idea that understanding is inseparable from certain habits of mind.

Habit is a word rarely used to describe academic mastery. We tend to reserve it now for the more pressing and oppressing concerns of affective issues or personal addictions. That is a pity, because a case can be made that academic learning and our assessment of it cannot be understood unless we see our aim as the formation of good habits of mind in each subject.[7] Yet we continue to do large-scale testing in a one-event format—a format inherently incapable of revealing whether a student is in the habit of performing up to standards—at our students' peril.[8]

Through the work of Piaget, David Hawkins, and Eleanor Duckworth and in the literature on naive misconceptions in science (all well summed up and extended by Howard Gardner in *The Unschooled Mind*), we are reminded that many "obvious" adult ideas are countertuitive.[9] Dewey, for example, was adamant that our ideas—even logical rules of inference—should be thought of as habits, sometimes not easily given up even when wrong: "The history of scientific beliefs shows that when a wrong theory once gets general acceptance, men will expend ingenuity of thought in buttressing it with additional errors rather than surrender it."[10]

The word *habit* suggests what assessment needs to become if it is to be directed toward thoughtful and effective understanding.[11] A higher-order habit is an intelligent *proneness*, not a reflex, in an inherently ambiguous situation. To say that academic learning aims ultimately to develop the habit of employing knowledge effectively alerts us to the fact that we need more than an assessment of *learnedness*; we need to assess for intellectual *character*. Any test of understanding should make it possible for us to know whether the student can accurately and willingly adapt knowledge to varying situations. This requires forms of testing that evoke and require for success the disposition to be critical in an ill-structured situation. Consider, for example, such open-ended prompts as this one used in a recent 12th-grade performance assessment in Connecticut. "How much does it cost to take a shower?"

To become progressively self-disciplined as a thinker, one needs more than an imposed rigor and the fruits of someone else's studies. One needs to acquire the habit of inquiring and engaging in discourse with care and thoroughness. What follows for assessment should be clear to anyone who grasps such an objective. How can I ever assess such a disposition in a one-sitting event? How can I acquire evidence as to whether students have "discipline" in a discipline without asking them to conduct inquiries and present findings? How can I assess students' learning unless I see whether they have *learned how to learn* in the subject in question? How can I assess their understanding without assessing their ability to ask and persist in trying to answer the right questions? Thus it is clear why a predominance of ill-structured tasks is essential for assessment of understanding: the lack of structure in the answering process is the only way I can discern whether a student has the necessary intellectual habits. If a focus on *understanding* is our goal, then secure, one-event, well-structured tasks with arbitrary criteria are at best dysfunctional.

It is one thing to learn how to respond to an unambiguous stimulus; it is another to become disposed to invoke the right habits of mind in a fluid performance context. Good teacher/coaches have students constantly moving back and forth between drill and a "whole" performance. In this way, students can learn what it feels like to be in the habit of skillful performing and can see the value of developing the newer, more difficult habits. We develop a repertoire of habits by continually practicing strategies in performance contexts, by using our judgment as to what works (and when and why), and by being constantly tested (through real or simulated performances).

UNDERSTANDING AS REVEALED THROUGH GOOD JUDGMENT

If performance requires a larger purpose, a rich context, and a repertoire wisely used, then effective performance is impossible without good judgment. Thus competence is testable only through tasks that demand good judgment in the use of knowledge. To test for understanding is to see if knowledge can be thoughtfully adapted. "Acquiring information can never develop the power of judgment," according to Dewey. "Development of judgment is in spite of, not because of, methods of instruction that emphasize simple learning.... [The student] cannot get power of judgment excepting as he is continually exercised in forming and testing judgments."[12] Rather than merely having knowledge of general principles and of unambiguous cases to which they apply, "to be a good judge is to have a sense of the relative values of the various features of a *perplexing* situation."[13]

Judgment involves effective adaptation to *specific* roles and situations; that is what we mean by *competence*.[14] We should recall that Binet defined intelligence as good judgment, "practical sense, initiative, the faculty of adapting one's self to circumstances"—what the French call *bon sens*, or good sense.[15] To develop a thoughtful control over performance depends not so much on learning and employing "knowledge and skills" but on having our judgment awakened and empowered through problems that demand judgment.

Judgment certainly does not involve the unthinking application of rules or algorithms—the stock in trade of all conventional tests. The effective performer, like the good judge, never loses sight of either relative importance or the difference between the "spirit" and the "letter" of the law or rules that apply. Neither ability is testable by one-dimensional items.

All performers must be judges. In a new case, how do we know which rules to apply? The performer, like the judge, "has to innovate, and where he innovates he is not operating from habit."[16] That is precisely what the soccer player mentioned above could *not* do: she could not discern when her "2 on 1" knowledge should be applied. Unending drill tests prevent the development of the perception and adaptive intelligence needed to meet that sort of challenge.

Consider a different perspective on good judgment in the employment of skills—the account by the OSS (Office of Strategic Services) staff of what they called behavior "of the highest order of effectiveness." In the view of the OSS, effective use of knowledge and skill requires someone to "perceive and interpret properly the whole situation that confronts him... and... to coordinate his acts and direct them in proper sequence.... [T]hey all require organization.... Consequently, [a test for effectiveness requires] tasks and situations which cannot be properly solved without organization." The OSS staff elsewhere described these tasks as requiring "mental operations on a higher integrative level; and since there is a difference between 'know-how' and 'can-do' we made the candidates actually attempt the tasks with their muscles or spoken words."[17]

In other words, any test must be judgment-based. After all, when asked to evaluate the correctness of an answer in real-world settings, we typically respond, "Well, it depends on...." But this response is the antithesis of testing as we know it, where the aim is to use well-defined, unambiguous problems with a single apparent variable and a single correct answer so that we can ensure reliability and cost-effectiveness.

Let us now consider two tests—both designed for use in a general science course for middle school students, both from published texts/curricula. The first, an ill-structured test that requires thoughtful performance, is known as the "Sludge." In the Introductory Physical Science course, it is one of the major events.

In this multiday test, students have to chemically analyze a sludgelike mixture of unknown solids and liquids. (In one New Jersey school district, the Sludge takes up the last two weeks of class in June, serving as a very elaborate performance test of the year's work.) This is an ill-structured and authentic task par excellence: though the methods and criteria are quite clear to all students in the course, there are no pat routines, procedures, or recipes for solving the problem. Thus the test faithfully simulates a wide range of real-world "tests" of chemical analysis.

By contrast, consider a brief sampling of traditional items taken from a summative test of 200 items in a science textbook, to be given in a 90-minute period at the end of the eighth grade:

2. A general statement based on a hypothesis that has been tested many times is

    a. a conclusion
    b. scientific law
    c. scientific knowledge
    d. a theory

125. Green plants and algae are

    a. omnivores
    b. herbivores
    c. consumers
    d. producers

191. The level in the classification that is broader than species but narrower than family is

    a. class
    b. order
    c. genus
    d. phylum

Such exhaustiveness may well provide a certain superficial "content" validity, but the test bears little relationship to the practice of science, which is the ultimate "test" of one's knowledge.

Norman Frederiksen made this point a decade ago in writing about the "real bias" that exists in testing.[18] His point was that the "tests" of life are more like the "Sludge" or the cost-of-the-shower problem than any neat and clean multiple-choice item. The "real bias" in testing is that tests are inherently restricted to unambiguous items, and their design ends up influencing what is taught and what is thought to be a problem.

A critic might respond, "But surely, before students can perform, we must give them drills and then tests concerning their mastery of the drills." This logical fallacy has probably done more harm than any other operant principle in American education. Look how Bloom's Taxonomy was (and still is) improperly construed as a chronology, though its authors warned against regarding it as such. Look how often syllabi unendingly postpone the student's exposure to genuine performance with knowledge in the name of "lessons" whose meaning is opaque and whose interest value is minimal.

All one has to do to see the fallacy of this way of thinking is to look at the adult performance world: musicians, athletes, architects, and doctors learn how to "perform with knowledge" by practicing the criterion performance. The Little Leaguer gets to play baseball; the medical student makes hospital rounds; the young artist starts by drawing. Any drill testing for these young performers is a means to an end; it is certainly not to be confused with the important performance itself.

Some roles and activities common to professional life might serve as possible "templates" for better test design. Perhaps a school district or state agency might store them in a nonsecure "bank." For example, to give students a taste of the role of museum curator, they might be asked to design an exhibit on a given topic or to compete with one another in designing grant proposals. To sample the problems faced by engineers, students might be given projects that require them to bid and meet specifications or to design and build a working catapult or herbarium. As a sample of the world of design and marketing, students might be asked to design an advertising campaign for a product (real or imaginary) or to design book jackets, blurbs, and so on for the books used in class. The possibilities are endless.

For assessment purposes, similar roles and situational challenges might be generalized into a more sophisticated and feasible classification system (or set of *representative* tasks), linked to role-based research such as that by Robert Gagné.[19] Many school districts are now developing sets of learner-outcome criteria and standards that point in the same direction. Situational accuracy depends on the kind of "job analysis" rarely applied to K–12 education. Yet this kind of "role analysis" is at the heart of competency-based education: "The competency-based approach begins with the definition of the knowledge, skills, and attitudes required for successful performance in a particular role."[20] Or, as Gerald Grant put it in a book thoroughly analyzing competency-based education at the collegiate level, "Competence-based education... derives a curriculum from an analysis of a prospective or actual role in modern society."[21] Distinguished psychometricians have been making these points for years.[22]

Persistent unwillingness to design K–12 tests to match ultimate criterion situations was at the heart of David McClelland's influential critique of standardized testing 20 years ago. He argued that validity coefficients for tests were too often derived from other indirect tests or from such predictors as college grades, which are still not the real measure. The best testing, he argued, is "criterion sampling.... [T]here are almost no occupations that require a person to do word analogies. The point is so obvious that it would scarcely be worth mentioning, if it had not been obscured so often by psychologists." The solution? "Criterion sampling means that testers have to get out of their offices...

and into the field where they actually analyze performance into its components. If you want to test who will be a good policeman, go find what a policeman does." McClelland knew well the difficulty of getting testers to honor his concern, however: "The task will not be easy. It will require psychological skills not ordinarily in the repertoire of the traditional tester. What is called for is nothing less than a revision of the role itself—moving it away from word games and statistics toward behavioral analysis."[23]

Frederiksen made the same point a decade ago: "We need a much broader conception of what a test is if we are to use test information in improving educational outcomes," he argued.[24] Or, as the OSS staff put it, anticipating all the discussion well: "The best that can be done [given the limits of predictive testing] is to expose a man to a variety of situations of the same type as those he will find in the field."[25]

The OSS staff noted particularly that traditional forms of paper-and-pencil tests failed to test for "effective intelligence"—the ability to select goals and to recognize the best means in context for attaining them coupled with quick resourceful thinking or good judgment. They were "prompted to introduce realistic tests of ability" when they observed inconsistencies between paper-and-pencil tests of real-world abilities and performance in the world on problems of the same sort. However, they added ruefully that few of their colleagues "seem to have been disquieted by the fact that taking a paper-and-pencil test is very different from solving a problem in everyday life."[26]

In fact, my claim about the tendency in testing to sacrifice validity for reliability was assumed to be a problem by the OSS team of researchers: "In retrospect it seems a little peculiar that we psychologists should have devoted so much time to improving the reliability of our tests and so little time to improving their validity.... Surely the essential criterion of a good test is its congruence with reality; its coherence with other tests is a matter of secondary concern." They went so far as to recommend that we *reverse* typical validation procedure: "Tests that are being developed should be administered only to persons who have been thoroughly studied, persons about whose activities sufficient data have already been collected."[27]

Finally, in a review of these issues, Lee Cronbach noted that "a bad criterion may make inappropriate tests look good. Tests that predict training criteria differ from those that best predict job performance."[28] Our school-based tests are inauthentic and inappropriate as predictors for the same reason. It is time that test-makers were held more accountable for their methods of validation and required to do more careful trait and job analyses to justify both the form and content of tests they design.

AUTHENTICITY

What we require, therefore, are more general design criteria that can be used to frame challenges that are psychometrically useful but also more "authentic" —that is, that require performance faithful to criterion situations. But first we need to be clear about what we mean by *authenticity*. Here is my latest version of a much-revised set of criteria for judging the authenticity of a test.[29] Authentic tests of intellectual performance involve the following factors.

- Engaging and worthy problems or questions of importance, in which students must use knowledge to fashion performances effectively and creatively. The tasks are either replicas of or analogous to the kinds of problems faced by adult citizens and consumers or professionals in the field.
- Faithful representation of the contexts encountered in a field of study or in the real-life "tests" of adult life. The formal *options, constraints,* and *access to resources* are apt rather than arbitrary. In particular, the use of excessive secrecy, limits on methods, the imposition of arbitrary deadlines or restrains on the use of resources to rethink, consult, revise, and so on—all with the aim of making testing more efficient—should be evaluated and minimized.
- Nonroutine and multistage tasks—*real* problems. Recall or "plugging in" is insufficient or irrelevant. Problems require a repertoire of knowledge, good judgment in determining which knowledge is apt when and where, and skill in prioritizing and organizing the phases of problem clarification and solution.
- Tasks that require the student to produce a *quality* product and/or performance.
- Transparent or demystified criteria and standards. The test allows for thorough preparation as well as accurate self-assessment and self-adjustment by the student; questions and tasks may be discussed, clarified, and even appropriately modified, through discussion with the assessor and/or one's peers.
- Interactions between assessor and assessee. Tests ask the student to *justify* answers or choices and often to respond to follow-up or probing questions.
- Response-contingent challenges in which the effect of both process and product/performance determines the quality of the result. Thus there is concurrent feedback and the possibility of self-adjustment during the test.
- Trained assessor judgment, in reference to clear and appropriate criteria. An oversight or auditing function exists: there is always the possibility of questioning and perhaps altering a result, given the open and fallible nature of the formal judgment.
- The search for *patterns* of response in diverse settings. Emphasis is on the consistency of student work—the assessment of *habits* of mind in performance.

We might summarize these points by using the perhaps oxymoronic term "authentic simulations" to describe what we should be after in the design of educative tests. As Robert Fitzpatrick and Edward Morrison put it 20 years ago in their comprehensive review of issues in performance testing, we seek two things in authentic simulations: the "fidelity" of a simulation and the "comprehensiveness" with which the many different aspects of situations are replicated.

Of course, any simulation, like any test, involves choices and compromises, and the purposes and budgetary or logistical constraints under which we test may cause us to settle for a lesser degree of each than is optimal.

But the problems are more than just practical. As Fitzpatrick and Morrison put it, "The dilemma of simulation is that increasing fidelity and comprehensiveness appear to increase validity but on the other hand with decreasing control [over the situation and possible responses] and thus reliability."[30] Tests are simplified of contextual "noise" to make scores more reliable; yet we need to maximize the fidelity and comprehensiveness of the simulation for reasons of validity.

We can thus learn to negotiate the dilemma in a way that is educationally sound only by gaining better insight into what it is we must be more faithful to: the setting in which the challenge is embedded or the constraints under which the student is expected to operate. If "generic performance" is a contradiction in terms and if judgment-based performance should be a major part of testing, then testers are going to have to think through the role of context in testing.

CONTEXT, CONSTRAINTS, AND AUTHENTICITY

In real life we use our intellect and acquired knowledge and skills in particular contexts to solve particular problems. As Arthur Chickering and Charles Claxton, researchers of competency-based learning, put it:

> Competence is... situational and personal. This is the most critical principle. Competence levels and qualities are dependent upon situations and contexts. Particular contexts and situations interact with particular clusters of predispositions and abilities brought by the person. The outcomes depend upon these complex interactions.... A person who is "literate" in one culture can at the same time be "illiterate" in another.[31]

Over the past few years of thinking these matters through, I have come to believe that this claim is so true that testers should pay most attention to the second of my nine criteria of authenticity—that is, replicating or simulating the diverse and rich contexts of performance.

As I noted in talking about judgment, being competent requires sensitivity to context. For example, a doctor is not expert merely because he or she possesses a set of general rules and propositions or habits in the muscles—rules and habits called "medicine." The doctor knows (or does not know) how to adapt relatively abstract guidelines of pathology and technique to each individual patient.

Support for heightened attention to contextual detail can be found in a variety of research sources. In addition to the report of the OSS staff, the competency-based model used at Alverno College makes "contextual validity" an essential part of the design problem.[32] And John Seely Brown, Allan Collins, and Paul Duguid have argued the more comprehensive point that all cognition is "situated" in cultures and contexts, rendering decontextualized learning and assessment invalid and dysfunctional—"not fully productive of useful learning." Since schoolwork is "very different from what authentic practitioners do" and since learning and testing tend to reflect the culture of school and not the culture represented by the field of study, "contrary to the aim of schooling, success within this culture often has little bearing on performance elsewhere."[33]

A test may always be a contrivance, then, but it should not feel like one. Consider the best professional training and testing. Doctors and pilots are confronted with situations that replicate the challenges to be faced later, including vital complexities of human interaction. (For example, many of the simulations used for recertification of professional airline pilots involve working effectively with other crew members, because no one crew member has all the necessary information.) A context is thus realistic to the extent that we so accept the premises, constraints, and "feel" of the challenge that our desire to master it makes us lose sight of any contrivances or extrinsic factors—factors such as the reality that someone is evaluating us—in the same way that Outward Bound exercises and the publishing of a school newspaper for a journalism course do not feel contrived. Researchers have consistently found that this verisimilitude and the chance to feel efficacious are essential not only to producing one's best performance but to student motivation.

Here is a simple example of one high school teacher's initial attempt to design a performance task and of how the task evolved as a concern for context was introduced. The original task (in a global studies course) required students to design a trip to China or Japan. The purpose was to determine whether they had learned from their reading the most important things about one of the countries. But what kind of trip should be designed? For what customers? With what constraints of budget or time?

The teacher then refined the task: each student had a $10,000 budget to design a one-month cultural-exchange trip for students his or her age. Okay. But the purpose was still too abstract. What must the tour designers accomplish? Are they trying to design a tour in the abstract or a tour to really attract young people? The students were finally charged to be travel agents who would develop an extensive brochure, fully researching the cost and logistical information using the SABRE computer-reservations system (available through the school computers). One student noted during the project, "Boy, this is hard. Is this what real life is like?"

Paradoxically, the complexity of context is made manageable by contextual clues. For the students to have a clear sense of what kind of answer fits the problem at hand, detail is essential. Think how difficult it would have been for students to design a trip with no contextual clues. Put differently, in the best case studies, the problem is solvable only within the context provided. This is why business and law school cases are so difficult to write: they must be as faithful as possible to both the important and the unimportant facts of the situation. "A case typically is a record of a business issue which actually has been faced by business executives, together with surrounding facts, opinions, and prejudices upon which executive decisions depend."[34] In other words, any criteria and standards required by a performance task should be clear and natural to the situation.

THE AUTHENTICITY OF CONTEXTUAL CONSTRAINTS

The most vital aspect of contextual fidelity has to do with the authenticity of the constraints placed on performance by the demands of mass testing. But most educational testing involves constraints that have little to do with fidelity to the criterion situation and everything to do with maintaining standardization of task and procedure. It is time that we looked at the validity questions raised by this unbalanced trade-off.

There are typically four kinds of constraints facing any performer. There are demands placed on us by others, whether or not we would make such demands of ourselves; there are limits on the time available to complete the task; there are limits (sometimes because of the situation and sometimes because of the time limits) on the human and material resources at our disposal; and there are limits on our ability to get guidance and feedback as we proceed.

We can pose the following, then, as a set of design questions: What are *appropriate* limits on the availability of time, of reference materials and resource people, and of prior knowledge of the tasks, criteria, and standards to be mastered? I am certainly not arguing that students should have unlimited access to all resources during testing. But let us ask, What kinds of constraints authentically simulate or replicate the constraints and opportunities facing the performer in context? When are constraints authentic, and when are they inauthentic? It is often a matter of degree, but the principle needs to be maintained and defended.

Consider the following guidelines for testing for synthesis from Benjamin Bloom, George Madaus, and Thomas Hastings:

> The student may attack the problem with a variety of references or other available materials as they are needed. Thus, synthesis problems may be open-book examinations, in which the student may use notes, references, the library, and other resources as appropriate. *Ideally synthesis problems should be as close as possible to the situation in which a scholar (or artist, or engineer, etc.) attacks a problem he or she is interested in. The time allowed, conditions of work, and other stipulations should be as far from the typical, controlled examination situation as possible.*[35] (Emphasis added.)

Thus whatever assessors are testing in a 20-minute essay, it most certainly is *not* the ability to write. As those of us who write for a living know, writing is revision, a constant returning to the basic questions of audience and purpose—a process that is missing from standard writing tests (where there is no audience, no opportunity to reflect on each draft, and no *real* purpose).

The amount of time allowed for performing is not always what determines whether time constraints are reasonable or unreasonable; sometimes the issue is how that time is allotted. Is the limiting of a test to one sitting authentic? If writing is indeed revision, why not allow the writing assessment to occur over three or four days, with each draft graded? Many districts now do so, including such large school districts as those in Jefferson County, Kentucky, and Cherry Creek, Colorado.[36]

Restrictions on access to texts and human resources, on time for revision and reflection, and on opportunities to ensure that one's answer is apt and understood would seem to change what a test is measuring. What are we really testing in, say, the Advanced Placement exams, in which we deny students access to reference materials and human resources—despite the obvious availability of such things in almost all criterion situations that could be imagined in the particular subject matters? What can the exam results possibly tell us about students' ability to bring research to fruition, to sift through facts to discern the significant from the insignificant, or to use knowledge to good effect?

We do not need to keep all books and other materials from students if the task is genuinely authentic. For example, in many of Connecticut's performance tasks in mathematics, the key formulas are given to the students as background to the problem. And why not allow students to bring notes to an exam? Is this not precisely the sort of thing we really want to find out about students—whether they are organized, well-prepared, and effective at using what they know? (The test-makers' defense—that I am seeking to measure something different from what they claim to be measuring—is a dodge. What they are measuring is inappropriate if our aim is to see what students *understand*.)

Authenticity in testing, then, might well be thought of as an obligation to make the student experience questions and tasks under constraints as they typically and "naturally" occur, with access to the tools that are usually available for solving such problems.

THE RELATIONSHIP BETWEEN AUTHENTICITY AND VALIDITY

Attention to the authenticity of purposes and constraints in context and to the nature of understanding makes clear why a performance-based *task* is not necessarily a valid or authentic *test*. Have we sampled the performance domain fairly or comprehensively? Would scores be different if we used different prompts or different kinds of tasks? Have we gathered sufficient evidence, using diverse forms and diverse settings, of the *pattern* of responses that indicates competence? These questions demand every test-maker's attention.

And the problem is not limited to the selection of tasks. Most of the scoring rubrics that I have encountered seem invalid to me. In English classes, we score what is easy, uncontroversial, and typical—not necessarily what is apt for identifying exemplary writing or apt for the situational demands of real-world writing.

Consider New Jersey's scoring criteria for essay writing and the descriptor for the top score on the scale. (New Jersey's writing assessment is typical of many state and district rubrics now in use.) The criteria are: organization/content, usage, sentence construction, and mechanics. The descriptor for a top score reads as follows:

Organization/Content: Samples have an opening and closing. The responses relate to the topic and have a single focus. They are well-developed, complete compositions that are organized and progress logically from beginning to end. A variety of cohesive devices are present, resulting in a fluent response. Many of these writers take compositional risks resulting in highly effective, vivid responses.

Sentence Construction: Samples demonstrate syntactic and verbal sophistication through an effective variety of sentences and/or rhetorical modes. There will be very few, if any, errors in sentence construction.

Mechanics & Usage: Few, if any, errors.

What a bore. Little in this scoring system places a premium on style, imagination, or ability to keep the reader interested. Only the top score description mentions "effective and vivid" responses, instead of those criteria being woven through the whole rubric. Yet we see this limitation in almost every writing assessment, including those of the National Assessment of Educational Progress (NAEP). For example, in a review of student stories contained in portfolios as part of a pilot project to score locally completed work, assessors using the NAEP rubric were restricted to formal criteria. Here is a descriptor for a story that merits a score of 6 (the top level): "Paper describes a sequence of episodes in which almost all story elements are well developed (i.e., setting, episodes, characters' goals, or problems to be solved). The resolution of the goals or problems at the end are [sic] elaborated. The events are presented and elaborated in a cohesive way."[37] Surely this is not the best description possible of a good story.

But habits of testing for merely formal problems run deep. In working with an English department on some schoolwide scoring rubrics, it took me two long sessions to get the teachers to admit that whether or not a paper was "interesting" was of primary importance. But they had never been willing to grade on that criterion, nor were they confident that such a criterion should be in a formal rubric.

The reader should not infer that I believe that criteria of the sort listed above do not matter. Of course, they are important. But they are merely necessary, not sufficient. As examples of better criteria that are more closely linked to the reason writers write and the effects writers hope to have on an audience, while still being mindful of formal criteria, consider *clarity, persuasiveness, memorability,* and *enticingness,* criteria offered by Allan Collins and Dieter Gentner.[38] Note that these criteria, which flow from a careful analysis of the purpose of the task, will probably not be met if there are distracting errors of organization or mechanics. Yet these criteria correctly alert the writer to the fact that writing ought to be worth reading, not merely formally "correct."

For scoring rubrics to be valid, the criteria have to be more than "face authentic." A test should enable us to effectively and validly discriminate between performances of different degrees of quality. As a result, scoring rubrics must be based on a careful analysis of existing performances of varying quality. We must possess models of exemplary and not-so-exemplary performance and be able to tell the two apart on the basis of apt reasons. Our discriminations must be valid, not merely reliable. Thus we should be basing our judgments on the most salient and educative distinctions—not on those that are easiest and most uncontroversial to score.

Rubrics that rely heavily on value-laden or comparative words are also guilty of sacrificing validity for reliability. For example, to say that a 6 is a "good" paper while a 5 is "average" or that the better essays support their positions with "more" reasons than the not-so-good essays is to make the judgment arbitrary—more like a norm-referenced test than a criterion-referenced test. The explanation is simple enough: weight does not equal quality. Many fine essays offer few reasons for the author's position; many dissertations with 400 footnotes have nothing to say.

The foreign-language proficiency guidelines of the American Council on the Teaching of Foreign Languages (ACTFL) show what scoring systems should strive to achieve. In their scoring descriptors, the scores reflect *empirically grounded traits* that characterize a speaker's performance, based on years of categorizing particular performances into levels of competence. Thus the guidelines identify typical errors for each stage of language performance. For example, the mistake of responding to *"Quel sport preferez-vous?"* with *"Vous preferez le sport tennis"* is noted as "an error characteristic of speakers" at the midnovice level, where "utterances are marked and often flawed by repetition of an interlocutor's words."[39]

Here again we see that the most valid design procedure involves working backward from the criterion performance and from concrete models of diverse levels of performance. What too few practitioners seem to understand is that scoring rubrics must be derived *after* we have a range of performances in hand, so as to ensure that our descriptors and discrimination procedures are not arbitrary.

THE CONTEXT OF TESTING

Contextual issues also relate to test administration itself. There is no such thing as an invariant and generic test situation—one in which students can be assumed to always reveal what they "know." Contextual factors in the test situation itself can affect what is *really* being measured—especially if the test does not permit the student to explain answers. Messick and others have argued the issue more broadly by making the point that validity must be analyzed in terms of the context in which testing occurs and the consequences that accrue from it. Not only is the meaning of test scores important, but so are the "relevance, utility, import ... and the functional worth of scores in terms of the social consequences of their use."[40]

Once we grasp the fact that student responses are colored by the particular task and setting, the implications, according to Messick, are considerable: "We are thus confronted with the fundamental question of whether the meaning of a measure is context-specific or whether it generalizes across contexts [since the] very nature of the task might be altered by the operation of constraining or facilitating factors in the specific situation." That is why validity inheres in the *interpretation* of a score and is not truly a property of the test itself. Messick soberly concludes by urging that "the role of context in test interpretation and test use be repeatedly investigated or monitored as a recurrent issue."[41] Can test-makers honestly say that they do such monitoring regularly?

Consider the following example of what happens when the context of testing is not considered. The kindergarten teachers in Ellenville, New York, were puzzled by the results of a commercial standardized test used in the district. Almost every student had gotten one simple question wrong. The question that caused the students so much trouble seemed easy enough: "Which one of the animals is a farm animal?" (In standardized testing for young children, the multiple choices are in the form of pictures, the "right" one to be selected after the test administrator reads each question.[42]) The choices: pictures of a whale (or a porpoise?) diving in the water, a giraffe, and a chicken. Why didn't the students select the chicken? Because not more than 20 miles from Ellenville is the Catskill Game Farm, where the star attraction (also represented on its large billboards in the area) is—you guessed it—a giraffe.

What seemed the most reasonable answer to the students was correct in context; what seemed the only apt answer to the test-maker turned out to be wrong in a specific context. Therein lies an inherent problem with tests that are both generic and nonresponsive. In a country with no agreed-upon universal syllabi or texts, test questions must be stripped from their natural setting. Yet, by depriving students of situational feedback and detail, we violate one of the most basic norms of social interaction. All questions are normally asked in context, often assuming a purpose, a culture, an audience, and various situational constraints. Suppose your math teacher says, "Do the odd problems for tonight's homework." We assume that she means the odd-numbered ones, not the most bizarre ones (though students can be masters at exploiting such inherent ambiguity to their benefit).

If we view the giraffe story as evidence of a mistake by the test company, we fail to grasp the danger of traditional generic testing. As Messick's argument about context suggests, we may be assuming far too much about the stability and transferability of student knowledge and too little about the influence of testing conditions. The particular "mistake" concerning the giraffe may be a sign that important arguments about the fundamental question of context have not gotten an adequate hearing. Tests that are designed to yield stable scores—without regard to the local syllabus, culture, and milieu—may end up testing only a trivial residue of a context-bound education.

Ironically, tests of this sort make test items harder for students than they normally would be, because all typical contextual cues and responses are removed. And those researchers who caution us in the use of performance tests—advising that there is inadequate generalizability when tasks vary slightly—may be looking through the wrong end of the telescope. Intellectual performance may be more contextually sensitive—and hence unstable—than we have heretofore been able to see or willing to admit.

Thus it is not proper to say that a student either does or does not "possess" knowledge. Rather, the test-taker acts knowledgeably or ignorantly—*in context*.[43] Context not only enables the student to know whether "chicken" or "giraffe" is the right answer in this case; it also lets the scorer know whether an answer is right or wrong in this case. What, then, is being assessed when the student answers a question but the judge and the environment are mute? Certainly not competence.

The use of the word *understand* as opposed to *know* makes the point more clearly: we do not understand things in general; we understand (or misunderstand) a person or an answer in *context*. Perfectly bright and able people who are effective in one setting or job can screw up in another: competency is context-bound. There is an obligation on testers, therefore, to seek each test-taker's rationale for answers. If they do so, there is no good epistemological or cognitive reason to assume that test scores *should* be stable (as most test programs tacitly assume) if we vary the task or context even slightly.

The argument for authenticity that I and others have made should thus be understood as something more substantial and less naive than some measurement folks would have us believe.[44] If validity refers to the implications or consequences of the inferences made, these issues cannot be ignored. As Messick puts it, in quoting Cronbach:

> "The bottom line is that validators have an obligation to review whether a practice has appropriate consequences for individuals and institutions, and especially to guard against adverse consequences. You ... may prefer to exclude reflection on consequences from meanings of the word *validation,* but you cannot deny the obligation." But we would prefer a somewhat stronger phrasing, because the meaning of validation should not be considered a preference.[45]

TASK WORTHINESS AND INCENTIVES: FACE VALIDITY REVISITED

In a student-centered view of assessment, perhaps we ought to resurrect an old concept that is now often pooh-poohed by psychometricians: face validity. Is the test, "on the face of it," a proper test of the ability or knowledge in question? Though this concept was once dignified enough to warrant discussion in measurement texts, few experts give any formal consideration to the matter these days.

In one standard educational measurement textbook that addresses the issue, the authors state that, in determining criterion-related validity, "we care very little what a test looks like." Yet a footnote to this sentence adds that the claim is not "entirely true," since what the test looks like "may be of importance in determining its acceptability and reasonableness to those who will be tested." Ironically, in discussing the legal issues surrounding validity, the example chosen by the authors concerns adult pilots, not young students: "Thus, a group of would-be pilots may be more ready to accept an arithmetic test dealing with wind drift and fuel consumption than they would the same problems phrased in terms of cost of crops or of recipes for baking cookies. This appearance of reasonableness is sometimes spoken of as face validity."[46]

In his analysis of the concept of validity and its history, Messick notes that, although "in the technical sense" face validity is not a form of validity, "whether the test is judged relevant to its objectives ... can affect examinee cooperation and motivation.... Therefore, it is argued that face invalidity should be avoided whenever possible."[47]

Anna Anastasi has probably written the most about face validity and its role in validation: In the most recent edition of her textbook on psychological testing, she argues that, while face validity "is not validity in the technical sense" (since it refers "not to what the test actually measures but to what it appears to measure"), it is vital for "rapport and public relations." In fact, she argues that "face validity itself is a desirable feature of tests." She too cites examples of the negative reactions of adults to items that were too much like school items; they were "frequently met with resistance and criticism." She goes on to say more forcefully that, "if test content appears irrelevant, inappropriate, silly, or childish, the result will be poor cooperation, *regardless of the actual validity of the test*"[48] (emphasis added).

It is this last phrase that needs to be pondered. To take an extreme case, why would we assume that a test is "technically valid" if it is universally ridiculed and resisted by those who take it? How can an inference about a score *not* be conditioned by the user's response to the test? For example, if performance tasks are in fact "far more likely to elicit a student's full repertoire of skills," as Howard Gardner's research shows, then why is the validity of tests that do not evoke these responses not open to question?[49] What if indirect forms of assessment so distance some students from contextual "tests" of understanding that they lose interest in the ultimate criterion? While the relative merits of directness and indirectness in test construction have been argued on technical grounds in the testing literature, there is no mention of the possible effect of this technical factor on the test-takers.[50]

Although face validity should be considered, to focus only on it is to miss a more important point about the incentives to perform well that might inhere in more authentic forms of assessment and that might change the implications of scores. For example, Gardner observes that assessment in the context of students' working "on problems, projects, or products which genuinely engage them" can "hold their interest and motivate them to do well," suggesting that a more substantive question about validity is at stake.[51] And John Raven is prepared to question the validity of any test that ignores motivational issues: "Important abilities demand time, energy, and effort. As a result, people only display them when they are undertaking activities which are important to them. It is meaningless to attempt to assess a person's abilities except in relation to their valued goals."[52] Raven acknowledges that such views are in "sharp conflict" with traditional views, but there is a commonsense appeal here that deserves better exploration at least.

It therefore seems not only reasonable and fair but also contributive to more comprehensive validation to give the (older), student and/or the teacher a chance to judge a test's appropriateness. (New York does give teachers this opportunity in the Regents Examinations.) I have devised a simple questionnaire to enable teachers to assess their students' sense of a test's aptness and fairness. It can be given out after every major test in middle or high school.[53]

I am not proposing that students have the final say, nor would I claim that their judgment is necessarily accurate or technically informed. What I am asking is that we take account of the test-taker's point of view as one factor in considering the matter of validity. Many respected testing specialists have advocated such techniques as part of all pilot testing.[54]

How one's work and talents are judged is of paramount concern to everyone. Thus fairness demands that the test-taker's responses be solicited and pondered. We routinely assume that adults have the right to some say in performance appraisal—often through formal negotiations. So why should students be perpetually shut out of the discussion?

THE 'VALUE' IN CONCERNS ABOUT VALIDITY

One reason that concerns about validity are so easily finessed is that they demand more than technical expertise in measurement. Any inference drawn about test results is a complex act of judgment that involves the consideration of different kinds of data and our intellectual values.

I am not arguing that indirect tests are inherently defective or prone to invalid inferences about performance. I am fully aware that certain constructs, such as critical thinking or reading comprehension, do not easily admit of direct testing. I am also aware that an indirect test can yield positive correlations with some criterion situations (e.g., vocabulary tests as predictors of verbal-role success). My fear is that validity in mass educational testing has deteriorated into an excessive concern with *content* validity, the use of questionable methods for obtaining responses that illustrate certain constructs, and mere correlations with other indirect tests (in an endless circle of results on questionable tests being used to validate other questionable tests).

At bottom is a major philosophical problem about the purpose of schooling—and hence of testing. Is schooling meant to yield common knowledge? If so, then it makes perfect sense to think of tests as properly focusing on what students hold in common. But what if education is seen to be a personal, idiosyncratic affair, where the meaning and personal effectiveness that I derive from coursework is more important than what knowledge we all hold in common? In that case, any kind of standardized, indirect test would make no sense. What could we possibly mean by a standardized test of the meaning of educational experience?

Consider Albert Shanker's view that we should think about achievement as scouts think of merit badges: achievement should be validated by a person's demonstrated ability to use knowledge in the field. "That's the kind of knowledge that doesn't leave you," according to Shanker.[55] The result would be a personalized collection of badges—even if each badge requirement is standardized.

This is the deeper issue raised by the report of the Secretary's Commission on Achieving Necessary Skills with regard to the meaning of a transcript.[56] If a transcript is really better thought of as a résumé, as the SCANS report claims, then what does that suggest about testing, about teaching, about curriculum design, and about the current myopic search for national standards? At the very least it suggests that a penchant for testing everyone on the same things is misguided. While the issue is debated further, let us at least demand that test-makers recognize their obligation to link their tests to the tasks, contexts, and "feel" of real-world challenges—in all their messiness.

NOTES

1. Lauren B. Resnick, "Tests as Standards of Achievement in School," in *The Uses of Standardized Tests in American Education: Proceedings of the 1989 ETS Invitational Conference* (Princeton, N.J.: Educational Testing Service, 1990), pp. 63–80.

2. Readers who want to review the most up-to-date thinking on validity are encouraged to review Jason Millman and J. Greene, "The Specification and Development of Tests of Achievement and Ability," in Robert L. Linn, ed., *Educational Measurement*, 3rd ed. (New York: American Council on Education/Macmillan, 1989); Lee J. Cronbach, *Essentials of Psychological Testing*, 5th ed. (New York: HarperCollins, 1989); and Robert Linn, Eva Baker, and Stephen Dunbar, "Complex, Performance-Based Assessment: Expectations and Validation Criteria," *Educational Researcher*, November 1991, pp. 15–21.

3. Robert Glaser, "Expertise and Assessment," in Merlin C. Wittrock and Eva L. Baker, eds., *Testing and Cognition* (Englewood Cliffs, N.J.: Prentice-Hall, 1991), p. 28.

4. William G. Perry, Jr., *Forms of Intellectual and Ethical Development in the College Years*, rev. ed. (Troy, Mo., Holt, Rinehart & Winston, 1970).

5. Robert Glaser, "Cognitive and Environmental Perspectives on Assessing Achievement," in *Assessment in the Service of Learning: Proceedings of the 1987 ETS Invitational Conference* (Princeton, N.J.: Educational Testing Service, 1988), p. 47.

6. William C. Ward, "Measurement Research That Will Change Test Design for the Future," in *Assessment in the Service of Learning: Proceedings of the 1985 ETS Invitational Conference* (Princeton, N.J.: Educational Testing Service, 1986), pp. 25–34; and C. V. Bunderson, D. Inouye, and J. Olsen, "The Four Generations of Computerized Educational Measurement," in Linn, pp. 367–408.

7. William James made this same point nearly a century ago in *Talks to Teachers* (1899; reprint, New York: Norton, 1958).

8. Readers might think I am forgetting about test reliability. On the contrary, the standard psychometric conception of reliability assumes that the *performer* is always reliable and that only *scores* can be unreliable. This is a fundamental epistemological error as well as a violation of common sense.

9. M. McCloskey, A. Carramazza, and B. Green, "Curvilinear Motion in the Absence of External Forces," *Science*, vol. 210, 1980, pp. 1139–41; and Howard Gardner, *The Unschooled Mind: How Children Think and How Schools Should Teach* (New York: Basic Books, 1991). As the history of such "fantastic" ideas as calculus shows, a new conceptual insight is often resisted by sophistical adult professionals.

10. John Dewey, *How We Think* (Lexington, Mass.: D. C. Heath, 1933), p. 24.

11. Let me offer a caution to the language-sensitive reader: I am speaking about higher-order habits—what are often referred to as "dispositions." For a good account of the technical differences between "habits" and "dispositions," see Gilbert Ryle, *The Concept of Mind* (London: Hutchinson House, 1949); and J. Passmore, *The Philosophy of Teaching* (Cambridge, Mass.: Harvard University Press, 1980).

12. John Dewey, "Moral Principles in Education" (1909), in J. A. Boydston, ed., *The Middle Works of John Dewey: 1899–1924* (Carbondale: Southern Illinois University Press, 1977), p. 290.

13. John Dewey, *How We Think: A Restatement of the Relation of Reflective Thinking to the Educative Process* (Lexington, Mass.: Heath, 1933), pp. 119–120.

14. See Arthur Chickering and Carl Claxton, "What Is Competence?," in R. Nickse et al., eds., *Competency-Based Education* (New York: Teachers College Press, 1981), pp. 9–11.

15. Alfred Binet and Theodore Simon, "The Development of Intelligence in the Child," in *The Development of Intelligence in Children* (1916; reprint, Salem, N.H.: Ayer, 1983), p. 42.

16. Ryle, p. 47.

17. Office of Strategic Services, *Assessment of Men: Selection of Personnel for the Office of Strategic Services* (Troy, Mo.: Holt, Rinehart & Winston, 1948), pp. 39, 49.

18. Norman Frederiksen, "The Real Test Bias," *American Psychologist*, vol. 39, 1984, pp. 193–202.

19. See Robert Gagné, "Learning Outcomes and Their Effects: Useful Categories of Human Performance," *American Psychologist*, vol. 39, 1984, pp. 377–85.

20. This definition, used by the Fund for the Improvement of Post-Secondary Education, was formulated by T. Corcorarf and is quoted in Nickse et al., p. 10.

21. Gerald Grant et al., *On Competence: A Critical Analysis of Competence-Based Reforms in Higher Education* (San Francisco: Jossey-Bass, 1979), p. 6.

22. Samuel Messick, "Meaning and Values in Test Validation: The Science and Ethics of Assessment," *Educational Researcher*, March 1989, p. 10; and R. Bond, "Making Innovative Assessment Fair and Valid," in *What We Can Learn from Performance Assessment for the Professions: Proceedings of the 1992 ETS Invitational Conference* (Princeton, N.J.: Educational Testing Service, 1993), pp. 64–65.

23. David McClelland, "Testing for Competence Rather Than for 'Intelligence,' " *American Psychologist*, vol. 28, 1973, pp. 1–14.

24. Frederiksen, p. 199.

25. Office of Strategic Services, p. 42.

26. Ibid.

27. Ibid.

28. Cronbach, pp. 414–15.

29. See Grant Wiggins, "A True Test: Toward More Authentic and Equitable Assessment," *Phi Delta Kappan*, May 1989, pp. 703–13.

30. Robert Fitzpatrick and Edward J. Morrison, "Performance and Product Evaluation," in F. L. Finch, ed., *Educational Performance Assessment* (1971; reprint, Chicago: Riverside/Houghton Mifflin, 1991), pp. 92–93.

31. Chickering and Claxton, p. 11.

32. See G. Rogers, *Validating College Outcomes with Institutionally Developed Instruments: Issues in Maximizing Contextual Validity* (Milwaukee: Office of Research and Evaluation, Alverno College, 1988).

33. John Seelv Brown, Allan Collins, and Paul Duguid, "Situated Cognition and the Culture of Learning," *Educational Researcher*, January/February 1989, p. 34.

34. C. Gragg, "Because Wisdom Can't Be Told," in M. P. McNair and A. Hersum, eds., *The Case Method at the Harvard Business School* (New York: McGraw-Hill, 1954), p. 6. This chapter is available as a reprint (HBS Case 9-451-005) from the Harvard Business School Publishing Division, Boston, Mass.

35. Benjamin S. Bloom, George F. Madaus, and J. Thomas Hastings, *Evaluation to Improve Learning* (New York: McGraw-Hill, 1981), p. 268.

36. Yes, yes, I know that the issue is really one of cheating. Let the teacher "sign off" on the papers, then, certifying authorship, as schools have long done in Australia (and now in Vermont) where the state assessment is built, in part, out of local work submitted to external examiners.

37. C. Gentile, *Exploring New Methods for Collecting Students' School-Based Writing* (Washington, D.C.: U.S. Department of Education, 1991), p. 20.

38. Allan C. Collins and Dieter G. Gentner, cited in John R. Fredriksen and Allan C. Collins, "A Systems Approach to Educational Testing," *Educational Researcher*, December 1989, pp. 27–32.

39. American Council on the Teaching of Foreign Languages, *ACTFL Provisional Proficiency Guidelines* (Hastings-on-Hudson, N.Y.: ACTFL Materials Center, 1982), p. 7.

40. Messick, "Meaning and Values," p. 5.

41. Messick, "Validity," in Linn, pp. 14–15.

42. Reliability problems abound in testing our youngest children this way (e.g., one must constantly make sure that the students are looking at the right line of pictures), which is why many districts and states have banned such testing.

43. For the definitive account of "knowledge" as intelligent performance, not as the "mental" application of declarative propositions to situations, see Ryle, op. cit.

44. For the view that the idea of authenticity is a big fuss about a naive idea, see F. L. Finch, "Issues in Educational Performance Evaluation," in idem, pp. 89–138.

45. Messick, "Meaning and Values," p. 11.

46. Robert L. Thorndike and E. P. Hagen, *Measurement and Evaluation in Psychology and Education*, 4th ed. (New York: Wiley, 1955), p. 60.

47. Messick, "Validity," in Linn, p. 19.

48. Anna Anastasi, *Psychological Testing*, 6th ed. (New York: Macmillan, 1988), p. 144.

49. Gardner, p. 93.

50. Millman and Greene, p. 348.

51. Gardner, p. 93.

52. John Raven, "A Model of Competence, Motivation, and Behavior, and a Paradigm for Assessment," in Harold Berlak et al., *Toward a New Science of Educational Testing and Assessment* (Baltimore: Johns Hopkins University Press, 1992), pp. 89–90.

53. This questionnaire appears on page 246 of *Assessing Student Performance*, the book from which this article is adapted.

54. Anastasi, *Psychological Testing*, 4th ed. See also Walter Haney and L. Scott, "Talking with Children About Tests: An Exploratory Study of Test Item Ambiguity," in K. O. Freedle and R. P. Duran, eds., *Cognitive and Linguistic Analyses of Test Performance* (Norwood, N.J.: Ablex, 1987), pp. 289–368.

55. Albert Shanker, "The Social and Educational Dilemmas of Test Use," in *The Uses of Standardized Tests*, p. 10.

56. U.S. Department of Labor, *What Work Requires of Schools: A SCANS Report for America 2000* (Washington, D.C.: U.S. Government Printing Office, 1991).

PART SIX

Motivation and Classroom Management

Chapter 11 Motivation and Discipline 327

On the Internet . . .

Sites appropriate to Part Six

This Big Sur Tapes site contains an archive of audiotapes recorded from Abraham Maslow's lectures at the Esalen Institute in California. Topic headings include Self-Actualization, Criteria for Judging, Psychology of Religious Awareness, Farther Reaches of Human Nature, and The Eupsychian Ethic.

http://www.bigsurtapes.com/tex7b.html

This site lists articles from the *Journal for Reality Therapy,* the official publication of the William Glasser Institute.

http://indigo.ie/~irti/journal.htm

Links on the Quality School and William Glasser Links Page include the William Glasser Institute, a discussion page, and a workshops and presentations page.

http://www.geocities.com/Athens/Acropolis/
    6499/quality.html

CHAPTER 11 Motivation and Discipline

11.1 ABRAHAM H. MASLOW

A Theory of Human Motivation

Abraham H. Maslow (1908–1970) was born in Brooklyn, New York, and studied at the City College of New York and the University of Wisconsin. He spent the majority of his research and teaching career at Brandeis University in Waltham, Massachusetts. Maslow was a leading exponent of the humanistic school of psychology, sometimes referred to as the "third force" (Sigmund Freud's psychoanalysis and B. F. Skinner's behaviorism being the first and second "forces").

Humanistic psychology judges orthodox behaviorism and psychoanalysis to be too rigidly theoretical and overly concerned with mental illness instead of psychological health. Maslow developed a theory of motivation, describing the process by which an individual progresses from basic needs, such as food and shelter, to social needs, such as belongingness (love) and esteem, and finally to self-actualization. This high-level need, self-actualization, is the self-directed fulfillment of one's inner potential, he asserts. Furthermore, humanistic psychotherapy, usually in the form of group therapy, seeks to help the individual progress through these stages. Maslow's writings include *Toward a Psychology of Being* (Van Nostrand, 1962) and *The Farther Reaches of Human Nature* (Viking Press, 1971).

Among the most famous theories in the field of psychology is Maslow's "hierarchy of needs." His theory of needs has extraordinarily high face validity. Few things concern teachers more than motivating their students.

Maslow's approach gives teachers an easy way to gauge their students' motivations and to help teachers analyze students' motivational problems, as well as come up with solutions to those problems. The following selection explains this hierarchy of needs. It is taken from chapter 2 of the third edition of Maslow's most frequently cited book, *Motivation and Personality* (Harper & Row, 1970).

Key Concept: a hierarchy of needs

This [selection] is an attempt to formulate a positive theory of motivation that will satisfy [certain] theoretical demands... and at the same time conform to the known facts, clinical and observational as well as experimental. It derives most directly, however, from clinical experience. This theory is in the functionalist tradition of James and Dewey, and is fused with the holism of Wertheimer, Goldstein, and Gestalt psychology and with the dynamism of Freud, Fromm, Horney, Reich, Jung, and Adler. This integration or synthesis may be called a holistic-dynamic theory.

THE BASIC NEED HIERARCHY

The Physiological Needs

The needs that are usually taken as the starting point for motivation theory are the so-called physiological drives. Two lines of research make it necessary to revise our customary notions about these needs: first, the development of the concept of homeostasis and second, the finding that appetites (preferential choices among foods) are a fairly efficient indication of actual needs or lacks in the body.

Homeostasis refers to the body's automatic efforts to maintain a constant, normal state of the blood stream. Cannon (1932) described this process for (1) the water content of the blood, (2) salt content, (3) sugar content, (4) protein content, (5) fat content, (6) calcium content, (7) oxygen content, (8) constant hydrogen-ion level (acid-base balance), and (9) constant temperature of the blood. Obviously this list could be extended to include other minerals, the hormones, vitamins, and so on.

Young (1941, 1948) summarized the work on appetite in its relation to body needs. If the body lacks some chemical, the individual will tend (in an imperfect way) to develop a specific appetite or partial hunger for that missing food element.

Thus it seems impossible as well as useless to make any list of fundamental physiological needs, for they can come to almost any number one might wish, depending on the degree of specificity of description. We cannot identify all physiological needs as homeostatic. That sexual desire, sleepiness, sheer activity and exercise, and maternal behavior in animals are homeostatic has not yet been demonstrated. Furthermore, this list would not include the various sensory pleasures (tastes, smells, tickling, stroking), which are probably physiological and which may become the goals of motivated behavior. Nor do we know what to make of the fact that the organism has simultaneously a tendency to inertia, laziness, and least effort and *also* a need for activity, stimulation, and excitement.

... [T]hese physiological drives or needs are to be considered unusual rather than typical because they are isolable and because they are localizable somatically. That is to say, they are relatively independent of each other, of other motivations, and of the organism as a whole, and, in many cases, it is possible to demonstrate a localized, underlying somatic base for the drive. This is true less generally than has been thought (exceptions are fatigue, sleepiness, maternal responses) but it is still true in the classic instances of hunger, sex, and thirst.

It should be pointed out again that any of the physiological needs and the consummatory behavior involved with them serve as channels for all sorts of other needs as well. That is to say, the person who thinks he or she is hungry may actually be seeking more for comfort, or dependence, than for vitamins or proteins. Conversely, it is possible to satisfy the hunger need in part by other activities such as drinking water or smoking cigarettes. In other words, relatively isolable as these physiological needs are, they are not completely so.

Undoubtedly these physiological needs are the most prepotent of all needs. What this means specifically is that in the human being who is missing everything in life in an extreme fashion, it is most likely that the major motivation would be the physiological needs rather than any others. A person who is lacking food, safety, love, and esteem would most probably hunger for food more strongly than for anything else.

If all the needs are unsatisfied, and the organism is then dominated by the physiological needs, all other needs may become simply nonexistent or be pushed into the background. It is then fair to characterize the whole organism by saying simply that it is hungry, for consciousness is almost completely preempted by hunger. All capacities are put into the service of hunger satisfaction, and the organization of these capacities is almost entirely determined by the one purpose of satisfying hunger. The receptors and effectors, the intelligence, memory, habits, all may now be defined simply as hunger-gratifying tools. Capacities that are not useful for this purpose lie dormant, or are pushed into the background. The urge to write poetry, the desire to acquire an automobile, the interest in American history, the desire for a new pair of shoes are, in the extreme case, forgotten or become of secondary importance. For the human who is extremely and dangerously hungry, no other interests exist but food. He or she dreams food, remembers food, thinks about food, emotes only about food, perceives only food, and wants only food. The more subtle determinants that ordinarily fuse with the physiological drives in organizing even feeding, drinking, or sexual behavior, may now be so completely overwhelmed as to allow us to speak at this time (but *only* at this time) of pure hunger drive and behavior, with the one unqualified aim of relief.

Another peculiar characteristic of the human organism when it is dominated by a certain need is that the whole philosophy of the future tends also to change. For our chronically and extremely hungry person, Utopia can be defined simply as a place where there is plenty of food. He or she tends to think that, if only guaranteed food for the rest of life, he or she will be perfectly happy and will never want anything more. Life itself tends to be defined in terms of eating. Anything else will be defined as unimportant. Freedom, love, community feeling, respect, philosophy, may all be waved aside as fripperies that are useless, since they fail to fill the stomach. Such a person may fairly be said to live by bread alone.

It cannot possibly be denied that such things are true, but their *generality* can be denied. Emergency conditions are, almost by definition, rare in the normally functioning peaceful society. That this truism can be forgotten is attributable mainly to two reasons. First, rats have few motivations other than physiological ones, and since so much of the research on motivation has been made with these animals, it is easy to carry the rat picture over to the human being. Second, it is too often not realized that culture itself is an adaptive tool, one of whose main functions is to make the physiological emergencies come less and less often. In the United States, chronic extreme hunger of the emergency type is rare, rather than common. Average American citizens are experiencing appetite rather than hunger when they say, "I am hungry." They are apt to experience sheer life-and-death hunger only by accident and then only a few times through their entire lives.

Obviously a good way to obscure the higher motivations, and to get a lopsided view of human capacities and human nature, is to make the organism extremely and chronically hungry or thirsty. Anyone who attempts to make an emergency picture into a typical one and who will measure all of humanity's goals and desires by behavior during extreme physiological deprivation is certainly being blind to many things. It is quite true that humans live by bread alone—when there is no bread. But what happens to their desires when there *is* plenty of bread and when their bellies are chronically filled?

Dynamics of the Need Hierarchy

At once other (and higher) needs emerge and these, rather than physiological hungers, dominate the organism. And when these in turn are satisfied, again new (and still higher) needs emerge, and so on. This is what we mean by saying that the basic human needs are organized into a hierarchy of relative prepotency.

One main implication of this phrasing is that gratification becomes as important a concept as deprivation in motivation theory, for it releases the organism from the domination of a relatively more physiological need, permitting thereby the emergence of other more social goals. The physiological needs, along with their partial goals, when chronically gratified cease to exist as active determinants or organizers of behavior. They now exist only in a potential fashion in the sense that they may emerge again to dominate the organism if they are thwarted. But a want that is satisfied is no longer a want. The organism is dominated and its behavior organized only by unsatisfied needs. If hunger is satisfied, it becomes unimportant in the current dynamics of the individual.

This statement is somewhat qualified by a hypothesis... that it is precisely those individuals in whom a certain need has always been satisfied who are best equipped to tolerate deprivation of that need in the future and that, furthermore, those who have been deprived in the past will react differently to current satisfactions from the one who has never been deprived.

The Safety Needs

If the physiological needs are relatively well gratified, there then emerges a new set of needs, which we may categorize roughly as the safety needs (security; stability; dependency; protection; freedom from fear, anxiety, and chaos; need for structure, order, law, and limits; strength in the protector; and so on). All that has been said of the physiological needs is equally true, although in less degree, of these desires. The organism may equally well be wholly dominated by them. They may serve as the almost exclusive organizers of behavior, recruiting all the capacities of the organism in their service, and we may then fairly describe the whole organism as a safety-seeking mechanism. Again we may say of the receptors, the effectors, the intellect, and the other capacities that they are primarily safety-seeking tools. Again, as in the hungry human, we find that the dominating goal is a strong determinant not only of their current world outlook and philosophy but also of their philosophy of the future and of values. Practically everything looks less important than safety and protection (even sometimes the physiological needs, which, being satisfied, are now underestimated). A person in this state, if it is extreme enough and chronic enough, may be characterized as living almost for safety alone.

However, the healthy and fortunate adults in our culture are largely satisfied in their safety needs. The peaceful, smoothly running, stable, good society ordinarily makes its members feel safe enough from wild animals, extremes of temperature, criminal assault, murder, chaos, tyranny, and so on. Therefore, in a very real sense, they no longer have any safety needs as active motivators. Just as a sated person no longer feels hungry, a safe one no longer feels endangered. If we wish to see these needs directly and clearly we must turn to neurotic or near-neurotic individuals, and to the economic and social underdogs, or else to social chaos, revolution, or breakdown of authority. In between these extremes, we can perceive the expressions of safety needs only in such phenomena as, for instance, the common preference for a job with tenure and protection, the desire for a saving account, and for insurance of various kinds (medical, dental, unemployment, disability, old age).

Other, broader aspects of the attempt to seek safety and stability in the world are seen in the very common preference for familiar rather than unfamiliar things (Maslow, 1937), or for the known rather than the unknown. The tendency to have some religion or world philosophy that organizes the universe and the people in it into some sort of satisfactorily coherent, meaningful whole is also in part motivated by safety seeking. Here too we may list science and philosophy in general as partially motivated by the safety needs....

Otherwise the need for safety is seen as an active and dominant mobilizer of the organism's resources only in real emergencies, such as war, disease, natural catastrophes, crime waves, societal disorganization, neurosis, brain injury, breakdown of authority, or chronically bad situations. Some neurotic adults in our society are, in many ways, like unsafe children in their desire for safety. Their reactions are often to unknown psychological dangers in a world that is perceived to be hostile, overwhelming, and threatening. Such people behave as if a great catastrophe were almost always impending—they are usually responding as if to an emergency. Their safety needs often find specific expression in a search for a protector, or a stronger person or system, on whom they may depend. It is as if their childish attitudes of fear and threat reaction to a dangerous world have gone underground and, untouched by the growing-up and learning processes, remain ready even now to be called out by any stimulus that would make a child feel endangered. . . .

The neurosis in which the search for safety takes its clearest form is in the compulsive-obsessive neurosis. Compulsive-obsessives try frantically to order and stabilize the world so that no unmanageable, unexpected, or unfamiliar dangers will ever appear. They hedge themselves about with all sorts of ceremonials, rules, and formulas so that every possible contingency may be provided for and so that no new contingencies may appear. They manage to maintain their equilibrium by avoiding everything unfamiliar and strange and by ordering their restricted world in such a neat, disciplined, orderly fashion that everything in the world can be counted on. They try to arrange the world so that anything unexpected (dangers) cannot possibly occur. If, through no fault of their own, something unexpected does occur, they go into a panic reaction as if this unexpected occurrence constituted a grave danger. What we can see only as a none-too-strong preference in the healthy person (e.g., preference for the familiar) becomes a life-and-death necessity in abnormal cases. The healthy taste for the novel and unknown is missing or at a minimum in the average neurotic.

The safety needs can become very urgent on the social scene whenever there are real threats to law, to order, to the authority of society. The threat of chaos or of nihilism can be expected in most human beings to produce a regression from any higher needs to the more prepotent safety needs. A common, almost an expectable reaction, is the easier acceptance of dictatorship or of military rule. This tends to be true for all human beings, including healthy ones, since they too will tend to respond to danger with realistic regression to the safety need level and will prepare to defend themselves. But it seems to be most true of people who are living near the safety line. They are particularly disturbed by threats to authority, to legality, and to the representatives of the law.

The Belongingness and Love Needs

If both the physiological and the safety needs are fairly well gratified, there will emerge the love and affection and belongingness needs, and the whole cycle already described will repeat itself with this new center. The love needs involve giving and receiving affection. When they are unsatisfied, a person will feel keenly the absence of friends, mate, or children. Such a person will hunger for relations with people in general—for a place in the group or family

—and will strive with great intensity to achieve this goal. Attaining such a place will matter more than anything else in the world and he or she may even forget that once, when hunger was foremost, love seemed unreal, unnecessary, and unimportant. Now the pangs of loneliness, ostracism, rejection, friendlessness, and rootlessness are preeminent.

We have very little scientific information about the belongingness need, although this is a common theme in novels, autobiographies, poems, and plays and also in the newer sociological literature. From these we know in a general way the destructive effects on children of moving too often; of disorientation; of the general overmobility that is forced by industrialization; of being without roots, or of despising one's roots, one's origins, one's group; of being torn from one's home and family, friends, and neighbors; of being a transient or a newcomer rather than a native. We still underplay the deep importance of the neighborhood, of one's territory, of one's clan, of one's own "kind," one's class, one's gang, one's familiar working colleagues. And we have largely forgotten our deep animal tendencies to herd, to flock, to join, to belong.

I believe that the tremendous and rapid increase in training groups (T-groups), personal growth groups, and intentional communities may in part by motivated by this unsatisfied hunger for contact, intimacy, and belongingness. Such social phenomena may arise to overcome the widespread feelings of alienation, strangeness, and loneliness that have been worsened by increasing mobility, the breakdown of traditional groupings, the scattering of families, the generation gap, and steady urbanization. My strong impression is also that *some* proportion of youth rebellion groups—I don't know how many or how much —is motivated by the profound hunger for group feelings, for contact, for real togetherness in the face of a common enemy, *any* enemy that can serve to form an amity group simply by posing an external threat. The same kind of thing has been observed in groups of soldiers who were pushed into an unwonted brotherliness and intimacy by their common external danger, and who may stick together throughout a lifetime as a consequence. Any good society must satisfy this need, one way or another, if it is to survive and be healthy.

In our society the thwarting of these needs is the most commonly found core in cases of maladjustment and more severe pathology. Love and affection, as well as their possible expression in sexuality, are generally looked upon with ambivalence and are customarily hedged about with many restrictions and inhibitions. Practically all theorists of psychopathology have stressed thwarting of the love needs as basic in the picture of maladjustment. Many clinical studies have therefore been made of this need, and we know more about it perhaps than any of the other needs except the physiological ones....

One thing that must be stressed at this point is that love is not synonymous with sex. Sex may be studied as a purely physiological need, although ordinarily human sexual behavior is multidetermined. That is to say, it is determined not only by sexual but also by other needs, chief among which are the love and affection needs. Also not to be overlooked is the fact that the love needs involve both giving *and* receiving love.

All people in our society (with a few pathological exceptions) have a need or desire for a stable, firmly based, usually high evaluation of themselves, for self-respect or self-esteem, and for the esteem of others. These needs may therefore be classified into two subsidiary sets. These are, first, the desire for strength, achievement, adequacy, mastery and competence, confidence in the face of the world, and independence and freedom. Second, we have what we may call the desire for reputation or prestige (defining it as respect or esteem from other people), status, fame and glory, dominance, recognition, attention, importance, dignity, or appreciation. These needs have been relatively stressed by Alfred Adler and his followers, and have been relatively neglected by Freud. More and more today, however, there is appearing widespread appreciation of their central importance among psychoanalysts as well as among clinical psychologists.

Satisfaction of the self-esteem need leads to feelings of self-confidence, worth, strength, capability, and adequacy, of being useful and necessary in the world. But thwarting of these needs produces feelings of inferiority, of weakness, and of helplessness. These feelings in turn give rise to either basic discouragement or else compensatory or neurotic trends.

From the theologians' discussion of pride and *hubris,* from the Frommian theories about the self-perception of untruth to one's own nature, from the Rogerian work with self, from essayists like Ayn Rand (1943), and from other sources as well, we have been learning more and more of the dangers of basing self-esteem on the opinions of others rather than on real capacity, competence, and adequacy to the task. The most stable and therefore most healthy self-esteem is based on *deserved* respect from others rather than on external fame or celebrity and unwarranted adulation. Even here it is helpful to distinguish the actual competence and achievement that is based on sheer will power, determination, and responsibility from that which comes naturally and easily out of one's own true inner nature, one's constitution, one's biological fate or destiny, or, as Horney puts it, out of one's Real Self rather than out of the idealized pseudo-self (1950).

The Self-Actualization Need

Even if all these needs are satisfied, we may still often (if not always) expect that a new discontent and restlessness will soon develop, unless the individual is doing what *he* or *she,* individually, is fitted for. Musicians must make music, artists must paint, poets must write if they are to be ultimately at peace with themselves. What humans *can* be, they *must* be. They must be true to their own nature. This need we may call self-actualization....

This term, first coined by Kurt Goldstein (1939), is being used [here] in a much more specific and limited fashion. It refers to people's desire for self-fulfillment, namely, the tendency for them to become actualized in what they are potentially. This tendency might be phrased as the desire to become more and more what one idiosyncratically is, to become everything that one is capable of becoming.

The specific form that these needs will take of course vary greatly from person to person. In one individual they may take the form of the desire to be an excellent parent, in another they may be expressed athletically, and in still another they may be expressed in painting pictures or in inventing things. At this level, individual differences are greatest. However, the common feature of the needs for self-actualization is that their emergence usually rests upon some prior satisfaction of the physiological, safety, love, and esteem needs.

REFERENCES

Cannon, W. G. (1932). *Wisdom of the body.* New York: Norton.

Goldstein, K. (1939). *The organism.* New York: American Book.

Horney, K. (1950). *Neurosis and human growth.* New York: Norton.

Maslow, A. H. (1937). The influence of familiarization on preference. *Journal of Experimental Psychology, 21,* 162–180.

Rand, A. (1943). *The fountainhead.* Indianapolis: Bobbs-Merrill.

Young, P. T. (1941). The experimental analysis of appetite. *Psychological Bulletin, 38,* 129–164.

Young, P. T. (1948). Appetite, palatability and feeding habit: A critical review. *Psychological Bulletin, 45.* 289–320.

Teacher Praise: A Functional Analysis

Jere Brophy was born in 1940 in Chicago, Illinois. He received his B.S. in 1962, his M.A. in 1965, and his Ph.D. in 1967, all from the University of Chicago. He has taught at the University of Chicago and in the Department of Educational Psychology at the University of Texas in Austin, Texas. Brophy currently is the University Distinguished Professor of Teacher Education at Michigan State University. He was originally educated as a developmental and clinical psychologist, but he has spent most of his career conducting research on the critical topic of teachers' strategies for motivating students to learn. Brophy has also studied and written about such topics as teachers' attitudes toward individual students and the dynamics of teacher-student relationships, teachers' achievement expectations and related self-fulfilling prophecy effects, students' personal characteristics and their effects on teachers, relationships between classroom processes and student achievement, and teachers' strategies for managing classrooms and coping with problem students. His latest work is on the topic of curricular content and instructional method issues involved in teaching social studies for understanding, appreciation, and life application.

Brophy is the author of *Motivating Students to Learn* (McGraw-Hill, 1998), *Teaching Problem Students* (Guilford Press, 1996), *Human Development and Behavior* (St. Martin's Press, 1981), *Student Characteristics and Teaching* (Longman, 1981), *Teacher-Student Relationships: Causes and Consequences* (Holt, Rinehart & Winston, 1974), and *Teaching in the Preschool* (Harper & Row, 1975). He is coauthor of *Looking in Classrooms* (Longman, 1997), *Contemporary Educational Psychology,* 5th ed. (Longman, 1995), and *Teaching and Learning History in Elementary Schools* (Teachers College Press, 1997).

The following selection has been taken from "Teacher Praise: A Functional Analysis," *Review of Educational Research* (Spring 1981). In schools of education praise is touted as one of the most effective reinforcers, yet Brophy's review of it indicates that it seldom functions as a reinforcer. Besides reviewing the applicable empirical research, he offers suggestions about how teachers can more effectively reinforce and use praise with their students.

Key Concept: teacher praise

Most educational psychologists and other sources of advice to classroom teachers stress the value of reinforcement of good conduct or successful performance, and single out teacher praise as a particularly valuable and desirable form of such reinforcement. Until recently, my own thinking and research was no exception; I assumed that teachers' statements of praise were intended and received as reinforcers. However, in study after study, measures of teacher praise failed to correlate with other classroom process variables, or with outcome variables, in ways that would be expected if such praise were in fact functioning as reinforcement. This led me to study the matter more systematically, and to draw conclusions sharply at variance with the common view. In this paper, I argue that teacher praise typically does not function as a reinforcer and that much of it is not even intended as reinforcement, at least not in the usual sense of the term. Further, I believe that much teacher praise is reactive to and under the control of student behavior rather than vice versa, and that when praise does have effects on student behavior, those effects must be understood using concepts from attribution theory in addition to concepts from social learning/reinforcement theory.

DEFINITIONS

In this paper, the term "praise" has the same meaning and connotations as it does in everyday language: to commend the worth of or to express approval or admiration. It connotes a more intense or detailed teacher response to student behavior than terms such as "feedback" or "affirmation of correct response" do. When teachers praise students, they do not merely tell them the degree of success they achieved (by nodding or repeating answers, by saying "okay," "right," or "correct," or giving a letter grade or percentage score). In addition to such feedback, praise statements express positive teacher affect (surprise, delight, excitement) and/or place the student's behavior in context by giving information about its value or its implications about the student's status....

THE CHARACTERISTICS OF REINFORCERS

Reinforcement theorists (c.f. Premack, 1965) apply the term "reinforcer" to any consequence that increases frequency of a behavior when performance of that behavior is made contingent upon presentation of the consequence. Individuals differ from one another, and even within themselves over time, in their responsiveness to potential reinforcers. Consequences capable of controlling the behavior of most people will not work with certain individuals, and thus will not function as reinforcers for those individuals. Also, reinforcers are subject to satiation effects, losing their potency if used too often or too long.

If they are to control behavior, reinforcers must be delivered contingently: the reinforcer is not delivered until the behavioral criterion has been met. In training animals, this contingency relationship is communicated primarily by minimizing the time between performance of expected behavior and delivery of the reinforcement. With humans old enough to understand language, the contingency relationship can be communicated verbally, so that reinforcement need not be immediate. However, the contingency between performance of the expected behavior and presentation of the reinforcer must be clear if reinforcement is to be effective.

PRAISE AS REINFORCEMENT

Praise is widely recommended as a reinforcement method for use by teachers. One reason is that it does not have the disadvantages associated with concrete reinforcers. The latter can be expensive to purchase and time-consuming to apply regularly in the classroom, and their use engenders objections ranging from nutritional fears to concerns about bribing students to learn. Praise is free, and is usually seen as desirable not only because it can be an effective reinforcer but because it is thought to provide encouragement to students, to help build self-esteem, to help build a close teacher-student relationship, and so forth.

A more specific potential advantage is that praise allows a direct statement of the contingency between the behavior and the reinforcement. That is, in the very act of praising, teachers can identify the specific behavior they are trying to reinforce.

Not everyone favors praise, however. Some oppose it on principle. Most of these are individuals who believe that learning is intrinsically worthwhile and rewarding, at least when learners are allowed to follow their own interests at their own pace (Montessori, 1964; Moore & Anderson, 1969; Piaget, 1952). Individuals who believe this look upon all attempts to control though extrinsic reinforcement as unnecessary, intrusive, and perhaps harmful.

This point of view has received support from research indicating that the introduction of extrinsic rewards (of which praise is one) can reduce rather than increase motivation, at least when the person has previously been performing the behavior in question for its intrinsic value (Deci, 1975; Lepper & Greene, 1978). Recent research in this area indicates that these undesirable effects of praise vary with several qualitative aspects of the praise itself, and can be minimized with appropriate praise. This point will be discussed in a later section. For now, let us note that praise is not necessarily desirable even in theory.

Others dislike praise because it implies differential status: the person distributing praise takes the role of expert or authority figure who is judging the behavior of the person being praised. Teachers who want a more egalitarian relationship with their students may minimize praise, especially contingent praise, for this reason. Similarly, some teachers avoid praise because they want to train their students to think for themselves rather than depend on them (the teachers) for guidance. Thus, there are philosophical objections to praise, despite its popularity.

Even so, a great many studies have made it clear that praise can function as a reinforcer by increasing specific student behavior when made contingent upon performance of that behavior (see Lipe & Jung, 1971; O'Leary & O'Leary, 1977). I do not dispute this. However, the fact that praise *can* function as a reinforcer does not necessarily mean that it always or even usually *does*. Nor does it mean that praise has inherent value (many students find it embarrassing or otherwise undesirable) or that it is synonymous with encouragement (we all know about "damning with faint praise"). Thus, praise is not always and necessarily reinforcing....

FREQUENCY OF CLASSROOM PRAISE

The fact that teachers are not systematically trying to reinforce through praise can be seen by looking at its frequency, both in its own right and in its relationship to criticism or punishment. Classroom studies of praise indicate that it occurs relatively infrequently, although precise figures are elusive in the published literature (Thomas, Presland, Grant, & Glynn, 1978). Dunkin and Biddle (1974) could find only 10 studies, most of which used some version of the Flanders Interaction Analysis Categories system (Flanders, 1970), which included information on the rate of praise observed. Dunkin and Biddle concluded that teachers use praise "no more than six percent of the total time on the average" (p. 121). That is, only an average of six percent of the total codes from a given study are likely to include teacher praise. Actually, this estimate is inflated because Flanders' praise category includes not only praise as defined here but also encouragement, jokes that release tension, statements like "go on," and head nodding or other simple feedback....

Figure 1 presents data from six studies that used the Brophy-Good dyadic interaction coding system (Brophy & Good, 1970a). This system defines praise and criticism as defined in this paper, and allows separate coding of teachers' responses to academic performance versus classroom conduct. Data from the original studies were converted to a common metric of mean rate per-teacher-per-hour (assuming an average of 25 students per class for data organized by student rather than by teacher). The data consistently indicate that teachers are more likely to praise good answers or good work than to criticize poor answers or poor work, but are more likely to criticize poor conduct than to praise good conduct. The absolute rates of praise and criticism are low, however....

QUALITY OF TEACHER PRAISE

O'Leary and O'Leary (1977) indicate that teacher praise must have the following qualities to function effectively as reinforcement:

1. Contingency: The praise must be contingent on performance of the behavior to be reinforced.
2. Specificity: The praise should specify the particulars of the behavior being reinforced.

FIGURE 1

Mean Rates of Teacher Praise and Criticism of Student Behavior (Per Teacher Per Hour) in Six Studies

Reference	Description of the Research Context	Sample or Subsample	Praise of Good Answers or Good Work	Criticism of Poor Answers or Poor Work	Praise of Good Conduct	Criticism of Poor Conduct
Evertson, Brophy, & Good, 1973a	Nine first-grade classes observed for 40 hours each in a naturalistic study of teacher expectations as related to teacher-student interactions	Total Group	4.38	1.19	0.05	2.19
Anderson, Evertson, & Brophy, 1979	Ten experimental and 10 control first-grade classrooms observed 15 to 20 times each during reading instruction as part of a treatment study of the effects of several small-group organization and questioning/feedback variables	Control Group Treatment Group	3.25 2.00	0.25 0.25	0.10 0.10	0.75 0.50
Brophy, Evertson, Anderson, Baum, & Crawford, 1976, in press	Twenty seven classes in grades 2–5 observed for 20 hours each in a naturalistic study of teachers' attitudes and students' attributes as related to teacher-student interaction	Total Group	3.28	0.80	0.55	0.95
Good & Grouws, Note 4	Nine high effective and 9 low effective fourth-grade teachers observed 5 to 7 times each during mathematics instruction, in a naturalistic process-product study of teachers selected as high or low in effectiveness in producing student learning gains in mathematics	Highs Lows	4.16 16.08	1.01 1.13	0.05 0.07	0.30 0.67
Brophy, Evertson, Harris, & Good, 1973	Nine fifth-grade classes observed for 15 hours each in a naturalistic study of teacher expectations as related to teacher-student interaction	Total Group	3.25	0.25	0.01	1.50
Evertson, Anderson, Anderson, & Brophy, 1980	Fifty eight mathematics and 78 English classes in grades 7 and 8 observed for 16 to 22 hours each in a naturalistic process-product study	Math English	2.09 2.16	0.58 0.54	0.01 0.01	0.96 0.85

3. Sincerity/variety/credibility: The praise should sound sincere. Among other things, this means that the content will be varied according to the situation and the preferences of the student being praised.

Contingency

It may be that teachers specially trained in behavior modification praise this way, but observational data indicate that more ordinary teachers do not. Harris and Kapche (1978) list failure to praise contingently as one of the most common problems they encounter in trying to train teachers to use behavior modification in the classroom....

Specificity

Lack of contingency or inappropriate contingency is not the only problem in the quality of typical classroom praise. Specificity is remarkably low. Anderson et al. (1979) found that teachers were specific in only 5 per cent of their praise statements following good work or good answers by the students. This is not as bad as it seems, because in many of these situations it was clear to the student, or to all concerned, what was being praised. Even so, 5 percent seems unacceptably low....

Credibility

Teacher praise often lacks credibility, as well. Sometimes, this is because of the problems of lack of contingency or specificity mentioned above. Also, the verbal content frequently is not backed by or is even contradicted by nonverbal expressive behavior (Feldman & Donohoe, 1978; Feldman & Orchowsky, 1979; Friedman, 1976).

...Sometimes... praise appeared to be a not very credible attempt to reinforce student behavior, and sometimes it appeared to be a generally credible, spontaneous reaction to student behavior, depending on the type of student and the context in which the interaction occurred. *Praise during student-initiated approval-seeking contacts* was likely to go to mature, high-achieving, confident students who showed positive affect toward the teacher and elicited a generally positive pattern of treatment from the teacher. In contrast, *teacher praise occurring during student-initiated work contacts* was usually directed to the more immature and teacher-dependent students, particularly students lacking in self-confidence which the teachers were trying to encourage. Such praise correlated positively with a broad pattern of positive teacher treatment: Other measures of praise, making a good example of the student in front of the class, physical affection toward the student, and flattery of the student. On the other hand, the teachers were more likely than usual to refuse the requests of these students for permission to do classroom housekeeping tasks, and the teachers were likely to show negative nonverbal reactions during personal and social contacts with these students. Thus, their reinforcement of these students was more deliberate and less spontaneous, and it did not carry over from academic contacts to personal and social contacts....

Praise of students for good behavior was rare but did occur frequently enough to analyze, and the patterns of correlation make it clear that teachers were using this praise in an attempt to motivate other students by vicarious reinforcement effects rather than to directly reinforce the students being praised. Behavioral praise of this kind went to students described as high achieving, quiet, conforming, and hard working, clearly those least in need of reinforcement for such behavior. Unfortunately for the teachers, the admirable qualities of these students did not extend to include peer leadership and popularity. That is, the teachers might have been successful to a degree in using the vicarious reinforcement principle if they had praised students who were looked up to by their peers, but instead they intended to praise "teacher's pet" types.

Taken together, the data on praise from this and other studies suggest that (1) much teacher praise is not even intended as reinforcement but instead is reactive behavior elicited and reinforced by students themselves; and (2) most of the teacher praise that apparently is intended as reinforcement probably does not function very effectively as such, because it is not systematically contingent on desirable behavior, lacks specification of the behavioral elements to be reinforced, and/or lacks credibility.

PRAISE AND STUDENT ACHIEVEMENT GAINS

Given what has been said so far, it should not be surprising that praise does not correlate with student achievement gains as it would if it were functioning as reinforcement. In analyses based on class means (comparing teachers), correlations between praise and student achievement gains are weak....

In any case, it is only with low-SES [socioeconomic status] low-ability students in the early grades that praise seems to have genuine reinforcing effects on student learning. It is true that rates of praise of good student answers tend to correlate weakly but positively with student learning in the upper elementary grades and in the junior high and high school grades (Evertson et al., 1980; Flanders, 1970). However, it appears that these correlations appear simply because praise of good student answers is part of a more fundamental teaching pattern involving concentration on classroom recitation and group discussion. Measures of time spent in these activities tend to correlate with achievement more strongly than praise rates do, and in general, process-product data suggest that structuring the classroom in order to elicit good student answers in the first place is far more important for producing achievement than praising those answers after they have been elicited. Teacher praise appears to have little or no causal role in its own right, at least in typical everyday classroom interactions (c.f. Brophy, 1979)....

Teachers typically do not systematically use praise as a reinforcer. Should they? If so, how, and with whom? I find these questions difficult to answer, because I believe that praise has been seriously oversold.

Potency of Praise as a Reinforcer

Teacher praise is a weak reinforcer (Walker, 1979), at least after the first few grades in school. Until they are age 7 or 8, children are very oriented toward pleasing adults, and have what Kohlberg (1969) calls a "good boy" or "good girl" sense of morality. For these children, praise constitutes guidance from an authority figure and feedback indicating that one is pleasing that authority figure.

Once this childish concern about pleasing adult authority figures recedes in favor of peer orientation or other motives, however, teacher praise usually becomes a very weak reinforcer for most students. This is especially true with respect to its potential for controlling disruptive behavior or other unacceptable classroom conduct (in contrast to its potential for reinforcing achievement), because students who were concerned about pleasing the teacher would not be behaving disruptively in the first place. Ironically, then, teacher praise is likely to be least useful for the kinds of students and behavior problems that teachers are most concerned about (Walker, 1979).

Teachers seem to be aware of this. Ware (1978) had high school students and their teachers rate a list of 15 potential rewards drawn up on the basis of previous pilot work. Students asked to rank the rewards for desirability and effectiveness ranked the opportunity to reach a personal goal first, followed by: school scholarships; compliments and encouragement from friends; being accepted as a person or having their opinion sought; trophies, certificates, medals, and ribbons; job-related rewards such as raises and vacations; special privileges or responsibilities; formal letters of recognition or appreciation; having their names printed in the newspapers or repeated on a loud speaker; teacher or employer compliments and encouragement; money for specific accomplishments; parties, picnics, trips, or banquets; election to office; being chosen to be on special programs; or being a winner in a contest. Thus, students ranked teacher praise and encouragement only 10th out of the 15 potential reinforcements listed. Interestingly, teachers ranked it even lower, almost at the bottom. Thus, it appears that teachers are aware that their praise is not very reinforcing to most students even though it is stressed so widely.

Feasibility of Praise as a Reinforcer

Even if teachers were convinced of the value of praise as a reinforcer and tried to use it as such, it is questionable whether they could do so successfully in anything other than one-to-one situations. The complexities of trying to reinforce the specific behaviors of the different students in the class would quickly exceed the teacher's time and ingenuity, even if compromise methods like contract systems or token economies were used. Teachers dealing with classes of 25 or 30 students are not even going to notice all of the relevant specific behaviors that students perform, let alone be able to reinforce them effectively.

FIGURE 2

Guidelines for Effective Praise

Effective Praise	Ineffective Praise
1. Is delivered contingently	1. Is delivered randomly or unsystematically
2. Specifies the particulars of the accomplishment	2. Is restricted to global positive reactions
3. Shows spontaneity, variety, and other signs of credibility; suggests clear attention to the student's accomplishment	3. Shows a bland uniformity, which suggests a conditioned response made with minimal attention
4. Rewards attainment of specified performance criteria (which can include effort criteria, however)	4. Rewards mere participation, without consideration of performance processes or outcomes
5. Provides information to students about their competence or the value of their accomplishments	5. Provides no information at all or gives students information about their status
6. Orients students towards better appreciation of their own task-related behavior and thinking about problem solving	6. Orients students toward comparing themselves with others and thinking about competing
7. Uses students' own prior accomplishments as the context for describing present accomplishments	7. Uses the accomplishments of peers as the context for describing students' present accomplishments
8. Is given in recognition of noteworthy effort or success at difficult (for *this* student) tasks	8. Is given without regard to the effort expended or the meaning of the accomplishment (for *this* student)
9. Attributes success to effort and ability, implying that similar successes can be expected in the future	9. Attributes success to ability alone or to external factors such as luck or easy task
10. Fosters endogenous attributions (students believe that they expend effort on the task because they enjoy the task and/or want to develop task-relevant skills)	10. Fosters exogenous attributions (students believe that they expend effort on the task for external reasons—to please the teacher, win a competition or reward, etc.)
11. Focuses students' attention on their own task-relevant behavior	11. Focuses students' attention on the teacher as an external authority figure who is manipulating them
12. Fosters appreciation of and desirable attributions about task relevant behavior after the process is completed	12. Intrudes into the ongoing process, distracting attention from task relevant behavior

Reinforcement of specific behaviors in an ongoing class situation simply is not feasible, even with praise as the reinforcer (assuming its effectiveness). At most, the teacher can concentrate on a few specific behaviors for the class as a whole, or on a larger number of specific behaviors for a few individuals. Beyond this, however, the teacher must function by obtaining the general cooperation of the students rather than by continually reinforcing their specific behaviors.

Student response to teacher praise can be expected to vary from highly positive through neutral to highly negative. That is, praise will act as a reinforcer for some students, but other students will be indifferent to it and still other students will actually experience it as punishment (perhaps to the point that they will become *less* likely to repeat the behavior that was praised). The latter outcome is especially likely in the case of a student who is fighting a "teacher's pet" image who gets singled out publicly as an example to the rest of the class.

Rather than just assume the effectiveness of praise, teachers should monitor students for their apparent reaction to it, and respond accordingly. Classroom interaction data suggest that most teachers do this to at least some degree, although not necessarily consciously and systematically. Existing theory and data provide some clues to the kinds of students who will respond positively to praise. In general, it appears that young students in the early grades are likely to find praise reinforcing, particularly those who are most oriented toward pleasing the adult authority figures rather than toward impressing their peers. Also, at any grade level, but perhaps especially in the earlier grades, students who are low in ability, who came from low-SES backgrounds, or who come from minority groups may be especially responsive to praise and encouragement from teachers. Finally, introverts apparently are more responsive than extroverts (Kennedy & Willcutt, 1964; Leith & Davis, 1969), individuals with external loci of control are more responsive than individuals with internal loci of control (Hammer, 1972; Henry, Medway, & Scarbro, 1979), and field dependent individuals are more responsive than field independent individuals (Witkin, Moore, Goodenough, & Cox, 1977).

With students who have the opposite traits, and especially with field independent students who also happen to be high achievers accustomed to success, praise may be not only ineffective but actually counter-productive, at least if overused. Eden (1975) provides a theoretical explanation of how this can be. He notes that rewards can be classified according to whether or not they are commensurate with the desires or preferences of the person to be rewarded. If one receives the kind of reward that one expects and desires following performance of some behavior, one is likely to experience reinforcement and an increment in motivation. However, this will not occur if the expected and desired rewards are not obtained, even if performance of the behavior results in some consequence that other individuals would find rewarding.

Reviewing many studies, Eden offers evidence that providing the individual with the "wrong" reward not only fails to bring about an increment in motivation, but actually results in a decrease. The decrease attributable to presentation of the "wrong" reward not only fails to bring about an increment in motivation, but actually results in a decrease. The decrease attributable to presentation of the "wrong" reward is considerably smaller than the increase likely to result if the individual is presented with the "right" reward, but it is a decrement nevertheless (this apparently is the reason why overall motivation apparently decreases when individuals who have been operating on the basis of intrinsic motivation are presented with extrinsic rewards). Thus, praise delivered to the wrong person, or in the wrong way, or under the wrong circumstances may be not only ineffective but counterproductive. Of course, the danger here is not nearly as great as it might be for something like publicly ridiculing a student. Even so, there appears to be good reason to urge teachers not to be indiscriminantly positive in their evaluative remarks toward students, but instead to pick their spots and choose their words carefully....

CONCLUSION

This analysis indicates that teacher praise may have a variety of intended and actual functions in addition to reinforcement of student conduct or academic performance. Classroom research on praise seems unlikely to reveal much unless these different types and meanings of praise are built into coding systems. In any case, it seems clear that praise cannot simply be equated with reinforcement.

Pending such improvements in research methodology, the data suggest qualifications on our enthusiasm in recommending praise to teachers (who, in any case, seem to be intuitively aware of its limitations). Infrequent but contingent, specific, and credible praise seems more likely to be encouraging (and perhaps reinforcing, although more with respect to general effort than to specific behaviors) than frequent but trivial or inappropriate praise. Rather than just assume its effectiveness, teachers who wish to praise effectively will have to assess how individual students respond to praise, and in particular, how they mediate its meanings and use it to make attributions about their abilities and about the linkages between their efforts and the outcomes of those efforts.

REFERENCES

Anderson, L., Evertson, C., & Brophy, J. An experimental study of effective teaching in first-grade reading groups. *Elementary School Journal*, 1979, 79, 193–223.

Brophy, J. E. Teacher behavior and its effects. *Journal of Educational Psychology*, 1979, 71, 733–750.

Brophy, J., Evertson, C., Anderson, L. Baum, M., & Crawford, J. *Student personality and teaching: Final report of the Student Attribute Study.* Educational Resources Information Center, 1976. (ERIC Document Reproduction Service No. ED 121 799).

Brophy, J., & Evertson, C., with Anderson, L., Baum, M., & Crawford, J. *Student characteristics and teaching.* New York: Longman, in press.

Brophy, J. E., & Good, T. L. Brophy-Good System (Teacher-child Dyadic Interaction). In A. Simon & E. G. Boyer (Eds.), *Mirrors for behavior: An anthology of observation instruments continued, 1970 supplement. Volume A.* Philadelphia: Research for Better Schools, 1970. (a)

Deci, E. *Intrinsic motivation.* New York: Plenum, 1975.

Dunkin, M., & Biddle, B. *The study of teaching*. New York: Holt, Rinehart, & Winston, 1974.

Eden, D. Intrinsic and extrinsic rewards and motives: Replication and extension with Kibbutz workers. *Journal of Applied Social Psychology*, 1975, 5, 348–361.

Evertson, C., Anderson, C., Anderson, L., & Brophy, J. Relationships between classroom behaviors and student outcomes in junior high mathematics and English classes. *American Educational Research Journal*, 1980, 17, 43–60.

Evertson, C. M., Brophy, J. E., & Good, T. L. Communication of teacher expectations: First grade. *Catalog of Selected Documents in Psychology*, 1973, 3, 60–61. (a)

Feldman, R., & Donohoe, L. Nonverbal communication of affect in interracial dyads. *Journal of Educational Psychology*, 1978, 70, 979–987.

Feldman, R., & Orchowsky, S. Race and performance of students as determinants of teacher nonverbal behavior. *Contemporary Educational Psychology*, 1979, 4, 324–333.

Flanders, N. *Analyzing teaching behavior*. Reading, Mass: Addison-Wesley, 1970.

Forness, S. R. The reinforcement hierarchy. *Psychology in the Schools*, 1973, 10, 168–177.

Friedman, P. Comparisons of teacher reinforcement schedules for students with different social class backgrounds. *Journal of Educational Psychology*, 1976, 68, 286–292.

Good, T., & Grouws, D. Teaching effects. A process-product study in fourth grade mathematics classrooms. *Journal of Teacher Education*, 1977, 28, 49–54.

Hammer, B. Grade expectations, differential teacher comments, and student performance. *Journal of Educational Psychology*, 1972, 63, 454–458.

Harris, A., & Kapche, R. Problems of quality control in the development and the use of behavior change techniques in public school settings. *Education and Treatment of Children*, 1978, 1, 43–51.

Henry, S. E., Medway, F. J., & Scarbro, H. A. Sex and locus of control as determinants of children's responses to peer versus adult praise. *Journal of Educational Psychology*, 1979, 71, 604–612.

Kennedy, W., & Willcutt, H. Praise and blame as incentives. *Psychological Bulletin*, 1964, 62, 323–332.

Kohlberg, L. Stage and sequence: The cognitive-developmental approach to socialization. In D. Goslin (Ed.), *Handbook of socialization theory and research*. Chicago: Rand McNally, 1969.

Leith, G., & Davis, T. The influence of social reinforcement on achievement. *Educational Research*, 1969, 2, 132–137.

Lepper, M., & Greene, D. (Eds.). *The hidden costs of reward: New perspectives on the psychology of human motivation*. Hillsdale, N.J.: Erlbaum, 1978.

Lipe, D., & Jung, S. Manipulating incentives to enhance school learning. *Review of Educational Research*, 1971, 41, 249–280.

Montessori, M. *The Montessori method*. New York: Schocken, 1964.

Moore, O., & Anderson, A. Some principles for design of clarifying educational environments. In D. Goslin (Ed.). *Handbook of socialization theory and research*. Chicago: University of Chicago Press, 1969.

O'Leary, K., & O'Leary, S. (Eds.). *Classroom management: The successful use of behavior modification* (2nd ed.). New York: Pergamon, 1977.

Piaget, J. *The origins of intelligence in children*. New York: International Universities Press, 1952.

Premack, D. Reinforcement theory. In Levine, D. (Ed.). *Nebraska symposium on motivation*. Vol. 13. Lincoln: University of Nebraska Press, 1965.

Thomas, J., Presland, I., Grant, M., & Glynn, T. Natural rates of teacher approval and disapproval in grade-7 classrooms. *Journal of Applied Behavior Analysis,* 1978, *11,* 91–94.

Walker, H. *The acting-out child: Coping with classroom disruption.* Boston: Allyn & Bacon, 1979.

Ware, B. What rewards do students want? *Phi Delta Kappan,* 1978, *59,* 355–356.

Witkin, H., Moore, C., Goodenough, D., & Cox, P. Field-dependent and field-independent cognitive styles and their implications. *Review of Educational Research,* 1977, *47,* 1–64.

Assertive Discipline—More Than Names on the Board and Marbles in a Jar

In the 1970s Lee Canter and his wife, Marlene Canter, developed a way that Marlene could cope with the difficult discipline problems she was encountering as a public school teacher. They published their ideas in 1976 in the now-famous text *Assertive Discipline.* The book became very popular among teachers, as the Canters formed their consulting business, Canter and Associates, and began offering workshops on assertive discipline to teachers all across America. By the late 1980s more than 1 million teachers had participated in these workshops. The Canter and Associates Web site states that the company developed "course materials for distance-learning video-based education classes. Each course included videocassettes as well as study guides. Canter added staff members to respond to these needs and within a year, the Canter family grew to 50 people. By 1995, 17 universities were collaborating with Canter to offer courses nationwide."

The Canters have published many books on classroom management and related skills, including *Assertive Discipline Positive Behavior,* 3rd ed. (1997), *The High-Performing Teacher* (1996), and *Lee Canter's Assertive Discipline for Parents,* rev. ed. (1990). These books have been read by thousands, perhaps millions, of teachers. In the following selection, which has been taken from "Assertive Discipline—More Than Names on the Board and Marbles in a Jar," *Phi Delta Kappan* (September 1989), Lee Canter asserts that his system is the only discipline and classroom management program that is supported by research articles. He cites a few studies to support his theory that assertive discipline is effective.

Key Concept: assertive discipline

About a year ago I was on an airline flight, seated next to a university professor. When he found out that I had developed the Assertive Discipline program, he said, "Oh, that's where all you do is write the kids' names on the board when they're bad and drop marbles in the jar when they're good."

The university professor's response disturbed me. For some time I've been concerned about a small percentage of educators—this professor apparently among them—who have interpreted my program in a way that makes behavior management sound simplistic. More important, I'm concerned with their misguided emphasis on providing only negative consequences when students misbehave. The key to dealing effectively with student behavior is not negative —but positive—consequences. To clarify my views, . . . I would like to explain the background of the program and address some of the issues that are often raised about Assertive Discipline.

I developed the program about 14 years ago, when I first became aware that teachers were not trained to deal with student behavior. Teachers were taught such concepts as "Don't smile until Christmas" or "If your curriculum is good enough, you will have no behavior problems." Those concepts were out of step with the reality of student behavior in the 1970s.

When I discovered this lack of training, I began to study how effective teachers dealt with student behavior. I found that, above all, the master teachers were assertive; that is, they *taught* students how to behave. They established clear rules for the classroom, they communicated those rules to the students, and they taught the students how to follow them. These effective teachers had also mastered skills in positive reinforcement, and they praised every student at least once a day. Finally, when students chose to break the rules, these teachers used firm and consistent negative consequences—but only as a last resort.

It troubles me to find my work interpreted as suggesting that teachers need only provide negative consequences—check marks or demerits—when students misbehave. That interpretation is wrong. The key to Assertive Discipline is catching students being good: recognizing and supporting them when they behave appropriately and letting them know you like it, day in and day out.

THE DISCIPLINE PLAN

It is vital for classroom teachers to have a systematic discipline plan that explains exactly what will happen when students choose to misbehave. By telling the students at the beginning of the school year what the consequences will be, teachers insure that all students know what to expect in the classroom. Without a plan, teachers must choose an appropriate consequence at the moment when a student misbehaves. They must stop the lesson, talk to the misbehaving student, and do whatever else the situation requires, while 25 to 30 students look on. That is not an effective way to teach—or to deal with misbehavior.

Most important, without a plan teachers tend to be inconsistent. One day they may ignore students who are talking, yelling, or disrupting the class. The next day they may severely discipline students for the same behaviors. In addition, teachers may respond differently to students from different socioeconomic, ethnic, or racial backgrounds.

An effective discipline plan is applied fairly to all students. Every student who willfully disrupts the classroom and stops the teacher from teaching suffers the same consequence. And a written plan can be sent home to parents, who then know beforehand what the teacher's standards are and what will be done when students choose to misbehave. When a teacher calls a parent, there should be no surprises.

351

Lee Canter

MISBEHAVIOR AND CONSEQUENCES

I suggest that a discipline plan include a maximum of five consequences for misbehavior, but teachers must choose consequences with which they are comfortable. For example, the first time a student breaks a rule, the student is warned. The second infraction brings a 10-minute timeout; the third infraction, a 15-minute timeout. The fourth time a student breaks a rule, the teacher calls the parents; the fifth time, the student goes to the principal.

No teacher should have a plan that is not appropriate for his or her needs and that is not in the best interests of the students. Most important, the consequences should never by psychologically or physically harmful to the students. Students should never be made to stand in front of the class as objects of ridicule or be degraded in any other way. Nor should they be given consequences that are inappropriate for their grade levels. I also feel strongly that corporal punishment should *never* be administered. There are more effective ways of dealing with students than hitting them.

Names and checks on the board are sometimes said to be essential to an Assertive Discipline program, but they are not. I originally suggested this particular practice because I had seen teachers interrupt their lessons to make such negative comments to misbehaving students as, "You talked out again. I've had it. You're impossible. That's 20 minutes after school." I wanted to eliminate the need to stop the lesson and issue reprimands. Writing a student's name on the board would warn the student in a calm, nondegrading manner. It would also provide a record-keeping system for the teacher.

Unfortunately, some parents have misinterpreted the use of names and checks on the board as a way of humiliating students. I now suggest that teachers instead write an offending student's name on a clipboard or in the roll book and say to the student, "You talked out, you disrupted the class, you broke a rule. That's a warning. That's a check."

In addition to parents, some teachers have misinterpreted elements of the Assertive Discipline program. The vast majority of teachers—my staff and I have probably trained close to 750,000 teachers—have used the program to dramatically increase their reliance on positive reinforcement and verbal praise. But a small percentage of teachers have interpreted the program in a negative manner.

There are several reasons for this. First, Assertive Discipline has become a generic term, like Xerox or Kleenex. A number of educators are now conducting training in what they call Assertive Discipline without teaching *all* the competencies essential to my program. For example, I have heard reports of teachers who were taught that they had only to stand in front of their students, tell them that there were rules and consequences, display a chart listing those rules and consequences, and write the names of misbehaving students on the board. That was it. Those teachers were never introduced to the concept that positive reinforcement is the key to dealing with students. Such programs are not in the best interests of students.

Negative interpretations have also come from burned-out, overwhelmed teachers who feel they do not get the support that they need from parents or administrators and who take out their frustrations on students. Assertive Discipline is not a negative program, but it can be misused by negative teachers. The answer is not to change the program, but to change the teachers. We need to train administrators, mentor teachers, and staff developers to coach negative teachers in the use of positive reinforcement. If these teachers cannot become more positive, they should not be teaching.

POSITIVE DISCIPLINE

I recommend a three-step cycle of behavior management to establish a positive discipline system.

First, whenever teachers want students to follow certain directions, they must *teach* the specific behaviors. Teachers too often assume that students know how they are expected to behave. Teachers first need to establish specific directions for each activity during the day—lectures, small-group work, transitions between activities, and so forth. For each situation, teachers must determine the *exact* behaviors they expect from the students.

For example, teachers may want students to stay in their seats during a lecture, focusing their eyes on the lecturer, clearing their desks of all materials except paper and pencil, raising their hands when they have questions or comments, and waiting to be called on before speaking. Once teachers have determined the specific behaviors for each situation, they must teach the students how to follow the directions. They must first state the directions and, with younger students, write the behaviors on the board or on a flip chart. Then they must model the behaviors, ask the students to *restate* the directions, question the students to make sure they understand the directions, and immediately engage the students in the activity to make sure that they understand the directions.

Second, after teaching the specific directions, teachers—especially at the elementary level—must use *positive repetition* to reinforce the students when they follow the directions. Typically, teachers give directions to the students and then focus attention only on those students who do *not* obey. ("Bobby, you didn't go back to your seat. Teddy, what's wrong with you? Get back to work.") Instead, teachers should focus on those students who do follow the directions, rephrasing the original directions as a positive comment. For example, "Jason went back to his seat and got right to work."

Third, if a student is still misbehaving after a teacher has taught specific directions and has used positive repetition, only then should the teacher use the negative consequences outlined in his or her Assertive Discipline plan. As a general rule, a teacher shouldn't administer a disciplinary consequence to a student until the teacher has reinforced at least two students for the appropriate behavior. Effective teachers are always positive first. Focusing on negative behavior teaches students that negative behavior gets attention, that the teacher is a negative person, and that the classroom is a negative place.

An effective behavior management program must be built on choice. Students must know beforehand what is expected of them in the classroom, what will happen if they choose to behave, and what will happen if they choose not to behave. Students learn self-discipline and responsible behavior by being given clear, consistent choices. They learn that their actions have an impact and that they themselves control the consequences.

I wish teachers did not need to use negative consequences at all. I wish all students came to school motivated to learn. I wish all parents supported teachers and administrators. But that's not the reality today. Many children do not come to school intrinsically motivated to behave. Their parents have never taken the time or don't have the knowledge or skills to teach them how to behave. Given these circumstances, teachers need to set firm and consistent limits in their classrooms. However, those limits must be fair, and the consequences must be seen as outcomes of behaviors that students have *chosen*.

Students need teachers who can create classroom environments in which teaching and learning can take place. Every student has the right to a learning environment that is free from disruption. Students also need teachers who help them learn how to behave appropriately in school. Many students who are categorized as behavior problems would not be so labeled if their teachers had taught them how to behave appropriately in the classroom and had raised their self-esteem.

WHY ASSERTIVE DISCIPLINE?

The average teacher never receives in-depth, competency-based training in managing the behavior of 30 students. No one teaches teachers how to keep students in their seats long enough for teachers to make good use of the skills they learned in their education classes. In most instances, behavior management is taught through a smorgasbord approach—a little bit of William Glasser, a little bit of Thomas Gordon, a little bit of Rudolf Dreikurs, a little bit of Lee Canter. The teachers are told to find an approach that works for them.

Such an approach to training teachers in behavior management is analogous to a swimming class in which nonswimmers are briefly introduced—without practice—to the crawl stroke, the breast stroke, the back stroke, and the side stroke; then they are rowed to the middle of a lake, tossed overboard, and told to swim to shore, using whatever stroke works for them. In effect, we're telling teachers to sink or swim, and too many teachers are sinking.

The lack of ability to manage student behavior is one of the key reasons why beginning teachers drop out of teaching. Teachers must be trained thoroughly in classroom management skills. It is not sufficient for them to know how to teach content. They will never get to the content unless they know how to create a positive environment in which students know how to behave.

Assertive Discipline is not a cure-all. It is a starting point. Every teacher should also know how to use counseling skills, how to use group process skills, and how to help students with behavioral deficits learn appropriate classroom behaviors. In addition, classroom management must be part of an educator's continuing professional development. Teachers routinely attend workshops, enroll in college courses, receive feedback from administrators, and take part in regular inservice training to refine their teaching skills. Classroom management skills deserve the same attention. Unfortunately, some educators view training in Assertive Discipline as a one-shot process; they attend a one-day workshop, and that's supposed to take care of their training needs for the rest of their careers.

One day is not enough. It takes a great deal of effort and continuing training for a teacher to master the skills of classroom management. A teacher also needs support from the building administrator. Without an administrator backing a teacher's efforts to improve behavior management, without an administrator to coach and clinically supervise a teacher's behavior management skills, that teacher is not going to receive the necessary feedback and assistance to master those skills.

Parental support for teachers' disciplinary efforts is equally important. Many teachers become frustrated and give up when they don't receive such support. We must train teachers to guarantee the support of parents by teaching teachers how to communicate effectively with parents. In teacher training programs, participants are led to believe that today's parents will act as parents did in the past and give absolute support to the school. That is rarely the case. Today's teachers call parents and are told, "He's your problem at school. You handle it. You're the professional. You take care of him. I don't know what to do. Leave me alone."

RESEARCH AND ASSERTIVE DISCIPLINE

Over the last several years, a number of dissertations, master's theses, and research projects have dealt with Assertive Discipline. The results have consistently shown that teachers dramatically improve student behavior when they use the skills as prescribed. Teachers who use Assertive Discipline reduce the frequency of disruptive behavior in their classrooms, greatly reduce the number of students they refer to administrators, and dramatically increase their students' time-on-task.[1] Other research has demonstrated that student teachers trained in Assertive Discipline are evaluated by their master teachers as more effective in classroom management.[2] Research conducted in school districts in California, Oregon, Ohio, and Arizona has shown that an overwhelming majority of teachers believe that Assertive Discipline helps to improve the climate in the schools and the behavior of students.[3]

No one should be surprised that research has verified the success of the program when teachers use the skills properly. Numerous research studies have shown that teachers need to teach students the specific behaviors that they expect from them. Research also shows that student behavior improves when teachers use positive reinforcement effectively and that the pairing of positive reinforcement with consistent disciplinary consequences effectively motivates students to behave appropriately.[4]

Any behavior management program that is taught to teachers today must have a solid foundation in research. Many so-called "experts" advocate programs that are based solely on their own opinions regarding what constitutes a proper classroom environment. When pressed, many of these experts have no research validating their opinions or perceptions, and many of their programs have never been validated for effectiveness in classrooms. We can't afford to train educators in programs based only on whim or untested theory. We have an obligation to insure that any training program in behavior management be based solidly on techniques that have been validated by research and that have been shown to work in the classroom.

Research has demonstrated that Assertive Discipline works and that it isn't just a quick-fix solution. In school districts in Lennox, California, and Troy, Ohio, teachers who were trained 10 years ago still use the program effectively.[5] The program works because it is based on practices that effective teachers have followed instinctively for a long time. It's not new to have rules in a classroom. It's not new to use positive reinforcement. It's not new to have disciplinary consequences.

Teachers who are effective year after year take the basic Assertive Discipline competencies and mold them to their individual teaching styles. They may stop using certain techniques, such as putting marbles in a jar or writing names on the board. That's fine. I don't want the legacy of Assertive Discipline to be—and I don't want teachers to believe they have to use—names and checks on the board or marbles in a jar. I want teachers to learn that they have to take charge, explain their expectations, be positive with students, and consistently employ both positive reinforcement and negative consequences. These are the skills that form the basis of Assertive Discipline and of any effective program of classroom management.

NOTES

1. Linda H. Mandlebaum et al., "Assertive Discipline: An Effective Behavior Management Program," *Behavioral Disorders Journal*, vol. 8, 1983, pp. 258–64; Carl L. Fereira, "A Positive Approach to Assertive Discipline," Martinez (Calif.) Unified School District, ERIC ED 240 058, 1983; and Sammie McCormack, "Students' Off-Task Behavior and Assertive Discipline" (Doctoral dissertation, University of Oregon, 1985).

2. Susan Smith, "The Effects of Assertive Discipline Training on Student Teachers' Self Concept and Classroom Management Skills" (Doctoral dissertation, University of South Carolina, 1983).

3. Kenneth L. Moffett et al., "Assertive Discipline," *California School Board Journal*, June/July/August 1982, pp. 24–27; Mark Y. Swanson, "Assessment of the Assertive Discipline Program," Compton (Calif.) Unified School District, Spring 1984; "Discipline Report," Cartwright (Ariz.) Elementary School District, 10 February 1982; and Confederation of Oregon School Administrators, personal letter, 28 April 1980.

4. Helen Hair et al., "Development of Internal Structure in Elementary Students: A System of Classroom Management and Class Control," ERIC ED 189 067, 1980; Edmund Emmer and Carolyn Everston, "Effective Management: At the Beginning of the School Year in Junior High Classes," Research and Development Center for Teacher Education, University of Texas, Austin, 1980; Marcia Broden et al., "Effects of Teacher Attention on Attending Behavior of Two Boys at Adjacent Desks," *Journal of Applied Behavioral Analysis,* vol. 3, 1970, pp. 205–11; Hill Walker et al., "The Use of Normative Peer Data as a Standard for Evaluating Treatment Effects," *Journal of Applied Behavior Analysis,* vol. 37, 1976, pp. 145–55; Jere Brophy, "Classroom Organization and Management," *Elementary School Journal,* vol. 83, 1983, pp. 265–85; Hill Walker et al., "Experiments with Response Cost in Playground and Classroom Settings," Center for Research in Behavioral Education of the Handicapped, University of Oregon, Eugene, 1977; Thomas McLaughlin and John Malaby, "Reducing and Measuring Inappropriate Verbalizations," *Journal of Applied Behavior Analysis,* vol. 5, 1972, pp. 329–33; Charles Madsen et al., "Rules, Praise, and Ignoring: Elements of Elementary Classroom Control," *Journal of Applied Behavior Analysis,* vol. 1, 1968, pp. 139–50; Charles Greenwood et al., "Group Contingencies for Group Consequences in Classroom Management: A Further Analysis," *Journal of Applied Behavior Analysis,* vol. 7, 1974, pp. 413–25; and K. Daniel O'Leary et al., "A Token Reinforcement Program in a Public School: A Replication and Systematic Analysis," *Journal of Applied Behavior Analysis,* vol. 2, 1969, pp. 3–13.

5. Kenneth L. Moffett et al., "Training and Coaching Beginning Teachers: An Antidote to Reality Shock," *Educational Leadership,* February 1987, pp. 34–46; and Bob Murphy, "Troy High School: An Assertive Model," *Miami Valley Sunday News,* Troy, Ohio, 12 March 1989, p. 1.

PART SEVEN

Special Needs and Socioeconomic Issues

Chapter 12 Special Needs 359

Chapter 13 Socioeconomic and Cultural Issues 385

On the Internet . . .

Sites appropriate to Part Seven

This site features an *ERIC Digest* article by sociologist Harriett Romo, an associate professor in the Department of Curriculum and Instruction at the University of Texas at Austin, on improving ethnic and racial relations in the schools.

    http://aelliot.ael.org/~eric/digests/
        edorc975.html

This is a Children's Express (CE) news story in which Jonathan Kozol is interviewed.

    http://www.ce.org/topnews/kozol.htm

This is the site of the National Association of School Psychologists (NASP). The association's mission is to promote educationally and psychologically healthy environments for all children and youth by implementing research-based, effective programs that prevent problems, enhance independence, and promote optimal learning.

    http://www.naspweb.org

This site of the Office of Special Education offers numerous links to sources of information on special education and disabilities.

    http://curry.edschool.virginia.edu/go/
        cise/ose/resources/

12.1 DANIEL J. RESCHLY

Identification and Assessment of Students With Disabilities

Daniel J. Reschly was born in Iowa in 1943. He earned his B.S. in 1966 and his M.A. in 1968, both from Iowa State University, and he received his Ph.D. in school psychology from the University of Oregon. He has been a school psychologist in Iowa, Oregon, and Arizona. From 1975 to 1998 Reschly directed the Iowa State University School Psychology Program, where he achieved the rank of Distinguished Professor of Psychology and Education. Currently, he is a professor of education and psychology in Peabody College at Vanderbilt University, where he is chair of the Department of Special Education.

Reschly has been active in state and national leadership roles, including president of the National Association of School Psychologists (NASP), editor of the *School Psychology Review,* and chair of NASP Graduate Program Approval. He has received three NASP Distinguished Service Awards and appointments as fellow of the American Psychological Association and the American Psychological Society.

Reschly has published widely on the topics of school psychology professional practices, system reform, the assessment of disabilities in minority children and youth, behavioral consultation, and legal issues in special education. He is coauthor of *School Psychology: A Blueprint for Training and Practice II* (1997), and he has contributed chapters to *Beyond Traditional Intellectual Assessment: Contemporary and Emerging Theories, Tests, and Issues* (1997), *Best Practices in School Psychology III,* 3rd ed. (1995), and many others. The following selection comes from "Identification and Assessment of Students With Disabilities," *The Future of Children* (Spring 1996). In it, Reschly summarizes his knowledge regarding the identification of students with disabilities.

Key Concept: identifying and assessing disabilities

IDENTIFICATION AND ASSESSMENT

Purposes

The two main purposes of identification and assessment of students with disabilities are to determine whether they are eligible for special education services and, if they are eligible, to determine what those services will be.

Eligibility for special education services requires two findings: first, the student must meet the criteria for at least one of the thirteen disabilities recognized in the federal Individuals with Disabilities Education Act (IDEA) or the counterparts thereof in state law,[1,2] and second, special education and/or related services must be required for the student to receive an appropriate education.[2,3] It is true that some students are eligible for special education and/or related services but do not need them, while other students need the services but are not eligible according to federal or state classification criteria.

If the disability diagnosis and special education need are confirmed, the student then has certain important rights to individualized programming designed to improve educational performance and expand opportunities. These rights are established through several layers of legal requirements based on federal and state statutes, federal regulations, state rules, and state and federal litigation.[2]

Chief among these rights are the requirements that eligible students with disabilities must receive an individualized educational program (IEP) based on needs identified in an individualized, full, and complete evaluation. The needs identified during the evaluation form the basis for the student's personal and educational goals, the specially designed instruction and related services (for example, psychological consultation or physical therapy), and the methods to evaluate progress toward the student's goals.

The classification system used in special education identification also serves numerous other functions that are not discussed here (for example, organization of research; communication among scholars, lay public, and policymakers; differential training and licensing of specialists such as special education teachers; and advocacy for expanded rights and support for programs).

CURRENT PRACTICES

A number of comprehensive classification systems exist and influence, to varying degrees, classification in special education.[4-6] There is, however, no official special education classification system that is used uniformly across states and regions. For statistical purposes, students are classified by their primary disability, though it is not unusual for a student to have disabilities in more than one category.

Federal and State Disability Categories. Thirteen disabilities are briefly defined in the federal IDEA regulations: autism, deaf-blindness, deafness, hearing impairment, mental retardation, multiple disabilities, orthopedic impairment, other health impairment, serious emotional disturbance, learning disability, speech or language impairment, traumatic brain injury, and visual impairment. Federal law does not provide classification criteria for any of these disabilities except learning disability.[1]

These disability categories are based to varying degrees on eight dimensions of behavior or ability: intelligence, achievement, adaptive behavior, social behavior and emotional adjustment, communication/language, sensory status, motor skills, and health status.[7] About 90% of the students who are found eligible for special education have disabilities that fall primarily within the first five of those dimensions.

Although all states must provide special education to all students with disabilities, states may or may not adopt the disability categories recognized in the federal regulations. In fact, there are significant differences across the states in the categorical designations, conceptual definitions, and classification criteria.[8,9] These differences have their greatest impact on the students who will be described later as mildly disabled. It is entirely possible for students with identical characteristics to be diagnosed as disabled in one state, but not in another, or to have the categorical designation change with a move across state or school district lines.

The category of mental retardation (MR)[10] illustrates the diverse classification practices in special education. The IDEA regulations define mental retardation as "significantly subaverage general intellectual functioning existing concurrently with deficits in adaptive behavior."[1] Mental retardation has been recognized as one of the disabilities for which special education was provided throughout this century.[6,11] Despite the longevity and nearly universal recognition of this category, enormous differences exist among states in terminology,[10] key dimensions (for example, some states do not include adaptive behavior in the conceptual definition), and classification criteria (for example, the intelligence quotient [IQ] "ceiling" for this category varies from 69 to 85). The variations in criteria have the most effect on the mild level of mental retardation.

TABLE 1

Comparison of Medical and Social System Models of Disabilities

Characteristic	Medical Model	Social System Model
Definition of problem	Biological anomaly	Discrepancies between expected and observed behavior in a specific context
Focus of treatment	Focus on cause with purpose of curing or compensating for underlying problem	Eliminate symptoms through direct educational or behavioral interventions
Initial diagnosis	In preschool years by medical professionals	During school-age years by professionals in education or psychology
Incidence	Low (about 1% of school-age population)	High (about 9% of school-age population)
Prognosis	Life-long disabilities	Disabilities may be recognized officially only in school years
Cultural context	Cross-cultural	Arguably, culturally specific
Comprehensiveness	Usually affects performance in most roles in most contexts	May affect one or a few roles in a few or multiple contexts

Similar variations among states exist for other disability categories, especially serious emotional disturbance (SED), learning disability (LD), and speech or language impairment (SP/L).

Medical and Social System Models.   Historically, the special education classification system involved a mixture of medical and social system models of deviance.[7-9] The least ambiguous disabilities are the clearly medical disabilities (such as visual impairment or orthopedic disabilities), often recognized by the child's physician soon after birth or during the preschool years. In contrast, the disabilities defined by social system models represent behavior, intelligence, communication abilities, or other characteristics that deviate significantly from the norm, and which are generally diagnosed during the school years (see Table 1). The initial identification of a student with social system disabilities usually occurs because of a teacher-initiated referral of the child as a result of severe and chronic achievement or behavioral problems.[7]

In the social system model, the question of where to draw the line between normal and "significantly different" characteristics is somewhat subjective, and has properly been considered a matter within the discretion of local or state authorities.... In addition, knowledge about the possible underlying physical causes of some social system disabilities (such as learning disabilities and attention-deficit disorder) is changing rapidly. There is research linking biological factors to mild disabilities such as learning disability, and in particular reading disabilities.... These links involve possible differences in brain functions among readers with and without disabilities as well as a possible genetic link to severe reading disabilities. The differences are, however, correlational as noted by a writer in a recent *Science* News and Comment.[12] Further research is needed to determine (1) if these biological correlates are replicated with new samples of students with learning disability; (2) whether the presence or absence of the correlates reliably distinguishes between those with and without learning disability; and (3) whether treatments work differently depending on the presence, amount, and kind of biological correlates. Until these questions are answered, little practical utility exists for the research on the biological correlates of learning disability.

Mental retardation is perhaps the clearest example of the mixture of medical and social system models. The current prevalence of mental retardation among school-age children and youth is 1.1%.[13] Approximately one-half of these persons have moderate to severe disabilities (IQ below 55) characterized by identifiable anomalies (such as Down's Syndrome) that are the cause of their significantly lower performance in adaptive behavior and intelligence.[6,11] A second group of persons with mental retardation who typically perform at the mild level (IQ about 55 to 70 or 75) do not exhibit any biological anomalies that can be posited as the cause of their lower performance.[14,15] Indeed, the etiology of this form of mental retardation has been called cultural-familial or psychosocial as a means of acknowledging that social system factors may be preeminent.[16] Persons with mild mental retardation rather than moderate or severe mental retardation have markedly different levels and patterns of educational needs and adult adjustment. Unfortunately, the current classification system uses the same term to refer to both groups of persons,[5] leading to frequent confusion over what mental retardation means and unnecessary stigmatization of persons with mild mental retardation.[6]

The paucity of clear evidence of a medical basis for many disabilities and the fact that most disabilities are at the mild level... does not diminish the importance of early recognition of problems and the implementation of effective treatments. For example, problems with attaining literacy skills as reflected in very low reading achievement or poor behavioral competencies as reflected in aggressive behaviors often interfere significantly with normal development and seriously impair the individual's opportunities to become a competent, self-supporting citizen....

DIAGNOSIS, CLASSIFICATION, AND TREATMENT

Elaborate legal requirements govern the procedures whereby a student is diagnosed as disabled and placed in special education. The process can be divided into several states, each reflecting legally enforceable safeguards that are designed to ensure that students with disabilities are identified and provided special education and, at the same time, nondisabled students are protected from inappropriate placement. The stages are prereferral, referral, preplacement evaluation, eligibility determination, IEP development, determination of the placement, provision of services, annual evaluation of progress, and triennial reevaluation.

Progress from prereferral to the provision of services can be interrupted and halted at any one of the stages depending on the nature of the assessment information, professional judgment, and the decisions of parents. Informed parental consent is required prior to the initiation of the preplacement evaluation and again prior to the provision of services. It is at the preplacement and triennial reevaluation stages that decisions are made about eligibility for services under the IDEA. . . .

Of all disability categories, mild learning disability may be the most difficult to diagnose. Yet, given the prevalence of this diagnosis, it is crucial that the process be examined. Eligibility for learning disability typically involves teacher or parent referral because of concerns about achievement lagging behind the child's apparent intelligence or measured IQ. The evaluation typically includes observation in the regular classroom, review of the child's educational history including past test scores, assessment with standardized tests of achievement and intellectual functioning, determination if there are any discrepancies between achievement and intellectual ability, and elimination of other possible causes of the learning problem (for example, sensory deficits).

In recent years increasing concern has been expressed regarding the dominance of standardized tests at the expense of assessment that is related to interventions in evaluations for learning disability and mild mental retardation. The administration of a comprehensive, individually administered IQ test and one or more standardized, individually administered achievement tests nearly always dominates the learning disability eligibility process. Such testing is virtually mandated by federal guidelines to establish a "severe discrepancy between achievement and intellectual ability."[1]

Problems

Problems with the current classification system were recognized at least 20 years ago in the large, federally-funded exceptional child classification project. Prevalent problems include stigma to the child, poor reliability for traditional categories, poor relation of categorization to treatment, obsolete assumptions still in use in treatment, and disproportionate representation of minority students.

Stigma.   The degree to which lifelong, permanent negative effects of classification (labeling) occur is disputed. Certainly, the more extreme claims made in the late 1960s, such as that labels create deviant behavior rather than vice-versa,[18] are heard less often now. Nevertheless, the common names used for students with mild disabilities have negative connotations. An earlier, now classic, review[19] reported that there is widespread misunderstanding of the meanings of traditional classifications by both professionals and the lay public;[20] and the bearers of labels find the classification uncomfortable and, very often, objectionable.[21] Concerns about the effects of classification on individuals have led to calls for the elimination of the common classification categories.[22]

Although this literature is complex, one conservative conclusion is that categorical classification should be used as sparingly as possible and, when used, should focus on skills rather than on presumed internal attributes of the individual. Current reforms that emphasize classification based on the specific skill deficits (low reading decoding skills) and the services needed (tutoring in phonological awareness) rather than presumed internal attributes may lessen the negative connotations.

Reliability.   Current diagnoses using traditional categories are frequently unreliable. Although it is virtually impossible for a student performing at the average level or above to be classified as learning disabled or mildly mentally retarded, differentiating between these categories or between these categories and other classifications such as slow learner, economically disadvantaged, and at risk for poor educational outcomes is often difficult. The reasons for this difficulty include (1) overlapping characteristics among students in these categories,[23-25] (2) variations in teacher tolerance for student diversity,... (3) differences in screening and placement practices among districts, and (4) variations in the quality of assessment measures used by professionals.[26]

Researchers[17] have noted the diagnosis of dyslexia is not stable for children in the elementary grade levels. The instability from year to year further aggravates the reliability of the diagnosis of dyslexia, an important subcategory of learning disability.

Relation of Classification to Treatment.   A disability category is useful to the degree that it is related to the determination of treatment, to treatment outcome, and/or to prevention. The information needed to determine whether or not a student is eligible to be classified as learning disabled, mildly mentally retarded, or seriously emotionally disturbed typically does not relate closely to treatment decisions regarding individual goals, objectives, monitoring of interventions, or evaluating outcomes. Furthermore, considerable evidence now suggests that the educational interventions provided to students in the different disability categories are more alike than different.[21,27,29] Effective instructional programming utilizes the same principles and often the same procedures (intensive individual instruction, along with close monitoring and feedback) regardless of whether the student is classified as learning disabled, mildly mentally retarded, seriously emotionally disturbed, a slow learner, or educationally disadvantaged.[28]

Another criterion for usefulness is relation to prognosis or outcomes. The research has indicated that traditional categories do not have a demonstrable relationship to specific outcomes or to prognoses.[28-30]

Obsolete Assumption: Homogeneous, Segregated Groups. A subtle, but important, premise of the current categorical system is that students must be classified into categories so that homogeneous groups can be formed. The efficacy of programming by handicapping condition has been questioned since the 1960s and continues to be a subject of concern with regard to the current categorical system.[21,27,29-31] Many education agencies and practitioners are moving away from the assumption that student services can be determined by category; it is time for the categorical system to reflect this change in practice.

Obsolete Assumption: Aptitude by Treatment Interaction. Perhaps the most widely accepted traditional assumption is that special intervention techniques, instructional methods, and instructional materials must be carefully matched to precisely diagnosed learning styles or processes. The underlying assumption in this matching process was that of an aptitude by treatment interaction (ATI).[32] The ATI evidence, however, has been uniformly negative in special education applications using disability categories, modality preferences, learning styles, cognitive processing, or neuropsychologically "intact" areas.[29,31,33-36] The process- or style-matching justification for the current categorical system has little empirical support.

Disproportionate Minority Placement. One of the most controversial aspects of the current system is the disproportionate placement of minority students in various categories of disability. Recent data regarding the participation of various groups of students in special education programs are summarized in Table 2. The data are subject to differing interpretations; however, the principal conclusions are (1) both African-American and Hispanic students are disproportionately represented in special education but in opposite directions, and (2) the disproportionately high number of African Americans in special education reflects the fact that more black students than white students are categorized as having mild mental retardation. Regardless of the actual proportions, there is widespread belief that special education has been used as a dumping ground for minority students.[37]

Commonly suggested causes of disproportionate minority representation in special education include (1) poverty, (2) discrimination or cultural bias in referral and assessment, and (3) unique factors related directly to race or ethnicity. Wagner's[38] analyses implicated poverty as the principal reason African-American students are overrepresented in special education. A similar conclusion was published by Reschly[39] in an analysis of a large sample of African-American and white students in Delaware who were classified as learning disabled. However, other studies have produced different results, and it cannot be assumed that poverty is the only, or primary, causative agent. Other factors, such as the increased prevalence of low birth weight among African Americans,[40] should also be considered.

Daniel J.
Reschly

The overall goal of the special education disability classification system should be to enhance the quality of interventions and improve outcomes for children and youth with disabilities. At the same time, the categories used should be as free as possible of negative connotations, recognizing that no disability classification system will be totally free of negative connotations. This section recommends the development of systems organized around the supports and services needed by children and youth, with further designation, if needed, of the dimensions of behavior in which supports and services are provided.[22,41]

Dimensional, Not Typological.   Classification systems should be based on dimensions of behavior (reading, social conduct, and the like) rather than on typologies of persons. Typologies involving dichotomies such as disabled–nondisabled, retarded–not retarded, and learning disabled–not learning disabled are never accurate reflections of the diversity of student aptitudes and achievement. As discussed earlier, students vary on broad continua by fine gradations. However, dichotomous decisions are imposed by the current classification system.

Current eligibility rules require educators to decide that virtually identical students have very different educational needs. These decisions are inaccurate. What is needed is a classification system that reflects the reality of student differences. A classification system based on broad dimensions with fine gradations would allow accurate description of the status of students without imposing false, either-or dichotomies.

In the meantime, there is some merit to the position taken by advocates for the learning disabled, calling for preservation of the full continuum of services. For the student diagnosed with mild learning disability, the school district, in combination with the parents, might be best advised to experiment with intense interventions (for example, temporary or long-term placement in a separate classroom), limited intervention (for example, small-group tutoring two or three times a week), or simply a wait-and-see approach (for example, no changes at school but intensive tutoring support from parents at home) based upon the family's preferences, the student's motivation, and the results of intervention. When the degree of disability can be measured but response to treatment cannot be predicted, the best choice may be to offer multiple treatment options.

Functional, Not Etiological.   The current classification system is based primarily on etiology or presumed internal attributes of individuals. These etiological formulations are not useful in that they are not closely related to treatment.

For the vast majority of students now classified as mildly disabled, functional classification will mean emphasis on skills related to the school academic curriculum and to essential social competencies. Attempts to use functional classification criteria and programming have been successful and represent enormous promise for improving the current delivery system.[42–45] This trend is by no means universal, nor even present in a majority of school districts.

TABLE 2

Comparison of Ethnic Representation in Three Categories of Disabilities Based on a 1990 Survey by the Office of Civil Rights

Disability	Of All African-American Students, Percentage Who Have Been Given This Diagnosis	Of All Hispanic Students, Percentage Who Have Been Given This Diagnosis	Of All White Students, Percentage Who Have Been Given This Diagnosis
Mild mental retardation	2.1%	0.6%	0.8%
Learning disability	5.0%	4.7%	5.0%
Serious emotional disturbance	0.9%	0.3%	0.7%
Total	8.0%	5.6%	6.5%
	African American	Hispanic	White
Of the total (disabled and nondisabled) student population in 1990 OCR survey, percentage from each ethnic group	16%	12%	68%
Of students with Mild Mental Retardation, percentage from each ethnic group	35%	8%	56%
Of students with Learning Disabilities, percentage from each ethnic group	17%	11%	70%
Of students with Serious Emotional Disturbance, percentage from each ethnic group	21%	6%	71%

Source: Author using data from Office of Special Education Programs. *Implementation of the Individuals with Disabilities Education Act: Sixteenth annual report to Congress.* Washington, DC: U.S. Department of Education, 1994, pp. 198, 201-202.

Important barriers in the forms of funding mechanisms and disability eligibility criteria exist in most states. However, these impediments have been placed under careful scrutiny in recent policy papers[41] sponsored by the Federal Office of Special Education Programs.

Multidimensional. All professionals and parents realize that students with disabilities are complex human beings with a wide range of assets and limitations. Unfortunately, the current classification system suggests that persons with disabilities are different from the norm on one or two salient dimensions such as intelligence or achievement. The focus on one or two dimensions rather than on the broad range of assets and limitations often leads to undesirable restrictions of programming to those dimensions. For example, although it is well known that a significant proportion of students with learning disability have difficulties with social skills, or that the adult adjustment of persons with mild mental retardation will be determined to a greater degree by social rather than by academic competencies, current educational programs often ignore the vital areas of social skills and social competencies.[46]

Reliable Technology.   Over the past 20 years, a reliable technology has been developed for direct measurement of student behavior in natural settings.[44,47–48] When an assessment reveals reliable and precise information about a student's deviations from the average on relevant dimensions, this information can be used in measuring the effectiveness of interventions (for example, assessment of current status in relation to target objectives, monitoring progress, and evaluating outcomes). Such detailed data on the degree of student variance from the norm could also be used in allocating services to students with the greatest needs, but it should be noted that this approach may encourage the assignment of limited resources primarily to students with the more severe behavioral problems, giving a lower priority to early intervention for students whose problems are not yet extreme.

Knowledge Based on Effective Intervention.   Clearly, there is a body of knowledge related to the effectiveness of instructional interventions. Classification systems that focus on functional dimensions of behavior will facilitate the application of that knowledge base. In contrast, a classification system that focuses on presumed etiology, or on factors such as underlying neuropsychological processes or learning modalities that have no relationship to treatment outcomes, interferes with the provision of effective treatment.

NOTES

1. *Code of Federal Regulations,* Title 34, *Individuals with Disabilities Education Act.* § 300 (1991).

2. Reschly, D.J. Assessing educational handicaps. In *The handbook of forensic psychology.* A. Hess and I. Weiner, eds. New York: Wiley, 1987, pp. 155–87.

3. *Hendrick Hudson District Board of Education v. Rowley,* 73 L.Ed.2d 690, 102 S.Ct. 3034, 1982.

4. American Psychiatric Association. *Diagnostic and statistical manual of mental disorders.* 4th ed. Washington, DC: APA, 1994.

5. Luckasson, R., Coulter, D.L., Polloway, E.A., et al. *Mental retardation: Definition, classification, and systems of support.* 9th ed. Washington, DC: American Association on Mental Retardation, 1992.

6. Reschly, D.J. Mental retardation: Conceptual foundations, definitional criteria, and diagnostic operations. In *Developmental disorders: Diagnostic criteria and clinical assessment.* S.R. Hooper, G.W. Hynd, and R.E. Mattison, eds. Hillsdale, NJ: Erlbaum, 1992, pp. 23–67.

7. Reschly, D.J. Learning characteristics of mildly handicapped students: Implications for classification, placement, and programming. In *The handbook of special education:*

Research and practice. Vol. I. M.C. Wang, M.C. Reynolds, and H.J. Walberg, eds. Oxford, England: Pergamon Press, 1987, pp. 35–58.

8. Mercer, C.D., King-Sears, P., and Mercer, A.R. Learning disabilities definitions and criteria used by state education departments. *Learning Disability Quarterly* (1990) 13,2:141–52; Mercer, J. *Labeling the mentally retarded.* Berkeley, CA: University of California Press, 1973.

9. Patrick, J., and Reschly, D. Relationship of state educational criteria and demographic variables to school-system prevalence of mental retardation. *American Journal of Mental Deficiency* (1982) 86,4:351–60.

10. The federal IDEA statute and regulations continue to use the term "mental retardation," although many professionals, clients, and families have long preferred the term "developmental disability," and state statutes may use terms such as "mental disability" or "significantly limited intellectual capacity."

11. MacMillan, D. *Mental retardation in school and society.* 2d ed. Boston, MA: Little Brown, 1982.

12. Roush, W. Arguing over why Johnny can't read. *Science* (1995) 267:1896–98.

13. Office of Special Education Programs. *Implementation of the Individuals with Disabilities Education Act: Sixteenth annual report to Congress.* Washington, DC: U.S. Department of Education, 1994.

14. Zigler, E. Familial mental retardation: A continuing dilemma. *Science* (1967) 155:292–98.

15. Zigler, E., Balla, D., and Hodapp, R. On the definition and classification of mental retardation. *American Journal of Mental Deficiency* (1984) 89:215–30.

16. Grossman, H.J., ed. *Classification in mental retardation.* Washington DC: American Association on Mental Deficiency, 1983.

17. Shaywitz, S.E., Escobar, M.D., Shaywitz, B.A., et al. Distribution and temporal stability of dyslexia in an epidemiological sample of 414 children followed longitudinally. *New England Journal of Medicine* (1992) 326:145–50.

18. See note no. 8, Mercer J.

19. MacMillan, D., Jones, R., and Aloia, G. The mentally retarded label: A theoretical analysis and review of research. *American Journal of Mental Deficiency* (1974) 79:241–61.

20. Goodman, J.F. Does retardation mean dumb? Children's perceptions of the nature, cause, and course of mental retardation. *Journal of Special Education* (1989) 23:313–29.

21. Jenkins, J.R., and Heinen, A. Students' preferences for service delivery: Pull-out, in-class, or integrated models. *Exceptional Children* (1989) 55:516–23.

22. National Association of School Psychologists. *Rights Without Labels.* Washington, DC: NASP, 1986. Reprinted in *School Psychology Review* (1989)18,4.

23. Epps, S., Ysseldyke, J., and McGue, M. Differentiating LD and non-LD students: "I know one when I see one." *Learning Disability Quarterly* (1984) 7:89–101.

24. Gajar, A. Educable mentally retarded, learning disabled, and emotionally disturbed: Similarities and differences. *Exceptional Children* (1979) 45:470–72.

25. Shinn, M.R., Ysseldyke, J.E., Deno, S.L., and Tindal, G.A. A comparison of differences between students labeled learning disabled and low achieving on measures of classroom performance. *Journal of Learning Disabilities* (1986) 19:545–52.

26. Ysseldyke, J.E., Thurlow, M., Graden, J., et al. Generalizations from five years of research on assessment and decision making: The University of Minnesota Institute. *Exceptional Education Quarterly* (1983) 4:75–93.

27. Algozzine, B., Morsink, C.V., and Algozzine, K.M. What's happening in self-contained special education classrooms. *Exceptional Children* (1988) 55:259–65.

28. Epps, S., and Tindal, G. The effectiveness of differential programming in serving students with mild handicaps. In *Handbook of special education: Research and practice.* Vol. I. M.C. Wang, M.C. Reynolds, and H.J. Walberg, eds. Oxford, England: Pergamon Press, 1987, pp. 213–48.

29. Kavale, K. The effectiveness of special education. In *The handbook of school psychology.* 2d ed. T.B. Gutkin and C.R. Reynolds, eds. New York: Wiley, 1990, pp. 868–98.

30. Kavale, K.A., and Glass, G.V. The efficacy of special education interventions and practices: A compendium of meta-analysis findings. *Focus on Exceptional Children* (1982) 15,4:1–14.

31. Colarusso, R.P. Diagnostic-prescriptive teaching. In *The handbook of special education: Research and practice.* Vol. I. M.C. Wang, M.C. Reynolds, and H.J. Walberg, eds. Oxford, England: Pergamon Press, 1987, pp. 155–66.

32. Reynolds, C.R. Two key concepts in the diagnosis of learning disabilities and the habilitation of learning. *Learning Disability Quarterly* (1992) 15:2–12.

33. Arter, J.A., and Jenkins, J. R. Differential diagnosis—prescriptive teaching: A critical appraisal. *Review of Educational Research* (1979) 49:517–55.

34. Good, R.H., Vollmer, M., Creek, R.J., et al. Treatment utility of the Kaufman Assessment Battery for Children: Effects of matching instruction and student processing strength. *School Psychology Review* (1993) 22:8–26.

35. Kavale, K.A., and Forness, S.R. Substance over style: Assessing the efficacy of modality testing and teaching. *Exceptional Children* (1987) 54:228–39.

36. Teeter, P.A. Neuropsychological approaches to the remediation of educational deficits. In *Handbook of clinical child neuropsychology.* C.R. Reynolds, and E. Fletcher-Janzen, eds. New York: Plenum Press, 1989, pp. 357–76.

37. Artiles, A.L., and Trent, S.C. Overrepresentation of minority students in special education: A continuing debate. *Journal of Special Education* (1994) 27:410–37.

38. Wagner, M. *The Contributions of poverty and ethnic background to the participation of secondary school students in special education.* Menlo Park, CA: SRI International, 1995.

39. Reschly, D.J. *IQ and special education: History, current status, and alternatives.* Washington, DC: National Research Council, Commission on Social Sciences and Education, Board on Testing and Assessment, 1995.

40. Paneth, N. The problem of low birth weight. *The Future of Children* (Spring 1995) 5,1:19–34.

41. NASP/NASDE/OSEP. *Assessment and eligibility in special education: An examination of policy and practice with proposals for change.* Alexandria, VA: National Association of State Directors of Special Education, 1994.

42. Hewett, F.M., Taylor, G.D., and Artuso, A.A. The Santa Monica Project: Evaluation of an engineered classroom design with emotionally disturbed children. *Exceptional Children* (1969) 35:523–29.

43. Reschly, D.J., and Tilly, W.D. The WHY of system reform. *Communique* (1993) 22,1:1, 4–6.

44. Shinn, M.R., ed. *Curriculum-based measurement: Assessing special children.* New York: Guilford Press, 1989.

45. Tilly, W.D., Grimes, J.P., and Reschly, D.J. Special education system reform: The Iowa story. *Communique* (1993) 22, insert.

46. Morrison, G.M. Relationship among academic, social, and career education in programming for handicapped students. In *Handbook of special education research and practice*. Vol. I. M.C. Wang, M.C. Reynolds, H.J. Walberg, eds. Oxford, England: Pergamon Press, 1987, pp. 133–54.

47. Shapiro, E.S., ed. *Academic skills problems: Direct assessment and intervention*. New York: Guilford Press, 1989.

48. Shapiro, E.S., and Kratochwill, T.R., eds. *Behavioral assessment in schools: Conceptual foundations and practical applications*. New York: Guilford Press, 1988.

12.2 JOSEPH S. RENZULLI

What Makes Giftedness? Reexamining a Definition

Joseph S. Renzulli earned his B.A. in math/science education at Glassboro State College in New Jersey in 1958; his M.Ed. in educational psychology from Rutgers, the State University of New Jersey, in 1962; and his Ed.D. in educational psychology from the University of Virginia in 1966. Since then his teaching and research interest have focused on "giftedness" and creativity, learning style, assessment, and curriculum development models. Currently, he is a professor at the University of Connecticut and director of the National Research Center on the Gifted and Talented.

Renzulli has published many journal articles on giftedness and creativity, and he has authored several books on the subject, including *The Enrichment Triad Model* (Creative Learning Press, 1977), *The Revolving Door Identification Model* (Creative Learning Press, 1981), *Scales for Rating Behavioral Characteristics of Superior Students* (Creative Learning Press, 1977), *Systems and Models for Developing Programs for the Gifted and Talented* (Creative Learning Press, 1986), and *Building a Bridge Between Gifted Education and Total School Improvement* (DIANE, 1996). Renzulli is also coauthor of several texts in this area, including *A Guidebook for Developing Individualized Educational Programs for Gifted and Talented Students* (Creative Learning Press, 1979) and *The Schoolwide Enrichment Model: A Comprehensive Plan for Educational Excellence* (Creative Learning Press, 1985).

A thorny and complex theoretical debate has raged concerning the definition of giftedness. Besides its theoretical importance, such a definition has practical and resource implications in schools that identify and provide special services for gifted students. The following article, "What Makes Giftedness? Reexamining a Definition," *Phi Delta Kappan* (November 1978), is Renzulli's seminal contribution to this debate.

Key Concept: definition of giftedness

*T*hroughout recorded history and undoubtedly even before records were kept, people have always been interested in men and women who display superior ability. As early as 2200 B.C. the Chinese had developed an elaborate system of competitive examinations to select outstanding persons for government positions,[1] and down through the ages almost every culture has been fascinated by its most able citizens. Although the areas of performance in which one might be recognized as a gifted person are determined by the needs and values of the prevailing culture, scholars and laypersons alike have debated (and continue to debate) the age-old question: What makes giftedness?

The purpose of this article is therefore threefold. First, I shall analyze some past and current definitions of giftedness. Second, I shall review studies that deal with characteristics of gifted individuals. Finally, I shall present a new definition of giftedness that is operational, i.e., useful to school personnel, and defensible in terms of research findings.

THE DEFINITION CONTINUUM

Numerous conceptions and countless definitions of giftedness have been put forth over the years. One way of analyzing existing definitions is to view them along a continuum ranging from "conservative" to "liberal," i.e., according to the degree of restrictiveness used in determining who is eligible for special programs and services.

Restrictiveness can be expressed in two ways. First, a definition can limit the number of performance areas that are considered in determining eligibility for special programs. A conservative definition, for example, might limit eligibility to academic performance only and exclude other areas such as music, art, drama, leadership, public speaking, social service, and creative writing. Second, a definition may specify the degree or level of excellence one must attain to be considered gifted.

At the conservative end of the continuum is Lewis Terman's definition of giftedness, "the top 1% level in general intellectual ability, as measured by the Stanford-Binet Intelligence Scale or a comparable instrument."[2]

In this definition restrictiveness is present in terms of both the type of performance specified (i.e., how well one scores on an intelligence test) and the level of performance one must attain to be considered gifted (top 1%). At the other end of the continuum may be found more liberal definitions, such as the following one by Paul Witty:

> There are children whose outstanding potentialities in art, in writing, or in social leadership can be recognized largely by their performance. Hence, we have recommended that the definition of giftedness be expanded and that we consider any child gifted whose performance, in a potentially valuable line of human activity, is consistently remarkable.[3]

Although liberal definitions have the obvious advantage of expanding the conception of giftedness, they also open up two "cans of worms" by introducing the values issue (What are the potentially valuable lines of human activity?) and the age-old problem of subjectivity in measurement.

In recent years the values issue has been largely resolved. There are very few educators who cling to a "straight IQ" or purely academic definition of giftedness. "Multiple talent" and "multiple criteria" are almost the bywords of the present-day gifted student movement, and most educators would have little difficulty in accepting a definition that includes almost every area of human activity that manifests itself in a socially useful form.

The problem of subjectivity in measurement is not as easily resolved. As the definition of giftedness is extended beyond those abilities clearly reflected in tests of intelligence, achievement, and academic aptitude, it becomes necessary to put less emphasis on precise estimates of performance and potential and more emphasis on the opinions of qualified human judges in making decisions about admission to special programs. The issue boils down to a simple and yet very important question: How much of a trade-off are we willing to make on the objective/subjective continuum in order to allow recognition of a broader spectrum of human abilities? If some degree of subjectivity cannot be tolerated, then our definition of giftedness and the resulting programs will logically be limited to abilities that can only be measured by objective tests.

THE USOE DEFINITION

In recent years the following definition set forth by the U.S. Office of Education (USOE) has grown in popularity, and numerous states and school districts throughout the nation have adopted it for their programs:

> Gifted and talented children are those... who by virtue of outstanding abilities are capable of high performance. These... children... require differentiated educational programs and/or services beyond those normally provided by the regular school program in order to realize their [potential] contribution to self and society.
>
> Children capable of high performance include those who have demonstrated any of the following abilities or aptitudes, singly or in combination: 1) general intellectual ability, 2) specific academic aptitude, 3) creative or productive thinking, 4) leadership ability, 5) visual and performing arts aptitude, 6) psychomotor ability.[4]

The USOE definition has served the very useful purpose of calling attention to a wider variety of abilities that should be included in a definition of giftedness, but at the same time it has presented some major problems. The first lies in its failure to include nonintellective (motivational) factors. That these factors are important is borne out by an overwhelming body of research, which I shall consider later.

A second and equally important problem relates to the nonparallel nature of the six categories included in the definition. Two of the six categories (specific academic aptitude and visual and performing arts aptitude) call attention to fields of human endeavor or general performance areas in which talents and abilities are manifested. The remaining four categories are more nearly processes that may be brought to bear on performance areas. For example, a person may bring the process of creativity to bear on a specific aptitude (e.g., chemistry) or a visual art (e.g., photography). Or the processes of leadership and general intelligence might be applied to a performance area such as choreography or the management of a high school yearbook. In fact, it can be said that processes such as creativity and leadership do not exist apart from a performance area to which they can be applied. A third problem with the definition is that it tends to be misinterpreted and misused by practitioners. It is not uncommon to find educators developing entire identification systems based on the six USOE categories and in the process treating them as if they were mutually exclusive. What is equally distressing is that many people "talk a good game" about the six categories but continue to use a relatively high intelligence or aptitude score as a minimum requirement for entrance into a special program. Although both of these problems result from misapplication rather than from the definition itself, the definition is not entirely without fault, because it fails to give the kind of guidance necessary for practitioners to avoid such pitfalls.

THE THREE-RING CONCEPTION

Research on creative/productive people has consistently shown that although no single criterion should be used to identify giftedness, persons who have achieved recognition because of their unique accomplishments and creative contributions possess a relatively well-defined set of three interlocking clusters of traits. These clusters consist of above-average though not necessarily superior general ability, task commitment, and creativity (see Figure 1). It is important to point out that no single cluster "makes giftedness." Rather, it is the interaction among the three clusters that research has shown to be the necessary ingredient for creative/productive accomplishment. This interaction is represented by the shaded portion of Figure 1. It is also important to point out that each cluster is an "equal partner" in contributing to giftedness. This point is important. One of the major errors that continues to be made in identification procedures is overemphasis on superior abilities at the expense of the other two clusters of traits.

ABOVE-AVERAGE GENERAL ABILITY

Although the influence of intelligence, as traditionally measured, quite obviously varies with areas of achievement, many researchers have found that creative accomplishment is not necessarily a function of measured intelligence. In a review of several research studies dealing with the relationship between academic aptitude tests and professional achievement, M. A. Wallach has concluded that:

> Above intermediate score levels, academic skills assessments are found to show so little criterion validity as to be a questionable basis on which to make consequential decisions about students' futures. What the academic tests do predict are the results a person will obtain on other tests of the same kind.[5]

*Joseph S.
Renzulli*

FIGURE 1

The Ingredients of Giftedness

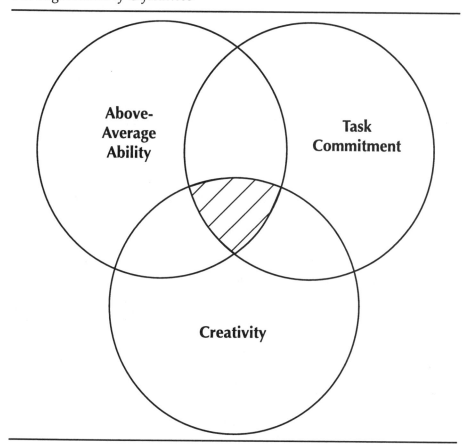

Wallach goes on to point out that academic test scores at the upper ranges
—precisely the score levels that are most often used for selecting persons for
entrance into special programs—do not necessarily reflect the potential for
creative/productive accomplishment. He suggests that test scores be used to
screen out persons who score in the lower ranges and that beyond this point
decisions be based on other indicators of potential for superior performance.

Numerous research studies support Wallach's finding that there is little
relationship between test scores and school grades on the one hand and real
world accomplishments on the other.[6] In fact, a study dealing with the prediction of various dimensions of achievement among college students, made by
J. L. Holland and A. W. Astin, found that

> ...getting good grades in college has little connection with more remote and more
> socially relevant kinds of achievement; indeed, in some colleges, the higher the

student's grades, the less likely it is that he is a person with creative potential. So it seems desirable to extend our criteria of talented performance.[7]

A study by the American College Testing Program titled "Varieties of Accomplishment After College: Perspectives on the Meaning of Academic Talent" concluded:

> The adult accomplishments were found to be uncorrelated with academic talent, including test scores, high school grades, and college grades. However, the adult accomplishments were related to comparable high school nonacademic (extracurricular) accomplishments. This suggests that there are many kinds of talents related to later success which might be identified and nurtured by educational institutions.[8]

The pervasiveness of this general finding is demonstrated by D. P. Hoyt, who reviewed 46 studies dealing with the relationship between traditional indications of academic success and post-college performance in the fields of business, teaching, engineering, medicine, scientific research, and other areas such as the ministry, journalism, government, and miscellaneous professions.[9] From this extensive review, Hoyt concluded that traditional indications of academic success have no more than a very modest correlation with various indicators of success in the adult world. He observes, "There is good reason to believe that academic achievement (knowledge) and other types of educational growth and development are relatively independent of each other."

These studies raise some basic questions about the use of tests in making selection decisions. The studies clearly indicate that vast numbers *and* proportions of our most productive persons are *not* those who scored at the ninety-fifth or above percentile on standardized tests, nor were they necessarily straight-A students who discovered early how to play the lesson-learning game. In other words, more creative/productive persons come from below the ninety-fifth percentile than above it, and if such cut-off scores are needed to determine entrance into special programs, we may be guilty of actually discriminating against persons who have the greatest potential for high levels of accomplishment.

TASK COMMITMENT

A second cluster of traits that are consistently found in creative/productive persons constitutes a refined or focused form of motivation known as task commitment. Whereas motivation is usually defined in terms of a general energizing process that triggers responses in organisms, task commitment represents energy brought to bear on a particular problem (task) or specific performance area.

The argument for including this nonintellective cluster of traits in a definition of giftedness is nothing short of overwhelming. From popular maxims and autobiographical accounts to hard-core research findings, one of the key ingredients that has characterized the work of gifted persons is the ability to involve oneself totally in a problem or area for an extended period of time.

The legacy of both Sir Francis Galton and Lewis Terman clearly indicates that task commitment is an important part of the making of a gifted person. Although Galton was a strong proponent of the hereditary basis for what he called "natural ability," he nevertheless subscribed strongly to the belief that hard work was part and parcel of giftedness:

> By natural ability I mean those qualities of intellect and disposition which urge and qualify a man to perform acts that lead to reputation. I do not mean capacity without zeal, nor zeal without capacity, nor even a combination of both of them, without an adequate power of doing a great deal of very laborious work. But I mean a nature which, when left to itself, will, urged by an inherent stimulus, climb the path that leads to eminence and has strength to reach the summit—on which, if hindered or thwarted, it will fret and strive until the hindrance is overcome, and it is again free to follow its laboring instinct.[10]

Terman's monumental studies undoubtedly represent the most widely recognized and frequently quoted research on the characteristics of gifted persons. Terman's studies, however, have unintentionally left a mixed legacy, because most persons have dwelt (and continue to dwell) on "early Terman" rather than on the conclusions he reached after several decades of intensive research. Therefore it is important to consider the following conclusion, reached after 30 years of follow-up studies on his initial population:

> ...[A] detailed analysis was made of the 150 most successful and 150 least successful men among the gifted subjects in an attempt to identify some of the nonintellectual factors that affect life success.... Since the less successful subjects do not differ to any extent in intelligence as measured by tests, it is clear that notable achievement calls for more than a high order of intelligence.
>
> The results [of the follow-up] indicated that personality factors are extremely important determiners of achievement.... The four traits on which [the most and least successful groups] differed most widely were *persistence in the accomplishment of ends, integration toward goals, self-confidence,* and *freedom from inferiority feelings.* In the total picture the greatest contrast between the two groups was in all-round emotional and social adjustment and in *drive to achieve.*[11] (Emphasis added)

Although Terman never suggested that task commitment should replace intelligence in our conception of giftedness, he did state that "intellect and achievement are far from perfectly correlated."

Several more recent studies support the findings of Galton and Terman and have shown that creative/productive persons are far more task oriented and involved in their work than are people in the general population. Perhaps the best known of these studies is the work of A. Roe and D. W. MacKinnon. Roe conducted an intensive study of the characteristics of 64 eminent scientists and found that *all* of her subjects had a high level of commitment to their work.[12] MacKinnon pointed out traits that were important in creative accomplishments: "It is clear that creative architects more often stress their inventiveness, independence, and individuality, their *enthusiasm, determination,* and *industry*"[13] (emphasis added).

Extensive reviews of research carried out by J. C. Nicholls[14] and H. G. McCurdy[15] found patterns of characteristics that were consistently similar to the findings reported by Roe and MacKinnon. Although the researchers cited thus far used different procedures and dealt with a variety of populations, there is a striking similarity in their major conclusions. First, academic ability (as traditionally measured by tests or grade-point averages) showed limited relationships to creative/productive accomplishment. Second, nonintellectual factors, and especially those that relate to task commitment, consistently played an important part in the cluster of traits that characterize highly productive people. Although this second cluster of traits is not as easily and objectively identifiable as are general cognitive abilities, they are nevertheless a major component of giftedness and should therefore be reflected in our definition.

CREATIVITY

The third cluster of traits that characterize gifted persons consists of factors that have usually been lumped together under the general heading of "creativity." As one reviews the literature in this area, it becomes readily apparent that the words "gifted," "genius," and "eminent creators" or "highly creative persons" are used synonymously. In many of the research projects discussed above, the persons ultimately selected for intensive study were in fact recognized *because* of their creative accomplishments. In MacKinnon's study, for example, panels of qualified judges (professors of architecture and editors of major American architectural journals) were asked first to nominate and later to rate an initial pool of nominees, using the following dimensions of creativity: 1) originality of thinking and freshness of approaches to architectural problems, 2) constructive ingenuity, 3) ability to set aside established conventions and procedures when appropriate, and 4) a flair for devising effective and original fulfillments of the major demands of architecture: namely, technology (firmness), visual form (delight), planning (commodity), and human awareness and social purpose.[16]

When discussing creativity, it is important to consider the problems researchers have encountered in establishing relationships between scores on creativity tests and other more substantial accomplishments. A major issue that has been raised by several investigators deals with whether or not tests of divergent thinking actually measure "true" creativity. Although some validation studies have reported limited relationships between measures of divergent thinking and creative performance criteria,[17] the research evidence for the predictive validity of such tests has been limited. Unfortunately, very few tests have been validated against real-life criteria of creative accomplishment, and in cases where such studies have been conducted the creativity tests have done poorly.[18] Thus, although divergent thinking is indeed a characteristic of highly creative persons, caution should be exercised in the use and interpretation of tests designed to measure this capacity.

Given the inherent limitations of creativity tests, a number of writers have focused attention on alternative methods for assessing creativity. Among others, Nicholls suggests that an analysis of creative products is preferable to the trait-based approach in making predictions about creative potential,[19] and Wallach proposes that student self-reports about creative accomplishment are sufficiently accurate to provide a usable source of data.[20]

Although few persons would argue against the importance of including creativity in a definition of giftedness, the conclusions and recommendations discussed above raise the haunting issue of subjectivity in measurement. In view of what the research suggests about the questionable value of more objective measures of divergent thinking, perhaps the time has come for persons in all areas of endeavor to develop more careful procedures for evaluating the products of candidates for special programs.

DISCUSSION AND GENERALIZATIONS

The studies reviewed above lend support to a small number of basic generalizations that can be used to develop an operational definition of giftedness. The first is that giftedness consists of an interaction among three clusters of traits—above-average but not necessarily superior general abilities, task commitment, and creativity. Any definition or set of identification procedures that does not give equal attention to all three clusters is simply ignoring the results of the best available research dealing with this topic.

Related to this generalization is the need to make a distinction between traditional indicators of academic proficiency and creative productivity. A sad but true fact is that special programs have favored proficient lesson learners and test takers at the expense of persons who may score somewhat lower on tests but who more than compensate for such scores by having high levels of task commitment and creativity. Research has shown that members of this group ultimately make the most creative/productive contributions to their respective fields of endeavor.

A second generalization is that an operational definition should be applicable to all socially useful performance areas. The one thing that the three clusters discussed above have in common is that each can be brought to bear on a multitude of specific performance areas. As was indicated earlier, the interaction or overlap among the clusters "makes giftedness," but giftedness does not exist in a vacuum. Our definition must, therefore, reflect yet another interaction; but in this case it is the interaction between the overlap of the clusters and any performance area to which the overlap might be applied. This interaction is represented by the large arrow in Figure 2.

A third and final generalization is concerned with the types of information that should be used to identify superior performance in specific areas. Although it is a relatively easy task to include specific performance areas in a definition, developing identification procedures that will enable us to recognize specific areas of superior performance is more difficult. Test developers have thus far devoted most of their energy to producing measures of general ability, and this emphasis is undoubtedly why these tests are relied upon so heavily in identification. However, an operational definition should give direction to needed research and development, especially as these activities relate to instruments and procedures for student selection. A defensible definition can thus become a model that will generate vast amounts of appropriate research in the years ahead.

A DEFINITION OF GIFTEDNESS

Although no single statement can effectively integrate the many ramifications of the research studies described above, the following definition of giftedness attempts to summarize the major conclusions and generalizations resulting from this review of research:

> Giftedness consists of an interaction among three basic clusters of human traits—these clusters being above-average general abilities, high levels of task commitment, and high levels of creativity. Gifted and talented children are those possessing or capable of developing this composite set of traits and applying them to any potentially valuable area of human performance. Children who manifest or are capable of developing an interaction among the three clusters require a wide variety of educational opportunities and services that are not ordinarily provided through regular instructional programs.

A graphic representation of this definition is presented in Figure 2. The definition is an operational one because it meets three important criteria. First, it is derived from the best available research studies dealing with characteristics of gifted and talented individuals. Second, it provides guidance for the

FIGURE 2

A Graphic Definition of Giftedness

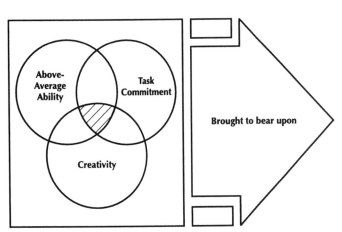

GENERAL PERFORMANCE AREAS
Mathematics • Visual Arts • Physical Sciences • Philosophy • Social Sciences • Law • Religion • Language Arts • Music • Life Sciences • Movement Arts

SPECIFIC PERFORMANCE AREAS
Cartooning • Astronomy • Public Opinion Polling • Jewelry Design • Map Making • Choreography • Biography • Film Making • Statistics • Local History • Electronics • Musical Composition • Landscape Architecture • Chemistry • Demography • Microphotography • City Planning • Pollution Control • Poetry • Fashion Design • Weaving • Play Writing • Advertising • Costume Design • Meteorology • Puppetry • Marketing • Game Design • Journalism • Electronic Music • Child Care • Consumer Protection • Cooking • Ornithology • Furniture Design • Navigation • Genealogy • Sculpture • Wildlife Management • Set Design • Agricultural Research • Animal Learning • Film Criticism • Etc. • Etc. • Etc.

Above-Average Ability

Task Commitment

Creativity

Brought to bear upon

selection and/or development of instruments and procedures that can be used to design defensible identification systems. And finally, the definition provides direction for programming practices that will capitalize upon the characteristics that bring gifted youngsters to our attention as learners with special needs.

NOTES

1. P. H. DuBois, *A History of Psychological Testing* (Boston: Allyn & Bacon; 1970).

2. L. M. Terman et al., *Genetic Studies of Genius: Mental and Physical Traits of a Thousand Gifted Children* (Stanford, Calif.: Stanford University Press, 1926), p. 43.

3. P. A. Witty, "Who Are the Gifted?" N. B. Henry, ed., *Education of the Gifted*, Fifty-seventh Yearbook of the National Society for the Study of Education, Part II (Chicago: University of Chicago Press, 1958), p. 62.

4. S. P. Marland, *Education of the Gifted and Talented*, Report to the Congress of the United States by the U.S. Commissioner of Education and Background Papers Submitted to the U.S. Office of Education (Washington, D.C.: U.S. Government Printing Office, 1972). (Definition edited for clarity.)

5. M. A. Wallach, "Tests Tell Us Little About Talent," *American Scientist*, vol. 64, 1976, p. 57.

6. M. B. Parloff et al., "Personality Characteristics Which Differentiate Creative Male Adolescents and Adults," *Journal of Personality*, vol. 36, 1968, pp. 528–52; M. T. Mednick, "Research Creativity in Psychology Graduate Students," *Journal of Consulting Psychology*, vol. 27, 1963, pp. 265, 266; M. A. Wallach and C. W. Wing, Jr., *The Talented Students: A Validation of the Creativity Intelligence Distinction* (New York: Holt, Rinehart and Winston, 1969); J. M. Richards, Jr. et al., "Prediction of Student Accomplishment in College," *Journal of Educational Psychology*, vol. 58, 1967, pp. 343–55; L. R. Harmon, "The Development of a Criterion of Scientific Competence," in C. W. Taylor and F. Barron, eds., *Scientific Creativity: Its Recognition and Development* (New York: John Wiley and Sons, 1963), pp. 44–52; B. S. Bloom, "Report on Creativity Research by the Examiner's Office of the University of Chicago," in Taylor and Barron, op. cit.; and L. Hudson, "Degree Class and Attainment in Scientific Research," *British Journal of Psychology*, vol. 51, 1960, pp. 67–73.

7. J. L. Holland and A. W. Astin, "The Prediction of the Academic, Artistic, Scientific, and Social Achievement of Undergraduates of Superior Scholastic Aptitude," *Journal of Educational Psychology*, vol. 53, 1962, pp. 132, 133.

8. L. A. Munday and J. C. Davis, *Varieties of Accomplishment After College: Perspectives on the Meaning of Academic Talent*, Research Report No. 62 (Iowa City, Ia.: American College Testing Program, 1974), p. 2.

9. D. P. Hoyt, *The Relationship Between College Grades and Adult Achievement: A Review of the Literature*, Research Report No. 7 (Iowa City, Ia.: American College Testing Program, 1965).

10. Francis Galton, as quoted in R. S. Albert, "Toward a Behavioral Definition of Genius," *American Psychologist*, vol. 30, 1975, p. 142.

11. L. M. Terman, *Genetic Studies of Genius: The Gifted Group at Mid-Life* (Stanford, Calif.: Stanford University Press, 1959), p. 148.

12. A. Roe, *The Making of a Scientist* (New York: Dodd, Mead, 1952).

13. D. W. MacKinnon, "Personality and the Realization of Creative Potential," *American Psychologist*, vol. 20, 1965, p. 365.

14. J. C. Nicholls, "Creativity in the Person Who Will Never Produce Anything Original and Useful: The Concept of Creativity as a Normally Distributed Trait," *American Psychologist*, vol. 27, 1972, pp. 717–27.

15. H. G. McCurdy, "The Childhood Pattern of Genius," *Horizon*, vol. 2, 1960, pp. 33–38.

16. D. W. MacKinnon, "The Creativity of Architects," in C. W. Taylor, ed., *Widening Horizons in Creativity* (New York: John Wiley and Sons, 1964), p. 360.

17. E. P. Torrance, "Prediction of Adult Creative Achievement Among High School Seniors," *Gifted Child Quarterly*, vol. 13, 1969, pp. 223–29; R. J. Shapiro, "Creative Research Scientists," *Psychologia Africana*, 1968, Supplement No. 4; M. Dellas and E. L. Gaier, "Identification of Creativity: The Individual," *Psychological Bulletin*, vol. 73, 1970, pp. 55–73; and J. P. Guilford, "Some New Looks at the Nature of Creative Processes," in M. Frederickson and H. Gilliksen, eds., *Contributions to Mathematical Psychology* (New York: Holt, Rinehart and Winston, 1964).

18. S. B. Crockenburg, "Creativity Tests: A Boon or Boondoggle for Education?" *Review of Educational Research*, vol. 42, 1972, pp. 27–45.

19. Nicholls, op. cit., p. 721.

20. Wallach, op. cit.

CHAPTER 13 Socioeconomic and Cultural Issues

13.1 MARGE SCHERER AND JONATHAN KOZOL

On Savage Inequalities: A Conversation With Jonathan Kozol

Jonathan Kozol's first teaching job was in a segregated Boston, Massachusetts, public school in 1964. Most of his students there were African Americans. Due to his propensity to teach outside the curriculum, he was fired after the first year and was then given a new teaching post in a rich Boston suburb. This experience, going from one of the poorest schools to one of the wealthiest, led Kozol to publish his first book, *Death at an Early Age* (Houghton Mifflin, 1967). Since that time he has traveled throughout America and Cuba, observing educational practices. His latest, highly influential book is *Amazing Grace: The Lives of Children and the Conscience of a Nation* (Crown, 1995). It describes the consequences of the AIDS epidemic on the youth of the South Bronx, New York. The students in the Bronx have extremely high rates of anxiety, depression, and asthma—all of which are at least partially caused by the horrible levels of poverty there.

The following selection comes from an interview by Marge Scherer, managing editor of the journal *Educational Leadership,* with Kozol concerning his best-selling book *Savage Inequalities: Children in America's Schools* (Crown, 1991). *Savage Inequalities,* as the title indicates, describes the unconscionable differences between rich and poor neighboring school districts and documents the psychological devastation of trying to get an education in a poverty-stricken school.

Key Concept: poverty and psychology

In Savage Inequalities, *you describe East St. Louis as the saddest place in the world. For the benefit of those who haven't read your book, would you please describe the conditions that you found there?*

Well, when I visited there a couple of years ago, East St. Louis was the poorest small city in America, virtually 100 percent black, a monument to apartheid in America. The city was so poor, there had been no garbage pickup for four years. There were heaps of garbage in the backyards of children's homes and thousands of abandoned automobile tires in empty lots.

On the edge of the city is a large chemical plant, Monsanto. There is also a very large toxic waste incinerator, as well as a huge sewage treatment plant. If you go there at night you see this orange-brownish smoke belching out of the smokestacks descending on the city. The soil is so toxic with mercury, lead, and zinc, as well as arsenic from the factories, that the city has one of the highest rates of infant mortality in Illinois, the highest rate of fetal death, and also a very high rate of childhood asthma.

The schools, not surprisingly, are utterly impoverished. East St. Louis High School, one of the two schools I visited, had a faint smell of water rot and sewage because not long before I visited, the entire school system had been shut down after being flooded with sewage from the city's antiquated sewage system. The physics teacher had no water in his physics lab—I remember that vividly. I was certainly stunned by that. In a city poisoned by several chemical plants, the science labs had very few chemicals. It was a scene of utter destitution.

I did meet several wonderful teachers in the school, and I thought the principal of the school was excellent. The superintendent of East St. Louis is also a very impressive person. In a sense, that sort of sums up the situation in many cities where I find great teachers and often very courageous administrators struggling against formidable odds, and then finding themselves condemned by venomous politicians in Washington for failing to promote excellence.

You say that a primary reason that such conditions exist in public schools is inequitable funding. What kind of funding do you think would rectify the shocking conditions in the poorest schools? Are taxes too low? Are Americans not spending enough for public education?

East St. Louis, like many poor cities in America, taxes itself at a very high rate. It's one of the most heavily taxed school districts in Illinois. In New Jersey, its counterpart is Camden. Camden has almost the highest property tax rate in New Jersey. But in both cases, because the property is virtually worthless, even with a high property tax, they cannot provide adequate revenues for their schools.

Marge Scherer and Jonathan Kozol

What we ought to do ultimately is get rid of the property tax completely as the primary means of funding public education, because it is inherently unjust. To use the local property tax as even a portion of school funding is unjust because it will always benefit the children of the most privileged people. The present system guarantees that those who can buy a $1 million home in an affluent suburb will also be able to provide their children with superior schools. That is a persistent betrayal of the whole idea of equal opportunity in America. It's a betrayal of democracy.

We ought to finance the education of every child in America equitably, with adjustments made only for the greater or lesser needs of certain children. And that funding should all come from the collective wealth of our society, mainly from a steeply graduated progressive income tax.

Don't you think that financially able parents will always want to pay extra for the education of their children?

Oh, sure. And if rich parents are afraid to let their children compete on an equal playing field, that's their right. But they ought to know what they're doing. They ought to recognize that they are protecting their children against democracy. And if they want to do that, they have a perfect right. They can pay $20,000 and send their kids to prep school. But they should not have that right within the public school system.

Even very conservative businessmen out in rich suburbs have in weak moments looked at me and said, "Well, you're right, we would never play Little League baseball this way." They wouldn't dream of sending their kids out with baseball mitts to play ball against a team that had to field the ball with bare hands. They'd regard that as being without honor. I say to them, "It's interesting. You wouldn't play baseball that way but you run the school system that way."

A point that you make very clearly in your book is that the foundation program for schools provides a level of subsistence—a minimum, or basic education, but not an education on the level found in the rich or middle-class districts. What we have is not equal funding, but an equal minimum, and the rest of the funding is decided at the local level. You're saying that there's something very wrong with that?

There are several things wrong with that. First of all, you guarantee every district—let's say, hypothetically, a basic minimum of $4,000. Then let's say a district that has enormous local wealth adds on another $4,000. That immediately invalidates the minimum $4,000 guarantee to the poor district because as soon as you double per-pupil spending, you raise the stakes. Now the rich district can steal away any teacher it wants. Many affluent people look at me and say, "Are you seriously telling us that if we want to spend more, we can't?" And I say: "That's right. Not in the public system. It isn't fair."

Do you think that public schools are being abandoned today? For example, there are funding caps, arguments for vouchers for private schools, and efforts to create business-operated schools. Is support for public schools eroding?

Absolutely. It's all part of the drive for privatizing the public sphere in the United States. It's a radical movement and it's very powerful. And it's not just in public education. It's part of a national pattern. In many big cities nowadays, affluent people vote against the taxes it would take to maintain good public parks and playgrounds. And then they spend the tax money they saved to join private health clubs, which they alone can enjoy. They vote against funds for citywide sanitation but then raise private funds to provide private sanitation simply for their exclusive neighborhood. They vote against taxation to increase citywide police protection and then hire expensive private security for their condominium. It's part of a pattern. The proposed voucher system is a larger extension of this pattern: cap the money for public schools and pull your own kids out.

And you don't think the voucher system would help poor people in any way?

No. Of course not. The voucher system is the most vicious possible device by which to enable affluent people and middle class people to flee the public system and to bring tax money with them into the private sector.

A $1,000 voucher, or even a $2,500 voucher, what will that buy a person? Can you buy tuition to Andover or Exeter or any other good prep school for that? Of course not. What can you do with that money? Well, if you're affluent, you could use that money to subsidize Andover tuition. If you're marginal middle class, that might just tip the balance and give you enough to pull off the tuition of a middle-grade private or parochial school. But if you're the poorest of the poor, you can't buy anything with $1,000. It's a sham to pretend to offer something to the poor when you're really offering a means for the middle class to rescue their children from the taint of the poor. The way I've heard it described is "save the best, and warehouse the rest."

What I find particularly bitter is that so many of the voucher advocates say, "Well, look. If these inner-city public schools were doing a good job, then we wouldn't be talking about vouchers." They say, "Look at these decrepit school buildings in East St. Louis. Look at these schools in Chicago that can't even afford toilet paper. That's why we need vouchers." But this is very cynical because the very same people who say this are the ones who voted for the politicians who starved our schools of adequate finances.

I want to talk about practices that, in addition to equal funding, would improve the odds for low-income children in urban schools. What would make a difference for at-risk students?

Well, let me just say parenthetically, while visiting urban schools, I saw some simply terrific teachers, some really wonderful school principals, and some excellent superintendents. But I purposely did not write a book where I highlighted these great exceptions because I've seen terrific exceptions for 25 years, and I don't want to waste my time pretending any longer that terrific exceptions represent a systemic answer to these problems. There are thousands of small victories every day in America, but I've seen too many small victories washed away by larger losses. School principals are always grateful if you write that kind of book, but I just didn't want to do it.

What would make a significant difference? Number 1: We ought to stop fooling around about preschool and do it at last after a quarter century. We ought to be providing full-day Head Start to every low-income child starting at the age of $2\frac{1}{2}$. And make sure that every child gets that for at least two years, *every* low-income child. That's one thing.

Number 2: I would abolish the property tax as the basic means of funding and replace it, as I said before, by equitable funding for every American child deriving from a single federal source.

Number 3: I would provide an increment in funding for the low-income inner-city and rural schools. I would go even further and provide at least a $10,000 increment for any really superb, experienced teacher who agrees to teach in the inner city, not for one or two years when they're just out of college and it's sort of fun and exciting, but for a lifetime.

I would enact a one-time federal school reconstruction bill of about $100 billion to tear down all these decrepit school buildings and put up schools that children wouldn't be ashamed to enter in the morning. I would encourage the present drive for site-based management to increase local school autonomy. I would encourage the decentralization of school systems so that teachers, principals, parents, and sometimes students themselves could have more input into determination of curriculum, for example.

I would like to see a more sweeping decentralization of school administration, but in saying that, I want to be very cautious. I'm not implying that most of our school superintendents are incompetent, and I'm certainly not implying that inefficiency is the major problem in the public school system. There is a lot of inefficiency, but the big issue is abject destitution. It's a lack of enough money.

It's interesting. People will tell you big inner-city school systems are poorly administered and that there's a lot of waste. They never say that about the rich suburban school districts. The reason, of course, is that when you have $16,000 per pupil as they have in Great Neck, New York, for example, no one will ever know how inefficient you may be because there's plenty of money to waste. The spotlight shines only on the impoverished district.

You mentioned site-based management. Many educators are urging that schools be restructured. They believe that site-based management offers communities a chance to run schools more efficiently. Do you agree?

I encourage more site-based management, but to me that's a secondary issue. The fact is that restructuring without addressing the extreme poverty of the inner-city schools—what will it get us? It will give us restructured destitution. And that's not a very significant gain. If the New York City schools were administered with maximum efficiency, without a single dollar wasted, they would still be separate and unequal schools. They would be more efficient segregated and unequal schools. But that's not a very worthy goal.

Let's talk a little bit about curriculum innovations—for instance, the idea of reaching at-risk kids in ways that are usually reserved for the gifted. Teaching algebra to remedial students, for instance. Dissolving the tracking system. What are your opinions about these solutions to problems of inequity?

Tracking! When I was a teacher, tracking had been thoroughly discredited. But during the past 12 years, tracking has come back with a vengeance. Virtually every school system I visit, with a few exceptions, is entirely tracked, although they don't use that word anymore. We have these cosmetic phrases like "homogeneous grouping." It's tracking, by whatever name, and I regret that very much. It's not just that tracking damages the children who are doing poorly, but it also damages the children who are doing very well, because, by separating the most successful students—who are often also affluent, white children—we deny them the opportunity to learn something about decency and unselfishness. We deny them the opportunity to learn the virtues of helping other kids. All the wonderful possibilities of peer teaching are swept away when we track our schools as severely as we are doing today.

The other thing, of course, is that tracking is so utterly predictive. The little girl who gets shoved into the low reading group in 2nd grade is very likely to be the child who is urged to take cosmetology instead of algebra in the 8th grade, and most likely to be in vocational courses, not college courses, in the 10th grade, if she hasn't dropped out by then. So, it's cruelly predictive. There's also a racist aspect to tracking. Black children are three times as likely as white children to be tracked into special-needs classes but only half as likely to be put in gifted programs. That's an intolerable statistic in a democracy. It's a shameful statistic. There's no possible way to explain it other than pure racism. It's one of the great, great scandals of American education.

Some say that the real problem is not equity but excellence. What's your reaction to those who say we must not spend money until we know what really works in education?

The problem is not that we don't know what works. The problem is that we are not willing to pay the bill to provide the things that work for the poorest children in America. And we have not been willing for many, many years. After all, if poor black parents on the South Side of Chicago want to know what works, they really don't need a $2 million grant from Exxon to set up another network of essential schools. All they need to do is to take a bus trip out to a high school in Wilmette and see what money pays for. All they need to do is go out and see schools where there are 16 children in a class with one very experienced teacher. All they need to do is visit a school with 200 IBMs; a school where the roof doesn't leak; a school that is surrounded by green lawns, where the architecture and atmosphere of the school entice people to feel welcome; a school in which the prosperity of the school creates the relaxed atmosphere in which the teachers feel free to innovate, which they seldom do under the conditions of filth and desperation.

What I'm saying is rather irreverent, I realize, but this is why I always sigh with weariness when I hear about the newest network of effective, essential, or accelerated schools. I say, I've seen these prototype models come and go for years and they sure do make reputations for the people who sponsor them. Foundations will support them and business partners will get on board so long as it's in fashion. If the issue in America were truly that we don't yet know what works, what arrogance would lead us to believe that we are just now on the verge of finding out?

But critics of our schools are saying that there are schools that have all kinds of equipment and materials and resources but where the academic curriculum isn't very good, where kids aren't learning that much. There are those who say the schools don't need to be fixed for the poor children only; they need to be systemically reformed to benefit all children. What about that argument?

I don't subscribe to the fashionable notion these days that all our schools are failing. I don't buy the argument that it isn't just the poor kids, it's all our kids; that suburban kids have it bad, too, and we need to make these changes for everybody. I don't really think that's true. It's a wonderfully consoling notion, because so long as it prevails, we have a perfect justification for postponing any efforts toward equality. After all, if these kids in Great Neck are suffering as much as the kids in the South Bronx, if all our schools are bad, if there's no way of discriminating between lesser and greater forms of injustice, then we can perpetuate the present inequalities for another century. I find that a very disturbing notion.

Certainly, even at a top-rated, highly funded suburban high school, there are a lot of things that I would like to change. There are kids at such schools whose individuality is not adequately respected. There are kids who suffer emotionally or don't get the challenging courses of which they are capable. But let's put things in perspective. These children are not by and large being destroyed for life. These children by and large are not going to end up in homeless shelters.

When people tell me that the schools in affluent suburbs are not doing the job that they could do, I ask, "Well, what do you mean by that?" Typically, they say, "Well, our daughter, Susan, went to our local school and she was bitterly short-changed academically. It did her real harm." And, I say, "What harm did it do her? Is she on welfare now?" "No," they say, "but she's having the devil of a time at Sarah Lawrence."

We've got to distinguish between injustice and inconvenience. Before we deal with an affluent child's existential angst, let's deal with the kid in Chicago who has not had a permanent teacher for the past five years.

It's a funny thing. After I give speeches, people will come up to me and say, "Good job." They seem to like me, but then a moment comes when they step away and I can tell something different is coming. That's the point where the question comes and the question is always the same. They ask, "Can you really solve this kind of problem with money? Is money really the answer?" I always think it's an amazing question. As though it's bizarre to suggest that money would be the solution to poverty. As though it's a bizarre idea that it would really take dollars to put a new roof on Morris High School in the Bronx and get the sewage out of the schools in East St. Louis; that it would take real money to hire and keep good teachers so they would stay for a lifetime in the schools that need them most; that it would take real money to buy computers. But that's what I always hear. They say, "Can you really solve this kind of problem by throwing money at it?" Conservatives love that word *throwing*. They never speak of throwing money at the Pentagon. We *allocate* money for the Pentagon. We throw money at anything that has to do with human pain. When they say that to me, I look them right in the eyes and say, "Sure. That's a great way to do it. Throw it. Dump it from a helicopter. Put it in my pocket and I'll bring it to the school myself." I don't know a better way to fix the root problem.

What is it that got you involved in public schools—and fighting injustice?

Oh, who knows? My mother read the Bible to me when I was a child. She's a very religious Jewish woman. My father is a physician; he spent much of his life healing poor people. My entire education was in English literature at Harvard and Oxford, and I got into teaching quite by accident. It was the spring of 1964. Three young men were murdered in Mississippi: Schwerner, Chaney, and Goodman. I was shaken by that, particularly by the death of Michael Schwerner, since he was from a background very much like mine, middle-class Jewish family from the North. So I got on the train at Harvard Square and went to the end of the line to Roxbury, the ghetto of Boston, and signed up to teach a Freedom School, run by the Civil Rights Movement.

That was in the summer, and in the fall, I signed up as a teacher in the Boston public schools. Although I wasn't certified, I was told that if I did not mind teaching black children, I could go into the classroom. That was a quick introduction to American racism. The year ended with my being fired.

Because you tried to teach Robert Frost and Langston Hughes and they weren't in the curriculum?

Yes. I was hired a couple of years later to teach in one of the wealthiest suburban school districts outside of Boston. There I saw what good education can be, what wonderful conditions can exist for privileged children. That's when, in a sense, this book that I just published, began. I saw how unfairly our schools are financed and governed. That hasn't changed. It's very much the same today. It's worse in many ways because there are so few political leaders even questioning these inequalities. I might just say parenthetically, the reason I made some critical references before to some of those pedagogic figures who get a lot of money to set up networks of excellent, accelerated, essential, or effective schools, the reason I refer to that with a sense of reservation, is that these people would not get that kind of foundation money if they were speaking candidly about racism and inequality. In order to make their programs palatable, they have substituted an agenda of innovation for an agenda of justice.

Listen, I've been invited to probably 100 conferences on education since this book was published. I've been to conferences on "quality" in education, on "more effective" education, on "excellence in education." I have not been invited to one conference on *equality in education*. There are no such conferences. And yet that remains the central issue in American education, as it does in

American democracy. That troubles me very much. To be honest, I'm surprised this book became a bestseller. I don't know why it did.

Where did you get the title, Savage Inequalities?

I chose that title because I was sick of powerful people suggesting that there was some kind of essential savagery in poor black children in America. I wanted to make clear that if there is something savage in America, it is in the powerful people who are willing to tolerate these injustices. That's why I chose it. I agree it's a tough title, and some people tried to talk me out of it, but I stuck with it.

Understanding Cultural Diversity and Learning

John U. Ogbu was born in 1939 and earned his teaching certificate at the Methodist Teachers College in Uzuakoli, Nigeria, in 1958. He studied at Princeton University and Princeton Theological Seminary in the early 1960s and received his A.B., with honors, from the University of California, Berkeley, in 1965. Ogub also received his M.A. (1969) and Ph.D. in anthropology (1971) from Berkeley, where he is currently a professor of anthropology. He has taught high school in Calabar, Nigeria, and college at San Francisco Theological Seminary and the University of Delaware. Ogbu's interests and research have focused upon psychological anthropology, education and culture, contemporary American society, and cross-cultural human development. His research has helped to explain, in a powerful and meaningful manner, the causes of differential success in American schools of various ethnic groups. He has also offered advice about how teachers and school administrators can assist low-achieving students to gain whatever American schools have to offer them.

Texts authored by Ogbu include *Minority Education and Caste: The American System in Cross-Cultural Perspective,* a Carnegie Council on Children Monograph (Academic Press, 1978) and *The Next Generation: An Ethnography of Education in an Urban Neighborhood* (Academic Press, 1974). He has coauthored *Reconstructing 'Drop-Out': A Critical Ethnography of the Dynamics of Black Students' Disengagement from School* (1997) and *Minority Status and Schooling: A Comparative Study of Immigrant and Involuntary Minorities* (Garland, 1991). In the following selection from his article "Understanding Cultural Diversity and Learning," *Educational Researcher* (November 1992), Ogbu explains the contrast between voluntary and involuntary minorities and the different approaches that are necessary for effectively educating these students.

Key Concept: cultural diversity and learning

Cultural diversity has become a household phrase in education, especially minority education. I suspect, however, that there is some misunderstanding about what it means and its relevance to minority education. As an anthropologist, I am sensitive to the use of the phrase *cultural diversity;* as a student of minority education, I am concerned about its application or misapplication with respect to the school adjustment and performance of minority children.

This article addresses two contrasting educational responses to the cultural diversity: (a) a core curriculum education movement and (b) a multicultural education movement. I argue that neither of the two responses will have an appreciable impact on the school-learning problems of those minorities who have not traditionally done well in school. The reason is that they are not based on a good understanding of the nature of the cultural diversity or cultural differences of minority groups....

CULTURAL DIVERSITY AND DIFFERENTIAL SCHOOL SUCCESS

Societal and School Influences on Minority Education

The school learning and performance of minority children are influenced by complex social, economic, historical, and cultural factors. Therefore, before describing the cultural forces, I want to make it categorically clear that I am focusing on only one group of forces. I have described elsewhere other forces at work, namely, how American society at large, the local communities, and the schools all contribute to minority problems in school learning and performance. Societal contributions include denying the minorities equal access to good education through societal and community educational policies and practices and denying them adequate and/or equal rewards with Whites for their educational accomplishments through a job ceiling and other mechanisms. Schools contribute to the educational problems through subtle and not so subtle policies and practices. The latter include tracking, "biased" testing and curriculum, and misclassification (see Ogbu, 1974, 1977, 1978, 1991). Here we are focusing on cultural forces, specifically, on the relationship between minority cultures and mainstream culture and the implications of that relationship for minority schooling.

Differential Influence of Cultural Forces

There is evidence from comparative research suggesting that differences in school learning and performance among minorities are not due merely to cultural and language differences. Some minority groups do well in school even though they do not share the language and cultural backgrounds of the dominant group that are reflected in the curriculum, instructional style, and other practices of the schools. Such minorities may initially experience problems due to the cultural and language difference, but the problems do not persist.

The reason some minorities do well in school is not necessarily because their cultures are similar to the mainstream culture. For example, Gibson (1988) reports that in Valleyside, California, the Punjabis do well even though judged by mainstream culture they would be regarded as being academically at risk.

One cultural feature, namely, differential interpretation of eye contacts by White teachers and minority-group members, has been offered as an explanation for the learning difficulties among Puerto Rican children in New York (Byers & Byers, 1972) but has not had similar adverse effects on the Punjabis. Other examples of differential academic influence of minority cultural differences have been found in studies of minority education in Stockton (Ogbu, 1974), Watsonville (Matute-Bianchi, 1986; see also Woolard, 1981), and San Francisco (Suarez-Orozco, 1988).

Studies outside the United States have also found that minority children do not fail in school because of mere cultural/language differences or succeed in school because they share the culture and language of the dominant group. In Britain, students of East Asian origins, for whom the British language and culture are different, do considerably better in school than West Indian students, who have much longer been privy to the British language and culture (Ogbu, 1978; Taylor & Hegarty, 1985). In Japan (DeVos & Lee, 1981) and New Zealand (Penfold, conversation with author, 1981), minority groups—even if they have similar cultures and languages but different histories—differ in school learning and academic success.

There are cases where a minority group does better in school when it is away from its country of origin, residing in a host society where its language and culture differ greatly from the language and culture of the dominant group. Take the case of the Japanese Buraku outcaste. In Japan itself, Buraku students continue to do poorly in school when compared with the dominant Ippan students (Hirasawa, 1989; Shimahara, 1991). But the Buraku immigrants in the United States are doing just as well as the Ippan immigrants (DeVos, 1973; Ito, 1967). The Koreans in Japan are another example. In Japan, where they went originally as colonial forced labor, they do very poorly in school. But in Hawaii and the continental United States, Korean students do as well as other Asians; yet Korean culture is more similar to Japanese culture than to American mainstream culture (DeVos, 1984; DeVos & Lee, 1981; Lee, 1991; Rohlen, 1981). The Koreans' case is further instructive because of their differential school success as a minority group in the United States, Japan, and China (see Kristoff, 1992, for Koreans in China). Korean peasants relocated to these three countries about the same time as emigrants, except the group that went to Japan. The Koreans are academically successful in China and Hawaii, but not in Japan. West Indians are a similar example. They are academically successful in the continental United States and in the U.S. Virgin Islands, where they regard themselves as "immigrants" (Fordham, 1984; Gibson, 1991); less successful in Canada, where they regard themselves as members of "the Commonwealth" (Solomon, 1992); and least successful in Britain, which they regard as their "motherland" (Ogbu, 1978; Tomlinson, 1982).

As these studies suggest, mere cultural and language differences cannot account for the relative school failure of some minorities and the school success of others. Minority status involves complex realities that affect the relationship between the culture and language of the minority and those of the dominant groups and thereby influence the school adjustment and learning of the minority.

TYPES OF MINORITY STATUS: A PREREQUISITE FOR UNDERSTANDING CULTURAL DIVERSITY AND LEARNING

To understand what it is about minority groups, their cultures and languages that makes crossing cultural boundaries and school learning difficult for some but not for others, we must recognize that there are different types of minority groups or minority status. Our comparative study has led us to classify minority groups into (a) autonomous, (b) immigrant or voluntary, and (c) castelike or involuntary minorities.

1. Autonomous minorities are people who are minorities primarily in a numerical sense. American examples are Jews, Mormons, and the Amish. There are no non-White autonomous minorities in the United States, so we will not discuss this type further (see Ogbu, 1978).
2. Immigrant or voluntary minorities are people who have moved more or less voluntarily to the United States—or any other society—because they desire more economic well-being, better overall opportunities, and/or greater political freedom. Their expectations continue to influence the way they perceive and respond to events, including schooling, in the host society. Voluntary minorities usually experience initial problems in school due to cultural and language differences as well as lack of understanding of how the education system works. But they do not experience lingering, disproportionate school failure. The Chinese and Punjabi Indians are representative U.S. examples. Refugees are not voluntary minorities; they are not a part of this classification or the subject of this paper (see Ogbu, 1990, for a full discussion of the distinction).
3. Castelike or involuntary minorities are people who were originally brought into the United States or any other society against their will. For example, through slavery, conquest, colonization, or forced labor. Thereafter, these minorities were often relegated to menial positions and denied true assimilation into the mainstream society. American Indians, Black Americans, early Mexican-Americans in the Southwest, and native Hawaiians are U.S. examples. Puerto Ricans may qualify for membership in this category if they consider themselves "a colonized people." The Burakumin and Koreans in Japan and the Maoris in New Zealand are examples outside the United States. It is involuntary minorities that usually experience greater and more persistent difficulties with school learning.

MINORITY STATUS, CULTURE, AND IDENTITY

The different types of minorities are characterized by different types of cultural differences as well as social or collective identities. Voluntary minorities are characterized by primary cultural differences and involuntary minorities by secondary cultural differences.

Primary cultural differences are differences that existed before two groups came in contact, such as before immigrant minorities came to the United States. For example, Punjabi Indians in Valleyside, California, spoke Punjabi; practiced the Sikh, Hindu, or Muslim religion; had arranged marriages, and wore turbans, if they were male, before they came to the United States. In Valleyside they continue these beliefs and practices to some extent (Gibson, 1988). The Punjabis also brought with them their distinctive way of raising children, including teaching children how to make decisions and how to manage money....

Secondary cultural differences are differences that arose after two populations came into contact or after members of a given population began to participate in an institution controlled by members of another population, such as the schools controlled by the dominant group. Thus, secondary cultural differences develop as a response to a contact situation, especially one involving the domination of one group by another.

At the beginning of the culture contact the two groups are characterized by primary cultural differences; later, the minorities develop secondary cultural differences to cope with their subordination. The secondary culture develops in several ways: from a reinterpretation of previous primary cultural differences or through the emergence of new types of cultural norms and behaviors.

Several features of secondary cultural differences are worth noting for their effects on schooling. First, it is the differences in style rather than in content that involuntary minorities emphasize: cognitive style (Ramirez & Castenada, 1974; Shade, 1982), communication style (Gumperz, 1981; Kochman, 1982; Philips, 1972, 1983), interaction style (Erickson & Mohatt, 1982), and learning style (Au, 1981; Boykin, 1980; Philips, 1976).

Another feature is cultural inversion. Cultural inversion is the tendency for involuntary minorities to regard certain forms of behavior, events, symbols, and meanings as inappropriate for them because these are characteristic of White Americans. At the same time the minorities value other forms of behavior, events, symbols and meanings, often the opposite, as more appropriate for themselves. Thus, what is appropriate or even legitimate behavior for in-group members may be defined in opposition to White out-group members' practices and preferences....

Secondary cultural differences seem to be associated with ambivalent or oppositional social or collective identities vis-a-vis the White American social identity. Voluntary minorities seem to bring to the United States a sense of who they are from their homeland and seem to retain this different but non-oppositional social identity at least during the first generation. Involuntary minorities, in contrast, develop a new sense of social or collective identity that is in opposition to the social identity of the dominant group after they have become subordinated. They do so in response to their treatment by White Americans in economic, political, social, psychological, cultural, and language domains.

Whites' treatment included deliberate exclusion from true assimilation or the reverse, namely, forced superficial assimilation (Castile & Kushner, 1981; DeVos, 1967, 1984; Spicer, 1966, 1971). Involuntary minorities, such as Black Americans, developed oppositional identity because for many generations they realized and believed that the White treatment was both collective and enduring. They were (and still are) not treated like White Americans regardless of their individual differences in ability, training, education, place of origin or residence, economic status, or physical appearance. They could not (and still cannot) easily escape from their birth-ascribed membership in a subordinate and disparaged group by "passing" for White or by returning to a "homeland" (Green, 1981). Native Americans and native Hawaiians have no other "homeland" to return to. In the past some Black Americans sought an escape by returning to Africa (Hall, 1978) and, more recently, by converting to the Muslim religion (Essien-Udom, 1964).

CULTURAL DIFFERENCES, IDENTITY, AND SCHOOL LEARNING

... The primary cultural differences of voluntary minorities and the secondary cultural differences of involuntary minorities affect minority school learning differently. My comparative research suggests that involuntary minorities experience more difficulties in school learning and performance partly because of the relationship between their cultures and the mainstream culture. As I have come to understand it, they have greater difficulty with school learning and performance partly because they have greater difficulty crossing cultural/language boundaries in school than voluntary minorities with primary cultural differences.

Primary Cultural Differences and Schooling

What kinds of school problems are associated with primary cultural differences and why do the bearers of these differences overcome these problems and learn more or less successfully? Why do voluntary minorities successfully cross cultural boundaries?

In school, primary cultural differences may initially cause problems in interpersonal and intergroup relations as well as difficulties in academic work for several reasons. One is that children from different cultural backgrounds may begin school with different cultural assumptions about the world and human relations. Another is that the minorities may come to school lacking certain concepts necessary to learn math and science, for instance, because their own cultures do not have or use such concepts. Still another problem is that the children may be non-English speaking. Finally, there may be differences in teaching and learning styles.

However, the relationship between the primary cultural differences and White American mainstream culture helps voluntary minority children to eventually overcome the initial problems, adjust socially, and learn and perform academically more or less successfully. First, the cultural differences existed before the minorities came to the United States or entered the public schools; the differences did not arise to maintain boundaries between them and White Americans. They are different from, but not necessarily oppositional to, equivalent features in mainstream culture in the schools.

Furthermore, because primary cultural differences did not develop in opposition or to protect their collective identity and sense of security and self-worth, voluntary minorities do not perceive learning the attitudes and behaviors required for school success as threatening their own culture, language, and identities. Instead, they interpret such learning (e.g., English) instrumentally and as additive, as adding to what they already have (their own language), for use in the appropriate context (Chung, 1992). They also believe that the learning will help them succeed in school and later in the labor market. Voluntary minorities, therefore, tend to adopt the strategy of "accommodation without assimilation" (Gibson, 1988) or "alternation strategy" (Ogbu, 1987). That is, while they may not give up their own cultural beliefs and practices, voluntary minorities are willing, and may even strive, to play the classroom game by the rules and try to overcome all kinds of schooling difficulties because they believe so strongly that there will be a payoff later (Gibson, 1987). With this kind of attitude, they are able to cross cultural boundaries and do relatively well in school. . . .

Secondary Cultural Differences and Schooling

Many of the "cultural problems" caused by secondary cultural differences are on the surface similar to those caused by primary cultural differences: conflicts in interpersonal/intergroup relations due to cultural misunderstandings, conceptual problems due to absence of certain concepts in the ethnic-group cultures, lack of fluency in standard English, and conflicts in teaching and learning style.

However, the underlying factor that distinguishes these problems from those of primary cultural differences is the style, not the content. Sociolinguists stress differences in communication style; cognitive researchers emphasize cognitive styles, styles of thought, or a mismatch between teacher and minority students in cognitive maps; interactionists and transactionists locate the problem in differences in interactional style. Researchers working among native Hawaiians traced their reading problems to differences in learning style.

What needs to be stressed is that secondary cultural differences do not merely cause initial problems in the social adjustment and academic performance of involuntary minorities but the problems appear to be extensive and persistent. One reason for this is that these minorities find it harder to cross cultural and language boundaries. . . .

Among involuntary minorities, school learning tends to be equated with the learning of the culture and language of White Americans, that is, the learning of the cultural and language frames of reference of their "enemy" or "oppressors." Consider the current argument by some that school curriculum and textbooks are reflective of White culture. (Note that for their part, White Americans also define minority school learning in terms of learning White culture and language as reflected in the school curriculum and practices.) Thus, involuntary minorities may consciously or unconsciously interpret school learning as a displacement process detrimental to their school identity, sense of security, and self-worth. They fear that by learning the White cultural frame of reference, they will cease to act like minorities and lose their identity as minorities and their sense of community and self-worth. Furthermore, reality has demonstrated that those who successfully learn to act White or who succeed in school are not fully accepted by the Whites; nor do such people receive rewards or opportunity for advancement equal to those open to Whites with similar education.

The important point here is that unlike voluntary minorities, involuntary minorities do not seem to be able or willing to separate attitudes and behaviors that result in academic success from those that may result in linear acculturation or replacement of their cultural identity with White American cultural identity.

There are social pressures discouraging involuntary minority students from adopting the standard attitudes and behavior practices that enhance school learning because such attitudes and behaviors are considered "White." In the case of Black students, for example, the social pressures against "acting White" include accusations of Uncle Tomism or disloyalty to the Black cause and to the Black community, fear of losing one's friends and one's sense of community (Fordham & Ogbu, 1986; Luster, 1992; Ogbu, 1974; Petroni, 1970).

The same phenomenon has been described for American Indian students —the tendency to "resist" adopting and following school rules of behavior and standard practices (Deyhle, 1989; Dumont, 1972; Kramer, 1991; Philips, 1972, 1983). According to some studies, Indian students enter the classroom with a cultural convention that dictates that they should not adopt the expected classroom rules of behavior and standard practices. A good illustration is Philips's study of Indian children in Warm Springs Reservation in Oregon referred to earlier. She found that the Indian students and their White teachers in an elementary school held different views about how students should interact with teachers and among themselves; they also held different views about how students should participate in classroom activities. Although the teachers' views apparently prevailed, the teachers were not particularly effective in classroom management and in getting the children to learn and perform. . . .

THE INDIVIDUAL IN COLLECTIVE ADAPTATION

We have described what appears to be the dominant pattern for each type of minority. But when we enter a minority community, whether of voluntary or involuntary minorities, we usually find some students who are doing well in school and other students who are not. We also find that the members of each community know that some strategies enhance school success and other strategies do not. We may even learn about the kinds of individuals and subgroups who use the different strategies. However, the strategies of a voluntary minority community are not necessarily the same as those of the involuntary minorities (Ogbu, 1989).

...[I]nvoluntary minority youths who want to succeed academically often consciously choose from a variety of secondary strategies to shield them from the peer pressures and other detracting forces of the community. The secondary strategies are over and above the conventional strategy of adopting proper academic attitudes, hard work, and perseverance. These strategies provide the context in which the student can practice the conventional strategy.

I will use Black students as an example of involuntary minorities employing secondary strategies. I have identified among them the following strategies, some promoting school success, some not.

1. Emulation of Whites or cultural passing (i.e., adopting "White" academic attitudes and behaviors or trying to behave like middle-class White students). Some students say, "If it takes acting like White people to do well in school, I'll do that." Such students get good grades. The problem is, however, that they usually experience isolation from other Black students, resulting in high psychological costs.

2. Accommodation without assimilation—an alternation model—a characteristic strategy among voluntary minorities. A student adopting this strategy behaves according to school norms while at school, but at home in the community behaves according to Black norms. One school counselor in Stockton described this strategy this way: "Their motto seems to be 'Do your Black thing [in the community] but know the White man thing [at school].'" Black students who adopt this strategy do not pay the psychological costs that attend White emulators.

3. Camouflage (i.e., disguising true academic attitudes and behaviors), using a variety of techniques. One technique is to become a jester or class clown. Since peer group members are not particularly interested in how well a student is doing academically, the student claims to lack interest in school, that schoolwork/homework or getting good grades is not important. The camouflaging student studies in secret. The good grades of camouflaging students are attributed to their "natural smartness." Another way of camouflaging is to become involved in "Black activities." If a Black athlete gets As, there's no harm done.

4. Involvement in church activities. This also promotes school success.

5. Attending private schools. For some, this is a successful way to get away from peer groups.

6. Mentors. Having a mentor is another success-enhancing strategy.

7. Protection. A few students secure the protection of bullies from peer pressures in return for helping the bullies with their homework.

8. Remedial and intervention programs. Some students succeed because they participate in such a program.

9. Encapsulation. Many Black youths, unfortunately, become encapsulated in peer group logic and activities. These students don't want to do the White man's thing or don't consider schooling important for a variety of reasons. They don't do their schoolwork. Many fail.

WHAT CAN BE DONE

Prerequisites

Recognize that there are different kinds of cultural/language differences and that the different types arise for different reasons or circumstances.

Recognize that there are different types of minority groups and that the minority types are associated with the different types of cultural/language differences.

Recognize that all minority children face problems of social adjustment and academic performance in school because of cultural/language differences. However, while problems faced by bearers of primary cultural differences are superficially similar to those of bearers of secondary cultural differences, they are fundamentally different. The reason lies in the difference in the relationship between the two types of cultural differences and White American mainstream culture.

Helping Children With Primary Cultural/Language Differences

Most problems caused by primary cultural differences are due to differences in cultural content and practice. One solution is for teachers and interventionists to learn about the students' cultural backgrounds and use this knowledge to organize their classrooms and programs, to help students learn what they teach, to help students get along with one another, to communicate with parents, and the like. Teachers and interventionists can learn about the students' cultures through (a) observation of children's behavior in the classroom and on playgrounds, (b) asking children questions about their cultural practices and preferences, (c) talking with parents about their cultural practices and preferences, (d) doing research on various ethnic groups with children in school, and (e) studying published works on children's ethnic groups.

Some problems caused by primary cultural differences can also be solved through well-designed and implemented multicultural education. Such multicultural education must be based on actual knowledge of the cultures and languages of the children's ethnic groups, how they differ from mainstream culture and language, and the kinds of problems they generate.

Helping Children With Secondary Cultural/Language Differences

First, teachers and interventionists must recognize that involuntary minority children come to school with cultural and language frames of reference that are not only different from but probably oppositional to those of the mainstream and school. Second, teachers and interventionists should study the histories and cultural adaptations of involuntary minorities in order to understand the bases and nature of the groups' cultural and language frames of reference as well as the children's sense of social identity. This knowledge will help them understand why these factors affect the process of minority schooling, particularly their school orientations and behaviors.

Third, special counseling and related programs should be used (a) to help involuntary minority students learn to separate attitudes and behaviors enhancing school success from those that lead to linear acculturation or "acting White" and (b) to help the students to avoid interpreting the former as a threat to their social identity and sense of security.

Fourth, programs are needed to increase students' adoption of the strategy of "accommodation without assimilation," "alternation model," or "playing the classroom game." The essence of this strategy is that students should recognize and accept the fact that they can participate in two cultural or language frames of reference for different purposes without losing their own cultural and language identity or undermining their loyalty to the minority community. They should learn to practice "when in Rome, do as the Romans do," without becoming Romans.

We have found from ethnographic studies (Ogbu & Hickerson, 1980) that whereas voluntary minority students try to learn to act according to school norms and expectations, involuntary minority students do not necessarily do so. Instead, they emphasize learning how to manipulate "the system," how to deal with or respond to White people and schools controlled by White people or their minority representatives. This problem should be addressed. A related approach that can be built into multicultural education programs is teaching the students their own responsibility for their academic performance and school adjustment.

Finally, society can help reorient minority youths toward more academic striving for school credentials for future employment by (a) creating more jobs in general, (b) eliminating the job ceiling against minorities, and (c) providing better employment opportunities for minorities.

The Role of the Involuntary Minority Community

The involuntary minority community can and should play an important part in changing the situation for three reasons. First, some of the needed changes can be most effectively brought about through community effort. Second, minority children do not succeed or fail only because of what schools do or do not do, but also because of what the community does. Third, our comparative research suggests that the social structure and relationship within the minority communities could be a significant influence on students' educational orientations and behaviors.

At this point in my research I suggest four ways in which the involuntary minority community can encourage academic striving and success among its children. One is to teach the children to separate attitudes and behaviors that lead to academic success from attitudes and behaviors that lead to a loss of ethnic identity and culture or language. This can be achieved partly by successful members of the group retaining their social membership in the community and not dissociating themselves from the neighborhood, labeling the less successful invidiously as "underclass," and so on. Second, the involuntary minority community should provide the children with concrete evidence that its members appreciate and value academic success as much as they appreciate and value achievements in sports, athletics, and entertainment.

Third, the involuntary minority community must teach the children to recognize and accept the responsibility for their school adjustment and academic performance. One difference between voluntary and involuntary minorities is that the former place a good deal of responsibility on the children for their school behavior and academic performance (Gibson, 1988).

Finally, the involuntary minority middle class needs to reevaluate and change its role vis-a-vis the community. We have discovered in our comparative research two contrasting models of middle class relationship with minority community which we suspect have differential effects on minority school success. The first model is, apparently, characteristic of voluntary minorities. Here successful, educated, and professional individuals, such as business people, doctors, engineers, lawyers, social workers, and university professors, appear to retain their social membership in the community, although they generally reside outside predominantly minority neighborhoods. Such people regard their accomplishments as a positive contribution to their community, a community, not just individual, achievement. The community, in turn, interprets their accomplishments in a similar manner. The successful members participate in community events where they interact with the youth and less successful adults informally and outside their official roles as representatives of the welfare, police, school district, or White-controlled companies. In this community, the middle class provides concrete evidence to young people that school success pays *and* that school success and economic and professional success in the wider society are compatible with collective identity and bona fide membership in the minority community.

In contrast, involuntary minorities seem to have a model that probably does not have much positive influence on schooling. Members of involuntary minorities seem to view professional success as "a ticket" to leave their community both physically and socially, to get away from those who have not "made it." People seek education and professional success, as it were, in order to leave their minority community. White Americans and their media reinforce this by praising those who have made their way out of the ghetto, barrio, or reservation. The middle-class minorities do not generally interpret their achievements as an indication that "their community is making it"; neither does the community interpret their achievements as an evidence of the "development" or "progress" of its members. The middle class may later return to or visit the community with "programs," or as "advocates" for those left behind or as representatives of White institutions. They rarely participate in community events where they interact outside these roles with the youth and the less successful community members. Thus, the involuntary minority middle class does not provide adequate concrete evidence to the youth and the less successful that school success leads to social and economic success in later adult life. The involuntary minority middle class must rethink its role vis-a-vis the minority youth. What is needed is for the middle class to go beyond programs, advocacy, and institutional representation to reaffiliate with the community socially.

REFERENCES

Au, K. H. (1981). Participant structure in a reading lesson with Hawaiian children: Analysis of a culturally appropriate instructional event. *Anthropology and Education Quarterly, 10*(2), 91–115.

Boykin, A. W. (1980, November). *Reading achievement and the sociocultural frame of reference of Afro American children.* Paper presented at NIE Roundtable Discussion on Issues in Urban Reading. Washington, DC: The National Institute of Education.

Byers, P., & Byers, H. (1972). Non-verbal communication and the education of children. In C. B. Cazden, D. Hymes, & V. John (Eds.), *Functions of language in the classroom.* New York: Teachers College Press.

Castile, G. P., & Kushner, G. (Eds.). (1981). *Persistent peoples: Cultural enclaves in perspective.* Tucson, AZ: University of Arizona Press.

Chung, J. P-L. (1992) *The out-of-class language and social experience of a clique of Chinese immigrant students: An ethnography of a process of social identity formation.* Unpublished Doctoral Dissertation, State University of New York at Buffalo.

DeVos, G. A. (1967). Essential elements of caste: Psychological determinants in structural theory. In G. A. DeVos & H. Wagatsuma (Eds.), *Japan's invisible race: Caste in culture and personality* (pp. 332–384). Berkeley, CA: University of California Press.

DeVos, G. A. (1984, April). *Ethnic persistence and role degradation: An illustration from Japan.* Paper presented at the American-Soviet Symposium on Contemporary Ethnic Processes in the USA and the USSR. New Orleans, LA.

DeVos, G. A., & Lee, C. (1981). *Koreans in Japan.* Berkeley, CA: University of California Press.

Dumont, R. V., Jr. (1972). Learning English and how to be silent: Studies in Sioux and Cherokee classrooms. In C. B. Cazden, D. Hymes, & V. John (Eds.), *Functions of language in the classroom.* New York: Teachers College Press.

Essien-Udom, E. U. (1964). *Black nationalism: A search for identity in America.* New York: Dell.

Erickson, F., & Mohatt, G. (1982). Cultural organization of participant structure in two classrooms of Indian students. In G. D. Spindler (Ed.), *Doing the ethnography of schooling: Educational anthropology in action* (pp. 132–175). New York: Holt.

Fordham, S. (1984, November). *Ethnography in a Black high school: Learning not to be a native.* Paper presented at the 83rd Annual Meeting of the American Anthropological Association, Denver.

Fordham, S., & Ogbu, J. U. (1986). Black students' school success: Coping with the "burden of 'acting white.'" *The Urban Review, 18*(3), 176–206.

Gibson, M. A. (1987). Playing by the Rules. In G. D. Spindler (Ed.), *Education and cultural process* (2nd ed., pp. 274–281). Prospect Heights, IL: Waveland Press.

Gibson, M. A. (1988). *Accommodation without assimilation: Sikh immigrants in an American high school.* Ithaca, NY: Cornell University Press.

Gibson, M. A. (1991). Ethnicity, gender and social class: The social adaptation patterns of West Indian youths. In M. A. Gibson & J. U. Ogbu (Eds.), *Minority status and schooling: A comparative study of immigrants and involuntary minorities* (pp. 169–203). New York: Garland.

Green, V. (1981). Blacks in the United States: The creation of an enduring people? In G. P. Castile & G. Kushner (Eds.), *Persistent peoples: Cultural enclaves in perspective* (pp. 69–77). Tucson, AZ: University of Arizona Press.

Gumperz, J. J. (1981). Conversational inference and classroom learning. In J. Green & C. Wallat (Eds.), *Ethnographic approaches to face-to-face interaction* (pp. 3–23). Norwood, NJ: Ablex.

Hall, R. A. (1978). *Black separatism in the United States.* Hanover, NH: The New England University Press.

Hirasawa, Y. (1989). *A policy study of the evolution of Dowa education in Japan.* Unpublished Doctoral Dissertation, Harvard University.

Ito, H. (1967). Japan's outcastes in the United States. In G. A. DeVos & H. Wagatasuma (Eds.), *Japan's invisible race: Caste in culture and personality* (pp. 200–221). Berkeley, CA: University of California Press.

Kochman, T. (1982). *Black and White styles in conflict.* Chicago: University of Chicago Press.

Kramer, B. J. (1991). Education and American Indians: The experience of the Ute Indian tribe. In M. A. Gibson & J. U. Ogbu (Eds.), *Minority status and schooling: A comparative study of immigrants and involuntary minorities* (pp. 287–307). New York: Garland.

Kristof, N. D. (1992, February 7). In China, the Koreans shine ("It's Our Custom"). *New York Times,* p. A7.

Lee, Y. (1991). *Koreans in Japan and United States.* In M. A. Gibson & J. U. Ogbu (Eds.), *Minority status and schooling: A comparative study of immigrants and involuntary minorities* (pp. 131–167). New York: Garland.

Luster, L. (1992). *Schooling, survival, and struggle: Black women and the GED.* Unpublished Doctoral Dissertation, Stanford University.

Matute-Bianchi, M. E. (1986). Ethnic identities and patterns of school success and failure among Mexican-descent and Japanese-American students in a California high school: An ethnographic analysis. *American Journal of Education, 95*(1), 233–255.

Ogbu, J. U. (1974). *The next generation: An ethnography of education in an urban neighborhood.* New York: Academic Press.

Ogbu, J. U. (1977). Racial stratification and education: The case of Stockton, California. *ICRD Bulletin, 12*(3), 1–26.

Ogbu, J. U. (1978). *Minority education and caste: The American system in cross-cultural perspective.* New York: Academic Press.

Ogbu, J. U. (1987). Variability in minority school performance: A problem in search of an explanation. *Anthropology and Education Quarterly, 18*(4), 312–334.

Ogbu, J. U. (1989). The individual in collective adaptation: A framework for focusing on academic underperformance and dropping out among involuntary minorities. In L. Weis, E. Farrar, & H. G. Petrie (Eds.), *Dropouts from schools: Issues, dilemmas and solutions* (pp. 181–204). Buffalo, NY: State University of New York Press.

Ogbu, J. U. (1990). Minority status and literacy in comparative perspective. *Daedalus, 119*(2), 141–168.

Ogbu, J. U. (1991). Low school performance as an adaptation: The case of Blacks in Stockton, California. In M. A. Gibson & J. U. Ogbu (Eds.), *Minority status and schooling: A comparative study of immigrants and involuntary minorities* (pp. 249–285). New York: Garland.

Ogbu, J. U., & Hickerson, R. (1980). *Survival strategies and role models in the ghetto.* University of California-Berkeley, Department of Anthropology, Special Project.

Petroni, F. A. (1970). Uncle Toms: White stereotypes in the Black movement. *Human Organization, 29,* 260–266.

Philips, S. U. (1972). Participant structure and communicative competence: Warm Springs children in community and classroom. In C. B. Cazden, D. Hymes, & V. John (Eds.), *Functions of language in the classroom.* New York: Teachers College Press.

Philips, S. U. (1976). Commentary: Access to power and maintenance of ethnic identity as goals of multi-cultural education. *Anthropology and Education Quarterly, 7*(4), 30–32.

Philips, S. U. (1983). *The invisible culture: Communication is classroom and community on the Warm Springs Indian Reservation.* New York: Longman.

Ramirez, M., & Castenada, A. (1974). *Cultural democracy, bicognitive development and education.* New York: Academic Press.

Rohlen, T. (1981). Education: Policies and prospects. In C. Lee & G. A. DeVos (Eds.), *Koreans in Japan: Ethnic conflicts and accommodation* (pp. 182–222). Berkeley, CA: University of California Press.

Shade, B. J. (1982). *Afro-American patterns of cognition.* Unpublished manuscript, Wisconsin Center for Educational Research, Madison, WI.

Shimahara, N. K. (1991). *Social mobility and education: Buraku in Japan.* In M. A. Gibson & J. U. Ogbu (Eds.), *Minority status and schooling: A comparative study of immigrants and involuntary minorities* (pp. 249–285). New York: Garland.

Solomon, R. P. (1992). *The creation of separation: Black culture and struggle in an American high school.* Albany, NY: State University of New York Press.

Spicer, E. H. (1966). The process of cultural enslavement in Middle America. *36th Congress of International de Americanistas, Seville, 3,* 267–279.

Spicer, E. H. (1971). Persistent cultural systems: A comparative study of identity systems that can adapt to contrasting environments. *Science, 174,* 795–800.

Suarez-Orozco, M. M. (1987). Becoming somebody: Central American immigrants in U.S. inner-city schools. *Anthropology & Education Quarterly, 18*(4), 287–299.

Taylor, M. J. & Hegarty, S. (1985). *The best of both worlds: A review of research into the education of pupils of South Asian origin.* Windsor, UK: National Foundation for Educational Research-Nelson.

Tomlinson, S. (1982). *A sociology of special education.* London, UK: Routledge & Kegan Paul.

Woolard, K. A. (1981). *Ethnicity in education: Some problems of language and identity in Spain and the United States.* Unpublished manuscript, University of California-Berkeley, Department of Anthropology.

ACKNOWLEDGMENTS

1.1 From John Dewey, *John Dewey on Education: Selected Writings,* ed. Reginald D. Archambault (University of Chicago Press, 1974). Copyright © 1974 by The University of Chicago. Reprinted by permission.

1.2 From Maxine Greene, "Metaphors and Multiples: Representation, the Arts, and History," *Phi Delta Kappan,* vol. 78 (January 1997). Copyright © 1997 by *Phi Delta Kappan.* Reprinted by permission of Phi Delta Kappa International.

1.3 From William James, *Talks to Teachers on Psychology: And to Students on Some of Life's Ideals* (1899).

1.4 From Edward L. Thorndike, *Educational Psychology, vol. 2: The Psychology of Learning* (Teachers College, Columbia University, 1913).

1.5 From Carol Gilligan, *In a Different Voice: Psychological Theory and Women's Development* (Harvard University Press, 1982). Copyright © 1982, 1993 by Carol Gilligan. Reprinted by permission of Harvard University Press. References omitted.

2.1 From Krishna, The Bhagavad Gita, trans. Juan Mascaró (Penguin Books, 1962). Copyright © 1962 by Juan Mascaró.

2.2 From The Holy Bible, Authorized King James Version (1611).

2.3 From K'ung Fu-Tzu (Confucius), *The Great Learning,* in Wing-Tsit Chan, comp. and trans., *A Source Book in Chinese Philosophy* (Princeton University Press, 1963). Copyright © 1963; renewed 1991 by Princeton University Press. Reprinted by permission. Notes omitted.

2.4 From The Holy Bible, Authorized King James Version (1611).

2.5 From The Koran, trans. M. H. Shakir.

2.6 From 'Abdu'l-Bahá, *The Promulgation of Universal Peace* (Bahá'í Publishing Trust, 1982). Copyright © 1982 by The National Spiritual Assembly of the Bahá'ís of the United States. Reprinted by permission of The Bahá'í Publishing Trust.

3.1 From Jean Piaget, *Six Psychological Studies,* trans. Anita Tenzer (Vintage Books, 1967). Copyright © 1967 by Random House, Inc. Reprinted by permission. Notes and references omitted.

3.2 From David Wechsler, *Wechsler Intelligence Scale for Children* (Psychological Corporation, 1949). Copyright © 1949 by The Psychological Corporation, a Harcourt Assessment Company. Reprinted by permission. Notes omitted. "Wechsler Intelligence Scale for Children" and "WISC" are registered trademarks of The Psychological Corporation.

3.3 From Robert J. Sternberg, "What Does It Mean to Be Smart?" *Educational Leadership,* vol. 54, no. 6 (March 1997). Copyright © 1997 by The Association for Supervision and Curriculum Development. Reprinted by permission of The Association for Supervision and Curriculum Development.

3.4 From Kathy Checkley, "The First Seven... and the Eighth: A Conversation With Howard Gardner," *Educational Leadership,* vol. 55, no. 1 (September 1997). Copyright © 1997 by The Association for Supervision and Curriculum Development. Reprinted by permission of The Association for Supervision and Curriculum Development.

3.5 From Hossain B. Danesh and William S. Hatcher, "Errors in Jensen's Analysis," *World Order,* vol. 11, no. 1 (Fall 1976). Copyright © 1976 by The National Spiritual Assembly of the Bahá'ís of the United States. Reprinted by permission of The Bahá'í Publishing Trust. Some references omitted.

4.1 From Erik Erikson, *Childhood and Society*, 2d ed. (W. W. Norton, 1963). Copyright © 1950, 1963 by W. W. Norton & Company, Inc.; renewed 1978, 1991 by Erik H. Erikson. Reprinted by permission of W. W. Norton & Company, Inc.

4.2 From James E. Marcia, "Development and Validation of Ego-Identity Status," *Journal of Personality and Social Psychology*, vol. 3 (1966). Copyright © 1966 by The American Psychological Corporation. Reprinted by permission of The American Psychological Corporation.

5.1 From Lawrence Kohlberg, "The Child as a Moral Philosopher," *Psychology Today*, vol. 214 (1968). Copyright © 1968 by Sussex Publishers, Inc. Reprinted by permission of *Psychology Today*.

5.2 From John R. Snarey, "Cross-Cultural Universality of Social–Moral Development: A Critical Review of Kohlbergian Research," *Psychological Bulletin*, vol. 97, no. 2 (1985). Copyright © 1985 by The American Psychological Association. Reprinted by permission of The American Psychological Association.

5.3 From Nel Noddings, "Teaching Themes of Care," *Phi Delta Kappan*, vol. 76 (May 1995). Copyright © 1995 by *Phi Delta Kappan*. Reprinted by permission of Phi Delta Kappa International.

6.1 From B. F. Skinner, "The Science of Learning and the Art of Teaching," *Harvard Educational Review*, vol. 24, no. 2 (Spring 1954). Copyright © 1954 by the President and Fellows of Harvard College. Reprinted by permission of *Harvard Educational Review*.

6.2 From Robert M. Gagné and Walter Dick, "Instructional Psychology," *Annual Review of Psychology*, vol. 34 (1983). Copyright © 1983 by Annual Reviews, Inc. Reprinted by permission of Annual Reviews, Inc., http://www.AnnualReviews.org.

6.3 From Albert Bandura, "Social Cognitive Theory," in Ross Vasta, ed., *Annals of Child Development, vol. 6* (JAI Press, 1989). Copyright © 1989 by JAI Press, Inc. Reprinted by permission of Taylor & Francis, Inc.

7.1 From Jerome S. Bruner, "The Act of Discovery," *Harvard Educational Review*, vol. 31, no. 1 (Winter 1961). Copyright © 1961 by the President and Fellows of Harvard College. Reprinted by permission of *Harvard Educational Review*.

7.2 From Lev Vygotsky, "The Development of Academic Concepts in School Aged Children," in René van der Veer and Jaan Valsiner, eds., *The Vygotsky Reader*, trans. Theresa Prout and René van der Veer (Blackwell, 1994). Copyright © 1994 by Basil Blackwell, Ltd. Reprinted by permission of Blackwell Publishers, Ltd.

8.1 From Herbert A. Simon, "The Information Processing Explanation of Gestalt Phenomena," *Computers in Human Behavior*, vol. 2 (1986). Copyright © 1986 by Pergamon Journals, Inc. Reprinted by permission of Elsevier Science.

8.2 From Endel Tulving, "How Many Memory Systems Are There?" *American Psychologist*, vol. 40 (1985). Copyright © 1985 by The American Psychological Association. Reprinted by permission of The American Psychological Association and the author.

9.1 From Nel Noddings, "A Morally Defensible Mission for Schools in the Twenty-First Century," *Phi Delta Kappan*, vol. 76 (January 1995). Copyright © 1995 by *Phi Delta Kappan*. Reprinted by permission of Phi Delta Kappa International.

9.2 From Robert E. Slavin, "Synthesis of Research on Cooperative Learning," *Educational Leadership*, vol. 48, no. 5 (February 1991). Copyright © 1991 by The Association for Supervision and Curriculum Development. Reprinted by permission of The Association for Supervision and Curriculum Development.

9.3   From F. Clark Power, Ann Higgins, and Lawrence Kohlberg, *Lawrence Kohlberg's Approach to Moral Education* (Columbia University Press, 1989). Copyright © 1989 by Columbia University Press. Reprinted by permission of the publisher. References omitted.

10.1   From Robert L. Linn, "Educational Testing and Assessment: Research Needs and Policy Issues," *American Psychologist*, vol. 41, no. 10 (October 1986). Copyright © 1986 by The American Psychological Association. Reprinted by permission of The American Psychological Association.

10.2   From Grant Wiggins, "Assessment: Authenticity, Context, and Validity," *Phi Delta Kappan*, vol. 75, no. 3 (November 1993). Copyright © 1993 by Grant Wiggins. Reprinted by permission of the author.

11.1   From Abraham H. Maslow, *Motivation and Personality*, 3rd ed. (Harper & Row, 1970). Copyright © 1970 by Abraham H. Maslow. Reprinted by permission of Prentice-Hall, Inc., Upper Saddle River, NJ. Notes omitted.

11.2   From Jere Brophy, "Teacher Praise: A Functional Analysis," *Review of Educational Research*, vol. 51, no. 1 (1981). Copyright © 1981 by The American Educational Research Association. Reprinted by permission of the publisher and the author. Notes omitted.

11.3   From Lee Canter, "Assertive Discipline—More Than Names on the Board and Marbles in a Jar," *Phi Delta Kappan* (September 1989). Copyright © 1989 by *Phi Delta Kappan*. Reprinted by permission of Phi Delta Kappa International.

12.1   From Daniel J. Reschly, "Identification and Assessment of Students With Disabilities," *The Future of Children*, vol. 6, no. 1 (Spring 1996). Copyright © 1996 by *The Future of Children*. Reprinted by permission of The David and Lucile Packard Foundation. *The Future of Children* journals and executive summaries are available free of charge by faxing information to: Circulation Department (650) 948-6498.

12.2   From Joseph S. Renzulli, "What Makes Giftedness? Reexamining a Definition," *Phi Delta Kappan*, vol. 60, no. 3 (November 1978). Copyright © 1978 by Joseph S. Renzulli. Reprinted by permission of the author.

13.1   From Marge Scherer, "On Savage Inequalities: A Conversation With Jonathan Kozol," *Educational Leadership*, vol. 50, no. 4 (December 1992/January 1993). Copyright © 1993 by The Association for Supervision and Curriculum Development. Reprinted by permission of The Association for Supervision and Curriculum Development.

13.2   From John U. Ogbu, "Understanding Cultural Diversity and Learning," *Educational Researcher*, vol. 21, no. 8 (1992). Copyright © 1992 by The American Educational Research Association. Reprinted by permission of The American Educational Research Association and the author. Notes omitted.

Index

'Abdu'l-Bahá, on education for peace, 76–82

above-average general ability, giftedness and, 376–378

abstract modeling, observational learning and, 211–213

academic achievement, cooperative learning and, 272–275

academic concepts, development of nonacademic concepts and, 228–236

accommodation without assimilation, 402, 404

Adventures of Huckleberry Finn, The (Twain), 22–23

"aha" phenomenon, 241–243

alternation model, 402, 404

American College Testing Program, 378

American Council on the Teaching of Foreign Languages (ACTFL), 317

American Indians, 401

analysis, as a component of intelligence, 99–105

analytic learning, 36–40

Anastasi, Anna, 320

anoetic consciousness, 251

aptitude of treatment interaction (ATI), 366

Aristotle, 261–262

Aronson, Elliot, 271

arts, integration of, in teaching, 14–27

assertive discipline, 349–356

assessment: authentic, 301–324; multiple intelligences and, 112–113; standardized testing and, 289–300

associative learning, 34–36

Astin, A. W., 377–378

Atayal, moral development of, 157

attention processes, observational learning and, 210, 212–213

autonoetic consciousness, 251

autonomous minorities, 397

autonomy, versus shame and doubt, in psychosocial development, 130–131

Bandura, Albert, on four basic processes of observational learning, 209–215

behavior management, assertive discipline and, 349–356

behavioral production processes, observational learning and, 210, 213–214

belongingness needs, hierarchy of needs and, 332–333

blacks, 399, 401; race and intelligence and, 115–124

blindsight, 247

Bloom, Benjamin, 314

Blough, Donald S., 192

bodily kinesthetic intelligence, 111

Book of Odes, 60–61

brain damage, multiple intelligences and, 114

Brophy, Jere, on teacher praise, 336–348

Bruner, Jerome S., 26; on discovery learning, 216–227

Buber, Martin, 178–179

Buraku, 396

Camden, New Jersey, 386–387

camouflage, 402

Canter, Lee, on assertive discipline, 349–356

caring: teaching as, 257–265; teaching themes of, 177–185

castelike minorities, cultural diversity and, 397, 398–399, 400–401, 403–406

"castration complex," in psychosocial development, 132

Checkley, Kathy, on multiple intelligences, 106–114

Chickering, Arthur, 312

Chodorow, Nancy, 43–44

classroom management, assertive discipline and, 349–356

Claxton, Charles, 312

Cluster School, just community and, 281–288

cognitive strategies, for instruction, 202–203

cognitive-developmental stage, 85–91

collective adaptation, cultural diversity and, 401–403

competition, reinforcement and, 191

computer-administered testing, 297–298

computer-assisted instruction (CAI), 204–205

concepts, development of spontaneous and nonspontaneous, 228–236

Confucius. *See* K'ung Fu-tzu

connection forming, associative learning and, 34

consciousness, functions of the stream of, 28–32

conservation, cognitive development and, 87–88, 89

Contact Theory, cooperative learning and, 275

context, authentic assessment and, 302, 312–315, 317–319

contingency, quality of teacher praise and, 339, 341

cooperation, reinforcement and, 191–192

Cooperative Integrated Reading and Composition (CIRC), cooperative learning and, 269, 270–271, 273, 274

cooperative learning, 266–280

creativity: as a component of intelligence, 99–105; giftedness and, 380–381

credibility, quality of teacher praise and, 341–342

crimes, unit on, and teaching themes of caring, 180–181

Cronbach, Lee, 310, 319

cross-cultural moral reasoning, 157–158, 161–176

cultural diversity, learning and, 394–408

cultural inversion, 398

cultural literacy, 178; integration of arts in teaching, 14–27

cultural passing, 402

culture, moral development and, 157–158, 161–176

culture-biased tests, 116

culture-loaded tests, 116

cumulative constructionism, discovery learning and, 220

Danesh, Hossain B., on race and intelligence, 115–124

Debra v. Turlington, 294

Demeter, 48

despair, versus ego integrity, in psychosocial development, 136–137

Dewey, John, 19–20, 23, 305–306, 307; on psychology and experience, 3–13

Dick, Walter, on taxonomy of learning outcomes, 200–208

Dickinson, Emily, 26

disabilities, identifying and assessing, 359–372

discipline: assertive, 349–356; positive, 352–353

discovery learning, 216–227

doubt, versus autonomy, in psychosocial development, 130–131

Douglass, Frederick, 18

Eakins, Thomas, 24

East St. Louis, Illinois, 386

ego integrity, versus despair, in psychosocial development, 136–137

ego-identity statuses, development and validation of, 138–148

elderly, caring and, 260

Elementary Perceiver and Memorizer (EPAM) program, 240–241

Emerson, Ralph Waldo, 17, 18

encapsulation, 403

England, 32

episodic empiricism, discovery learning and, 220–221

episodic memory, 246–253

equal opportunities for success, cooperative learning and, 268, 269

Erikson, Erik, 45–46, 139–140; on psychosocial stages, 127–137

esteem needs, hierarchy of needs and, 334

existential intelligence, 108

experience, as a resource for teaching, 7–8

extrinsic rewards, discovery learning and, 221–224

Ferster, Charles B., 191, 192

Fitzgerald, F. Scott, 23

"fixed ratio" reinforcement, 192

"fixed-interval" reinforcement, 192

foreclosure subjects, development and validation of identity statuses and, 140, 147

foreign-language proficiency, authentic assessment and, 317

Frederiksen, Norman, 308, 310

Freud, Sigmund, 42–43, 45, 47

friendship, 261–262

Fuller, Margaret, 18

Gagné, Robert M., 309; on a taxonomy of learning outcomes, 200–208

Gagné-Briggs theory of instruction, 201–202

Galton, Francis, 379

Gardner, Howard, 261, 320; on multiple intelligences, 106–114

Geertz, Clifford, 24

gender differences. *See* sex differences

generativity, versus stagnation, in psychosocial development, 135–136

generic mediation, 226

Germany, 32

Gestalt phenomenon, information processing and, 237–245

giftedness, definition of, 373–384

Gilligan, Carol, on women's distinct developmental path, 41–49

Glaser, Robert, 304–305

Great Gatsby, The (Fitzgerald), 23

Greene, Maxine, on integration of the arts in teaching, 14–27

Group Investigation, cooperative learning and, 272, 273, 274, 275

Guide for the Perplexed (Maimonides), 217

guilt, 130; versus initiative, in psychosocial development, 131–132

habit, 305–306; laws of, 35–36

Hartshorne, Hugh, 153

Hastings, Thomas, 314

Hatcher, William S., on race and intelligence, 115–124

Hawthorne, Nathaniel, 17, 19, 20–21

hierarchy of needs, motivation and, 327–335

Holland, J. L., 377–378

Homer, Winslow, 24

honesty, 153

Hoyt, D. P., 378

identity achievement, 139, 147

identity diffusion, 139, 147

identity statuses, development and validation of, 138–148

identity, versus role confusion, in psychosocial development, 134 immigrants, cultural diversity and, 397, 398, 399–400, 403

individual accountability, cooperative learning and, 268–269, 273

individualized educational programs (IEPs), 360, 364

Individuals with Disabilities Education Act (IDEA), 360, 361, 364

industry, versus inferiority, in psychosocial development, 133–134

inequalities, poverty and psychology and, 385–393

inferiority, versus industry, in psychosocial development, 133–134

information processing: explanation of Gestalt phenomenon, 237–245; memory systems and, 246–253

initiative, versus guilt, in psychosocial development, 131–132

insight: information processing and, 238–241; planning as sudden, 241; sudden, after incubation, 242–243

instructional psychology, 200–203

intellectual potency, discovery learning and, 219–221

intelligence: four components of, 99–105; race and, 115–124; verbal and nonverbal, 92–98; Wechsler Intelligence Scale for Children and, 92–98

intelligences, multiple, 106–114

intergroup relations, cooperative learning and, 275

interpersonal intelligence, 111

intimacy, versus isolation, in psychosocial development, 135

intrapersonal intelligence, 112

intrinsic rewards, discovery learning and, 221–224

intuition, information processing and, 238–241

involuntary minorities, cultural diversity and, 397, 398–399, 400–401, 403–406

isolation, versus intimacy, in psychosocial development, 135

James, William, on functions of the stream of consciousness, 28–32

Japan, 396

Jazz (Morrison), 24–25

Jefferson, Thomas, 16

Jensen, Arthur, criticism of views of, on race and intelligence, 115–124

Jesus Christ, on instruction in spiritual and moral development, 66–70

Jigsaw, cooperative learning and, 271, 274–275, 276

Johnson, David, 272

Johnson, Roger, 272

judgment, authentic assessment and, 302, 307

just community, Cluster School and, 281–288

Katona, George, 243–244

knowing consciousness, 251

Kohlberg Lawrence, 45, 47; creation of a just community at the Cluster School and, 281–288; on stages of moral reasoning, 149–160; study of cross-cultural moral reasoning and, 161–176

Koreans, 396

Kozol, Jonathan, on poverty and psychology, 385–393

Krishna, on Yogi, 50–53

K'ung Fu-tzu, on the way of the great learning, 58–65

Larry P. v. Riles, 292, 293

Law of Effect, reinforcement and, 190

laws of habit, 35–36

learning: by analysis and selection, 36–40; associative, 34–36; discovery, 216–227; four basic processes of observational, 209–215

learning styles, versus multiple intelligences, 113

Learning Together, cooperative learning and, 272, 274, 275

learning with understanding, 243–244

Lever, Janet, 44

linguistic intelligence, 111

Linn, Robert L., on standardized testing, 289–300

logical-mathematical intelligence, 111

love needs, hierarchy of needs and, 332–333

MacKinnon, D. W., 379, 380

Madaus, George, 314

Maimonides, 217

mainstreaming, cooperative learning and, 276

Mann, Horace, 16–17, 19

Marcia, James E., on identity statuses, 138–148

Maslow, Abraham H., on hierarchy of needs, 327–335

mathematics classes, teaching themes of caring and, 180, 182

May, Mark, 153

"May-Pole of Merry Mount, The" (Hawthorne), 20–21

McClelland, David, 309–310

mediation, discovery learning and, 226

medical model, of disabilities, 362–363

Melville, Herman, 22

memory: as a component of intelligence, 99–105; conservation of, and discovery learning, 225–226

memory systems, 246–253

mental retardation (MR), 361, 363

mentors, 402

Messick, Samuel, 317, 318, 319–320

metacognition, instruction and, 203–204

metaphor, 21–22

minimum competency testing (MCT) programs, standardized testing and, 294 minorities: cultural diversity and learning and, 394–408; disproportionate placement of, in special education programs, 366–367

mistrust, versus trust, in psychosocial development, 128–130

Moby Dick (Melville), 22

modeling, observational learning and, 211–213

moral development, 66–70, 149–160; cross-cultural, 157–158, 161–176

moral instruction, 54–57

moral laws, 54–57

moratorium subjects, development and validation of identity statuses and, 140, 147

Morrison, Toni, 24–25

Moses, on moral law and moral instruction, 54–57

motivation: discovery learning and, 222; hierarchy of needs and, 327–335; teacher praise and, 336–348

motivational processes, observational learning and, 210–211, 214

Muhammad, on submission of the psyche's will to God, 71–75

multiple intelligences, 106–114

multiple-matrix sampling, 296–297

musical intelligence, 111

National Assessment of Educational Progress (NAEP), 316

naturalistic intelligence, 107, 112

Nicholls, J. C., 380–381

Nicomachean Ethics (Aristotle), 261–262

Noddings, Nel: on teaching as caring, 257–265; on teaching themes of caring, 177–185

nonacademic concepts, development of academic concepts and, 228–236

nonknowing consciousness, 251

nonspontaneous concepts, development of spontaneous concepts and, 228–236

observational learning, four basic processes of, 209–215

oedipus complex, 42–43, 132

Ogbu, John U., on cultural diversity and learning, 394–408

Ontario Institute for Studies in Education (OISE), 204–205, 206

Organizing and Memorizing (Katona), 243–244

Ozick, Cynthia, 21–22

part-whole mediation, 226

PASE v. Hannon, 293

Pavlov, Ivan, 223

peace, education for, 76–82

perfection, Maimonides on, 217

Persephone, 48

Pettigrew, Thomas F., 122

physiological needs, hierarchy of needs and, 328–330

Piaget, Jean, 44–45, 47, 232–234; on cognitive-developmental stages, 85–91

positive discipline, 352–353

poverty, inequalities and, 385–393

Power, F. Clark, on the just community, 281–288

practicality, as a component of intelligence, 99–105

praise, teacher, 336–348

primary cultural differences, 398, 399–400, 403

problem solving, discovery learning and, 224–225

procedural memory, 246–253

production processes, observational learning and, 210, 213–214

property taxes, school funding and, 386–387, 389

psychosocial stages, of Erikson, 127–137

Public and Its Problems, The (Dewey), 23

Punjabi Indians, 396, 398

race, intelligence and, 115–124

rationalism, 15–16

Ratliff, Floyd, 192

Raven, John, 320

recognition, intuition as, 240–241

reinforcement, 189–199; teacher praise and, 336–348

religion: teaching themes of caring in mathematics classes and, 182; trust versus mistrust and, 129

Renzulli, Joseph S., on defining giftedness, 373–384

representational processes, observational learning and, 210, 213

Reschly, Daniel J., on identifying and assessing disabilities, 359–372

retention processes, observational learning and, 210, 213

Roe, A., 379

role confusion, versus identity, in psychosocial development, 134

safety needs, hierarchy of needs and, 331–332

schedules, reinforcement and, 192

Scherer, Marge, on poverty and psychology, 385–393

secondary cultural differences, 398–399, 400–401, 403–404

Secretary's Commission on Achieving Necessary Skills (SCANS), 321–322

self-actualization need, hierarchy of needs and, 334–335

self-esteem: cooperative learning and, 276; development and validation of identity statuses and, 147; hierarchy of needs and, 331

self-knowing consciousness, 251

semantic memory, 246–253

sex differences: distinct developmental path for women and, 41–49; in friendship, 262 shame, versus autonomy, in psychosocial development, 130–131

Sharan, Shlomo, 272

Sharan, Yael, 272

Shaw, George Bernard, 46

Simon, Herbert A., on information processing and intuition, 237–245

Simpson, Elizabeth, 166

site-based management, of schools, 399

Skinner, B. F., on reinforcement, 189–199

Slavin, Robert E., on cooperative learning, 266–280

"Sludge," authentic assessment and, 308

Snarey, John R., on cross-cultural moral reasoning, 161–176

social cognitive theory, four basic processes of observational learning and, 209–215

social system model, of disabilities, 362–363

socioeconomic status (SES), race and intelligence and, 115–124

spatial intelligence, 111

special education: identifying and assessing students with disabilities and, 359–372; standardized testing and, 292–294

specificity, quality of teacher praise and, 339, 341

speed, cognitive development and conceptualization of, 90–91

spiritual development, 66–70

spontaneous concepts, development of nonspontaneous concepts and, 228–236

standardized testing, 289–300; authentic assessment and, 301–324

Steffens, Lincoln, 224

Sternberg, Robert J., on memory, analysis, creativity, and practicality, 99–105

Stevens, Wallace, 15–16

strokes, multiple intelligences and, 114

student certification, standardized testing and, 294

Student Team Learning (STL) techniques, cooperative learning and, 268–271, 273, 274, 275, 276, 277

Student Teams-Achievement Divisions (STAD), cooperative learning and, 269, 270, 273, 274, 275, 277

students with disabilities, identifying and assessing, 359–372

Taiwanese, moral development of, 157

task commitment, giftedness and, 378–380

teacher praise, 336–348

teacher testing, 294–296

teaching: as caring, 257–265; resources for, 3–13; themes for caring, 177–185

Team Assisted Individualization (TAI), cooperative learning and, 269, 270, 273, 274, 275, 276

team rewards, cooperative learning and, 268, 269

Teams-Games-Tournament (TGT), cooperative learning and, 269–270, 273, 274, 275, 276, 277

Terman, Lewis, 374, 379

testing: authentic assessment and, 301–324; standardized, 289–300

thematic mediation, 226

themes of caring, teaching, 177–185

Thoreau, Henry David, 17–18

Thorndike, Edward L., on connection forming and analytic learning, 33–40

three-ring conception, of giftedness, 376–383

time, cognitive development and conceptualization of, 90–91

Tolstoy, Leo, 230–232

tracking, 390

trust, versus mistrust, in psychosocial development, 128–130

Truth, Sojourner, 18

Tulving, Endel, on procedural, episodic, and semantic memory systems, 246–253

understanding, 243–244

U.S. Navy, 205–206

U.S. Office of Education (USOE), 375

validity, authentic assessment and, 302, 315–317, 319–322

voluntary minorities, cultural diversity and, 397, 398, 399–400, 403

vouchers, 388

Vygotsky, Lev, 222–223; on development of spontaneous and nonspontaneous concepts, 228–236

Wallach, M. A., 376–377

Wechsler, David, on IQ and verbal and nonverbal intelligence, 92–98

Wechsler Intelligence Scale for Children (WISC), 92–98, 293

Wertheimer, Max, 243, 244–245

West Indians, 396

White, Robert, 222

Wiggins, Grant, on authentic assessment, 301–324

Witty, Paul, 374

women: caring and, 260, 262; distinct development path of, 41–49

Woolf, Virginia, 46–47

writing assessment, 315–316

Wyckoff, L. B., Jr., 192

Yogi, 50–53

Young Man Luther (Erikson), 114